KU-052-587

The Diaries of A. L. Rowse

The Diaries of A. L. Rowse

EDITED BY
RICHARD OLLARD

ALLEN LANE
an imprint of
PENGUIN BOOKS

ALLEN LANE
THE PENGUIN PRESS

Published by the Penguin Group
Penguin Books Ltd, 80 Strand, London, WC2R 0RL, England
Penguin Putnam Inc., 375 Hudson Street, New York, New York 10014, USA
Penguin Books Australia Ltd, 250 Camberwell Road, Camberwell, Victoria 3124, Australia
Penguin Books Canada Ltd, 10 Alcorn Avenue, Toronto, Ontario, Canada M4V 3B2
Penguin Books India (P) Ltd, 11, Community Centre, Panchsheel Park, New Delhi – 110 017, India
Penguin Books (NZ) Ltd, Cnr Rosedale and Airborne Roads, Albany, Auckland, New Zealand
Penguin Books (South Africa) (Pty) Ltd, 24 Sturdee Avenue, Rosebank 2196, South Africa

Penguin Books Ltd, Registered Offices: 80 Strand, London, WC2R 0RL, England

www.penguin.com

First published 2003
1

Set in 9.75/13pt PostScript Linotype Sabon
Typeset by Rowland Phototypesetting Ltd, Bury St Edmunds, Suffolk
Printed and bound in England by Clays Ltd, St Ives plc

ISBN 0-71399-572-6

To Raleigh Trevelyan and Norman Scarfe,
friends and writers,
valued in both capacities by A.L.R.
as by his editor

Contents

Preface

A. L. Rowse's journals – or diaries: he used both terms indifferently – cover a long period and exist in several forms. He re-read them several times, often deleting or emending, often commenting and sometimes dating his comments. Most of the text exists in manuscript – all his long life he wrote a beautiful hand and never himself learned to type – as well as in typescript, meticulously, often abusively corrected by the author, enraged by the typist's ignorance of Cornish topography or of English literature. With a view to publication Rowse himself prepared a few abridged texts of these ample originals, again freshly typed, again embellished with angry marginalia, and he made full use of them in writing his volumes of autobiography.

What prompted this powerful and persistent impulse? First, no doubt, the egocentricity (a term by which no moral censure is here implied) common to all diarists and, in some degree, to almost all authors. Second, perhaps, the instinct to record which dominated his consciousness. 'Memory and Desire, the twin pillars of existence' to quote his own words. Beyond these were others, some given, some acquired. Among the first were his observant nature and his active curiosity: he was not a bookish historian, in spite of his exceptionally wide reading and his passionate love of books. The world of nature, of light and landscape, of plants and trees, of birds and domestic animals, never passed unnoticed. Still less did that of humanity, much as he might execrate it *en masse*: society and the individuals who composed it were of absorbing interest: above all, their arts; literature, music, painting, architecture. From boyhood to old age he thrilled to them.

Secondary motives which became at various stages of his career overwhelming were his alarming and long undiagnosed ill-health and his obsessional resentment at what he considered his want of proper recognition. The first of these two converted itself, as it did with the young Winston Churchill, into the conviction that his life-span was going to be short and that everything must be crammed in in double-quick time. To make sure that nothing was missed, to catch life upon the wing (as he put it), he kept pocket books from which the diary proper was later written up. Often in pencil and sometimes difficult to read I have included a few entries taken from different periods, authentic specimens of a consciousness which, from the first strongly individual, was anything but impassive. These pocket books exist in large numbers and I make no claim to have examined them all.

The diaries themselves are, as might be expected, unequal in quality and notably so in quantity. Some of the earlier ones were destroyed by the author because of their bitterness. In his later years, roughly from the 1980s, he more or less abandoned keeping a diary in favour of notebooks in which he recorded what he was reading or feeling. First, last, and all the time Rowse thought of himself as a writer, conscious of his craft and ready, when young, to accept criticism. The later volumes of his diaries are therefore not only richer in experience, more varied in content, more mature in perception, but also much more readable.

As to the subject matter, the early years with their contrast of an intensely Cornish, intensely working-class upbringing with the sudden beauty and liberality of Oxford between the wars sharpen the delineation of both and confront the writer with choices that stimulate his imagination as well as his intellect. Young men of intellectual tastes and aspirations are much more alive to ideas than to people. Rowse often records that from boyhood his favourite reading had been biography, and especially autobiography. Both were fields in which he was himself to perform with distinction. But it is worth noting that his first two books were about ideas: the very brief *On History* (1927) and his real literary début *Politics and the Younger Generation* (1931). It was not that he was insensitive to, or unobservant of, people; still less that he saw himself as a philosopher, preferring abstract ratiocination to investigation of the concrete. But, bent on academic success which was in his situation the prerequisite of any other, he lived and moved in a world where ideas and argument made up both work and play. Not for a grammar-school boy of working-class origins were Commem – balls or dining-clubs where everyone wore a dinner-jacket. Relaxation was found – and how pleasurably – in argument and discussion in one's college rooms of an evening or on long walks in the country which then lay within easy distance of the University.

At All Souls the pattern of existence was much the same, except that formal dinner and subsequent attendance at Common Room meant that one was no longer entirely free to choose one's company or the topic of conversation. Living at close quarters with men of different generations from his own and of much wider experience intensified Rowse's natural bias to the personal. It was now the people rather than what they said that really interested him. To some extent of course the two were intertwined.

To take one instance conspicuous in the diaries, the personality of E. L. Woodward repelled Rowse in exactly the same way and to the same degree as his politics and his general ideas. Perceptibly at first and then more and more strongly the matter of the diaries becomes increasingly personal.

Curiously, as it does so, so does Rowse's protestation, faint at first but by the end of his life positively raucous, that he cannot stand people at any price. Solitude and solipsism is the only way to happiness, a precarious state at best, and to sanity. These outbursts, to judge from the abundantly documented history of his life, are rather explosions of frustration, of annoyance or of wounded feelings, than maxims of conduct on which he acted. He was extremely hospitable, generous to friends and acquaintances, a diligent correspondent, driven above all by the insatiable curiosity of the born historian. Intermittently aware of some self-contradiction he qualifies his professions by expressing a strong preference for the past over the present in personal relations. He can sympathize more easily, more pleasurably, more completely, with someone who cannot irritate or bore or repel by their actual physical presence. All the same the living have undeniable fascination: he wants to know about their social background, their religious and political affiliation, their tastes and affections, their sexuality, perhaps above all their local roots.

This chimes with another leading characteristic of the diaries: their sense of place. As with the poetry of Sir John Betjeman (a close friend) or the historical insights of Richard Cobb the apprehension of personality is interpenetrated by that of social milieu and of physical location. The eagerness with which Rowse observes the surroundings of D. H. Lawrence's early life in Eastwood or pursues the traces of his last phase in Taos are as good examples as any. The poetic side of his own nature (he wrote poetry from boyhood to old age) is evident in his imaginative reaction to place and to physical phenomena generally, smells, sounds, colour, light. This irradiated but was distinct from another quality: his extraordinarily powerful memory. In conversation, even in his eighties, he was rarely at a loss for a name or the title of a book which might crop up unexpectedly. His visual memory was no less remarkable. As a young man he travelled a good deal in western Europe, generally to the great cities rather than out of the way. His visits to the churches, art galleries, cathedrals and palaces are recorded with thoroughness and enthusiasm, an appetite that is never jaded. He resumed these travels after the interruption of the war of 1939–1945. But after his defeat in the contest for the Wardenship in 1952 he took to spending a great part of the year, usually from October to March, in the U.S.A. His journeys were often made by train or bus or car (not, fortunately, driven by himself: he was dangerous and aggressive at the wheel). He always enjoyed walking about the places he was staying in and had a real eye for the American landscape on which Edmund Wilson, by no means an indulgent critic, complimented him. Here again it was the human element as much as the physical that engaged him. His likes and dislikes of American life are outspoken and vivid. Whatever else one finds in Rowse's writings there is none of that grey neutrality that the Impressionists were determined to avoid. Consequently he excels as a descriptive reporter and he made many well-observed friendships.

During the war he travelled a good deal in England and always made the most of his opportunities. Both then and before and after the war he was often accompanied by a friend, sometimes Jack Simmons, sometimes Norman Scarfe, but more often and, it must be said, more hegemonically by Bruce McFarlane, the brilliantly successful History tutor at Magdalen. Hegemonically (hideous word!) because it was generally McFarlane who arranged these expeditions and always, if they were by car, he who drove. It was he, indeed, who initiated their friendship in which he maintained the dominant role. A medievalist of unrivalled learning in the field of England in the fourteenth and fifteenth centuries he wrote no books[1] and let it be seen, by scorn and by silence, that he didn't think much of Rowse's. Such an attitude in anyone else would have led to instant anathema and exclusion from the presence. That he remained all his life a close friend and after his death was often recalled with affection and regret shows the special place he held.

As a medievalist McFarlane's knowledge of English parish churches and of the wealth of tombs and brasses they contained was comprehensive and lively. He knew who the families were and what had been their relationships. This contributed to, if it did not form, what became Rowse's approach to history and to the life of his own time, underlying, reinforcing, the apprehension of locality already emphasized.

McFarlane also, by Rowse's account, developed another power of understanding himself and other people, the sexual. This element plays little or no part in the diaries of adolescence and young manhood. By the prime of life and the onset of middle age it is rarely far from the centre of the stage. Rowse asserts that it was McFarlane who alerted him to the fact of his own homosexuality, an aspect of his personality that the readers of his published works as well as of his personal papers are never long allowed to ignore. Perhaps early reticence on the subject prompted a compensatory expansiveness in later years. Whatever the reason, hardly any character of any

1. Except for one short volume in Rowse's *Teach Yourself History* series: *John Wycliffe and the Beginnings of English Non-conformity* (1952). A number of his articles and papers have been posthumously published.

importance is left without anecdote or speculation or, sometimes, retailed confidences on the topic. What should an editor do about these?

Libel, of course, solves any problem where the living are concerned. But most of Rowse's contemporaries and all of his seniors are now dead. They have, however, often left behind family or friends who might be hurt by exposure of matters that up to the day before yesterday were considered private. There is also the simple question of taste. The concept may provoke superior titters or even the moral censure of those who know that such a concept is mere camouflage for the hidden batteries of the class war. In his early days and in some later moods Rowse would have agreed with them. But his position here, as in many other matters, was equivocal. Derived, originally, from Marxism it owed, as time went on, more and more to the idea of the artist, committed to a no-holds-barred exposition of the truth. Gentlemanliness is explicitly disavowed where it obstructs this often painful duty. Yet, just as explicitly, the highest terms which Rowse can find to praise the writers whom he most admired and loved – for example T. S. Eliot and Quiller-Couch – are these: 'What a gent!' 'The greatest gentleman I have ever known.' So whatever line one takes, support could be found, emphatically expressed, in his writings.

An editor, anyhow, whether he be high- or low-minded, by definition employs his own taste and his own judgement. Objective he may try to be, subjectivity he can't escape. All diaries present the flavour of a personality, even if it is only that of insipidity. Selections from them are similarly idiosyncratic.

The text itself presents an editor with questions to which there are no wholly satisfactory answers. Where Rowse amends or excises, should one follow the original or the corrected version? Where the editor omits a phrase or even a sentence or two, should he indicate this? My practice has not been uniformly consistent, but I have tended towards the earlier of two or more versions and I have not, as a rule, indicated minor excisions.

Of the footnote indicators those that bear numbers are mine, the others Rowse's. The identification of persons has been sparing. Any who are simply figures and make no further appearance in the text are usually left undescribed. On the other hand identifying notes are sometimes repeated to save the reader the trouble of turning back. Passages in square brackets are editorial insertions.

RICHARD OLLARD

Acknowledgements

I should like to express my thanks to E. C. Hodgkin for giving me a vivid portrait of Helen Sutherland, reduced in this book to a bare two-line identification, and to Brendan Lehane for his enlivening account of the people Rowse met in the Dublin of the late twenties. And I am once again indebted to Mary Edmond for her guidance in the world of Shakespearean scholarship.

Finally I am, as so often before, indebted to my indexer Douglas Matthews for the safety net of his omniscience.

Some Dates

1903 4 December. Alfred Leslie Rowse born at Tregonissey
1907 Autumn. Starts going to school at Carclaze
1915 Wins minor scholarship to St Austell Grammar School
1921 Elected Douglas Jerrold scholar in English Literature at Christ Church
1925 First-class Degree in History
Elected Fellow of All Souls
His parents move to council house, 24 Robartes Place, Slades, St Austell
1926 Travels in Germany
1931–5 Part-time work at London School of Economics. Research at Public Record Office and British Museum
1931 Fights Penryn and Falmouth as Labour candidate in General Election
1933 October. Death of Charles Henderson
1934 5 March. Death of ALR's father, Richard Rowse
1935 Fights Penryn and Falmouth for the second and last time
1938 A serious illness, followed by surgery
1940 Moves from 24 Robartes Place to Polmear Mine on the outskirts of St Austell
1945 Succeeds Sir Arthur Salter in beautiful rooms in All Souls
1951 First visit to U.S.A. (Huntington Library, Pasadena)
Presides as Sub-Warden but does not stand as candidate at the election of a new Warden of All Souls
1952 New Warden, incapacitated by ill-health, resigns. ALR stands and is defeated by John Sparrow
1953 August. Moves to Trenarren, his home for the rest of his life
1953 27 September. Death of ALR's mother
1958 March. Death of Richard Pares
1960 May. Hon. Doctorate at Exeter University
1966 July. Death of Bruce McFarlane

1972	Elected to Athenaeum under Rule II – a great distinction
1982	Receives Benson Medal of Royal Society of Literature
1996	July. Severe stroke. In autumn made Companion of Honour
1997	3 October. Death

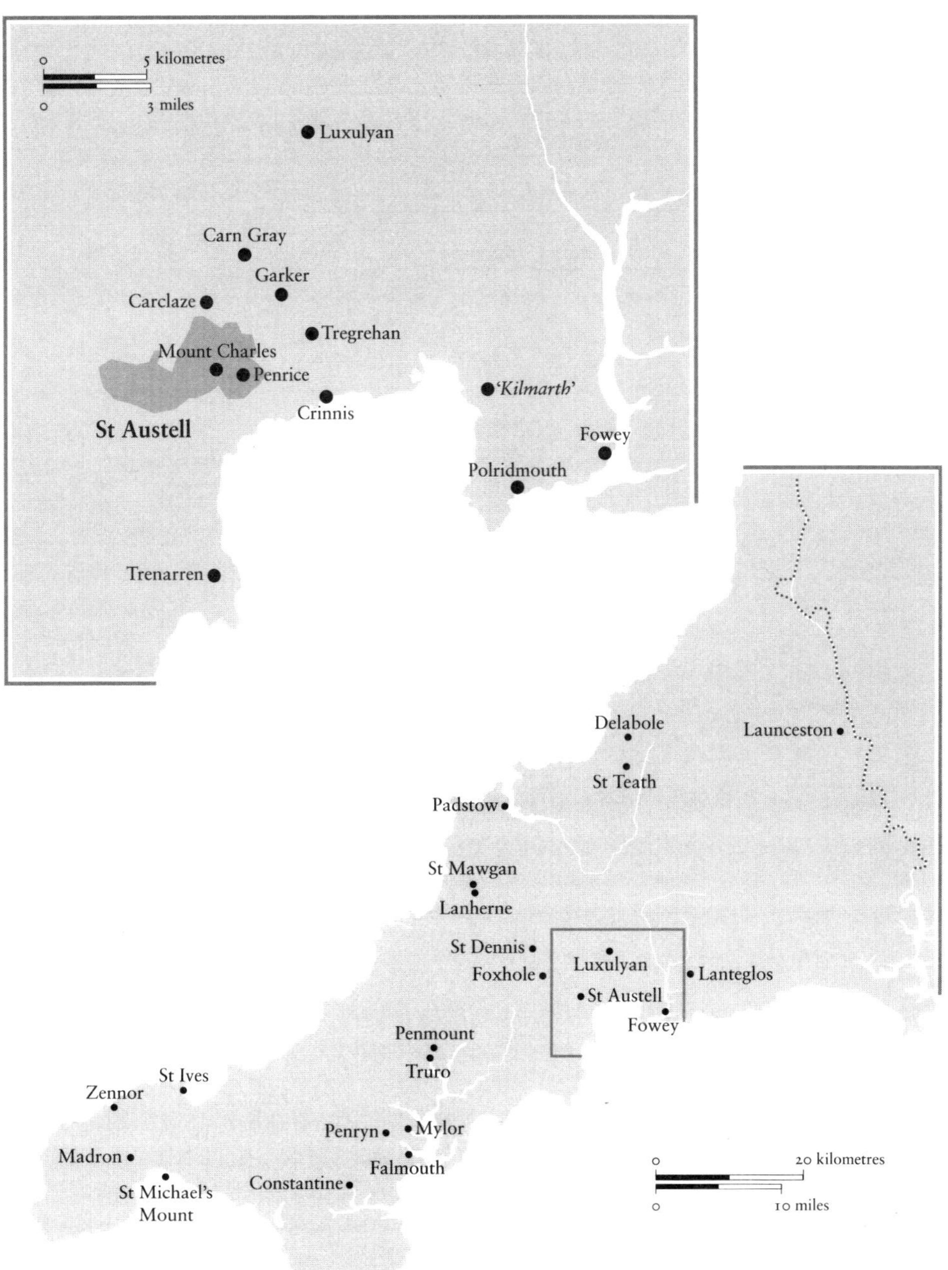

o
5 kilometres
o
3 miles
Luxulyan
Carn Gray
Garker
Carclaze
Tregrehan
Mount Charles
Penrice
Crinnis
'Kilmarth'
St Austell
Fowey
Polridmouth
Trenarren
Delabole
Launceston
St Teath
Padstow
St Mawgan
Lanherne
St Dennis
Luxulyan
Foxhole
Lanteglos
St Austell
Fowey
Penmount
Truro
St Ives
Zennor
Penryn
Mylor
Madron
Falmouth
Constantine
St Michael's
Mount
o
20 kilometres
o
10 miles

The Twenties

The thinnest of the decades for Rowse's journals was the most eventful for the development of his personality – when it opened he was a clever, impressionable teenager. When it closed he had established himself as a formidable left-wing intellectual, unusual in the fact that his antecedents were as emphatically working-class as his tastes and pleasures were those of the educated bourgeoisie or even the aristocracy. His election to the Fellowship at All Souls in 1925 was the hinge on which his life turned. It is from that moment the journals begin to assume a tone and a manner that, for all their changes of mood and matter and opinion, persist to old age.

It seems appropriate, therefore, to open these selections at that point. Some flavour of the earlier years is conveyed by the brief extracts I have transcribed from the pocket books, or notebooks, in which throughout his life he jotted down thoughts, impressions of people and places, of books, sensations, ideas to be examined and followed up in the journals themselves. I have not expanded abbreviations. The first extracts, dated 1921 and 1922, were written at St Austell.

18 December 1921

The gas lamp outside our door has been lit again for the first time since 1914. There was great jubilation when the lamplighter arrived at teatime. Lennie skipped about and did his best to persuade father to come out into the court and have a look . . . To me the lighting of the lamp meant much more than conveniency [*sic*]. I thought of the years that followed 1914; and all that the war means the relighting of our lamp this evg. has meant to me.

Tomorrow I go to Truro to sit for the County Scholarship. The examn. will last from Tues. to Thurs. I can't say that I have worked at the syllabus at all thoroughly. My knowledge of Eng. History is sketchy. I probably have a better knowledge of Eng. Lit. than most boys of my age – but that is saying v. little; while my reading of Ruskin has not been extensive. Still – what will happen if I *don't* get the scholarship, I can't say . . .

[*ALR goes to a choral concert in Truro Cathedral and attends a W.E.A. lecture*]

Tuesday evg. was one of the happiest I have ever spent. I met Mr Bennett[1] at Treleaven's Restaurant and we had tea together there. We had heaps of things to discuss and made the most of our time, staying I believe over an hour. We went on to the Technical Schools where T.C.B. was to give a lecture on the Renaissance and the Reformation – one of the course he is giving for the W.E.A. Afterwards we stayed so long discussing points arising from the lecture that T.C.B. had to run to catch his train! Most of those present were socialists and I felt much at home . . .

Thurs. aftn. I spent in Jordan's bookshop. Boscawen St. from here looks something like Broad St. Oxford[2] from Blackwell's. I stood on the steps of Jordan's and tried to persuade myself that it was Blackwell's and that Boscawen St. really was the Broad. I intended to go home to St A. by the 3.15 train but the books in the upper rooms of the bookshop held me . . . My interest was chiefly in the Poetry and Cornish books . . .

1. Workers' Educational Association lecturer.

2. Rowse had visited Oxford to sit, unsuccessfully, for a scholarship to Exeter College.

3 January 1922

I've done nothing for the morning except weigh flour and do housework for mother. Yesterday I read half of *Mansfield Park*. I hope to finish this aftn. and evg. Did not think I shd. appreciate Jane Austen so much. I remember *Sense & Sensibility* and giving it up before I'd read a quarter of it. With *Mansfield Park* I was not enthralled but it interests me to trace the satirical outlook of the authoress upon society . . . The Bertrams, the Grants, the Crawfords, even Fanny Price never seem to get down to the depths of life in the way that Rochester and Jane Eyre do. All my admiration is for Charlotte and Emily Brontë. I have just interest in Miss Austen, and that has only developed recently.

[*Much pain, sickness, sleeplessness, the beginning of ulcers*]

10 January

Again I am sitting up late to write a short entry in my diary before going to bed. Father and I have been to a mtg. of the Labour Party in Carclaze Council School. Came home about an hour ago, had supper and discussed the meeting and the speeches. Father is still reading a pamphlet issued by the Lab. Party in 1920, 'An Appeal to the British Nation'.

I come away from a mtg. such as that held tonight in deep despair. There wasn't a soul except Joe Harris, the chairman, Millman the organizer *and myself*, who understood a thing about the Labour programme, the cause of the present state of affairs, or the necessity for the altering of our social system. I watched the face of each man that came into the room; and upon every one was an expression of sheer, stupid ignorance. Perhaps there was one man who had a faint glimmering of intelligence and whose face was less blindly stupid than the rest – and he said he was not converted to the Labour Party! Oh God! How can these people grumble about the present state? They won't make one move themselves and there is such work to be done – such leeway to be made up! [*repeatedly endorsed in later readings in 1935 and 1938*]

Oxford, 1928

To the bank in the morning sun. The light v. sharp and clear upon the busy street. The Midland Railway carrier van halted with restive horses chafing before the Home & Colonial Stores. Mrs Rawlinson[1] rushes by in a fury,

1. Wife of a Christ Church don.

pushing her perambulator like a weapon, into Webber's Drapery Stores. There is a sudden rush of people along the squalid pavement. A dog fight on the other side of the road: a chatter of snarls, and all the people hurrying turn their heads to watch. Then the patter of a greyhound's feet, swift and clean, like rain, upon the roadway.

A young man pretending to be a Tory is either a poseur or a nincompoop. No: there is a third possibility: he may be an intelligent young man, with a keen eye to his own interest.

To Corpus with Henderson:[1] a storm of wind and rain while I watch from a window looking on to the garden. A volley of wind bursts upon the trees and strips them of their leaves driving them in a cloud across the grass. Then for a second it looks as if the tall trees twisted in the wind were gathering their skirts of a myriad leaves around them, as they go swishing in great waves at their feet . . .

Now everything still in the garden: and for a moment just now there was a lovely cross light, bright lemon colour cutting across the roofs and into the garden's murky greenness. Glowed for a moment athwart the trees and on the summit of the scarlet creeper: then passed.

[France,] 1928

N. portal of Chartres. Tympanum of W. side the scene of Solomon deciding between two women, appealing for possession of baby. One of them, a brazen strumpet welcoming the suggestion; the other full of dejection and grief at the thought of the baby being killed. Behind Solomon, who is seated on throne, an attendant is drawing sword from its sheath. Central pillar between main doorway of portal. This portal richer and more original in design than South, probably later. The impression of incredible richness of plastic imagination heightened by foliage designs on flat stones at base of capitals and perfect luxury of foliation inside the canopies over the figures.

The chatter of jackdaws among the buttresses mingles with the steady drone of an aeroplane flying high. A group of children in a high window under a gable in the Cloître Notre Dame. The silver chime of the clock beyond the old Bishop's Palace. People passing on their eternal rounds.

A perfect picture in the clear morning light of the spring. One stands on the S. side towards the E., beyond the transept and its portal: there is the charming little chapel of S. Pyat, beyond the apse of the cathedral; its lines v. slender and aspiring and with bright sunlight cutting the silver-grey stone

1. Charles Henderson, Fellow of Corpus and one of ALR's closest friends: the early patron of Isaiah Berlin.

with darker lines of grey shadow. The buttresses lead the eye up to the steep slope of the chapel roof the red irregular tiles speckled with green lichens gleaming in the sun. Above, the sky of a clear blue and all the clearer as it appears through the fresh green foliage of the young beeches of the terrace.

M. Houvet[1] in his little den by the chapel of S. Pyat, who only cares for the 12th and 13th centuries. The C18 altar of the choir 'Mais, c'est ignoble'. His views on altars and grief at a new one going up. 'C'est du XXme siècle. L'autel, c'est une table: ce n'est pas un monument.'

Dublin, 1929

Gathering at 84 Merrion Sq.[2] Friday tea.

Lennox Robinson[3] just going, a little hot and bothered. Katherine [properly Katharine] Tynan[4] apparently has been running down the *Observer* and St John Ervine,[5] esp. latter for his atrocious book on Parnell. Atmosphere a little strained. I had just time to shake Robinson by the hand and compliment him on his play. At this he cheers up and goes out, pricking up his ears.

K.T. goes on against T. P. O'Connor and Tim Healy. They had always been taken in England to represent all that was noblest and best in Ireland. Then a long rigmarole about T.P. and Tim Healy getting up some book on the basis of Parnell's letters, these letters however having been saved from getting into the hands of T.P. by some words K.T. spoke to Mrs O'Shea's daughter[6] who possessed them. What a good thing it wd. be to have them.

AE seized the opportunity to turn the discussion away from the polemical into the general. Such letters written by a man who falls in love in middle age are usually pretty poor. He has, just like a boy making love, to go

1. Author of the standard monograph on Chartres.
2. This describes a typical gathering in the top-floor office, in Dublin's handsome and always fashionable Merrion Square, of 'AE', pen-name of George Russell (1867–1935), poet, editor of the *Irish Statesman*, mystic, painter, (the walls were covered with his representations of Irish *sidhe* or fairies), conversationalist and host – here and at his home in Rathgar – to literary Dublin.
3. Lennox Robinson (1886–1958), playwright and manager of the Abbey Theatre.
4. Katharine Tynan (1861–1931), author of 105 novels and much else, was a life-long friend of AE and of W. B. Yeats. She would object to Parnell's letters being used by the journalist and newspaper publisher T. P. O'Connor (1848–1929) and the politician and first Governor-General of the Irish Free State Tim Healy (1855–1931) since both had turned against Parnell over the O'Shea scandal in 1890 (when Captain William O'Shea won a divorce from his wife Kitty on the grounds of her adultery with Parnell), and because of what many considered their later abject accommodation with the English government.
5. St John Ervine (1883–1971), playwright, critic and biographer. He settled for the rest of his life in Devon shortly after this meeting.
6. The issue of the adulterous affair with Parnell.

through all the same process and express himself, saying all the same things without any barriers; and all his greater experience and his cleverness don't make any difference, or it any easier for him. Then it reads so ridiculous, you know, afterwards. There were Shaw's letters to Mrs Pat Campbell, did you ever read them? Well here you had a man fifty or fifty-five pouring himself out, and what nonsense it sounded like, you know.

Then he went off into a long and lovely and rounded digression on Tolstoy. How it all went by contraries. Did you ever read Tolstoy's diary? Here you have the strangest man in Russia, you know, entering his notes: the morning wasted; cards in the afternoon and then dots which they say mean women, and at night, the day wasted; must do better with my life. And so, always this swing from one to the other.

A curious rat-looking little man, very dirty and intelligent, called Hegarty, interrupted to say that Tolstoy was always like a Salvationist in continual process of Conversion.

And all the time K.T. daughter or daughter-in-law, chattering in the best society style, modelled on the Asquiths and the Bowras. Very hard and glittering, unemotional and throaty; cutting, but not going anywhere in particular, rather like a razor being slashed about by somebody without much rational control.

Then Jimmy Goode, charming man comes in, and takes the burden of the female off me.

Mrs Hinkson[1] becomes sentimental and starts 'AE you're a dear man: and I want to say . . .' holding his hand, while he blinks a little, large and elephantine.

[*Two pages follow on the prevalence of spitting in Dublin; among both sexes*: 'an old woman, coming over the bridge in the Green, who hawked with a voluptuous fullness and spat several times with great velocity and directness, to her evident relief and satisfaction'.]

Last day of October, 1925

Here begins the XXth volume of my diary; that is nominally the XXth, for the first half-dozen volumes having been burned, this must actually be somewhere about the XVth.

Not that I am as careless about this diary as that would suggest: but for the last few weeks, my not having a fresh book in which to write the impressions of the moment when the old volume was filled out, has given me a feeling of dissatisfaction. And during the last few days, when I have

1. Katharine Tynan: she was the widow of H. A. Hinkson, a barrister.

been freed of both All Souls and illness, I have felt a real need to continue this diary.

This evening, now that I have time to fill up the gap since my last entry in the old, I am too tired to do it. I spent the morning with Burn[1] and lunched with him; all the afternoon and part of the evening with David Cecil. David told me of his plans for a story he is going to write; I was thrilled about it, as he told it me this evening, walking up and down the Broad opposite Blackwell's. When we went in and stayed a long time, I suddenly found he had gone. Queer to find he had flitted in that way!

Later:

I have been revived somewhat by supper, and can now go on to some of the things that have long been overflowing. My head has been bothered by the old doubts whether this awful concentration on academic work, which has been going on unrelieved for the last two years (and with especial emphasis for the last eight months), will not end in the atrophy of what is imaginative in me. So few have been the poetical ideas and images that I have had time for; and so much thought has been devoted to pure theory on history, economics and art. I am reading Trotsky's *Literature and Revolution* with the ardour of a disciple; that puts the finish on to my own thoughts on the matter. The materialist conception of history obsesses me; my historical theories come in and colour whatever I am thinking about. My friends must be bored at my bringing this into all discussions; however, I can hardly help myself. Is it that I am mentally tired out, and should have a rest? I have no doubt that I have found a philosophy which gives me intellectual satisfaction; but may it be that the effort of construction (for that's what it amounts to: I have to piece out each step for myself; there is no guidance to be had, but only stray suggestions which have to be made consistent and systematized), is it too great a drain on one's energy? Perhaps I ought to have a rest; but how to do it? My brain goes on and on like a steamroller, and there's ever more stones in the way to crush into order. There's German and Italian to learn; philosophy for me to read; my own lines of historical criticism to work out; besides the old schemes for poems and writings, which though overlaid have always been nearest my heart. Never more than now when it is becoming inevitable that I should throw in my lot with the historians, and when I have been straining every nerve to make myself competent as a historian.

There is an odd sequence of ideas which I must work at. In the vacation

1. A. R. Burn of Christ Church. Subsequently Head of Classics at Uppingham and author of works on Greek history.

when I used to sit all day working at my bedroom window, the same people passed and re-passed day after day in clockwork regularity; the insurance clerks, the barber, the shop-girls, and last the roadman. What makes life bearable for them? The same round year in, year out, like mother drudging in the house for the family (but then she has had her glorious hour of crowded life; I wonder if she felt that life was an anti-climax after that all too short a time at St Michael's Mount. What a story it is: When I first heard of it, my head swam for days; now at times, it seems as if such a story in our family was meant for me to make something out of it.) I have a thought for a Sonnet On the Progress of All Men towards Death; and, more rare and infrequent, the idea of an Ode on Love; for I have at last seen that it is only love that gives meaning to life. A strange approach to Love after all, for I have never been in love, only struck for a time with the beauty of some one particular face. Sometimes I feel that I shall go through life without ever feeling what love is. But there is this rarer approach – an intellectual conception of love, *amor intellectualis dei* – which might lead from philosophy to a reconciliation with life itself. I know what a struggle it would be to follow that path; and I am not really sanguine that things will take that course. But I can at least be proud of having caught a glimpse of it.

I have never put down anything like this before. But I talked about it for the first time to David Cecil this afternoon; he said something that has made me think highly of him. He had felt really afraid only on realizing the horror of Death; but if he cared very much for someone, it made him feel that he wouldn't be afraid to die. There's a curious connection between Love and Death in his mind, and Death and Love in mine. I felt after my talk with him (the first time I have ever gone so far beneath the surface) that I had at length come to appreciate for myself the ideas that inspire poets like Shelley, and have never before meant anything to my mind save coldly and externally.

Wednesday, 24 February 1926

No mood of indignation tonight, but a feeling of regret for Edgeworth.[1] (D. H.) Macgregor's remarks about the Marshall–Edgeworth correspondence brought his image back to me, as on that afternoon walk in the Parks when the snow on the ground was thawing. That remote look in his eyes, as if lost in thinking of something else and conversation with me was a game which could be carried on by rote, it had been played so many times before with others. I recognize that my acquaintance with him was no more than

1. F. Y. Edgeworth (1845–1926), the senior Fellow living in college. He pioneered the application of mathematics to the then new study of Economics.

most other people's. Though all the people who came here to his funeral had their tributes; I have at least been faithful: not a day has passed without some thoughts of him, since we buried him in that quiet corner in Holywell cemetery.

I miss him in the evenings in Common Room, for his was a mind I had more in common with than any of the others there now.

Old Arthur Johnson in the buttery last Wednesday held forth on the difficulty of approaching Edgeworth: 'I could not put up with the indefiniteness and the indecisiveness of him; never a straight answer to a plain question.' Edgeworth was as young as our own generation. He always left much to be inferred from his remarks; because his attitude was not explicitly stated in so many words, it didn't mean that there wasn't a definite outlook. But it was always subtly suggested. He loved to see the duplicity in things, he told Jacob.[1] I always *felt* that I knew where he stood with regard to an opinion, after he had stated both sides and come to no obvious conclusion; on some subjects, it might even be said beforehand what his real opinion would be.*

There must be hundreds of his letters abroad in the world. Keynes told Macgregor[2] that for ten years he had received almost a daily letter from him; and scarcely one without some gem of expression, some original phrase. I hope these letters will not be lost to the world, any more than that Edgeworth's injunctions that his papers be burned are construed to mean his correspondence too. There is a whole budget of Marshall's letters apparently, lasting over years; and Edgeworth had put them in order, docketed them and labelled the parcel 'Marshall on himself'. And mighty enlightening, Macgregor thinks them. It is a pity that these too should be turned into ashes.

Monday, 1 March

What an amazing new experience: Past midnight, but I must write a few words. David Cecil took me out to dine with Lady Ottoline Morrell at Garsington Manor: an extraordinary woman and an extraordinary place. We arrived in a dark courtyard, with the house standing up high and black, and a line of tall trees before the gateway. Deep country stillness everywhere: it could almost be breathed. The house a paradise of beautiful things and

1. E. F. Jacob, Fellow of All Souls and subsequently Chichele Professor of History. A medievalist who had briefly tutored and encouraged Rowse as an undergraduate.

* He was very positive against Marx, for example.

2. D. H. MacGregor, academic economist who held a chair at All Souls. ALR usually, and correctly, gives him a capital 'G'.

smelling of some rich aromatic scent. The lady might have been out of a Pre-Raphaelite romance: a striking pallid face with strange eyes and bronze hair; a flowing grey satin dress, great pearls in her ears and round her neck. What an evening to sentimentalize over! The people she knows and has known – a step down when it comes to inviting me. But I admire her as much as I am struck by her; of all people really sincere about the war, horror of which is the one fixed star in my firmament.

Late at night a long talk with David about his family, which interests him as how can it fail to do?* And many curious things I never knew about the end of the Coalition and the Tory defeat in 1923.

Monday, 8 March

A hurried weekend in which I have been so busy that I am quite upset; have spent the morning in my room with a thick head and in a state of nervous indigestion. Yesterday, rushed about abominably. Breakfast with a crowd here; then spent all the morning drafting rules with a Labour Club committee; lunch with Pares[1] and his mother and Roger Mynors[2] of Balliol; in the afternoon a walk through Magdalen and round the Parks with the Archbishop of York, most interesting talk but exhausting; bus to North Oxford and tea with the Joseph Wrights and another crowd of people; hurried back to my rooms and on to the hotel to find Booth and Jessop. Unsuccessful, I ran on to New College Chapel where they were; arrived in time to hear the anthem; an enormous dinner with two meat-courses at the Eastgate, and a rush to the Cathedral to hear Wood's Passion Music. I sat it out as long as I could and then hurried out to be sick. What could be more ignominious than to be sick in a cathedral?**

So I'm done for, for a day or two. In this state I don't look forward to going abroad as I ought. I only feel like going home; two months is long enough to be away from home, and just about now I want to go back and refresh myself at Carn Grey and Trenarren and all the places that seeing Booth makes me think of.

* *All* Cecils are interested in their family.

1. Richard Pares, ALR's closest friend at All Souls. Perhaps the most brilliant and irreverent of the young Fellows of his time.

2. Classical scholar with remarkable breadth of reading in medieval and Renaissance Latin literature. Subsequently held chairs at both Cambridge and Oxford.

** Once, later, I was.

Thursday, 11 March

A day in which I have again been far too busy and bothered; but at last I feel calmer in mind because a decision has formed itself. I will give up Italy this vacation, and not venture any farther than Paris. And I won't set out until my piece of work on History[1] is finished; and that means spending a fortnight here. It's hardly worth the expense to go to Italy for so short a time; and I'd prefer my first stay abroad to be in a country whose language at least I know. (Not that I'm likely to understand it when spoken.) Three weeks in France ought to provide the required break between terms, and without the hurry and bother of journeys beyond.* The summer will be time enough.

Canon Cooke has sent me a photo of the lovely Parmigiano drawing of Christ in the Library at Christ Church. I have set it up on top the bookcase and against the panelling: it serves as a spell against the ghosts and the loneliness of this place.

Friday, 12 March

The end of my first term's teaching this morning. I celebrated the occasion by a little lunch, to which my last batch of St Edmund Hall men were bidden. Quite affecting when we came to take leave of each other; I believe they enjoyed my tutorials, or they wouldn't have thanked me for them as they did. My teaching has been a real success, and I have taken to it like a duck to water; but it exhausts one's brain as well as developing it, and I must be careful.

What a day yesterday was, through those innumerable engagements which tired me out. I must rest just a little: not much more work today, but a walk. Received a cheque from Christ Church this afternoon; and went out and bought exultingly Tawney's long-awaited *Religion and the Rise of Capitalism*.

Monday, 16 [?15] March

Am just back from another visit to Lady Ottoline Morrell at Garsington; the place beautiful by day as ever by night. A glorious walk, full of sensuous impressions and thoughts, from Cowley village onwards. Along that road was my first walk with Wadleigh,[2] my first Sunday in Oxford. Beyond

1. *On History* (1927), ALR's first (very brief) book.

* What a pity to have forgone Italy then!

2. Undergraduate friend at Christ Church. Subsequently prosecuted in the Alger Hiss case. See Alistair Cooke, *A Generation on Trial* (1950).

Cowley it hasn't changed, but Cowley itself has sprung up like a mushroom in the night. I don't remember Morris's immense motor works there three years ago; now they are being made still more vast; a great field was being ploughed up by steam-engines and foundations of stone and brick being laid. On the other side of the road a motor tractor was harrowing. What extraordinary activity: men going in and out of the works and hundreds of cars, the cars being tested on the roads; the men looking like children playing with toys. One wonders how long the mushroom growth will last, compared with what goes on on the other side of the road. The fields were full of birds; I have never noticed such a chatter of chaffinches and rooks; in the marshy places big birds flying together in couples and chaffing each other with their wings and whistling cries, they must have been lapwings. As I drew near to Garsington men were working in the fields, a little beyond the wood.

A much-occupied weekend, what with J. H. Thomas[1] staying in college, reading Tawney with excitement, and my talk with Lady Ottoline. Of Thomas we didn't see much, though I should have liked to talk of Labour's prospects and of Easton Lodge and the Trade Unions. But Coupland[2] kept him much to himself, while J.H. played bridge with ardour and drank an incredible amount of whiskey, on Saturday night. On Sunday night he spoke at the Raleigh Club, and I made an effort to hear him. I broke away from dinner, and in my haste to approach the Warden, got to the door in front of the Sub-Warden. One would have thought an elephant had trodden on the Sub-Warden's toes. Not that the old things really take these customs any more seriously than I do, at bottom; but it is curious to behold the mummery with which mediocrity surrounds itself. I was thunderously impatient at it, but went to J.H.T.'s meeting all the same and without permission to leave.

Thomas was not at his best; but he struck the right note for a club of imperialists and they all got on very well together. I asked one or two respectable questions; but refrained from asking whether Thomas's aim was the restoration of prosperity to capitalism or its reconstruction. He is not even confused as to the two: he stops at the first. His lack of education or a disciplined mind has made him a mere opportunist. Any conception of a general objective has escaped him. Impressive in his mastery of detail and knowledge of the facts of the job, he has been forced into a false position by his lack of real intellect and character. He looks rather like H. G. Wells, the incarnation of the common.

1. Labour Cabinet Minister, subsequently disgraced over a Budget scandal.
2. Sir Reginald Coupland, imperial historian.

While sitting in that lovely panelled parlour at Garsington, I read the poems of Padraic Pearse, revelation of a nobler mind.*

Saturday, 20 March

A clear spring morning with a high wind; not much work to be done, for this is the morning of Cleary's[1] funeral. I have just come back from chapel where the coffin is resting, the chancel steps covered with flowers. Sad to think that Cleary's dead: almost as hard as to believe that Edgeworth is. Sharp** and I were sitting together in the Common Room, when the Manciple[2] came in and told us how Cleary had had a stroke outside Brazenose, and died almost immediately. With what distant respect I used to watch him at his job as Porter when I came here for lectures; he was at the top of his form during the week of the Fellowship examination, when he directed us all about with the air of the old Army man. He was only just older than father, which gives me a fearful thought. It will be strange to think of anyone else usurping his place in chapel in the evenings, lighting all the candles and ringing the bell for service at quarter past seven.

The essay on History moves forward but slowly, but as fast as it ought.

Afternoon:

Cleary's funeral over, I went for a walk round Magdalen and Meadows with Cruttwell,[3] who is a wonder. Last night he was at his best with Chelmsford about the origins and causes of the war, and the events leading up to it. It is a vast picture to fill in, the various attitudes towards the war which I am getting to know in conversation. Chelmsford let us in for a bit of secret history: the protest of the Indian government to the Mesopotamian Commission, which was never allowed to be published, nor were its criticisms replied to. Cruttwell must know an incredible amount about the documentation of the war: he told us about the agreement as early as 1909 between England and Italy (and Russia too?) about Tripoli and Constantinople.

Must return to my labour now, though I have been excited by thinking too much over Max Beer's guide to Marx, and by hearing Magdalen bells

* But sillier. 1981.

1. Head Porter of the College.

** Sir Henry Sharp, ex-Indian Civil Service, Secretary to the University Commission, and I were much alone together in those days when the College was blissfully empty.

2. College officer in charge of the servants and general administration. A kind of Regimental Sergeant-Major.

3. Fellow and subsequently Principal of Hertford College, mercilessly misrepresented by Evelyn Waugh. Author of a remarkable one-volume history of the war of 1914–1918.

ringing. They rang a peal of eight, which made me think of St Austell, and of autumn evenings in the lanes between Penrice and Porthpean. It made me almost too happy. Then David Cecil came to say goodbye. After that tea, and a hurried dash to a bookshop where I reconnoitred Joseph on Marx's Theory of Value.

Sunday, 21 March

I was displeased with yesterday's entry and yesterday's work. So many fine ideas besieged my head that it was hard to concentrate on the prosaic drudgery of the argument which is my booklet. But a sense of duty to it prevented me from working up the romanticism seething all the time under the surface. Today has been more satisfactory: in a whole day I have produced about three pages. What hard going it is: I never thought it would be so hard to write, after all the experience of this diary. But writing this is more congenial. A highly abstract argument freezes one; and yet I've plenty of ideas to go on with. There's a rarefied excitement in working these ideas into logical form: not a humanistic art. I fancy it must be the particular pleasure of B. Russell. So far I've just reached the Salute to Marx, or the Invocation of the Name of Marx; the difficulty is to keep from making it more than a Salute or Invocation. It would be fatal to write a whole excursus on Marx; it will probably be fatal enough to my chances of getting the House Lectureship[1] to have written at all. Perhaps that's unwarranted: I hope it is.

My head full of an essay on 'The Idea of a Labour University' (*à la* Newman); and a great edition of Marx in English (*à la* Jowett's *Plato*).

Thursday afternoon

After the morning's work, three hours in which I produced three pages of my little book, my afternoon walk around Magdalen and Christ Church Meadow tired me, and I went into St Mary's for rest and quietness. A refreshing experience in spite of the mustiness. I went down into the chapel which had been the old Convocation house; there were the old statues from the tower, St Edmund Rich[2] and St Hugh of Lincoln. A strange experience to live in medieval times; here am I writing an indictment of imaginative history, and yet there is the real thing. I must be careful to allow a place for it in my summing-up. I lingered in the chancel before the spot where

1. The History Lectureship at Christ Church (in Oxford slang 'the House') for which ALR was a candidate.

2. Patron Saint of St Edmund Hall.

Newman's mother is buried. It makes a curious impression on one's mind to linger in a place where the life of centuries has flowed through, but now is left high and dry; it is so obviously forgotten by our generation, and counts for nothing much. Yet the spire of St Mary's is enduring; I see it all day from my windows, and when I look up from writing there it is always. I am made uneasy by the gargoyles that crane their necks out from the coigns; I don't believe they are intended to be humorous; they reveal a haunted imagination. My final impression of the interior of St Mary's is depressing: all the tablets, bits of glass and sculpture, the gravestones that line the floor, are just the deposit of time that nobody cares for.

Thursday: no, some Saturday in mid-April

The previous entry was written in the middle of my labours at the *parvum libellum*; now I am in Paris, and have been here for a week.

A year ago I should have grasped the opportunity of a free evening to sit and write verses. But the desire to make a single line seems to have vanished. There's some undercurrent going in my mind, I don't know what. The feeling for words hasn't gone, but my real interest has shifted to ideas;* and not even as good or true in themselves, but as interesting or curious. It may be a good sign; this interest in theories and logical methods may denote development upon more masculine and independent lines.

In France just now there is much discussion in the circle around André Gide of the *nouveau mal de siècle*. In company I decry the stuff written about the modern malaise; but I know in myself, no-one better, what are the roots of this disquiet. But the gospel which I preach to other people must serve for myself. Some solution must be found; and I don't believe that a solution on Gide's lines is satisfactory. Would that it were; in some moments it would best suit my emotional inclinations. But there are other inclinations also; it will involve a strenuous struggle to develop them. How to develop them, when a stronger feeling than all others – that of my work in the future – runs counter to that development? Later on, my work in the world may run counter to my emotional nature. I am not attracted to women; nor do I believe that any women are attracted to me when there's anybody else about. But if what is distasteful is necessitated by my future, I must make myself accept that solution.

Anyway, what is the future to be? All the time I have been in Paris, I have been filled with such questionings. I have worked myself into a state where

* i.e. the historian forming.

it is impossible to enjoy what has been achieved. Has it really been done by concentration and willing the end? It has taken the strength and hope out of me, and here I am, with the steepest problem yet to face – my own wretched self. Two things are before me: either to face this problem of how to live my life as a man, or to take the line of least resistance. The one means great achievement and still more strain; the other to sit tight in Oxford, making myself comfortable with what has been already won and, instead of struggling to read and read until someday I become a savant and an authority. Everything hangs by this choice for me. Perhaps during these weeks in Paris the decision has been forming itself under the surface.

Friday, 23 April

Only a day at home, and already the sense of Paris is loosening. Till the business of the morning, I continued in the cocoon of the past three weeks; but all the bother of arrangements for tutorials and the score of things to be done before settling in again put an end to my dream of Paris. The pull that Oxford has upon the mind is so much stronger; in the course of the morning only, I have slipped back into the groove.

Late on Saturday night, 1 May

News of a general strike ordered for Monday; what to think, or still more what to do? It is a helpless kind of feeling to be here and doing nothing, when at last one ought to be up and doing. Not that one ought to take a cataclysmic view of things, revolution has been threatened before. What is impressive is the *solidarity* in the trade-union ranks; there seems no sign of its being broken. But the government appears equally determined; the preparations were already made for running essential services, and for drafting soldiers into South Wales. What are the chances of our taking over and running the mines? What are the practical prospects? We could get the coal out, but could we organize the distributing agencies, and rally sufficient technical ability to our side? Anything rather than a passive struggle, digging our toes in while the spirit of the miners is worn down by a lower standard of living during a long strike. We must have something to fight for: the mines and the railways would be our fighting lines. What would a general strike involve after four or five days, I wonder? Should we have to take over the government of the country? or would the possessing classes fight to the end?

I couldn't rest tonight in my rooms; I couldn't stand the talk in the

Common Room. There was Woodward[1] – vulgar petit bourgeois that he is, aping the attitude of the man of affairs, hoping that the general strike wouldn't come off through dry-rot in the trade unions. I went to see Ayerst[2] to get him to move the Labour Club and keep me informed of what the Committee will do in raising money etc.; then I went down to G. D. H. Cole's[3] house in Holywell, but hadn't the brazenness to persist in ringing at nearly 11 p.m.

Now I'd better write to my people and send them some money.

Wednesday, 5 May

The second day of the general strike: a curious silence over all the land and upon everybody, one can't say whether ominous or not. So far there doesn't seem to be any ugly temper in the people; but it is unthinkable what might happen if the general strike hangs on for a fortnight, and supplies begin to fail, while the government defeats the strikers bit by bit. That would lead to an appalling spirit in the strikers who remain. Perhaps the best sign is the solidarity in the ranks of the unions; if they can maintain their cohesion, there is less likelihood of head-on conflicts on both sides.

I wonder what they are thinking of us on the continent? The lack of news must be regarded as a dangerous and revolutionary sign; but what strikes us is the calmness and friendly spirit. One can't really tell as yet, or from the atmosphere in Oxford.

Last night the University Labour Club held a meeting to pledge members against blacklegging, and the Master of Balliol* came to make a statement about the attitude of the authorities. Two lots of rowdies from the House and Hertford came and held up the meeting for a long time. At first there was an attempt to keep them out of the hall; but when they came in, led by an enormous brute who turned out to be full of good-will, they shouted down Lindsay and sang 'God save the King'. After that, things went very well; except that Lindsay, tremendously on his dignity and white with indignation, made a very short statement and left.

Afterwards Ayerst made a clever humanitarian appeal to the divided audience, which got under the skin of the well-intentioned young men at

1. E. L. Woodward, historian and Domestic Bursar of the college, much disliked by ALR and Richard Pares.

2. David Ayerst, undergraduate friend at Christ Church, subsequently consigned to outer darkness for his review of ALR's *Politics and the Younger Generation* in the *Manchester Guardian*.

3. Academic economist, patriarch and patron saint of left-wing intellectuals between the wars. Co-author with his wife Margaret of a number of detective stories.

* A. D. Lindsay.

the back. I borrowed somebody's hat, went back and collected money from them for a 'special fund for women and children'. It had a wonderful effect on the House rowdies, who put their money into the hat and went out like lambs! I didn't catch the horrible little toad from the House called Phillips, who had instigated the business, and then went to report to the Proctors.

(Long interruption: first Le Bras* with whom I go out to buy paper in a shop; then to the Union to read the telegrams and the BBC bulletins which are all we have for news. The people in the Union lobby in a kind of gloomy silence. Then G. D. H. Cole to tell me about his successful discussions with the ecclesiastics: he's moving them via Lindsay and Sadler[1] and Father Waggett** to put pressure on public opinion to urge reopening negotiations. I am very well in such excitement: only wish at this time I were in the real centre of things. Now must rush to Exeter,[2] where I am reading a part of my book on History to a College society.)

Late on Saturday, 8 May

Still no news, and the situation still no clearer. People are settling in to the tug-of-war with a certain grimness. One hopes that the government's hand will be forced, but is the pressure of moderate opinion for negotiations likely to be strong enough? For our part, if the Labour movement as a whole has remained solid as we have here in Oxford, all would be well.

Our leaflet committee which was mainly the heir of my invention is proceeding well, and this evening produced No. 8 of its leaflets on 'Sir John Simon and the Strike'. I wrote also No. 2, on 'The Strikers and the Community': an argument on the issue of sovereignty, though not too explicit as it attempts to side-track the issue; and also No. 5 on 'The *Daily Mail* and the Strike', answering the argument about interference with freedom of the press. I had a hand in others, and made suggestions for the rest of the series. Not a bad contribution,*** what with meetings and the spiritual consolation I offer to the nervous who resort to my rooms. Tomorrow night I have to hold forth to the waverers in Webster's rooms at Christ Church. But how to get out of the Curtis[3] lunch at Kidlington and Mrs Beazley's[4] tea tomorrow?

* Gustave le Bras, Breton jurist, visiting at All Souls, later head of the Sorbonne.

1. Master of University College.

** A popular Cowley Father.

2. The Oxford college, not the Devon city.

*** All to what point? A waste of time. 1981.

3. Lionel Curtis, pillar of All Souls.

4. Wife of the Christ Church don who single-handed developed the study of Greek vase painting.

Today a hurried morning, looking up the Trades Disputes Act in the Codrington, pondering Simon's wily speech to reply to it; lunch with the Master at Balliol: the household seemed distraught. Lindsay himself fairly calm, though interrupted again and again by callers. Mrs Lindsay almost frantic, I feared tears, with two silent children, both charming and rather grave. What a big barrack the Lodge is: no opportunity today to think of Jowett and his parties. Outside the bay-window the chestnuts in full leaf and bloom; on the front door a notice of a united religious service for tomorrow.

Midnight has just struck on all the bells.

Wednesday afternoon

Just after lunch came the news that the strike had ended. A great relief: I feel insanely glad, though a bit tired; but we must wait to see what the terms of the settlement are before being rationally glad. The last two days have been a strain: unpleasantness in the air, and I got weary of the ceaseless barrage with which Holdsworth,[1] Swinton and Co. have defended the rights of constitutional government, etc. As if the precious heritage of Parliament was ever in danger from the leaders of the T.U.C.!

It has been difficult to make out a logical case for both Parliament and the T.U.C. – when writing pamphlets for the Labour Club, it exercised my wits to ward off such arguments as Simon's without giving the show away for the left wing. However the middle position, though uncomfortable, is honest enough, and not completely untenable.

This morning I made arrangements to be taught German during the interval of my pupils' absence; having taken the plunge, I had better persist. Went out, and joyfully bought several expensive books; Hancock's *Ricasoli* among them, beautifully produced.

A relic of the agitation of the last few days: the All Souls copy of the petition supporting the Archbishop's proposal for negotiations. The names of the signatories I sent in to Webster; but the copy itself I kept to obtain other signatures. Now that it has no further use I shall keep it in the end of this book, for posterity.*

Wednesday night

It's impossible to settle down to reading straight away tonight. I drank a glass of sherry and a glass of port at dinner. I felt jubilant both before and

1. Sir William Holdsworth, historian of English law.

* Where is it?

after G. M. Trevelyan's lecture in the Sheldonian – not during it. I am tired of people's obscurantism with regard to the obvious roots of party politics in economic interests; the fact that there was a certain cleavage inside the XVIII century governing class between the landed and the commercial interests seems to blind people to the class distinctions upon which political parties rested. They regard that governing class as homogeneous, and the divisions within it as one of opinion, not interest.

My little book on that score is well on its way now – part of this evening's good humour was due to that. It looks as if I must give myself up to intellectual work: staying here will make anything else impossible. If I am to declare myself, I must resolve upon some plan of work worth doing: perhaps after many other studies and books, a History of the English People, which shall really be about *them*.

Good heavens! I hear the newspaper boys calling out in the streets as usual!

26 May

Another disappointment: this time the most serious that I have ever suffered. It seems to close one path of advance to me; but perhaps that is an advantage.* Christ Church has appointed the younger Myres[1] to the History Lectureship over my head – and after having asked me to stand for it! It remains now to think over the future anew. It is obvious that I am not going to be *given* anything: I must extract it myself. That is something in common between my father's experience and my own. What has embittered him may serve to strengthen me.

In this matter I have been led astray by the temptation of money. Security is desirable, but not above all things. I should have been willing to give myself up to the academic life (for the next ten years at least), in order to lay by a surplus of money. Not that I had the slightest intention, in allowing my name to go forward at Christ Church, of committing myself to teaching all my life. The Christ Church dons may have acted wisely in choosing Myres: after all his father was a don before him at the House, and I am still an unknown quantity. But they may have done me a good turn too. It is obvious that I must never expect plums to fall into *my* lap; I had better buckle to now and make myself proficient in German and Marx, not in the kind of history that may be in demand at some lesser college here.

The plan of campaign then must be: first, not too much miscellaneous

* It turned out to be so.

1. Subsequently Bodley's Librarian, Sir J. N. L. Myres.

teaching; then, acquiring German and Italian, with tuition and travelling abroad; working up my research thesis into a book; other writing, not so much in journalism as in little books on 'The Idea of a Labour University' and 'History and Literature'. Cornish studies as a by-path, essays and portraits for example; not impossibly, a book of poems and one of selections from this diary. It will keep me fully occupied; though not immediately remunerative, will go towards a more enduring reputation than any drudgery as a tutor would achieve.

Friday, 28 May

Just before going up to bed, and in a rather more benevolent mood towards the House than has prevailed in my mind these last three days. As with all disappointments, the element of personal pique wears off quickly;[1] and I am left only vaguely regretful for prospective comfort. I know in my heart of hearts that the best course is not the easiest; and I have been providentially fortunate in my defeats.* It was a great advantage not to have got the early scholarships at Exeter and St John's I tried for.

I have been sitting near the open window, reading, and there's a fresh breeze up from the west; so I could hear the two bells chiming the quarters from the belfry at Christ Church, just as I used to hear them at night from my room when I lived nearby in Meadows. That made me a little sad to think I shall never go back there again. But I know that ultimately I shall not regret – as indeed I regret nothing, when I think of the future. It would have been easy, and quite fatal to the ideas and plans which are all I care for, to have settled down in the life of security that Christ Church offers. But Christ Church didn't offer that security to me; that makes the problem simpler.

Colleges sometimes make mistakes, however. Here at All Souls at our last meeting we turned down T. S. Eliot, for a Research Fellowship. Now that is irreparable, and unforgivable. The spectacle in Hall was a sight to see. The two bishops were anxious only for a theological Fellow, Headlam[2] consumed with impatience, and gnawing not only his knuckles but his whole hand. Several sensible speeches in favour of Eliot from Grant Robertson, Malcolm[3] and Brand[4]. Then came a thunderbolt from the blue, just when

1. In fact it lasted for several decades.

* This pattern went on all through life.

2. Bishop of Gloucester.

3. Sir Dougal Malcolm.

4. Lord Brand: both Malcolm and Brand had been among Milner's Young Men in South Africa who went on to successful careers in the City.

one might have thought Eliot had a chance in spite of his poetry. Doddering old Sir Charles Lucas[1] got up and said he'd never heard of Eliot before his name was brought before the College; that he'd read two poems the night before, and he thought them indecent, obscene and blasphemous; why such a man should be regarded with approval, or rather singled out for high honour he didn't know, and he hoped he had not lived to see the College make such an election. This obviously shook the Archbishop. The fat was in the fire over this. There got up in a row three high-minded and narrow-minded Scots, Lucas, Adams and Macgregor,[2] none of whom had read any of Eliot's work until that weekend, when they singled out a few of the more comprehensible but questionable poems as a text for moral denunciation. After that, there could be no doubt. On those grounds there is no literary man of distinction who could achieve a two-thirds majority of the College. And that's the way Oxford fails to exert the intellectual leadership beyond its walls which at many times in the past it has had.

9 August

It is a long time ago since the last entry; and my days have been so filled with a more serious affair, that the subject of the foregoing has passed safely into the middle distance of memory. My friend[3] was much in my thoughts for a fortnight, and then came with an awful suddenness another terrible illness. Looking back upon the previous weeks, I saw after the operation how they were leading to it, I felt myself sinking.

After the end of term, I went straight on reading and reading, taking no exercise in the day and cheating myself with nearly three hours' hard concentration upon Beethoven by way of relaxation in the afternoons. A pall of staleness hung over me, and yet I went on feverishly with my German and the half-a-dozen books I was reading at the time. It all has a curious fatality as I look at it now.

I am told I was fortunate to have come through.* It doesn't console me for the bitter feeling that my plans have been all postponed while other people are going ahead in health and happiness. This I feel the more keenly as I recover. Is this really going to be the end of my troubles, and the beginning of new health which will enable me to do all that I want to do in my life? Or am I to be hampered at every turn by ill-health which is the result of my efforts to make my way alone in the world?

1. Retired civil servant and historian of the British Empire.
2. All Professorial Fellows of the College.
3. Adam von Trott.
* Perforated ulcer, and a *second* experience of peritonitis!

10 August

Idea for a poem on recovering from illness: Return from the darkness that has revealed the treachery of the universe. The delicious sensation of living comes back, as I watch the sunlight on the wall. But in the next room a woman lies dying. Now and then in the watches of the night I hear the long-drawn sigh of agony and a stifled murmur. Not to her returns day or the hope of life renewed. The blinds are drawn; in the dim light of the room there is only the long slow stupor of deadened pain.

15 October

Three months after my illness, which was due to a duodenal ulcer. It must have been poisoning me for the last four years, and at last broke through into my stomach and nearly killed me. It was fortunate to be here when it happened, and to have the best surgeon and the best nursing at the Acland Home –

When I went home in the summer* I began a new volume of diary, without finishing the present, and now there's a gap to fill.

2 November

11.30 p.m. So I have kept my first All Souls' Day; and not so badly – I kept it with champagne and madeira at dinner.** And this entry is in despite of it, rather than because of it!

What a day: two hours of the morning spent in old-fashioned High Matins with a sermon by Headlam and Pontifical Low Mass, also by Headlam. A pathetic figure has glided in and out the doings of the day, Sir Arthur Hardinge[1] apparently a shadow of his former self. A brilliant man, not so old, obviously breaking up; they say, because of the death of his son in a cycling accident not long ago. I haven't been able to keep my eyes off him all day: from his behaviour in chapel this morning, wandering up to the altar to make his offering and then forgetting, kneeling down at the pew as if to receive communion, and on to the last thing in Common Room where he stayed, not drinking, with the latest, an inane look on his face and his sight so poor I had to lead him out. Kenneth Bell[2] played me a trick, though.

* Thus was the summer of 1926 spent, while my contemporaries, Connolly and Co., were frolicking abroad.

** Not the thing for an ulcer.

1. Elected Fellow in 1881. A distinguished diplomatic career, culminating in the embassy to Madrid, 1913–1919.

2. Famous History tutor at Balliol.

It's my duty to be last out of the room, and as I led Hardinge out K.B. was left behind. I came back to search and he wasn't there; I looked behind the thick curtains and screens and under the tables. Not finding him there I wondered whether I wasn't a little drunk. But no; my head is stronger than any strain I put on it in that way. (He had got out of the window.)

What I can't stand is the smoke-room after. The atmosphere is blinding and pungent; the chatter so loud as to be more intoxicating than all the drink. So I left them in their little groups in conversation; I felt outside. That is as usual; they like me well enough and I like them; but it's as well that I'm not lost in the mêlée.

Look at them: it's amusing enough. On the outskirts of one group I hovered for a moment: Gwyer, Spencer Wilkinson and Swinton[1] placidly on the sofa, with Kenneth Bell on the arm of a chair holding forth on the virtues of Balliol, while Feiling[2] makes up to him with a remark that the combination of Christ Church and Balliol (his own) isn't a bad one. Woodward sits by, waiting for the opportunity to corner Feiling and perhaps to sound him about Ayerst's election. It would be funny for them both to have Ayerst elected tomorrow, and that might quite well happen. The old fogies and crusted Tories are getting restive: Charles Fletcher[3] made a speech after dessert in praise of the great days whose memory they must cherish more and more as the challenge of a greater menace than they had faced in the past loomed before them. Another group: Alington standing up grandly before the fire and saying Floreat Etona to his audience; magnificent man to look at, very consciously Head Master of Eton and a prospective bishop. Wee Gee Macgregor, as they called him at Trinity, Cambridge, rushes impulsively into the circle, and treads upon the magisterial Etonian toe. And so on. It's not even really funny – as well to be outside it!*

3 November

After the comedy yesterday, a worse farce was perpetrated today. They did not elect Ayerst after all. So Woodward's little game, whatever its motive, succeeded; I am sure he had talked over the Warden and Sub-Warden. I have been consumed with impatience, but it has been interesting to see which Fellow votes which way. Oh these old men! The more I see of them the more I observe an implicit struggle between generations. The old ones have been so long in possession, with no middle generation to take their

1. General Sir Ernest Swinton, Professor of Military History, co-inventor of the tank.
2. Historian of the Tory Party; ALR's tutor at Christ Church.
3. C. R. L. Fletcher, historian and co-author with Kipling of a popular history of England.
* Always an Outsider everywhere.

places: they are all dead, in the old men's war. And so their day is unnaturally prolonged, and they have face to face with them only the youngest, without experience and without confidence.

The moral of the event is not to expect too much from men and institutions. I have been so happy in college since I came back from my illness, that I have been in danger of sinking into its comfort. It's as well to have an occasional jolt. Experiences of this kind will teach me not to set too much store by its doings, nor to care so much when they go wrong. In short, to use this place as a resting place for my body, while the things that I most care for I must keep to myself for the outside world.*

Monday, 8 November

David Cecil had come along to meet Osborne, and during tea David Ayerst came too. The interesting thing to watch was the gradual concentration of the talk along my lines; that was followed, as in a previous conversation with D. Cecil and Ayerst (which exasperated me the more), by a coalition to bait me.** It was like a captious offensive on their part, which I refused to draw on my energy to meet. Osborne explained it afterwards as the natural coalition of two good dialecticians to attack any position which was strongly taken up. It is a disadvantage to hold a system of thought with conviction, in the hope of building up other systems around it. Neither D.C. nor Ayerst cared two pins for the truth or not of what we were discussing, but were simply out to score points. Perhaps my anger was because, in those circumstances, the two did score.

Tonight I have been through another little storm of indignation: a mere triviality, not worth a rational man's thought. In the crowd of people dining tonight (among them that hog Holdsworth) more port and claret were called for, and I decanted claret into the port decanter, to be detected by Sharp, whose exquisite senses were a little shocked. Then people went on soaking port till nearly 9 o'clock, and I as 'screw' had to sit them out. These little things fill me with impatience, and reduce me to sullenness. Any pleasure evaporates along with my confidence.

* How oddly this has been borne out in the end.

** Natural enough. I was much too positive, full of ideas but, not good at expressing them, needed an interpreter. When Richard Pares came back to College, he interpreted the more original, less conventional ideas than these Public School men had.

Vienna, Easter Day, 1927

A full day after the easy-going week I have had – getting up late in the mornings, messing about in the afternoons and nothing definite in the evenings. But I've got to know my way about Vienna, down every one of the numerous little streets in the old part of the town; and often into the inner courtyards of the eighteenth-century palaces crowded together in the narrow *Gassen*. I've been over the Hofburg, paid two lengthy visits to the chief gallery, been to the Opera three times and into a score of churches. Reading: Baudelaire and a life of Baudelaire. But I've dropped keeping up diary in the ten days I've been here.

The plain record of the day then: out of bed at ten to nine, to get to High Mass at the Cathedral at nine. Taxied down to Stefansdom, in time to hear the Kyrie of Beethoven's Mass in C. The procession of the Cardinal from his palace across the street (the ground storey occupied by shops!) had taken time, and then dressing him up in white and gold in the sanctuary. It was a splendid ceremony, what with the music and the hundred lights and vestments, putting on and taking off of mitres.

The afternoon to letters, a longish one home; and to a hurried reading of the *Meistersingers*. All the evening from six to eleven hearing the *Meistersingers* under Weingartner at the Opera. I loved the Nürnberg night scene – something of the flavour of Shakespeare. Turning the corner into Hörlgasse I was solicited by a prostitute, for the first time in my life. The woman came down the side-street where I was standing in the shelter of the doorway ringing the bell for the concierge. She had large dark eyes like Hilda's.[1] We hadn't much time anyway, I was surprised by a second attempt and had rung again. I could scarcely find any words in German; as the door opened, she went off with a friendly 'Auf Wiedersehen'; I might at least have said she was an optimist. A wretched cold night to be waiting about at that bitter corner.

Tuesday, 19 April

I am spending my first morning at home since my early days here: in need of rest after two whole days afoot. Yesterday morning I spent in the Kunsthistorisches Museum, the Venetian Room brilliant with Easter sun lighting up one side; I watched the light passing across the pictures, gleaming and fading. At one moment of illumination, the Palma Vecchio 'Madonna and Child' was the glory of the room. Among all the Titians with their rich

1. ALR's elder sister.

colouring and impressionism, this picture stands out by its clarity and quietude. I sat there a long time before it, and made a few notes; but making notes on pictures is to realize the hopelessness of translating from one art into another. The humiliating feeling of one's life being too short and one's capacity too limited oppresses one; it becomes a nervous obsession, such as I have with books, obsessed with the desire to know everything. Never admit that there is a limit to my faculty of learning! Yet such a limitation is essential. Moreover, the ideal of universality is the greatest danger for the instinct of creation.

Len Tippett told me, as we were walking along the brow of the hill towards Carn Grey, that he had come at last (at twenty-three, say!) to recognize that there was a limit to his faculties; one of his greatest disappointments was to have to admit that he had no originality. In his research in physics he had been successful up to the point where a leap of the mind was necessary. Just where the leap with him never came was the point where with me certainty began. I have always felt that I could rise to the occasion. I have relied upon that in any number of examinations, and in the two critical examinations when it has been a question of life or death, in both my operations my mental attitude was just that before an examination, only with every faculty trained on the end of surviving. A similar confession that he had come to realize limitation of his capacities was made to me by *David Ayerst* during one of the *recurrent strains in our friendship*.

What is curious is the inversion of confidence that appears in me, and the reverse with regard to them. Len is the solidest and most normal of us; when he dreams, he is always successful and applauded. That's natural; his sexual vitality expresses itself in confidence in himself. But Ayerst is a problem; he outwardly has every confidence, and is thought brilliant. At the Labour Club, he was really more successful than I, I considered; at Christ Church, in the Essay Club and in undergraduate society he appeared at a great advantage over me because of his being at ease in society. He is at his best in company; it excites him to be the centre of interest. That ran counter to my plan; not that I wanted the centre of the stage for itself, but to influence other people. In private I could always bring him round; out of society and alone, he was nervous and without confidence; alone with me he could always be twisted round my finger. He hates being by himself, it is because of nerves that he has to go out into society.

Where he has this outer confidence, I have an inner; my happiest times are when I am alone, I think independently by myself, without help except that of reading.

But outer confidence is lacking. I am never sure of my effect on people; I cannot depend on it as I can on myself. I see clearly the part played by my struggle against circumstances and the sense of social inferiority. This uncertainty, I tell myself, will disappear with the justification by work. But there was also an inner uncertainty to be fought down, probably unconsciously, as the outer uncertainty had to be fought consciously. In my dreams nothing ever goes right with me. The form my characteristic dream takes is some ceremony, a service in church or a public meeting, at which I have to speak. In contrast with actuality, where I always have enough or too much to say, in my dreams I am without words. Much excitement and everybody waiting, I have only a few halting sentences or nothing at all. The feeling of dissatisfaction usually wakes me, while the dilemma is unsolved.

Some of the elements, including sex, I spot. But why it should come about in that way I can't think. Perhaps the dissatisfaction which permeates the half-light of my dream may not only be due to my *hesitation before the secrets of sex* but also to the long waiting for responsibility and achievement, where only I can find full development.

1990: The naïveté of this! But I was at least thinking things out for myself . . .

20 April

My days abroad are drawing to a close. So many times I have looked forward to going back to Oxford, often with impetuosity to be getting on with the plans I have in hand. Yet tonight, before settling down to a few hours' reading and writing (it is now ten o'clock) I went to my bay window and looked down the street to the square, where the trees are now coming into leaf and the dark mass of the Votivkirche, its spires gleaming in the night-lights, closing the view, and I felt that I don't want to go away from this place that I have come to care for: I don't want to give up my loneliness.

At the same time, I noticed the silence in the next room with an odd sort of regret. There is a high doorway between my room and the next; though it is blocked by cupboards on both sides, it makes for a certain intimacy between the inhabitants on either side. The woman who lived next door was an Englishwoman, who had spent most of her youth, until the middle of the war, in Falmouth. So there was a good deal to talk to her about, an interesting character to observe. Her father had been a Yorkshire manufacturer, who made money and retired at forty-two to Falmouth; after his death the money was divided between Miss V. and another sister, who built a house in Cowes and settled there. Miss V. was determined to see the world. An enormous woman with plenty of pluck, she is capable of fending for herself in most countries.

When I talked to her, I felt as if I had been bathed in ink; there hadn't been anybody to whom I could express everything for months; nor in the company of such a typical ordinary person for years. With this large creature I heard the tale of all her friendships, courtships, disappointments in love and failures to marry; all her prejudices, views about Society, the Working Classes, Strikes and diminished dividends; her acquaintances and relatives, their histories and circumstances: the story of her life was open for me like a Thomas Mann novel. Though I disliked the sentiments, I ended by having respect for the woman. When all is silent in the next room, in place of footsteps on the creaking floor or the snip-snip of scissors as she made a carpet for her new flat or the hoarse voice as she talked fluent German to her Viennese 'cousin', I think of her with a friendliness hardly in keeping with academic Oxford.

I can't transcribe her life here, it would take the rest of the book.

Today, one of the best of my days in Vienna, like one of those Munich days when I came back content with the experience brimmed into so short a space. In the morning, a longish visit to the Kunsthistorisches Museum, most of my time with the Velasquez, Rembrandts and Van Dycks. The afternoon to reading the *Nouvelle Revue Française*, and pondering the letter of David Ayerst which arrived the day after my thinking about him. In the evening a charming walk through the oldest part of the town between Stefansdom and the Post, where I sent off Hugh Walpole's *Jeremy and Hamlet* to her.* In one of the crowded squares, a sudden burst of song from a woman's voice at an open window high up above the street fell like rain on the sultry square. After posting my parcel, back into the sombre court before the Old University; its baroque front, built by Francis I and Maria Theresa, on one side, the University Church on the other. In the church a little crowd kneeling in the pews and before the side-altars. A bell began to ring, the agile figure of a young fellow pulling at the bell-rope before a window of the tower. Tea and papers in a café in the Graben. Last, an organ recital in Stefansdom; I haven't heard such playing since I last heard Henry Ley:[1] a longish Passacaglia by Max Reger, a Mozart Adagio, a Bach cantata 'Ich will den Kreuzstab gerne tragen', and the Toccata in F which fills me with exultation whenever I hear it.

* The woman on the preceding page.

1. Appointed organist at Christ Church while still an undergraduate, the outstanding performer of his generation.

Saturday, 23 April

A red-letter day in England now: St George's Day or Shakespeare's birthday, perhaps both. In the Hofburg this morning to look at the two treasuries, the Weltliche and the Geistliche Schatzkammer. In the first the Habsburg coronation jewels (except for a crown and a few items carried off to Madeira by Karl and Zita) and their robes are kept. An elderly woman with something English about her was showing another about the place. In passing we exchanged glances, her eyes weak and red. I went dutifully through the pleasant rooms, lined with walnut panelling, with the Habsburg paraphernalia in cases and wardrobes. I noted the little ribbon and cross of the Order of St Stephen which Maria Theresa wore every day. Among the robes was a splendid mantle covered with tongues of scarlet and gold, that of the French Ordre du Saint Esprit. The coronation cope of the Holy Roman Emperors, beautiful Saracen work, was made in the twelfth century at Palermo: far the most interesting artistically, the oriental pattern wrought in gold on a background of plum-coloured silk.

Going out of the first Treasury we were dubious as to the whereabouts of the second; there was my good lady again, nothing for it but to speak. She reminded me of Miss Maunder who used to impose on us at home with her ladylike manners. Overjoyed at meeting somebody from England, she began 'Sie sind kein Amerikaner?' She said, with no trace of foreign accent, that she had been English, though she wasn't born in England, and hadn't been there for nearly half a century; but she still liked to think she was English.

She had married an Austrian officer, who was dead, and she was living on a pension from the Austrian Government and what little she had saved. Had she found it difficult living in Austria all through the war? She said it had been; many of her best friends had been nasty to her, she could hardly bear it – 'it was so uncalled for'. I said as a comforter that the Germans living in England had probably had a bad time. She said the Austrians had turned like that in imitation of the Germans, for it didn't really lie in their character. The Germans after all were responsible for a great part of the trouble and for the war. William II she thought no better than 'a clown'. He was always making so much of the army. Then there was all this nationalist boasting. It was just what my New Englander thought, at the pension in the Rue Honoré Chevalier, and what Miss V. thinks too. I asked her a cruel question, which almost hurt her to answer. Did she ever go back to England now? No; she was a pensioner and couldn't very well leave Austria; besides she had no-one in England now, all her friends were dead. But she had a son, a doctor. I said, I owed my life to the doctors. This pleased her, not many had a good word to say for them. When I told her that her English was perfect, she was touched, she never had any opportunity to speak English now and often words failed her; but she would never forget it. She said what joy it had been to meet somebody from England again; I promised her that we would try to meet whenever I came back to Vienna.

A poor little friendliness that; for we know neither the name nor the address of the other, and I may never come back. At the gate of the Hofburg we said a few parting words and went different ways. From the pavement before the Michaelskirche I saw the couple going along the opposite side of the square, my friend in her light grey costume, walking along with short uneven steps. They turned the corner; and went for ever out of my life as I from theirs.

[Oxford,] 18 June

Last night at dinner an amazing story of the war was told us suddenly by a quiet little man, a guest. An Englishman who spoke German very well crossed the lines and got behind the German trenches. There he passed himself off as from another German unit which had been ordered away, leaving him in liaison. In the officers' mess he made a friend, a German who was very sympathetic: they liked each other and talked philosophy and literature. One night in the excitement of discussion he broke into English; and saw in a flash that he had betrayed himself and that his friend realized. When the friend turned his back, he shot him and made his escape back to the English lines. Now years after, he lives a life of remorse, wondering whether he ought not to have shot himself too.

Everybody was struck at hearing this and leapt to discuss the moral guilt involved. Woodward pronounced solemnly that he ought to have considered shooting himself, after performing his duty and bringing back information to the English lines. Moon[1] submitted all sorts of clever dilemmas, looking over his spectacles in the supercilious old man's way he has. Headlam, the Bishop, said that killing himself would not make it any better; he must live out his life and if possible live it down. The moral guilt was the same, and anyhow it was his duty to escape, though other means might have been possible. It sounded rum to me sitting next to him, to hear never a word as to the horror of killing his friend.

Here is my room with the things about just as he and I left it: they all have the impress of his personality. I had only just left him and gone into Common Room for a moment: when I came back the scene gave me such a feeling of immediacy and pain, I could have cried out in my dream.

1. Young Fellow of All Souls, about to join the Indian Civil Service in which he had a distinguished career.

A. v. T., his initials and his name[1] I shall always remember. He didn't want me to write mine: he said he couldn't forget it or All Souls. Perhaps he won't forget All Souls; but for the rest, I have no illusions, even though I am possessed by him. I know well enough by now not to expect, nor to encourage a dream. He has a beautiful head delicate as a girl, with a high arched nose, and fine texture of skin; red sensuous lips, with a cut on the side of the mouth, got in fencing to prove his masculinity; eyes deep violet and liquid, with long lashes and an expression of extreme sensitiveness.

This was only the third time I met him: no, the fourth. Once with Swinton;[2] twice here when he came to tea, and to lunch, then tonight. It was only then that I got to know him. He told me how glad he was to get my note, that he thought I had been disappointed by him and that he had made no impression on me.

The evening went in talking one each side of the fireplace. I had thought of him as charming and sensitive, radiant with his looks and, naturally, happiness. But no: he was everything except the last, and to an extreme degree. He has based his outlook on life upon his acute, even morbid sensibility, upon his feelings and intuitions of others. Personal relations are the stuff of his mental universe, which seems incredible to me. It made me go back a long way in my own emotions to achieve a state in sympathy and in tune with his. His defeatism for one so young was so difficult to comprehend, it took constant intellectual effort to follow him. I made it, for I was willing at last to fall in love: here is the one whom I have always hoped to find: someone who could go along with me the way I want to go.

I don't think I shall forget him, though I am quite prepared to get a card and hear no more. It is a sort of fatalism which I expressed to him; he called it cynicism, which he didn't approve. But it is better to have no illusions; I asked him if he had felt how the irrevocability of things put a price on them, that our talk had not the value which it *would* have when it was past and over, a creation of memory. He talked of life based on memory and desire: as if I didn't know these twin chords – how they echo through all my solitude!

I came back from my walk into the night with him, sick at heart to see the room with everything as it had been while we were together. My top row of German books knocked a little askew where he had picked out Rilke's *Stundenbuch* to read while I dressed for dinner; the cigarettes on the mantelpiece, the china ashtray by his side; the cushion fallen back over his

1. Adam von Trott zu Solz. For ALR's relations with this controversial figure, executed for his part in the plot to assassinate Hitler in July 1944, see my biography of ALR, *A Man of Contradictions* (1999). The bibliography of von Trott, already large, is still growing.
2. See page 25.

chair while talking; the reading lamp where I placed it to read a sonnet of Shakespeare's by. Already the surfaces of things have lost that impress which caught at my heart when I came in. He has gone: his image haunts my mind and adds only now to my feverishness. Only a card he has left: Adam v. Trott zu Solz, Imshausen, b. Bebra, Germany. Shall I ever hear of him again?

Saturday

I have lived all this day in a waking dream. Perhaps I have been more ill than I know; for apart from the thought of him which has never left me for a moment, I have felt sick-hearted and in a trance all day. When I got up, I couldn't eat anything: that was merely the effect of the fever; but my mind was held rigid in the frame of last night as if the hours of sleep had never intervened. I mightn't have been asleep at all: I woke from a night of stupor, to find myself just where I was when I went to bed, and the illusion of his presence as strong as ever. Perhaps, if I hadn't been ill, last evening would never have made such an overwhelming impression; even now it seems that I, so proud of keeping my head above water, have been submerged at last. He said once or twice last night that we belonged to a generation that was mad. When he told me all his doubt of himself, the lack of any purpose in living, or even any interest in what he does, he couldn't stand much longer like that. It is an impossible sense of defeat to have got hold of such a young man; he said one wouldn't have thought that that was his state of mind judging from his appearance. One certainly wouldn't.

I thought of him the first times we met as a typical young German, sanguine, enthusiastic for social service and other Student Christian objectives, with a passion for romantic literature, philosophy, all that. I've never been so mistaken in external appearances. He looks more like a child pleased to open his eyes upon the delightful world. And yet, there is a young man out of Dostoievsky – I shouldn't have thought that such existed outside of Russia and the books. He asked if I had read *The Idiot*, and wanted to tell me about it. Why he should be fascinated by madness? – perhaps it is something to do with his family. His father is an old man, and there has always been a strain between his father and his mother. He has no feeling for his home: he has lived away from it a good deal and regards his going back with fear rather than any pleasure.

Sunday: the dream continues, but not so feverishly. Indeed it could not go on like that, it was bound to burn down to a dull glow. I shall watch the process as has happened before: passionate possession becoming bearable as remembered emotion.

Yesterday in my solitary walk he was with me every step I took: I could see him out of the corner of my eye. His voice I tried to conjure up, soft with little hesitancies for words. I picture him at table here, bending over because of his tallness, or talking excitedly to Richard Hare* who was dazzled by him at lunch, and wanted to meet him again either here or in Germany. I met him first when Swinton brought him into the smoking-room, where he was a little stranded. People talked to him about his grandfather who was ambassador to Russia in the eighties; Moon couldn't think of anything to talk to him about, though he was the first to notice how exceptional his looks were. When I talked to him about Thomas Mann and Werfel his eyes lit up in sympathy.

I have never met such sensibility: he told me that his senses reacted immediately to the slightest changes in contact of feeling. He was much against the domination of contemporary German literature by the Jews: I was surprised to hear that Mann was a Jew, but Werfel and the Zweigs I know are, and Wasserman too. They didn't really represent the German tradition; a new German movement would have to take Goethe for its starting-point, the way of advance for the novel would be to learn from Dostoievsky. He admired Hölderlin above all – that would fall in with his fascination for madness.

Already I see it in the distance: I have written a few lines by which to remember him. On his youth and the innocence of spring, for he will lose perfection *if he lives*.

> Summer will come, and make you brave to war
> And harden you . . .
>
> And Autumn will lay a still, cold finger
> On your beauty, and dim your liquid eyes
> And suck the juices of your lips.
> This living dream you are shall see eclipse
> And I'll not mourn you in my waking state,
> Wide-eyed and frozen of heart.

These lines are the nearest thing to a dream-poem, and have more of him than the three sonnets I have been thinking of. He said that a poem after all was a dead thing: what was really alive was the experience in the mind.

Since I am already detached, I can collect every scrap that I saw, so that even if I would, I shall not forget him.

*

* Hon. Richard Hare; wrote about philosophy.

In Oxford he became fond of 'a little German girl', but what was so painful was that he could not retain his affection for her, he hadn't the stability. It began by being a dream, like every other of his loves for girls, and then he couldn't hold to it. It was always like that: he no longer had any confidence in himself, though it had meant a great deal to him to know her. He still believed that the only solution for his problem was desire: he had only to remain true to it and love would follow. I told him that there was nothing for him to complain about; he was beautiful, and women would always respond, he would be sure to find someone whom he could love and that would be the solution of all this uncertainty.

He said that he wasn't sure of himself, that he would ever find anyone with whom he would always be in love. Women would be attracted to him, there always were people who were; he found that a greater trouble than if they weren't. He seemed filled with impatience at it; they liked him for his looks; he never knew anyone to love him for what he was, when once the other really saw. I was bound to be happier, for there could not but be women who would be attracted by my mind, and what I thought and wrote. I said it wasn't what one really wanted: one longed to find comradeship in mind as well as personality, and I had never found the two united in any woman: nor perhaps would he. That was not what he wanted; he wanted to solve the problem of his own personality first, and to hold fast to desire was the only way for him. Desire and memory were the pillars of life; and once they failed him there would be no further purpose in living.

I couldn't make it out, nor can I now; he told me at the beginning he was disappointed at not having made an impression on me the first times we met. Perhaps he was treating me as the elder brother whom he is accustomed to rely on as philosopher and friend; anyway I took up the role.

– Though it's a Sunday night, I have stolen out between Hall and Common Room, to be away from all the chatter and alone with my memory, before it fades into grey common experience. I don't want to go on recalling our talk, it is so hard, though I was glad to find I remembered it exactly when I tried. I want to note how he looked: his eyes for example. Moon said he could tell from them he wasn't the ordinary intelligent young student but above all things reflective. They are a rare violet colour, but of a liquid softness I have never seen before. When he came up my stairs that night I was just going up to dress, I looked over the banister into his eyes turned to me brimming with light.

We walked together to Beaumont Street to return a book there and say goodbye to a man he knew. I asked him if he was going to stay, and he said not, he despised him! Why such a strong reaction I couldn't think. He said once or twice what a pity it was that we had met so late, it was only when he was going that he had come to know what there might be for him in Oxford. He had no use for the Student Christian Movement which had brought him to Mansfield College. At least that night he had found someone who stood to him in a 'pedagogisch' relation, when usually it was he who stood in that situation towards others. How could he make such a recommendation to others of the course they should follow, if he was so uncertain of his own? That brought another change of feeling and a return to the uncertainty from which he had raised himself on the basis of desire and memory. The irony of his recommending them to me of all people!

What was the secret of expression in writing, if salvation for him lay that way? I said that one had above all to grip the vision of what one saw in one's mind, and express it as simply and directly as one could. And that this took time. He said he never had tried to write; perhaps his family tradition or his school was against it. He felt the visual picture melting away from him as he tried to put it into words. He always associated certain thoughts and words with pictures of the landscape at home. A walk he takes across country comes into his mind with one train of thought; and a girl whom he used to know in Germany recalls a meeting of the ways in a wood near his home. A phrase of music my mind associates with him – the tune with which the Rondo begins in Beethoven's Op. 22 Sonata.

Is there much more to glean before consigning him to the slow oblivion of memory? Not much. He hadn't been taken in by Oxford, he was only just beginning to see what the place could be for one. He wondered if there wasn't some way of coming here for a full three years at a college, or of getting into English life for a time. I suggested the diplomatic service, or failing it to go on to the staff of a big German paper. He had been in London and tried to interest the *Frankfurter Zeitung* correspondent in him, in which he had completely failed. I tried to console him with 'he would always be received in English life as an Englishman'.

It was a vain courtesy, if nothing else, that led him to ask when was I coming to Germany. I would go if I could find in him the companion I have longed to find. He said that if I would come, we should have a good time together: a phrase he must have used to many others, no doubt. He would take one about and show one the place, he said. He strode along in the lamplight, the skirt of his full coat swinging in military fashion. I noticed his set profile, and a suggestion of fanaticism when his lip drew back from clenched teeth. There was a light in the window in Beaumont Street. He went up to it and, more Dostoievsky than ever, peered in: his great height was just above the level. His friend was there, and I said he ought to say goodbye and that I would go. So I held out my hand and shook his, which gave a limp unresponsive return.

Monday

I have watched the progress of this obsession day by day, as if it were a disease. And now at this late stage there is an odd phenomenon to record: today I can't recall his face however much I try. Another face comes in the way. A pupil of mine at St Edmund Hall is the same physical type, very tall and slender, full lips and long hands, and a fine fair head poised above throat and shoulders, though nothing of the variety and subtlety of expression of Adam: something rigid in his features, his eyes are cold and as much grey as blue. However this is the face that comes blurring the picture whenever I try to recreate the image of Adam. I wondered if this would happen: and behold it has.

It is as if the impression he had made had burnt itself out with its intensity. Perhaps it won't be long before his image has sobered down to the cool grey tone of experience; and I shall wonder at the state of mind which was ever induced by his passing my way.

Wednesday, 20 [? July]

Near midnight. Today there came a letter from him: it seems he has been filled with thoughts of me all these last days as I of him. A strange providence that led to that crossing of our paths: could I have known, or he, that we should make such an impression on each other? It seems incredible that it should ever have happened; it might so easily have not, and life would have been infinitely the poorer. At the moment it makes me happy to have my love returned in that undreamed-of way. When he wrote, it was for the same reasons that haunted my mind: he could not hold on to what he called the 'adventure' of the soul that night, and I the 'experience'. He feared he might forget it and asked for some picture to remember me by.

I can't think what happened to each other that night. We dined in perfect sobriety: we merely sat all evening each side of the fire, I a bit feverish with my cold and he with what emotion he was going through. He says in his letter, 'our souls loved each other' in that hour.

It's a distressing experience, which for my part I am prepared to go through with, though it can bring only unhappiness in the end. He can never hold to love for me: we can ultimately make nothing of it. So I have given him perfect freedom: he can rest assured of my devotion to that memory.

This forecast turned out true over the years ahead. He was a colossal German egoist: we were all his victims. All the same it made an *historic* experience in the end.

Oxford, Saturday, 23 March 1929

I begin my Irish diary, which I had not intended until I was across the Channel, here in the familiar room. Room where I have my comfortable things about me, room of such a strange story, and still more entangled with my own fate. Here I have passed hours of pain – even the physical torture of earlier years endears the place to me; of unhappiness and longing; of dull work and exciting, day after day; and at length two precious hours, worth a life to me, of unfulfilled desire afterwards fulfilled only in memory.*

Yesterday and today I went into Mansfield College. In the two months he spent there only once did I see him near the place: that raw day when I went to put him off dining that night, I was unwell with a cold. I met him coming along the road and we went back together along Holywell, to Blackwell's where we parted.

*Bruce*** and I got into Mansfield yesterday from the lane that follows the boundary of Wadham garden. A spring sky, clear and blue, with white clouds billowing across, the afternoon quiet and deserted. How empty the place was; I felt acutely the sense of his being absent from it.

Today too, Stonier (G.W.) said,*** returning up Parks Road, 'Let's go down by Mansfield.' At the gate we went in; I wandered inside the entrance hall, hoping there might be a list of those in residence this term. No, not the name I hoped for. From the steps one can see the twin towers of All Souls, as he must have seen them.

I wonder how much, if anything, they meant to him? (Adam was ambitious to enter All Souls.)

Dublin, Wednesday, 27 March

How I hate hotels! Here I am in a not particularly bad one, and yet its unhomeliness has driven me to bed at ten o'clock. However, I counterfeit comfort by ordering pen and ink, drawing the writing table up to the bedside, putting myself to bed, shoving my shoulders into my dressing-gown. The electric light is in the far corner behind the washstand; I've no room for anything and the window doesn't look out on St Stephen's Green, but on to a Dogs' Rest Home.

The dogs are rather comic, except in the early mornings when I hear them for hours in my sleep, grrr-ing and yelping and growling. They may be there for a rest, but they certainly don't take it.

* My first acquaintance with Adam von Trott.

** K. B. McFarlane.

*** A rather tepid reviewer on the *New Statesman*, who annoyed Edith Sitwell.

Holy Thursday

My initiation into Dublin began today. Quite early Mrs Fitzgibbon arrived, with fresh red face like the skin of a peach: an Irish type, for Mrs Adams has it, rather sharp in feature with intense grey eyes. She motored me down to the Parliament House, to see Grattan's House of Commons, with its marble floor encumbered with bank-counters, and into the House of Lords less altered in appearance. It's a fine room, eighteenth-century magnificence in small: a splendid fireplace, and tapestries of William III at the Boyne. At the dais-end a statue of George III; Americans make remarks about him, the attendant informed us.

To lunch in Trinity with Robin Gwynn,* a man of charm, his rooms in confusion and squalor. Hasn't he got a wife to put his rooms in order? Anyhow he is oblivious of surroundings, *distrait*, very deaf, a gentlemanly don of old-fashioned courtesy.

In the afternoon to Merrion Square to call on the great AE.[1] I lumbered up many stairs of a Georgian mansion but was not prepared for the mountain of flesh which filled the chair at the untidy desk. He started to talk immediately and went on and on, until I thought I should never get a word in. He got on to a story of how James Joyce first came to see him and was difficult to get going, arrogant and silent, while himself blathered away until Joyce was ready to say something. He was playing the same game with me. He blathered while I recovered my breath and my legs, and mutely got the office young man from the room. That done, I had AE to myself and all was well.

Good Friday

Today a delightful visit to yet another of the Gwynns, at Dollymount. A strongly entrenched family – this is the third of them, counting the Provost whom I was to have met; Stephen makes a fourth, and the Jesuit son fifth. Judging from two members, it is a family with its own marked characteristics: a negligent distinction, affability, courtesy, yet wrapped up in their own interests, giving the impression of aloofness. Charm! Yet I don't wonder that they lost the game: they have a kind of ineffectiveness with their easygoing ways. This Gwynn today had never washed his car or his dog since he had them. They are no leaders.

* A foremost Dublin family at the time, Stephen Gwynn, writer, its best-known member.

1. See p. 6.

Saturday, I suppose 30 March

My Swift doesn't advance much,[1] nor my diary. Dublin fascinates me too much, I become so interested in its atmosphere of revolution and politics. It's an uncanny place to be in; I find myself instinctively on guard in what I say – it gives one the creeps.

The first night I went down to a political meeting in O'Connell Street (formerly Sackville Street). The speakers, Republicans, were just fanatics abstracted from political reality, yet the crowd took them seriously. They laughed at the jokes and took points quickly enough: but where was the famous Irish sense of humour with regard to the main issue? An old woman,* dressed in cape and bonnet with a cultured accent and no voice, acted funny parts with a policeman's truncheon and tried to conduct the crowd into singing political songs she had composed: 'Ba, Ba, Black Sheep' one was called, and they were all agin the C.I.D. Nobody sang, they listened in silence: about a quarter of the crowd cheered the Republic. Afterwards someone told me the reason for the silence: if you laughed in the wrong place, it mightn't be so well for you. There was sure to be one or two men with guns about them.

The police behaved well through it all. One handsome young fellow next to me stood quite composed, but that the shafts went home one could tell from the gleam in his eye. Half-a-dozen other C.I.D. were disposed about the place. At the end the crowd remained knotted together, not at all moved to get away as they would be in England. I heard the Inspector say to the younger constables, 'Best thing to get away from it', and they went off.

One doesn't need incidents like that to remind one: all Dublin is a reminder: it has seen revolution, and the look of it remains. The Four Courts and the Customs House have scaffolding still around them; the lower side of Sackville Street is being rebuilt, many gaps show in the houses here and there. The Castle is a rabbit warren for the Free State bureaucracy by day, and a desert by night where memories stalk in the silence of defeat.

Today was the second time I have been there towards evening. The first time, the civil servants were pouring out of the Viceregal gates; today they had gone and I had the place to myself, all except the garden where the usual Dublin brats, dirty and unkempt, were at play.

The Castle is a monument of departed glory, the more romantic for its desertion: not unlike the Hofburg in Vienna in its situation, straddling

1. A biography of Swift which ALR intended to enter for a prize offered by the *Atlantic Monthly*. It was ultimately written nearly fifty years later.

* This was Mrs Despard, sister of Governor-General Lord French.

across unequal levels, in period and style, in the wings it thrusts out like bastions, in its impression of departed grandeur. The grand staircase was made for entrance to a palace, the pillared and gilt corridors for grandeur; desks and chairs were crammed into reception rooms that still had their long mirrors and Georgian fireplaces. Here were the maids with mop and pail. The woman in charge was full of regret for former days, how good it was for Ireland that the grand people had brought money into the country and now it was poor. Several such folk have expressed similar regrets to me.

The attendant at the Parliament House, for one; then the bookseller on the quay, particularly his wife, who said, 'The people of this country are mad; they're mad!' Attendants at the National Gallery this morning quoted swathes out of the *Daily Mail* with appropriate sentiments. And yet, there were those people in O'Connell Street, determined – and rather mad.

Easter Sunday

The place fills me more and more with alarm. Not that – as yet – there has been an Easter outbreak again; but the atmosphere of the place is so unquiet, full of nervousness and expectancy. Tonight a little gathering at AE's: Walter Starkie (I never knew he was Shamus O'Sullivan) and his wife, and two other young men, one a deputy by name Esmond——, and the other O'Reilly. They gave me the creeps: only AE and Walter Starkie could one feel at home with. Of the others Mrs Starkie is a Republican, though she listened unmoved to the anti-Republican talk. The deputy belonged to the Government Party; strong man as he looked, his nerves were on edge. A broad-shouldered fellow, with a face full of strong lines, but amazing hands, white and powerful and murderous, he looked in his double-breasted suit and his trench coat like the fighter he probably was in the Troubles. Now he appeared to be rattled by the situation. He couldn't bear the thought of De Valera coming into power with the gunmen behind him. He says that De Valera would throw in his lot with a Republic proclaimed by force of arms, and there'd be civil war again.

Even the other man, less noticeable, made a sinister impression: a Catholic fanatic, with a violent hatred of England – though he went to Oxford and enjoyed English hospitality. Anyway both were fanatically in favour of the Censorship Bill, and both looked forward to Fianna Fail getting control, one in hope and the other in despair. What a people! and what a future!

P.S. Just as I came to the end, there were cheers outside in the street for the Republic and De Valera.

2 April

A good theme for a story occurred to me today in the Cathedral, as the Dean was showing me the place where Swift lies by one of the pillars at the bottom of the nave.

3 April

When some Scientific Association came to hold its conference in Dublin in the thirties of last century, they got up Swift's skull for examination. William Maguire the sexton fetched it out, and it went the round of Dublin at-homes, particularly at the Deanery.

A good theme, the return of Swift – a night-scene, himself cursing the disturbers of his peace in eighteenth-century language. The skull left out on the sideboard into the night: a summons of the present occupant of the Deanery down to the dining-room, and his terror. Curse and his death.

All my days busy. I have written two letters in one to Adam: the first last night in bed, full of feeling, and this morning a more reasonable one. It seems at last as if his side of the infatuation has caved in.

A degree of sympathy binds us together even at this distance. For just when I was thinking that life had become quite tolerable without him and love had passed into a pleasant memory, there came this morning a letter in which he expressed the same thought. He could now look back upon it as upon a landscape from which a storm had passed. It is best this way. What more could one expect? In two or three short hours I got to know him: how could it last from that?

Thursday, it must be the 11th [April]

My Dublin diary hardly exists, I have become so caught up in social life for once. Every day I have engagements to lunch out or take tea with somebody, or go for a drive out of Dublin. What time I can spare from the neglect of my Swift studies, I spend in the hotel lounge. A motley collection – I've got a few notes of one personality, though I'd like to sketch them all. A charming young man in green, Sarsfield by name, has intelligence, English manner and speech; he was in the Army in India, invalided home with lung trouble. He's good-looking, fine golden hair, little military moustache, and round blue eyes. All the women follow him round with their glances. He is the heart's-ache of poor Dr O'Leary, who's getting up in the thirties and wants a man badly. She chooses me for confidant; I encourage her maliciously, and then withdraw, leaving her exposed. She wants him, that's clear; but Sarsfield doesn't want her. He's diffident, tells me he suffers from inferiority complex.

Anyhow that's been a good card to play. With another man, a Northcliffe-cum-Napoleon type in appearance, over forty and unsure of his attraction for women, the psychoanalysis gambit has been very successful. Vain, he wants to hear about himself in dubious psychological terms, so I gave him a dose. Talking about the kind of Napoleon-mania some people get, I blundered upon his own fixation: it gave him into my hands at once.

– Then the women! One is a beauty specialist, correct head and profile, a fixed smile revealing large dentures. Her conversation is punctuated by 'If you can understand', or 'If you know what I mean', 'We ought to have got over somebody from Mademoiselle's in Bond Street. She's very good at her job, if you can understand, but there's too much of the Jewess in her. She's too forward in her manner, like standing in a market-place, if you can understand.'

Sunday, 20 [?21] April

A fatal day: I missed three engagements and offended four people. I was to be taken to lunch with Lady Fingall by Gogarty. Young Frank O'Connor came and we walked in St Stephen's Green, watching the tiny ducks just hatched like midges on the water. When I came back, it was late: Gogarty had phoned and was gone from home. I waited until two, and then went to my superfluous lunch, having breakfasted at twelve. Already in the morning I had put off Harold Williams who is studying Swift manuscripts here, and Joseph Hone (dear man) who asked me to lunch and/or tea.

I set out towards four for the station intending to go to Killiney which must have been heavenly today: I imagined the plumy eucalyptus trees waving against the brilliant sky and the sea. When I got to Westland Row, the train was just going out and I was too late. So I came home to have tea and post letters. Worst of all, I insulted an old lady who saved my life with a stamp – by paying for it.

Finally to AE, who made up by charm and sweetness for all the disappointments of the day.

Monday night, 22 April

Tonight one of the most interesting nights I have spent in Dublin. Myles Dillon asked me up to the Dillon house in North Great George Street, at the upper end of one of the Georgian streets now eaten into by tenements. All the way up from the Pro-Cathedral is a mange of slums, where once was order and decency. At the bend of the streets there a slum funeral crossed my line of advance. It was amusing to make myself one with the lounging creatures at the corner, stopping and taking off my hat.

The house is distinguished: a flight of steps with wrought-iron lamp-posts, a fine hall and staircase; inside, spacious rooms. Since his father's death,[1] Myles Dillon has lived on his bachelor existence there with a brother, and half the house is shut up. He has one servant in a house that needs four; in the front a fine room dismantled of everything save books. In one room are cases full of the best books: nineteenth-century literature, rare books on politics, like privately published things on Parnell, masses of letters and documents. In this room had been a Whistler, now handed over to the sister in the division of family property.

I got a vivid sense of the dominance of the dead man – the portraits showed him young-looking, with sensitive features and a beard. Pathetic too: a man of culture and distinction, whose life was wasted on sterile nationalism, and who might have been a first or second minister in his own parliament.

A large collection: Desmond Coffey whom I knew, Professor Tierney whom I had met, a young man called Binchy, another called Hogan, and two older, Burgan and Best, Librarian of the National Library. Things didn't wake up till after our tea, and I became involved in an argument with Tierney and Hogan. The point was whether the preservation of the Irish language was essential to preserving the distinctive memories, traditions, legends, turns of speech and phrase which have given such character and life to the Irish contribution to English literature. I argued that the actual linguistic element was small; what was important was the whole background, whose existence did not depend upon Gaelic. In the case of a poet, what is of most value to him in creation is what excites his mind to expression; these things are often dependent upon chance or whim, or perhaps upon a deliberate choice, both of which may have nothing to do with his cultural background. The fact that Keats did not know Greek did not prevent him from writing the 'Grecian Urn'; and Eliot's being an American has not interfered with his intention to build upon the Browningesque content and late Shakespearean free-verse form.

A second argument seems to me important to put forward in Ireland; that if the Irish were oppressed right up to and into the nineteenth century, so were the English. The oppression in both countries was that of the lower classes by the aristocracy. The game-laws acted just as savagely in England

1. John Dillon, Home Rule leader.

as in Ireland; and what about the transportation of 437 agricultural labourers from Hants and Dorset after the riots of 1831?

Tuesday morning

Frank O'Connor* and I at the play the other night: he told me he is going to write a sort of Schwalbenbuch of his days in prison: but the first two lines were so beautiful he had not been able to find anything to go on with. He wrote them on the programme for me, and I said I would try and complete them. Out of that arose the idea of our both writing a poem beginning with these same two lines, though I don't think them so wonderful:

> A honey-coloured flick of sunlight on the white wall
> Is, Natalie, this bright bewildering day in spring.

The second poem is a ballad-parody to the tune of 'When I play on my fiddle in Dooney', which came into my head at tea-time in the Bonne Bouche talking with Sean O'Sullivan,** and I wrote it walking back through St Stephen's Green in the intervals of watching the ducks.

Towards the evening I went for a walk in Phoenix Park, one of those solitary walks when I renew my resolutions and regain vigour in my intentions. This evening it was a return to politics which occupied me, and wondering when and how it may come about. The best time would be next winter, after my book on Swift. Or if a Tory government goes on, it won't hurt to wait longer.

Some part of my walk along the rides under the trees was given up to Adam. I haven't heard from him since his *cri de cœur* to write to him. He sent me a postcard of Van Dyck's head of Charles I: that was like his responsive sensitiveness. I had told him about the visual image of Charles on horseback spanning the eastern horizon, which I often see when at Carn Grey I look towards the hills beyond Fowey river and the Gribbin headland.

I went as far as the old Chief Secretary's Lodge – a long way off I saw its dark orange walls through the trees. It looks not unlike Porthpean House, grander and looking out over the plain away to the mountains. The trees were at their best, beeches fringing the lawn, dipping fans of new foliage out over the dyke that surrounds the property. Smoke went up from a chimney, but the blinds drawn in the glasshouse gave the appearance of

* Became best known for his short stories.

** He painted the first portrait of me.

desertedness. I thought of the Fenian murders here, and Birrell's secretaryship, and Dillon going up to the Lodge for consultation.

At night to the theatre with Sean O'Sullivan, where I met Lennox Robinson again and Dermot O'Brien. The more I see of Sean, the better I like him. He has distinction and integrity. All kinds of things he has told me in the course of my sittings for my portrait – I hope I may not forget them. Tonight, of a man among the rebels in St Stephen's Green who crept out of the bushes and lying flat bent his head down to drink at the pond; a shot from the Club side of the Green got him in the head, and he lay there half in and half out of the water, nobody daring to venture out to him.

Saturday, 26 April

In Oxford again, heaven but a prison. I cherish the chains that bind me. The night that I came back from Ireland, silvery bells welcomed me coming down the High: that lovely peal from All Saints, the church at the corner of the Turl and the High. All its enchantments are put forward to lure me into submission. Even Ireland put up hardly any resistance in my mind. When I come back from Paris, or Germany or home, the spell goes on and on; but coming back from Dublin, there was no such hold. Is it that the influence of this place is getting such a grip on me after all?

Still I don't think I am submitting: I would go away from it all tomorrow, if the chance I look for offered.

Saturday, 11 May

These are divine days – summer at its earliest and loveliest. Every walk out is a revelation. Coming back from North Oxford I took the path through the Parks where the flowering trees are: one so beautiful, I stood back from the path to take in all its points, so thick with white blossom one could hardly see any green of leaves. I then stood under it, and let the tree spread its flowery crinoline over me; I looked up under – into the delicate matchwork of black trunk and branches starred with blossom.

On my walk at Magdalen I stopped to admire a fruit-tree in bloom, just where in autumn Bruce and I find crab-apples strewn on the ground. This made a picture with the copper-gold tree behind it and fresh green on the other side of the path.

At night, when David [Cecil] and I were shut in Wadham Garden we went round to the little cloister to see the cherry with its pink boughs, in the angle of the grey building. A gravestone nearby has a date, 1676, on it. David chose just that place to say that he sometimes thought he ought to leave Oxford if he wanted to be really good as a writer. It is just what I have felt; nothing would keep me back if I had his independence of circumstances. Yet, whenever he came back to it he felt that there was nothing in the world like it, even coming back from Venice; in Wadham Garden on a summer night he felt that he would be a fool to leave it.

He went on about politics, wondering why it was I was attracted by it: he thought I should so dislike the life of practical compromise. David doesn't think me suited for politics:* he sees so much the literary and the hermit-intellectual side of my life. The other side he doesn't see much when I am with him.

I'm elated tonight, for I have been hammering at a poem the last few days, and it is this moment finished.

I've been to one of Rudler's lunch parties when a French poet was present: Paul Valéry and now Fernand Gregh. Quite a to-do about getting there: I'd forgotten, and at ten to two was enjoying my abstemious cup of coffee in the smoking-room, over a general conversation in which Moon's father and Oman[1] and Ernest Jacob joined. Then a telephone message arrived and I went careering in a taxi up to North Oxford, tying up my shoes and putting myself to rights as I went. Arrived; people not very far advanced; my salmon mayonnaise waiting for me, and a seat between two middle-aged ladies of whom one looked rather English but with Italian eyes, and the other very French-Jewish: the one was Madame Halévy, the other Madame Gregh. Both took extraordinary pain to bridge the circumstances of my arrival. The room echoed with chatter: a lot of people speaking French gives a vulgar impression. Perhaps the hardness and precision of the language.

Madame Halévy was informative about John Dillon: he had said to her in despair, after a lifetime in the service of his cause, 'Now I think we were happier under the English than as we are.' With Madame Gregh I carried on a heavy conversation, overcast by mutual incomprehensibility. She rattled off a speech with eloquent gestures and dark eyes cast up to the ceiling; I responded with equal enthusiasm and inability to make myself understood. It made me think of the disputation of Thomas More and Gargantua in Rabelais – without the humiliating consequences. The lady had heard of Katherine Mansfield from Louis Gillet's article in the *Revue des Deux Mondes*. She was voluble about André Maurois, talked of the *Discours du Colonel Bramble*; I haven't [read it], so I couldn't respond with the 'Silences du Docteur O'Grady'.

* How right he was! Old Lord William Cecil at Exeter made the same point about the conscienceless compromises of politics. The Cecils certainly found them difficult to make.

1. Sir Charles Oman (1860–1946), a stalwart of All Souls, where besides being a Prize Fellow he held the Chichele chair of Modern History for forty years.

Wednesday, 4 September. At home

No letter from Adam; day after day I have been collecting every scrap of memory of our Berlin days. Something to fall back on, in case something should happen to him or to our friendship.

My feeling is that it is not love that he feels for me, nor ever will, and that we can make nothing ultimately of it – even if we were of one mind. He has the greatest affection and, he adds, admiration. In the beginning, there was more to it than this: he felt the same emotion that night as I, and we both lived in its shadow though separated in space those early days. He told me so, a little unwilling to say any more about it, for it would do injustice to a past experience to speak about it later when it had changed. He shared my experience at first, and was the first to write; without that first move on his part I should have made myself forget him.

He said that he too had gone through those days of anguish, and then of misery because it was past. Why had it vanished? Because of what I had said about the hopelessness of my own attitude to love? He said, once or twice, at Neu Babelsberg and our last night in the Tiergarten, that he was sure the future would bring him nearer to me; when he got rid of his present bewilderment and uncertainties, he would have come nearer to my point of view. He would be able to follow better the movements of my thought and with more complete sympathy; we should be brought closer by time, not carried further away. In our last hour together he said that he believed I cared for him more than anybody in the world had cared for him before. As he lay on the sofa he was silent, as if waiting passively without wanting or not wanting, but I would not commit myself at the last moment.

He fears a relationship in which he would be passive. He is too masculine for that, and I have too much respect for him, so I held aloof. But the moment I was leaving, *he* turned back to me in the passage with an unconscious movement, a second in which we leaned together to say goodbye. That was the nearest we attained to an embrace, though not the fullest moment of sympathy; its incompleteness revenges itself upon me, as its completion would have done also.

8 September, Sunday night

I've got up from my bed to write a note of memory: Adam has gone to bed and got up again to write a letter to me, and this is only a vain return. While reading Hölderlin's *Hyperion* which he gave me, I kept seeing in my mind's eye the picture of Moritzburg where we went together from Dresden. Perhaps it was because of the reference to a visit there by Frederick the

Great in Catt's *Memoirs* which I was reading this afternoon; a fortnight today we were there together.

We went out from Dresden in a motor coach, after waiting a long time in the boiling heat of the Altmarkt. We talked about dialects of home: he is on good terms with the youths of the village and can talk their dialect with them. His young brother, who reacts against the family, always speaks dialect and won't speak correct German.*

It was sweltering in the bus, full of courting couples and young women off to the country: we crept up the long hill out of Dresden on the north bank of the Elbe at a snail's pace. Arrived, we decided not to be shown round the Schloss, and sat on the low wall of the avenue leading up to the castle gate. A lake fills the marshy low-lying ground and almost surrounds the castle. Later we went round the lake and into the woods. Walking over the paths and ditches, I told him the story of Swift and Stella and Vanessa, which fascinated him. By a bathing place were a few nude figures sunning themselves; sitting on the bench, Adam looking towards the wood and I towards the lake, he told me about the girl he met one evening in the streets of Berlin. He had already told me in a letter what a strong feeling it had created. Now he was disappointed. I said I had never found a woman from whom one got intellectual response, as from him, or others of my friends. One could get a lot from them, he found: sympathy and understanding of one's difficulties;** but at last one saw that they didn't really care for one's heart-searchings, these were not ultimately serious matters to them. He said he had never cared sexually for this 'bourgeois girl', except for the first two or three days when he thought he was in love with her. In the end he felt as I did, that one lived one's life in isolation: one had to grapple with one's difficulties by oneself alone.

I kept thinking that perhaps I was guilty of imperfect sympathy for him; I haven't that perfect gift of sympathy which he has, by which he knows intuitively what is going on in the other's mind. I wondered if I hadn't stifled something of this sensitiveness in myself, instead of perfecting it as he has done by his way of life and his belief in personal relations as the only reality. Then too I was unhappy at the glimpse of his caring so much for me in those early days after our first meeting: then he had been as much in love as I, and had lived those days in anguish. That had changed, and 'it does an injustice to the experience to talk about it at a later time when it has become something different'. This was what I would most

* After the war he came to see me at Oxford, as tall and gangling as Adam, but dark. He would have made no difficulties.

** What an egoist Adam was – I too; he was an instinctive seducer of the heart. Did David Astor find this? – as Diana Hubback did.

have liked to know: his side of the mutual experience, and why it had changed.

He had already had a woman, though only once, a long time ago and since then he never had. The other students in Berlin and people like Hans all did; he was exceptional in not having relations with women.

In the journey back to Berlin, just a fortnight ago, we had a half-compartment to ourselves: he was in the corner, like a tired child with a flush on his face. As the journey went on, he became more and more tired and got hoarse in the throat: so we stopped talking and sat together. People passing up and down the corridor were interested in us, he said, and suggested we draw the blinds. But one didn't need to shut out the world: the world of our own feeling was enough, for me at least.

Cornwall, Thursday, 12 September

Trying to write my wretched book* all day is agony in the hot weather. But yesterday I had a good day, wrote a third of a chapter by intense application in the morning, and going on at night till two next morning. The result nothing today: this morning I sat hopefully at my desk a long time, wrote some notes for later chapters, then relapsed into reading Browning by way of experiment, to see what he was really like. I didn't like it. So I read 'Thyrsis' to comfort myself. This was so touching, I found myself crying over the end of it, reading it aloud. Then more notes.

In the afternoon at my window it was so nice with the sea breeze blowing up gently from the bay, that went to sleep in the draught. From five to six, my walk to Carn Grey where I meditated on what life would be at Methrose, if I bought it and set up house there. The evening I dawdled away at the piano and looking into books, Carlyle, Browning and Cobbett.

I haven't heard from Adam. However I feel more resigned about him since I got my mind back into the groove of my work. *There* lies the future for me, and not in any love. Still, he has such a sense of one's being, and such sensitiveness of response, I can't but recognize that we have some special relation. It is impossible to define it – better to let it take its course, naturally and without pressing. There was never any intimate relation established or love created without some effort, I suppose. I could argue myself into anything I wanted: better to reserve the faculty for arguing other people into things they don't want.

Because my day has been so empty and unsatisfying I call up some memory

* *Politics and the Younger Generation.*

of Adam, an oasis at the end of the day. On the last night, not the best, when we were together in the Tiergarten, he was in a mood like that of the night in Oxford: gloomy and moved in a disturbed way, rather outside my sphere. As if I existed less for him when he was so filled with despair about the future for himself and Germany. Though I was critical, I loved my country – it was possible to be content in England and with the possibilities of its future, it was so highly organized a community, its traditions and values so firmly established. But for Germany what was there? Or for a German like himself in that environment? He hated the horror of Berlin life, yet that was what the Germany of the future was going to be like: shallow and materialist, talking about art but never caring for the values of life nor understanding them, godless and pleasure-seeking, subsisting on American money, and holding on to power so that the people like him would never have a chance of changing things.* He seemed filled with gloom, a kind of passionate melancholy, which – as an attitude in face of what has to be done – I haven't much sympathy with. It makes me uncertain of his capacity to rise above the situation and help to form a new order. He has intelligence enough and understanding and subtlety; he needs only strength of purpose. But this too, he told me another time, he has at bottom.

24 September

The constant chatter of children outside my window makes it hopeless to try and concentrate on the book. So I took up *War and Peace* which has occupied this summer in its way. I began the Preface in the train from Oxford, going to Germany. I was in doubt whether it was the right thing to do, half-thinking I ought to be going back to Cornwall to write my book and arrange about the constituency. Going to see Adam took a secondary place in all this welter.

And so it remained the first two or three days in Berlin. I felt master of the situation because less affected emotionally than he! The evening I arrived he was rather overwhelmed, jolted out of his command of English. He came to the station to meet me: a screen of people prevented us from seeing each other and the train glided on till I caught a glimpse of him, tall above all the others and with that nervous turn of the head. Coming to Pariser Strasse through the Tiergarten, he was excited, told me how much he had waited for my coming, while I as usual was expecting to settle myself in. At such times he seemed so much younger than I, at others I felt

* What a contrast this was with the Berlin enjoyed by the carefree Isherwood, of *Mr Norris Changes Trains*, Auden, Spender and Co.!

he had more experience and was altogether more mature and disillusioned.*

He sat astraddle the bedroom chair, with the glass door open on to my balcony. He wasn't at ease, he was too much moved. We stayed talking until we had each found footing, then went out to dine at one of the little Russian *émigré* restaurants he likes to go to. It took us all that evening to recover the fullness of sympathy we found at once in Oxford. I felt uncommitted at first, half-amused: a good thing, for it enabled me to lay down a programme, by which we would be apart in the daytime, when he worked and I saw Berlin, and devote the evenings to each other, for 'night is the best time for friendship'.

Next evening we went up to the Schloss to supper with his uncle;** when we had his uncle's rooms to ourselves we established the same relations as our letters had maintained. Perhaps that was at the back of my amusement, the feeling of restraint at being with one to whom I had written in such an unrestrained way. However it was he and not I who broke that down: by the hours of talk we had together in the room in the Schloss, while the evening grew darker and the room black all round Adam lying on the sofa. I console myself with the thought that he took the initiative at two important points: it was he who wrote to me from London after the evening in Oxford, and he again in Berlin who led us on to real intimacy.

Now, after it has all gone by, I play the pathetic Proustian game with myself – taking out the three little photos and reconstructing how he looked from them. This evening I took up *War and Peace* not to finish it, but to recapture some essence of the nights in my room on the Pariser Strasse, when under the green lamp I would read a bit and then look out on the lamplit street where he too was living.

Saturday, 28 September

I have said nothing of our visit to Potsdam, though that was one of the best of our times together. A grey misty evening, autumnal dampness in the woods. We went out from the little station not far from the Kurfürstendamm, in the Savigny Strasse; going through the gardens and woods of Charlottenburg and Grünewald: stretches of pine and fir on the sandy soil, glimpses of water and lakes as we went by. At last we saw the green dome of the church across the fields from the railway before drawing in to the station.

* Of course he was: for me, maturing was a long and painful process, emerging from such *in*experience.

** Von Schweinitz, grandson of Bismarck's ambassador to Russia, had an apartment in the Kaiser's Schloss.

Going up the avenue to Sans-Souci he told me that his mother had come back to Potsdam not long ago, and cried to think of the memories the place had for her. Adam was born in a house looking out on the Paradenplatz, and from there was taken to the house in Unter den Linden where he lived till he was seven. He wondered how I should like her, and told me about her strength of character and religious devotion. He had sent an Indian friend to stay at his home, while he was away; his mother and the Indian found common ground in their religious sense and their liking for Browning! He supposed I didn't care for Browning, any more than I should approve of the interest in religion?

('Oh, it's in vain to remember it all. The light is fading, I can hardly see to write; the awful kids are outside in the avenue, shouting, kicking a ball, quarrelling, as usual.)

That evening we walked up to the great fountain which throws a jet of water higher than the trees. As we went up the terraces every step took us higher above the woods that stretch away to the town. A few people were waiting in the colonnade at the back of the palace: we went back up the hill to a sort of folly. Adam told me that his father, as Governor of Potsdam, had had all the palaces in his keeping: odd for him to be seeing Sans-Souci on the same footing as any other sightseer. We talked about national qualities; he thought that there was a great deal of the Roman qualities in the English.* He thought that I had something of them: self-sacrifice, the ability to subject what was not in keeping with my deliberate plans. This must be more evident in my relations with other people than it is to myself.

We went into the palace, following his uncle's advice to keep at the end of the crowd. All these rooms looking out over the terraces form one long corridor – one can see from one end to the other – we went through by ourselves as belatedly as possible. In Frederick the Great's room at the end, everything that surrounded him in life still remained: if one collected it all, his plum-coloured coat and satin waistcoat from the Zeughaus, his flute and music-stand from another room, his books and papers, one could reconstruct the life of all those years ago. There was the chair he died in, his writing-desk towards the window, and the alcove with his bed. A most vivid impression passed over me, while Adam went over to the alcove and bent over the dividing rope.

We arrived at the end of the other wing, Voltaire's room decorated with parrots and flowers on the panelling. While the others delayed with the guide Adam wanted to go back through the rooms again, so that we might have them to ourselves and recapture their atmosphere. We were pressed

* Nothing of them in evidence today, 1979.

for time, doors were being shut behind us, people leaving. This was an added excitement to me; I enjoyed the feverishness of hurrying through the silent rooms, all one's senses heightened so that I heard the clocks ticking; I had the feeling of having stolen in upon their continuous, secret life. Now Frederick's room was locked; we had to scurry back along the main corridor.

While we walked in the gardens, I suggested that Sans-Souci would make a background for our friendship as well as for Frederick's with Voltaire. I offered myself as Voltaire to his Frederick; he was unconvinced. We talked about the savagery of nationalism compared with the spirit Sans-Souci witnessed to, conceived in imitation of the France of Louis XV and choosing French taste to express itself. I went on to talk about the *grand siècle*, and Versailles through the eyes of Saint-Simon, and how much the English were indebted to French taste.

We passed in and out arbours of clipped trees, with basins and fountains, and seats among the statues. We came to a large formal garden with a palace in imitation of an Italian villa: here we stayed until Adam wanted to find a spot away from people. In the park we found a seat where few came by: he wanted to talk as we did in the dark in the Schloss, intimately, as if to oneself. He has the gift of leading into such intimacy: I couldn't achieve it by myself. No doubt what he could do so easily with me he must often have done with others; still, I am grateful for these hours which were pure gifts from him. The rarity of those hours we created together; whatever he may have shared with others would not be the same thing. That preserves some uniqueness out of the end I foresee.

Late evening came down over the park, open spaces of grass, only a tree here and there, mists filling the hollows and stealing across the flats. A vesper bell was ringing in the town; out here the notes were soft and soothing. He told me about his family, the influence his elder brother had on his mind, and the anxiety his extraordinary ways caused his mother and father. It must be unsettling for Adam: his brother has reached bottom; disillusioned has given up any occupation and gone to live in a peasant's hut in Bavaria. A life of abnegation, from which he discourages Adam from any activity and reproaches him for a life of compromise. I don't understand the strength of such an influence; evidently the brother is a strong personality, Adam said of great acuteness of mind. He was a favourite pupil of Max Scheler's at Heidelberg, then threw it all up in despair. One of the war generation.

We came to Adam's own difficulties. There again I don't quite understand their intensity; partly because I have forgotten the depth and depression of my own adolescent moods, I find it hard to realize his. He would repudiate the idea of their being adolescent, no doubt.

Monday, 11 November

I can't go on with my work this morning, for Moon has just gone. His last weekend in college before going to India, nothing but a round of goodbyes for him. I don't know what to do, but gaze out of the window, vainly, as I ran out into the street because I couldn't resist seeing him away safely. I was too late, the car had already gone. He rushed up the very last moment to say goodbye, and wouldn't let me go down to see him off. So I waited by my window looking on to the quad; he didn't emerge for a minute or two, then I knew he was saying goodbye to his own room down below, already occupied by somebody else, though it will always for me be occupied by him. He was a dear, an odd companion to have had in that room below, a high-minded, noble nature. I hope he'll come home safely.

There are the signal bells for the silence: it's Armistice Day, and the leaves blowing across my window.

The silence is over, Tom bell has rung out his deep strokes: footsteps sound in the quad and the buses are beginning again in the High.

18 November

A week after, and the character of the occupation down below has greatly changed. As I write I hear Maurice Bowra's shrill laugh alternate with the ceaseless dialogue: a night or two ago there was a large crowd, and a voice reading a paper to a society, with one joke a paragraph, judging from the punctuated laughter. The quiet presence of the little Moon was more domestic and intimate. But he is now on the high seas, another* takes his place.

Several things, I can't say what, have combined to make the past week melancholy. Last night, an upsetting episode when Oman asked me to look up the St Aubyns in Burke's *Peerage*, to see when they first occupied St Michael's Mount, I came upon the name of 'the Captain'.[1] 'Francis Michael' I found his name: Captain in the Rifle Brigade, had fought in the Burmese War. His birthday, 3 November 1859; after being invalided home he died unmarried in March 1895.

So he was thirty-five when he died: I shall be able to tell Mabel, who likes to have every scrap about him, and mother will tell her nothing. Once she had a photo of the Captain, which she carried everywhere with her: a

* John Sparrow.

1. The father of ALR's illegitimate half-sister.

handsome young fellow, no doubt felt towards him like a lover rather than a daughter. And then, careless and lackadaisical as she is, she lost it: that's like her, and I daresay like him.

I can well imagine the type: the Peckwater hunting type. Yet the whole story, and the effect it has had on my mind, make it impossible not to think of him as a romantic figure. To have died so young, for one thing: in the prime of life. And what was it he died of? Everything about him I'd like to know: what wouldn't I give to find out from his brother before the old peer dies; there's more chance of knowing from him than of getting her to open her lips. She has said a word now and again, but worse than useless, a part that she was playing, she wanted me to think him a bad man. 'He was fast; still he had to pay for it, didn'a!' was all she said: the last with a kind of resentment that seemed genuine, though what it meant I am not sure even now.

At first I thought it was resentment at the thing coming up in her mind; that seemed a poor sort of reaction, as if nothing in it but a persecution for which he had to pay. It is clear she has never forgiven herself. Perhaps that accounts for the iron in her character which Mrs T. sees, but which I had never thought of. It must be so: about everything else she is open and natural. On that one point, or anything like it, there's the silence of a coffin. Besides, how could she have kept those tight-fastened lips – which have retained their beautiful lines – if it had not been through years of determined silence?

What a life to have lived around me, all through the years of childhood, the years of security. No wonder there was no feeling of love, even though there was security and we were all well cared for: but when I think of it, my childhood was empty of love.*

At home again: Boxing Day

Last night I heard some stories from mother worth preserving: like that Cornish story of Lawrence's about the man who returned to his wife after years of desertion, the scene the Tinners' Arms at Zennor.

There's Aunt Emily's case too. Particularly mean – Joe Anstis went off with every penny she had: £150 she had saved while he was working in the iron-mines. In Northamptonshire he fell in with a Mrs Abbot, and in two years out of love for his wife. (When I was a child I remember how fond and proud of each other they were.) Every time he came home he was colder,

* The discovery of the story was a great blow and made for an almighty complex. It was followed by another concerning myself. Not good for duodenal ulcer. I inherited the iron.

and turned his back on her in bed. Letters came and were addressed to his old parents' at Holmbush. They couldn't read and wondered why so many came: he said they were from the captain of the mine and probably he would have to go back. In the end, Emily pieced together scraps of letter torn up in the shit-house, and found Mrs Abbot putting him against her, your 'old wife', and 'the old woman' in the way.

Son Russell one night went down and found her letter in his pocket: 'My dear, I can't live without you. I am dying for you to come back.' Aunt Emily knew that something was afoot, and when he asked her to get out their money, she suspected he would cheat her. She said, 'Joe, you know you can't serve two masters, nor two women'; but she let him have the money. He went to America and once sent back a pound. Then she knew it was all over, and wrote to tell him she had no money to pay the rent, and there was a year's to pay. He wrote back: 'Your children are married and grown up, and there's only your mouth to feed. You can go out to work to provide for yourself.' She was not to write any more, for he was going up into the country. There came a letter from Northants from Mrs Abbot's children, two girls working in a factory, asking for news of Joe, for their mother had left home and they thought must have gone to America. Nobody knows where; that was seven years ago, Aunt Emily says bravely nobody seems to be able to tell her any news of her 'beauty', where he is or what he is doing, whether living or dead.*

31 December

I'm dead tired, I was up so late last night after a long day coming home from Truro and going out to St Dennis and Foxhole in the evening.** But I always write a little in this diary on the last day of the old year; and now something would be lacking if I missed it this year.

Perhaps it would be a good omen if I did, so little seems to come from the other line. Four years at All Souls and nothing achieved; it's hard to defend myself and harder to know how the time has gone. There's no such consolation as Richard Pares finds in the thought of Julius Caesar at twenty-six crying because Alexander the Great at that age had conquered the world.

There are only the bells for consolation: I am happy to be in sound of them. Yet they tell me how the years go on; and I remember other New Year's Eves. Always first I think of that one some time just after the war –

* She had pride and dignity – and died in agony, of cancer; I once sat by her bedside, trying to console.

** To speak at boring Labour Party meetings.

1919 or 1920, when I sat up alone with the lamp in the old kitchen at Tregonissey, reading the first war memoirs – Col. Repington's and Margot Asquith's. And in Germany too – already three years ago, when I heard the chorales being played in the square.

The Thirties

The thirties, Rowse complained in moments of passion throughout his later life, had not afforded him a moment of happiness. The decade saw the ruin of all his larger hopes. The financial crash of 1929 that led to the collapse and division of the Labour Party in 1931, worse, far worse and worst of all the triumph of Hitler in 1933 and the futility of British policy in the face of this terrible threat to everything he loved and valued – all this coloured Rowse's vision and no doubt weakened his physical resistance to the disease that nearly killed him in 1938.

On the other hand it was the richest period in both his emotional and his intellectual life. The overheated but strangely evanescent affair with Adam von Trott, ended by Trott's apparently pro-Nazi letter to the Manchester Guardian *in 1934, was succeeded by the three great formative friendships of Rowse's mature life, those with Charles Henderson, Richard Pares and Bruce McFarlane. Some account of these people and of their effect on Rowse is given in my biography of him,* A Man of Contraditions *(1999).*

Professionally and intellectually this was the decade in which he found his feet. His passion for Cornwall, notably refined and deepened by his friendship with Charles Henderson, a Cornish antiquary of unrivalled range and erudition, led him to think of focusing a study of the Reformation on that limited and distinctive geographical entity. A conversation with Sir Charles Firth determined him to mould it in the form of a social history, the book that ultimately was to be published as Tudor Cornwall *(1941). That necessitated prolonged research in the Public Record Office, the Library of the British Museum and the Institute of Historical Research, which meant finding lodgings and, if possible, some part-time academic post in London.*

This brought him into direct contact with a number of scholars such as R. H. Tawney, Eileen Power, L. B. Namier and J. E. Neale at the Institute of Historical Research, and with luminaries such as Sir William Beveridge and Lionel Robbins at the London School of Economics where he briefly occupied a temporary teaching post. It also strengthened his intimacy with

Richard Pares who for much of the time was doing his own research in the Public Record Office and found Rowse his lodgings.

Yet for all this Rowse never became a metropolitan figure, although a regular contributor to the Spectator, *the* Criterion *and other journals. Much of his time was taken up with work for the Labour Party, lecturing, reporting on Congresses, speaking at meetings (he stood for Parliament in Penryn and Falmouth in both the 1931 and 1935 elections).*

He also, as some of these extracts make clear, was an enthusiastic and observant traveller on the continent, of which this fragment from one of his pocket books is evidence:

Rome, April 1937

My morning with M.S. [?Sarfatti, Mussolini's Jewish mistress]. M's m. holding her hands etc. My hands afterwards smelling of scent – horrible – a form of prostitution. Glad for a stronger scent of orange to put it away. Even then not quite – it remains in my nostrils bringing back that flat with the pictures and books, the Sirones and Chiricos, the false intimacy – ugh. The smell of lunch cooking. What a morning!

[Oxford,] 12 March 1930

Nothing for months. I suppose because I have stifled a good deal of my private life in work, and disappointment and work again. A separation from Adam: memory of him gives way to work. Letters from him, but I harden my heart against writing. So I take no notice of his endless changes of feeling, but work until I am tired. Now I have come out the other side of tiredness, which a week ago I thought impossible for weeks. I have replied because he wrote so hopelessly. Anyway being abroad with him spoiled going abroad for me without him. So the choice is still his.

Meanwhile the drudgery of the 'prison' has been almost unbearable. I sit in my blue chair, listening to the essays droning on, catching a word here and there, but it means nothing. Outside in the garden spring is coming.

30 May

Unhappy days these are, and today least tolerable. I have been plodding laboriously through the ante-penultimate chapter of my book, put off by tutorials, callers, worrying letters from the constituency[1] and the innumerable distractions that take one's mind away from the one thing (at the moment) I care for.

So much has it become this, that I haven't even regretted Adam much, though it looks as if we have lost each other, partly through my fault, irrecoverably now. Sometimes, the image of his head turned this way or that, or his beautiful melancholy eyes, or some charming trait of his character, natural and grave, passes across my mind. I hardly have the energy to visualize him so completely as in the earlier days. Perhaps it all goes into my book, leastways it should.

But this afternoon I paid him the tribute of a few moments in the quad at Mansfield. Nothing vivid about it, just hopeless. It was looking sad, a dark day of summer cloud and rain; young men in white were playing tennis on

1. Penryn and Falmouth had adopted him as Labour candidate.

the lawn. C.H.* wanted to go down that road, where I hardly ever go; we went by, but I came back and stood there waiting. He kept saying, 'I don't think very much of the buildings, do you? Who is it, Champneys I suppose.' Or 'Have you ever been into the chapel? I went in once and it has such funny windows.' Then 'Did you ever know anybody here?' I seemed to hear myself saying, 'Yes. I once knew somebody who was here for a short time.'

But I wonder, all the same, what Adam is doing now. Whether he has got to Göttingen all right? I think at times he may be ill. He is probably settling into a new environment, making friends with his usual facility, and sometime will write. I should like him to, just now: it would be comforting to hear *happily* from him.

The last letters I had he was worrying about his love for a girl, who was so like him that people mistook them for brother and sister. Unsatisfying for him, as usual, though I wasn't clear why. He complained that she was incapable of understanding him beyond a certain point. He wanted to tell me more about her, which I didn't want to hear.

I had the suspicion that he never would be happy however much he was in love, or thought himself to be, there are such depths of uncertainty in him. That, I believe, was what appealed to him in being loved by someone whose own certainty was much greater – so firm as to remain unshaken. At the same time as he is irresistible, what would the poor woman have to rely on? She would be made to fall in love with him but it wouldn't last; he would become restlessly unsure again, and find some other attraction. So much so that to myself, I called him a Don Juan of friendship.**

Still, he may grow up and find someone who will help to develop some certainty and confidence, and exorcize his doubts; or again, who will provide him with repose and a sense of security. Then he might marry happily, have children and be content; the role I played in his life will have been useful to his development.

We might even meet again, years later. How altered he would be: it would not be the same Adam I loved as a youth. We should find it in ourselves to be friends, with so many things in common still to talk about.***

* Dear Charles Henderson, soon to die.

** This was apt. Under the spell he exerted on others he was evidently a colossal egoist. We were all his victims.

*** Alas, alas! Plötzensee, the disaster and ruin of our time.

2 September 1931. At home

A mixed evening. Going through the squalor of Union Road, Mount Charles, somebody called me in to see an old man who was anxious to see me. His neighbour had been showing me the old man's aviary. For years he had kept canaries, but now he was getting past looking after them. He had cancer of the throat. I went in to see him. A little frail old man, Billy Morshead: I've often heard father mention his name. Yellow and parchmenty to a degree that looked Chinese; he got up from his chair to receive me, poor old man; that dreadful look in his eyes, the terror always before them, the eyes looked frantic and appealing, yet passive and accepting. Nothing to be done.

I asked him if he had any pain. Not much, he said. Glad for that.

He knew my father and had worked with him for years. I told him father wasn't very well either. He had been to Plymouth twice for radium treatment. 'You see this lump here has got to go,' he said, the frail finger pointing. It was a hopeful frame of words; for a moment I thought he imagined it would go. Then I realized it was just a form of words suggested early in his illness, which he now repeated without belief. He said that the doctor at the Devon and Cornwall Hospital at Plymouth sent him back saying he was cured. But he could see that his own doctor didn't think so.

'Where 'twas,' he said, 'when I went up the second time, it was going on all right; then I had radium on the old wound' – he pronounced it 'w*ow*nd'. There was a stale smell in the room. Was it ordure, an old sick man's uncleanliness; or old age; or cancer? It was just as if Fate had him visibly by the throat, sitting in his chair, waiting for death. I was afraid to be there, to be near him; yet I had shaken his hand on entering.

'They want me to go up for treatment again,' he said; 'but where 'tis, I don't feel I can. You see, I'm over seventy; good many years older than your father.'

I wanted to rush from the poor room, so desolate, so full of this third presence. He made a pathetic attempt to keep me:

'You know, I've been away a good many years,' he said. 'I've been in a good many countries: Canada, America, Australia.'

I thought of the forlorn birds out in the hut, and said that they were beautiful. He was only sad about them. 'You see, I used to show them. It's nothing to what I used to have; I've had a hundred and fifty of them before now.'

This clearly was his specialty, his gift, his love; the clue to the man lay somewhere here. Since he was a lone man, breeding these birds, watching over them and caring for them answered some deep need.

I would have stayed; but I couldn't; it was too hopeless. I said that I would tell my father I had seen him, and went gloomily on my errand to Fred's.

It had given me a strange turn; I couldn't help telling Fred. Then I said, there were people who believed in the goodness of the universe, while there was Fate with its fingers round that man's throat. Fred, a staunch Methodist, said it was a great mystery; he had seen his father-in-law die of the same thing, and he wished never to see another man die like that.*

Then on to the coast, the sea calm and pure, the colours clear after rain, the clouds ragged, but gentle and grand. I stopped at favourite spots and looked up at Duporth House, so longed for and for so long, now to be sold again. But O so unattainable; the lights in all the front of the house looked cosy.

Coming downhill to the basin, I watched a ship going out in the darkness; a three-masted schooner, with an oil-lamp at mast, that left a pinkish patch of light on the water of the outer basin. I thought I would use the image of the ship leaving harbour for unknown waters. Perhaps the end should come this way, going out and out into the darkness of the sea. The lines right at the end of the poem came into my head:

These shall remain
Only this hope,
Only this star.

Coming through the copse on the cliff was terrifying: I kept thinking there were hoofs following me, a horse tracking me down. Perhaps the end would be like that: hundreds of horses, the horses of the Judgement, like thunder upon the earth so that it shook.

The ship's going-out was comforting after that. The soft voices of the men calling out from the quayside to the vessel: 'Easy', 'easier!' 'All right.' 'All right now.' 'So long,' as they manoeuvred out of the narrow mouth into the night.

Saturday, 5 September

Today a unique experience. Doran Webb, whom I went to St Mawgan to meet, took me to the convent at Lanherne to call on the Mother Prioress. After a tea with the priest, a nondescript Irishman, Doran Webb and I were shown up to a shabby room (the whole house was down-at-heel) with two chairs set for us before an iron grille with black muslin drawn across.

* My uncle, Sam Vanson.

Doran Webb, completely at ease (he had been there often before), said 'I've brought Mr Rowse to see you, who's a Fellow of All Souls College, Oxford.' 'We're very pleased to see him.' 'We're very glad,' said the voices from behind the veil. 'He's interested in the Arundells,' he explained. 'Oh,' said they, their voices in a little flutter of interest; 'then he's interested in Lanherne. It's a wonderful old place with a most interesting history. Have you seen the chapel yet?'

No, I hadn't; I should be glad to, if I might.

'Oh certainly.' It had been the ballroom, the sacristy a banqueting room (more likely the chapel was the hall, the sacristy a dining parlour at the dais end). The latter had a low plaster ceiling, with a room above; when altered, they had to re-roof it. But perhaps it was a providence, for they found the roof badly needed repair and in twenty years or so it might have fallen in. All this with a sort of eagerness; half the nervousness of meeting a stranger, half suppressed excitement.

I went on this tack for a bit and asked if the house had had a chapel. Yes, said they, both together. Then one, I suppose the Mother Prioress, 'We call it now the Chapel Cells. We had it made into cells for the sisters, but you can see the roof decoration and the plasterwork still.'

They fell in with Doran Webb's small-talk about counties. Some king had referred to the western counties as being Wilts, Dorset and Devon.

What about Cornwall, supplied one of the voices. 'They reckon themselves outside of England,' he said. Subdued amusement on the part of the ladies, followed by both:

'They're all so proud of their counties.'

I began to feel more at ease, though I couldn't relax in my chair and sit back at ease like Doran Webb.

'Mr Rowse knows Father D'Arcy at Oxford,' he went on.

'Oh!' again the eager interest.

I told them I knew Martindale a little and what clever men they both are. This pleased them and they launched forth about D'Arcy's new book *The Nature of Faith*. I tantalized them a bit by telling them how much it was praised by the Dean of St Paul's, what he had written appearing everywhere in the advertisements.

Then, quietly introduced: 'Are you a Catholic?'

'No, but I've a great many Catholic friends in Oxford.' I told them of some, that my first pupil was a young Benedictine, that I knew Father McCann, the Master of St Benet's. This rather established me with the ladies.

I spoke of D'Arcy's book, and what he had told me of its closeness to Newman, and the story he told me of Newman at the Oratory. This led on to Newman. I asked if they had read a brilliant book on him by a French abbé – and forgetting the name, they supplied it: 'Brémond.' And so to whether it wasn't rather unfair to Newman.

Doran Webb contributed some Oratory stories, all conflicting as to evidence. How one father said the clue to Newman was music; another would say he never got a tune right, and so on.

Said one voice, 'Perhaps it was because he was so simple.' We all stopped at this; I wanted to say it was because he was so complex, but didn't.

What a wonderful man, said the voice; and then – '*He was a great loss to your side*.'

And so back to Arundell history. I told them a little of the Elizabethan period, the time of persecution for them. One of them got a little muddled when I talked of Sir Richard Grenville as under Elizabeth; they thought for a moment it was the time of Henry VIII. But no, the 1570s, this was the age of Cuthbert Mayne: he was the great figure to them, by whom they fixed their dates.

They told me they had his skull, with the hole where they drove in the pike; and 'you can imagine it is our greatest treasure'. Would I like to see it? They would have it fetched from the reliquary down to the sacristy for me, when the Father would show it me. I thanked them and told them what I knew of Cuthbert Mayne.

Here I drew near the centre of their life's interest. They were quite excited, you could almost hear them lean forward on the other side. One said it was their greatest hope to find some clue to the whereabouts of his body. It was quartered, you know, and the parts disposed at Wadebridge, Launceston, etc. Dorothy Arundell, who was a great relic-hunter, secured his skull. There was a story at Lanherne of treasure buried there, and they wondered if some part of his body might not be buried there. If ever I came on any clue, would I let them know?

'I would willingly, but it is so unlikely,' I said.

'Oh, but it's the unexpected that happens so often.'

What a world they live in: of providences, of the unexpected happening, of compensation for their forlorn hope of a victory here and there. Doran Webb was telling them a wild tale of a Captain Scott, who had been a British spy in Russia, was captured by the Bolsheviks and inoculated with twenty different diseases. Now crippled and aged, though a young man in years.

'How dreadful,' they said, a ring of innocent horror in the voices; 'How can they do such things!'*

I offered the suggestion that the Russians always had done these things, and haven't the same respect for human life as we.

* The nuns were not so far out after all.

More about the relations of Newman and Manning. Webb told a good story of Father William Nevill, and Manning's trying to worm out of him what Newman meant by his last letter to him. Also of the numbers of Newman letters that he had destroyed unread under pledge, as Arundell trustee I suppose; for 'it is unjust to judge a man by his letters'. A politic comment by the voice to the effect that it was good that Nevill had said nothing; he knew too much!

I took up with how Oxford was on the losing side at the Reformation, and with it Cambridge came up. Cranmer and Matthew Parker and the Cecils, as against Cardinal Allen, Parsons, Mayne, etc. 'The Blessed Edmund Campion was at Oxford too,' the voice supplied.

'Perhaps it was our Blessed Lady. Do you know the story how at the Reformation a workman was employed to demolish a beautiful stained glass window; but, a Catholic at heart, he was determined that our Blessed Lady who had been there so long should not be left out of the window. And they say right at the top there is a little light and there she is. Do you know that window?'

They seemed disappointed when I said No; so I went on to tell them of the All Souls windows left, the Women Saints, the Kings, and that of the Fathers and Doctors of the Church, including a Pope, Gregory the Great. This bucked them up. They seemed to entertain not only superstitious beliefs about roofs, Cuthbert Mayne's quarters, our Blessed Lady, but also about Charles Henderson whom they know and revere.

They were so sweet and naive, and in spite of being enclosed in their own little world so lively and intelligent, they made a marked impression on my mind. I thought of them all the evening; their voices were so candid and gentle: something more purely feminine than anything I have ever heard. They clearly have the secret of the good life. They are quite happy, the young farmer at the barton told me. I can well believe it; for they have renounced desire. He told me of the wonderful old Rev. Mother Christophers and how when he came home from the Balkans she had asked him in to tell her what things were like there, for she had been in Greece forty years ago. At her jubilee she was allowed to see people without the veil; she had had four or five of the people around in to talk to her. She said that all the years had gone by as nothing, her life a dream.

1 Brunswick Square, WC1. 6 November

Several times since coming to London I have wondered if I am not verging on neurasthenia. There is more excuse for me this time than last, since coming back from three weeks' strenuous election-fighting at home. Last time, I was worn out and tired, as I seem to be always anyhow. I can't stand the nervous exhaustion of the ceaseless solicitations of town life. I shall be broken in to being as dull and unobservant as the rest. For a countryman it is hard not to notice everything; and I have trained myself to take note of everything that interests me. It has become second nature; but the strain is unbearable.

4 December: Perhaps the first edge of that is already wearing away – a symptom of exhaustion which I shall recover from. When I first came to London it was such a strain: everything wrought upon my nervous system immediately, as if I had no protection. I couldn't bear – even if I can now – the restlessness of the street signs, newspaper posters, hoardings.

7 November

The soft quarter-chime of an Augustan church comes intermittently into the room on the wing of the spring wind. The lights gleam and wink and gleam in the square because of the wind; branches go bobbing up and down, in and out the traffic and among the winking lights and voices.

But the chime is of another world: so rare as to be irrecoverable except intermittently, in odd catches of the heart. The chime buffets clearly with the wind across the square; just as clearly as they who were alive in the days of Caroline or Anne would hear when the wind was this way. Those few sweet notes! And in turn, the field of Blenheim, and the Peace, and Swift, and Anne dying at Kensington. A few more years – they are all one to the chime that strikes over the changed city – and it is the time of the Regent; the stucco in the Regent's Park is fresh above the bottle-green grass. In his phaeton the bedizened old roué rolls round Windsor Great Park and dreams he won Waterloo. Back a few years – backward and forward is all one – to Pitt in the lonely years, nose turned up at all the world, and the ships of Trafalgar sweeping the seas. The chime rings out eleven o'clock, the lights blink, the spring wind stirs the night-trees and the echoes.*

[1932]

A new film: 'Mädchen in Uniform', life in a school for officers' daughters at Potsdam. All day I have been under its impact, as with the thought of Adam, with the thought of whom it mingled to make me unhappy. Here was this school under the shadow of the Military Church at Potsdam, among the

* I suppose all this was by way of learning to write and learning to be an historian. 1979. Much influenced by Virginia Woolf.

gardens and colonnades of Frederick's time – I heard the chime again last night, and the soldiers exercising on the Paradenplatz. The theme was the love between E. v. B., the mistress whose initials the girls marked upon their arms or embroidered with a heart upon their clothes, and the new girl who falls in love with her. The older woman struggles against it, telling the girl she must be reasonable, when she cannot be reasonable herself. They exchanged a look of recognition at first meeting; when the young mistress makes her rounds, kissing them all goodnight, the girl throws herself into her arms. It has quite distracted me.*

[Oxford, n.d.]

I thought of Adam at Bablockhythe this afternoon, by the river.** Last night I spoke to him over the telephone. He is there, over the fields from the city. I think he too might hear Magdalen bells from there, if he listens.

O lovely city! It would be easy to change what should be changed, if this place were not so beautiful.*** One must save what is irreplaceable, even if it is bound up with an order that must be transformed.

Morning in Paris [n.d.]

Here I am, as three years ago, up at a window in the Hotel du Quai Voltaire. Not the same window – that was higher up in an attic – but much the same view. At night the same image occurs of Eugénie hurrying down the length of the Tuileries and the Louvre, just across the river from my window. I spent last night mooning about the *emplacements* of the Tuileries – making out where the palace was. It is all so easily reconstructed, the balustrades that approached the palace from the Place du Carrousel undisturbed, and the deserted sentry-boxes in the pedestals of Second-Empire goddesses; then the gates and railings on the other side where the private garden of the palace ended. Were the gates closed at night, so that there was that large area of quietness in the middle of Paris?

Not much change since I was here last. I was going to say noisier, but that could hardly be. The green motor-omnibuses go at a furious pace, crashing on the brakes at corners. The traffic of Paris has a different character from London traffic: rapid, excitable, varying in speeds, wilful, dashing, disordered; yet it gets through somehow, and quicker than in London. From here I watch a more regular flow, over the bridge that takes it through the

* All too obvious what the young man *needed*. 1979.

** I helped to get him to Balliol as a Rhodes Scholar.

*** Still thinking of a new social order evidently!

Carrousel, through the heart of the palace. Last night I went up to the windows of the Pavillon de Flore, where the nursery of the Prince Impérial was, thinking of his longing in exile in England to see the horse-bus that went up to the Place de Clichy debouching from the Rue du Bac.

Paris is so dreamlike to me – I knew it long before I knew London – that I cannot take its traffic seriously. I cross streets, with motor-cars bearing down in all directions, in a way I should never dream of in London, where I regard the traffic with more respect. Here it is haphazard, rather comic. The men are comic too, at any rate looking down on them, I see them strutting along like game-cocks, so self-satisfied and self-assured: no doubts about themselves and their place in the order of things. I was first struck by the insect-appearance of motor-cars seen from above: black oblong objects like big beetles with legs at the corners creeping by in the night, the antennae of their lamps feeling their way forward.

The human element provides a farce: it is so unaware of itself, so possessed with its own concerns, from the outside one can see it as a menagerie. In England, they would have a different humour, more self-aware, ready to catch your eye and laugh or look surly, but including one in the game. But the game does not wholly possess them, they are too little immersed in what they are doing.

I watched a long old-fashioned cart coming slowly down the Quai Voltaire, an old grey nag led by a fat man in sloppy brown slippers. The horse was decorated with a wooden collar painted green and garnished with a frame of bells that tinkled; at the back, fastened on, was a green tub that swung in rhythm. He stopped outside our door. What is he going to do? I read on the back of the waggon: Armand Cornet, Dêpot Marché de la Madeleine. A trickle of water leaks out under the doors. The man comes back, knocks up the iron bar that fastens the doors; the van is filled with big blocks of ice. He slides one out, hacks at it with an iron hook, then carves as if with a knife; the block splits into three. I admire his skill, splitting the pieces so regularly, no cross-splitting or bits broken off. He wraps two of them in a piece of sacking and carries them on his head into the hotel; emerges, elbows his horse out into the street, and repeats the process at a house lower down. Everybody is buying ice along the Quai Voltaire today. I watch him go slowly down the street, leading the old grey horse, towards the dome of the Institut and the spire of the Sainte Chapelle, where the river bends.

While I write, the barges and little launches go gaily up and down the Seine; the green omnibuses come and go under the arches of the Carrousel.

[Oxford,] 4 November, Friday evening

I don't know how many dreams are pursuing me at this moment. I am tired, not only with the day's work, but with so many things; I am tired *out*. Perhaps the long hot summer I worked through in London without break, perhaps the ceaseless agitation of meetings to attend to, speeches to make, lectures to compose, articles to write, researches to catch up with; perhaps a secret worm gnawing at my insides; perhaps the increasing disillusionment with politics that hit me first at the General Election, the blow of which I have never been able to forget. Tonight, for the first time, it struck me with force how paradoxical is my way of life, or rather the sources from which I draw my subsistence, and the world I am always arguing for and to which I am pledged, are. Going down the Blue Boar side-street in the rain to the post-box, I thought, here I am bent upon rooting out these interests living upon surplus value that others produce – and my living is provided out of the unearned increment of north London at All Souls; and out of subsidies from capitalists to the School of Economics.*

Then, too, save for a small group of realist, sensible people – Morrison and Ernest Bevin above all; Dalton it is impossible to like and Cole ridiculous to think of following – I cannot collaborate with the people I most agree with. I think of the Adelphi group, Middleton Murry's lot of Pharisees; the Communists might be better, but are hopelessly ineffective; those infected by MacDonaldism have done the unforgivable thing. And so it goes on. It is worse with the People. They suffer; but it is largely their own fault, especially since they have never properly supported their own cause. Poor fools: half of them voted for the National Government. I have never forgiven them that; nor shall I. It was a lesson to me, if not to them.

One cannot trust the people; one can trust only one or two rare individuals: in the end, there is oneself alone. There is hardly a soul I can really consult, in the sense of opening to him my own troubles of mind. Once and again, I have been candid with someone, thinking he would understand that, whatever my doubts and disappointment, I was reliable at bottom. But you dare not let anybody see what you think beyond a point. Not even Claude.** You cannot share your doubts with them. You have to keep a poker face. The run of Labour people are longing for a genuine grip on things: they get it from me, if in an exasperated form. They lap it up; they batten on it, but the virtue goes out of one.

[Somebody coming: even now, to see me.]

*

* The dilemma I was caught in.

** Claude Berry, editor of the *West Briton*, my closest political friend in Cornwall.

An old pupil, one of my earliest, from St Edmund Hall: a nice fresh-faced lad, not much changed, crisp, attractive brown hair, already streaked with some grey ones!*

Talking with him has driven away some of the troubles that haunted me. But did it though? Nothing could drive away this undercurrent of hopelessness about the People, the futility of our efforts, the bitterness that poisons my personal relations. Nor need I blame myself much for it; either on the public side, or the private. It is hardly a question of blame; it goes beyond that. The people are utter fools: the revelation of that at every turn in politics renders one's public activity pointless. As for the private – as a child I looked for affection and rarely received it, and it has gone on like that ever since. But then I'm not the only one; there's C.H., and J.S.,[1] and R.P. – all of us with that common bond at least. Only there is a further frustration – early training in starved affection has the result that now one desires affection only from those who cannot or will not respond. Then, when affection is offered, one now spurns it.

O what a change! Tonight's few minutes in the garden was so refreshing, because it took me back to youth and boyhood, in the way that I haven't thought of for a long time. I am now too busy. Whereas earlier, I used to spend a lot of time thinking regretfully of my childhood.

Some of the things I have been doing lately:

The last few days re-writing my Fabian Lecture for the press; revising has been as much trouble as if I were writing it.

There was all the fuss and nervousness of delivering the lecture. Wrote also a résumé for the *New Clarion.*

Also a *Clarion* article, about Youth and Politics. (I'm now sick of the theme. But the new League of Youth bulletin wants an article this week.)

The Clarion Rally – of youth elements in the Labour movement – took place at Transport House last Saturday, which I spoke at, probably annoying Shepherd, the National Agent, who was there taking notes.

The weekend before I went up to Birmingham to start off their Socialist Forum, which was a success; I daresay it will go with a swing now this winter.

I gave two of Morrison's[2] London Labour Party lectures at Hackney and Southwark; the first a great success. One afternoon I spent with Morrison at County Hall, supposedly over my Fabian Lecture, but ranging over

* C. R. Hiscocks, who became a professor.

1. Not Jack Simmons, whom ALR had not yet met.

2. Herbert Morrison, long thought of by many, including Rowse, as the obvious leader for the Labour Party.

everything. He asked me whether I'd like to come on to the County Council; but attractive as it is, it would be too absorptive of time.

Last night, I lectured to the London Cornish Association on 'Cornwall in the days of the Armada': *that* didn't need preparing.

I have had to put in some preparation for my BBC talk on Marx – writing synopsis, bibliography, etc. It has turned my mind to the old man again with interest.

Various articles I've written, one on the Oxford Press Autumn Catalogue, which everybody says is 'charming' but nobody cares to publish; reviews of Shaw and Cole and a new Life of Bacon for *The Listener*. Earlier in term, a long attack on MacDonald, analysing his statement in the *News Letter*, which like everything to do with that paper, infuriated me.

All in addition to my usual vast correspondence, and to my full-time job, researching two or sometimes three days in the British Museum, and giving two courses of lectures at the School of Economics.

On the whole I am pleased; but when two more articles, one on bloody Youth, the other for Germany – the *Neue Blätter für den Socialismus** – are finished, I shall feel more relieved.

4 December

I realized it was my birthday only by accident in Trafalgar Square tonight. Somebody said it was December 4th, when I had thought it was tomorrow. Besides being tired with writing at a *Clarion* article all day in reply to Lord Melchett, I am not at all satisfied to be twenty-nine – and so little done. Perhaps especially the past year. Last year I wrote my book. This year I have written nothing but innumerable ephemeral articles for innumerable febrile people. I say innumerable? A dozen for the *Clarion*; three for our *Cornish Labour News*; a dozen reviews or so; a long article like that on Keynes, short ones on a few books. My time really goes into copying hundreds of pages of sixteenth-century mss. – it's what I'm really paid for: to be a scribe in the British Museum, a drudge in the Public Record Office. Such is historical research, into which I seem to have wandered; and, like William James in philosophy, what I'm looking for is the way out.

What is the way out? Is it politics? Is it marriage, I sometimes wonder in the course of a particularly painful night? I wish I had more *Ahnung* for the latter; I am so little qualified for it. But it might be a way out.**

What is wrong with politics is the bloody people. They clearly won't

* Adam von Trott arranged this.

** It would have killed me.

allow one a way out if they can help it. If I got into Parliament, it would be merely an accident. It is humiliating to engage in a course that is so dependent on other people. I regard myself as unlikely to fail where I depend upon myself; to depend on others is an open invitation to failure.*

However, politically, I see some signs of establishing myself. Not rapidly, that is the curious thing – I am more capable of making an effective impression than it would seem. Perhaps I left coming to London rather late; but my emergence on the horizon is being noticed. Still, I am only on the margin, like any other don, not *in* politics.

Meanwhile the years pass. I wonder when on earth we are going to get our chance? 1929–31 was a chance for some of us but, unhappily, for the MacDonalds, the men in the sixties. And they have put off our chance for years. I don't repine much, for my passive side wants to postpone the decision about going into politics. More livable is this university cum writing cum margin-of-politics life. Not that I should hesitate if the chance came – but it depends on other people and outside circumstances. I don't want so many years to pass in the British Museum that at last I am fit for nothing else, a Museum specimen. I console myself by recalling the years that Marx and Lenin spent there, and yet were capable of a Revolution.

26 December

When I consider one aspect of my character, I recognize that there is a kind of fatality in my family. The men in my mother's family are women; the women are very much women. I don't know whether owing to the dominance of Grandmother Vanson, but the family is overwhelmingly feminine. This is where I get my emotional side from. When I was a child I was all feeling: I learned all from feeling. I remember how strongly things affected me: being frowned on for being too 'forward', or speaking when I wasn't spoken to, or being too bright for them, asking too many questions they couldn't answer. The unhappy thing was the guilt-complex that this repression produced. On the other side was responsiveness to affection, rarely received, almost entirely from my sister, whom in consequence I adored. This reinforced the feminine characteristics I had inherited. Right up to the time of going to Oxford, I was dependent on intuition and the emotions for what I knew and was. I felt everything keenly, emotionally alive to the fingertips. I was shaken by passions, anger and love – I fell for my school-friends. A prey to self-pity, for there was never any response. I was acutely upset by cruelty to animals. And so I still remain: cruelty to

* This was borne out at every turn all the way along.

animals appals me, but experience has taught me to look away, for I cannot bear it; my reaction to cruelty to human beings has remained patchy and undependable. Perhaps now I recognize it, I may remedy it.*

Oxford made a profound difference. Up to that time I felt so strongly that I could never argue a case for myself or my convictions. I could only convince other people by the force of emotion. At Oxford I learned to defend myself intellectually; I remember my vexation at not being able to defend my point of view with logic and reason. It was an unpleasant surprise to come up against Wadleigh at Christ Church, who knew better how to argue; and again later, Moon at All Souls, who was my junior. In the end I learned the tricks of the game. I sometimes feel now that there is no case I could not defend.

I am grateful to Oxford for this development. Formerly at the mercy of emotion, and others, I now have a defence-mechanism. It has given me the power to dominate others and, if necessary, to throw others off the track. It was perhaps an inevitable change. But it may ultimately have damaged the poet for the benefit of the politician.**

The process has not gone far enough. Control over myself must be absolute; or I become 'The Cracked Vase' – this phrase comes into my head to describe myself, whenever I am walking down to the sea, or along the lanes, in the field of the dead, or alone in my room. 'The Cracked Vase' I say to myself, thinking to write a poem under that title.

But can the control be absolute? It must be; or this fatality in my blood will undo me – this conjunction of pride with faulty self-control. If the self-control were perfected, the pride might be justified. Self-control, with simplicity and integrity (not pride, but I will not say humility), must be my aim. Or else I shall not achieve what I want to achieve.

You have to put what they think or say over the numerator of what they are: the woman who talks lightly of virtue is somebody's mistress, or would be; another who defends having illegitimate children had one herself; a man who is physically weak favours intellect against physique. They believe what they *want*.

Make the adjustment.

If only people *could* catch themselves out – what relief! How refreshing after all the sameness of people's views not worth considering, not worth listening to, a waste of precious time.***

* I did not. The realization of human idiocy forfeited sympathy for them. After all, animals cannot help themselves; humans can and should.

** Disingenuousness would have been useful in politics. All politicians are disingenuous – have to be. 1979.

*** After giving up on politics I adhered to that principle – and saved a lot of time that way.

[London,] 29 March 1933

Tonight to the theatre with Lady Pares to see *Richard of Bordeaux*. Something of a gala night: I might have known that something was in the air. Just before the performance the manager himself entered in full evening-dress to try the lighting and arrange the chairs in the royal box. While I was deep in talk with Lady Pares, everybody began to clap, and lo the royal party was there. Queen Mary in the corner nearest, very regal in a blue velvet wrap, then the Duke of York with a white buttonhole, the Duchess charming and schoolgirl-like; a gentleman-in-waiting in the far corner where he can have seen nothing.

It was fascinating to watch the effect on the theatre. The clapping was very friendly, but polite. The audience developed a perceptible unity: a beehive of British bourgeois, with their Queen among them. It all pivoted upon that box, on the Queen especially. Not a discordant note was observable.

O what a wonderful sensation – all of us one family, the hearts of all beating as one. I was more intent on watching the behaviour of the insects for future use. I was as curious about that box as anybody else. Nearly everybody was too well-behaved to take more than an occasional glance.

The behaviour of the audience was the thing to register – it keyed them up – though they behaved with restraint: weren't they British?

22 July

London has a peculiar effect on me – it makes me work like hell, it exhausts me, and then it makes me peculiarly sensitive and unhappy at one and the same time. As if my nerves were frayed out, but as such are all the more in a condition to catch all the impressions that are abroad, and to weigh me down with them.

It is the noise and the people more than anything that do it: the unceasing noise and the omnipresence of people, so that one is never to oneself, and yet one is always to oneself in it. As François Mauriac says: in Paris a desert amid innumerable people, in the country never alone though in a desert.

'I've done my best . . . according to a certain scale . . . And I've tried to keep up to it, haven't I?' A loud man's voice comes up into my room even now. He is speaking to his woman, who hastens, for he speaks with the tone of deliberate self-pity, to assure him: 'Yes, you 'ave.'

The people are my greatest problem. I can't say what damage the miserable population of this part of London has done to my political confidence. They are such wretches, so feeble, so mentally-defective, even when not criminal.

Coming along the Euston Road tonight, two or three rows were in progress on the pavement. One between two middle-aged men, of whom one, very fat and boss-eyed, was drunk. The worst was between two women over a sodden youth named Gerry. One of them had apparently smacked his face, the red-faced, bleary-eyed lout. The women were fair devils, white to the gills; one screamed, 'You smack his face again then, and I'll see . . .' The other fury: 'I *will* smack his face, you see if I don't.' The first, returning: 'You smack his face then, and see what I'll do to you.' The two women drew themselves up, breasts bridling, then clashed. The one who had smacked the young man's face drew back with, 'Here, you take my bag,' handing over her bag and fur, preparatory to a fight. The other white, eyes flashing, false teeth gleaming. They might have been two animals – except that animals would have been better looking. 'I'll fetch the police for you,' said somebody. The crowd lurched on.

In Tottenham Court Road a handsome young policeman was having all he could do with the traffic in the heat and the noise. Sweat ran down his face: he was very red and hot, his clothes sticking to his figure, which remained elegant and efficient amid it all. All my sympathies were with him: one must never let down these men for the sake of the scum.

These are the people. How to get out of it?

Well, they are only a section of the people, debased and urbanized. These creatures can never be allowed to come on top; cf. Trotsky on the scum that popped up their head during the Revolution – to get shot down.

[Paris,] Sunday, 7 January 1934

Today, after writing in the morning till I remember that my object was not to come to Paris to write, I went for a walk on the other bank of the river. Through the garden of the Tuileries, more formal than ever in winter with the trees straight black lines and no grass to relieve the stony places at the western end. The great fountain was playing, and so was the lesser at the Palace end: – it always oppresses me to look at the gaping space between the Pavillons de Flore et de Marsan, where the long range of the Palace went. André Le Nôtre is remembered: 'l'auteur de ce jardin, de ceux de Versailles, Chantilly, Saint Cloud, Meudon, et des plus beaux parcs de France. 1613–1700'. That was the great age of France; I used to think the 'grand siècle' meant the eighteenth century and Voltaire. But no; the great age would be an age of faith, I reflected, looking at a volume of Pascal's Letters on the quays, and again this afternoon in the Île Saint Louis.

Le Nôtre is commemorated again in the church of Saint Roch, where he is buried. Saint Roch was in the centre of fashion in the eighteenth century, from the notabilities buried there. Wicked old Cardinal Dubois, with a propitiatory smile on his face, biretta in hand, making up to Heaven pliably upon his knees; aristocrats like the Comte d'Harcourt, 'lieutenant-général des armées du Roi'; princes of the church, Bossuet, the eagle of Meaux, a cardinal-archbishop of Besançon, princesses of the blood – Marie Princesse de Conti, the Admiral de Grasse, one of the founders of the United States. It is an impressive company; for all that one thinks, when the monarchy fell something grand went out of the life of France.

I spent so much of the afternoon in Saint Roch that I was too late to go and see one of the contemporary notabilities of Paris, André Siegfried. But I did try to see Léon Blum, and found that he inhabits the most intellectual corner a man could find: a shuttered hôtel of the seventeenth century in the Île Saint Louis, not far from the Hôtel de Lauzun. A glimpse of his open door (he is away speaking in the country) revealed an entrance hall filled with books, all the latest and best, with a charming statue and *objects d'art* on the tables. Not an impression of a leader of the people, but of an intellectual; what an argument for *not* having one's desire to live in similar surroundings!

I spent my afternoon in even less socialist sort, listening to vespers and saying of the Rosary at Saint Roch. The old enchantment was rather lost by the raucousness of the voices, of the organ (which seemed to be all reeds) and the slatternliness of the eldest of the three acolytes. He kept fidgeting, dropping cards out of his book, pulling up his socks and tying his bootlaces under his red cassock and cotta. He *could* not attend, but got through his performances somehow. At the proper places he bobbed his head to the priest as abruptly as a grimace – he is evidently at the restless sexy age. The officiating priest behaved very well with him, though he was clearly irked. There he sat in a gold cope falling round and about his chair, following the service in his book, occasionally getting up and chanting a sentence or two. Very much the priest, thin and ascetic, his eyes dark and mild, the expression of his face keen and pointed, the eyebrows puckered with suppressed annoyance. His voice was feeble; he kept close to the Gregorian chant with accurate sensitiveness, not with any force or fire.

Catholicism was in the ritual. After all, the Catholic Church is the heart of France, not Léon Blum whom I was going to see; if one were French one would wish to have been brought up a Catholic as a child. Then one could find one's own feet and move away as an adult.

I was glad, then, to have been brought up in the English church; and to have had that tradition behind me. In a half-conscious way I seemed to see St Paul's on a Sunday afternoon – this same Sunday afternoon that I was in Saint Roch – as this older tradition was behind them: the priest, the acolytes, the clergy in the choir stalls, the girls in their veils who sang the hymns of the Rosary, and, in their tombs, the historic dead.

[After the sudden death of his father, 5 March 1934. Cornwall]

I am writing now in the sun, up in my bedroom window that overlooks the gate, and whenever the gate clangs I find myself looking – it has just shut to, it is George, who is like him: he looked just as his father used to do, his quick footsteps echoed down the passage, just like father's: you cannot tell the difference. I am glad he has left some image of himself in the world. Mother was comforting herself with the thought a few days ago: Aunt Bess said: 'As long as George is alive, his father will never die.' He used always to look up to my bedroom window; he liked to see me working away in my room. Usually he would smile that shy smile of his, with a lively glance of his grey eyes.*

Monday 12th. A week today since he died. A lovely spring day, sun and light spring air that propels the white clouds across the sky ('the orchestrated clouds,' I said aloud in the Field of the Dead, watching their ranges moving down from the uplands to the sea). Last Monday there was rain and wind that beat down upon the car as they went up, after seeing him die, to the station to meet me.

I never came by that train. I didn't get George's letter until that afternoon when I came back from Oxford. I phoned at once to the infirmary and heard he was dead. At first I was in perfect control, and was surprised at myself. This is the second time this has happened to me: coming back to 1 Brunswick Square, opening my letters in the hall, to hear first that Charles was dead – and now that my father was. I shall not open my letters at that table again. What was I to do? – there was no need to hurry home, too late. I was expected to go to the theatre with Lady Cripps and Veronica. Should I tell them that he was worse, leaving them early after the theatre to catch the midnight train? I was distracted: I didn't realize that until I telephoned them.

All the way home in the train I was in the same state: not so much stunned, as frozen. In my sleeper I tried to go on reading my book on the archaeology of Cornwall. I had been reading about the megalithic chamber-graves of Cornwall, the pots containing human ashes, the cult of the dead, this weekend in Oxford while father was dying. I ought to have known something was wrong: he hadn't written to me for a week, and earlier he had been writing nearly every other day. All that weekend I was in a dazed

* He was proud of me, and can never have thought that I might not be his son. My mother not, became even jealous – nasty spirit. O the duplicity of women! 1979.

condition, not knowing what to do with myself, though there was as usual plenty to do: I put it down to being fagged. I went on reading my grim book about the graves I had seen with Charles in the Scilly Islands.

On the homeward journey, I could not read, nor could I sleep. My mind went round and round trying to accustom itself to the idea that father was dead; I still find it difficult after these days, the agitation of seeing his body (like a child), his funeral, the emptiness in his bedroom and about the house. By the first stations, Reading and Swindon, I had not slept; afterwards I woke up at each one and remember Taunton, Exeter, Newton Abbot and Plymouth. I was still numbed and got up after Liskeard to look out in the early morning. The trees alongside the railway were dripping with rain. By Par there was light enough to see the line of the Gribben and the bay, calm and grey; lights in the flour-mill by the harbour, smoke going up from the stack, a few small vessels in the basin.

Then came St Austell; George had come to meet me in a downpour of rain. We met in silence and then carried on a conversation about the arrangements for the funeral. Not even the sight of mother in misery, standing at the stove, broken and crying, moved me much. Nor all that morning. George wanted me to go with him to Truro to pick up father's things; but it would never do to leave mother there alone for hours.

Trenarren House,[1] 12 June

I have broken off in the middle of writing at my book,[2] because there came into my mind too powerfully the haunting image of how the road looks at Trenarren just where it turns in to the house, that narrow neck where the trees open and you come suddenly into full view of the bay. There is anguish in thinking of it so much: is it that I shall never live there after all? So much of my effort nowadays, working hard to make money and saving, is directed towards someday going there to live. I used to entice father with the idea, so that sometimes he may have half-thought we should go there; in the end he knew, and one day on his last drive there, looking over the gate he said to mother that someday when they were in the grave, I might live there, but that he never should.

The pathos of that memory and how I used to talk to him about it has entered into my thought of the place. I see it so frequently, never more clearly than when I am away from home (wherever I am, it seems I am away from home): the bend of the road and the wall, starred with primroses in

1. The house which ALR was to lease from the Hext family from 1953 till his death. It was at this time unoccupied.
2. *Sir Richard Grenville of the Revenge* (1937).

the spring, the fringe of beeches leaning away from the south-west; the granite pillars on each side of the shut gate with a 'gentility ball' on each; inside, the desertedness of the house, always empty, except occasionally for a thin straggle of smoke ascending among the trees, always waiting; the garden shelving and hollowed to the south, the rhododendrons and the tunnel of stunted oaks, the tumbledown wall at the bottom of the kitchen-garden towards the tiny hamlet.

O what a place it is: in summer when the flowers in the cottage gardens are out, when the smell of the sea is over everything and the nights are white, or in autumn when the open space of the leddra above is grey and silver; best of all, in spring when the shoots of fern are coming out in the crevices and crannies, and the paddock is carpeted with spring flowers: I love every stone and corner and tree in the place. When I think of it waiting there, and its rather ghostly loneliness. At the same time it makes me afraid, for by the time I shall be able to go there, shall I not be alone (my father already gone) and too lonely myself to be able to support its own loneliness?*

[Oxford,] Saturday, 23 March 1935

Unable to work much today, because ill again last night, I had a little supper in my room alone and afterwards Geoffrey** came up to talk with me. He was fascinating as usual, with so original an angle he sees things from. And I have heard so little comment on the momentous things that have been happening this week – since Germany's springing universal conscription upon us last Saturday. I heard the news of it in Cornwall, not until I had got on to the platform at a 'Peace or War' meeting at Falmouth. The chairman, Jack Hieatt of the Transport Workers' Union, had heard the news that evening on the wireless.

Geoffrey told me about Flandin's speech in reply to Hitler's *coup*. He held up Germany as an example for France to imitate: look at the unity of Germany on this issue, while in France there is dissension. From now on propaganda against the army and military service is treason. Thus, Geoffrey said, the militants in Germany play into the hands of the militants in France, and the militants in France play into the hands of those in Germany. To the destruction of us all, the French papers had quoted Austen Chamberlain's attack on Attlee: if London were bombed, insufficiently protected, he and his friends would be hanged from the next lamp-posts – quoted under the headline 'La Lanterne les Travaillistes'.

Geoffrey was good about the difficulties a Labour foreign policy would

* I managed it only when my mother was off my hands in 1953.

** G. F. Hudson, expert on the Far East.

have to face if it came into the present mess – that our foreign policy would need to be extremely skilfully conducted over the next few years, what with the pacifists and women's associations on one side, and on the other the Beaverbrook isolationists ready to exploit the slightest mistake to raise a scare. He said: 'The clever politician knows that it is more than his seat is worth to say anything against the League; but that it is equally more than his seat is worth to be in favour of doing anything to carry out our obligations under the League.'

Very true. I told him what I consider the Labour line to be. Instead of the fantastic speech of Stafford Cripps in the House contemplating a League war against Japan, it is not for us to take the responsibility for the mess that they have landed us in. They are responsible for it: they have defeated and crushed, in practically every country, the people who stand for moderation, peace and civilization. Why should we pull the chestnuts out of the fire for them? Why should we take the responsibility for it, when they have had everything their own way for so long? The Reaction in Europe has won and this is what it means; if you like it, vote for it; on the other hand, if you want some international order which can give us peace, the Left in Europe is the only foundation for it.

This line may escape the dilemma they force us into. Either you are in favour of armaments and national security, in which case we lose support of the peace movement in the country; if people realize that there is going to be a war, they will rather fight it under the leadership of the Tories than under us – and I don't wonder at that. On the other hand, if we cry Peace, Peace, when there is no peace, oblivious of our own security, we open the way to a Nazi victory on the continent and that means the end of internationalism and peace for this century.

I read Geoffrey a few extracts from the flood of speeches by European statesmen during the last day or two.* Richard (Pares) says, there are times when things are so bad, all one can do is just giggle. It is enough to make me think what J. A. Spender said, that, after a long lifetime's experience of public affairs, *things really are as silly as they seem*. There is Mussolini: 'Let it be clear that our desire for peace by collaboration in Europe is backed by several million bayonets . . . We will overcome all obstacles placed to prevent us fulfilling our destiny.'

* After citing Laval, I gave up with Blomberg – ominous names. With Nazi Germany war *was* inevitable. I note the recurring illness: constant growth of scar-tissue from continued ulcers was blocking the duodenal passage and responsible for frequent sickness and pain. Only a short-circuiting operation could save me – I didn't know this, and went on hoping against hope, until forced to it, when nearly dead. [This note, evidently written much later, is undated. Probably 1979.]

Sunday, 24 March

Today, in pursuit of health and to steady my nerves, I went for a day-walk with Geoffrey from which just returned sunned and refreshed, ready for work again. Oxford's quadrangles and gardens (it being Sunday) are full of bells and birds singing. The place is a paradise to come back to. David Cecil used to say that Oxford, like Venice, was a place to be always coming back to; if you lived there all the time you became dulled to the enchantment.

I remember the first excitement on coming back to Christ Church as an undergraduate, entering Tom Gate from the noise of St Aldate's; the stillness of the quad, the splashing of Mercury, the rippling of the bells around the walls, through the cloisters and echoing about the Hall staircase. Oxford has never lost this magic for me. Tonight after a dozen years it is still as magical. The light is going from the garden; blue dusk has descended upon the long line of Queen's beyond the garden. Every moment the trees grow darker; the bells are very far away, ringing somewhere for evensong; a boy in the kitchen is whistling happily.

I feel the need to catch every detail, for time is flying, as if this moment were my last. 'Look thy last on all things lovely every hour', I have remembered since a boy at school, when it made a great impression on me. Or again, two lines that I first read then – as if these things

> may never come,
> This side the tomb.

Geoffrey and I walked most of the way to Kidlington, after hanging about by the Castle for a bus which never came. While waiting, we walked about the streets of this poor quarter,[1] which never fails to interest me with its Grey Friars Building, rehashed in the seventeenth century with a baroque doorway in plaster. And Paradise Square, with trees and sunshine on such a day, and the slums about it. The people here a low lot – *lumpen proletariat* – all voting Tory, no doubt. We passed degraded-looking young men at the corners of the streets; a cripple boy with a half-wit face. I said to Geoffrey, what can we hope from the people, if they're like this? On the other hand, the more respectable middle classes stand for Fascism, nationalism and the mentality that leads to war. It's a hopeless dilemma we're in. In St Ebbe's Street, a dark alley, a congregation was enclosed in that box of a church singing their hymns – in darkness – on a morning like this!

At Kidlington we lunched in a pub, after wandering about trying

1. Now demolished and unrecognizably redeveloped.

hopelessly to find the way to Hampton Poyle. Lionel Curtis absent from the house at the corner, in South Africa: he would have put us on the right road, in more ways than one! Geoffrey sat as usual with his rather oriental dignity – he must have caught the habit in the East, living so much first in Turkey, then in China – munching cheese with his draught beer. I, in pursuit of time on the wing, jotted down a few notes, having finished my milk before he his beer. 'Curtis absent in S. Africa, the sun bright upon his willow-field while the great man is away. Larks singing over the Cherwell and in the fields – the voices of men, thick and masculine outside in the bar.' I in the middle of quoting La Rochefoucauld to G. – 'Les querelles ne dureraient pas longtemps' – when interrupted by the innkeeper, a stocky, potent type, attended by a little boy, who had been summoned by his wife to describe to us the way to Hampton Poyle and Hampton Gay.

Rustics have difficulty in expressing themselves or explaining anything, even the way to the next village. Or it may be the difficulty the rational mind has in following the wamblings of the uneducated: I can never even listen when they begin to explain anything to me. My brother, for example, I could never be taught to drive the car by him: his mind is so little rational. G. illustrated this from a farmer in Devonshire (he often walks on Dartmoor) explaining: you go up to where the mill used to be, and then on to Farmer Guise's farm that was, etc. Because I belong to them, I can't bear it. The same idiocy is what enables them to be exploited economically and politically.*

Sometimes it is simply due to their never having been anywhere. Our people at home hardly ever went anywhere; some there never go even out of the village; my Uncle Harry, with whom our family was at daggers drawn (also typical of human idiocy) hardly went out of his house: he had a morbid fear of being seen. It makes them all the more curious about every little thing that happens in the village: it is astonishing how they can reconstruct what is going on in the house across the way by the moving of blinds, twitching of curtains, appearances at window or door, lights upstairs or downstairs, etc. Like Proust's picture of life in Combrai and of Tante Eulalie, who though an invalid in her bedroom recognized all the dogs in the town – 'Comme si je ne connais pas le chien de M.—.' At a school near Padstow, about five miles away, of a class of quite senior children, not a single one had ever been into Padstow.**

Thanks to the innkeeper we got on to the right road; walking up it in the sun, I thought of John Simon at this hour closeted with Hitler, or going to

* And *now*, 1979, when they have everything their way, they are wrecking their own show.

** All this has changed with the social revolution.

the musical tea-party at the Kaiserhof. The music would be entirely lost upon him, and he would infallibly get it wrong.

Hampton Poyle a pleasant village to the north of Kidlington, the spire of which dominates this river landscape for miles. There was a diminutive church, empty and countrified – few houses around – hardly a church at all, more like a family chapel.

In the little north aisle were a few of the Poyles, a family that has entirely disappeared.* A recumbent knight of the fourteenth century, with crossed legs; a lady under a canopy; a brass to John Poyle armiger and his wife, who died in 1434. I have never heard of anything the Poyles did or were; they gave their name to this village, and for the rest vanished out of remembrance. Their manor house, a stone's throw from the church, is now a farm with substantial buildings.

Saturday, 6 April

Today, having written up to late last night, I couldn't write at *Grenville*[1] this morning; anyhow I had arrived at a suitable place to break off, having dealt with the episode of Cuthbert Mayne's capture and the crushing out of the Catholic remnant in Cornwall. I think it's done well; am on tenterhooks before undertaking a new chapter lest it should not go well; when I get down to it, it comes off all right. This gives me confidence – I feel I have altogether more power these days in writing, and what I set myself to do, I can bring off. Yet each time anew, with a new section, I hesitate and work myself up into a state: that's what must be so nervously exhausting. For here I am, in the middle of the vacation, alternately writing my book and being ill, and I won't give up so long as it is going well.

That story of Grenville's hunting out the seminary priest at Golden was the subject of one of the earliest stories I ever wrote, when I was a boy at school. It won a prize, £4 or £5, I think; and how disgusted I was when it had to go in buying myself a new pair of boots. I resented intensely the lucky devils who, if they won a prize (they never did), would not have had to buy themselves boots with it. All my youth I was seared with resentment – all those black moods my early diaries bear witness to, if they remain. I tore up the earliest, they were so bitter; there was even a poem of mine, I believe in *Public School Verse*, under the title 'Black Mood', at least I wrote one.

Perhaps it was a good thing that my people took no notice of all these little schoolboy achievements: they just were not interested in what happened to

* The name comes from Apulia, with a Simon of Apulia.

1. The biography of Sir Richard Grenville (1937), to which ALR had been directed by a remarkable find during his research for *Tudor Cornwall*.

me at school. It was not deliberate, it was just stupidity: they didn't know enough to take any interest. Perhaps it was better than having foolish parents fretting and fussing over their offspring, who never came to anything much. I used to watch them, as a boy, having their girls taught the piano with not a scrap of music in them; no such chance for me.

It is curious how far back one's interests really go. Cuthbert Mayne, for instance – I called him Carnsew in my story; I have found out a lot about the real Carnsews, and even discovered in the Public Record Office the diary of an Elizabethan Carnsew.*

My interest in Tudor history goes back earlier than anything else in my mental life, far earlier than politics, before poetry, even earlier than my interest in the Church. When a boy of nine or ten, I used to call in at Aunt Rowe's on my way home from the elementary school at Carclaze, where was an old book on English history. (No books at all in our house. How I have avenged that since: as I look round here the room is crowded with books, in the bookcases, on top of them, on all the tables, filling up the window-sills, stacked in heaps on the floor.) I used to be fascinated by the middle chapters in it about 'Bloody Mary' – Mary Tudor: Aunt Rowe was vexed at never being able 'to get a word out of me', that book was so absorbing.

What is it that modern music, our age, our time lacks? A moment after, listening to a Mozart pianoforte concerto was pure enjoyment. It is joy that is lacking in the music of our time. Bruce thought it was because it was so strenuous; but there is more in it than that. It is impossible in our time to know what pure joy like that is: always something that overshadows the best of us. It is impossible for elect spirits who see things clearly to feel happy; even when they remove themselves, as Vaughan Williams has, from the pressure of common things, and sought to return to the simplicity of the pastoral Earth. But he has not succeeded; apart from the meditative and religious element in him, he is stark and tragic.

And no wonder.

A moment later I listened to the short description of the grand wedding in Berlin today (Göring's). There were I don't know how many troops in the street; and 200 of Hitler's new air force flew overhead; Reichsbischof Müller preached in the Cathedral. Hitler was one of the two witnesses to sign the register.

The B.B.C. continued. The last wedding ceremony that took place there was that of Group-Leader Ernst, who was murdered on 30 June 1934.

* Many years later I wrote this up in *Court and Country*.

Further news from Berlin is that today were executed by the axe two Communists who had been condemned for their part in the death of the pimp Horst Wessel, whose appeal the Supreme Court at Leipzig disallowed.

The grand wedding – aeroplanes overhead – the axe!

The barbarians!!

Not to forget, a week or so ago, the day's lunacy from Germany. Reported late, a slop-over from Hitler's birthday, celebrated with the biggest military parade in Berlin since the days of the Kaiser, great brilliance of uniforms, bands, tanks, new armoured cars, new titles for Göring and other criminals – all the things the German soul would delight in – a few days after, the modest tribute of the German Officials' Association: *Mein Kampf* handwritten upon 965 pages of parchment for the Führer.

The simple German soul! On a par with the sausages, the *würstchen* – the middle-aged widow of a professor who stood beside O'Neill* at Heidelberg in an ecstasy of tears and joy at the spectacle of the soldiers returning into the Rhineland, broke down and said: 'When Hitler dies, we'll all die too: we don't want to survive our Leader.' Bloody idiots.

[Oxford, 1936]

In Geoffrey Hudson's view certain economic conditions had to be fulfilled before civilization could be said to exist. I said it seemed to need a certain complexity of social and economic organization, some class differentiation. Plato and Aristotle, reflecting upon the emergence of Greeks from primitive to civilized society, began their state with the division of labour between the husbandman, artisan and soldier. Geoffrey said that a surplus over and above subsistence level was a necessity. So long as the whole energies of the tribe were taken up by the struggle to get food, you could not get civilization.

I agreed. But these were only the prerequisites of civilization, not the actual *differential*. The essence of civilization seemed to consist in a *self-conscious* cultural tradition, created by the dominant class, emancipated from spending all its energies upon the pursuit of food. That self-consciousness was part of its very nature – something partly external, created and handed down (not merely in writing – Geoffrey interposed: writing is not a *differentia*; for example, the poems of Homer were handed down a long time by oral tradition before being written down). Civilization is thus the creation of the dominant classes, not the creation of the proletariat, though it may have

* Con O'Neill, a Junior Fellow, in the Foreign Office, carpeted by Sir Horace Wilson for expressing his views on the danger from Hitler.

been squeezed out of the surplus value of their labour. Their unselfawareness, compared with the selfawareness the dominant classes have of their position, tradition, etc., is one of the things I despise most about the people. It is what enables the poor fools to be ruled so easily, and makes them incapable of ruling. They can't rule themselves; how can they hope to rule others? The upper classes know this only too well. It is a comparatively late discovery for me and a bitter one, for after all I belong to the fools, not to the other side.

But unselfawareness is the characteristic mark of the people: they cannot see. They literally do not see what is about them: the hideousness of their surroundings and appointments, their houses and furniture, their hideous ornaments, the enlarged photographs on the wall, the cheap colours, the tawdryness of carpets; no sense of the simple, they automatically take to what is pretentious and gaudy: they do not *see* the horror of their streets, the shambles they make of the countryside. When Q. protested against the disfigurement of the cliffs at home with an eczema of bungalows, some Rural or Urban Council answered back that they knew what was beautiful as well as Sir Arthur Quiller-Couch.[1] Who was he to tell them what was what? This is the *petit bourgeois* mentality that is behind Fascism and Nazism.

Well, the lower middle classes do not see; so how can they be expected to have foresight? Nor does the working class *see* any better; the natural trend upwards is for them to become *petit bourgeois*. There is *something* that saves them politically: they are on the side of right causes.

Anyhow, anthropology will be the right subject for me, as a second or third string in the intervals of work next year.

In the evening I sat in the sun and read Previté-Orton's summing-up at the end of the *Cambridge Medieval History*. It and the sun, the spring evening and the bells, filled me with thought. I wanted to sit down and write an essay on 'The Modernity of Medievalism', I was so struck with the parallel between the end of the Middle Ages and our own time. The fifteenth century witnessed the decline of the Church – the greatest example of international government since the Roman Empire. The Conciliar Movement wanted to liberalize the Church, make the papacy dependent upon the episcopate and so on – so like the ineffective doctrinaires of the League of Nations. The old women of international liberalism have refused ever to put themselves into effective relation with the one big popular force making for internationalism, namely social democracy. Until too late, too late to save any liberalism,

1. The doyen of Cornish writers, early patron and friend of ALR. Editor of *The Oxford Book of English Verse* and first Professor of English Literature in the University of Cambridge.

perhaps too late to save socialism. The world meanwhile handed over to all too effective Thugs.

When they produce the catastrophe they're manufacturing now at top speed,* I shall take to anthropology. Perhaps South America, Patagonia.

At dinner, a discussion about the parallel between the Nazi regime and the Second Empire in France sprang up.

Methods of keeping up the population without the necessity of marriage. State institutions – stud-farms where the persons most suitable for breeding from might be chosen to keep the population going. Here Isaiah got back with a popular question: suppose you were chosen as a most suitable person for breeding purposes? Would *you* do your duty? It was generally thought unlikely to be an attractive proposition. In fact, existing family arrangements are leading to a decline in the population. I am in favour of giving income-tax rebates to people with families. This was regarded as a broad-minded turn; it was intended to appear so, but had an edge – that marriage and children were so disadvantageous that discrimination in favour of the married was a form of compensation. This escaped their notice.

In the midst of this ragging, all very good-tempered and full of quips, a momentary silence fell; the sound of bells came into the room from the city, with evening sun upon the grass and rich tawny colour upon the stone. I suddenly saw them all, as if with love, as if for the last time. Holdsworth, absurd old figure with vast moustaches fringed by a little salmon-trout and egg-sauce; kindly and simple, Dick's** father – stroke of the University boat, of whom he is inordinately proud. At the end of the table, Ian Bowen, looking like an early-Victorian statesman with his enormous head and long lank hair; racing late through the quad with open-neck shirt and sports jacket, his dog Judy beside him, up to his rooms to rush on a suit, the only one not dressed for dinner. No-one more casual, more dissatisfied; Richard (Pares) charmingly comforting him because his wife is having a baby, and they are poor and worried. At the same time as ragging I saw them all *sub specie aeternitatis*, as no-one else, unless perhaps Richard, saw them. I think they were enjoying the evening, the summeriness of it, the summer food, *salade de volaille*, *coupes à la belle Hélène*, the comfort and intimacy.

But I was listening to the intermittences of the heart in the bells of the city, the quieter talk when I fell out of it, to listen to the silence. And so afterwards. They grouped themselves now in one way, now in another. Ian and Richard, one married and slipped away, the other about to be married

* This was not far out either.

** Dear Dick, in so few years to be killed in the war.

and slipping away, every day, little by little. It is as well not even to try to reverse the process: it must happen. But I saw them tonight, as if I, more even than they, were in a dream. When I withdrew from the group and went to lean against a buttress of the tower, Isaiah laughed – propitiatingly as if I were up to some game again. But I was not: I was too much moved for that; the dream went on.

So it continued for the half-hour in which we played about. I played too, though my mind was not in the game, but in the dream. There Richard was, as if I at some future time when all was over or different or changed, should see him then as he was now; there Ian, unhappy, perplexed, pathetic, a charm about him – all question of his not liking or not understanding me as I am, of no relevance now; the dull domestic Jones,* reliable and uxorious, as intimate a part of the dream as those two associated now on the other side, when I am now outside.

The evening sun was moving round to the north face of St Mary's, the hands of the clock made bright by it; I thought of all the summer evenings like this, of that summer when Adam was first here and the successive summers when he was no longer here; how many summer evenings would be like this again; which of us would depart, which move to another place, within the association or outside it; of the pattern the figures made to me outside, as I am outside every association: I thought of them no less with love.**

9 July 1936

Such an extraordinary dream about Charles[1] last night; an atmosphere of poignant grief, so that I woke up crying.

I dreamed that, though I knew Charles was dead, I had re-established contact with him, by sheer force of devotion had thought his presence back from the dead. It gave me great satisfaction to see him and be with him again. We were together walking somewhere in Cornwall, he for the most part dumb as if he couldn't get through to me. I had the sensation that he had come back from the dead. And then his family got to know of it: he had come back to them. It was a cause of grief to them, for they knew him to be dead. I met old Major Henderson coming down Tregonissey Hill into the town by the vicarage; I laid a hand on his arm, to let him understand that Charles was with us. He was only grieved by it all – Charles's spirit moaned disconsolately at Penmount – none of the happiness that I felt in having his

* A. H. M. Jones became an eminent Roman historian.

** How much I loved the place. 1979.

1. Charles Henderson, who had died in 1933.

company once again. This was the end; I woke up crying and with the words 'I have been loyal, too late?' in my mind. A good deal came before which I can't remember – about where we were journeying together: it may have been the Scilly Islands again as three – was it four or five? – years ago. The place, it comes back to me, was the fields around Tregonissey: it is a long time since I dreamed of the village.

August, I think the 20th, at any rate a Thursday

So this is Brussels. I came on here this morning after a last ghastly night of sickness and pain at Bruges. Fatigued and hungry after a whole day's touring Ghent, I came back to eat a most excellent dinner. Duck, which I never eat at All Souls – never was duck better cooked, two tiny succulent morsels with orange and a delicious compote of apple; followed by the lightest, puffiest soufflé that ever was. I complimented the manager afterwards on his chef. But it did for me. I was awake every hour listening to the belfry of Bruges strike the hours, until in the morning the full chime returned to remind me another night wasted.

Consequence: a journey here this morning more dead than alive; after seeing St Gudule, I came back really done-up. Indeed I felt it all the afternoon, sitting down three or four times in the church, having to rest a long time in a café on the Place de la Monnaie, and again in the Park on my way back. At five o'clock I went to bed and didn't get up till 8 a.m.

Perhaps I have been sightseeing too vigorously – I certainly have done my duty by Bruges and Ghent and have started on Brussels, *working* at it, seeing the churches, picture galleries etc. thoroughly. But I have hardly ever known what it was to be so dead-done as this evening, except after the Election,* climbing up the hill at Hartland with Bruce, when I used to think I was going to collapse.

It puts all sorts of ideas into my head – whether I am not crocked for life, etc. – this stomach affliction now seems permanent, whether I *can* go on as I am; whether not to reconcile myself to a quiet don's life, not ceaselessly straining myself for ambition's sake. But I think not: ambition *is* my life: I think I shall go on till I drop.

After my light supper, out into the town: down the Rue du Midi, attracted, as always, by the lights and sounds of the Fair: *le goût de la vie* in spite of everything.

I thought, hardly consciously, of the Fair at Plymouth. How outside it all

* I fought in the General Election of 1935, and should have given up *then* – but did too well, second in the poll.

I was then! I felt less so tonight. But I *was* all the same. Always condemned by circumstances, my way of life, the determination to be free, to have no commitments, to be a spectator of other people's lives. The result is at any rate a trained, a hungry, Eye: nothing escaped me. The oldish man in charge of a loop-the-loop: you tested your strength (or knack) by thrusting a machine in a track that, if successful, made a complete circle. The usual young men (how they are the same whether abroad or at home, Plymouth or Brussels), amateurs of strength, anxious to test their own, had several tries at it. First one, without any success, the old man showing him how to do it with a vigorous push, looping the loop sometimes twice. The second young man evidently thought he'd do it better than the first. No better success, he quickly went away self-conscious and crestfallen.

[Cornwall,] New Year, 1937

Returned late from a full day at Penmount – Launceston – Truro to hear the end of the B.B.C. programme with mother for whom I turned it on. An accumulation of letters while I have been away, supper and today's *Times* at 11.30 p.m., after full account rendered to mother of all doings while away. At the end of it all, George VI's pathetic message, the Chelsea Arts Ball like a beehive humming, I opened the front door for mother to hear our own church bells ringing from over the hillside. How much longer shall we hear them together? I wonder as I open the door from the clamour of the ball away in London, to hear the regular peal of the church I have known since childhood. I have moved away from that anchorage since those days. The church I went to as a boy regularly every Sunday for years, that I sang in and prayed in – I remember how hard on those Wednesday evening services of intercession for the men on service during the war, when the list of young men, some of whom I knew as seniors in the choir, killed or wounded, was read out and grew constantly longer. I remember all the intimate experiences connected with the singing, which I have never wanted to write about, the loss of my singing voice meant so much to me – my first effective mode of self-expression.

There were those walks down the road, then a narrow lane between trees, in summer dust, summer evenings when the sun was still hot, or winter evenings when the cold was sharp and we arrived with frozen hands to warm before the vestry fire and tell stories until the choirmaster came; or coming home up the hill under the stars, that clear night of stars when I lay in bed and wrote my first poem. Or coming up the road frightened and alone, always waiting for someone. Sometimes someone emerged from the shadows, some man waiting for the boy, excited, with senses on the alert, never more tingling with desire. Or afraid, afraid of ghosts, of shadows, of being alone, again all the senses alert along the spine: sometimes running helter-skelter, blood pulsing, or whistling to warn whoever lurked in the hedge not to come out.

All this is more than I can ever express – the faces of boys I knew then, all dead, in a sense all, dead, myself included – though I have tried so hard in the years to keep what I was as a boy alone, this diary is witness of that – the faces of boy after boy I knew and not one forgotten, the distinct personality indestructible. The very days and hours, Mondays and Wednesdays choir practice; the smell of the church, the annunciation-lilies, the western sunlight coming in through the tower window, shafts of colour falling upon the choir stalls; the prefiguring dreams of history I used to dream after service, listening to the organ from the dark Lady Chapel among the monuments to departed Sawles,[1] from Joseph Sawle of the time of William and Mary onward. All this in my mind in listening to the bells.

Oxford, 6 February

Recovering from flu, my mind has been wandering all day in a haze of images, mostly of home. Too enfeebled to work, I sat in the large armchair with a book in my hand, or the large folio of Vivian's *Visitations of Cornwall* open on the arm, while the images swam in and out of my mind, glimpses of places, a turn in the road, a hedge in spring, a ploughed field with the gulls upon it, or idly read the names of the generations who once lived at Trenarren or Penrice. Curious how infertile a stock the Sawles have been: once before they died out, in the eighteenth century, with a bachelor and two sisters, the family of Admiral Graves took the name of Sawle. Now with the present owner their name dies again, the heir having been killed in the war.

The Hexts at Trenarren seem on the other hand to have been prolific. I looked up their pedigree, following it back from the old Colonel who was born in 1847 and survived to be a name in my youth up to the war: last of the Hexts to live continuously at Trenarren. Vivian gives the impression of a house crowded with children: the Colonel was one of a band of six brothers and five sisters; they must have been a full house at Trenarren in those days. I fancy the voices of children in that enclosed valley where everything echoes. It gives me pleasure to read all the names, the dates of their births, baptisms, marriage and burial. I cannot say in what the fascination consists: if only I could, that would be to yield up the secret of history. It

1. Local landowning family with naval connections.

has some relation to life itself: as if Time is standing still for a bit, and I am watching life pass by.

It is not, at its most intense, the people themselves that I visualize: this other pleasure does not take place at that level of experience, but at a deeper one: where things are less differentiated. It approaches more the aesthetic experience of music and poetry: the real (and partly secret) values of my life.

So I read on all the morning, feeling guilty because I wasn't working. I noted that elder brother of the Sir Charles Graves-Sawle of my time, the last, Sir Francis, whom I remember to have been commemorated by a tablet at Padbury, where All Souls owns most of the village. Why there? He evidently died there; I never heard of him at home; it was always a Sir Charles who lived at Penrice. Their names call up to me monuments in the church at St Austell, the arms, the white gate on the road to Trenarren, the 'Lovers' Lane', the long drive and the deer.

Trenarren and the generations of its occupants should have a more intimate interest, since I always think of myself some day living there, that exquisite view between the two screens of trees to the sea mine, the shelving lawn from the front of the house, the hedges with the first primroses and the sound of the sea outside everything. But about the family I know hardly anything: they left little trace of themselves. All through the last century they seem to have kept up an unexciting connection with the Army. One brother of the Colonel, a first lieutenant in the Royal Middlesex(?) Light Infantry, served on the Gold Coast in the Ashanti War of 1873–4; another was a second lieutenant in the Royal Cornwall Rangers. The Colonel's grandfather, John Hext, who was born 15 November 1766 and died 30 June 1838 at Restormel, entered the Army as ensign in the 22nd Foot in 1783, became captain and sold out in 1826, becoming colonel commanding the Royal Cornwall Militia. They were evidently a family of soldiers – still are, for the young man who is the owner of Trenarren, though he has never lived there, is an officer in the D.C.L.I. at Bodmin.*

Generation after generation, never rising above a certain level but going about their concerns, riding, shooting, serving abroad, coming home again to Trenarren. They seem to have been fond of coming home to Trenarren, or at least the women do: one or two of them who were married, and then widowed, came to spend their last years under the family roof there. Nor do I wonder at them; it has become almost the chief passion of my life to achieve my last years there too.[1]

One woman of the family intrigues me, a woman of spirit: Gertrude, aunt

* David Hext became my landlord there in 1953.

1. Fulfilled.

of the Colonel, became a convert to Rome and married the son of a Fellow of Oriel – perhaps he was the cause of the mischief and was also a convert. They were married at the Roman Catholic chapel of St Nicholas at Exeter – probably by the antiquary, Dr Oliver of the *Monasticon Exoniensis*. No fine wedding from Trenarren at St Austell church for her: one can imagine the shock, the scandal. She must have added to it later by the novels she wrote (I have never even seen one); they were all the novels of a convert, very much of the fifties and sixties. She must have had character: I should like to know whether it was made hard for her.*

The family seems to have come from Devon, but to St Austell from west of Cornwall, from Constantine and Madron. An Arthur Hext of Constantine was baptized at Madron 17 February 1593 and buried at St Austell 22 February 1650. His son, Samuel Hext, who was baptized at St Buryan in 1616, is described 'of Trenarren' and was buried at St Austell 28 December 1680. That would be a few years before Celia Fiennes, riding through the county, stayed a night at St Austell. So through all the eighteenth-century Samuels and Francises, baptized and buried in the church at St Austell. My father remembered when all their bones, innumerable cartloads of them, were carried away from the old churchyard around the church which had become heaped up with so many generations of the dead.

There is no crowded family of Hexts at Trenarren now. For some years the house stood empty, or with a succession of short-term tenants. Often in the past ten years since I have been devotedly watching it, no smoke comes from the chimneys, the place shut up, empty, silent. Now new people from South Africa are living there: the windows are opened once more to the sea air and the scents of the shrubs and trees (there is a eucalyptus-tree in the garden, feather-plumed, for ever moving to and fro with the least movement of the wind). But in one sense, the place is mine: it is identified with my dreams, the sense of my own life. It is the house of my imagination: the chimneys, the gate I have never been inside** – where my father stopped the very last time he was there and said that though I might live there some day he should never live to see it – the spring flowers, ferns and mosses in the crannies of the hedges, the sea-clouds sailing over the tops of the trees, and everywhere the sense of the sea.

So much for the morning. This afternoon no less the subject, the victim of these images, these sense-pictures. The lapse and return of the sea, the sparkle and ripple, the white edge of foam under a hot blue summer sky off the rocks right out between Polridmouth and Fowey, where the cliff-walk

* Yes, she was disapproved of.

** Re-reading this in 1990, I have lived there longer now than anywhere, except All Souls.

goes down to the water and the waves break among the rocks. Or again, Luxulyan when the daffodils are out, the parson's garden sheltering behind the screen of beeches copper-coloured in the autumn; and the grey granite church, my first passion among village churches, decorated with spring flowers for Easter. Or the gentle heave of sea into the mouth of the Helford River.

What else of all the innumerable images? Largely of summer expeditions with Bruce, the capacious old Fiat waiting outside of Magdalen to take us through Northampton and into Lincolnshire, to draw up in the evening at the door of the best hotel in some cathedral town.

8 March

Today is ugly with black east wind. 'Black east wind' my father and mother used always to say; never 'grey', and always with the suggestion of something sinister about the 'black', not with any colour-connotation attaching to it. It usually is so with folk speech; the vividness of it, the impression of freshness, are undeserved; they are merely inherited characteristics handed down from generation to generation. It is as much pure cliché with them as the speech-forms of urban life are. When my grandmother said she had often come home from town 'loaded like a bee', she was not really phrase-making, vivid as the phrase was; she was merely repeating the phrase her mother had used before her, and hers before her. 'You'm so blue as a dyin' winnard,' my mother used to say when we came home from school on a bitter March day like this; 'black as a craw', 'maazed as a sheep' – all these phrases, good as they are and direct as are their comparisons, are not in the least original. In the mouths of those who use them they are as much divorced from the concrete reality as the stale phrases of the modern press.

But the black east wind has brought back to mind the anguish of a year ago, when my father died. I haven't been able to write much about him even here, though I think of him often, always with tenderness and pity; not too often – sometimes I check myself when it makes me so miserable as to prevent me from working. For a few moments after tea alone, I went through it all again: to think that I never went down to see him while he was in hospital, for he was getting better! I ought to have known during that last week when his letters to me ceased that there was something wrong. I remember hanging about here all that weekend of our Spring Meeting and Bursars' Dinner, and going back to Brunswick Square late on Monday to get George's two letters telling me to come home at once. I telephoned and heard he was already dead. 'Passed away this afternoon,' they said over the phone, lugubrious, fatal phrase. I felt an unnatural calm which lasted all the days till I went to see him for the last time and then everything broke.

The black east wind which killed him – why did I not think of these things myself and have his operation postponed until the early summer? he would have had so much better a chance – why do the doctors never think of such things? An ounce of brainwork would be worth all the comforting words in the world; the wind which gave him pneumonia and carried him off, blowing through the bitter wards of that dreary building had by then given way to spring sunlight over the hills around Truro. It wrung my heart to see him, like a little child, a wax doll in his small coffin. I thought of him as a baby, of his mother who had borne him seventy years ago and whom I never knew – she died not old, heroic soul, bringing up her family of nine boys, her husband a tin-miner having died of miners' phthisis in his early forties.

Then I thought that he saw me; I felt I had seen the eyelids move. I bent down to touch him and took his hand, so small and delicate now – he was proud of the small shapely hands he had – after all those years of work; I laid my hand on his brow and along his hair, still not yet quite grey. His hand was cold and clay-like, his face quite beautiful, the flesh fallen back revealing the fine lines of the nose. But oh 'what pain, what pain' I kept on saying to myself, what agony he must have gone through in that last week to die; and I not there to be near, to help him. I had been glad to be spared that; and yet now in the little chapel alone with him, I wished I had been there every moment. It must be so difficult to die; one must want every consolation and aid. He was a simple man and perhaps he never knew he was going to die. But the nurse told me that all through the last day he was asking for his young son – I can't believe it – he would have asked for Les, and she couldn't remember my name. And mother said that he was asking all the time for George who was with him most of that last month and to whom he was more closely bound, by mutual likeness. But to think I was not there! I have been miserable about it ever since. I take no consolation in the thought that I was a good son to him and looked after him in his latter years and saw that he had security. It was all no use: I had not been with him at the end.

I stayed in the little chapel as long as ever I dared. When I was crouching down by the coffin to be near him, one of the young assistants came gaily in – he may even have been whistling. To him it was all a matter of trade – I suppose one gets used to being a mortician. He was horror-struck at the sight of me and did not come back again. There was everything finished – 'Richard Rowse died March 5th 1934. Aged 70 years' – the bright plate on the lid, and just a label to show who he had been.

It was true that he was no longer there. I remembered the phrase Isobel

Henderson wrote me about Charles – dear Charlie – how on his deathbed he looked like an Angevin king; but it was no good, he simply wasn't there any more. I thought of them together: they became one in my mind owing to their having suffered death and to my love for them. Though indeed they hardly knew each other and would have been surprised at so close a union in my mind.

How mysterious a thing it seemed, that life should just have gone out of my father – it could not be just that some physical function had ceased? His personality was so definite a thing, so much his, to be extinguished like this. But when I looked, it was not he – it was just the shell of what he had been, the mask that expressed what he had in those last days suffered.

In a way, that thought consoled me: what he was essentially remained where it had ever been in my mind and in the minds of those, few enough, who loved him. I got up and left the place, came back again, went out to see that nobody was looking, then down the hill to the town. The March wind blew the sunlight along the hills and the daffodils down the green slopes of that ghastly place. Crying out for comfort I went to find Claude,* who didn't even know my father, but who knew me. I cried my heart out as we went along the streets, till I came to the Cathedral.

It was not until I reached the little chapel at the back, in a remote corner, with the picture of Christ blessing Cornish Industry, that I was overcome by grief, finding words for what I felt. I had the place to myself; I need fear nobody; only once did anybody come near and stole away again without breaking in upon me. All his life, the hardness of it, the unending labour, so little consolation, little enough of joy passed in review before me. If only he could have lived a little longer – ten years – to have enjoyed something of the success that might come more fully to him through me. He had worked at china clay all his days; at the end nothing but pain, and this was absolutely the end. It was this that was written in the lines upon the face I had seen. I had been glad to see him once more; I was determined to see him for a last time; but alas, that image of him lying there is how I always see him now. For it was thus that his life summed itself up and came to its close.

Next day the black wind returned; he came home once more and we buried him; on just such a day as this is now outside, blackness in the green quad and this bitter memory awakened.

* Claude Berry, a staunch friend, editor of the *West Briton*. Together we ran the *Cornish Labour News*, a monthly.

17 August

Half-past ten, and I have difficulty in making myself get down to write. I am so tired – staying on in Oxford into the depths of vacation when the college is officially closed; so disturbed – the papers are full of world-order breaking down, this hideous Japanese action in Shanghai, the incompetent Chinese bombing their own civilians in reply, Franco continuing his advance into Basque territory, a Spanish Government steamer torpedoed in the Mediterranean by an Italian submarine; meanwhile the Spanish Government forces paralysed, the weakness and hopelessness of the Left everywhere. The breakdown of the European order is partly due to the British governing classes. They have sold pass after pass since 1931 – or not even sold it, for what have they gained? Well, I suppose, the frustration of the Left everywhere. Yet the interests of Britain are identified with the Left, as in the nineteenth century; the governing classes are selling the interests of their country. As the disintegration goes further, there will be a shocking price to pay: perhaps the eventual break-up of our position as a first-class power.*

The effect of this endless anguish I have been living in since 1931 is curious: I believe the whole of the Left feels it: hopelessness. There is nothing we can do. You can't arouse public opinion: the whole thing is deadened by four years of 'National' Government, and practically all the organs of opinion are in the hands of the governing classes. *They* know what the situation is, but the bloody people understand nothing.

[Afterthought,] New Year, 1979

Some few (very few) Fellows have loved the College as I did – notably Grant Robertson, who as Domestic Bursar had it in its keeping – certainly not Woodward who followed. I have seen Robertson coming out from his (and my) staircase to feast his eyes on the lovely scene: the majesty of the Camera, St Mary's spire, All Saints' spire further off, framed by Hawksmoor's arcade. During the war, when Oxford might have been bombed, I heard Robertson say, 'If anything happened to this place, it would kill me.'

It was *love*, as with me.

But he couldn't express it. I fancy no-one has, except me. Curious that it should be the young proletarian outsider to whom it has fallen to leave this account of the life of the College to posterity. For myself, mine at this time was 'An Arrested Life' – I was working, teaching, examining, lecturing, researching, politicizing, but life itself was arrested by illness. I was watching,

* This was percipient for a young man in 1937.

watching, for ever watching, while others went forward with their lives, not only their careers but their loves, marriages, families and family chores.

Like me, Robertson was a bachelor and had no other love but the College. He did get forward with his career as Vice-Chancellor at Birmingham, where he did a fine job. But his writing was clotted with clichés: he wrote historical jargon. Woodward put something of what he felt in his prose poems, *The Twelve Winded Sky*; but there was little poet in him, for there was no love in his composition.

How much there was in mine the diary itself is witness of: because it was thwarted and repressed – I could not find or accept the proper outlet for it – it increased the inner tension and the illness. I had a Manichean cult of heightening the sensibility at every point, every moment I could catch, in case the illness ended my life before I could fulfil what I had in me.

Watching my life go by – the title for those years might be 'The Arrested Life'.

A further reflection: the constant discipline of the diary made me a writer, not only a writer of academic history like my friends – Richard Pares, Geoffrey Hudson, Bruce McFarlane – but taught me to compete with contemporaries who, altogether more sophisticated, as Etonians, like Cyril Connolly or Orwell, or Graham Greene, were already making their mark as writers. *That* achievement was held up for me, partly by my immersion in academic life, partly by my innocence and naïveté; holding apart from life.

It is ironical that, in the end, after decades I have caught up with them – though they, and literary life, have even yet not caught up with the fact.

[Reflecting on Adam von Trott, ?1937]

A new direction, the later movement of my temperament, the disillusionment, came out of the unsatisfactoriness of my relations with him. Half-dozing, I thought of him back in this room again, sitting in the usual chair opposite me, and the dialogue that would ensue: how ill I behaved in never writing to him, that he would not be patronized by me (as he said when he was last in the room);* that my excuse was that he was the one person with whom I had once been passionately in love.

Then, a completely different scene came into mind, such a contrast of an interior. When last at Roche for a meeting before Christmas, one of our men there, a china-clay worker with a smallholding, took me home with

* Here was the typical German inferiority complex.

him for a cup of tea 'to warm me up' before catching the bus back. A low snug Cornish cottage crouching down in the fold of the windswept moor; a warm yellow blind on the hillside as you clatter by in a bus, or walk the road on a winter's night. The two of us sploshed off the high-road up a lane that was half a stream, the wife opened the door of the storm-porch to us. In a minute we were in the front-kitchen, cosy and snug, bright fire burning, a heavy curtain hung over the door to keep out draughts, low ceiling with open rafters, a lamp on the table strewn with the wife's sewing. While the tea was being made, Samuel Johns told me the story of how he had met his wife: during the war at the Workhouse at Truro when it was a naval hospital. He was on duty there and she was one of the cooks. So his wife was a 'splendid cook'. Hearing voices downstairs, a little girl's voice said immediately over our heads: 'Can us come down, daddy?' 'Yes, if you like,' he said slowly and tenderly, in his deep Cornish voice.

In the middle of our chat, his wife brought in the tea for the two men, hot and steaming, with nice fresh bread and butter and cake all laid (Samuel was right: she was a good cook!). She herself pleased and proud to have me there sitting high up on the settle next the fire. Then the two little girls came down too to join the circle: well-behaved and clearly enjoying being allowed up, no beauties either, as so frequently with the Cornish out on the moors, a stony soil, for centuries a hard struggle with the rocks for a living. It has left its mark on them. The elder extraordinarily long-faced, long-nosed like Samuel, but fortunately without his squint; both of them quiet, interested, which fixed itself in my mind with an unexpected hold, for suddenly here in Oxford tonight, dozing by my own fireside, it came back to me with its quiet charm, warming my heart and filling up my loneliness.* From far down his throat, large Adam's apple moving as he speaks, Samuel is no beauty: he must be years older than his wife, perhaps fifty-five when she is still in the forties. He is tall for a Cornishman, one eye askew. (This brings him back to me. 1979.)

He has a fine character, strong as a horse and as gentle; generous, yet careful; public-spirited and willing to do his duty for his neighbours. His ambition is to become a J.P., there being no J.P. in the parish and people have to go down to Bugle, a couple of miles off, to have their papers signed. A hard worker; for he works regularly at clay-work and in addition farms his smallholding, and is ready to take on more if only he can get the farmer to lease the fields next door.

* Nor have I ever forgotten it. Passing by the house, I still remember. 1979.

[Oxford,] 11 May 1938

The phrase 'evening . . . quiet as a nun' has been at the back of my mind these last evenings. This, for instance: it is the chestnut-time in May, when the sun has gone from the garden, and the trees are very still, holding up their candles, heavy and full with flower and leaf. Everything seems expectant: roofs and chimneys as clearly defined as on those summer mornings of pain just before dawn years ago when I began first to write of these things. Now it is so many years later, and still pain hangs about me, half-exhausts my life, half-stimulates me and keeps all my senses nervously on the *qui vive*.

Tomorrow I leave Oxford for a London nursing home, and almost certainly an operation, yet another. Leaving Oxford in May, the loveliest time of the year, to be mewed up in blankets and sheets when one wants to be out in the country. Or rather, for I have hardly had the strength to go far of late, when one's mind floats out over the downs beyond Wantage and Faringdon; or I fancy myself with Bruce in the car running up the cliff road to Lincoln, the summer air rushing by, evening sinking across midland shires and the fenland withdrawing into the distant haze. Or I think of our delicious summer walk, a little later, to Rycote and across several fields home, I don't know how.

The bells have been ringing out in Oxford, an almost necessary accompaniment of my dream. They too, no less than the phrase of Wordsworth's, induce this mood of suspension, suspension of pain, an enchanted moment full of expectancy, expectant of what? Everything is so still now, even what noises there were have sunk to a magic silence, even the sleepy birds, the sounds of the street over the roofs. I can see the mortar lines between the red bricks of the chimney across the garden quite clearly in the gathering dusk. A frightened thrush rushes richly across the lawn, full-throat.

I have the poem open before me:

> It is a beauteous evening, calm and free,
> The holy time is quiet as a Nun
> Breathless with adoration; the broad sun
> Is sinking down in its tranquillity;
> The gentleness of heaven broods o'er the sea.

Why should that carry me so surely back to that evening over a hundred years ago? Something in its atmosphere makes it part of history, and yet this evening brings it back as if now.

Brings back also other evenings, thoughts of another place. I have been thinking of Cornwall, of the smell of summer hedges full of vetch and foxglove and honeysuckle with the dew upon them, rushing back in the car with George from bathing on the north coast. Or of Penmount,[1] the cornfield at the back of the house behind the trees, the steep lane planted with bright gorse coming up from Idless. I have been thinking of Charles of late and of what summer meant to him: as if the thought of summer connected up with him and the mystery of life and death, as if one were on the verge of understanding. Charles – how he loved life, and summer bathing, a long blue fish, in the Wiltshire Avon in the meadows below Amesbury; or again in the cold waters of the Teign, a rich clear brown, at Fingle Bridge; or in the landlocked little bay at Porthellick on St Mary's in the Scilly Isles. And I see myself, an accompanying figure, always under some pressure of time or circumstance, or half in pain, part of this lovely pattern that life makes and of which we are part.

Life! Life! there is only life –

I found myself crying a night or two ago in one of those watches when pain keeps me awake, excites my mind so that I cannot sleep.

Amid all these thoughts the half-realized images of home have been about my mind comforting me, as I hope they will in London: this evening the recurring thought of the headland at Trenarren, the fine smell of sea-laden turf and camomile and gorse, the scrambling lane among the blackberries to the Black Head, the deep water breaking at the point, the little cove where I love to bathe. All this associated longingly with thoughts of health, to be as others are, with no pain, rid of this burden that I have borne so long.

Tuesday, 24 May

My last evening of freedom for some time: the night before my operation. I see myself in the mirror of the dressing-table, sitting up in bed, looking pretty well for me, decent colour, knees propped up under the eiderdown, writing, as always, writing.

Len[2] and I went for a walk, visiting old haunts, about Bloomsbury and the Strand. We looked for a moment inside the quadrangle of University College, then along to Tavistock Square where I put the large fat article I have been writing while here, in the intervals of stomach wash-outs and rectal salines, into the chaste Leonard and Virginia Woolf's letter-box.[3] Thence by old habit to Brunswick Square; looking up the road with the

1. The family home of his friend Charles Henderson.
2. Len Tippett, son of ALR's half-sister.
3. Probably for the *Political Quarterly* which Leonard Woolf edited.

tower of St Pancras station at the end of it – how often I had paused at that corner before crossing and looked up that vista.

The square was very quiet and the garden in its summer dress, the lawns green, the nets out for tennis, as during those summers when I was an inhabitant – I became quite an old inhabitant among that floating population – and sat there in the evenings in the garden. Tonight I leaned on the gate for a bit and thought of the night or rather early dawn when I walked the garden of the square for hours barefoot with the agony of an ulcer on me. I took off my slippers in desperation – I was in pyjamas and dressing-gown – to feel the dew upon my feet. That kind of mad idea comes to you when you are in pain, some sort of consolation. No doubt I had Paul Valéry in mind; yes, I remember now thinking of his doing the same thing at the time he was writing 'La Jeune Parque'.

Wednesday 25th. This is to be the day of my operation, and I am writing about midday a few hours before it takes place. A succession of minor attentions has preluded the event: the usual stomach wash-out, which – difficult and nasty as it is – I have become used to; a rectal injection of glucose for the benefit of the blood; a blood test from my ear; an injection into my arm, and a drug they gave me to drink. I can feel the effects of this last: my head is heavy and slightly headachey in a way it never is. It is always clear, but here I am writing away with this drowsy feeling stealing over me. If I persist, I might write it away, which I don't want to do.

This morning Warden Adams came to see me and told me all about the College quincentenary celebrations. I had a letter from Isobel,[1] too: a brilliant letter describing the pre-Waterloo atmosphere of the evening party in the Codrington on Saturday night, when first Halifax, the Foreign Secretary, was called away and then Sir John Simon. The Czecho-Slovak crisis. How I hope nothing more will come of that while I am lying helpless here in hospital! There were several mass formations of aeroplanes flying ever London yesterday: reminder of how horrid it would be to be here unable to move and the bombs dropping.

Len very affectionate and concerned last night, he stood a long time on the pavement of Trafalgar Square waiting until the bus started off for Tottenham Court Road. We had done a little tour of Mecklenburg Square, Doughty Street, Bedford Row, Chancery Lane past the Record Office. Going down the lower end of Chancery Lane, I had the sensation of Crompton walking down beside me, as he had done several times on our way to lunch

1. Charles Henderson's widow. Much of the letter is printed in *A Man of Contradictions*, p. 133.

together – as on the last occasion when he gave me lunch in Fleet Street.* Then to the Embankment down Essex stairs and across the gardens, hating the new Adelphi building rising there. The evening fresh and summer-like; while I felt so well, that I thought how nice it would be, walking out into the town, to walk straight back to Oxford.

Wednesday, 29 June. University College Hospital, London

It must be five – or is it six? – weeks from my first operation, (altogether my third) today. I felt so fine that after dinner this evening I went up to the solarium and spent a delicious hour in the evening sun, drinking in the fresh air, pretending that the place was Carn Grey. It was just such summer evenings as this that I used to spend up by the Rock, lying on the big army mackintosh I used to carry with me, and reading Daudet or Hazlitt or Stevenson, until the sun went down, the evening grew cold, the trees that run like a ridge along by Luxulyan church-tower grew very clear, then dark, and at last blue in the distance, mist came over and veiled the sea, and the dogs all round the moor began to bark and answer each other. Then I knew it was time to go home. Drawing the voluminous mackintosh over my arm and with my books under the other, I made my way down the hill – that dear, remembered road: I feel I know every gateway, every stone in the hedge, every patch of stonecrop and heather, every bush of gorse, every thorn-tree. There is the view down over the moor to the left to Garker, the china-clay dry there, the woods of Tregrehan and Crinnis, the darkening, withdrawing sea. Then the bend in the road, the old stone and brick stack, and the view of Carclaze and Tregonissey, the plain, the road descending into what remains of the sunset, the village, home.

Oh, how many times when I was a boy!

But I didn't intend to write about that at all. It was pleasant though up there on the roof this morning, looking out in the placid sunlight over the roofs of this part of London. In the background the roofs of the cinema next door and the flats around, the little turret and dome of Maple's in Tottenham Court Road. In the distance the tower of the Abbey Investment Trust building in Baker Street, the long line of new flats looking over Regent's Park, the turret of that Regency church at the entrance to the Park; by screwing my neck round in my chair I could see the massed trees of the Park itself. There I sat wrapped up this time not in an old mackintosh sheet, but in blankets, thinking of home, of summer evenings at Carn Grey, of the sea and summer passing; of the difference between then and now. (And yet how

* A young official in the Record Office, very tall and masculine, kind and helpful.

much the same person I have remained.) I thought too, what has often struck me in bed here listening to the quieter, more distant traffic of London in the evenings, how like the noise of the sea it is, sibilant, lapsing and retreating. It is a comfortable thought to cherish and go to sleep on.

[Looking at St Paul's from the hospital roof.]
How many times Wren worked over his plans before this creation came off – I took that as a moral, which I haven't been much willing to observe; yet perhaps there is encouragement in it. I remembered with a passing sense of the familiar *feeling* for history, that Pepys saw the dome which I saw now rising day by day and stone by stone before him. The view to the south was obscured by thunder-cloud: I could just see the Victoria Tower at Westminster swathed in scaffolding. The north was bright, open and sunny, the view to Hampstead and Highgate very clear and close at hand: a comfortable, suburban view. I had never realized it before as a ridge, a line of hills terminating London proper to the north: Keats's and Coleridge's London.

Even more, I was fascinated by the life of the hospital going on around me: the organization and working of a great hospital is most impressive, and here it was displayed ward by ward below me. In the top men's ward a fat middle-aged man in a bed by a window was washing himself meticulously, and brushing his hair. He was baldish with a round bare patch on the crown, like a monk. He wore blue-stripey pyjamas; a jar of bright orange marigolds in the window. I felt so pleased with life, or with life returning, that I felt filled with a sense of camaraderie and waved across to him; to which he replied rather perfunctorily. At the end was an open-air balcony with two cases: one a rather good-looking fair young man, with something wrong to his left leg or foot; the other a negro, coal-black and rather fine, a good deal older. It was wash-time in the hospital and a nurse appeared to put screens around while they were washed and beds made. From my perch I could see all, the so familiar routine administered over there. The only difference was that their top-blankets are a geranium red. (I had seen patients from the General Hospital wrapped up in these down below, waiting in the corridor to be X-rayed.) I saw the beds being made; the negro sat on the edge of his meanwhile, though for the most part he lay still, rather motionless, much less restless than the whites. The fair young man had fine muscular arms which he used a good deal to swing himself about, his nurse evidently found him attractive. She played with him a bit, pushing the towel at him; he didn't respond much; perhaps he was shy. But when there came a burst of brilliant thundery sunshine he suddenly began to make shadows with his hands upon the bed; she joined in the game, leaning her hand against the well-developed arms and hands to make a figure upon the blankets. At the end of the building are evidently all the lavatories; behind a frosted window a man in red pyjamas was standing up at the w.c. for a moment, then giving himself a shake went out; a nurse was emptying a bedpan behind another of these windows.

In a lower ward the children were playing about in their pyjamas before going to bed. Lower still and at an angle were the women's wards: they appeared altogether more helpful. A woman in a pink dressing-gown was making her bed, she made it and made it, running round like a mouse in an oxygen chamber. Somewhere else a woman in a purple dressing-gown was washing up at a sink before the window.

Presiding over all was the queer silent transeptal building high up over the junction of the wings, with a dingy spire above it: either the chapel or mortuary. Perhaps both. But I am bound to say that so remote was it from all that life, so silent and neglected-looking, that it was not the presiding spirit of the place. That was to be seen, as vivid an object-lesson as ever I had, spread out before me in the life, the bustle of the wards, the nurses moving quickly in and out, bringing all together in their devotion to duty.

The joys of proletarian life: [St Austell,] 29 July

Tonight coming up the hill from the pleasure of seeing a sick relative to whom I had given a pound, after so many previous ones in the same direction, I was accosted by a neighbour's wife, of a respectable family. I didn't know her name from Adam (or Eve), nor very clearly who she was; but I listened to her chatter in my usual candidate's manner, putting in suitable comments and interjections such as 'Is your husband well?' 'I hope you're better', etc., all the fatuities which with these fools pass for conversation.

Arrived at her gate she suddenly seized my arm and, with a dotty look in her eyes, said, 'What a wonderful personality you have, Mr Rowse, if only you were on the side of the Lord. I'll say it to you now, what I've often said behind your back: if only you would do the work of the Lord, you would have a wonderful influence.'

I was too taken aback to say anything; being a political candidate so cramps my style here, I couldn't tell her she was taking a liberty – she wouldn't have heard me: she was deaf. I called attention politely to the little boy waiting for her, to the locket with an inset photograph she was wearing – evasively. He was her little grandchild, she said; he was her son's child, (whispering) her son didn't live with his wife: she had had the child two and a half years. What a pity wasn't it?

I might have told her to call the attention of the Lord to her own family affairs. I thought the corner safely turned. But no, at that moment her husband came up. 'I've been lecturing Mr Rowse,' she said, rather proud of herself; 'I've been telling him what a wonderful work he could do if he were on the side of the Lord. I've often said so to you, haven't I?' 'Yes,' he said submissively. All kinds of thoughts besieged my head, already upset by the idiocy of politics. She was wearing a badge, 'Worthy of the Lamb'. (But these fools have votes.)

When I came in, seething with annoyance, I learned that that was Mrs Mingo. Then I remembered that one Saturday evening they were holding one of their idiot services outside the Labour Party Rooms in the town. Mrs Mingo was playing a harmonium in the street, making so much noise that people couldn't be heard inside the Town Hall. One of our men went out to ask them if they would move further up the street. To which Mrs Mingo thought sagely for a moment before replying: 'Well, I'll see; you see the Devil is abroad and the word of the Lord must go forth.'

When they say 'the Lord' they mean themselves.

Oxford, 14 July 1939

Conversation after lunch with Salter yesterday of great interest. The nefarious influence that Montague Norman has had behind the scenes.* At floating of League loan to Austria, Geneva anxious to appoint as Commissioner Boyden, an American, who would cooperate with the Left, the intention at the League being to get non-socialists and socialists to work together. Montague Norman wanted Zimmerman, a reactionary Dutchman with Norman's point of view, very antagonistic to Left. Boyden's appointment nearly got through; then through his misunderstanding with the U.S. government withdrawn and Zimmerman had to be appointed. Too late for anything else. But his influence fatal all the way through in Austrian affair. Result . . .

Brüning told Hudson and Salter that *all* the big German banks had put money on Hitler, including one big Jewish bank. Brüning was clearly convinced that Albert Thomas was got out of the way. The Comité des Forges did their best to wreck – and succeeded – any arms limitation agreement on the French side. Thomas at last got evidence of their activity which, he said, would blast them for ever from having any influence in French politics – evidence so damning – evidently of complicity with the Germans. (French individuals – along with the Comité des Forges too – had

* Governor of the Bank of England, consistently pro-German and anti-French.

money on Hitler.) Albert Thomas was coming to Paris with this evidence on him. Arrived in Paris, after a meal he was found dead in the restaurant, *and his case containing papers was missing*. Brüning clearly thought he had been poisoned . . .

This is the world they have brought us to.

15 July

Two afternoons ago I went for a walk down the towpath with G. N. Clark.[1] Beautiful day with sun and spring-wind across the wide spaces, the river meadows, and on the long line of ugly houses across the river that become transformed into a picture of the French nineteenth century for me, perhaps a Boudin, no a Seurat, with all their crude colour softened. One or two men were sculling, one in particular a fine bronzed body beautifully muscled, impelling the slender, feminine boat along the water, the edges lapping a little with the wind.

G.N. told me about the emotional experience he had on a beautiful May morning in the trenches in 1915, getting up at dawn, breastwork with men shaving, washing, happy together, men of all classes. G.N. was suddenly overcome with the sense of comradeship and said to himself: 'After this things never can be the same again; the old bad days and ways have gone. There will be a great change surely.'

Shortly after he had a letter from his brother-in-law in England, who later went out and was killed. He wrote: 'The country has had its great change of heart and you won't like it when you see it.' This was *à propos* of R. H. Tawney, who told me that the Army of 1914 to 1916 really had a great deal of idealism in it; in the course of fighting it developed a certain *esprit de corps*; it was not fighting to keep the old order going, but for something better. When they came back in 1918 – those who did come back – they found a world in the hands of Northcliffe and Rothermere and Beaverbrook and Horatio Bottomley.

To this I must add Salter on the shipowners in the war, especially the Runcimans. Those Wesleyan Liberals – humbugs – made a shipping fortune out of Britain's dire necessity in 1914–18; sold their ships at the top of the post-war shipping boom; in the slump bought them back again at half-price. But it was a work of supererogation on old Runciman's part to do Hitler's work for him and sell Czecho-Slovakia down the road to 1939.

1. Eminent historian, ALR's senior by fourteen years at All Souls, who held chairs at both Oxford and Cambridge and was General Editor of the *Oxford History of England*.

22 July. Dannreuther's funeral

Today is Saturday. On Thursday the Warden, Geoffrey Hudson and I made a melancholy pilgrimage, rain, rain all the way, to Denis Dannreuther's funeral at Golders Green Crematorium. The news of his death was a blow, more so than in the case of all but a few of my innermost friends here. For I felt intimately about him; I liked him, as I know that he liked me. We were exactly of an age; we came up in the same year: he from a brilliant career as Captain of the School at Eton, a Balliol classical scholar, and I from St A.C.S. Then I was elected here two years before him. I remember very well his papers, written in that careful, scholarly hand: they were not brilliant, like Douglas Jay's, or Penderel Moon's, or J. L. Austin's, of all of which I have a distinct impression. That wasn't really Denis's line; he was a careful, excellent scholar. I remember too his election in Common Room: Warden Pember saying that he was ultimately of Jewish extraction, but that the extraction was complete – or words to that effect. His mother was a beautiful Miss Ionides. So that altogether he wasn't very English.

And yet school and training had made him a very English type. He was upright and just-minded. He was a reformer. Cyril Connolly has a lot to say about Denis's year as Captain of the School at Eton: he made an important contribution. Denis took a strong reforming line, against beating and such traditional amenities. At Balliol there was an emotional bond between Denis and Cyril, though the latter let Denis down in the end, as he did everybody. Denis talked to me a bit about Cyril's book,* said that he had forgotten it all, but that as he read it came back; and it was very much as things had been.

In later years, Denis had two breakdowns – he had an epileptic tendency; this put an end to his career at the Bar. He then went into the parliamentary draughtsman's office, where he was ideally placed – he had the civil servant's temperament, with a strong strain of the reformer – he was very much of a law-reformer. When the question of his establishment came up he was turned down for health reasons. He had again drawn blank. Only recently things had taken a brighter turn for him. He was becoming legal consultant to the L.N.E.R., had just become engaged and was happy. Then came this last stroke, double pneumonia, and he died in a few days.

It was as if he were dedicated to death. When I think of him, I see someone with a pathetically precarious hold on life. He had a noble face, with a look of strain in its lines, fine eyes with a speaking awareness about him. He surely *knew*. It gave me a feeling of kinship with him that we were so much

* *Enemies of Promise*.

ill together. We had few contacts – though hardly anyone had more with him; but I always felt that underneath there was understanding which did not need words.

Well, we went to his funeral. I had never been to a crematorium before, nor Warden Adams. The incongruity of it was depressing in the extreme. We three wore gowns, at the instance of the Warden: in itself odd. The attendant, one of the numerous young men in funeral habiliments and with an air of business, thought we might be taking the service: 'Dannr*oo*ther?' said he. 'In the small chapel, 2.45.' I had never seen death turned into a commercial concern before. Mourners were constantly arriving for different funerals, the businesslike precision, the attendants, the lavatories provided for 'gentlemen' and 'undertakers', even a tea-room on the premises. The service was, if possible, worse. The thought of Denis lying there, waiting to be burned, the clergyman with sanctimonious voice, the form of words which he recited without book, being so professional, addressing the poor dead Fellow by name, 'Denis', as if he knew him, the pretence that there was nothing to be regretted, that death is an armchair affair.

The chapel was got up like a hotel lounge, over-decorated with palms and hydrangeas for a succession of anonymous visitors passing through. The Warden was appalled by it; I was horrified, Richard Pares and Roger Mynors indignant. I wasn't very sure of myself and too unhappy to care; but I felt the added pathos in seeing these few friends of his Eton days, good-looking men in young middle age whom I didn't know, James Gibson and one or two more, besides Bobby Longden* and Roger (Cyril, of course, didn't come), there in that gruesome place watching the last of Denis. In my half-frozen mind, some sense of the playing-fields at Eton, the river, College and Chapel, summer and books, the vividness and gaiety of youth, all mingled and hardly conscious passed in my mind. All come now to this!

August Bank Holiday

I live my life in a dream these days, here in deserted Oxford with nobody about, Bruce away, Richard away, everybody away. I am so fatigued, the workings all slowing down like a machine, that I do less and less each day, yet will not go away until I have done my next chapter. My head is full all day of Arundells and Godolphins and Killigrews, dead these hundreds of years, and monasteries and chantries dissolved any time from 1536 to 1547. I go out for a brief potter in the Meadows or around Magdalen, no further. Sometimes I meet some similar belated bird, like Father D'Arcy last week,

* Became Headmaster of Wellington, where he was killed by a German bomb.

who was up for some eight days' spiritual exercise which the Jesuits have at this time of year, when they do not accept invitations out, are not supposed to converse with the outside world. He wasn't supposed to be talking with me then, he said sweetly, just there under the great hornbeam. For a moment I felt a sudden impulse of sympathy for him: life going by, life never tested, a life submitting to the torture of this discipline one well knows why.* I felt sorry for him, and affectionately towards him. I noticed the black hair which grows on the outside, the lobes of his ears!

Today some kind of Town Regatta going on on the river. A loudspeaker crooning American songs – how irresistible we find them – floating out over the river and across the Meadows, with the peewits and the placid cattle, to Magdalen tower whence the bells have been ringing all day.

After all this rain, I felt on entering the Meadows, the vivid colours, all washed greens and blues, the trees shimmering elegantly in wind and sun. This was one of the days when life has a bloom upon it. There were the young men in shorts, flies bulging, arms firm and muscular, waiting their turn for the races.

I turned in at Magdalen and looked for a moment at the porch of the chapel, which has been cleaned and restored: the little statues speak of the fifteenth century, the quaint gestures and poses of body: St John the Baptist with hand raised in blessing and the Lamb of God in the crook of his arm; a medieval worthy, king or something, next to Mary Magdalen in the centre, with her vase of ointment; a bishop with crozier next her, and another fat, stocky little bishop without crozier at the end. This was Waynflete; who was the other, I wondered. I must ask Bruce – but he is away careering over the roads of France with his Gerald Burdon, I remembered with more nostalgia for France and being abroad than anything else.

The bells are faint and far away now: the wind must have changed. I am distracted with the beauty of the world and of life, this dream I live. The garden is all shades of green, tinged with September-yellow on the crab-apple (it was struck by lightning a year ago and is dying on one side). There are the footsteps of a few visitors outside; the thrush that lives in our garden flutes away to himself the same inquiring notes up the scale. Everything is very quiet, and my head a jumble of Sir Thomas Arundell and Chideock and the great park at Wardour, and walking there one summer day in the rain years ago and getting lost, while old Lady Arundell and Doran Webb were still alive, and the thought of the lane out to the sea at Trenarren, the honeysuckle and blackberries, the first glimpse of the headland at that gate when the lane twists round; and history again, Dorset, and Plymouth and

* A similar temperament, a private tragedy in his life.

the sea, and the longing to go home and hear my mother speak, to have tea in the little front room and go up to Carn Grey after tea, that divine fresh air and the view towards Fowey and Luxulyan, the thought of my father and the fact that I cannot hear him speak: all in a jumble in my tired mind. But my will tells me that if I am to realize the life I wish, I must go on with my work.* I suppose then it will be too late.

12 August

Yesterday Lionel Curtis, Bruce Richmond** and I lunching. I got them on to Kipling, whose autobiography I had just come down from reading: enjoying it greatly, I was struck by the adolescence of his political views – the prejudices of an old school-boy. Richmond told a story very much *à propos*. When Leo Maxse was dangerously ill, he was given a blood transfusion. It didn't do any good, and as he lay there he said: 'They've been and injected the blood of a believer in the League of Nations into my veins.' When this came to Kipling's ears he rushed off to the post-office and sent him a telegram: 'Quite all right. No believer in the League of Nations ever gave his blood for anything.'

Curtis knew Kipling very well in South Africa: the latter stayed with him a month in Pretoria. After wrote him a Collins from somewhere in the Karoo, 'There we are stuck like flies in a pot of treacle', which Curtis said exactly described what it was like crossing the Karoo – he had to do it often as dispatch-rider during the Boer War. When Campbell-Bannerman granted self-government, Kipling was flabbergasted to find that a number of the younger men out in South Africa were in favour. And Lionel became known in that particular circle as 'The Traitor'.

In spite of difference of views etc. Kipling had an enormous respect for Thomas Hardy. After Hardy's death, Kipling was elected to the Fellowship at Magdalene, Cambridge, which he had held. Richmond went up in the train with him, and had never seen a man so pleased: he regarded it as a great honour, and was very humble and modest towards Hardy.

Then Curtis told a story of Kipling's visit to Rhodes House, when he was shown over by the door-keeper there, a well-known figure. After this, Kipling said kindly, 'You may like to know who it is you have been showing round. I am Mr Kipling.'

Pause. Then the janitor said: 'I'm sorry, sir . . . But I don't know who Mr Kipling is.'

* I was writing *Tudor Cornwall*.

** Editor of *The Times Literary Supplement* in its best days.

Richmond told us of an interesting coincidence in his family history after 500 years. His brother on retiring bought a small manor-house which he found somewhere in the Cotswolds: an interesting old house, Threopham or some such name which he had never heard of before.

An American cousin who knew the whole history of the family was able to tell him that 500 years before, in 1430, their ancestor William Richmond had been in negotiation for that house, and was unable to buy it because somebody stepped in between and bought it. Half a thousand years after his descendant was able to complete the negotiations and live there.

The Forties

The forties, by far the richest decade of Rowse's literary production, are not well represented in his journals. Physically though in much better health than he had been he was, like everyone else, circumscribed by the war. Foreign travel was impossible until 1946, and even then currency restrictions, not eased until the fifties, imposed severe limits. Wartime train and bus services were surprisingly good but often crowded and delayed. Cornwall and Oxford divided his time.

Cornwall indeed became an increasing delight because for the first time he acquired a house of his own, in which he could entertain and have friends to stay. He had a large light room to work in and even adequate space for his books. The house was on the outskirts of St Austell, on the road leading out to Trenarren, which had itself been vacated by its peacetime tenants. Their place was taken by the Headmaster of King's School, Canterbury, which had been evacuated to avoid the bombing. As a contribution to the national effort (Rowse was of course unfit for any form of service) he lent a hand with the Sixth Form history teaching and brought down other writers and scholars to address the school. An unexpected reward was the beginning of his last and greatest affair of the heart, his love for Norman Scarfe, then in the Sixth Form but shortly to go up to Oxford and then into the Army, where he was among the first to land in France on the D-Day assault.

The depth of the emotion, their consonance of taste and sensibility, their shared gift for topographical writing, absorbed Rowse to an extent he had never experienced or imagined. In the old inexplicable but expressive phrase, it took him out of himself. Perhaps that, together with the multiplicity of his literary commitments, explains the absence of diaries, though he continued to keep up his pocket books and, on occasion, to expand these to cover a few consecutive days, for instance when visiting Norman Scarfe in camp in Yorkshire or in the anxiety preceding and following D-Day.

As these extracts are drawn from the pocket books I have included one or two pieces from the late thirties which I found there rather than interpolating them into the diaries proper for the period.

Towards the end of the forties the diaries are, fitfully, resumed.

Whitsunday, 1939, at 24 Robartes Place [St Austell]

Only now at the end of the day writing in bed that I have a few moments to myself to reflect on Noreen's[1] wedding today. Here in the same bed, the big brass one which stood in my sister's room at Tregonissey, in which I have written so many reflections on New Year's Nights, have had so much pain and one or two serious illnesses. Only now that I am beginning, belatedly, to enjoy life – so much so that today was not unenjoyable though a little poignant, where last year I should not have been able to endure it.

The church was at its Whitsun best, high bright sun coming in at the little porch from the churchyard rosy with rhododendrons. Inside the candles lighted on the altar, the sun again shining in the chancel, and the church already well filled with simple people so much more used to attending weddings than I. I sat in the last pew on the bride's side, straight in from the porch where I should first see her arriving. Behind me a little light burned and there was some of that honeysuckle-like flower which was Charles's favourite – embothrium, only yellow not red. I thought of that other wedding, of the pathos of all weddings, the fidelity of all the country people who had passed through this church. Here they were, and this one spectator, this ironical observer in an equivocal position (not a few must think he should have been the bridegroom), determined to do his duty and see her properly married. The organ played softly; a bird cheeped outside in the churchyard, the sun came in at the porch; the choirboys and parson assembled.

But when the bride came on the arm of her brother, and halted in the doorway, a charming picture framed by the arch. I felt a tug at the heart. It should have been I that was marrying her. She gave me so charming a smile, so kind and understanding as always; I watched her walk up the aisle looking so fresh and pretty under her dark blue hat, the lovely line of the Renaissance gown she had told me I should like clinging to her figure and

1. Life-long friend from schooldays when they had acted opposite each other as Malvolio and Olivia.

rippling round her feet, arms white under high puffed sleeves. Then she was joined by Christopher, the new man I am not yet used to, and stood there between him and her brother, and the service began, sun shining brightly all through in the chancel.

But how much better a husband he will make than I: straight and strong, a man's man – not the incalculable odd creature they do not know that I am – drives a car, a good swimmer and cricketer, a strong arm for her to lean upon. All is well with her, I hope and have no doubt. The fantasy that occurs in all this is that some day something may happen to Chris, and I may then humbly take his place, Noreen having enjoyed the best of her life with him; and I may console her latter days, and she look after me as she has always done, with patience, and sympathy, and so much wisdom.

Some people in church were thinking what a mistake I had made in letting another man marry Noreen, or that Noreen was making when it should have been me. (Her brother told me as much.) I do not think so. She will be happy with him – think of the midnight now at Hartland where they are, with a Whitsun moon high up over the sea; in my favourite place to which I introduced Noreen, she will be unable not to think of me; – and she will (I think) always have me to fall back on.*

> Somehow I should have lost a gesture and a pose
> Sometimes these reflections amaze the midnight and trouble the
> noon's repose

Norman Lyne (to whom I once thought of marrying her) came to rescue me and carry me off for an evening by the sea at Kilmarth, along the Gribben by the cliff path close to the water with drifts of bluebell and pink campion below, around the point to Polridmouth beach. Norman remembered young Harford Pethybridge striking out across the cove and out to sea in the summer before he died of TB; up into the grounds of Menabilly.[1] We walked up between banks of rhododendrons to peer into the windows of the deserted house, the family portraits up in the dining-room, the big fireplaces, firedogs, Sheraton chairs, china, the confusion of the library, no-one there, the cupola falling in.

One unframed thought lurked round the corner as we walked through deserted avenues and walks, between ilexes and dracaenas, eucalyptuses and ferns, talking of Freud's view of Moses and Monotheism, the nature of

* 28 December 1978. Rather touching and sentimental. Something did happen to Chris – he died eight or ten years ago. Noreen had a happy life with him, a conventional family life. Today I take her for a drive in the car, with Phyllis who looks after me.

1. Subsequently the house of Daphne du Maurier.

religion, whether it was a neurosis of the race comparable to that of the individual, or whether the symbolism of religion reveals more of the truth about our lives than reason does – one thought lurked there which I did not have the opportunity to frame:

Had I after all been a fool?

I do not think so; but only time can tell.*

Oxford, Friday, 25(?) May 1940

Today, for half an hour after lunch, an interesting chat with Laurence Binyon under the trees in the Warden's garden: the sun coming through leaves of Siberian crab-apple, the chestnut candles upstanding. Binyon charming and simple as ever – such strange china-blue eyes. I got him to talk about the '90s and Q. He said that it was a pity Q. had not taken himself seriously as a novelist – he had all the gifts for it – with delightful humour and fantasy. Perhaps it was due to want of money – he had done so much journalism, then got into a groove, hard to get out. So many people had done it. He wondered whether he wasn't a victim of his own facility. When up here, he turned out any amount of light verse for the *Oxford Magazine*, awfully good and fluent. When doing so much journalism he used to come up to London three times a week – much too much.

Arthur Symons – B. had known him quite well, but Symons was antipathetic to him, antagonistic. S. all in favour of French models (I must say he proved to have been right). S.'s father a Methodist minister. His breakdown – he went to Venice with the Edmund Davieses and disappeared. Couldn't be found. At last tracked him down to the gaol at Ferrara where he was chained down, raving mad. B. had seen him a few years ago in a shop in London like a ghost of himself, a dead man walking, something *spectral*. Not so amorous as he made out – Rothenstein said S. was always making bad resolutions in the morning which he broke at night. S. taken up by Pater. Left isolated by the death of friends of '90s. Lionel Johnson pathetic – go to see him and there he'd be sitting alone with a bottle of absinthe – no conviviality – heaps of books all round – he was very well-read. Son of a squire, undersized – had always from a child had to have drugs to sleep, etc. Fell down drunk in the Strand and cracked his skull.

Richard Middleton committed suicide. But no-one knew that his father had hanged himself and mother taken poison next day.

* 1978. Of course I was right to let this, and every such, opportunity slip – free to live *my* life, follow my own bent, not subserve the purposes of nature or other people. Cynthia Carew-Pole saw: 'AL would never marry any body.' How could I? And there, this afternoon, there will still be Noreen waiting at the corner for me to pick her up at Mevagissey.

An article of Symons in *Life and Letters* describes his experience of going mad.

1978: Q. was antipathetic to Symons too, told me that he belonged to the 'other school'. He had read through Symons' poems to see if there was something for the *Oxford Book of Verse*, but 'I could do nothing for him'. Understandable – I don't think much of Symons' poetry.

But Q. knew Lord Alfred Douglas – who asked himself down to stay at Fowey. Lady Q. wouldn't have him, 'with young children in the house'. Q. had accepted, and then had to cry off. So he must have met Wilde in those London days.

March 1941. Accidie and Bachelordom

All the latter half of this term I have been tired and stale, unable to work – no lift in it, no chance of a fresh wind in the climate of Oxford. I wished for a cottage in the purer air of Boar's Hill, but hadn't the energy to make a change. I came to the conclusion that I was suffering from the accidie which medieval monks suffered from. The day after I diagnosed my case I came upon a book which W. P. Ker had presented to Charles Plummer (the beloved bachelor 'W.P.', of All Souls stories, soul of Common Room, dominated by his bust). Inside was a letter in that exquisite, scholarly hand: 'This book would have been sent before, if it had not been for *accidie*.'

So W.P.K. had it, leading the same kind of life, without excitement or companionship, without bed-mate – without love. But perhaps it is a condition incident to the end of a winter term's teaching after all?

[?1942]

My German-exile dentist's interior: a vast cupboard with ecclesiastical stained glass and corkscrew pillars. A light depends from the ceiling of some metal, the colour of iridescent vomit, and of Teutonic complexity of design. A mud-coloured painting of a Westphalian *bauern-hof*, all set to touch the sentimental German heart. On the table a lamp with vast parchment shade that fills the room as Hitler fills Europe.

Yet it was at this dentist's today that I had a meeting I had wished for for years. I have long been interested in the Cornish Godolphins, thought of writing their history, and loved that sad, half-ruined remnant of their great house – and wanted to meet the heir to all that history. While upstairs closeted with the dentist, under a hot lamp, his pretty assistant came in and said *sotto voce*, 'The Duke of Leeds'. I said, 'I've just been writing to him.' And am rather psychic, accustomed to these Koestler-coincidences.

Going down after my treatment, I had a moment in the waiting-room alone with the Duke, whom I had wanted to get in touch with over his Godolphin archives. An odd figure arose behind that enormous shade obliterating him, evidently the fag-end of an old stock. In spite of the seedy appearance perhaps a look of his ancestors, even of the Lord Treasurer: those extraordinary dark eyes, round and bulging out of a puny, insignificant face – the face of a young man prematurely old.

'I've had a wisdom tooth out,' he said.

'So have I.'

'And haven't been able to eat,' he added.

I had heard before that he was nervous and elusive; with me he was not so much nervous as jerky, like a jockey or man of the turf. Dr Munz now entered, large as an elephant, white overalls and white skull-cap as usual, with elephantine courtesy holding the door open for us to go out. But who was to go out first? It was plainly my right. I was before the Duke, my treatment over. I moved towards the door, the Duke behind me. Then I hesitated, reflecting that a duke after all was a duke, however seedy, and had precedence over a commoner – and with all that Godolphin–Osborne history behind him (though only the Godolphin half of it interested me).

Dr Munz observed the state of play with interest, not without a little concern that etiquette should be observed. I motioned the Duke towards the door before me; he whipped through like a whippet, while Dr Munz held the door open for me, beaming that the proprieties had been observed.

Reading this passage over to David (Cecil), he returned with one from Boswell's *Tour of the Hebrides*. The Duke of Argyll ordered one of the *gentlemen* present to fetch something from another room. He blenched but he obeyed, whistling as he went to show his independence all the same.

The ducal encounter in the dentist's waiting-room led to nothing: the family story was too sad. The Duke had sold the Osborne family seat, Hornby Castle in Yorkshire, everything, lock, stock and barrel – even, what annoyed King George V, the ducal coronet. Apparently the mother preferred the Mediterranean, leaving the heir rootless and nobody to follow on. End of the family – as of so much else in our squalid society.

Monday, 15 March 1943

Sudden inspiration in the midst of reading Horace Walpole's Letters. 'I'm going to travel – like Hell. I'm going to travel when the war is over,' I say aloud, surprising myself. Copenhagen – it was the thought of eighteenth-century Copenhagen undestroyed, unspoiled that brought the thought up to the surface. Then Stockholm, perhaps Leningrad. Certainly Danzig, Königsberg. But above all Italy – Ravello, the Amalfi peninsula, Naples, Sicily. And Spain! And Portugal! I want to see Lisbon and Coimbra and Oporto. And Madrid, Burgos, Santiago, Toledo and Malaga.

I believe I shall do no work at all, but revolve round and round the Continent, after these years of being mewed up in this island accumulating staleness, at times an acute sense of mingled claustrophobia and nostalgia for abroad.

Wednesday, 30 June

Helmsley: the long succession of the Rooses all through the vicissitudes, quiet and tumult, of the Middle Ages. The sense of it like a dream, as I sit on the earth ramparts while Bruce reads out a long list of the owners of the castle: the Roos of Magna Carta, Rooses of the Wars of the Roses, the one who sold it to Richard, Duke of Gloucester – to come to an end with an heiress who married a Manners.

The sense of all that life vanished, as if it had never been: the champing horses, clatter of armour, clamour and clangour of so many men at arms; the great ladies and their maids; bustle of kitchen and buttery and pantry; the services of chapel; smells of the moat; the comings and goings – all still, all vanished utterly, only rubble and stone. And the memory of the Duke,* broken in health and fortune, rusticated from the gaieties and follies of Charles II's Court, dying in an inn at Kirkbymoorside.

These thoughts and a cluster of harebells – the Scottish bluebells – growing upon the wall under the ruined gatehouse.

Byland Abbey: the Romanesque last decades of the twelfth century, where Rievaulx is the very end of the twelfth and early thirteenth century – Early English. One can see the transition at both. Walking down over the steep Wass Bank from the moor, to come upon this long and lovely shell.

Coxwold: Laurence Sterne's living – attractive street climbing uphill to a highly decorated Perpendicular church on top, octagonal tower and many-pinnacled nave. Inside, the chancel full of big Bellasis monuments. On the north side a very ornate affair to Sir William Bellasis who married a Fairfax,

* This was that clever ass, the second Duke of Buckingham, who ran through all his property: Dryden's Zimri, who

> in the course of one revolving moon
> Was chemist, fiddler, statesman, and buffoon.

d. 1603: two fine effigies in good repair: he in armour, ruff, with pointed beard. Underneath three sons in odd kneeling posture, in jerkins with coats-of-arms. The whole thing painted and piled up with obelisks on either side. Opposite, a classical monument of 1618: black and white marble, two figures in parallel compartments, framed within columns, pedimented. The transition from ornate and rather vulgar luxuriant Elizabethan to classical restraint and proportion in these two monuments. (N. B. for my Elizabethan Age.)

The family became Lords Fauconberg: the F. Arms the pub in the village street; opposite, early seventeenth-century almshouses. Higher up, small Elizabethan hall with big windows overlooking valley and across to woods between Sutton Bank and Wass Bank. Beyond the church another small seventeenth-century hall. Then, opposite a line of sycamores and beeches, Shandy Hall, where Sterne wrote *Tristram Shandy* and *A Sentimental Journey*. A ramshackle seventeenth-century house with huge chimney at end in farmyard: brick pleasantly washed, an eighteenth-century front added, looking on garden – great dead tree that must have known Sterne at corner. Tablet over the door saying that he died in London, aged fifty-five. No memorial of him in the church, so much of which remembers him all the same: Georgian two-decker pulpit, from which he preached those sermons, the notes of which we have; horseshoe-shaped communion rails projecting down into the chancel.

Beyond the village the lake and grounds of Newburgh Priory: interesting house with Elizabethan wing, main block seventeenth century uncompleted, right wing irregular, part-medieval buildings. The Priory produced a chronicler in William de Newburgh. Sterne a frequent visitor here – Lord Fauconberg a fellow toper and companion in conviviality (*v.* the Letters).

And wasn't there a Cromwell marriage? And a lugubrious memento, preserved in the house, of Oliver's head?

Walking over Scawton Moor and Wass Moor we had in view the immense mound of High Paradise.

Kirkbymoorside: King's Head has an interesting picture, late seventeenth or early eighteenth century, Marriage of the Virgin, Italian in style. Whence come? Worth buying.

2 July

Coming over the moor from Lastingham Bruce and I stop by the bridge to paddle in the beck – our hot weary feet, with ice-cold moor-water running over them. When we go on our way a delicious scent assails us from over the moor. What is it? – scent of limes: it must be from young bracken shoots. So down to Hutton le Hole, stream making a ravine through the village, houses rising on either side.

Farms of Helmsley: Rising Sun, Flower o' May, Peep o' Day, Throstles' Nest. Was one of them the farm of Herbert Read's admirable autobiography, *The Innocent Eye*?

Characteristic of Yorkshire: the mellow sound of whistle of L.N.E.R. engines echoing softly in the valleys, so unlike the shrill note of G.W.R. engines. I notice it in all those dales, Wensleydale, Swaledale, making their remoteness even more remote. And here again in the Vale of Pickering, sitting beside the beck in Gilling.

Coming down a side-road on the way – a whole patch of rosebay willowherb and foxgloves, bordered by elder in flower: an extraordinary rich smell like blackberry jam-making when I was a boy at home. We scrambled down a steep side into Oswaldkirk – do the Yorkshire people call it a scar or a hauk? Thick vegetation, shoots of plants, stripling trees, thistles, flowers: among these a wild campanula, almost as big as Canterbury Bells. In field beside the valley running down to Helmsley purple orchis and mullein.

Oswaldkirk: a fine seventeenth-century house and good Georgian rectory. Little church on valleyside has delightful Georgian tablets. One to a Thompson, Commissioner of Customs in Ireland for seventeen years (he must have made a pretty pile out of that) who became a Lord of the Admiralty: charming white marble medallion of him.

On the roads all day troops moving: Guards, Coldstream and Irish, Corps of Signals putting up their telephone connections, enormous lorries and carriers; in Oswaldkirk little tanks being stowed away in the innyard. (What a deflection of human energies – all due to the idiocy of Germans following Hitler.) All that mass of sweltering, good-tempered humanity, sunburned, sweating, many bare-bodied, moving arms and limbs and vehicles, whenever we came to the road from our cross-country route, across field, up paths and tracks, by wood and copse, pursued by clouds of flies, along edges of hay fields, hay lying in swathes, corn fields not yet ripe, and at last down that precipitous bank across the plain to Gilling.

3 July

St Mary's, Beverley: charming pillar given by the minstrels of the church; five figures with their instruments and 'Orate pro animabus misteriorum'. Tablet in chancel aisle, oval with crossed swords above:

Here two young Danish Souldiers lye,
The one in quarrell chanc'd to die;
The others Head, by their own Law
With Sword was Sever'd at one Blow.

1689 – bloody young fools, two good lives lost by human foolery. I suppose from Danish troops recruited to aid William of Orange to boot out James II, a more exalted fool.

Bishop Fisher born at Beverley 1459, son of Robert Fisher, mercer, buried before the Crucifix. Another kind of fool, executed for his convictions – or masculine intellectual conceit – against Henry VIII. The church full of matrices of magnificent brasses – all gone. In the human foolery of Reformation or Civil War – though why should the admirable works of men's hands be the victims of the nonsense they *think* they think?

On a piano in church a Penguin of Maupassant's *Boule de Suif* – more to the point.

The bells of Beverley ring their strange chime at the quarters, such as I have never heard anywhere else.

The Percy tomb[1] the most perfect masterpiece of medieval stonework, *c.* 1350: I have never seen anything to equal it. Grand Gothic canopy in shape like Edward II's at Gloucester, but so richly carved. The whole rises up to a splendid bloom of a finial; majestic figure of Christ blesses a female figure, a naked soul in the wrappings of the tomb. In spandrels knights carrying shields with the Percy lion and their own arms alternately. The smallest spaces made use of to contain angel or flower design, the tiniest bosses finished off with a head or animal.

The wooden screens of the same period – how much lovelier and freer, more delicate, than later woodwork: wood being transformed into a flower. To think of the losses through the iconoclasm of Reformation or Civil War, even of eighteenth or nineteenth century – the idiocy of it! However, they created other forms of beauty for their time. Today's the streamlines of motor-cars, aeroplanes. The stalls later, Perpendicular; one misericord to Johannes Webbe, 1520, 'thesaurarius huius ecclesie'. They portray late medieval life vividly: hunting, activities of field and farm, along with joyous humour, *joy* in life. Here a man milking a cow, there one spearing a boar; a fox carrying off geese, then fox hanged on a gibbet. A man in armour spears a dragon, St George or St Michael? Bear-wrestling appears as a subject.

I am struck by the names of the shopkeepers in Beverley: Uriah Butters conjures up the picture of an eminent Nonc.; Irene Bloom and Miss Tiplady;

1. In the Minster.

Mr Cattle's Stores; Mr Richard Care and Mr Fussey; Messrs Heaps, Baggs, Potts. All very Yorkshire down-to-earth. Nothing so idiosyncratic as our Cornish Hoskin, Trevithick and Polkinghorne of Truro or Button, Menhennit and Mutton of Wadebridge.

The Slingsby family lived at Belton, looking across the Nidd valley to Knaresborough, where they are buried in their chapel. Sir Henry, who fought in the Netherlands, has a curious Caroline memorial-portrait in a niche. The re-discoverer of the springs of Harrogate. (N.B. for the Elizabethan Age.)

Ripon – lime trees in flower, alders by the bridge over the Skell.

Fountains: the great yew hedge, sweet-smelling in sun. Exquisite Fountains Hall, built out of stone from the Abbot's lodging; central oriel, long lighted windows as at Trerice, broad gables either side ended by two slender towers. 1611 – but looks earlier Elizabethan from its simplicity; excellent situation facing south, better than the Abbot's on top of the river. Elizabethan houses more comfortable, with light and large windows.

A masterly sentence by Queenie D. Leavis, on Hardy: 'With Meredith, the then current comparison, he could of course only be compared to his advantage in every respect.' A woman who writes like that should be a kitchen-maid washing dishes – as I told her. Characteristic of the Leavises: they couldn't commend one writer without depreciating another. Note the style: 'then' used adjectivally, and 'of course' pontifically. Incorrect too: for, though I vastly prefer Hardy, he cannot be compared advantageously to Meredith in point of style. Anyway the Leavises have no sense of style, can hardly write the language; the texture of their writing the texture of coke. Fancy a whole generation of innocents being taken in by their nonsense – and the damage to the study of English Literature, through all the naif secondary-school teachers, their pupils.

Here is the husband – whom dear Q. got his job for him at Downing: 'Milton's dislodgement, *in the past decade*, after his two centuries of predominance, was effected with remarkably little fuss. The irresistible argument was, *of course*, Mr Eliot's creative adjustment; it gave his few critical asides – potent, it is true, by context – their finality and made it unnecessary to elaborate a case.' The vacuity of this! It says nothing, except that this second-rater can't appreciate the greatest poet in the language, after Shakespeare. 'In the past decade' is a complete giveaway – it shows the myopia of those who have no historic sense.

8 December 1949

A useful day in Glasgow, and even enjoyable. It did not rain. I breakfasted off tea, toast and butter, a small portion of bacon and scrambled egg, a roll, marmalade; meanwhile reading *The Scotsman*. Then up to Kelvingrove to the Art Gallery, where I had the good fortune to run into a fascinating exhibition illustrating Medicine in History. For two hours I worked at making notes, which will come in very useful for my chapter on Science in volume II. I was fascinated by the portrait of Vesalius and the early books – one of his and of Paracelsus along with the English writers. An unexpected portrait of Smollett too – the converse of what one would have expected: not jovial, coarse, or brutal, but sensitive, almost finicking, with small upcurved mouth and oval face like a lady of the period.

Then I went to look for pure pleasure at the French pictures: a couple of magnificent Daumiers, 'The Good Samaritan' and 'The Miller, his Donkey and Son'. A moving Delacroix – Adam and Eve expelled from Paradise – a most original composition, unlike no other of the subject: Eve in her shame exposed and suppliant, right hand open outwards, Adam like a man hiding his shame so that you cannot see his face, the Angel's blue robe forming a background for Adam's ruddy brown figure. I contemplated stealing an exquisite little Boudin – boats at Deauville: I should find it difficult, a young assistant assured me. There is the finest Guardi I have ever seen – San Giorgio and the Canal. At the end of the morning I was introduced to a Mr Hanna, keeper of the immense Burrell Collections: the old boy still alive at eighty-eight, as shrewd and dictatorial as ever. They are having a tough time trying to get him to agree to the Burrell Gallery being a little nearer and get-at-able from Glasgow. He has a daughter whose suitors he has chivvied off – a sad time for her at forty, still unmarried.

Back to lunch: chicken broth, roast lamb, potatoes with onion flavouring, an ice and coffee. Then off to perambulate the town: my idea to traverse Sauchiehall Street. First stop Porteous' bookshop, where a fine youngish fellow in naval blue raincoat distracted my attention for a bit. However I made forward, fulfilled more than my programme – walked the whole length of S. Street up to the Latin Quarter of Glasgow, good late Georgian and early Victorian terraces, Newton Place, Clifton Place, on into the Park and into the rabbit-warren of the University to call on Robin Burn. He not there. I could not bear to inhabit such a place: the thought of it oppressed me and made me grateful for Oxford.

In bed at St Enoch's after a successful lecture on the Elizabethan Age at Paisley – to a rather slow, cautious, appreciative audience. I find it a bit difficult to make immediate contact with a Scottish audience – perhaps because, with my Elizabethan background, I think of them as different. I remember last year being surprised at both Helensburgh and Greenock at the way in which they identified themselves with the English Tudor period – as if they had been part of it. It showed how much subsequent education has *verschmelzt* distinctions and made us one people. (Though my lecture was a success at the Ministers' Arts Club at Helensburgh, they haven't asked me again. I went down with the heterodox wise old minister, not with his young colleague, who had been an Army chaplain, knew about the world and took an opportunity to refer to 'social pests' – a convenient term by which to condemn what he disapproved of, Laodiceans, unbelievers, what not. No doubt he recognized what was what. Nasty type of a Calvinist inquisitor: there was the barbarism, the intolerance of a culture framed on John Knox.)

Bus to Paisley – only a short step over the black-wet pavements of Glasgow: this masculine city, pulsating with life and obviously – to the credit of the new social order – much improved in manners and morals, if less drunken, less diseased and murderous than in pre-1914 days. It must have been a rough house then.

After my lecture a *few* bodies got together; we drank tea and had a Y.M.C.A. cake. A Dr Watt, interested in whether Paisley's St Mirin is the Cornish St Merryn, whether St Mungo can have brought him and a St Constantine back with him from St Asaph. How I love these old antiquarian lunacies! Tomorrow I am to go and be shown around Paisley Abbey by him.

9 December

My last day in Glasgow. Early this morning a dream – my first on the subject of taxation. It took an archaeological form. I dreamed that I was presented with a demand for £91 on top of everything else – on the ground that the foundations of the nave of a chapel lay on my property. I denied that they existed: they were not above ground and could not be seen. At the same time I knew that they were – or fragments of them – there. But nothing would induce me to pay. One of my kind relations – the architectural Len – let me down. You know that they are there and you will have to pay was his line. Nothing would induce me: I'd rather sell the whole place at a bigger loss than pay the government's demand. With that resolution and in that temper I awoke.

This morning at breakfast – tea and toast, grilled herring, marmalade – a brother of Bill Collins* sat at the next table. He wanted my *Glasgow Herald*

* His twin, Ian, with whom he had played in the Men's Doubles at Wimbledon. Sir William Collins was always known as Billy, not Bill.

open at the Collins issue. 'You know who I am?' he said. I hadn't the remotest idea. I liked that piece of naïveté from him: so like the directness of Glasgow: nobody would have given themselves away like that in the English environment.

I spent the whole morning in Paisley Abbey, being shown every feature and almost every inch by Dr Watt, who evidently loves every stone. One unique feature: a large stone balustrade to carry the clerestory walk high up: it makes a heavy ungainly rhythm all round the nave. A fine church for Scotland, with three good Burne-Jones windows and some hideous modern glass. Woodwork of the choir by Lorimer – but God how such a place cries out for altars, colour, processions, ceremony. What interested me most was the mansion the Hamiltons made out of the monastic buildings. Outside grim grey-black seventeenth-century Scottish fortress – architecture, several storeys, entrance up defensible stone steps, high stepped gables. Inside sophisticated panelled rooms of William and Mary, modillions and door-cases, coved and painted ceilings. A town house fit for an earl – one saw the Scottish Reformation at a glance. Not the Crown, but the Hamiltons got the lands of Paisley Abbey. One saw the sombre background of seventeenth-century Scotland – Montrose and Argyll, Lauderdale, those homicidal aristocrats, with their veneer of civilization and their feuds.

Lunch with good Dr Watt who had got the organist to meet me, a Cornishman, Pearce Hosken. A good musician – I noticed how good the music they sing. Orlando Gibbons, Weelkes, Bach, Brahms. Hosken was Dr Orchard's organist at King's Weigh House chapel – unprepossessing, cross-eyed, but a man to respect. In the afternoon he played for me alone, showed me all the qualities of a grand organ, built up from the small French organ of the nave-church, with their beautiful reed-tone – a certain delicacy compared with the stolidity of the English manuals. I went down into the nave to listen while he improvised on plainsong themes, filled that bare Philistine building with the memories that still linger there, almost brought back the shadowy monks into the aisles and transepts: the music of another world. Two women were whispering and tispering in the back. Too much moved by the music for which those December-dark spaces were made I rose and made a deep genuflexion to where the high altar once was and its simulacrum now stood.

Back to tea, then off to Greenock; a good dinner in the Town club in the square: asparagus soup, roast beef, baked potatoes, but sweet? – it has gone utterly out of my head. I am afraid I make no hand at a Parson Woodforde.

15 December

Home from Oxford today. The usual flurry of packing: I *never* catch up completely with the hundred and one things I mean to do before leaving one place and going to another. Coming down in the train from Reading was a man whose appearance intrigued me immensely. Where had I seen him before? For he was a type that struck home – that family look about the eyes above all: the eyes of various members of my family. At first I thought of Tony Rowse – the same type of head, mouth, nose, moustache; the expression of the eyes Hilda's boy, Dick's. I was held by him. He took no notice whatever: that was characteristic of him I found. He had evidently come back from a hot climate – sun-burned complexion, summer suit, no waistcoat: he was cold and threw an American camel-hair coat over himself. I studied him, fascinated: hands small and finely made, like my own; small head well poised, small tight ears; nose with the hardly perceptible depression or division at the tip; brilliant expressive dark eyes; most striking – regular thickly waving hair carefully combed and just beginning to grey. He slept, woke up complaining of cold; I changed seats with him. He spoke like a Colonial. He was Cornish – came from St Ives. I was surprised to learn he was Scots on his father's side. 'Which do you consider yourself?' 'Oh, Cornish' – with emphasis. I discovered he had very Cornish characteristics, perhaps emphasized by his Scottishry. He was hard, unsentimental, self-satisfied and self-sufficient; he had the usual Cornish smugness and boastfulness; he took it for granted that his concerns were the most interesting on earth – I thought of those bores, my Charlestown cousins; he was out, not so much to impress – he didn't care enough for the person he was talking to for that – as to put himself across, the characteristic Cornish self-importance. (I recognize the traits in myself.) He travelled everywhere by plane. He had just that morning come from Paris. He had travelled from South America – done a round trip via New York and Iceland, etc. I noticed he never spoke of *leaving* the country, it was always *take off*. The natural desire of the homecoming Cornish to impress. I have observed it in the swaggering boasting Joe Anstis, as in my own egoistic absorption in my own concerns.

This man – named Elder – has a mother and brother at St Ives and comes home at intervals from his career as geophysicist, exploring for oil. Employed by a large American oil firm, paid in dollars, does well. Wherever he goes he has the local Cornish papers sent on – correct touch that. Camborne School of Mines, 1936–9, then in the R.E.s for seven years, ending up in Kiel where his job was blowing up submarine-pens. Had a good time in Germany. Has just entered on a two-year contract exploring for oil in the

Amazon. Had an offer through the F.O. to work in Soviet Russia at a large salary. On 28 December takes off for U.S., for two years will live with a few other men in the wilds of upper Brazil. Leave every three months in Rio. Or fly to New York, where a wonderful time could be had. Quite different from London. Before the war London used to be a wonderful place. Not so now.

I inquired in what way New York gave one such a good time. It appeared it was the usual vulgarian's idea of a good time: cinemas, clubs, night-clubs, shows. He commented with some surprise that the Vic-Wells ballet had proved a dollar goldmine. There were comparatively few in his profession: he was liable to knock up against them all over the world. One Christmas he had spent in Baghdad at the – hotel (he assumed I knew its importance); an American, another chap from the School of Mines and another cosmopolitan. Everything laid on: I supposed women too. All that side of life provided for more easily than at home. A mining engineer back from the wilds – oh, he'll need a bit of life, will need to go wild for a bit. In Damascus he had been put in gaol for a Jewish spy (the Cornish as one of the lost tribes no doubt) during the Arab–Jewish troubles. Kirkuk was mentioned. He liked the life. He liked being free and independent and individual. He had no ties. It wouldn't do to fall in love in his job. Not much danger I should say: too much of an egoist, too smug, too hard and impermeable. As hard as the mineral quartz he deals in. At the same time I was fascinated: for there was the age-old type of the Cornish adventurer before me. I told him the story of the Cornish Emigration, if only it were written properly, would make a wonderful book. He thought it wouldn't have much interest. Evidently – so enclosed in his own mining engineering world – no imagination: the perfect technician – adventurer. I do not think he even noticed how fascinated I was, or that I gave him no information as to who or what I was. That was quite OK by him: he wasn't even interested.

17 December

Today and yesterday might almost qualify as Woodforde days, so little external incident. And yet how different really! For yesterday morning, afternoon, evening, night I worked at revising, and finished revising the first three chapters of my book: some 150 typed pages. I was agreeably pleased with it – surprised in fact: I thought it would need a great deal more revising. One thinks the work that has gone out of one's head can't be any good; then one is pleasantly surprised to find that it is.

This morning and afternoon I spent on revising an immense chapter on 'The New Wealth' – 80 or 90 pages of it = 27,000 words. Then off into the town to look at an anthracite stove for my cold morgue of a hall. The squalid down-at-heel ugliness of every step into the town irritates me beyond belief: every step jars the nerves and sensibilities: – it is like a whip across the face to see the hideous 'villas' with their interiors exposed to the view: the coloured and frosted glass, the frilly-edged glazed earthenware tiles, the concrete edges like exposed nerves. To escape I fled up the backway across the railway bridge and along the edge of Willie Coode's once-desirable property.

The Fifties

This decade and its immediate successor provide the richest, most elaborate passages in the diary. The opening years are sparse. Rowse's involvement in the affairs of All Souls took up too high a proportion of his time and energy. He had become, by rotation, Sub-Warden, usually an unexacting office simply requiring its holder to deputize for the Warden in a few administrative and social duties. But Sumner, the then Warden, had a long run of serious ill-health which meant that Rowse found himself called on to do practically the whole job. In 1951, after an apparent recovery, Sumner died suddenly and Rowse, still Sub-Warden, had to preside over the election of his successor. Urged by some of his most senior colleagues to offer himself as a candidate, he steadily refused but could hardly avoid involvement in the caballing and backbiting that followed the last-minute withdrawal of the obvious, consensual candidate.

Unfortunately the new Warden, not robust at the time of his election, suffered a succession of heart-attacks which prevented him from coming into residence. He therefore resigned in 1952 and Rowse, still Sub-Warden, was faced with going through the whole circus again. This time he accepted the invitation of colleagues to stand for the Wardenship himself: his ensuing defeat by John Sparrow marked a turning-point in his career, as is abundantly attested by the pages that follow.

These matters are dealt with in my biography of Rowse, where such evidence as the diaries afford is fully cited. I have therefore omitted all such passages here. One obvious consequence of the 1952 Election was Rowse's determination to turn more and more to America and to distance himself from a country that had, in his view, rejected him.

15 January 1950

Back in college since Tuesday night, I have had so much to get through – 220,000 words of typescript twice over, other people's books too which have arrived on me, e.g. Sumner's *Peter the Great* which I have been through today, besides a lot of letters and oddments – that it was only this evening that the sheer joy of being back in Oxford caught me suddenly, came at me round the corner and pounced on me, as I emerged from a brief tea in the Common Room. There had been the familiar party of friends round the tea-table: G. M. Young, still rather at a standstill in his Life of Stanley Baldwin and whom I was trying to persuade to write a 'Queen Victoria and her Age' for my series; Lionel Curtis, who collapsed in New York this summer, was at death's door and made a marvellous recovery; now at seventy-six or seventy-seven looks a man of sixty, and is as loud and lays down the law as vigorously as ever; Cyril Falls, rather seriously unwell with colon trouble, brought on by incessant work over the past ten years – his Professorship, writing a weekly article for the *Illustrated London News*, *Times* military correspondent, and writing books – he has an expensive wife and couple of daughters to keep; nice Charles Monteith, just left living in college to begin at the Bar, and Stuart Hampshire, who comes down regularly at weekends.

I slipped away, and as I came out into the quadrangle was suddenly seized: a thrush singing in the corner of the old buildings, Spring in the air, making the veins in the stone from the old quarries in the Cotswolds to tingle and my heart to stop for a heart-beat; the bells all chimed the half-hour over the roofs of Oxford; a subdued murmur of the life of the city, though out beyond like a distant sea at the cliffs; here were my chosen cliffs, the dark arcade of the cloister, the darkening well of the quadrangle. The quietness of Sunday brings home this happiness to be alive, this sense of ecstasy, of savouring the moments as they pass, with this edge of propitiatory fear, the shadow of *angst*, that lies on everything, hoping that nothing occurs to shatter or disturb or even change my life. 'If only this moment of time might last' . . . the constant condition present at the back of my mind, the threat to such contentment. After such unhappiness as I have known it seems too much to hope: this is its legacy, the wound it has inflicted on the fabric of my mind. The underlying state is that expressed by Swift – the words I used to know: 'I could never take it that happiness was a state meant for this world.' And now that I find I am happy, it is always with some after-thoughts, fears that it may not last,* that something lies in wait round the corner,** anxiety. *Angst* – so fashionable a grief among the elect in our time – no-one is more marked by it, or with more reason, than I. Only I have kept it rather inside, turned the other side outward in my written work, not made a saleable article of it like Cyril Connolly, or even Uncle Tom Eliot. Not but what the obverse has not made a saleable article too: some consolation for which people seem grateful, for the time we live in. People are so obtuse: they do not know to what an extent I am marked by the demon, am a victim – but do not present that side to the world. One is very much out of fashion; but then I have never been in fashion.***

Moved by the evening, I paid a call on Geoffrey Hudson, mesmerized as usual by the accumulated evidences of his paralysis of will: standing amid the confusion of his new room – to which he moved six or eight weeks ago. The pictures are still on the floor, the books and papers, the tea-chests unpacked, the first chapter of his unfinished book on modern Japan – on the stocks the past fifteen years – on the table before him. I planted a few barbs and left to take Salter for a walk. He had a Very Urgent letter to post to Rab Butler: poor Salter, reduced to such consolations for lacking any influence or voice in affairs. We went to the Post Office, crossed Tom Quad where I expressed my own happiness with such lack of caution that I had to touch the wood of the Dean's door as we passed to avert nemesis; down through Merton Street with lighted rooms revealing some pleasant civilized interiors, across the High into Magdalen. 'We can't get in,' said Salter seeing the iron gates of the Walks closed; he was prepared to turn back. 'One can *always* get through,' I said, pushing them open. We had the Walks to ourselves, beautiful beyond hope in the strange light of January evening. I thought there must be a concealed moon, for the light gleamed strangely on my hands and face as we walked in brushwood darkness.

* It didn't.

** It was waiting all right – the fearful trauma of the Wardenship Election.

*** They thought I was an optimist, and a conformist, bloody idiots.

17 January

G. M. Young has been up for the weekend, bringing his own tang of scholarship and touchiness, distinction and naif conceit, friendliness and aloofness, perhaps accentuated by deafness. A curious figure, who stayed away from the College, offended, for twenty years and then suddenly arrived back one day within the gates and, liking it, returned more and more. Re-elected to a Fellowship, he is now one of the faithfuls, coming up regularly from the Old Oxyard, Great Oare which he has shared with Mona Wilson since the day, many years ago, when he went down there for the weekend and stayed for good. He always brings with him a store of Victorian stories – or is rather a store in himself, from which he can always reach down an anecdote, a quotation or a phrase. Good shopmanship in it – sometimes the action is a little too mechanical – a reach-me-down; but it goes well with his Victorian appearance, always dressed in the dark broadcloth of a clergyman or an undertaker, accentuated by a white tie; rimless glasses and that long turned-up, disdainful instrument – his nose.

A curious episode enacted itself *à propos* of his appearance. Quintin Hogg, who must have known Brand for years, laboured under the impression for a whole evening that Young was Brand. The situation was enjoyed by all in the beginning, not least by Young, who fed Quintin's illusion by throwing in little bits of wartime economic information such as might have come Brand's way, – e.g. that the rifles coming from U.S. were all made of elm. Quintin, so unlike him, was very deferential: and it was 'Of course, you will know so much better than I,' or 'Correct me if I am wrong,' etc. etc. In the end it became embarrassing, but Feiling and Hampshire hadn't the courage to make the *éclaircissement*. So like *them* too!

Young told me a story of Creighton, who gave someone some advice as to how to be a successful dean of a college, founded on his experience at Merton. 'Never send down the bloods. For the bloods you will always have with you. Send down some quiet little man who fell into temptation: it will have a good effect on the others.' G.M.'s spectacles sparkled with enjoyment. '*Wicked*, wasn't it?' he said. And then, pausing for effect – 'He confirmed me'; and walked out on the joke.

Friday – it must be 20 January

Last weekend Lionel Curtis signalized his return to health and College by a floater at lunch in buttery. A good deal of noisy banter was going on, mainly between him and me, when he said in his portentous way – *à propos* of a joke of mine about the Rhodes Scholar saying to Herbert Fisher's 'When I was in the Cabinet with Mr Lloyd George', 'Come, come Mr Fisher' – 'There's one thing Salter, you never boast about your having been in the Cabinet.' An awkward silence followed, which poor Salter himself had to end by saying he never had been.

Saturday, 11 February (Notts.)

I spent one of the most exciting days I have ever spent at Eastwood – D. H. Lawrence's birthplace. The morning with Jack[1] and David T.[2] sightseeing in Nottingham. At lunch-time I did not know where I was going in the afternoon. Jack and David were going to Wollaton, which I have seen. My idea was to see the University. They had no doubt where I was going, though I didn't know myself. I was drawn to Eastwood. The bus passed through Basford and Nuttall along the road D.H.L. knew so well. At Nuttall the Palladian Temple which was standing in good repair ten or fifteen years ago has been dynamited: only a shell of wall left, a ruin. But the Nuttall Temple petrol-filling station is there beside the gate pillars and the squalid drive.

By good luck the first man I met coming off the bus put me straight on the track of an old man, W. E. Hopkin, who had been a friend of D.H. from his boyhood. The working fellow himself told me something interesting. That D.H. resented Eastwood. He had been unhappy at school – no good at games, laughed at by the other boys, who thought him eff – eff – effo – what was the word? Effeminate? Exactly. (He didn't like to say 'sissy' to me evidently: the well-dressed stranger astray in the little mining town.)

It reminded me strongly – allowing for differences of colour, accent, geography – of a china-clay village at home, rather than a coal-mining area. For one thing, clean, blowy, healthy; then the same rawness and rudeness, the Philistine newness of houses and shops, the chapels in evidence; a working-class community. None of the graces of life: no taste, no culture. How he must have felt about it, just as I used to feel about Tregonissey and Carclaze.

They hadn't thought anything much of him, said the young man, until he became famous. But he seemed to resent Eastwood and his boyhood there. The last time he visited it he said he hoped never to see it again.

The usual story, I registered, but said nothing.

Old Mr Hopkin's sister lived at a nearby bungalow. She asked me in, and there were photographs of D.H.L. Her brother was away in Nottingham for the afternoon, but would return to his shoe-shop. At the shop his wife

1. Jack Simmons, Professor of History at Leicester.
2. David Treffry.

made out an itinerary for me to follow. All the afternoon I went over the ground. The little shop where he was born – not a miner's cottage: but a cottage over a tiny shop which Mrs Lawrence kept, with baby-clothes, ribbons and lace, to help out in early married days. In the squalid street – the house positively dirty now, a court beside it, with row of outdoor privies – I stood in the biting wind and occasional skiffs of rain, writing notes, while work people, mostly collier-folk, passed by. They looked as if they took me for someone to do with the election – the Conservative van blared to and fro in the main street with 'In 1945 Mr Aneurin Bevan said' and 'In 1945 the socialists made promises' – all the stock-in-trade that meant so much to me once, and surely was more important in 1931 and 1935?

From here I trudged back to Dovecot Lane, where was the Board School D.H. attended. I noticed it was the road that led to Hucknall and Byron's grave. On the way a curious experience: a man looked quizzingly at me out of a car: I thought it was Norman Lyne, those sloe-black eyes. Then back down Lynncroft, the last house the Lawrences moved to, where Mrs Lawrence died. Along Walker Street with its open side giving a wide view dominated by the big colliery tip, but still with trees – in the foreground there had been trees described by D.H. from the bay window which Mrs Lawrence had so eagerly aspired to (third along the row); and far away the trees behind which was the farm where Miriam lived. Down in the bottom the Breach – the rows of miners' cottages in pleasant valley surroundings – which was the Lawrences' first move.

All the way I wrote notes.

Back to the shop, Mr H. not yet back. So down the street to the church, which meant nothing in D.H.'s life – the more's the pity: it might have rubbed off some of the harshness, the pedalling iteration of the Nonconformist preacher – his regrettable introduction to culture.

Back to the shop I waited, chatting by the kitchen fireside where D.H. used to sit, in the same place, perhaps the same chair, innumerable times, for this was the house he came to – the one house outside his own home.

Mr Hopkin came in: eighty-seven, looking like a man of sixty-seven, bearded, bright as a bird, started talking straight away. He had known D.H. all his life: since he was two months old and, asking Mrs Lawrence how the latest arrival was, she drew back the shawl inside the pram and said: 'I am afraid I shall never rear him.'

She was a foolish woman – to think that she could alter her husband, bring him up in her ways. She had never seen him dirty before her marriage: met him one Saturday night at a dance in Nottingham. He was a really *beautiful* dancer, known for miles around. The first day he came home from the pit and insisted on eating his dinner without washing *appalled* her: she never got over it. Her folk were Leicestershire people, had never seen a coal mine.

When Bert was in his teens (I had made a mistake and said David. He was never David here, always Bert). You'd have thought he and his mother were more like a courting couple than mother and son. (Mrs Hopkin: she was a very possessive woman. It was she that prevented him from marrying Miriam (Jesse). Never wanted any courting around.) When she was dying I thought he would have gone off his head, clean off his head! He had written his first book *The White Peacock* and there is a story: there is a unique edition of that book consisting of only one copy. His mother was slowly dying of cancer and Bert sent message after message, telegrams to the publishers: the only thing she wanted to see before she died was Bert's book. It came, and half-an-hour before she died he rushed upstairs and put the book in her hand. It was a grief to him that he never knew whether she was conscious what she was holding.

The last walk Mr Hopkin had had with Bert – and therefore a sad one for him – he said to him, 'Why didn't you marry Miriam (Jesse)?' He burst out: 'Mind your own bloody business.' Then afterwards: 'I'm sorry. But she wasn't the one for me.' Then he said several words in German. I asked him to translate. The upshot was that she would have been just a 'bed-rabbit'. He needed something to fight. Miriam would have destroyed his genius.

(In other words, too much of a yes-woman. Like Noreen, I registered. No. D.H. was right.)

Miriam had married and had children. Mrs Hopkin: But she always loved Bert. The last time she had been over to see them (she died two years ago) they went up to Walker Street and looked into the distance to the trees behind which her father's farm was, where she had lived. There was a pause between them. The hard-looking, practical Mrs Hopkin's eyes glistened: 'She was very sad,' He: 'Yes. She always loved him.' The memory was too strong. He couldn't speak about it.

What D.H. wanted all his life long was a man-friend. Hopkin was the only friend he ever had that stayed his friend. Middleton Murry? The dirty dog. He isn't genuine. After that book of his came out, *Son of Woman*, I told him to his face what L. had said to me: 'Murry is my Judas Iscariot. And he will betray me. Not in my lifetime: he'd be afraid of what'd be coming to him. But after I am dead, you will see.' And Murry went as white as a sheet. L. never had the man-friend he was looking for all his life.

I said that that was partly, perhaps largely, his own fault.* You couldn't lacerate people's feelings and quarrel violently – and expect all to go on as

* Like A.L.R.? 1974.

it had been before. No friendship – no human relations could stand it. Curious that he never learned that, that he had no more self-control.

Hopkin said that he had a terrible temper. But it was like ginger pop, very effervescent, over in a minute. I said did he never try to tell him when he was younger? H: Oh dear No. I never interfere with people. I let them go their own way. I said that lads like D.H. as good as had no fathers and had no-one to tell them or help them. It might have been a good thing if he had been told when young.

It struck me while Hopkin was speaking that there was perhaps a parallel here too. It may be that if one has too much of a struggle in early days one needs unconsciously to perpetuate the struggle – to create enmities, antagonisms. Hopkin said that Lawrence had extreme antipathies. If he were sitting there where you are sitting and someone came in he took a dislike to – when the news went round that he was staying here, there'd be a lot of women school-teachers who'd come in in the hope of seeing him – he'd sit there and not say a single word. And yet – he was a wonderful conversationalist. (Oh, the usual story. How well one knows the symptoms. It is what I am engaged in doing to Cornwall.) D.H. said to me one day when I was putting out chairs for them to sit down, 'What are you putting out chairs for the bitches for? You know, Willie, you are making a great mistake. When you get to Heaven for your good works you'll be so busy putting out chairs for the bitches that you'll fall backward – into Hell.' Clearly the way D.H. went – following his own intuitions absolutely, with no attempt at control whatever, made him pay a heavy price – loneliness and friendlessness.

Of course there were his grand friends. D.H. liked it assumed that he had always known them and lived with them. H. once met Lady Ottoline – who complained characteristically of her brother's being unable to send her any flowers from Welbeck when asked, when he had thirteen bloody gardeners. She was always loyal to D. H. Hopkin had been to a grand party of D.H.'s friends – when D.H. himself was too ill to be brought from France: he wondered as he watched several famous names rolling about tight what their admirers would think if they could see them now.

Frieda was the right wife for D.H. They fought like tigers: but it never made any difference: they were very much in love with each other. Frieda was beautiful when young. On her honeymoon night with Weekley there was a pedestal in the room, which she stood on the top of stark naked, posing, and said 'Am I not a beautiful woman?' The professor said, 'Come down, you shameless woman.' Until Weekley died L.'s name could never be mentioned in the College at Nottingham, nor could the Library buy any of his books.

When the news of D.H.'s death came he could not believe it – there had been so many alarms before. The coat he was wearing when he died H. had now – they thought no-one else should have it. D.H. had always been fond of his daughter – she went about everywhere with him when he was here. She helped to edit the Letters – went out to New Mexico; she has one of his pictures – lives out there in Southern California.

Of the rest of the family, L.'s sister went on living at Ripley till two years ago, when she died: she had a wonderful collection of his books, and many of his pictures. The brothers had married and had children. But there was no talent – nothing left in the family – nothing to compare with Bert. It had all gone with him. Mr and Mrs L. were buried in Eastwood Cemetery, down below the church.

I told the old man he had been a most fortunate man. He said, simply, I have been. I said it was astonishing the way that a life like D.H.'s could light up the whole landscape, so that the place lived in him. It was obvious how these simple good people, through this man's kindness to the boy and the man, had been caught up in the intensity of the dead man's personality – so that it *made* life for them – as Shelley's life was all in all for E. J. Trelawny and nothing that happened after had any significance. There is the living power. This kind old shopkeeper was what John Poole had been to Coleridge at Nether Stowey and always after.

My last impression – so strong that the dream has gone on ever since – was of Eastwood: those raw streets and miners' terraces, the wind blowing along the ridges, the shops unchanged since he knew them, with their inscriptions 'Millinery, Drapery, Mantles'; the bookshop window with *Forever Amber*,[1] but no book by the man whose genius made the place glow in the imagination, every street and lane in it, the harsh corners and the Congregational Chapel in whose Sunday School he taught as a lad, the spire pricking up from the places where he lived, the little shop, the Breach, Walker Street, Lynncroft where his mother died. And the pathos of it all– all springing, like that first glance of Hardy's mother and father exchanged in the church at Stinsford, from that ill-assorted couple, the miner who was such a beautiful dancer and his wife who felt herself superior to the life she lived with him and yet gave birth to all this: both of them now together in the cemetery under the hill from Eastwood church.*

1. Bestseller of the late 1940s.

* And for me there was the charming experience in the little church, not forgotten. 1974.

14 February

What a character G. M. Young is! For the second day in succession he proposed a walk; and for the second time he donned his black fur-lined coat with astrakhan collar, white silk muffler, which with battered trilby and slightly askew rimless spectacles, make him look more than ever like a survivor of his own Victorian Age, the object of interested contemplation of the contemporary undergraduate. And not only the undergraduate either. As we walked across the grass a group of riveted spectators at the iron gate drew closer to observe the passing couple and moved along in flank to keep us in view as we went sideways to the Codrington entrance. 'They had their money's worth,' said G.M.Y., well satisfied, as if he had been a Prince Consort. (In the smoking-room after lunch he had been speculating on what would have happened if it had been Victoria who died and Albert who lived on. Quintin confessed that of all jobs in the world Prince Consort was what he'd most like to be. We had been very gay and cheerful.)

G.M. and I were out for a tour of unknown Oxford – spots that either he or I had never seen. First across to B.N.C. (Brasenose), still in disarray from the fire last night. (I knew nothing of it. Feiling, Falls, Ernest, Geoffrey Hudson, Raymond Carr were up from 5 a.m. observing it.) It was on an old staircase – G.M. thought Pater's. Firemen, fascinated undergraduates, water and reek of charred timber still about. We explored the chapel – a decent late seventeenth-century building, good oak pews with *trompe l'œil* panels. A Frodsham Hodson and other such monuments, but nothing to Pater. G.M.Y. quoted the inscription on Molière's bust in the French Academy, 'Ce n'est pas sa gloire qui manque, mais la nôtre.' I then got the key to the Hall – again late seventeenth century with wide-arched ceiling. Among the portraits good ones of Dean Nowell and Mrs Joyce Frankland[1] – one of which I must have in my book.

On through Christ Church, where we passed the Dean[2] in Tom gateway – whom G.M. recognized, since they have so recently been in session electing a new Chichele Professor – not me, I should say. (The encounter had its irony. I cannot think that Lowe would regard me with any favour. On the other hand G.M.'s friendliness should be a good omen.* So all candidates argue in such contingencies – to no purpose, or not much.) He was charmed with Pembroke, which he had never entered. And indeed it was charming: exploring the little court between the quad and the Master's house we

1. A sixteenth-century benefactress.
2. John Lowe, a distinguished Canadian academic.
* Of course it was not. He was personally responsible for forcing Jacob on the electors, making them sit a second time.

enjoyed the long crooked view right through two quadrangles to the hall. (Entering the inner quad I said I felt that this was the next college marked for combustion.) We enjoyed chapel and hall – the tables in the latter shining like glass.

This prompted G.M. to recall Anson's story of Henry, the butler's, mournful reflection on the Common Room boy who found no joy in his work. Anson on exploring the matter found that the boy was employed in rubbing the green baize over the mahogany tables of Common Room all day – this was the occupation he was expected to find 'joy' in.

We surreptitiously looked into the Common Room at the fine Reynolds of Dr Johnson – the famous portrait, so unflattering, so revealing; a handsome Lawrence, an Opie of a Vinicombe, a portrait of Sir Thomas Browne.

Thence next door along Brewer Street to Campion Hall. I cannot think this a very successful work of Lutyens – nor can I ever feel at ease in it: the atmosphere so very Counter-Reformation – portraits and reliefs of Ignatius Loyola, Christs in agony, sentimentalizing Virgins and *pietàs* and whatnot, the pervasive smell of incense, a claustrophobic hothouse atmosphere – all slightly sinister. It brings out the Protestant in me. We left it with relief.

So down Littlegate through mean streets till we came to King's Terrace – a pretty 'Fly – all is discovered'. We discovered some Franciscan walls with a tablet commemorating Roger Bacon who died there in 1292. In this quarter sloping down to the river were gardens and arbours in the eighteenth century, where the dons drank wine in the afternoons after dinner. We went round the south side of Paradise Square and into the second of Oxford's High Streets, along by the back of the gaol to Quaking Bridge and Fishers' Row. We looked with disfavour upon the new Nuffield College rising from its swamp, deploring this nondescript exercise in modern Gothic and the commonplace exercise in modern Georgian towering above it – St Peter's Hall.[1] Between them a piece of eighteenth-century elegance in Bath stone – headquarters of the old Canal Company. So along Bulwarks Lane into St Peter's Hall and into the church, which pleased G.M. as being Evangelical. Out into New Inn Hall Street and past the house in St Michael Street where he had had digs, to St Michael's church, our last call. An insensitive mule-faced undergraduate was pedalling Bach loudly, remorselessly, faultily: we were driven out after a brief tour, and I had to hurry back to meet a young poet who had sent me his poem and was coming to tea.

In the course of the walk G.M. gave me the wanting clue to Geoffrey Madan.[2] The handsomest man of his generation: people really would turn

1. Now St Peter's College.

2. Fainéant wit and scholar whose *Notebooks*, edited by John Sparrow and John Gere, were published by Oxford University Press.

round in the street to look at him. Married money and proceeded to live on it for the rest of his life, never doing a stroke of work. Her family at one time wanted her to leave him: he could always have whistled her back. She in love with him, he uninterested. An unsatisfactory life – a talented man who did nothing whatever with it. A difficult man, who had to be handled very carefully – like G.M.Y. himself.

One day when lunching with him Madan got out a bottle of Chartreuse – slowly they sipped it and finished it. Going out in the cold air for a walk G.M.Y. said, 'We must take care how we proceed.' Half-way across the Park they both felt the need to relieve nature. Looking around for somewhere they found a place – and discovered it was locked. 'Closed until May.' Trying the door, they were confronted by a park-keeper who told them the order.

'Who gave the order?' said Madan.

'The First Commissioner of Works,' said the man.

'This *is* the First Commissioner of Works,' said Madan pointing to G.M.Y.

They were ushered respectfully in.

14 April. Hôtel St Marie, Rue du Four, Paris

One thing has bothered me on this visit to France: the extent of people's devotion in the churches. On earlier visits, years ago, my attitude was rather different. First in 1926, when I had only quite recently ceased to believe in the Christian religion, I traipsed round in a melancholy lag-over frame of mind, wishing it might be true. Was sentimentally affected by the offices of the Church, touched by the sight of Renan's Seminaire de St Sulpice, reduced to tears by High Mass on Easter Sunday in Nôtre Dame, Stefans Dom, etc. Then in the more militant days of my Marxism, I regarded the evidences of people's beliefs as contemptible signs of their foolery, of *their* credulity and the Church's readiness to take advantage of it.

Now I think rather differently again. I am as shocked as ever at the signs of human infantilism. I have taken down in my notebooks some pretty examples of their childishness from the pencilled scribblings on the marble plaques of Reconnaissance à Marie, or Merci to St Joseph or to the odious Little Flower, Sœur Thérèse. *What* a cult! What a horrid little creature!

'St Joseph, faite (*sic* – they usually write faite for faites) que ma femme bien aimée et ma chère fille Sakie restent toujours près de moi et que nous soyons heureux, grâce à notre travail dès maintenant le 19/2/30 et conserve la santé à tous ceux que j'aime.'

There is something touching about that one – he sounds a nice fellow, thinking of those he loves rather than himself. Not so the man who calls upon St Joseph to see that he gets a good price for the house he has to sell and a good bargain in the property he is to buy. Or this – 'St Joseph, faite que mon travail me donne de bons résultats.' Or – 'St Joseph, faites que je réusisse dans mes études, que j'ai l'argent, que j'ai une bonne situation, que cez(?) aille bien pour mes dents, qu'il n'y ait pas de guerre et que tout aille bien avec celle que j'aime. RB.' Obviously a fool. No – an ordinary human.

But I am more puzzled now by these evidences of human foolery. Not so much by these simple children, but by other people I see in the churches, well dressed, apparently well educated, elderly, responsible people. It makes me feel very Protestant when I see them humbling themselves, crossing themselves, occasionally a fine upstanding man with hands joined in prayer before some image or before the Sacrament, oblivious of the world. What on earth is he doing? What are his mental processes? [Well, it's all dying now. 1974.]

Of course I know about the temptations of the flesh and spirit, the difficulty of knowing how to live one's life, unease of conscience, the tortures of *Angst* – for in one sense I am a religious type, never at ease with myself, striving to do or be better, always making some effort. All the same I do not understand what they think they are at, these people with their eyes closed, hands clasped, lost in reverie in dark chapels contemplating the Blessed Sacrament. I am more puzzled than angry.

It all comes back to the place of the Irrational in life. It is hopeless to expect of human beings the same adherence to rational standards that I expect of myself. All this beautiful myth about Jesus being the son of God, Mary the Mother of God, God Himself becoming incarnate in man, etc. etc. is quite untrue: a fabric of fable and parable and doctrine built up nearly two thousand years ago. On the other hand a great deal in the system of conduct, the guidance given in the difficulty of living one's life, is good. Is it that people can take it better if administered in this form? Or is there a deeper significance still: is it that the Irrational in the Christian Myth appeals to the eternally irrational in man? Is there some correlation between the nature of the story and the nature of man?

But that still says nothing as to the truth of the matter.

Can it be that in the nature of man the rational matters less? that the core of man is to be found in the irrational, the subconscious, the numinous, to which these watchings before the Sacrament, the prostrations, the unearthly silence maintained in vast churches at the moment of the consecration – the miracle – are all directed?

I cannot believe it. I remain stuck. My mind remains convinced that it is only on the basis of the rational that our experience can be correctly correlated, and that the rational enables us to guide and control the external world as no other principle can. The whole of modern science, the whole fabric of modern thought we owe to our adherence to the rational, the scientific, the susceptible to empirical tests. I favour the extension of these methods into the realm of the subconscious and irrational. Plenty of way to go there – and already some results appear – particularly in modern psychology.

But I am puzzled why these other people remain stuck there. There are the usual explanations – habit, training, indoctrination; simplicity, credulity, fear; the human need to confess, to be forgiven, of consolation and reassurance. But what the intellectually adult think they are doing still puzzles me. I wish someone would explain it to me as they see it. But I fear it is outside the possibility of explanation.

Cork, 19 October 1952

I woke up to see the lighthouse at the entrance to Cork harbour white through the port-hole; but, shaving, getting up, missed Queenstown. Later, coming up the river, I observed the pleasant Georgian houses, the green lawns; on the left bank one or two small estates, mounded trees all russet and pinks and gold – places that would just suit me.

I arrived on the quay to find no promised Mrs Treston of the Literary Society to meet me: a situation that always makes me impatient. A dark little man, all grey tweed and hearing apparatus, recognized me and came to the rescue: Denis Gwynn, of the great clan married to everybody – 'Sooner or later, everybody marries a Gwynn.' He arranged to show me something of the city. Then Mrs Treston arrived like a gale of wind, Paul Henry weather, all green and lavender and purple; explained to me breathlessly the situation in the society – a very old Protestant society now mainly Catholic. Denis Gwynn, ultramontane, turning Catholic had made a very unpleasant situation in the family. She then swept me off to the Metropole, which turned out a squalid commercial travellers' rest, was being rebuilt inside, full of draught, noise and hammering. She was a friend of the manager's; effusive introductions followed.

I expected a good Irish breakfast to freshen me up after my long journey and gave my order: cornflakes, bacon and *eggs*! The cornflakes and tea came; then a long pause, during which nobody came. Waitress after waitress passed, took no notice of my empty plate; the tea went cold, I very hot with anger and impatience. Nothing happened; everybody too busy chatting for me to attract any attention. At last I thought of the trick with which I once shamed the waitress in a hotel at Harrogate and made her scurry: I put my empty plate on the floor to attract attention. Here they thought it a joke.

They merely collected in a group to laugh. Then I blew up: the bacon and *two* eggs arrived when I was on the point of getting up and going.

An hour remained in which to write my lecture before the Professor arrived to show me the College, one of the three Queen's Colleges. It turned out a pleasant Victorian building, grey Cork limestone, three sides of a quadrangle. The interior of the President's former house still more Betjeman: the remains of Victorian drawing-room and dining-room with hideous furniture and pictures, going down at heel; a cheap lodging-house effect in rooms which could be fine. There were the portraits of unheard-of celebrities, the extinct professors of so many dead controversies, nationalist, linguistic and no doubt religious.

I saw everything, admired everything – as on so many occasions now; including the modern replica of an ancient Irish chapel with unbearable glass. I was on my best behaviour.

In the afternoon train to Mallow there was a young artist, with a fanatic Irish-American face, dead white with grey short-sighted eyes, thinnish lips, long hands and a mass of reddish-yellow hair: just returning from two or three years in Paris, to settle in Merrion Square and paint portraits: a son of an Irish sculptor: called Roderick O'Connor. He sounded as if he might make good.* Sean O'Sullivan, he told me, had practically come to an end through drink. He was already drinking far too much twenty years ago when he painted the portrait of me looking like an Irish ecclesiastic, in my grey-brown Franciscan dressing-gown. (I must retrieve that portrait from where it hangs in the Y.M.C.A. at St Austell!)

We had an interesting talk: he thought the Irish failing for drink part of their *fear* to face the world, their shrinking into themselves, their irresponsibility to their age-long being governed by the English so that they could blame everything on them, while themselves were free to be bad children.

The journey in the train was pleasant, the country green and gold, not many trees, a few plantations, a ruined abbey (perhaps Mourne abbey) beneath the lofty ruins of a castle on a hill.

At Mallow there was Elizabeth's[1] secretary to meet me and my nervousness began. While she shopped in the town I wandered along the street – a pre-1914 world – and down the lane between chestnuts dropping their leaves thick underfoot and then beeches to the Protestant church; boys playing football in the field below, the hills beyond. It was an autumnal moment full of pleasant melancholy, my mind turned back to the world of Somerville and Ross, Victorian Ireland, the Ascendancy gentry coming in

* Did he, I wonder?

1. Elizabeth Bowen.

to the little spa, the redcoats marching down this leafy lane to church, eyeing the girls. The smell of the piggeries over the wall was unchanged.

I was on my way to stay with one of the remnants of the Ascendancy gentry. A pretty road, with the trees all kinds of colour, lemon, rose and flesh-pink; then the long-embracing wall of the estate and Spenser's Ballyhoura Mountains behind. We drove up to a tall and largish grey limestone country house, with Elizabeth at the door to greet me, breathless in a burst of wind.

I was plunged at once into tea with four women, in a big hall with nice old furniture; the dauntingly clever Elizabeth presiding very handsome in black – Alan died in July; Lady Cynthia Asquith on my left, whom I had apparently met at the Buchans long ago – fancy her remembering! I hadn't the remotest recollection. I began by carefully putting my cup and saucer on what turned out to be a flat glass ashtray: Elizabeth removed it for me: I hadn't wanted to make a hot spot on the table. I was in a hot spot, between these two clever women machine-gunning across me. Miss Frost, the secretary, was unaware that I was nervous, thought I 'had kept my end up very well': there's the difference between her and the other two.

It seemed that Lady Cynthia fell for me: changed her mind about walking in the garden with the others to stay and talk to me alone in a window-embrasure. My heel scraped on the wooden floor: her whole body shrank at the sound: the too great nervous sensibility of the over-bred.

At last alone, I could take in the house: I recognized it all from Elizabeth's book I had read fifteen years before. Here was the library: the usual big Georgian room, of no beauty, but honest and capacious, with built-in book-shelves and several tall windows; a log fire burning brightly, but not enough to heat the room; the atmosphere just like a Cornish country house, it reminded me of Penmount – homely, *familial* or rather ancestral, slightly dank, melancholy, with a charm in the atmosphere. Outside was the park; the rooks were beginning to come home; day was ending over the Irish landscape.

Shown up to my room I recognized everything, from the book of fifteen years ago. Across the hall again with its poor portraits, the Georgian furniture, the tarnished mirror above the steel grate, up the wide staircase with the worn carpet to the lobby with its bookcases, whence the first-floor bedrooms open out; on up a second staircase to the gallery above running the whole length of the house, built to serve as a ballroom. Here was my bedroom, opposite Lady Cynthia's in the other high corner of the house. I refused to have the fire lighted, settled down to finish my lecture in remembered Penmount cold, faded white paint, a high coved ceiling flaking a little, a view out over the park and from the dressing-table down the slopes to gardens. I looked at the books – one of them, Maria Edgworth's *Castle Rackrent*, an Everyman edition inscribed 'Alan Cameron, Hertford College, Oxford: June 1914'. There was the story of his life, rounded and completed in this house only a few months before, all written down for me in this undergraduate's inscription just before the war broke out in which he served as a soldier.

At dinner and indeed through my stay Elizabeth seemed completely herself – though Lady Cynthia told me after that she was very unhappy now. But Elizabeth is in such control of herself that one could never tell. She has the finest breeding of any woman I know. Women, even of the best breeding, don't go in much for effacing themselves for another woman, even if she happens to be a guest. The consideration she instinctively shows to others, the standard she sets so that no-one could conceivably take liberties with her (that must cut her off,* disadvantageously for her as a writer), the absence of the usual personal edge women so boringly give to everything – all that belongs to the masculine element in her intellect, on the other side, nothing could be more feminine than her extreme sensibility, her X-ray perceptiveness, the sexiness of her imagination. She is a wonderful woman, a personality like no-one else's, with that extraordinary voice, darting along – influenced by David's a bit, in the way he has of influencing everybody near him (Isaiah's way of speaking, mine, John Buxton's gestures – an inappropriate femininity for so masculine a person) – her brain going too fast for her tongue so that she is frequently held up by an attractive stammer; then the voice going down into a male register, rich and golden-brown. In colouring like her hair, which is red-gold with a Viking wave of the sea, washed up here inland in an Irish park; grey-blue eyes and a strange mouth – large and straight lines, wide without being voluptuous, and a look as if it might be cruel – but is it not rather self-torture? (She speaks in *The Heat of the Day* I have been reading on my visit of the *wound* that underlies a stammer; towards the end of that book I notice such an agonized awareness, so fine that it reaches the point of dissociation, that I could not but detect the symptoms of madness.)

Her control is such that she gives hardly any indication in conversation of this daunting subtlety and sheer cleverness: she never lets on, as it seems, that she is taking in absolutely everything. Or does she invent all that she knows in the solitude of her imagination, slowly ripening? I think not. There she sat at dinner, at the head of the oval table in the hall, the tarnished mirror behind her, the portraits on either side, the silver candlesticks lighted, the long twisted-necked decanters of wine before her, while I sat in Alan's

* I was wrong about this – plenty of sex in her life apparently. Any with David C.? I doubt it.

place opposite – or was she sitting in his place now, and I in hers? After dinner, in the library, she sat on her legs gathered under her in her chair, looking not at me, but at Lady Cynthia, concentrating all the attention she could on her. (What other woman would do that? Unless, indeed, the wound is there? I think not, or hardly at all.) Certainly Lady Cynthia wanted attention. I talked about Lawrence and she was evidently happy to talk about him. I tried to shift the talk away from him, after it had begun to flag, she snatched it back to Lawrence, quite greedily, from Elizabeth. Elizabeth at once handed over once more to Lawrence.

In bed that night under the high coved ceiling, with the Victorian papered screen in the corner, the wind rushing at the windows, I had a horrible dream.

Often nowadays, with the trouble of my mother always on my mind, I have some ghastly dream about her. But this was of a son murdering his father. I was inside a hen-coop, and through the wire-netting I saw a young man with a chopper hewing down his father as if he were a tree. The father had his back turned and seemed half-kneeling. He was incredibly strong and the chopper stuck in his shoulders as if they were wood. The son got it out and gave another huge stroke, enough to fell an ox. Still the father remained upright. But when the son got the chopper out this time, the blood gushed out. I had come out from the coop and wondered, not very clearly, whether to intervene. With the gushing out of the blood, I woke.*

Before dinner, as the light was failing, I had been for a walk in the park. Through the trees and the cows out to the road and down along it to get a glimpse of the Ballyhouras back beyond the house, two crests with a pass between. It was getting dark as I made my way back, enormous crowds of rooks settling on the trees. I wondered a little what it would be like to take Alan's place and have to manage the estate. I didn't fancy it much. It was all too alien – in spite of the fact that the house, were it not too tall – might pass for a Cornish house. There was a soft low light in the Library windows, and another, firelight, in Lady Cynthia's high up in the corner. All that long front of the house unoccupied and, I think, unfurnished: it would hold me and my furniture very well: on the ground floor a big drawing-room, the old dining-room which would make a study; above, bedrooms, a little suite for secretary's workroom. Elizabeth on one side of the house; I on the other. A fantasy to occupy vacant moments of the mind. But, of course, it wouldn't work.

Though this time Elizabeth was a little more interested – or less unattracted – than ever before.

* Interpretation pretty clear. Oedipus. 1974.

I breakfasted in the hall in state alone, the ladies in their bedrooms. Elizabeth has an old-fashioned view about the authority of the male and made a point about my liking to come down: I sat at the head of her table.

I made off disconsolately in the rain to Cork, the apprehension as to my lecture before such a difficult audience dankly oppressing with the weather. I genuinely did not want Elizabeth and Lady Cynthia to come. Miss Bowen of Bowen's Court settled that: she *was* coming.

I arrived back, obedient to my Brünnhilde, at the Metropole – though I had written from Oxford asking for a room at the Imperial, the most comfortable hotel. Elizabeth was sure that Brünnhilde was bat-witted: the Metropole was, among other things, unlicensed. I struggled up the steep stairs – by this the rebuilding of the Ladies' Toilet had halved the passage, so that one could only get up sideways. Obedient to my sponsor, I signed the book and got my room. When the door opened I was confronted by an extraordinary spectacle of ladies' hats – fifteen or twenty of them on both beds. I said, this can't be my room. The porter said it didn't look like it. I couldn't have got into bed, if I wanted to, for the hats. It looked as if a traveller in hats had deposited all his stock there. But no: it was a wedding and the room was being used as a cloakroom. We changed into another – at the back of the house, so bleak with a view of galvanized roofs that, utterly dispirited, I sank down under the eiderdown and into a doze.

When I woke, I found a resolution steeled in my breast. I was damned if I would submit any more to Mrs Treston's dictation. Elizabeth was right: she was bat-witted or worse. Thud, thud, thus – listen to the hammering! I wouldn't stay a moment longer. I would go to the Imperial, where I had stayed in complete comfort before: why had I not been allowed to do what I wished? With my shoes in my hand I stole past the Reception office, made my way past the porter and got to the Imperial; where from the security of a decent room, I telephoned the Metropole to cancel my room as I was stopping with friends. When they said they would see about it, I hastily put down the receiver.

I was overjoyed. I had given La Trestonne the slip. Nobody knew where I was. I was in hiding; I was playing a game of hide-and-seek. That afternoon I went to bed and, sleeping soundly, laid up a stock of energy for the trial of the evening.

Happy as a boy I went down to tea by myself with a book – Elizabeth's. I was to meet them all three and give them dinner at 6.30. Plenty of time to prepare my lecture before then. I remained in the lounge too long: for about 5 p.m. I saw a figure enter and settle down in the further corner. Could it be – was it – Lady Cynthia? It was. Had she seen me? I was supposed to be at the Metropole. I sank lower and lower into my chair, hid behind my book – Caught! I should have to go and talk to her. No time to prepare my lecture.

She had certainly seen me. Next the secretary arrived; then Elizabeth: I had to go out and direct her where to park.

Dinner was a great success – made by the story of my adventure with the hats. I hadn't even seen the funny side of it, I was so bothered. This made it all the funnier: Elizabeth roared and said 'You quite snubbed me when I warned you about Mrs Treston.' Lady Cynthia thought that I had invented the hats and that I was a hat-fetichist. I said I couldn't have gone to bed with them in the same room.

When we arrived at the hall, we were greeted by La Trestonne, with *empressement*, when introduced to Lady Cynthia and Miss Bowen. A regular reception was held by Lady Cynthia in the private room: she did it beautifully, was gracious to everybody, everybody delighted to be presented. The old boy who was my Chairman – a R. C. Canon – asked me if this was Lady Asquith – Margot? I said she was dead. The tramp of people coming upstairs punctuated the seconds. I slunk away to a final look over my notes.

I came out on to the platform, a pre-1914 world before me, provincial, dowdy, interested, friendly. I did my best: within two minutes I had them in my hands. I took no risks and didn't put a foot wrong. I took the opportunity of paying a tribute to Elizabeth sitting there like a schoolgirl before me. It was a success and Elizabeth was very pleased. The old Chairman went one better still – with no very clear idea of who any of us was – paid a resounding tribute to the professor from Cambridge, Lady Asquith and Miss Marjorie Bowen. Elizabeth was not much amused.

Next day, Gwynn called for me, first at the wrong hotel, and showed me round the attractive water fronts of the city – mostly from 1830 on. One Regency Gothic church – Holy Trinity – with a tall open portal inspired by an Italian or Spanish original and sugar-icing spire. Another, the first Catholic church permitted – extraordinarily like a Methodist meeting-house, with wooden galleries and large flat ceiling. Then the Protestant Guinness-built cathedral, a Betjeman masterpiece with admirable Victorian glass. This whole area of the Cathedral very C. of I. with decayed canons' houses and a large bishop's palace suitable to the revenues of Georgian days.

To lunch at the Club with Horgan, the hospitable Chairman of the Harbour Commissioners, a Round Table man, important in the life of the city. Brought up in the Parnell tradition, a follower of Redmond, out at square with the new regime. Had dined at All Souls, impressed by the presence of Lang, Simon, Dawson, Amery, etc. Also at Blickling: then came the inevitable sense of inferiority to the surface – 'to think of a little country attorney like me among such people'. The Professor who was with us, as a

Gwynn, had no such feeling, commented afterwards on Horgan's innocent pride in his Round Table contacts.

Gwynn had taken me hospitably to his house that morning: a pretty 1830-ish house entered down steps into a pillared hall, with various things of interest: an appealing portrait of Burke by a young Cork artist he had befriended, Barry, Victorian paintings of his family, a Lavery landscape. And an old lady, Mrs Rickard, in bed because paralysed down one side, writing with her left hand. An elderly lady of distinction of manner, with boxes of picture postcards beside her; for, since her illness, Lord Wicklow sends her a p.c. every day. How very Irish it all was! these terraces rather like Falmouth, Regency stucco looking down the steep sides, silted with golden leaves, across the river to the Georgian houses being gradually given up, even here in Ireland.

After tea, I left the hotel for the ship, the wind fresh, autumn sun bright and clear. Almost the last person I saw had a curious affliction: enlarged tongue stuck full out of his mouth, as he walked along the pavement. How did he manage when he ate? Or perhaps, being Irish, he preferred to keep it out like that?

I boarded the *Inisfallen*, stayed on deck to watch the steeple of Shandon church – the bells of Shandon, indeed – fade in the evening grey, Regency terraces, Georgian houses, the green lawns by the river, slide away until we were past Queenstown with its Pugin cathedral, past Drake's Pool, past the little lighthouse so like St Anthony's, out into the dark, the open sea.

Yorks., 23 October [?1953]

My previous journeys were nothing like so interesting. The first of the season was to Bradford, on which carrying forward my Scott campaign (I had been reading *Redgauntlet* – the finest of any of Scott's I have read) I read *The Bride of Lammermoor*, with almost equal admiration. I arrived in time for dinner in a not bad hotel on a rainy evening, first of autumn, 24 September and sauntered in the fresh air about the square outside after. Next morning I went to see the parish church again, now cluttered up as a cathedral, but with sensible moderate plans for an extension to the east end by Maufe, self-effacing and right. Lunch in Betty's Café crowded to the door – I am a popular number with the lasses of Bradford and quite remunerative they are. I meet again the old Cornish girl who took the chair for me last time, a pince-nez'd headmistress, a dry vintage, but makes an excellent speech. Coffee and sandwiches and cakes, and I hold forth to the enraptured audience, receive my cheque and go. – To explore the Victorian churches of the town: uphill to St John the Evangelist. Here is my note: 'Not a soul to disturb my post-lecture meditations. Hideous Victorian interior, patterned brick, little columns like Victorian table-legs, pitchpine pews with brass umbrella-stands, the encaustic tile – all that could warm dear John Betj's heart. What would warm mine better would be such an adventure as befell in Eastwood church.'

What might have been an adventure but wasn't befell in the train on the way back late. At some place there got in a very attractive elongated young Australian, who was over here to buy bulls for his herd on a ranch outside Sydney. He was at a loose end and was going to stop the night at Nottingham. He was very anxious for me to break my journey and stop too. Should I? If I went on there'd be supper waiting for me on my arrival, but that would be 1 a.m. dog-tired. I got out on the platform. He was very appealing, tall, glamorous, forlorn. At the last moment I dashed back, got my grip and went with him. We got a room, had a damned good meal – and slept the chaste sleep of the just. It was very comic in a way: the immensely tall figure in flannelette pyjamas tucked into bedroom-booties, standing up towering over the washbasin washing his nylon shirt. We slept peacefully in a three-bedded room, not without some qualms – comic and fearful – on my part. In the morning we breakfasted and said goodbye; he wanted me to accompany him on his way to Loughborough – I stayed, correcting a typescript, till the fast direct train to Oxford.

Encore une expérience – not really very amusing; I laughed at myself.

On Saturday 27th I took train to Bournemouth West, where Arthur (Bryant) and Anne and Jimmy, the Cornish dog, came to meet me. On a golden autumn day we motored through blue Dorset landscape, past Creech Manor – classic front of cream stone looking up against the last sweep of hill before Kimmeridge bay – up and up and then a long swoop down upon Smedmore, demure, bow-fronted, blue-painted, very virginal and lovely, waiting at the end of the road beyond which there is no further.

It is a dream of a place Arthur has got; yet, having got it and furnished it, he isn't satisfied and wants somewhere else. I told him Chatsworth would soon be available. After tea in that congenial dark-panelled William and Mary parlour, we walked through the walled garden and the domain up the steep down-side, very Hardy and Nelson going down channel to Trafalgar – there was Portland in the mist on the western horizon. We talked, all Arthur's plans, the book he was bogged down in: it was clear that my work for the weekend was cut out. I began that evening, and slaved away all Sunday: nothing better to do, it rained most of the day.

In the morning we went out at a horrible moment – because Jimmy wanted a walk – ploughed uphill to the coast, got caught in a drenching shower and I returned angry – and wet. It makes me mad to be caught in heavy rain. I had to change into Arthur's clothes. I found our belly-girth was precisely the same. He lit the fire in the library – and what a fine room he has made of it: all rose and wine colour, Regency sofa-tables and Georgian mahogany and an Aubusson carpet. What luck he has had to pick up these things: what luck, and what taste!

There, in that attractive room, I quite happily wrestled with Arthur's much-corrected typescript all day. Anne took the day off in bed, saying how restful it was to have me for a guest, she wouldn't have to talk to a woman. In the late afternoon it cleared and we had another walk. I met one time or another the two nice fellows Arthur has, one as herdman, the other as bailiff. A blown-down top of a tree revealed a cache of honey with the exposed bees struggling blackly about it.

Next day, an excursion to Wincombe, the house and estate near Shaftesbury which Arthur has *bought*! All the way there in the car we wrangled about politics. Arthur said if there was one man who was responsible more than any other for the catastrophe of 1939, it was – Winston Churchill! And then trotted out the old stuff about the Ten-Year Rule.[1] I wasn't going to have that. And said that technical arrangements of that sort, however important, were secondary to policy, which was overriding; that if Baldwin and Chamberlain had got the policy right, the Ten Year Rule could be changed the moment it ceased to apply. When it was adopted in 1928 no enemy was on the horizon. Arthur was extremely obstinate, as emotional as I was, and intellectually confused. I was very vexed – and even shocked to hear such a line about Winston from Arthur who had been so profoundly wrong about the Germans in the thirties – *Unfinished Victory* and all that. I even went the length of reproaching him with that book, which had had to be withdrawn. He said it never had been. He was moved to admit that I had been right and he wrong about the danger from Germany in the thirties; then went on to attack the Labour Party, as if – poor fools that they were – they had been responsible during 1931–1939!

The row raged right across the county, and almost to Wincombe. Anne thought it would be the end of our friendship. I said No – if we had been two women, Yes; but we made a complete disjunction between intellectual disagreement and our private feeling. My feelings for Arthur remained unchanged, in spite of the heat generated. Anne told me that there wasn't anybody else to stand up to him; people all agreed or knuckled under; I was the only one to argue with him. (Actually, I think him on the purely intellectual plane, second-rate – in spite of his gifts, which are different.

1. 'No major war within the next ten years', a maxim governing Defence Policy Expenditure adopted during Churchill's time as Chancellor of the Exchequer, 1924–9.

That was what nettled me so much: the inability to see that logically policy must come first, and the technical steps to implement it second; that policy cannot be left to depend on the subordinate technical considerations. Precisely what Baldwin and Chamberlain did – of whom he was in those years very much a spokesman, defender, sycophant.) I couldn't help wondering whether there wasn't a slight emotional element of chagrin at not being 'in' with Winston, as he was with Baldwin and Chamberlain, in it all.* But then – I am 'in' with nobody! Nor do I care ultimately, compared with the importance of the issues.

So we arrived at Wincombe – an enchanting small estate around its combe – might almost be the country of *le grand Meaulnes*. I put on long stockings up to my thighs and waders to wade through the grass down in the valley where Arthur's precious Jerseys were cropping – one creature with mushroom muzzle, curious and friendly, followed me. There was a fine belt of yellowing beech-trees above us on the ridge, and at the end overlooking it all a pleasant, not large, Regency house with engaging verandahs south and west. It might have been a Cornish house in a Cornish situation, high up and sunny and cheerful.

Arthur told me the whole story. His aunt had lived there all her life and he had known it from childhood. (Here were the shrubberies he was always trying to persuade his girl-cousins to go into alone with him.) The owner, who had always refused to sell the property, suddenly gave her notice two years ago, thinking to come and live there himself. Greatly grieving, she left the place – Arthur had gone over to stay for the last time, expecting never to see it again. Meanwhile the aunt died. This year, a bolt from the blue, the owner wrote to Arthur asking if he'd buy it. Arthur took advantage of the situation – the fact that he did not intend to take on anything else on top of Smedmore – to beat him down to an absurdly low figure – the woods alone were practically worth it. At that figure, £10,000 less than he had asked originally, Arthur raised a mortgage on extremely favourable terms – and it was done.

Arthur had installed his mother there as caretaker, a spry old lady in a hat *à la* Mrs Clive of Brympton D'Evercy, widow of the Comptroller of George V's Household, and full of stories of the Royal Family. Arthur wanted some tips for an article he has to do on Queen Mary – no doubt well remunerated: they were forthcoming. The old lady dotes on her son: 'He is a genius,' she told me when he was out of the room. Over pleasant picnic lunch in the not yet furnished room she reminisced about Sandringham and Edward VII: – 'everybody loved him' (news to me) and her memory

* He soon jumped on the bandwagon.

of the young Duke of Windsor walking behind his governess, taking the opportunity when her back was turned to kick up every puddle of water he passed. The old lady thought that a symptom. He has certainly kicked up a good many puddles of dirty water since. Then, a charming memory of taking Arthur to Harrow and saying goodbye to him. A. 'Well, aren't you going to kiss me, mummy?' Lady B. 'I should dearly like to, but I didn't know if *you* would like me to in front of the other boys.' A. undaunted, 'Well, other boys have mummies too, I suppose?' So she kissed him goodbye.

This wrung my heart a little, as I sat there in the bright sunny room, all autumn ripening in the combe below the house – as it might be Cornwall. Nothing of that in my life, with the unloving bitch I had for mother. I never remember a single gesture of softness towards any of us, when we were children: always the hard, unyielding, self-absorbed egoism of a fine figure of a woman who only wanted men. And the inexpressible nuisance she has always been – to herself and everybody near her – has deeply damaged me as a human being and goes on and on deranging my mind, robbing me of all inner peace and security, tormenting my mind with the wish to be rid of her at last – but one will never, never be rid of the incubus, always a public humiliation so long as I can remember, a private torture. –

After lunch I helped Anne to wash up, and we had a hilarious drive through charming country to Salisbury to put me on the train. We were late, so I rushed – to find the nationalized train thirty-five minutes late, which started an anxiety at the other end, Chichester where I was due at 6.30 for a lecture.

A pleasant unfamiliar journey through Southern Railway country, at the end good old J. A. Williamson[1] waiting for me. I hadn't many minutes before my lecture was due at the Council Chamber. As I waited, I could hear the tramp-tramp of an unexpected crowd; seating exhausted, people standing on the staircase.* When I got into the room I took in with a glance the Georgian scene – portraits of old celebrities on the walls, city Members and Recorders, a bishop or two – one bearded and sardonic, looking very bilious (as well he might, the date 1641), turned out to be Bishop King;[2] at the end of the room was George I or George II. Everybody in Chichester seemed to be there – the Dean and a good sprinkling of clergy, cathedral or otherwise, some retired naval officers, headmasters and such. In the heat and crowd one young man fainted and was carried out; one silly old woman started to disturb the atmosphere with a cough: I gave her a look and she went out.

1. Naval historian, author of several excellent textbooks.

* I certainly was a draw in those days. Still am! 1978.

2. Henry King, poet.

Back to stop with Williamson. His wife, now an invalid, had gone to bed; but as a seaman, he was as handy as any woman at supper and looking after one. We had a good historical chat, and I told him what I felt about Treharne's behaviour over the attack on my *Use of History* in the organ of the Historical Association.* While living at Looe, Williamson, a confirmed bachelor, married his housekeeper. He wrote to me, 'We can't think why we didn't think of it before.' (I bet she did.) She has had nothing but illness since. First, an operation for duodenal perforation. This year, a stroke, so that she is paralysed down her right side. Getting up I saw a horrifying spectacle of a grey-haired woman, hair down, foot trailing, crossing the landing. She got down to see me off: talked with the pathetic futility of such cases of her fibrositis. So that was J.A.W.'s married life! He now has an invalid to look after and has to have a help to do the housework. I was shocked and, saddened, made her a present of the bunch of grapes from Wincombe I had been given. I left in a miserable downpour for the station and back to Oxford.

[Staying with Jack Simmons at Leicester, Autumn 1953]

From Uppingham before lunch we saw Stoke Dry of the Digbys – which should be called Stoke Wet as it now looks down on a reservoir. The Digby house has vanished from the east end of the church, owing to the activities of that young fool in the Gunpowder Plot. Up by the altar were his parents or grandparents – Kenelm Digby and his wife, Anne – who died but fifteen years before, in 1590. A family chapel near by had an earlier mutilated tomb, and other fragments, one with a lady outlined in the flat.

Thence to Lyddington, fine church with the remains of the fifteenth-century manor of the bishops of Lincoln – a range of good buildings with a long hall on the upper floor, chambers at either end, almshouse hutches for old women below and several garden closes. The whole now empty, growing desolate, the beautiful quarries in the windows going, in spite of the wire-netting. It won't be long, it won't be long – like everything, everywhere. If only one were a millionaire and could spend £10,000 on it! Think of the Texan fortunes that could easily do it.

Lunch in the Falcote, with a crowd of parents and their boys out for the meal from School. Last Sunday Marlborough with N., this Sunday Uppingham; the first golden autumn, today December blackness everywhere.

After lunch to Brooke church. It poured. The church small, but very

* I have forgotten about this, but just like what I've had to put up with all along.

interesting to me as an Elizabethan rarity – almost entirely rebuilt about 1579, like Standish. Evident that the tradition of medieval church building had been lost: this little church looked like a house, classical arches and arcade inside, a gable-end outside.

Thence to the high-water mark of Exton: a splendidly restored, largely rebuilt, church inside the park. Within a fine medieval table tomb, two admirable big Elizabethan tombs, both of alabaster and coloured marbles, from the Johnson workshop; a magnificent Grinling Gibbons affair, with marble reliefs and figures; a medieval alabaster tomb; and a Nicholas Stone masterpiece, a young lady in her shroud, a tear falling from her eyelid (she died in childbirth), on a table tomb of black and white marble. What a master he was!

Back to Oakham to tea, where I made up to a reluctant black and white cat in the shelter over the town pump. He was a fine cat, who refused to respond at first; but couldn't hold out against blandishments, and ended up with cold muddy paws in my arms purring and loving me.

It was an enjoyable day, in spite of the rain. Some of the lights occasionally beautiful, the atmosphere of Exton nostalgic. The ruined house a mound of ivy, where were so many festivities, a dripping wetness from the woods, the trees now stripped so that the boles gleamed in the gathering Decemberish darkness.

21 November

A Saturday, in the train standing in the station at Cambridge on my way back to Oxford from speaking to the undergraduate historical society last night, a packed meeting in the New Combination Room at St John's. Saltmarsh of King's put me up in that congenial Cambridge college: himself a very Cambridge type. One observes a contrast between Cambridge and Oxford dons. The ideal of the latter is to be men of the world; they don't *go in* for being donnish oddities, though some acquire them and look the part. At Cambridge the influence of the scholar-ideal, rather a recluse, unworldly, remains. Oxford is more anxious to shine in the world, to be of the world. Oxford dons prefer not to be taken for dons. Cambridge dons prefer to be dons.

Saltmarsh, I discovered, was a perfect specimen. On arriving in Cambridge I had slight apprehension, not being clear who he was, or what he had written. I wished I had looked him up in *Who's Who*, but had been far too busy, arriving back from Manchester to find a mass of literary business to deal with, about my new book, *An Elizabethan Garland*, proofs of the translation of Romier,[1] etc.

1. A bad, but bestselling, history of France.

A monastic figure came to meet me, hair stiff like a brush and unparted, sticking up like a monk or a convict; gentle voice, not well shaven, monkish-homo gestures, putting the hands together as if in prayer, intelligent eyes behind close spectacles, no figure of a man, baggy, almost Chaplin-trousers. I thought conversation was going to be sticky – it certainly was formal. Cold and damp evening, buildings looming up in the November dark, from the cliff of King's chapel came the sound of evensong – no light, only candles within. In the cold the monastic figure appeared without coat or hat, and led me across the soggy wet grass of the court. His rooms fine and large, Wilkins' rooms, sparsely furnished with extraordinary furniture: an enormous lamp stand six feet high, of Burmese bronze, daunted me. A few indecipherable chairs turned out to be Dutch, a horror of a Dutch dresser, and some bookcases with books that looked like the dead collection of a decayed schoolmaster. (Indeed, the Cambridge don is really a sort of schoolmaster.)

Led into the Combination Room, I met Shepherd[1] again after many years – inimitable, except that he imitates himself, is his own caricature. (All very self-aware, of course: no flies on Provost Shepherd: clever old thing, takes in everything.) There was the celebrated appearance – the brushed white hair, unchanged since his thirties, the stiff old-fashioned collar. He bowed twice, rather deeply, and then went out. He came in facetiously to announce dinner to his young men. It had just been announced to him outside; but in fact, he looked the part – the old-style family butler. Quite spry, with characteristic tottering walk he marched in, I following, up through the waiting ranks of undergraduates, the Provost beaming benevolently, while I felt I was taking part in a farce.

I said that as a Cornishman I felt proud of his second name – Tresidder. This launched us well on conversation that took us through most of dinner. 'Oh yes, you're a Cornishman. I've read several of your books, with great pleasure,' etc. (I don't suppose that he had read any.) There followed a story about a man who knew nothing about him but had recognized him as Cornish. 'Yes, there is a something; I feel myself to have that difference.' He certainly had: he had a strong streak of the Cornish – humbug, or perhaps just blarney. That's where he gets the art of putting it over. I said that it was an advantage; but to be 100 per cent Cornish was just *too much*. Later on, as he warmed up, I saw the full Shepherd laying himself out – to captivate, to charm, impress. It was on the subject of the portraits in hall. There was a rather good portrait of Francis Basset, Lord de Dunstanville. 'Ah,' said the Provost, 'the portraits in hall – d'you know, they move, *they bump each*

1. *sic. recte* Sheppard.

other in the night! We had a portrait of Charles Simeon at the bottom of the hall; and I said to Milner-White – now Dean of York – *you'll see*. And he did. Simeon bumped his way up the hall to the dais, until he came next to *that* portrait.' The Provost turned himself right round in his chair, eyes gleaming with mischief and glee – I recognized the slightly demonic element that put off people earlier, now mellowed and rendered acceptable by those venerable white hairs – and pointed out the portrait of the spotless Archbishop Sumner. 'I never knew what a good man he was until I went to New Zealand, etc. *That stopped Simeon*! He fled in the night, out of the hall altogether.'

The Provost drew himself up on his little hassock, carefully placed in his seat to give him height. We processed back again, the Provost pausing to enquire after the damaged hand of an elderly servant. 'Getting better, thank you, Mr Provost.' 'Glad to hear it, bless you.' 'Bless you' and 'Bless their hearts' were frequent expletives on the Provost's boyish, if septuagenarian, lips. He rose up in his chair to address me at one point as 'My dear boy'. I felt that I had not been a failure. The Provost had earlier informed me that his mother's people were Baptists from the vicinity of Falmouth.

There was E. M. Forster dining half-a-dozen places away. I made myself scarce and kept away from him. Not that he would have known who I was, but some kind friend would pretty certainly have drawn his attention to my recent 'Two Cheers for Mr Forster'. His appearance unmistakable – humorous, discontented or rather unsatisfied, kindness, petulance mingled into an expression of unease, the Monty James iron spectacles, the Cambridge disarrangement of the hair going sparse. In the Combination Room (horrid taste of the twenties, the grand period of King's and Bloomsbury: these were the relics) Forster lapsed into an armchair by the fire, hands together between his legs, legs sideways, in unconscious abandon: it made him look youthful, one saw the boy under the man of eighty, and that, after all, he had a touch of genius.

Then we taxied off to my talk. (The sun has come out quite warmly, lighting up the ruddy hips and haws along the pleasant banks of a Bedfordshire river, winding flatly through rich fields, black cattle, manure heaps. Now a harrowed field is red. We are at Willington: a fine church and medieval barn or dovecote with stepped gables.)

At my lecture it was so hot and stuffy one could hardly breathe, young men packed on the floor and sitting along the high window-sills.

Pleasant talks with Saltmarsh, who showed himself a kind man, attentive, perceptive, but defeated and dispirited. Another trait was revealed: outside his window is a little roof terrace with a cupola: this serves him as a summer-house. On hot summer nights he sleeps out there: he doesn't have a bed made up, he sleeps on cushions. He has no house or home. It is a perfect picture of the bachelor domesticity of the Cambridge don.

Later in the week. From Bletchley to Oxford I had pleasant, bucolic, if unforthcoming company. I arrived in the early afternoon; at 6 p.m. Simon, awaited with excitement, rang up to say that he had arrived, but might he come to my rooms at seven, as he was being taken to see someone. At my Cambridge meeting he looked like a young god, when he arose from the floor at the end of it – I could not see him when speaking – 6 ft. 3 or so of him, in pale corduroys, long hair golden, magnificent head, blue eyes like Adam's, liquid and expressive. I discovered in the course of the evening that he was still more like Adam than I could have imagined. I had thought of him as pure English aristocrat, and fell for his fearless way of saying exactly what he felt and thought: an appealing characteristic, in a bourgeois world where everybody is looking over everybody else's shoulder, afraid of being scored off, inhibited, boring. Simon gaily exposes himself. So do I.

But in the course of the evening, I found I was mistaken about him. On his mother's side he is American – Swiss – Jew. Very much Adam's combination, only English or Anglo-Irish, in place of Hessian. And what a background! *Two* brothers killed in the war; the third, heir to the peerage, slightly mad, behaving with cruelty to his mother – and Simon himself giving hostages to the enemy! I think he laid himself out to capture me – I resisted, oddly enough, with not so much difficulty. He could not have known that it was largely diffidence, himself too splendid a creature for me.

But I discovered how American-foreign he was: in his lack of reserve, his neurotic sensibility, his instability, the muddle of his ideas, all over the place. He has a passion for Greece, and this summer went to work in a bauxite mine on Mount Parnassus – what he likes are human relations, living in a community, the dionysiac, his 'enthusiasm for other boys'. And though he knows hardly anything of the subject, he has a real – foreign – responsiveness to the beauty of objects.

Sunday morning I took him round to sit at the feet of Jacky Beazley: he ought to see the great man at least. 100 Holywell was looking more exotic than ever: more Levantine draperies, more Greek tablecloths, rugs stretched across walls, more exquisite objects on mantelpieces, picked violets lying on an antique marble dish, etc. Nor have I ever seen Jacky looking so exotic: with increasing deafness and dependence on Marie, she now dresses him as she likes: her doll. He was wearing crimson corduroy baggy trousers, bright scarlet socks, red shoes; a large white knitted sweater more like a blouse, a red silk scarf: he was hardly distinguishable from her. And – like Philip to Ottoline Morrell – he has got to look more like her: grey hair parted in the middle and loping down over the ears; he only needed some of the numerous rings she had put on her fingers – and perhaps bells on his toes – or a ring through his nose. But *nothing* of the bull – not even a sacred one – about Jacky.

The interesting thing psychologically was that though he is dependent on her and everything has to go through her, he could really hear the beautiful Simon better than her. (Prieto got that point in his drawing of Jacky with a vista of a Greek boy, like an athlete in a dream, behind him.) Conversation was difficult, but once launched, I devoted myself to Marie to give Simon a better chance with the great man. To my horror I heard Simon asking Beazley whether he was interested in Greek vases. 'I should think so!' said Marie, affronted. I was amused, but weighed in and got the talk around that rock. Simon wanted to tell the greatest master of the subject in the world that *he* didn't care for Greek vases, he preferred archaic sculpture. But he was fascinated by, and responded exquisitely to a seventh-century marble lamp with a head. Both Marie and he fondled it with love – I was unmoved, except by Marie saying 'You should see it in the evening with the firelight playing on it.'

Then she and I went upstairs to bring down her horse – the finest horse in the world: a bronze figurine of a foal with long tail slightly arched, as if whinnying, with head raised for its mother; tiny wasp-like body joining the two parts together. The figure perfect, still standing on its legs. Simon was thrilled. Marie held it lovingly, sheltering it with her fingers, shifting them round to show the different lights on the patina. It was an interesting scene: Jacky like a learned old crone giving out precious information, like bits of jewels, or slightly crusty precious stones jutted out into the discursive, halting, not perfectly flowing stream.

All the same, the stream flowed away not badly: there *was* a flow between the great man and Simon, if sometimes arrested; there was Simon's eager impetuosity and enthusiasm. There was a flow, amused, flirtatious between Marie and me – and all the years of the past, since I was a difficult, shy, proud undergraduate whom Jacky picked for the English scholarship at the House. And Marie's devotion to Jacky. 'I am dedicated. My husband is a great man,' etc.*

* He was a man of genius.

16 December

On Oxford railway platform yesterday were the Beveridges,[1] who have come back to add new terrors to the Oxford winter: two old scarecrows, lost without their former entourage, now vanished, and themselves ceased to be important. Should I speak to them? Or would they speak to me? Since they had left Oxford I ceased to have any purpose for them (and they for me), and some rumour of my disapprobation of Beveridgism and of my reference to Beveridge as an old Daddy Christmas must have penetrated those vain and alert ears.

But he, sharp as ever, caught sight of me and informed her who I was – those fine dark eyes growing dimmer, both of them looking much older, pathetic figures. I was bidden up by Lady Beveridge, determined to be friendly; I took her hand and at once resumed the old flirtatious relations. I took hardly any notice of him: I have never forgotten the inconsiderate way he ended my lectureship at the London School of Economics. (Not that I set any store by being a member of that establishment: it happened to be a convenience when I was doing my research for *Sir Richard Grenville* and *Tudor Cornwall* at the P.R.O. and the British Museum. Mrs Mair[2] was friendly, ready to make up to a young Fellow of All Souls. I always mark a difference in my behaviour to her and that to him.) They have now come back to Oxford, of all places, where he was an important figure and where they have so many enemies – without a job, without any of the 'Power and Influence'* they attached so much importance to, generally disliked, on the shelf.

Lady Beveridge began by putting things in the right perspective: they hated Edinburgh, so far away. (They always hate what they are leaving, for the next place that offers, and that is their attitude to people too. No doubt it is the same with others; but everything in *their* case is so crude – it is what I chiefly object to in them.) Lady Beveridge had read my books with so much pleasure – she couldn't remember the names of any of them: I offered the name of *The England of Elizabeth*, rather absentmindedly as to a member of a lecture audience. No, it was the one about your Cornish—; *A Cornish Childhood*, I supplied. Lady Beveridge was ten years behind. 'But have you read *his* book?' she said, lighting up and pointing to the object of her devotion looking rather ridiculous standing there, having his praises sung

1. Sir William Beveridge, Director of the London School of Economics in the 1930s, author of the famous wartime blueprint for a Welfare State, subsequently Master of University College, Oxford.

2. Then Beveridge's secretary, not yet his wife.

* The egregious title of his book.

by a fond mistress. But he didn't object. Rather uncomfortable, embarrassed as only Lady Beveridge can embarrass me, I gradually edged us two away from the old nanny-goat, looking more unkempt than ever, positively shabby. I fancy he knows I do not like him: he gave no trouble.

I said I had not yet dared to read the book, deep as I was at the moment in the Elizabethan Age, etc. 'You must, Leslie; it's such an im*port*ant book.' 'And *I*'ve written a book too,' giving me a wide smile, with those powerful dentures. 'It's all about the Beveridge Plan. You see, we were going to write the book together in two volumes; and then the publisher said you couldn't have a book in two volumes. So then *he* wrote his big book and I have written mine, with all the photographs.' She ended with beaming bogus self-deprecation. Acutely uncomfortable for her, I came to her rescue, 'You have written the human side of the story.' 'Yes, that's it,' she affirmed.

She turned to the attitude of the younger generation – as for the youngest things of all, her grandchildren, she couldn't understand them at all. I said, according to the newspapers they were up to no good. This let loose a flood of Victorian moralizing – it is character that counts more than anything, good sterling character. 'Now there,' she pointed to Old Father William now standing somewhat further off along the platform, 'there's a *puir* mind, so upright, so devoted to other people's good' – words failing her, she stood back, arm outstretched in the manner of a huckster-woman selling her wares. (As, in a manner of speaking, she was – but such bad salesmanship!)

Then, turning to the subject so much to the fore in the newspapers and remembering that I was a highbrow, 'Leslie, I've been reading Proust – the book "Sodom"' (as if it were a book in the Bible) – with an assumed expression of horror, 'but I was so *outraged*. Leslie, so outraged.' Anyone would think that the book had been specially written to outrage Lady Beveridge; but, of course, this showed how *puir*, like Lord Beveridge's, her mind was. I took her hand: 'I'm surprised at you being so Victorian,' I said. 'I thought you had progressive ideas. I've never heard anything so girlish' – Lady Beveridge simpered. 'Now I'm so disillusioned, I don't mind what people do to each other: there's no end to human quirks and oddities.' The simper grew into a broad smile. 'I don't mind what they do, either,' said Lady Beveridge, with a woman's quick turn-round, revealing the feminine under such a strong masculine appearance and the essential woman's disconcern for morals. 'But I'm not disillusioned about human beings – they're so interesting and good at bottom. Now there's one –' she began again, pointing to Lord Beveridge by now a little further away along the platform, 'there is one who has devoted his whole life to the service of others. How can people compare a Churchill to a record like his?'

I couldn't allow her to continue along that line: more amusement to be got by teasing her about what I was going up to London for – to dine with the Queen Mother. 'Oh, Will: he's going up to dine with the Queen Mother. She's a *wond*erful woman.' I dared to say that she was irresistible and sweet. 'But it's not only that. She's a woman of sterling character: it's sterling character that counts.' It was necessary to recall Lady Beveridge to the present situation: she was evidently mixing me up with the inhabitants of Stevenage, who had no doubt been fed on this diet during their rule as lord and lady there.[1] ('But the people there adored William. They *ate* out of his hand,' etc. It was not my concern if his wife were making a fool of him and herself for my benefit: I did not look at Beveridge, I excluded him from the conversation, as if he did not exist – as for me he does not. He must have appreciated what was happening in a half-conscious way: even he could hardly be such a fool as not to know that she was being led on to make fools of them both. After all, he had once made a fool of me!)

I said that Nancy Astor was giving a party at which the Queen Mother was to be present. 'Oh, *dearr* Nancy, do give her our kindest regards – from us both. We were very close together in the first war, and he' – as it might be He – 'worked a great deal with Waldorf. Oh, yes, he was such a friend,' etc. 'We haven't seen Nancy for *such* a long time. *Do* give her kind wishes from us both.'

I said that I was lunching with Harold Macmillan. That produced an explosion, for it was Harold Macmillan who kicked Beveridge out of the job at Stevenage. I hadn't been aware of this, but it produced the whole story. 'He just wrote William a note, only three or four lines, saying that we were too old for the job. After all that He had done there – oh, it was fearfully *raw*, you know. I should never speak to Harold Macmillan again if I saw him.' 'Shall I give him a little bite in the bottom, at lunch, for you?' 'You can *kick* him in the bottom,' said her ladyship with a good will, but with no good humour.

It crossed my mind to mention Ernest Bevin, who had also kicked Beveridge out during the war;[2] but I refrained.

Lady Beveridge remembered Veronica, whom she always connected with me in her marriage-making mind: 'She is making a great name for herself,' said Lady Beveridge, displaying other wares. I told her that she had been down to grace my literary party this term, and that she would be coming down to my next, next term. 'Oh, *do* ask me, Leslie, to your next literary party: now that I have written a book, *do* ask me.'

1. As Chairman of the New Town Corporation.

2. As Under-Secretary at the Ministry of Labour, appointed in December 1940, Beveridge regarded himself as in charge of manpower policy. Ernest Bevin had other ideas.

It crossed my mind that I would ask her – or I might; but his lordship? Certainly not!

The pleasant conversation ended on a pathetic note: Lady Beveridge on the sacrifices they had made and now they had no money.* ('If *I* can be any use, tell the Warden, in helping him about the furnishing of the lodgings. He *must* bring the kitchen up out of the basement. People oughtn't to be expected to poot up with it, y'know: they won't anyway: you can't get them to come. I've a lot of exp*ee*rience about this, and if he wants any help, just tell him to come to me.' The Warden is already very well informed about her experience in the Master's Lodgings at Univ – and of her interfering in the running of the College the moment she installed herself there. I think I will pass on her generous offer to him.) I protested against any such idea as their being hard up: they must have made plenty of savings. 'Only a very little,' said Lady B. But he must have several pensions from his various jobs, Civil Service, London School of Economics, as Master of University; and she must have a good full pension from the L.S.E. 'No, we've got to live by our wits,' she said. Quite well as she has done by her wits so far, I do not think they are going to take her much further.

Anyway, the train was coming in. Leaving them to get into their first-class compartment, I hurried forward, a long way, to get into my third.

[Title – 'A Penny for the Old Guys: or the Beveridges on Oxford Railway Station']

At lunch with Harold Macmillan I said that I had run into two old guys, well known to him, on the railway platform at Oxford. He laughed and said, 'I knew you were going to say the Beveridges. They are a couple of old guys. The truth is that Beveridge isn't so bad, but she makes him ridiculous.' I said that I preferred her. He told me that it had twice fallen to him to get rid of Beveridge. The first time was during the war when Ernest Bevin came to him and said that he must get rid of this fellow Beveridge. Harold said it was nothing to do with him, it wasn't his department. But Ernest said, 'You must get rid of him: he's one of your sort, a university chap and you can do it.' He gave a broad grin and Harold did it. He had had to do it again over this new town; they were much too old for the job.

* That was rather nice – to be so candid.

This journal of Rowse's second visit to America (the first had been cut short by Warden Sumner's sudden death in 1951) is, like its successors, written with an amplitude and perspective that is only occasionally found in his English and continental diaries.

To his quality as a descriptive reporter with an ear for dialogue that Pepys and even Boswell would have appreciated he brings a social appetite remarkable in a man of his years who thought of himself as a misanthropic recluse. Plutocrats, casual acquaintance, academics, publishers, men of letters, political and other celebrities are all observed, judged and brought before the reader. His account of his stay at Urbana, Illinois is perhaps the fullest of his many descriptions of American university life. Never a metropolitan figure, he makes good use of his visits to the Middle West and the Deep South.

Sunday, 28 August 1955

Here I am well started on my second visit to America. It seemed that the omens were against my ever getting away. To get ahead early, I packed up at Trenarren[1] on Tuesday and left in broiling heat in the afternoon.

Thence on to Bodmin, across the moor looking coloured and a little autumnal already – dark green flanks, purple-grey outcrops, tors, homesteads, feathery ridges of Rowtor and Brown Willy – scooting by in scented evening wind. Never have I had such a sense of harvest countryside happiness, free and alone, fine naked bodies on top of corn-ricks, a carefree figure whistling round the bend on his tractor as I crossed the bridge, the frontier, into Devon.

No reason why I should stop, so on and on I went across Devon, past Exeter, to Honiton, where I was forced to stop for petrol. Too late: all garages shut. I considered whether I would stop the night there, or try and raise some petrol and get on further. When I looked for money, my coat, which I had taken off, was nowhere to be seen. Had it got out of the window in the through-draught? With my complex, I was sure it must have been stolen – with £20 in it and a gold watch. But I hadn't stopped anywhere, since calling in at Aunt Beat's.

At the call-box I couldn't get through either to her or to Beryl. In my agitation I left all the silver I had in the call-box and had to go back for it. A nice Suffolk man called Strake at the 'Angel' came to my rescue: let me telephone, fill up and gave me a meal on a cheque. Telephoning to Aunt Beat, I think I came to the wrong decision – to go back to St Austell for the night and pick up my coat, which I had left with her.

After eight o'clock I started back over the 100-mile course again, too sick and apprehensive to be angry. Serve me right, I felt; I must pay the penalty. The penance was not long in coming. Put off by a string of lorries, I made another wrong decision: to come back through the middle of the Moor, Moretonhampstead, Postbridge, Princetown. Darkness soon came down

1. ALR had moved into Trenarren in August 1953.

and I am unaccustomed to night-driving.* The hills were tremendous, sometimes one in six, and at other times it was difficult to judge what gear was necessary. Fortunately, there was little traffic; on the other hand, if anything had happened to the car I should have been stranded out on the moor.

The moor was impressively lovely. I had never driven this route before and was struck by the deep wooded valleys on the eastern side. A half-moon kept steadily in front of me on the road west; romantic shapes of hills rose on every side and sometimes threatened. On the unfenced part of the moor animals came out of the shadows to mess up one's gears – ponies and cows; the sheep were more sensible.[1]

Time went on: it was a long pull across Dartmoor. I kept promising myself, if only I can get to Tavistock it will be all right.

At about 10 p.m. I was passing through the main street of Tavistock and it was all right. Went to bed at Trenarren at midnight, utterly tired out with a couple of hundred miles' hard driving since the middle of the afternoon.

Leaving Trenarren all over again next morning, I caught sight of an owl – a little barn-owl – in broad sunlight sitting on a telegraph wire, and wondered what that portended. On top of the hill above the turning from the Lostwithiel road to Fowey, something awful happened to my accelerator – I didn't know what. A passing good Samaritan, a Jew who had lived in Oxford and knew my books, gave me a lift into Lostwithiel, where I was recognized by the garage proprietor – his wife had been at school with me (everybody in the neighbourhood increasingly was at school with me) – who sent out a mechanic at once to the horrid scene.

Inured to disaster by this time, I was again sick and philosophical rather than angry and agitated. The trouble was soon put right: a broken accelerator-spring. Tenderly, gingerly at first, but with increasing speed I went on – to lunch at Honiton, humiliatingly, where I had got as far the evening before.

All the same, I arrived at Oxford by five, and there Derek was awaiting me, gave me a hand with all my luggage and everything. I handed the little Minx of my various adventures over to him and the Manciple, and we went out together to a grand tea at the Mitre.

Next day, helped by Derek – indeed, driven in my own car to the station – I got off to Liverpool.

* I was new to driving.

1. No doubt aware of the sage's difficulties.

I spent the night at the Adelphi – this time without Norman. Before leaving, I wrote him a letter that I did not mean to be savage; though I must write Jack and Rupert* similarly. For I cannot stand – or understand – their inability to get forward with their writing. Year after year passes by without their producing their books. I would not be so unreasonable as to complain if they could *not* write. Most academics can't anyway. But these three can – and don't get forward with it. It took Jack eight years to do a little book of 60,000 words on Livingstone. (It took me five months to do a book of 180,000 words on the Churchills.) I don't expect them, I don't expect anybody, to get up to my standards of concentrated work. But I am astonished at their weakness of character, for that is all it is: they have the intelligence, the knowledge, the ability to write. Though they haven't the inspiration or the will-power, they are better educated. They go drifting on year after year without producing what they have it in them to produce; making all allowances for their teaching and lectures (Norman has little to do). I simply cannot understand it.

I suppose it is true that most academics are *like that* and are too soft to get their books written. It is the case with Geoffrey Hudson or Isaiah Berlin or John Sparrow. The fact that others are weaklings is no excuse for friends of mine; and if they go on in that way I cease to respect them.

They may regard this as presumption on my part. But it would be more assuming of me to take all that they have to give me – which I value greatly – without caring whether they achieve what they have it in them to achieve or no. It would be far easier for me not to have to exert will-power to drive them on to do what they should be able to do on their own steam.

What should I do? Go easy with them? Encourage gently, coax and persuade and forbear? They would then slack along and get hardly anything worth doing at all. Jack would give still more lectures, write still more letters, fuss about still more trivialities. He wanted to come and see me off at Liverpool. Fancy wasting a couple of days on that – it would only make me more sad to leave.

My first evening on board the *Britannic*, I wandered round and ended up in the Tourist Class Dining-Room, where I ate somebody else's dinner. A bright steely woman, with husband – evidently North Country – attacked me with a direct question: 'Are you travelling for work or pleasure?' Taken aback, I considered, and answered, 'Work.' That did not check her, however. She pursued, with insatiable curiosity, 'But perhaps work need not exclude pleasure?' I considered again, and then answered discouragingly, 'No – just

* Rupert Evans spent his life at Leicester, never wrote a thing.

work.' Her husband commented, 'He evidently doesn't derive pleasure from travelling.'

After that, I surreptitiously moved the tall vase of flowers so that she couldn't see any more of me, and settled down to *Martin Chuzzlewit* with my meal.

Jack suggested that I should take *Martin Chuzzlewit* with me. A quarter of the way through – just about where I am across the Atlantic – on the threshold of Martin's journey to America, it seems the least imperfect of Dickens' books. So many of them have slabs of the intolerable – either sentiment, or moralizing; but so far there is very little that I want to cut out – my usual wish in reading Dickens. I have been carried away by the exuberance of the poetry, the bounding imagination, the sheer joy of life of the young Dickens at the height of early success, when the world was good. Mr Pecksniff I had remembered, though not his horrid daughters – *Martin Chuzzlewit* used to be my favourite Dickens as a schoolboy.

But what creativeness, peculiarly about inanimate objects: they live and make gestures on their own, the faces of the clocks grin, the tables and chairs waltz about, parapets peer, chimneys totter, doors leer, glasses mirror the intense life of Dickens' aquarium. I love the scenes of the family gathering of Chuzzlewits at Mr Pecksniff's, the dinner party at Todgers', Mr Pecksniff ending up drunk, his rejection at the mansion where Tom Pinch's sister is employed as governess, the dinners in inns – John Westlock, Martin and Tom Pinch at the 'George' at Salisbury, Martin's meal in his squalid lodgings in London. The fun of it all! Dickens must have been exuberantly happy just at this time; sad to think of the experience of life that brought the sense of guilt, the murders, the evil that hangs over the later books. Like the sad progression in human knowledge from the joyous young Shakespeare to the old. And yet neither Dickens nor Shakespeare lived to be old.

2 September

The boring journey draws to an end: tomorrow we'll be in New York. But who would want to cross the Atlantic, if it were not for money or ambition, self-importance, getting a job or on with one's career? Not I. I hate the sea and being on board ship with the dull throbbing headache of the engines never still, the insistent musical note that the ship sounds, which drives one dotty when one once is aware of it, the heave and lurch and creaking of timbers when it is at all rough, the noise at night as of someone patiently rasping away at the ceiling with a file.

And when it is rough, I fear every motion of the boat. We went right out of our course to avoid a hurricane – I should be terrified to be in one. We simply got the tail-end of a heaving sea. Forewarned, I turned my back on the beastly sea and my face to the wall, took to bed and enjoyed teasing images of the way Bodmin Moor looked, the late summer in its colours, the line of hilly country one sees along the edge of the moor cross-ways to Callington – Hawk's Tor and the eastern ridge above Northill and Trebartha. Such images, and the thought of the little white shadow inhabiting the green glades of Trenarren.*

I have slept and rested a good deal and eaten too much, though careful. I have managed to read *Tudor Family Portrait* and write my review of it for *E.H.R.*; re-read Martyn Skinner's *Return of Arthur* and write a good article on it for *Time and Tide*. And a mass of overdue letters, though still not enough: one to Eliot, letters to Veronica and Cyril Falls and home to Beryl and Aunt B. And three resounding reproofs to Norman, Jack and Rupert for their failure to write their books – as above.

I have amused myself avoiding the company of the ship's passengers, and cultivating that of the ship's company. In the latter respect, going a little far. It has been not only more interesting in itself, but brought some insight into the kind of lives I want to know about. I don't want to know about conventional family lives: I long to have an intimate look into the lives of these seamen.

The first mystery about them is the extent to which they are driven by the pursuit of Cunt.

Cunnus teterrima, etc.

I suppose it is no different from the pursuit of Prick by us others, but naturally it is unintelligible – the experience of normal humanity from which one is outside. That is what all, or almost all, of the young men of the crew want. I am out to understand their ways, from the outside, since there can never be any inner sympathy. I talked on the top deck to a dark young engineer-officer last night, a Glasgow Scot, with lean hungry features of a greyhound. He was hungry for a woman, on edge, desperate. Nothing else would do.

5 September

I count my first twenty-four hours on my second visit to New York successful and enjoyable. It was pea-soup hot on arrival and the usual long incompetence at the Customs – impossible to get a rude porter to attend to one. The Cunard people had told off one of their men to look after me, and a casual

* This makes me sad sixteen years later – such love between Peter[1] and me.

1. ALR's cat.

sort of chap with a straw-band tied round with a coloured neck-band looked after me very well. I thought of Mr Jefferson Brick. Ian Mackenzie, head of St Martin's Press, turned up and saw me to the Wellington Hotel, with a complete programme for the week.

He turned out much what I expected, burly, competent, masculine Scot, better read and more of an academic than I supposed. Was in the Navy, in the Dieppe and D-day operations.

For the first hour or so, I felt *dépaysé* and glad to have him look after me: I had forgotten the currency and the way of things. Left to myself, I was astonished to find how it came back in a matter of minutes. I remembered the faces of two of the black porters, the wallpaper of the bedrooms, the carpeting. After tea, I went out by myself and the neighbourhood was as familiar as the West End. I walked down Fifth Avenue and into St Patrick's Cathedral, thronged as usual with the faithful: nice young man in uniform praying; a young sailor in white, with his girl – he, a non-Catholic, attendant upon her observances; at the Pietà, surrounded with large glass globes containing red roses, a coloured girl praying fervently, wanting something very badly, holding on to the arm of Christ, her hand occasionally smoothing the glass globe. Well, Mother Church provides well for the credulity of its simpler members.*

Behind the high altar was a statue of the Child, with an illuminated prayer in Cardinal Spellman's execrable prose style: all about Thee in Thy robe of rabbit-skin, protecting our beloved America – several times repeated – with its forests and flowers, and sunsets and sunrises and the innocence of Thy Childhood, etc.

The Rockefeller Center was packed on this warm evening. I ran straight into an out-of-work young poet, fed up with America, with New York, longing to get to Europe, to Paris. I detected a Slav streak. He turned out to be partly Polish. He came back to the hotel, where I gave him a meal and afterwards we went up for him to recite his poems to me. He recited three, each of them a genuine poem, good third-class.

Next morning, Sunday, I made for East Side, where I had never been – what different characters the Avenues have! Within a few blocks of each other, going across them, all the difference in the world: from the smartness and wealth, the skyscrapers, of Fifth Avenue to the seedy squalor of Third, Second, First. On Third Avenue I was already in the Jewish quarter; perhaps even in Fourth, with all the doctors, Rothbendler, Friedmann, Schlossman *und so weiter*.

* I have never forgotten this scene.

Tuesday, 6 September [?]

I *hope* a profitable business-day. At eleven I went down to St Martin's Press, inhabiting a small apartment on Park Avenue – very new, very contingent, but promising. I had a full discussion with Ian Mackenzie and Sherman Baker about the promotion and arrangements for publication of *The Expansion of Elizabethan England* over here; seemed satisfactory: they are spending $1,900 on promotion and advertising. I learned that, where both *The England of Elizabeth* and *The History of France*[1] had been chosen by the History Book-of-the-Month Club, *The Expansion* had been turned down by the Irish Roman Catholic who read it. At the same time, a Leftist Jew running another Book Club who was impressed by the book and thought it brilliant, turned it down because he didn't agree with my point of view! So much for justice of mind. – Behold the occult influences upon freedom of expression in the free United States. But nothing of the kind would make me change my expression of opinion. I am prepared to pay the price for independence of mind, here as in Britain.

There then appeared a brash and crude young man from the *Publishers' Weekly* to interview me. Little did he know it, but he was Mr Jefferson Brick out of *Martin Chuzzlewit*. His attitude the whole time was 'What do you want out of me?' Underneath this habit was a rather pathetic young man, slim and spinsterish. He wanted to know about *The Churchills*, which is the real purpose and problem of my visit: to decide who shall publish my one chance of a bestseller so far. St Martin's Press is merely the New York end of Macmillan's and on a very small scale;[2] on the other hand, they would go all out on this one book, are prepared to spend $3,500 on its promotion. Cass Canfield of Harper's is after it and has a personal interest in it. He asked me to call at Harper's: the nearest thing in New York to Macmillan's in London: old-fashioned, carpeted Victorian opulence, giving the impression of 'safe as the Bank of England'. I was introduced to Fischer, editor of *Harper's Magazine*, a lean, long-fingered, greyhound of a man; dark, mercurial, jumpy; very much on the pounce, an Oxford Rhodes scholar. At once wanted me to write an article.*

Cass Canfield took me to lunch at the Hotel Vanderbilt next door. He was slow, very fly, and friendly. The situation between us was clear. He made no bones that any of the big New York publishers would be delighted at the chance of publishing *The Churchills*. We talked about Winston and my day with him. Still no specific offer. He carefully revealed, on a side-wind,

1. Romier's book which ALR had translated.
2. Now (2002) a very different affair.
* Fischer, a German-American, turned out unfriendly.

how much he admired *The England of Elizabeth*. He talked of Alice Longworth Roosevelt[1] and her patronage of Joe MacCarthy.[2] I said the French Revolution had seen cases of horrid Jacobins patronized by *marquises*. He then threw out a fly – $10,000 for the two vols. of *The Churchills*. A derisory offer, really. I wasn't interested in any large lump sun: it would only go in tax. He said only a top-royalty would do. I said, Yes. He at once suggested a flat royalty of 15 per cent, where St Martin's Press had only been able to offer 10 per cent for the first 10,000.

There is, besides, the more important consideration that Harper's have a large sales organization covering the whole country. I am afraid Harper's have it, and that I ought to close with them, probably through the intermediary of Curtis Brown to make all watertight.

Sad for the young St Martin's Press, who have laid themselves out to entertain – and seduce – me here, no doubt under instructions from London.

From lunch I went on to the Macmillan Company, where I wanted to get a copy of *The England of Elizabeth* for my lectures at Urbana. I did not intend to bother George Brett, the almighty President of the largest publishing firm in the English-speaking world; but his secretary gave him my name and he breezily took me into his office, overlooking a busy corner of Fifth Avenue, an open space with trees and a church on the other side.

'What do you think of my desk?' he said, seating himself in the middle of a yellow-wood horseshoe with every conceivable gadget. Separate piles of papers on different subjects; little leaves you pull out all round the outer rim, to jot down a note when you came for conference with the great man. He propelled himself right back to show me one kind of dictaphone in one hide-out, another in another. He wasn't interested in me.

However, he gave me a mechanical smile. 'Let's look into the record of *The England of Elizabeth*,' he said – he wasn't very sure of the name. I deprecated bothering him. 'No, no,' he said; 'let's have fun.' He punctured a bell-push, held up a disk and spoke: 'Margaret Barton – Margaret Barton – Margaret Barton' (or whatever her surname was, against the noise of Fifth Avenue). 'Bring me the record of sales of Rowse. *The England of Elizabeth*.' A little later, 'Let's have more fun: let me have the complete record. Is the book in stock? If so, what stock have we left? What is the monthly rate of sale?' etc.

He wasn't minding me: he was 'having fun'. Later, he got the complete record of each of my books: a useful check on the London Macmillan's. I remember only that *The English Spirit* had sold 5,500 copies and was now

1. A notable political hostess, daughter of President Theodore Roosevelt.

2. *recte* McCarthy, demagogic U.S. senator who exploited Cold War fears of subversion to conduct a nationwide witchhunt in the 1950s.

right out: not worth a new edition decided Mr Brett. I agreed. A stock of 700 copies of *The English Past* remained: 'You might tell your pupils in Illinois about that book and get rid of some,' he suggested.

I had really had enough of him. I saw what a brash fellow he was, where the trouble with Macmillan's in London came from, who was responsible, and that this man was well capable of firing his Vice-President, Randall Williams, and giving him five minutes in which to go. From this point, I was only interested as a writer in Mr George P. Brett.

8 September

The last two days have been decisive from the business point of view here: I hope all turns out as it promises: the prospects look good. In any ease, the necessity of coming over to see for myself, get the hang of the situation, has been proved.

Yesterday I lunched with Commager[1] at the Century Club: my first within those portals – quintessence of New York upper-class, professional life. The atmosphere quiet; place not large, darkened rooms, portraits of nineteenth-century New Yorkers that spoke prosperity, exclusiveness, good standards, public spirit: the best element in American society.

Humorous-faced Commager, with his flattened features, round face and pimple of a nose, greeted me with his usual busy friendliness and warmth; with the buzz of one who is greeting one between trains. Which was, in fact, the case: he was passing through that morning on his way from his Vermont farm to Utah, for a couple of lectures. He is too busy, too restless, too much of a publicist to be a good historian. A full-time professor at Columbia, he is often in England or on the Continent, in the Middle West or the Far West, he pours forth articles, books, editions; he is editing a series covering America's history in forty-five volumes! He is a corporation. He too, appearance and all, might have come out of *Martin Chuzzlewit*. Bigger is better.

He is the soul of good nature. After finishing up his business talk with a Swedish professor – about a visit to Sweden – he took me to a table where congregated the elderly worthies, the crustaceans, of the club. I was settled with a handsome old gentleman named Cleland, a distinguished printer, impenetrably deaf. He made up for this by retailing a non-stop series of amusing anecdotes, which were not amusing.

After lunch I ran into Kenneth Lindsay – who has broadened into a handsome middle-aged man: a casualty from politics, having lost his seat, he makes his living by lecturing all over the States. (What a life! I must be careful not to come to that.) He used to be a figure in the undergraduate

1. Henry Steele Commager, one of the leading U.S. historians of his day.

world of my time: senior to me and already well known. He was rather pathetic about himself: I did my best to console him. He was with John Fischer, of *Harper's*.

Immediately after lunch I took my leave: Commager would want to get on to the next item in his schedule. And I had to go to Curtis Brown's, the literary agents.

I had not got in touch with them before leaving or let them know of my visit, merely rung up that morning. The lower down one makes one's contact, the less likely one is to be known. And that is what happened at Curtis Brown's. If I had been Herman Wouk, author of *Marjorie Morningstar*,[1] with which all the bookshops are stacked, my name would have been known. As it was, a young lady bade me to a chair, after I had waited humbly in the lobby (on a sterling basis, facing the dollar), and listened kindly to my stumbling story.

To her credit she said, 'I think you should see Mr Collins.' 'Who is he?' I said. 'The President.' She rang through, and, by a sheer fluke, he was there. A stroke of luck, for otherwise – drifting aimlessly into Curtis Brown's and out again – I might have missed clinching everything there and then, or even been too discouraged to explore any further.

When I got into Alan Collins' office, a little dazed, I said, 'You perhaps know my name?' The large, good sort of a fellow replied, 'But you gave me lunch at All Souls, don't you remember?' The bulky figure looked vaguely familiar; but I concentrate so much on my work that I forget the living people who recur, so much less real to me than the dead people I write about.

He was extremely interested by the prospect of the Churchills book. We got down to a business discussion. He corroborated my view all along that Harper's would be far better publishers for the book than St Martin's Press. That was what I wanted to be sure of, that I was making the right decision. A book with the possibility of a large sale should be handled by a firm with a large sales organization. An *American* firm has great advantages in dealing with the American public. There is Cass Canfield's personal interest in the book.

Alan Collins said that he had just been talking to Little Brown's, who were much interested in my work – and they had heaps of money. I said I had no wish to hold the book up to auction: I knew that any of the big New York publishers would willingly publish it; but for me, it was a choice between Harper's and St Martin's Press, the New York end of Macmillan's. At that he got down to the core of the matter. He would speak to Cass

1. And of the much better known *The Caine Mutiny*.

Canfield about the promotion of the book, its character, financial terms, etc. I decided then and there to let Curtis Brown handle all the American rights.

The news of my being in the building flew round. An intelligent young man came in: he wanted a word with me: he is handling the New York publication of *A Cornish Waif*.[1] I had forgotten all about that. It shows how engrossed I have been these past six months, and how much I need someone to look after my affairs, help me with the things that are getting beyond me.

It was a lucky visit to Curtis Brown, for there was a series of editorial questions from Dutton's about *A Cornish Waif* waiting for me to deal with. I dealt with them there and then. This young man settled my last remaining doubt, whether Houghton Mifflin wouldn't be the best publishers for *The Churchills* – as Rache[2] betrayed he thought in London – since they publish Winston's books over here. The young man said disinterestedly – and this was just what I wanted – that Houghton Mifflin had rather overdone their Churchill line. That settled my mind, all the doubts and contrary pulls that have been going on under the surface of my New York visit, obviously entertained with special intention by St Martin's Press.

I left the building with a load off my mind. This what I had come over to resolve. It had all worked out clearly, when I had drifted in haphazardly, unexpected and unprepared. I called in at the entrance office to thank the young woman, who had not known my name, for looking after me. She had done well.

I arrived, late, for a cup of tea with friendly Edward D'Arms of the Rockefeller Foundation, in his office on the 55th floor with that staggering view across New York and up the Hudson.

With him I did my best to forward getting Geoffrey Hudson over here for a short visit and or to the Far East; and talked up Ken Wheare's stock, which does not need any talking up: I found D'Arms had learned that Wheare's political science colleagues regarded him as the best on the subject in Britain.

As evening came on more lovers about, and a single young man, might be Puerto Rican, eyed me from his seat. I sat down at the other end of the line. He got up, passed me and sat down at the next line of chairs to do up a shoelace. I did not sit down beside him but passed right on, out of the Park, weary and bored, to dinner.

After my meal, I sat on in the intolerable heat, trying to catch up arrears of letter-writing.

1. *A Cornish Waif's Story: an autobiography*, anonymous with an introduction by ALR (Odhams Press, 1954). For the troubled history of this work see *A Man of Contradictions*, pp. 252–3.

2. Lovat Dickson. 'Rache' was an abbreviation of Horatio.

The well-got-up and expensively dressed young women filed in and out, attended by their obsequious young men. Fortunes had been spent on their clothes. This is a woman's civilization – at any rate, in its outward expressions. At last the hour came; Ian Mackenzie arrived, together we trundled my four bags into the taxi and off to Pennsylvania station. More dead than alive, longing for bed, I crept into mine, only sparing a few minutes for a last glimpse of the lights across the Hudson.

Urbana, Illinois

It is a good thing to have got away from the noises of Seventh Avenue. The skyscrapers reverberate them, so that on the 20th floor they rise up and hit one: the fiendish trumpets of the automobiles sounding now a sharp B, then flattened almost to A, answered by a higher note, C, which is then echoed more flatly by H: a more diabolic symphony on the name of Bach can hardly be conceived. Then there is the hiss of the buses starting up or rounding the corner. Fire-alarms or police cars are frequent, with sirens magnified several times. Even barking dogs sound like fiends in an Inferno; lesser noises would scale their way up and hiss at one like snakes.

But there was at least a breeze in the room. Here in my swept and garnished apartment – No. 13 on the sixth floor, I hope no ill-omen – there is *no* air. A breezy young woman said to me this morning, 'These apartments are not well ventilated, I guess.' They certainly are not: not a breath of air: twice as hot inside as out. In addition, the girl who cleans the apartment explained that my room is next to the incinerator. It will be very nice in two months' time, meanwhile I expire in a roaring crematorium.

Agitatedly, I got from Chicago-Pennsylvania station to Illinois Central, was kept waiting by No. 98 porter for my luggage until the very last aboard. I was so anxious – just what I hate – that I was almost without voice when this black turned casually up. He thanked me pleasantly for my dollar: I looked thunder at him, but did not speak. Everybody else was already well settled in.

When I got in, a blasted Radio voice was commenting on some baseball match in Boston, interspersed with advertisements of Oklahoma Gas. Enough to make one mad. The rest of the Pullman didn't notice it, so conditioned they are to the constant solicitations of eye and ear of the American Continent. I wasn't going to stand it: I told the attendant to turn it down. He turned it down. It was still intolerable: I shot up from my seat next it to the middle of the compartment, where there was peace. Then I went to dinner. The attendant turned the hideous voice completely off.

*

Professor Dietz and his wife were waiting for me at Champaign, and drove me to this hothouse, where there is every modern convenience except a breath of air. I slept naked, with the sheet hardly over me – the Professor's: I must buy some for myself tomorrow.

In the morning I sallied forth, to find the world outside distinctly fresher; had my breakfast in the drugstore, bought toilet-paper, a bath towel, face towels and two plastic mugs. It was like setting up as an undergraduate again.

And so it has been all day.

To the History Department at 10.30 to meet an indistinguishable company of colleagues: all smiling, all with the self-deprecating cynicism that expresses the American academic's sense of inferiority in a world where business success sets the key.

So far I have managed to kill time here successfully. Nobody disturbs me: I am left to myself: I work all day in the Library, dividing my time between the Elizabethan Age and The Later Churchills. In the evenings, I come back, relapse on to my bed and go on reading. In this way I am not wasting time here. Next week my lectures begin – and I hope not too much social life.

The early part of the week was overcast by a minatory cablegram from Rache Lovat Dickson, reminding me that Macmillan's hold all world rights in my books and ordering me so to inform Harper's. I was thunderstruck, thought I had asserted my freedom to place *The Churchills* in America in my showdown with him before leaving. The fact is he is determined to use me to make the grade with his St Martin's Press, to build them up with me as their star. One of my chief motives in going to Macmillan's in London was to be published in America by the Macmillan Company. No sooner was that achieved than the two Macmillans separated, leaving me as a casualty. Just my bloody luck! Rache took advantage of my ignorance, and the fact that owing to the tax situation at home I am in their hands,* to force me to publish my books in U.S. with his chick, the struggling S.M.P.

I have never been pleased about this, and a main motive in coming over was to see the situation and judge for myself – which I did in New York.

But he is determined to hold on. That night I wrote a furious letter asserting my freedom. All night my mind was upheaved about it, and next day. Next morning when I awoke, the right course stood clear before me: to write asking Macmillan's and Christopher Medley, my lawyer, to readjust

* I was not in their debt – the converse; I left a large balance accumulating with them, on which they received all the interest!

my agreement with them, confining it to English rights and leaving me free to control American rights myself.

What move will Macmillan's make now?

I shall be furious if they put *force majeure* on me, threaten to end the agreement and pay me the whole balance in my account – some £7,000 at one go: which, with my existing income of £3 or £4,000 for the year, would mean losing it practically all to the government. I have no intention, if I can help it, of handing over what I earn by the sweat of my brow, for the upkeep of the idiot people's perambulators, crowding the pavements wherever one goes. They who have the pleasure of begetting their unwanted offspring shall maintain them – as far as I can help it. I cannot avoid maintaining a number already, with the taxation I pay: the thought gives me no pleasure.

If Macmillan's make such a move, and *force* me – against my will – to publish with their small New York end-branch, I can foresee the sad train of consequences I have experienced with others who have, in my view, treated me unfairly: Christ Church, Cornwall, my old school, All Souls.

I wonder why?

Defects in my own character? No doubt: impatience, touchiness, pride; slow to understand the disingenuousness, the treacheries of ordinary people; myself too candid, it may be that life is impossible on the basis of a directness and candour other people find too much. Rosalie[1] once told me that she found it so refreshing; Veronica asked if I considered myself clever; Rache betrayed that he thought I was not good at business. Nor am I. And yet I get by: the odd fact is that I am worth more than any of these, and have had to make every penny of it myself. Perhaps I am not so simple as they think. For the independence I have won, from all and every, Macmillan's no less than All Souls, has been won by yielding not a jot of independence of mind or opinion, making no concessions to anybody. Yet – it is successful; I have made my way. Perhaps the combination of hard work, tenacity, readiness always to sacrifice in the present for the future, plus my own genius, is a stronger combination than all their sophistication and disingenuousness, their hypocrisies and caginess playing their game.

All the same, no-one has so lonely a road: the paradox is that, without powerful friends and with many enemies, saying exactly what I think and making no concessions at all, I have won a position with the public. And, paradoxically, am better off.

One advantage is that I am at least not *open*: nobody knows my affairs, if I am not very expert at conducting them myself.

*

1. Rosalie Glyn Grylls, subsequently Lady Mander.

The infernal heat-wave has gone off, and the campus is fresh and autumnal. I talk to everybody I can, make what contacts I can – on two levels, as usual.

My colleagues, the professors, ask me out to dinner. First the Dietzes, who have one of those tasteful houses of the best American professoriate – like the Johnsons at Stanford: placed in the quarter where all the other professors' houses are, all much alike, same size, type, etc. – nobody would dare to be very different from anybody else. No servants, and that imposes a regulation size on the houses: what can be managed by one woman. Mrs Dietz obviously manages him very well, a *hausfrau*: furniture good, a pleasant green shade made all round by the grass and the shrubs; within, the dining-room lit by candle-light.

I feel my way along, as in a foreign language – I hope not treading on too many toes, talking a lot, for that is partly what I am here for – I hope not patronizing. For one falls into that too easily: American academics somehow invite it by their inferiority complex, their good manners, their self-deprecation. So – *achtung*!

Last night I dined at a younger professor's, Arthur Bestor, where there were a couple of boys aged about five, tartars. The new professor here, Kenneth Porter, adopted a young German boy on his way back through Europe from Australia. His wife is in process of spoiling the brat, as Mrs Bestor spoils hers. It is the modern manner with children everywhere.* We ate our dinner, a party of eight, amid the fracas of two boys all over the place, crawling over the floor, toppling the screen over, all round us, interrupting, worrying. I wonder it was no worse than it was. Parents are terrified of administering a check, they proceed by a policy of inducements: 'If you are good, I will read you a story after dinner.' It worked after a fashion. But what a strain!

My other contacts are with the undergraduates, also feeling my way, trying to learn. The mystery is what these young men do about sex: precious little, I fancy, and according to the Greek Papa Dmitrion whom I've met and who is similarly nonplussed. It would seem that the young men and young women just hold hands, at the most kiss each other goodnight, after spending whole evenings together. P. thinks that the Puritan ethic prevails with them, and is astonished. I think the middle class really rule in America.

I am excruciatingly bored, but also intrigued: how much do they know, how much do they understand? I am liable to assume, too much with some; too little perhaps, with others. It is tricky but important to find out: after all, the centre of a people's experience of life. But, if there isn't any centre?

* Behold the consequences 10–15 years later.

31 October

The reviews of *The Expansion of Elizabethan England* are reaching me. One remembers Virginia Woolf's anguish, waiting for what the critics would say. I don't mind what they say for the most part; and for the most part I have no reason to complain. All the reviews have been favourable save one. By far the best was really Jack's, understood the book and its intention best, appreciated what was original, and – deservedly – made the one score against me: insufficient justice done to Philip II. There was a fine and favourable review in the *Glasgow Herald*, evidently by some academic hand who knew what he was talking about. Veronica was generous and perceptive as always, writing in the *Observer*. An extremely patient and sympathetic review by Templeman in the *Birmingham Post*. One outright hostile review in the *Listener* may be discounted, it was so evidently written by an enemy – G. R. Elton, whom I don't know: ignored the whole point of the book and its originality, made every possible hostile insinuation, every trite score not worth making – in one case humourlessly failing to see ('the usual reaction of the inferior to the superior') that the cap fitted him.

Hugh Trevor-Roper didn't fall for that one. He wrote me a letter on a first unwontedly generous impulse to say that he found 'the part about the Borders and the Celts absolutely fascinating: you really do re-create that Border world: I seem to be reading about the French pacification of the tribes of the Atlas Mountains: I am *sure* you are right.' This pleased me very much: I was even touched by such generosity from that ungenerous pen.

But I didn't write, for I knew it would be impossible for him to translate such generosity into print. And, sure enough, today came an unforgivable review. Half-admiring, half reluctant tribute; the rest reveals the jealous competitor – for he is not a rival. What is unforgivable from a supposed friend is that he twice uses the word 'falsity' about the book, and makes an impudent assertion about my past and present self, which is untrue. 'Can one, without an inner falsity, love an age and hate the mental substance of it?' That can be answered quite simply: I do not *like* Puritan Cartwright, it is true; but I share the point of view of Elizabeth I. Nothing false about that: it is quite simple. He goes on, 'And is there not also something false in thus defiantly making history into stepping-stones of one's own dead self?'

That is a shocking aspersion from a friend. In fact my present is continuous with my past: few people more consistent. I do not hold with religious belief. Nor does Trevor-Roper. I find much more falsity in his attacking me on this score. And accusing me of *irresponsibility*, of caricaturing people in history, is what offends me most of all – considering the efforts I make on behalf of responsibility, the sacrifices I have had to make, the attacks from intellectuals of the Left precisely on that score.

It is not worth going on answering such a 'friend'. Some people by reaction may take my side. But they won't see the point at issue: they won't see the injustice: they won't understand; they never do. And no-one will come to my defence: they never do.

Perhaps I ought to be pleased at the misunderstanding that has dogged me always, ever since I can remember: naturally in my family, and ever since I began to write. I should take it as a tribute to originality; I should welcome this live response to whatever I write, that keeps me a 'provocative', a 'controversial' figure, with a good effect on sales. I ought to laugh.

It would be a wry laugh, I fear. I feel as Elgar did about it all – the superciliousness of the academic second and third-rate, the refusal even to *try* to understand. When he became old and famous, the one thing he would never talk about or discuss, when people longed for him to, was – music, where they had most to learn from him. Games, bridge, chemistry, anything; but music, never.

Serve them right – the one thing that mattered to him. Shaw thought Elgar the greatest man he had ever known – something from him, who had known William Morris.

If I live to be old, I too may be famous. They shall never know me, any more than I allow them to know me in Oxford. There is so much they might learn: they shall not learn it from me. Like Thomas Hardy, with his peasant shrewdness, to Desmond MacCarthy at a grand party: 'Do you tell these people your ideas? I don't.'

Their responsibility: they cold-shouldered me all the way along. Now, even these enemies combine to say that I am a very learned historian. That is not quite so: hard-working, yes, but not a learned man. Accurate, yes – why don't they try and find some errors of fact in my work, as they could with Froude? Jack made a perceptive point in comparing me with him, save for his constitutional inaccuracy: excitement, vividness, colour, feeling on top; moral indifference below. If I am largely indifferent about humans – and the contempt is partly the obverse of pity for avoidable suffering (it is humiliating to have to explain) – is that very different from Gibbon, who was a 'great historian'? Or Hume? Or even the position Carlyle came to in the end?

This is the second time Trevor-Roper has urged that I am not a 'great historian'. Is he afraid that I might be? I do not claim to be. It takes me all my time and all the energy of body, mind and spirit I have to write my books: I have no time to waste on arguments with such people on such themes.

So I must not reply to Trevor-Roper or to any of these people. I must be content to be misrepresented, to be given an unjust account of, to be misunderstood all the way along, from the beginning perhaps to the end. Perhaps it is better than a dead and boring agreement, leading to being written off and discounted.

But it is sad all the same. My nature underneath always was an affectionate one. Jimmy Neale[1] wrote me while here – 'I always knew you had a heart of gold.' And for all my moral indifference I set a better example than these people of generosity and justice in the treatment of others who come under my notice. I should hope – however much of a Pharisee it makes me – to exemplify a better code of manners than Trevor-Roper's.

All the same, this has its effect in accentuating my loneliness, sharpening my isolation. As I walked the leaf-strewn streets here in the remote Middle West, where I have been telling students and crowded audiences (people sitting on the floor, standing ten deep at the door, turned away) all that I know, giving of my best – what a contrast with Oxford, where I live, yet no-one knows me. For years they took no notice; all round me, especially among the younger generation at All Souls, there was always jealousy, envy, questioning – they couldn't bear to hear my books mentioned, or me to talk about my work – when they might have picked up so many tips. It was the same with Woodward years ago, a mean attitude in someone a generation older; it was the same with Feiling, I discovered. G. M. Young who made special efforts, which were successful, to keep me out of the Chichele Professorship, and to put Jacob in, said afterwards, 'I don't see what you have to complain about' – because my own efforts are financially well rewarded, his not. And even darling Richard,[2] when I was pushing him round New College garden one day, wanted to make me say outright if I would accept the Regius Professorship, if it were offered me. I wasn't going to say: my experience makes me assume that it never would be offered to me. And dear Richard said, 'I am not willing that you should have that attribute too – giving you the opportunity to refuse it.' Why should *I* not have the opportunity to refuse it? – apparently it would be all right for anyone else to. I caught my breath a moment and registered, 'You too, Richard', though of course not holding it against him, in his condition.

I must be content to trudge on, saying exactly what I think, writing the best I can: expecting nothing. And I know that, even if anything were offered me, I ought not to accept it. To be consistent with my view of human beings, I must not mind being misrepresented; I mustn't reply or take any public

1. Professor J. E. Neale, the biographer of Queen Elizabeth I.
2. Pares, by then confined to a wheelchair.

notice, I must just go on. For I am largely, if not wholly, indifferent: it is all that, with my intellect, I expect of them, though my heart yearns for understanding and acceptance.*

[Chicago]

I taxied expensively along the sunlit South Shore to arrive at Zabel's University Club, heavily carpeted, plushed, prosperous. We went across to the Art Institute, and there, tired and rushed round as I was, I was dazzled more than ever by the sunlight of the French Impressionists. *There* was the world to inhabit! – later nineteenth-century France, Seurat's and Monet's Seine, Monet's garden blazing with flowers, Monet's Argenteuil, Seurat's 'La Grande Jatte' – like some paradisal symphony in colour and perspective, the ladies walking like goddesses, heads turned away, the children playing, the loafers reclining, the dogs and monkey prancing – all in soft blues and purples and greens, the colours of dream and evocation. A miracle.

Zabel brings all his European visitors to stand before this picture. He had last brought Eliot, who was properly impressed; but the aged eagle seems to have said nothing. I was moved to say a lot.

We hurried on, though how much of it all remains with me: the finest Corot portrait I've seen, a girl interrupted reading a book; a grand Courbet, 'Mère Grégoire', fat, solid owner of a bar, head thrown back, a flower in hand, shrewd and no doubt generous with her 'charms'. The finest of Sargent portraits, a small one of Mrs Dyer, over-sensitized, tragic woman – Sargent has seen that she would go off her head.

Scores of other things I caught sight of: seaside Boudins; a Degas of dancers, exquisite in colouring – and the famous Milliner's Shop, the hats flower in his garden. The gallery has a tempestuous Constable – Stoke-by-Nayland (to which N.[1] took me: alas, he does not write) – not over-finished but left raw and rich, one could lick the paint.

I must remember getting on for a hundred pictures: the El Greco 'Immaculate Conception', the small rounded 'Last Supper'; the early Velasquez with the tawny-golden youth. The stripey Mary Cassatt I had remembered from my last visit and, oddly enough, the Roger van der Weyden portrait. There was the remembered primness of Madame Cézanne, the blues of his Mediterranean landscapes; the ruddy sunlight of Renoir's late expansive nudes; but I don't respond – I love his earlier garden and flower pieces. A not first-class

* All this remains unchanged, worse if anything. 1972.

1978. I no longer yearn for understanding or acceptance. I live for myself alone.

1990. Even more so – and how right in such a society, and the world around us as it is!

1. Norman Scarfe.

Tintoretto 'Tarquin and Lucretia'; but I was immensely taken with Finsonius'* Resurrection. (Who was he? Some Flemish follower of Caravaggio) – the colouring of a rare range, harsh clear lines give an edge to his personality: rather a mystery picture, the top half a different hand from the bottom.

Of the American pictures – the Innes landscapes were pleasant enough, and the Eakins and the often reproduced 'American Gothic': two Spencerish portraits of prim sobriety. Quakerish, the farmer holding up his fork, spectacled and bald, his wife pinafored and puzzled: image of marital fidelity. I didn't waste time over the moderns – I don't like Fernand Léger and Co. There was a better Chagall portrait of a Jew – and a better Dali than most. I was only moderately taken with the Bracques, but I can see that they would be Eliot's choice: they have a keyed-down sobriety, all in browns and blacks and greys. Right for Eliot. Give me Monet's wonderful garden of colours, the tense and vibrant Van Goghs.

Last, I was rushed round the French drawings from the Louvre: so elegant – but not memorable, save for a few, like Seurat's studies for 'La Grande Jatte'. Not as memorable as second-rate painters like Cazin and Ribot, whom I'd never heard of, but would much like to own.

I really must go out and get my lunch. I am astonished to find how much of that crowded rush-round I remember: this is not a third, or a quarter of what I recollect – the fine Gainsborough, the poorish Reynolds and the fine one, the Rembrandt of the girl at the half-door I had remembered from before, the Giovanni da Paolo series, the uncouth German paintings of the sixteenth century, the Goya scenes, the Dutch painting that does not really speak to me. I simply must stop or go without lunch.**

[Indianapolis]

In every room was a children's class – lucky young Americans – noisily engaged in modelling, drawing, cutting out paper strips for Christmas decorations. I was much taken by a young teacher, tall, fine eyes and profile, with the irresistible combination of physical masculinity with feminine nature, who stood happily in the middle of the bustle, sissily putting hands to ears with a deprecatory smile. I was in the charge of a young professor from Butler university, R. G. Usher's son: square-set, ex-Navy type, with wide-apart dark eyes and four children. When I joined him at the entrance to leave, there was, unexpectedly, the young Arts teacher waiting for me, took my hand in both his, uninhibited, gay. Shall I ever see him again?***

* The painter dubious, the picture unforgettable.

** I have never been so taken with a gallery.

*** Of course I never did. One never does.

I had to go to the middle-aged meeting of the Indiana Historical Society, presided over by rich John G. Rauch – donor of a Gainsborough portrait (which I'd have kept) to the gallery. We were meeting in the big hotel, in the Riley room, named after the poet of Indianapolis: the city's favourite son, a character, a rhymer, whose rhymes everybody liked. There all round the room were the appalling rhymes with which he had won such popularity.

But life and love
Will soon come by
There! little girl
Don't cry!

It hain't no use to grumble and complain
It's jest as cheap and easy to rejoice.

It's the songs ye sing
an' the smiles ye wear
That's a'makin' the sun
Shine everywhere.

Riley went straight to people's hearts with his sentimentality, all about family life and children. Himself was a bachelor, who couldn't stand children. What he could stand was half a bottle of whisky a day. When the newspapers fixed it up to photograph him surrounded by children, after a bit he would growl, 'Take these goddam children out of the way! I can't stand 'em any longer.'

He made a pile of money by going round the country giving readings. He would come back with a suitcase full of dollar bills, five-dollar bills, quarters, nickels, whatnot; and, not bothering to count it, would hand the suitcase over to his brother-in-law at the bank to look after and invest for him. When he died, well off, his fellow-citizens raised a mound of stones in the cemetery, so that he should lie on the highest spot above them all.

Here I am a twentieth-century Riley traipsing about the country, garnering in the dollars.* I recognize something of a fellow-spirit with his dislike for children. I do not think my fellow-citizens of St Austell will raise a mound for me, to rest above them all.

* Now largely confiscated by penal taxation.

Tuesday, 20 December

My last few minutes in Apartment 613 of the Student-Staff Building, which might have been so unlucky a number, but has ultimately turned out better than expected. Where I spent in my first weeks some extremely bad moments, ill with the heat, anxious, so bored that I often felt I could not bear another moment of it. I was certainly put to a severe test.

Yet, this morning as I crossed the Campus for the last time to my office – No. 327 in Lincoln Hall – the Moment came for which life is most worth living: one strings them like jewels in the memory. The clock struck the three-quarters on the cold winter air; the boys and girls were crossing the spaces under the bare trees; the sun shone clear and there was some quality in the light that spoke of Italy, my dream of the East, boyhood on such mornings in the village, the youth of these folk who would one day look back on those glad years as I on mine. 'The moving finger of time.'

I looked back over the scene in which I have made a figure, been a spectator, these last months. I went into Lincoln Hall, along the corridors which have been my regular route day by day – students in the attitudes that have become so familiar: standing or sitting on top of the radiators, scribbling casually at their tasks, so unselfconsciously, on the marble benches at the entrance. One of my own students, a Kentucky boy, had just run up the path after me to say goodbye: he was leaving early, dark brown eyes friendly in the winter sun.

Washington, 29 December

Such a round of work and entertainment all through Christmas in New York that I had no time for my diary. Every interval I had free to myself was taken up with slimming and revising *The Early Churchills* for Harpers. I got to New York at 8.30 p.m. on 21 December, delayed by the snow along the line. But I like these long comfortable railway journeys in America, the slower-moving stately trains, well appointed and well warmed; waking up to breakfast at Buffalo, sun gleaming on snowy roofs.

22 December

I chiselled away at Churchills morning and evening, cutting and pruning. In the afternoon down to St Martin's Press, where I discovered the explanation of my friends not receiving copies of *The Expansion of Elizabethan England*. They had failed to send them out to about thirty friends and acquaintances

– people like Sam Morison, Admiral Nimitz and Notestein,[1] whose support would have greatly added to the book's impact on its appearance here. – If that doesn't justify all my doubts about being published by this stripling firm!

Friday, 23 December

I worked all day at the Churchill typescript and dined with the Canfields in their charming house behind a quiet patio with iron gate in East 38th Street. A house of rich good taste: flowers, china vases, French eighteenth-century furniture, an expensive second wife, wavy grey hair, well-groomed children – daughter in stiff silk Chinese evening dress, tall son in dinner jacket going out – even a butler and parlour-maid. What it is to be a successful publisher! Cass Canfield is also of good family. A clever Mrs Lutyens was there: haggard, intellectual face, Joan-of-Arc style of haircut – when Dylan Thomas (drunk) caught sight of her, he cried 'St John the Baptist.' She was too clever, too sophisticated, too unsatisfied for me: New Yorker married for a mere five years in England. Jack Fischer, editor of *Harper's*, and Scottish wife were there, and the Commagers, who were bound to make an odd impression in that well-bred, upper-class house: he, bustling, brimming over with friendliness, interrupting, elbowing his way along; she, odd to look at and odder to hear, with her exaggerated Southern accent, that made her sound like a natural.

I spent the whole of Christmas Eve with the Commagers, after finishing my work on the book. In late afternoon I made my way in crisp cold up the western side of Central Park, walking until within reasonable distance of Columbia, when I took a taxi. A party was going on when I entered the first floor of the old-fashioned house, walled high with books, both big rooms (library and drawing-room) and also across the wide landing. Commager – curious round-flat Danish face, with button nose and pimple – showed me all round his shelves, then introduced me to the party: his wife in a dress almost as curious as the night before, voluminous and sweeping like a queen's – 'My husband buys them for me' – their two daughters and the son I had heard of as brilliant: disturbing good looks, large dark eyes, fair hair and face of a faun; tall, large hands, inky and boyish; eager, highly-strung, a perfect young god. ('Do you know what the years will do to you?') On the sofa sat a Columbia Professor of Classics, iron-grey beard consciously brushed apart in Continental fashion of the nineteenth century.

Then came in a don, a Dean – who did not fail to let us know that he was

1. Wallace Notestein, leading authority on England in the early and mid-seventeenth century.

a Dean – from Harvard: to whom I did not take. He was too familiar a type at Oxford – used to being a large frog in a small pond, the centre of admiring undergraduates hanging on his jokes. His were stock jokes, at the expense of academics of the older school, without much point. Much pleased with himself. He had been the brilliant boy's tutor. (Never heard of since.)

After the other guests had gone I was taken possession of for the evening. We went across to another party where we all fed: turkey, ham, celery, Christmas cake, candy, coffee, and I chatted round to various people.

On our way back, Steele[1] was told off to show me the interior of the Cathedral nearby, which I had long wanted to see. We were alone: we talked eagerly, he perceptive, well-read, unselfconscious and unspoiled. Understands everything – Proust, Panofsky, the classics, Henry Adams, Henry James. He is the only American I have yet come across, of his age, who compares with the best young Englishmen. I hope nothing untoward happens to him – as to so many of ours, Humphrey Payne, Alan Blakeway, Michael Beaumont, Tom Dunbabin; and that nothing happens to frustrate the promise of this spring.*

We talked all round the dark aisles of the vast church, with that vivid sense of mutual discovery, which will, alas, lead nowhere – we are of such different generations, backgrounds, subjects and sympathies. Poised on that edge, there was no point in being unhappy. I accepted the fact that I should not see him again, or leave any impression on him: he has the world at his feet, he will go on – to what end? For that evening hour we were content; perhaps he was surprised: certainly I was.

We got back to the house in quieter mood, the carol service with the Nine Lessons in the room from King's College Chapel. It was touching to hear those gentle English voices coming on Christmas Eve across the Atlantic to Morningside Heights, the boys singing high in descant – one could hear the echo in the spaces of that far-off, familiar place. The Professor was settled in his corner of the library across the landing. I sat on the sofa in the drawing-room, with Mrs C. by this time in a different dress – a long blue silk Chinese garment, drinking beer and interrupting with her North Carolinian nonsense. Her younger daughter was reading, one leg tucked under the other, in the armchair opposite; a Millais picture, apple-green dress against purple chair, face shaded by hand. 'Could there be a mo' speaking example of intrinsic beauty?' Mrs C. said to me. I considered this: it seemed a silly thing to say in the little girl's presence. 'Heck,' said Mrs C., 'you are supposed to say "No, there is not."' I said peaceably, 'I was

1. Commager's son.

* I felt like Henry James on first meeting young Rupert Brooke. But he was no poet.

thinking over in my mind what "intrinsic beauty" meant.' The girl's face was in shadow anyway and I could not tell. I helped Mrs C. out by saying what I thought 'intrinsic beauty' could mean. Mrs C. descanted on her daughter's looks until the child protested; and no wonder.

Meanwhile I was under constant siege from the Commager dog, a woolly brown poodle. In spite of commands, pushes, blows, he returned again and again, worming round behind Mrs C. to get at me, up from under the sofa, etc. Nothing would stop him: like a spoilt child, he became a pest and a nuisance, and I had no peace.

Steele joined the reading party and was able to concentrate, isolate himself, amid the wireless, the infiltrations of Henry and the rebuffs administered, the nonsensical remarks of Mrs C. drinking beer beside me. The time came for the children and me to go out and have a snack at the bar round the corner. The C.s eat a good deal in this haphazard fashion apparently. One of the things Mrs C. confided to me was that she did not 'run this house very well'. To me it looked charming: lamps lighted in the corners, a subdued light, large Christmas tree in the corner, presents heaped up beneath it, delightful disarray of books, kindness everywhere, music coming from across the landing.

However, in such a family atmosphere, which I have not been in since I was a child, I could never concentrate.

In the milk-bar, away from Mrs C., Steele and I had some more serious talk: the horror and despair of the age we live in. The girls overheard. (In that clever family everybody overhears everything.) On our way back, at the door – a kind of farewell – I said, 'As you are just, be merciful. Think kindly of me.' 'How could I not think of you – with respect – and admiration?' he said, brilliant eyes gleaming in the street-light. It was not the point. He would not recognize it: from me it was a kind of farewell.*

We went in, and shortly after – Mrs C. having changed her dress once more – we all went out together, bundled one too many into a taxi, to go to the midnight Bach concert at the Carnegie Hall. I refrained from sitting next to Steele; I ensconced myself at the end with Mrs C., who had been confusingly lyrical earlier about the 'Shlogäduck' we were to hear. I could not imagine what this could be: it turned out to be Bach's 'Schlage Doch', sung by a young man with brilliant copper-coloured hair, announced as a counter-tenor but whose voice was really a soprano. The curious performance was enthusiastically received. I kept my thoughts to myself but, here at Washington, the innocent Professor confided to me that the young man he took to be a boy of eighteen is a well-known singer of thirty, of course

* Though a friend of his father, I never saw him again.

queer. I was not near Steele to share the odd experience of listening to him.

Of this crowded Christmas Eve, I have said nothing of the second party where we had our meal – all of us, at the expense of our hosts – and where I met professor after professor, wife after wife; for there, there was nothing significant. It was the moments alone with Steele, or observing the family scene – for that one Christmas Eve in my life a member of a family – that gave the evening its poignant happiness.

[Washington, 28 December]

I have never been to a conference of historians in England; my experience at Chicago was my first. But this was a far more formidable affair, on a vast scale: there must have been a couple of thousand historians here from all over the States. At its height it was like an eighteenth-century horse-fair, with an element of *Kuh-handel*. For here were the senior professors in pursuit of juniors, there the juniors in pursuit of jobs, and a good deal of bidding and offering on the side-line.

I was surprised to find how many people I knew or who had met me. There was a solid kernel from the University of Illinois: the Dietzes, the Swains, Marguerite Pease with her good heart and crashing loud voice; Starr, Genokoplis, little New England Miss Dunbar, Lucille Shay and her sister; wry, dry Bill Bowsma, who is hoping to leave for the climate of California (I don't wonder); kind-hearted, dull Eriksson and Stearns; angelic Bob Sutton, so hopelessly gone-to-the-good and with more charm and looks than any – very affectionate to me (but what's the use of that? well, better than nothing).

Then my visits around the Mid-West bore fruit: there were Pearson from De Pauw, Mullett from Missouri, people from Ann Arbor, Indianapolis, Wisconsin and a fair number I had met at the Chicago Conference. The Eastern contingent turned up – Commager, Nevins, Mattingly, Haller, Ferguson, Read; complete with publishers. My first evening Fred Dietz introduced me to the top salesman of Macmillan's, who had much the strongest force here. – It brought home to me how much I had lost by Macmillan's breach with the Macmillan Company. I came over here to size up the situation for myself and, my goodness, I have succeeded in doing so.

December 28th I gave a little lunch party for Margaret Swain, Marguerite Pease and Fred Dietz – Elsie was out sightseeing. I had been asked that day to lunch by Roger Makins at the Embassy, but put it off, since at 2.30 I had to read my paper on 'Tudor Expansion'. The room was a small one, and a lot of people could not get in to hear my paper. Very flattering; but a fool of a fan of mine turned up – a slightly dotty woman from Chapel Point at home, who would chip in with applause whenever possible. Afterwards I gave her three minutes and was whisked away by Giles Dawson to a tea going on at the Folger Library. The chatter was deafening. I had a few friendly words with Louis B. Wright, who wrote such a mean review of my book in the *American Historical Review*.

That evening I went to a party in the hotel – I already cannot remember whose. In bed I could not sleep till 2.30 a.m., an unusual state of affairs. So I slept in next morning and went to no session until the afternoon, with Caroline Robbins to hear Mattingly on 'Cold War or Co-existence under Elizabeth I?'. I thought the paper – much as I admire his book – second-rate; so were the comments. So, when called on, I made a warm defence of Elizabeth, which hotted things up and got a round of applause. On Conyers Read I made the comment of my footnote, without realizing that he was there in the front row. One more score in our regrettable breach – but he had no business to write such a crabbing review. Anybody who treats me unjustly must expect to get something back. Friendly criticism is quite a different thing. Something else happened to hurt Conyers Read, Caroline told me. Apparently, when he was at Oxford a year or two ago, he came to call on me and I never answered his message. It had quite gone out of my mind. My diary is witness of how much I am away and how such things get squeezed out. It is only now that I think the porter left Read's name on my table, without any address, and I assumed he had gone. I would not wittingly have missed him or the chance to talk to him. This is how breaches are made, more by accident than design.

All the same, the old buffer should have been generous about a younger man's work, instead of crabbing it in public and then saying *privately* to Neale, 'All the same, it's a great book.' Why couldn't he have had the generosity to say that in public, and give me privately the benefit of his criticisms? I can honestly say that my relations with him are my only casualty, by my default, in America. I have been incredibly careful, over here, not to quarrel with my bread and butter – partly because the audience is so warmly appreciative. At home I do not care: people are jealous and envious anyway.

Even so, Dietz and Marguerite Pease say that it is just like Read, that *he* is difficult; Dietz has apparently had experience of it. They blame him; but the sad thing is that I should like to be on good terms with Conyers Read, if only he had not begun meanly. So characteristically an academic squabble. He left the room early.*

Commager, Caroline and I had tea together. I had asked [ ] and his new

* I got my own back when I reviewed his long-winded, pedestrian *William Cecil*.

wife to dinner: nice to see him again, and he is rather sweet. In the American environment, the first marriage having broken up so unhappily, he has to be married again: everybody has to be married in America. The pressure of social conformism is the worst thing over here: everybody must think alike, do alike, be alike. Only in New York, or in holes and corners, is it possible to be one's self. However, I did my best for him in the horse-fair, introducing him round to seniors in the hope it might be useful. On the other hand, he does not have the drive to get his book written. And did he have to bring his wife to the Conference anyway? Most people, for once, were without their wives. (Nothing came of him either.)

Two more parties filled the evening: one with Wallace K. Ferguson, whose book *The Renaissance in Historical Thought* I so much admire and with whom I see eye to eye; the other with a party from Kenyon College, nice Americans and an egregious young Oxonian throwing his Oxford weight about. (It annoys me that he led me into doing the same.)

Next morning I was tired out and had to speak at the Luncheon of the Society of American Historians. Allan Nevins, who took the chair drily and well, produced a diplomat, Claude Bowers, to give an eloquent, old-fashioned address in defence of American liberties. Then came John Dos Passos, large-limbed, negro-featured, negro-voiced, with whom I got on extremely well. I like negroes: he evidently had a lot of negro in him, through his Portuguese ancestry. Then came my turn, and the speech, thank goodness, was an immense success: got so much applause I had to get up and make my bow, a thing I never do.

Immediately after, I went to bed, after a shower, for the atmosphere in the room had been torrid.

At six I went off to the Embassy to see Roger. It was all very natural to see him ensconced there: the last time, when I lunched with Oliver Franks, there was Roger. Now he is top-man, in control of the immense organization. Roger threw his noble profile at me in the old familiar way – what an actor he is, and what a superb appearance! And was as nice as ever, with more than ever the sense of complete confidence. In old days Roger was so sensitive that I didn't know what was behind it all, whether there really was solid ability or just a fine façade.

As his confidence has grown with his position and the exercise of power, he has become quite sure of himself and is less cagily discreet than he used to be. He made no secret of it to me that he was sorry about the changes in the government at home; that he thought the P.M. temperamental (Eden). He had conducted a correspondence with Winston over a long period now and, shut your eyes, it might be the same person you were dealing with. After long practice, he had found the knack of dealing with the predecessor and, knowing Anthony, by now he knew how to deal with him too. All the same, the government was a team, and the P.M. had to have the men where he wanted them.* This has the advantage of being the propaganda line as well as the truth.

I was struck by the Englishness of Roger's American wife: quiet, speaking only when called on to speak, she has conformed entirely to Roger's requirements. And this, in spite of being the daughter of an American politician, Davis of the Davis Cup, who must have a good deal of money of her own. Result: happy family. Wise Roger, never to have made a mistake or put a foot wrong – except when, as a young lad, his foot slipped and he killed his brother out shooting. I thought of that when his wife told me he was going to Georgia quail-shooting this weekend. He did not tell me that: did he know that I knew?

He chatted a good deal about All Souls and the losses among the senior Fellows this year: Simon, Dougie Malcolm, Lionel Curtis, Amery, Brierly. I said that the place was so much less interesting with the old boys gone – I loved talking to Oman, Lang, Robertson and such people, they had such interesting memories. Lady Makins said that now we were the seniors, perhaps the juniors similarly liked to hear us talk. Little does she know the situation in college. They certainly should not have the chance to hear me talk. This rather surprised them: I told them a little of what I had to put up with from Cooper, Carr, Holladay, Quinton, Dummett and that gang, but no more than a little. For the Kenyon young man's talk about All Souls brought back the old complex the other night and made me sleepless for hours. It has been out of my mind while in America: only twice have I had a recurrence of the 'old headache', with consequent sleeplessness.

On leaving the grandeur of the embassy I reflected, without envy, of the way our subsequent lives have diverged – Roger's and mine – as our beginnings were so different, after our brief convergence at Oxford: taught together by Feiling and Masterman at Christ Church, taking the same subjects, the same examinations, competing together and being elected at All Souls.

Roger was always Feiling's particular favourite, Masterman's less so. (Perhaps I'll send J.C. a signal tonight: he might appreciate it. I never have, after the happenings about the Studentship in 1926 or 1927.)** Roger, always rather grand and socially accomplished, but sensitive and highly-strung, was kind in an elder-brotherly fashion to me. When I was rather fussed by the big American Lohmeyer's attentions, with the sentimental heart and the big sexy nose, Roger warned him off. Once, when Roger and

* It didn't work. And, as to Roger, at the Suez crisis he was away duck-shooting in Carolina.

** This I did, which J.C. much appreciated.

Woodall were going away for the weekend, leaving me alone for the tutorial with Feiling, Roger said, rather clumsily, 'He won't have much of an audience.' I put in 'Oh, I dare say I shall be able to make up by my ignorance for your absence.'

He was always rather sweet. I remembered the embarrassment of his asking me for a weekend to his home, the big Norman Shaw house in South Kensington. His mother was angelic, but I must have been pretty far gone with exhaustion – it was just after our election at All Souls, and I was ill from the strain of it all – for I remember little about it. Except Roger's 'I always laugh at my guests' jokes', which seemed to me the height of sophistication; and his mother wanting him to take me for a walk in the Park, and his unwillingness: I thought, because of the shabbiness of my country overcoat, all I had then. It is always a mistake for friends from different social levels at Oxford to visit each other's homes. I was never asked to visit Roger again. Until he was Ambassador at Washington and I, also well known in my way, was invited to lunch at the embassy. As I went out through Lutyens's corridors, I saw Roger's secretary, who had followed him with a last telegram, eyeing me. At the door, Roger introduced him; the young man was very polite, 'I thought it was Mr Rowse,' he said deferentially. Myself, I do not set store by the name.

Roger was having to go on to a party at the State Department and in the car we chatted about politics. 'They amuse me,' he said. I said it was a good thing they did, or he would not be able to support the burden and the boredom.

Better him than me, I felt, taking leave of the Washington Embassy, on which so much depends in the shaping of our policy to confront the dangers of the age. Roger said that Ike was rather like Truman; both were simple men who had no difficulty in taking decisions. But what decisions, in what an age! I am quite happy to have no part nor lot in it; the age has never wanted me or my participation in it. I am content to touch only its margins and give my mind to the past.

That evening I gave dinner to Marguerite Pease and afterwards went with her to call on Ruth Anna Fisher, of the National Archives: a cultivated, part-negro lady, who lived for years in London and loved it. An attractive woman, life had been difficult for her: whom could she have married? Now life was over for her, she said, casting several sidelong glances at me. Easy to understand that life in London was more agreeable: no colour-bar there. Here, in their earlier days, Marguerite told me, they could only eat together in government restaurants. The war had driven her back from London, on the last ship the Americans would guarantee; and she had lost all her books and possessions in the Blitz. Very chic, she still got her clothes, her books and her tea from London. She would, if it were not for the thought of another war, retire there.

4 January 1956

Form-criticism deals with only one aspect of a totality. Panofsky's approach in terms of a reconstruction of the whole experience is in keeping with my view of the creative process in historical writing, making the thing *live* again.

It is rarely that I read books from which I really *learn* nowadays. My visit to America has been rewarding with Wallace K. Ferguson's *The Renaissance in Historical Thought*, a book to influence one's thinking. Books which have added to the *knowledge* of my period – T. W. Baldwin's outsize volumes, D. C. Allen's *The Star-Crossed Renaissance*, Mattingly's first-class *Renaissance Diplomacy* and the concentrated reading I did in the English Department Library at Urbana on Elizabethan literature, on Spenser, Donne, Sidney, Daniel, the poets and the dramatists.*

I finished reading Panofsky in two days, 2 and 3 January, and the result of this excitement: I could not go to sleep for thinking of a possible course of Ford Lectures which I should, but shall not, be asked to deliver. Fancy my 'friend' G. N. Clark and Co. inviting A. J. P. Taylor to deliver them – when his field has never been English, but European, history, and the Ford Lectures are supposed to be in English history. They have never asked me. I know all about my touchiness and making enemies; but this is the kind of treatment I have received all along.

Anyway I thought out a scheme of lectures on the theme 'Reflections on the English Reformation'.** The key would be a lecture on 'What England Lost at the Reformation' – suggested by the two damaged alabasters in the National Gallery here: the fourteenth-century representation of the Trinity, God the Father with the crucified Son on his lap, arms broken off; and the fifteenth-century St George killing the dragon – also damaged. Imagine the effect of a lighted candle before the Trinity, making the shadows move and live; or shifting sunlight suffusing the stone with the glow of life.

Think of all the other destruction, and the evidences, the scraps that survive: the buildings themselves, the choirs with their music, the frescos, painted glass, sculpture, wood-work, books, manuscripts, reliquaries, ivories, etc. etc. *What* destruction – hardly at all realized by the imagination! Bare ruined choirs.

* I had forgotten that, and thought I had wasted time at Urbana.

** Still in mind, still not asked. 1972.

The scheme would have to be balanced by a lecture on 'What England Gained *by* the Reformation' – economically, morally, even in (some) realms of the spirit. One should begin with a couple of lectures on 'The Nature of the English Reformation'; a third on 'The Significance of the Reign of Mary Tudor' as the dividing line. It would make a more interesting series of Ford Lectures than most. But I don't expect to be asked.

Is it any wonder I have reacted as I have done to this kind of thing all along?

I have spent the mornings in galleries: yesterday in the Corcoran, a second-class show, roomfuls of second-rate Corots and Monticellis, but with one lovely Sienese triptych of the Crucifixion and a couple of superb fifteenth-century French tapestries, the pleasures of country life, 'from an old castle in the forest of Loches'. For a touch of home, there were Gainsborough portraits of Francis Basset, Lord de Dunstanville, and his wife: he, long-headed, elegant, lounging against a tree for support, dark intelligent eyes; she, stupid-looking, a nonentity. How did they come there? When Tehidy was sold up, no doubt, by the hopeless Arthur Basset in our time.

This morning I spent in the Phillips Gallery. Not excited by the routine Degas *danseuses*, but immensely by one of the finest Renoirs: a boating party beside the river, seated round tables with fruits and wines. It made me think of the Chicago Seurat, so different a technique and mood: that, nostalgic and musical, a fresco of life caught on the wing; Renoir's a world of present enjoyment, flesh and blood.

Monday, 9 January

I write this from General Oglethorpe's Georgia, where I am modestly installed at the Atlantan Hotel, in Luckie Street, Atlanta. (The Mayflower at Washington would have been beyond my resources for long.) My first penetration of the Old South was very pleasant: waking up as the train neared Durham, North Carolina, to find we were going through pine-woods, frosted grey with hoar-frost, and a Breughel-green stream under thin ice arrested in the woods.* Gradually the light came on from behind, bringing out the rust-colour of dead leaves against the green of pine, and shortly there was a break of Tiepolo-blue sky above.

On the station awaiting me was an unknown professor, a crusty Mississippi-Scot, who turned out to be a man of some parts. He took me home to his widower's house in a clearing in the woods and cooked me breakfast. He had an American cocker-spaniel – dust-gold in colour and named Dusty – for company.

* I remember it still. 1972.

We spent the morning sightseeing at Duke University, the impressive Gothic layout owed to the fabulous $40 million gift of the tobacco-and-power Methodist tycoon. These people are the modern Chicheles, Waynfletes, William of Wykehams of America; their generosity is fantastic, their public spirit beyond anything. Also a good way to be remembered: there in the Lady chapel(!) of the Methodist University Chapel were the tombs of the Dukes.

For lunch we were joined by a taking young Southerner – of course married and family on the way – quizzical and observant, who took in everything and said nothing. A good deal of cross-grained banter between Hamilton and me, about Chatham and Newcastle.[1] Hamilton entirely shares Richard Pares's devotion to the latter and has more than his detestation of Chatham. This denigration of a great man provokes me. Young Durden said he had never seen Hamilton so effectively handled, and added that he was a 'mysterious' man. Under the prickly exterior was a kind, vulnerable man. I suspect that under the surface lies some tragedy. In addition, a man of good critical standards; a friend of Eudora Welty. An odd man, whom I would gladly know more about. Appearance of a self-aware 'character': short, thick-set; gruff, masculine voice; square spectacled head, black square-cut hair, grey eyes, the look of an intelligent black pug.

We were lunching at Chapel Hill, a few miles away from Duke, seat of the rival University of North Carolina. The places are in happy contrast. Duke has a fine situation on the edge of a ravine in the pine forest; the valley partly filled up to make a platform on which the Gothic buildings are laid out in symmetrical balance, the rest of the valley filled with flowering shrubs, gardens. Everywhere were Southern magnolias, trunks as large as trees.

Chapel Hill was not designed all of a piece and has a sedate Georgian flavour: some of their buildings go back to the 1830s. The campus made its impression: one could imagine the place earlier, the young men gone off to fight in the Confederate armies, Venetian blinds drawn all through the relentless summers of the sixties.

Back to tea with the Clarks, whom I had met on board the *Britannic* coming over: a hospitable couple who had achieved a more cultivated picture in their home, full of the things they had picked up on expeditions to the Middle East. He must be a good biblical scholar, is in on the Dead Sea Scrolls, and has catalogued the MSS. of the Greek monastery at the southern tip of the Sinai peninsula. At 6.30 a dinner party. There followed my lecture, in a room stiflingly hot. A charming audience.

1. The Duke of Newcastle, who was the nominal head of the Elder Pitt's great administration in the Seven Years War.

Afterwards to a party at the young Durdens, where some twenty people gathered and I talked too much. It is surprising how closely people in these remote places keep in touch with what goes on in England – or in Oxford. Several people knew the whole T. E. Lawrence saga; others knew about Milner's young men; another young man, a Celt, was much taken in by Aneurin Bevan. I hope I corrected that.

Atlanta, Georgia, January 1956

Taking things easy I went out late to the Capitol. It was bitterly cold as I stood there taking down inscriptions; it had been a park on the edge of town, where the 2nd Massachusetts Regiment had camped during Sherman's occupation. There were tablets reciting the hardships of the population during the siege; a statue of their General Gordon on horseback, with a relief of the episode at Spottsylvania, 12 May 1864, 'General Lee to the rear', when Lee wanted to lead the attack in person.

On the other side was a bearded gentleman standing, with his seated Victorian wife: Joseph Emerson Brown, War Governor of Georgia; Patriot, Statesman, Christian, 1821–1894; Governor of Georgia for four terms, 1857–1865; Chief Justice of the Supreme Court of Georgia, 1868–1870; United States Senator, 1880–1891. His lady was described as 'Devoted wife – loving mother – loyal patriot – a Christian obedient to God'. There is the *mystique* of the South: the unexpected Calvinism, the combination of belief in slavery with fanatical religiosity; the sentimental cult of Southern Womanhood (with its consequence in hundreds of lynchings of negroes for no more than a look at a white woman). I thought of Mrs Commager, with her exaggerated expectations of what was due to Southern womanhood.

Actually, Governor Brown was the chief opponent of President Jefferson Davis all through the struggle: Georgia looking out for herself – a nice demonstration of the impossibilism of the Confederacy, like the defeated side in the Spanish Civil War. They get what they deserve. But what a fate, to be involved with such people. They fought heroically, but all a mistake. The way the Southern cause commanded the devotion of its people shows that the South were an articulated nation of their own.

Above the centre portico the Stars and Stripes flew above the flag of Georgia. From a window of a wing of the building flapped the Confederate flag – blood-red, a diagonal cross with the stars of the Confederate states.

The wind whipped around the building and crackled in the leaves of the magnolias. I was glad to move round to the sunny rear, to note the inscription of a bronze tablet to 'William Ambrose Wright, 1844–1929. Soldier, Statesman and Christian Knight. A gallant officer in the Army of the Confederate

States of America, for fifty years Comptroller General of the Commonwealth, Guardian of its honor and its people's friend; a Gentleman in whom lived the graces, the virtues and the heroisms of the Old South. This tree is lovingly planted and this tablet reverently inscribed by the Atlanta Ladies Memorial Association, 19 January 1930.'

Other bronze tablets had been dedicated by the Daughters of the Confederacy: still going on about it before World War II. The Civil War is still *the* war to the South; hardly surprising, considering how much the South suffered by it. But, then, they should never have let themselves in for it. One notices the Southern addiction to oratory, the cant as from early Revolutionary days with the fatuous Patrick Henry, 'Give me liberty, or give me death' – as if anybody was going to give him death! Loud-mouthed humbug. Going back in a taxi, I noticed another large statue to a minimal orator, one Grady – Irish, no doubt.

Inside was a group of battle-flags, one of the 21st Georgia Regiment: a flag 'used in many bloody battles in Virginia, Maryland and Pennsylvania'. Another was the battle-flag of the 48th Georgia Regiment, captured by the 59th New York Volunteers; one of the Sumpter Flying Artillery, surrendered at Sailor's Creek near Appomattox, four days before Lee's surrender. Another was among those surrendered at Appomattox. An old tattered flag of the 9th Georgia Regiment had been returned to safe keeping, to the ladies who made it, when the Regiment was presented with a new flag: one of these, a Mrs M. E. Patton, had deposited the old one 'as an object lesson to further generations'. (What object?)

Nearby was a statue to Benjamin Harvey Hill, member of the Provisional Congress of the Confederate States, Senator of the Confederate States, 1861–5. 'He was at all times the champion of human liberty.' Quite so – unconscious of the irony in this, of course. A bust of the diminutive doctrinaire, Alexander Stephens, Vice-President of the Confederacy, bore the inscription, 'A great man because he was a good man.'

New York, 25 January

I am dog-tired and, after an evening of letter-writing, came unexpectedly upon a review of my book[1] by Angus Wilson in *Encounter*. I wondered why Stephen Spender had sent it: he has several times asked me for a contribution. There is the same incomprehension of the intellectual that makes me feel lonelier than ever and would discourage me, if I had no iron underneath, like my mother.

1. *The Expansion of Elizabethan England.*

Angus Wilson says that the narrative chapters on the Borders, Wales and Ireland are the 'finest pieces of narrative history' he has read; that the defeat of the Armada is 'beautifully told'. And yet finds my point of view 'a defensive, self-conscious intellectual Philistinism', which he synchronizes with healthy worldliness and robust *joie de vivre*! My diary is the best witness as to that. It's odd that they shouldn't detect the despair, the hopelessness as to humans, the abnormal sensibility, the exacerbation of nerves, the inner truth. I must go on putting up with it year in, year out; for I am not going to explain myself to the second-rate, whose business it should be to try to understand. It makes me sick and miserable. But I wouldn't dream of altering my ways, or considering them or anybody else in writing my books. I write them for myself alone.

There is evidently a line-up of the intellectuals as to my character and qualities – which is quite inaccurate. They allow that I have great erudition, for that doesn't hurt their vanity. (I am not very erudite.) Some think my gift is for narrative; others that I have no gift for narrative. I do not regard myself as particularly good at narrative. And so on.

What would be best? To ignore them, if I could. Not to be involved with them, for that might affect one's creativeness. My instinct is to hold aloof from all discussion, all acquaintance, with them.

They obviously do not understand, have not got the hang of my work, or a clue to me – even clever, perceptive Angus Wilson, who has once met me. Why shouldn't they *try* to understand? But that would not be like intellectuals, whose business is not to understand, but to tell people what they, in truth, do not understand. Their instinct is destructive, to carp and erode – so I must close myself to them, protect my essential creativeness and not allow them to get under my skin, when they cannot achieve their own work: for Connolly – sloth, Roper – vulgarity and conceit, Mortimer – sissiness, Crossman – A. J. P. Taylor – Kingsley Martin – incurable irresponsibility. No, just plough on alone, for my friends never speak up for me. David Cecil, my oldest at Oxford, never has once in his life; Bruce not once, he has never even thanked me for sending him my book* or written me while over here. Neale has written me an enthusiastic and generous letter in private; not a word in public. 'You have written, and must know that you have written, a great book.' No Clark Lectures or Ford Lectures – I see my juniors and inferiors preferred. My seniors and contemporaries will find themselves too late – not, I hope, in the sense that I shall be worn out; but that they will never catch up with my achievement.

* *The Expansion of Elizabethan England* – about which I had an extraordinary experience, see later.

[Written up on board *Queen Elizabeth* – homeward bound in early February]

16 January. In the morning Francis Berkeley, descendant of the Governor and of all the Berkeleys – whom I had met in my rooms at All Souls – showed me round. His small house had distinction with its eighteenth-century furniture and books, with the rewarding surprise of a blue jay and a crimson cardinal together outside. Followed the usual tour of library and everything, then lunch at the Old Ivy Inn outside the town, looking up against a hill with another old house unreachably on the top of it. (Farmington?)

A good turn-out for lunch, including elderly President Darden – whom I had met at Cliveden four years ago: was Governor of Virginia, married to a Dupont. I was rather nettled at lunch by a professor called Gooch, who was supercilious about Williamsburg. I was quite put out. I said that it was (1) beautiful, (2) scholarly – what more could anyone want? He said that it was 'artificial' – as if Mozart or Gluck weren't 'artificial'; he'd have no idea that 'artificial' was the highest praise with Elizabethans. It is always the third-rate with pretensions that I run up against, and can never resist putting down. I said that (3) the place was not a mere reconstruction, but a re-creation, a living centre of research and scholarship, and (4) educative – setting admirable standards of craft in the objects they make and sell, exemplifying good ideas for the people who come there to follow. I may have made an enemy of Professor Gooch. He was, of course, falling over backwards, anxious to be thought more sophisticated than to approve of anything so crude as Williamsburg.

5 February. Sexagesima Sunday. On deck I ran into Victor Gollancz, who descended from higher up to watch the departure. I hadn't seen him for many years – since the expensive lunch he gave me at the Savoy which shocked me when I was young. After which he turned down my essay, *Mr Keynes and the Labour Movement*, which was then published by Macmillan's:[1] actually my first Macmillan book. Much as I disapprove of both phases of Gollancz's activities since – the Left Book Club, no less than his recent Jesus Christ-like falling-over-backwards to forgive the Germans (it was one of the young women in his firm who referred to him as 'that Jesus Christ-like man, Victor Gollancz'), I was determined to be agreeable. He was present at the PEN Club party given in my honour on Monday evening: I went up to him, shook hands and said a few words before leaving.

On deck, against the panorama of skyscrapers, we talked about Rebecca

1. 1936.

West and the fuss over Anthony West's novel; Edith Sitwell and her recent conversion to Rome, in which V.G. says she is not happy; Daphne du Maurier, *his* greatest of bestsellers. I did not mention Elizabeth Bowen, whom he has lost to Cape. We talked of Uncle Jonathan. A professional literary man's conversation. At the party he had kindly invited me 'up' to see him on board, assuming, quite rightly, that I would be travelling a class below. This amused me: it was so naif and unaware; and it repeated the pattern of twenty years ago, when I had been shocked by the luxury of an *ethical* left-wing socialist – too left-wing to approve of my Keynes book, but lunching me at the Savoy.

New York Harbor was magnificent as ever – from Washington Bridge down Manhattan Island to Battery Point, where the view up the East River opens up with the Brooklyn bridges and Long Island. This time, because there were people with me, I got no such thrill as on arriving, when the out-going *Caronia* saluted the incoming *Britannic* and we watched the ship sail proudly outward and home, leaving me on the threshold of those unknown experiences which are now part of the past. The *Queen Elizabeth* herself gave me a sensation of pride as she slid quietly out from Berth 90, dwarfing the *Scythia* beside her and all the other ships, appearing to reach half-way across the mouth of the Hudson before she straightened out to face the open sea.

[Further recollections written up on the voyage home]

To Philadelphia, where Caroline Robbins[1] had engaged me a whole suite in the expensive Barclay, at the corner of Rittenhouse Square.

Though cold, Richmond had been sunny, no snow. I appreciated its defensible position, the bluff the old part is built on, falling sharp down an escarpment into a valley, Jeff Davis's house – the 'White House of the Confederacy' right on the edge. Philadelphia was grey and glum – the Quaker City.

Next morning, snow on the way, I was in favour of moving while we could, and we set out on our tour of the old town. Very well planned by Caroline, we went to the first settlement by the Delaware, the Swedish, and its pretty church, Gloria Dei, with white interior like King's Chapel, Boston. Through the churchyard, full of graves of people who went through the Revolution – it reminded me of that churchyard at the east end of Boston Common – we marched out into dirty, grimy streets, with slummy rows of nineteenth-

1. Sister of Lionel. A seventeenth-century historian, married and settled in the U.S.A.

century houses, with always a glimpse of the river at the end of the street. Past the tumbledown old Market with its cupola and Market-building at end, to St Peter's Church and, finest of the three, Christ Church: a sophisticated London church of the early Georges, with rich cornices and good brickwork; also bells, which I miss more than anything in America. We called into Carpenters' Hall where the Continental Congress was held; passed a porticoed bank, First Bank of the United States, and a Regency colonnaded Exchange. All leading up to the main showpiece, Independence Hall, which is under restoration, while whole streets in front have been pulled down to make a grand approach to the national shrine.

I duly took off my hat at Franklin's grave: covered with wreaths to mark his 250th birthday. I had noticed on my arrival, scooting down Legust Street – 'The Franklin Printing Works since Spring 1728'. After lunch at the Russian Inn, we visited the Historical Society and saw specimens of his printing, early editions of his book about Poor Richard and How to Get on in the World.

By the time we got back to Caroline's home at Ithan, out along the original Welsh settlement with names like Merion, Radnor, Bryn Mawr, Haverford, Narberth, the snow was beginning. There was just time to see the little Welsh church of the settlers here, with names like Roberts, Cadwallader, Lloyd, dark under the trees with winter evening coming down. Inside, Joe made a fine log-fire while all that evening and through the night it snowed.

Meanwhile Caroline was under observation. She is a thorough good sort, with her share of the Robbins' egoism which used to infuriate me in Lionel, when I was young and unnoticed at the L.S.E. and he was a big bombinating noise. What surprised me was that, with a woman, it should be so uninhibited.* Trudging the streets of Philadelphia, she said, 'I decided that there wasn't room in England for Lionel *and* me. Of course, Lionel is on a plane quite beyond me: he has genius and I've nothing like that. All the same, I decided that with my gifts – of course, only second-rate compared with him – I'd be better off over here.' The thought of the two Robbinses bestriding the two countries, not room enough for both of them in one! Where do they get it from – this total, *unconscious*, egoism? The strict Baptist background. Lionel had been made a Member of the Philosophical Society of Philadelphia – 'very much of an honour: you know, he has a great reputation over here. He mustn't take a mere knighthood: now a peerage is different. If they offer him a knighthood, I have told him he must turn it down.' She was kind enough to include me too. I said peaceably that I had no claim: I was not a

* She is phenomenally humourless, Baptist background, a good woman and a bore.

public figure and had no intention of doing any public work, far too disillusioned to raise a finger. With Lionel, it was different: head of an important department of Economics in London University, had done a lot of public work, served on many commissions, was a public figure.

Talk that evening revealed naif gulfs of egoism. Caroline has a small collection of old books. 'Yes,' she says with complacency, 'I've a lot of lovely books.' How had she got them? 'Well, you see, I'm very fond of booksellers and they're very fond of me, 'cause I *know about* books.' Libraries also like her, I forget why – I was so astonished at the unselfawareness. Caroline has little idea of what good writing means; however, she assured me that, whatever criticism might lie against her work on the score of insufficient research, 'I know that I *can* write.' The truth is the reverse: no real idea of writing, while she has difficulty in finishing a book for chasing irrelevant by-paths of research. She bores us all with tales of what she is doing, and nothing is ever completed: not a book, merely articles. She has amassed interesting material about the English Republicans. I told her that Trevor-Roper had thought of writing a book about them. 'I don't care what he's doing. I think I'm more intelligent than Trevor-Roper.'

I was flabbergasted.

On the other hand she did cook a good meal for us. But then, 'I'm a very good cook. No, I didn't learn it: you have to be interested in food to be good at it.'

The pure Robbins essence is intolerable; yet she has a good heart and I like her.

She was anxious not to let the group who run *Current History* get in touch with me. She was very off-putting on the telephone to the young people who had arranged a dinner party for me and naturally wanted to know whether I was coming. Perhaps there was a scintilla of femininity there, wanting to keep me to herself. When they got through to me they were greatly relieved. Then Caroline wanted to know who were these people in literary life – a touch of jealousy?

There had been a mix-up about my lecture at Bryn Mawr: it clashed with Charlottesville. I don't think this grieved Caroline – I think she wanted to keep me wholly to herself.

[After an argument with a young lawyer about the reasons for American unpopularity abroad]

I was troubled by this dispute, for it grazed the heart of the problem as I have glimpsed it on this visit: something that I do not understand, and certainly do not appreciate about Americans. Theirs is a middle-class society, so far as I have seen it; the standards are conformist and Puritan, respectability above all, doing the right thing, being like everybody else. Liberal progressivism imposed on others, who know better, as political wisdom; democratic illusions assumed as truth; everything seen in terms of ethics, moralizing, cant, humbug – ugh, intolerable! For a moment, in arguing with that tough young Philadelphia lawyer, I sympathized with George III: this, I felt, was what the makers of the American Revolution were like. (Not surprising that Caroline Robbins sympathizes with them.)

Unlike George III, I silenced the young man, though I did not convince him. He still did not see the point.

Afterwards I felt sorry. I remembered Logan Pearsall Smith's Trivia note about dining out, how brilliant he had been, what truths he had enunciated, what original thoughts he had brought forward, how he had sparkled and scintillated; then – 'God! what an ass I made of myself.'

It is men like the young Philadelphia lawyer who – however stupid of them – carry on the world's work; and, when the conflict comes, they will fight it.*

Next day I saw a different aspect of Philadelphia society and a very different type of man.

Most of the morning of Saturday, 21 January, I spent in a cold and dirty bookshop just out of Rittenhouse Square, run by a fat and dirty old lady – a character out of Dickens – who was beguilingly candid about the high prices of her books. 'Much too high,' she would say. 'I wouldn't pay it. But somebody else who is dumb enough will.' So I did, and ran up another bill of over $50.

I did, after all, enjoy the luxury of my Philadelphia hotel, had breakfast sent up to my room, pretended – on my hard-earned dollars – to be a plutocrat for once, loved looking down from a height on the snowy roofs of the Quaker city, across Rittenhouse Square, the people moving like black ants upon the white. Down in the restaurant I chatted with a Greek sailor turned waiter, now married and settled in America. Here, as everywhere, in evidence the wealth of America – the women with their pearls, their jewellery, furs, minks, clothes always new and chic. Across from me at lunch sat two old ladies with their mink stoles, their pearls, pince-nez waggling to and fro, settling down to their artichokes. I went off to feed the squirrels in the Square with a nice French roll. Not a bit of it! The squirrels were too well fed to eat bread: they turned up their noses: not one took a bite.

* America has experienced a great deception since then.

After lunch I went back along the Main Line to Devon, where I was met by Boies Penrose – a Wyndham kind of man:[1] eighteenth-century appearance, large Penrose nose through which he snuffled at intervals like a strangulated walrus. Here was a congenial scholar-gentleman, bookish, collector, good tastes, essentially a bachelor – how much more congenial. For the first time in all those months I found myself in a country house: full of books, fine furniture, pictures and china – all as should be.

But how American is this? Boies Penrose for many years lived half the year in England; he is more than half English in habits, outlook, tastes. Arrived at his house, set in a little snow-covered park, we sat down to tea: exquisite china tea, muffins in silver dish – all as it should be.

His wife was in bed with a heavy cold. For the evening's entertainment he took me off to a session of an extraordinary club – a revelation of upper-class American life I wouldn't have missed. For a century now an exclusive club – men of the best Philadelphia families – perhaps not more than fifty all told have met every quarter to spend the whole day together, doing their own cooking and washing-up, drinking and playing games in the intimacy of an eighteenth-century house in the country, which they own and run. It was like a weekend of Gaudy and General Meeting at All Souls – except that here a few guests were permitted. It was called the Rabbit Club.

We took off coats and donned aprons with big pockets over shirtsleeves. Big fires were blazing in every room; groups of men in shirtsleeves and aprons sitting in front of them, drinking and chatting cosily. I was introduced all round, then we looked over the pleasant old house, with its mementoes and photographs, rabbits everywhere, in silver, wood, china. The whole place lit by firelight and candle-light. In the big kitchen two or three members were getting forward with the dinner.

We had a good meal: excellent soup, a well-turned chop with vegetables and salad, an orange-ice. It was Boies's and my job to serve coffee: I was so engrossed by the Governor and my neighbours that I forgot. I made up for it by making the speech of the evening – about my day with Winston at Chartwell. It was followed by extraordinary twaddle: hardly anybody had any idea of making a speech; the usual form was to get up and tell a pointless dirty story, at which everybody laughed heartily.

1. i.e. like Wyndham Ketton-Cremer.

Rowse preferred to keep his U.S. and his English journals distinct. These extracts are from the English journals kept from the autumn of 1954 to the autumn of 1956.

Oxford, 6 November 1954

In the middle of the College Gaudy I have taken to bed, not unwell, but just to keep away from the crowd, happy with drink and smoke, atmosphere unbreathable. At the meeting this morning I was re-elected or admitted – I don't much care which, as long as the legal requirements were fulfilled – as Fellow for the fifth time since I was first elected in 1925. *That* was much the greatest event in my life. This morning's ceremony of re-admission didn't move me in any way, so long as I might have another five years in a convenient base from which to carry on my own work. The familiar scene – myself waiting in the smoking-room for the summons, young David Edwards, my King's Canterbury protégé from St Austell wartime, coming out to summon me, my successful rival for the Wardenship asking me to read the formula in friendly spirit, 'You must know it by heart by now.' I read it inaudibly, shook hands, 'Admitto te verum atque plenum socium,' and was rather surprised by quite a warmth of applause – I expected it would be very feeble and desultory. However, I took no notice and went straight to Richard sitting there paralysed in his chair.[1] How differently the years have treated us, since we were the radical junior Fellows, the *enfants terribles* of the Abbé Woodward[2] and Geoffrey Faber, joint Bursars then.

I sat out the Fellowship meeting, attending with one ear, while I studied more carefully the Halliday catalogue with a number of Elizabethan items.

The familiar scene, the familiar ritual. The Report of the Assistant Examiners read out and discussed. Apparently a poor field this year. And so it seems all over the country: the works must have gone wrong about the years 1929–35 and no wonder! Discussion centred on the candidate who had done best, a young man from New College, who was recommended by a majority of the Assistant Examiners, but sabotaged by Berlin in a lightweight, supercilious speech as being crude and vulgar. There was a line-up among this element, supported by the Warden and Leo Butler, who always

1. Victim of multiple sclerosis.
2. E. L. Woodward, nicknamed the Abbé by Richard Pares and G. N. Clark.

operates as his jackal, against the solid historians, Rohan Butler, Gibbs and Jacob.

It seems the young man isn't a Wykehamist or even a gentleman, a grammar-school boy of grit and determination, who had to teach nine months in an elementary school to make enough money to come here, lost his mother in his first year and has yet come through – to do the best in the examination. But not well enough to overcome the faults of taste so fatal to him in the eyes of Isaiah Berlin and John Sparrow, though neither of them has been able to produce a single book of any weight.

Rohan was concerned about it tonight. And I cannot think it right. But then I never take any line nowadays. So long as the institution provides a berth for me to do my work in, I really don't mind.

After the meeting was over I took Richard in his chair back along the pavements of the High, Longwall and Holywell, came back to lunch as far as I could on my own in the Buttery, then to bed, tired with so much entertaining the day before.

This evening an excellent Latin speech by young Morse – very competent, the best Latin speech I have ever heard: I remember this young man similarly snooted at by the same group last year. He is not popular with them, he is so able and impeccable, as clever as they are, but with a cool, sound judgement: he will make a great banker. An excellent dinner, traditional mallard and orange salad.

I went in late, hoping the Latin speech would be over and one could go straight to one's meal. But proceedings were late in beginning – the Warden couldn't find his gown. I stood apart from it all, eyes closed, no friends near. Then made my way to an end seat at high table with only Rohan to have to talk to – pleasurably – whence I could survey the whole scene, viewed once with mingled quizzical observation and pride, now with detachment and faint disdain. There was old Dougie Malcolm, aged eighty, singing the doggerel 'O by the blood of King Edward, it was a – swapping, swa-a-pping mallard.'

[Stokesay Castle, Shropshire] 20 November

My second visit to the hospitable home of Jewell Magnus Allcroft.[1] I am in the same bedroom as before. *Rien n'a changé.* There is the pincushion that was Sally's hoof facing me; and Jewell, looking cross and ill-tempered as a bride, with a dress up to her knees and a long veil – not very perceptive to

1. Wife of Sir Philip Magnus Allcroft, Bart., author of a number of historical biographies under the name Philip Magnus.

hang up *such* a photograph in a guest bedroom. This visit I have only had time to observe new the mustard-coloured, yellow carpet with brown flowers, and the coffee cups with foxes' masks and handles made to look like twigs.

The Salvator Rosa is still in the bathroom; the drawing-room glistening with late Victorian bric-à-brac, red cut-glass vases, innumerable vases on the glass and brass chiffonier that stands where a sideboard should be, under the Chinese mirror looted from the Summer Palace at Peking. My mantelpiece is still cluttered up with those two outsize vases looking like Levantine wine-flagons covered with ivy leaves; again I have not been able to resist arranging the pretty china urns at the ends with the travelling clock in the middle, instead of just off it. And I observe that those terrible udders of lamps hanging over the dressing-table are made of an oily substance like fish scales.

What a genius Jewell's mother must have had to bring all these objects together; and what a combination of piety and tastelessness keeps everything together untouched! When one thinks of their friends' houses – Wyndham's, for example – do they never notice?*

3 December, 12.20 a.m.

Yesterday a full and satisfying day in London. On the way up I revised my 'Nelson' article for *Everybody's*, sitting in close proximity to a fur-coated, froward woman who wanted to make contact – touched me with her furred elbow. I shrank from her touch, but had some difficulty in establishing impersonality. Then I worked.

From noon to two in the eighteenth-century Exhibition, which gave me more pleasure than any show since the French Landscapes. *Then* I was so held by the superb Poussins in the first room that, though I went twice, I never got any further, and hardly any further than the wonderful 'Ashes of Phocion'.

Yesterday I did better, went straight for what I wanted to see: the room with the Fragonard 'Fête at St Cloud' from the Banque de France. What a world of fantasy and sensibility Fragonard inhabited! – the feathery trees, the light clouds and plume of water rising from the fountain. On the right, a stage under the branches of a tree where a man in fancy costume demonstrates his marionettes. A group of figures languish in front, an exquisite parasol out like a round red mushroom. On the left, another stage with an actress declaiming before a backdrop, with red pennon flying above.

* Brinsley Ford refuses to stay there: 'I am an old-fashioned aesthete, and I cannot bear it.'

In the foreground a pretty group at a roulette table; at the back, booths with awnings draped and women buying *lingeries*.

O exquisite world of eighteenth-century sentiment, the fantasy world they inhabited – Fragonard, Watteau, Boucher, Hubert Robert – all to be shattered by the hideous realities of 1789!

I felt at once, as I always do with *French* painting of the seventeenth, eighteenth and nineteenth centuries, that *this* is what I really like – it arouses a response in me which Dutch painting does not. The little room of Fragonards and Chardins I lingered in: the exquisite cool colouring of Chardin: the *cabaretier* down in his cellar, a rose blush upon the solid pitcher, the tomato red of the three pails, the creamy white of the raga-muffin's headdress. One could lick the paint! Or again, the lady dressing up her child at the dressing-table: the little girl, eyes turned to the mirror, very serious about what will become the business of life, the mother with melancholy concentration bending over her.

It was a good empty hour in which to take the pictures in. Late, I dashed down to the restaurant, to share a table with a fine-looking man who had just retired from business, had never been to Burlington House before, was looking forward to doing the things he had been wanting to do. He had been taken by the little Lawrence roundels of the Hamilton children: sentimentalized, over-painted, – one sees where Victorianism in painting came from.

Trenarren, 18 December

A good many things have vanished out of my head since my last entry. But I meant to include an interesting addendum to the Westminster Hall proceedings.[1]

A day or so later, Somervell* was lunching in the Buttery and R. W. Lee asked him if he was present at the ceremony. 'No,' said S. without enthusiasm. 'I didn't go.' And then, thinking that this needed explanation, added, 'I meant to go to the other one – which I had subscribed to. But when I found that it meant standing three-quarters of an hour before it began, I decided better not.'

I have often wondered how the Chamberlainites feel towards Churchill and his government – especially this last year, when it has done so well, with Eden taking the lead in world affairs in the failure of the Americans.

1. In honour of Churchill.

* Lord Somervell was Chamberlain's Attorney-General and a consistent supporter of appeasement.

Rohan Butler has been fascinated by Sam Hoare's book[1] as an expression of the Chamberlainite mentality – an unrepentant Chamberlainite, smug as ever. 'Yes, we four ran the policy: Chamberlain, Simon, Halifax and I' – as if it were something to be proud of. 'Churchill did not want me in his government, nor did I wish to serve under him. Except that I should miss the routine work of a department, I was not sorry to go.' This in 1940 of a man and his government that saved the nation, and only at the last moment from the ruin *they* had brought on it!

Winston knows what [their deserts] are. He said to Isaiah Berlin during the war, 'Much as I like Edward (Halifax) as a man, one thing I will say – his attitude has always been Grovel, Grovel, Grovel: Grovel to the Indians, Grovel to the Germans, Grovel to the Russians.' And later, after Winston had given evidence to help Flandin from imprisonment, 'We do these things differently. There is Edward, wrapped round with every honour the British Empire can offer him.' It must have given Winston a wry pleasure to recommend 'Edward' for the O.M.

With all this in mind I deliberately took the opportunity of Lee's question to Somervell to find out what I had been longing to know.

'Oh, I listened,' I said, 'with fascination. I kept thinking, Goodness! this must make the Chamberlainites turn in their graves.'

Somervell reacted at once, emotionally, hotly. 'It didn't make *me* turn in my grave,' he said.

Now, in the old days, before his stroke, he would have been more careful to be as smooth as smooth.

Delighted to learn what I wanted in one go, I went on:

'But Sam Hoare?'

'Oh, I expect he listened in all right.'

But Somervell, hot in the face, went on:

'If there is one man who ought to be ashamed, it is Churchill.'

I think we were all astonished at this outburst and at a loss to know what Churchill, of all people, has to be ashamed of.

Somervell explained.

'In all the books he has written, never once does he give any credit to people who made the way for him – Swinton,[2] for example.'

This was all that I could have hoped for. Delighted to discover what they still feel – after all *we* had to put up with at their hands – I thought it best to appease a little. So I said conciliatorily –

1. *Nine Troubled Years*, a volume of memoirs covering 1931–1940.

2. As Sir Philip Cunliffe-Lister he overcame fierce Cabinet opposition to the building of the Spitfire and the Hurricane, indispensable to victory in the Battle of Britain.

'I don't know about the subject, but I've always understood that Winston *was* rather unfair to Wavell.'

'Yes, a thoroughly *mean* man,' said Somervell, with real hatred in his voice.

'So *that* is what they really think – still,' I registered, surprised at the extent of the feeling. And when they were so wrong! . . . Somervell was a minor member of the gang, but he was the smoothest of the lot! He thought Munich 'a miracle of timing'.

Richard Pares added a coda to this when I told him the story. He said how terrible the feeling was in the Civil Service at the beginning of the war, before Winston took over. There was a hopeless feeling; the papers went round and round; nobody had any conviction that the war could be won. When Winston took over, after a few months the spirit began to change: he somehow managed to convey the feeling that the war could be won. It was just like Chatham:[1] no-one can put his finger on precisely what it was that Chatham did; but he contrived to give a wholly different spirit to things, so that the war was won.

I am reporting Richard, with his slant on it: his curious psychological inhibition about dynamic characters in history, his (to me wrong) insistence that they in fact do nothing very much. The explanation lies in his reaction from Sir Bernard, who was so troublesome to him all through life. I have often wondered whether Richard's terrible sclerosis may have a psychological origin:* the constant struggle between his parents, so that when Richard was only a child his parents would often refuse to communicate except through him. The effect was to make him think that all adults were utter zanies. It certainly has had a lot to do with – what irritates me in his attitude to history – the determination to write down the brilliant, the coloured, the scintillating, and write up the dreary, the nondescript, the – Richard's own favourite word – *dim*. He detests Chatham; he has a real fondness for Newcastle, 'the *dear* Duke'.

My visit to Hughenden the other day made Dizzy all the more attractive to me: the fantasy, the taste – plumb in the Victorian age. And when one thinks of the courage, the entertainment value, the amusing things he said and wrote; I love his 'cynicism', the twist he gave to his sceptical view of life, the corrective to his own romanticism. When one thinks of the loneliness of his struggle, and the splendid show he put up, an alien and a Jew, for this country: what a tribute to the country no less than to Dizzy! I had brought

1. ALR here alludes to the electrifying effect of the older Pitt in the Seven Years War.

* But no: it is, like haemophilia, transmitted through the female to the male.

Richard round to the smoking-room for coffee; we stayed there talking to Isaiah, who knows what I think about Dizzy, though I said merely that I liked him. Richard, himself the sweetest nature: 'Oh, no, I can't bear him. He gives me goose-flesh all over, to read him solemnly writing to his sister how many Duchesses he dined with last night.'*

Now, isn't that unimaginative? To Dizzy, so much an outsider, it was romance, all part of the fantasy-world he was entering into, without belonging to it. Yet he was not taken in by it; it meant not all that much to him; he was perfectly aware of the situation.

It irritated me to hear such nonsense – middle-class inferiority complex.** But I didn't say a word, with Richard in his dreadful condition.

I wonder if Isaiah understood – I would never have made such a reflection on Dizzy in his presence. Actually Isaiah urged in pressing Richard's re-election, that he was 'the brightest jewel in our academic crown'.

A silly phrase . . . like Isaiah's commending Virginia Woolf's *A Writer's Journal* as a brilliant *creative* work: not a creative work at all.

Yet it is Isaiah whom the fashionables of the intellectual world regard as the cat's whiskers.***

27 January 1955

A quiet hour in the foyer of the Paddington Hotel, waiting for the 9.50 back to Oxford after a rackety couple of days away. I am straight from the party in honour of Veronica's new book[1] given by Bill Collins at St James's Place[2] – little unspoiled Caroline corner of London, narrow street of eighteenth- and seventeenth-century houses, the height of fashion in the time of the later Stuarts. Such a pretty house – though the panelling has been peeled in every room: it would be so much prettier painted.

I arrived early, hoping to leave in time for the 7.30. There was dear Veronica very chic in black, with a red, red rose – hair greying, like all of us as we become well known. (I knew her, taught her, as a girl.) Few there at first, so I had some chat with her – she is well into the middle of her second volume on the Civil War. Then the pretty room began to fill and there was a whirl of talk and I found myself – so unlike old shy, self-conscious days – with never a moment. I took my chance to talk to agreeable Jack Plumb, who is editing the Trevelyan volume in which my Roscarrock essay is

* It might be me – or Swift.

** Not at all David Cecil's attitude to Disraeli.

*** Now an O.M.! And what has he written?

1. *The King's Peace*, an account of the years leading up to the Civil War, 1637–1641.

2. From 1944 to 1980 the offices of Collins were at 14 St James's Place.

appearing. Feiling* came up to grasp my hand: I didn't get up from the sofa with Plumb. Talk with Elizabeth Bowen, looking magnificent as ever: she has finished her new novel and will be in America at the end of the year. We may meet; but there she'll be a big noise and I a feeble one or no noise at all. We laughed over my visit to her and the episode of all those hats; she remembered me going out to walk alone in the dark: it *was* melancholy and a bit eerie, mountains in the distance and clouds of rooks coming home to roost in the park. I'd have them much reduced in number – eating all the corn! Elizabeth regarded them with favour as a feature of the place. Now she is writing a short story about them. I at last invited her to Cornwall – a great risk: I have never aspired to such heights as to entertain a lady before. It might give her an inspiration, would be completely new territory for her.

Dear old Sir Ralph Wedgwood[1] was waiting in the background: I made my way across and we reminisced about my early teaching of Veronica. He was very proud: the bond between her and her father has always been close. Not so with her mother. There has always been tension there. In early days when I dined once or twice at the big expensive house on Campden Hill, and Lady W. regarded me as a possible candidate for her daughter, the mother with her beautifully dyed gold hair looked no older than the daughter. She frightened me then: sophisticated and insinuating, restless and uncertain, with unsatisfied literary ambitions. She was kind to put up with me, ill, haggard and unpromising as I was; for she cannot have approved of me, working-class and a Leftist. For a conventional and a snobbish woman she treated me very well. But I was never at ease with her. She must have been attracted to me, to put up with me as she did; and Sir Ralph must have liked me always. Secretly I always nursed a trump-card with Lady W.: she thought I was *after* her daughter, a good catch for an indigent young don; in fact I wasn't, though I thought of it and was fond of Veronica. If I hadn't been so ill something might have come of it. (For anything to have come of it, I should have been caught then. Any later, too late.)

Tonight Lady W. seemed touched to see me – summoned me by a message; when I got to her, I realized that I was *very* pleased to see *her*, after all the years. Her hair is now blue, and though she refuses to become an old woman, she is sweeter and less on edge. She was quite affectionate with me, and I with her: I kissed her hand and held her fur cape, made up to her a little to make up to her for not being what I was meant by her to be: her son-in-law, a member of *her* family. I promised I *would* this year go and see them at Leith Hill Place: I have promised before.**

* Keith Feiling, historian, my old tutor at Christ Church.

1. Retired Managing Director of the L.N.E.R.

** But never went to their grand house there.

Perhaps, after all, Veronica – a subterranean nature (needs must, from her difficult relations with her mother) has always been less keen, though fond of me, than her mother? I didn't say too much about Veronica, for I sensed the old jealousy: her mother's ambition was to shine as a literary figure herself. It is Veronica who has achieved it. Mothers are much less prepared to be satisfied vicariously in their daughters, than fathers are in their sons.

To resume the party. When I arrived, there were the brothers Mathew, whom I should be entertaining at dinner tonight, instead of wallowing in bed. There was Mark Bonham Carter on the hearth-rug, pale, supercilious and princely: Princess Margaret's friend, he must have found this small beer – he was to dine later at the P.M.'s farewell dinner to the little girl off to the West Indies. Mark is very handsome, but there is a certain meanness about his face; nobody seems to like him, Jack detests him – but no doubt that's unfair.

I had a flirtatious time with Rose Macaulay, noticeably aged, drier than ever, but good fun. She always flirts with me and I with her, laughing with her more than with anyone – teasing each other with our religious position, which we found to be the same: High Church unbelief. I said it was enough to make the Macaulays turn in their graves: she should be an Evangelical unbeliever.

A gross red-faced youngish man, with a red buttonhole as red as his face and a pretty wife, came up and took possession of me. He had had too much to drink. I was assumed to know him, but couldn't think who he was. I did my duty by his wife. (Can he have been one of the Collinses? Or a member of the firm?) – And I was snubbed by a good-looking *young* man, whom I have met here (a boy-friend of the Warden's: could it be Simon Raven?).

Milton Waldman[1] turned up – to my surprise, considering his breach with the firm of Collins and his going over to Rupert Hart-Davis. He was pleasant as ever, looking a bit more puffed and dropsical and, I thought, drinkier. (All these people drink too much.) He brought up Peggy to talk to me, looking completely Italian, all in black and with her hair-do – and pressing me to come and stay with them in their Italian villa. But I have never said I would: I don't know them well enough, and I don't like staying with people much.

There was a rumour that Collins's star as a bestseller – Arthur Bryant might not be able to come: he had been bitten on the nose by his beloved Jimmy. When one thinks of all the fuss Arthur makes about that dog, it was

1. The most brilliant publisher's editor of his day and author of two notable Tudor biographies.

only poetic justice. Neither Arthur nor Anne can ever go away for a holiday, because Jimmy doesn't like it. I have never liked that dog, with his habit of scrambling forward to sit on one's lap in the car, sitting bolt upright so that one can't see a thing, digging his sharp talons into one, vibrant with yapping and barking.

Arthur arrived and at once attached himself to Lord and Lady Hesketh. I gave him some time with them and then went up to say a word. His nose was a perfect pickle, all bloody. I didn't say a thing, for he knows my sentiments about Jimmy. Arthur was at once over-grateful for my boost of his book in the Reprint Society paper – 'the finest review I have ever had,' etc. He may have seen me wilt a little, for he couldn't think of anything else to say. Nor could I. I ought to have congratulated him on his knighthood, but I had already done that. He introduced me, somewhat reluctantly, to Lord Hesketh: whom I took away from him.

A comic young peer: fat and florid, with such an expanse of old-fashioned waistcoat – dressed to look like a peer. And talked like a caricature of one. Was he nervous among all these intellectuals? We talked about his house, Easton Neston, and Hawksmoor and All Souls; we invited each other to pay visits. Then his wife came up, whom Gervase Mathew brought over one day to see my rooms. Looking more beautiful and wide-eyed than ever: a gold coat matching her gold hair, a Georgian necklace of strung cameos and, within the coat, very *décolletée*. Again I caught a look in those eyes, which give the impression of being golden too. With such an exquisite piece for a wife, the young man oughtn't to let himself get so gross. She and I looked at each other. She was taking her leave, and collecting him like a piece of the furniture, she took him off.*

I had come on to the party from an afternoon in his suite at the Savoy with Leonard Brockington of Toronto, friend of Lionel Curtis, of the Astors, of John Buchan – an elderly, ginger and grey-haired, hump-backed Welshman with glistening spectacles and all the generosity (and slight unreliability, I suspect) of his race. Anyway, he is good-hearted, vain, intelligent, a marvellous raconteur and giver of good meals.

He shows signs of being very good to me. When he came over for the Coronation, he slipped in his bath here at Oxford and sprained a ligament. I looked after him, got him a doctor (with difficulty, for it was Whitmonday, and he was as frightened as a child) and got him into the Wingfield hospital. Problem: how could he report the Coronation? I volunteered to do it for him, since I was already doing it for the *W.M.N.*[1] So Brockington on the

* Kisty became a great friend – she was taking care of Freddie then.

1. *Western Morning News*.

day sat in his suite in the Savoy, broadcasting to Canada, while H. M. Tomlinson described the London streets and I the scene inside the Abbey. What an evening that was – dashing straight from Westminster to Fleet Street, sitting on my arse three hours and a half (after seven hours on it in the Abbey) writing direct home to the West Country, having a pot of tea and going on with the article for Canada till eleven. Then off to the Savoy with it.

Brockington was just finishing lunch, with the Dean of St Paul's and the Commissioner of Metropolitan Police, Nott-Bower, head of Scotland Yard. A good-looking, neat, clean-cut man, who showed me proudly the photographs of half a century ago, himself and three brothers as boys, policemen in *The Pirates of Penzance*. I sat on with Brockington, whose mind is an inexhaustible ragbag of reminiscences, quotations, stories, verses, jokes – a prodigy of a memory.

Another, exceedingly nice man came in – Sir Patrick Duff? was it? I couldn't place him, unless in the colonies. Then arrived a Mr Pemberton, handsome son of the Edwardian bestseller, Sir Max: descended from a doctor of Marie Antoinette's, who managed to escape the guillotine because he had some talent or other useful to Danton and Marat.

I had come on that morning from Bristol and gone straight to the show of English secular church plate at Christie's: homework in a way, for I always keep my eye on whatever is grist for my Elizabethan book. There were lovely things – chiefly the medieval cups. It pleased me that several beautiful things had come from Cornwall. What treasures there are still in England – to think of these things in obscure country parishes: we really oughtn't to grudge things going to America.

Outside in the sale-rooms furniture was fetching the usual high prices. Oddly enough, the furniture was Lady D'Abernon's, Cyril Falls's[1] sister or so, for whom he is (proudly) a trustee. I fancied a nice sofa-table: went for £95. A pair of dilapidated gilt eagle tables by Kent fetched 480 guineas. *À propos* of this a pansy young gentleman cottoned on to me and talked: I fenced and kept him at arm's length, until, with a sudden observation about a picture, gave myself away. He went off.

A good lunch at Martinez off Regent Street, then to the Lansdowne pictures at Agnew's. A dull lot, except for an exquisitely coloured Bronzino of a Medici boy – rose coloured curtain, nut-brown cropped hair, perfect modelling: the picture had belonged to William Beckford – of course, and no wonder! None of the pictures excited me much, though there was a

1. ALR's colleague at All Souls, as Professor of Military History.

splendid Mabuse of a young banker, and a magnificent sombre portrait of a Spanish cleric by Murillo – shows what a fine painter he was when he got away from the sentimentality of all those starry, milky Immaculadas.

The most interesting portrait for its associations was that of Horace Walpole. (It ought to be at Farmington, Conn.) Such a clever face, pointed and faun-like, with luminous brown eyes, lively, so intelligent and really rather kindly. Horace was wearing his own sparse brown hair, and a velvet suit of a colour that betrayed the aesthete – I suppose, murrey, too lavender-blue for mulberry. What excited cupidity more than the Lansdowne pictures were a couple of eighteenth-century moonlight paintings (in original frames) by T. Hastings. Never heard of him, but most charming – like a Wilson or a Vernet. An early nineteenth-century French coast scene that might have been a Bonington, if it had been a bit more luscious with the paint: a Bright. Never heard of *him*.*

If I were rich, I should go bust on pictures.

Cyril Connolly's profound thought for the week in last *Sunday*'s *Times*: 'the inevitable unpopularity of the true artist'. Like Shakespeare, I suppose, or Dante, or Goethe; or Dickens or Tennyson – or almost anyone one can think of. This week's thought: 'But sincerity? What is it? Are human beings more themselves when they are lying or when they are telling the truth?' Connolly is 'modern' all right: the basis of his appeal. As if being 'more themselves' were any criterion – apply it to criminals or lunatics, or the simply stupid, and one sees how fallacious that is. For the confusion of truth and lying, sincerity and insincerity, honesty and treachery, see *The Unquiet Grave*, that guide and companion to the pretentiously astray.

Truth, sincerity and honesty are essentially direct and simple matters; no amount of meretricious glamour confuses their essence.

This was *à propos* of Maclean and Burgess. Naturally these simple distinctions are not very clear to one who wrote the disloyal exposure of his friends for the Kemsley Press, to work his passage.

Sunday, 6 February

The bells have continued to rain away time: it is a week later. Hubris betrayed me: next day, after that long entry, I was much worse and continued ill several days: fever and an irritable scarlet rash all over me. I thought scarlet fever, but apparently conjunction of flu with food poisoning – that stuffed pimento out of a tin at Martinez, off Regent Street, would account

* Henry Bright. I now own one. 1973. Now two, 1990.

for it. Oddly enough, I had presentiments at the time; for my own fresh-complexioned, clean-faced waiter was seconded by an ill-favoured, unshaven baboon off the Rock of Gibraltar, who made me shudder to have anything.

Today I am better, after a whole week in bed – not for a long time have I had so long. The first days, too ill to do anything much, and worst of all was the way my mind *raced* at night. I wondered if it wasn't a bit the price I pay for incessant work, my mind always on the stretch; or just fever. The next days I managed a good many letters and a fair amount of reading: the sad and beautiful private Memoir of Michael McKenna, who so loved Menabilly in the years of the first war – cousin of Martin Mclaren, who turned up at Trenarren on New Year's Day and with whom I went up to the foot of Roche Rock in the howling gale on New Year's Night, afterwards dining in the snug cabin of the Victoria Inn, anchored out there on the heaving ocean of Goss Moor.

Read Sprigge's *Anglia Rediviva*, and Martyn Skinner's new long poem, 'The Return of Arthur' – for which C. S. Lewis and I have joint responsibility; for I said, 'Write an Arthurian poem' and C.S.L. said, 'Write about the *Return* of Arthur.' It is a strange work: visibly influenced by *1984*, but with its own flavour, rustic, wry, stoical, earthy, occasionally flower-scented, also musty with books. I couldn't but admire Martyn's spare, spry figure and the life-battle he has put up at Ipsden; nor fail to see, behind the pages, that exquisite summer morning – his garden full of roses, the hay cocked in the slope above it – when we went to bury his clever boy in the churchyard on the hill above.

One day I read Clara Vyvyan's new book about walking the length of the Rhône. I can't see that the book isn't as good as *Travels with a Donkey*. Her Cornish girl-friends come very well out of it: Daphne du Maurier, spirited and mettlesome; Oenone Johnson, very feminine and fragile-seeming, blown along like a leaf, yet daunted by nothing. It's the *spirit* of these two very feminine ones I fell for. (– If I had been exposed to girls like this when younger, I'd have fallen.) I knew before that Foy and Clara were staunch. Excellent book, full of knowledge of flowers, plants, birds I wish I had.

Clara has been going through trouble: handed the estate and beautiful Trelowarren over to the next young Vyvyan, who within eighteen months sold the furniture, the pictures, the library. – As if there were not enough devastation that is unavoidable, without adding to it weakly and irresponsibly.

Today I've read an eighteenth-century Diary, of Sylas Neville: of just such a misfit who might do such a thing. Who did nothing all his life long –

cultivated, talented as he was up to a point – but get through money, live on other people's, beget several bastards, fill several volumes with Republican cant and moralizing censoriousness about the enjoyments of others. Also I've been getting forward with the Churchills: read old Atkinson's *Marlborough and the Rise of the British Army*, very sound and lucid, and full of good ideas.

This morning Dougie Malcolm very kindly came to see me. Told me the pleasant story of the young man up with him who 'wasn't very economical', to whom an uncle left £5,000. 'This will keep the wolf from the door,' said a friend. 'It's done nothing but bring the wolves *to* the bloody door,' said the young man.

Then came Lady Evelyn,[1] very expensively dressed: coat of black astrakhan, bright red suit underneath of a Paris make, red spectacles to match. I believe Dougie, who always *was* of an economical turn himself, met more than his match in Lady Evelyn, with her passion for buying expensive Chinese *objets d'art*, getting earlier and more costly until – as Dougie sighed – they look just like something that has come out of Woolworth's.

14 February

My first trip out of Oxford since my illness. I was much looking forward to a change, though I found it hard to tear myself away from 'The Churchills' – the new book I have begun the moment I am better. My second day up I wrote 3,000 words, the next 2,000 and finished the first chapter. This week I want to write the second.

The car gave great difficulty: never such an unattractive journey. The Manciple had difficulty in starting her, suggested I took her to the garage before setting out. There in cold and boredom I waited three-quarters of an hour, while all the plugs were blown. I naturally thought all would then be well. Not a bit of it. I could hardly get up Holywell, stopping all the way, in second gear. I thought she would warm up. She did later, sufficiently to enable me to get up to 55 m.p.h. along the Bicester by-pass, where I usually do 70. Before half-way was reached I was in trouble. She fell down to 30 and even 20, would only go at all with the choke full out or in third or second gear. I had difficulty in getting up even the gentle hills of Bucks and Beds. Once I came to a sharp, hump-backed railway bridge, which I might have got over going at my regular pace. Of course there was a bloody lorry going at 10 m.p.h., which slowed me up so that I could not get over and

1. Malcolm's wife, daughter of the Earl of Donoughmore.

stopped short of the top. I started up four or five times, each time making a couple of feet until I was over.

The drive was hell, the dangerous skiddy character of the iced-up roads the least of my troubles. However, no question of giving up unless she stopped outright; when I put the accelerator down, she did. Driving skilfully, coaxing her along, choke out, sometimes in third, sometimes in fourth, with the accelerator in what I discovered to be the optimum position, I kept her going; and on the level roads of Cambridge, picked up to 40 and 50 m.p.h.

13 February

The taxi slushed across snowy Cambridge to a road behind the Library, to an Edwardian neo-Georgian house. G.M.T.[1] came to the door, looking an old man at last, after so many years of healthy walks keeping him fit and young. He was quite white and hadn't shaved well for days – a Victorian outcrop of white hair on his jaw and round his neck, adding to the distinction of his appearance. He was warm and welcoming, lithe and energetic as ever.

I had never met his wife – Janet Penrose Ward, Mrs Humphry Ward's daughter – and had derived an incorrect picture of a high and dry blue-stocking. Now, an invalid stricken with paralysis, she made quite a different impression, gay, very lively and intelligent, ready to giggle and chaff G.M.T. Over the chimneypiece was Will Arnold Forster's admirable portrait of her – 'The woman you married, George' – a luminous atmosphere of sunlight filtered through the sunshade under which she was sitting. One saw the whole cultivated circle, Cambridge of the early 1900s, superior and secure, given to high thoughts and good causes: Trevelyans, Arnold-Forsters, Penroses; Darwins, Sidgwicks, Keyneses, Marshalls, Butlers.

Lunch was very gay – Janet P. prepared to be amused and be flirted with. G.M.T. was in a good humour, helping us to large helpings of a plain lunch. Two nurses were in attendance, his wife being practically helpless. What an expense it all must be! He didn't know whether he would be able to keep Hallington. He goes there for four months in the summer – the same arrangement as I with Trenarren. After lunch he took me sharply away from Janet, for fear of exhausting her. She had had about enough excitement – I certainly had amused and pleased her. 'As brilliant as ever' – said G.M.T.: I remembered that with the older Cambridge, the word 'brilliant' has a questionable note. No-one could accuse G.M.T. of being 'brilliant': absolutely solid, big-minded sense, plumb right judgement, plus imagination and poetry, rather than sensibility or subtlety.

1. G. M. Trevelyan.

We talked in his study, history and politics, present and past. It must have been after Winston's H-bomb speech. Trevelyan hates the modern world – more completely and consistently than any of us; for he hates modern science and the world it has made. Rather piquant, for one who was the Master of the most distinguished scientific college in the world. I said that all these horrors sprang out of Cambridge and the Cavendish Laboratory, where they had split the atom. 'Yes,' said G.M. 'There are Rutherford and J.J.* buried in Westminster Abbey; when the atomic ash rains down on London, they will be well and truly buried under it.'

I said a word for science as the characteristic and most important development of rational thought in the past three centuries. 'But I don't like the world it has made – the world of the Industrial Revolution, with industrial development all over the country and all that has come with it.' I suddenly saw that G.M.T. is really an eighteenth-century figure: I hadn't thought of him as that; he would like to go back behind the whole development of modern industry to a world of coaches and carriages, smallpox and typhoid, a world of farms, villages and estates, of squires, farmers, labourers. He saw himself as a country squire in a stable country world. But he must have gone back into that from the nineteenth-century Liberal, or rather, Radical he was in his younger years.

Thence to history. What he had to say about Elizabethan Ireland sounded to me old-fashioned, coloured by the sentimental pro-Irish view of the Gladstonian Liberals. *There* his views hadn't kept pace with the rest. His whole attitude to history springs from the *general* point of view of a member of the old governing class, whose judgements came from proximity to government rather than from the specialist outlook of the historian. Therein lies its advantage, though creaking a bit.

At the end, when I asked if he was writing anything, he said sadly, 'No, I'm too old to write any more.' He had what will be, I suppose, his last book lying out before him, *A Layman's Love of Letters*. There was something touching about the scene.

As I walked away over the Cambridge snow I registered: 'Work while it is yet day, for the night cometh in which no man can work.'

Clapper Bridge, 31 March

On my way to lunch at Newton Ferrers – one of those places I longed for so long to penetrate, where I might *penetrate* all too easily nowadays.

The moment before belated Spring: sun gleaming on hollies and the river

* J. J. Thomson, scientist, Master of Trinity.

Lynher; woods purplish, about to burst into bud; ploughed slopes. Coming down the hill, in winter-bareness, I caught sight of the house that presides over this haunted valley – for the first time. It is country of the Grand Meaulnes, and has this in common with that: that though I have been here several times before, I can never be sure of finding my way. I am always foxed by the roads, it is so unfindable.

When first I came here with Gerald Berners, at the end of the war, I followed the map, which ended just where Newton Ferrers was. So we went all round the back of it; Gerald, who was in a state of acute melancholia, was sure we were lost. I got out to ask a man keeping cows, who answered me in an East European accent, that he didn't know. We were within two miles of it. Other times I have struck other roads, impossible ones: narrow lanes with corkscrew bends. And even today, on a sixth or seventh visit, I went a bit wrong at the top.

Here is a magic spot, now too well known to people, I fear. I have driven the car on to the tongue of land between the two streams, between the two old-world bridges, that will shortly be crowded with Morrises, Austins, motor-bikes, bicycles, girls in shorts, boys in shorts, an ice-cream stall.

So busy and hard at work these past six weeks that not one moment to record even the more amusing part of my doings. – (At night.)

It was a beautiful day at Newton – up that long drive through the enchanted, quite empty valley, where Bertie Abdy has planted cherry trees along the edge. Higher up, there were the series of pools, with *jets d'eaux* being drained and cleaned for their summer operations. The house, as always, gives one the feeling of melancholy, unhappy beauty. Once inside, Diane's gay salon was cheerful, filled with Spring sunshine. I was late, and was let in by Diane at the side-door in a leopard-skin coat and with a hug. The assembly consisted of Daphne Vivian-Bath-Fielding[1] ('From Marchioness to Mrs'), looking younger than ever I have seen her: a gipsy-like appearance given by her round red hat and her flower-like earrings. Her husband swarthy, masculine, sharp – the glint of the adventurer in his eye. Two strangers: Prince Chula of Siam, who lives at Tredethy, and his English wife. She a friendly, competent, middle-class girl, who has got him and is holding on to him.* Bertie was absent.

I was to be host and sit at head of table. O, the colours of the carpet in that room! dark honey-brown, lemon gold, magenta; the gold china, the coffee-cups; the glints of gold against sage-green. Daphne was eager, full of

1. i.e. wife successively to the Marquess of Bath and to Xan Fielding.

* They became my friends. Younger than I, alas both dead. 1973.

life, a great dear, as ever, evidently enjoying life with Xan – the Barbary coast, where they have been ploughing the sand in their Land-Rover, and bought a house in Tangier, *as an investment.* The middle-class Princess was a trifle dull, no *soufflet*, but – with all that money – had seen a great deal of the world. The Prince handed round his Fabergé cigarette case, given him by his father, with the crown 'so well placed on it'. Part Russian, he was more like a recent Balkan royalty.

After they had all gone, I stayed on with Diane alone to talk about Valentine [her son]. We walked down those marvellous terraces, to the grey stone piers that open upon the gorge. The slope was golden with daffodils. We sat and talked looking down on it; Diane told me how they had come upon it twenty years ago, and what difficulty they had in finding it, as everybody has. When they saw it, it had been empty for three years; every room had a bees' nest, and there were billiard tables about. Diane saw what could be made of it, and persuaded Bertie, who was averse and wanted beautiful architecture: something bigger and grander, with pillars. (He ought to have had Carclew.)

And what an exotic thing they *have* made of it. A whole train-load of French furniture came over from their house in Paris. Bertie's library reproduces a Louis Philippe interior, heavy red and green velvet tablecloths with bobbles; the finest of Hubert Roberts on the staircase, eighteenth-century French furniture everywhere; the salon hung with Winterhalters and Boldinis. Outside, Bertie has scooped out one valley to make a series of descending pools with fountains. The green court at the back has a tank of water with a fat woman by Rodin; the forecourt a Henry Moore torso, empty like a shirt (or a chemise, for it is a female).

I wouldn't have any of it. I quite understand what straightforward conventional Cynthia Carew-Pole said to me last week: 'They have spoiled it. It had such a wonderful atmosphere. Now, it gives the feeling of such an unhappy house.'

I was quite surprised by Rohan Butler saying, on coming back from a Princess Bibesco evening there, that he *much* preferred my house. The truth is that Newton Ferrers has been so Frenchified: one sees the old rustic Cornish house, mottled grey and green, humiliated underneath the sophistication. Why couldn't they have let it alone to be itself? I'd have the sound of the running stream down that valley, not the *petites eaux de Versailles.* The interior would remain just an old Cornish house, with portraits and plenty of books on the walls, the panelling restored. In fact, I'd have it as it was meant to be; as it is, it has been dolled up and deformed, for all their sense of beauty.

The house has always been unhappy. There is some story of a murder, of blood on the floor. Actually, I am the only person who knows the true story of parricide attached to it: the young Coryton who killed his father, with a pitchfork in the stable yard, because his father obstructed his love for a girl of a station below them. Somewhere, I have got all the documents, and the touching way it was transmitted, through a priest in prison in the Tower, a generation after, who had heard the young man's confession.

I have always meant to write it up. I doubt if I could now. One disadvantage from penetration.

When Diane and I got back to the house, there were Daphne and Xan back – Daphne had left her coat behind. It was an amusing situation; for, not a doubt of it, she had come back to see how Diane and I were getting on. Daphne and I had a very hilarious five minutes, while Xan recovered the coat. But dear Daphne, with her zest for life and her insatiable interest in human beings, was defeated. And probably baffled as well. She does not understand the relation in which Diane and I stand: two disillusioned beings,* who prefer solitude to the society of our fellow-creatures, for whom there is no point in approximating, or likelihood of it. (Quite apart from other considerations – no intention of providing Bertie with a co-respondent for a divorce.)

Easter Tuesday

An exceptional, odd, not unhappy Easter, for I have had George,[1] his two children and his intelligent little mongrel for the weekend. I hadn't intended all this: I had asked him to give him a change, thinking that the children might go with their aunt, and stay with Beryl[2] later at the cottage. As it turned out, I had the whole lot. He was pathetically pleased over the telephone at Beryl deciding we could have them all. I said I would collect them at St Dennis. 'Lovely chap,' he said at the other end of that grim telephone I used to hate to hear: the three pennies dropping, Mrs 'Tippett' on the line worrying me about my mother, news of her getting worse – never anything good where she was concerned. I said Beryl was ready to have them all three: 'Good Beryl,' he said, clearly touched.

So I went out for them, through the squalid china-clay area that was so faithful to me,[3] so raw and ugly I can't bear it. A beautiful evening, like those early autumn evenings last year when I used to go out to see my mother. I passed the house where she died and where I broke down when I

* No: Diane wanted me. See later.

1. ALR's brother.

2. ALR's housekeeper.

3. In the days of his Labour candidacy.

first saw her there. I said nothing to myself, but put on a little speed to pass it. There was the chapel where she could listen to the singing across the road and the place where I used to turn the car with such difficulty. Oh, the simplicity, the heart-ache of it all!

Now I was on a similar mission, which I had put off thinking about till the last moment.

In the narrow corkscrew village street there was my brother waiting for me, looking odd man out, nondescript, as always: old shabby trilby, raincoat and – in deference to me, who never wears them – shabby gloves! We said hardly a word, the situation too difficult on both sides. Anyhow, I had to attend to my driving: china-clay village, the females walking all over the street, don't get out of the way as in a town. Up to a Council houses settlement, which I have often enough written to this last year, sending books, papers to read, money for Christmas and for his wife's funeral.

Here was the house, the children – her children – all packed and waiting and, more than I had bargained for, a dog: poor little creature, a stray, intelligent and well trained, afraid he was going to be left behind. I didn't go in: the house the usual working man's dwelling, furniture, curtains, linoleum – the woman gone. It was all too much. We loaded up and set off, and arrived at Trenarren, the magic valley, the rhododendrons coming out, crimson, magenta, white and cream.

All went better than I could have expected: the children old enough to be sensible; Elizabeth, only thirteen, tall enough for a girl of sixteen and very helpful. The younger one, devoted to her father, a curious child – a Vanson,[1] shut up in herself, independent, self-sufficient, silent. The little dog, 'Gyp', was very good and obedient. My brother had taken him, not wanting him, because a fellow-workman, who was going to sea, wanted him to take the poor creature or else he would be 'thrown in a pool' – the usual way with these china-clay workers and their animals. 'I don't want 'ee to do that,' said George. Just like his father. Under the rough, masculine exterior, more sentimental than the feminine side of the family to which I belong.

The only person who detested the weekend was Peter, who was thoroughly put out. Sensed the presence of a dog in the house, *heard* the confident scramble of his footsteps up the stairs. On Monday he stayed away in the garden and had no meal until they had all gone and the place was clear.

(At this moment, he is on my lap: difficult to write: he has made me make two blots with my horrid Biro.)

*

1. ALR's mother's family.

Sunday evening, I had to leave them for two or three hours, for the party at Port Eliot – 'a tiny party', consisting of my friends and I *must* come, etc. Lady St G.'s[1] 'tiny' parties must be well known. There was the saloon thrown open, *en suite* with the drawing-room with the early Reynoldses (the Eliots were early patrons, like the Parkers at Saltram). It all looked rather fine, particularly the Red room we came through, with its soft lighting, two shades over big Chinese vases, old rugs and furniture and things that have always belonged. That is what I like – and what makes all the difference between Port Eliot or Saltram or Antony, and a 'made' place with all that wealth can do.

I had a swift drive up, irritated by finding yet one more bitch in the spinney picking primroses – I was so enraged I couldn't remember *who* she was, though I knew her face. Every Easter is rendered vexatious by people who will get over the hedge or unbar the gate and make a dead set at the primroses. It is always the bitches who do it, never a man: this is their idea of loving flowers – destroying them. However, they are all rather taken aback by what they hear from me, before I have finished with them. And this happened to be the wife of a 'friend', or a friend of George's. They were fearfully upset. Apparently she collapsed on getting home. Chased me in their car – but I went on too fast and furious.

It is, of course, 'a thing' with me: I hate it more as one more indication of human idiocy – that they *will*, *must*, destroy the flowers. Not if I can stop them! Most of the way to St Germans, I kept thinking what a mistake it is to know working people. No-one of a decent class would do such a thing – all the less since these were people I know. It's their stupidity I hate.

It is all part of my complex about human beings, that gets on my nerves – and, I fear, may sap my creative power as a writer, since I hate them too much to write about them living – I can only write about them dead.

I arrived first and was last to go – I wanted to have a word with Lady St Germain l'Auxerrois, whom I hadn't seen for a long time. The house-party was arrayed in front of the fire: Betty Somerset, beautiful, so sensitive. She had something good to say – as usual about her husband, who was arriving by boat up the river. I said did he ever land? She said he sometimes put a foot ashore, only to withdraw it. Cynthia Carew-Pole said he was only happy on the water.

There was Monty, looking taller, more peaked and blue-nosed than ever, not absolutely gaga – had totally forgotten who I was, small blame to him. I got him talking about his Oxford days. His father couldn't afford to send him to the House. So he sat for a scholarship and was given one at Exeter.

1. St Germans.

He gave the impression of not thinking much of that. I expect he has been an old silly most of his life – the brains of the show being Nelly St G. It was very much *her* party, not his.

She must be by nature sociable, expansive – and expensive. She gave about 180 people champagne and smoked salmon sandwiches! It must have cost a pretty penny, and she always cries poor. Really, how can people spend so much? This will be the end, I thought. *Look* while there is yet time.*

Alas, there was no time for looking; I was too much engaged. I moved into the big saloon, where out of the corner of my eye, while talking to John Tremayne, I noticed the portrait of the younger Pitt in the place of honour over the fireplace. Quite right, having married Pitt's sister, he made Edward Eliot a peer – liberal as he was with his peerages.

Easter Wednesday: again difficult to write for Peter the cat on my knee. I wish I could write about him like Colette.

A wasted day: weeding in the garden all the morning, so that I can hardly stand. Afternoon, into the horrid town for haircut and car-wash. I looked in to George Truscott's shop to apologize to Doris T. and him for my bad language on the subject of Bitches in the Spinney. He took it in good part – as surprised at my apologizing as he was at the original offence. Thence to Mrs Peters to bring her down in the car to picnic tea on the terrace in full view of the garden at its best, afterwards piloting her round each room on the ground floor. She can now hardly move, her limbs half paralysed: so it was quite a job.

Too busy before leaving Oxford, and down here since, to record my movements about the country.

Came down early here to present prizes at Torpoint School for Cynthia Carew-Pole – making me break a rule.** An early Spring day: I raced up with my exhaust pipe broken, making as much noise as a helicopter. Lunch *à deux* at Antony; the local cinema packed. Absurd occasion, the local grandees queued up to shake hands, including people from Truro – the Education Secretary, and Norman Lyne (again!) as Chairman.

That weekend a party at Antony for Mr Dupont – more like American royalty than anything I've ever seen: parchment-skinned, irritable old gentleman, interested only in old furniture, china, etc. and flowering shrubs, particularly azaleas. An odd party to meet him. But perhaps as good as

* I was wrong – they were rich.

** i.e. not to speak in Cornwall.

any other. An intelligent elderly General, Howard-Vyse: descended from Howard of Effingham, married to a tenacious, glum sort of woman who could talk about nothing but her *first* husband's relations, the Cokes, and the glories of Holkham. And it transpires, from Wyndham, that she is the nigger in the woodpile there, keeping eyes of a cat on the place – on behalf of her son in South Africa not a bit interested in it – to which he is next male heir. But *she* is. I can see that: a fixation with her: can think of nothing else. Meanwhile, the poor Leicesters have three daughters and can produce no more offspring. Lady H.-V. evidently sees herself as the *châtelaine* of Holkham. She ignored the present occupants, never mentioned their existence. Perhaps they will outlive her. I liked the old guardsman of a General: shrewd, well educated and knew everybody.

From Devon came the Heathcoat-Amorys, present baronet and his wife, Joyce Wethered, the champion golfer. A homely simple woman with a middle-class accent. He an enormous overgrown boy, fists like puddings (and no doubt everything else to match), pretty rich from their factory at Tiverton, does his duty for Blundell's; lives in an outré Burgess house, the more extreme Victorian manifestations of which he has reduced; collects paintings, mildly, sensibly – bought a Bonington, for example.

I suppose Cynthia asked them so that there might be suitable company for John. Actually I fell for them – and they rather for me: at any rate insisted on my calling in on them to or from Oxford. Shall I? I rather think not: dangerous getting to know people: they eat time.* They told me such a strange story of the way their cousin Dick has gone – whom I just knew at the House. Embarrassing law-suits with his in-laws, which he loses: some kink going back to hatred of his father, who was selfish about the boy – wouldn't give up hunting, so sent his son to Berkhamsted instead of Eton. His son mortified and furious. Once threatened to shoot his father, who was afraid of him and gave way. Ruthless, ambitious, vindictive, frightening. What an exciting character! I was much gratified to hear about it all: who'd have thought it of the pale, spectacled youth of thirty years ago? I have often wondered what happened to him.

The last member of the party, intended for me, I did not take to. Sonia Cubitt, daughter of Mrs Keppel – but not, I take it, of Edward VII. Had recently lost her husband. She looked a predatory type with prominent nose; intelligent taste, has a collection of blue-john.

On Sunday we went to tea at Saltram, where Lord Morley kept himself upright – though brain-sodden – for the occasion. One detected the pleasure it gave him to have survived a younger brother, whose funeral he had lately

* I never did, and now regret it. 1973.

attended, to whose son, the next heir, he has no intention of handing over. Instead, he has handed over to the National Trust, with a lot of fine objects – the family cannot make out what.

It must have been an even odder *ménage* when the oldest brother was alive, who couldn't bear seeing people: hence the preservation of the house, not a thing changed. The finest interior in the West Country: splendid Adam saloon and dining-room: I have never seen such a carpet, designed for the room: rich browns, honey colour and rose; blue silk and gilt chairs, early Reynoldses everywhere. Apparently Angelica Kaufmann worked in the house. But Sir Joshua never fell for her. Was there something interesting about Reynolds? No sex-life, sublimated into paint perhaps.

It tickled me to watch Sonia Cubitt making up to the rich, dipsomaniac, bachelor peer. Wouldn't she love to be the Countess of Morley, in spite of everything? It was 'Monty' this and 'Monty' that, and staying behind the party last in the room with the salacious old boy. All to *no* effect, as one could see. *He* had his Betty coming down the next weekend, when they were going to have a party in the saloon lit by candles in those blue-john candelabras. Not for all her taking thought could she add a cubitt to her stature with the absurd Earl.

Beneath the absurdity of the manner, the fuddle and muddle, he was still a shrewd old boy – where they affected his comforts, selfish as a bachelor.

The weekend was very enjoyable, cleverly organized by Cynthia. She enjoys life herself: buxom, fine figure of a woman, eupeptic, good complexion, candid, clear blue eyes; good-humoured, a hard worker. Underneath the low-brow, and in spite of the attitude of high-brows like Diane, Cynthia is an able woman, utterly competent. She has got John harnessed to work: to Antony, the market-gardening, a Guernsey herd, sheep; to the County Council and the county. She is at the back of it all: *she* will be responsible for his being made Lord-Lieutenant, if it comes about.*

On the Saturday she wanted me to join the party that was accompanying Mr Dupont to Caerhays. For a variety of reasons, obscure to myself, I wouldn't go. Chiefly because I never had been – though Mary Williams had asked me. (This was very much my area: *my* constituency that never was.) I don't much like the thought of Charlie Williams, dull man. I fancy he wouldn't much like the thought of me.** I don't know a thing about gardens. No, altogether, better to abstain.

So I worked all day, and only fled up east after tea, before the party had

* It did.

** He was a 100 per cent Chamberlainite, a rabid Appeaser – wouldn't admit Harold Nicolson to the garden, because he wasn't!

got back from Caerhays. Not a thing to be seen: everything a month late. Nothing out.

Oh, the pleasure of that house, with all the things that *belong*: the portraits of Carews and Poles right back to Elizabethan times. Richard Carew in the hall, at foot of the staircase; towards the top, Sir Gawen Carew, black-bearded buccaneer. Would there were one of Sir Peter! Along my corridor, all those eighteenth-century and late seventeenth-century Sir Coplestone Bamfyldes, Mr Ash, Sir Courtenay Pole (who got a *douceur* of £4 or £5,000 for proposing the chimney tax), Sir Nicholas Morice. There *he* was again in my bachelor bedroom, with his wife Elizabeth, daughter of Humphrey Prideaux, a sour-faced, unsatisfied-looking woman with a bad smell under her nose.

Next morning I awoke in bright Spring sun, still with east wind, to see the pink and rose of the front of Ince a couple of miles away across the blue haze of river. I never saw that romantic house so clear before: it always holds itself withdrawn, and later in the day it became merged into the landscape, was hardly decipherable, except a slightly darker grey or green against the bare trees of this late Spring.

On Sunday, Cynthia had laid on a large lunch: the Colvilles from Penheale with one of the Aosta stepsons, immensely tall and taking after the House of Savoy; for me, Cummings who directs the Plymouth Art Gallery, and the Editor of the *Western Morning News*. That afternoon we went to see the exhibition of Plymouth porcelain and the Clarendon pictures[1] – which I must go and see again, the Restoration so much in my mind with the early Churchills. And on to Saltram.

Looking back over it all, it is not the people, not the great Mr Dupont, in whose honour it was all organized, that remain with me; but the light in those tall Queen Anne rooms with the painted panelling, the portraits of the figures who are more touching to me than the living occupants of their former haunts. After all, *they* made them, made the life lived in them possible, by their prudent marriages, the bribes they took off Charles II, the provision they made for themselves at Restoration and Revolution. And perhaps not even that so much as the rare light of first Spring that lay upon it all.

Oxford, 13 June

As usual, as it has always been since I was a child, when some change of place has made a strong impression on my mind, I have not yet (at 10 p.m. the day of my return) recovered from the dream of where I have been this

1. Part of the collection of contemporary portraits made by the great Earl of Clarendon is usually on loan to the Plymouth City Art Gallery.

short weekend. My brain is still returning to that lovely, battered house I saw this morning – Great Milton, where Tony Muirhead (whom I remember as an acquaintance of Cruttwell's, friend of the Prince of Wales) shot himself. Now Nancy Lancaster[1] has bought it – found dry-rot all through the house and had to take floors, panelling, walls out. The place this morning was a hive of expensive activity, in the American manner. One arrived at a remote enough common, and beyond – where there was nothing – behind a devastated approach, trees down, road up, evidences of late military occupation, was this pale grey, dreaming stone house. Box hedge in front and sunk garden hidden, with its topiary and shaped trees. Behind that a stretch of moat, with an alley waiting for a lead statue at the end, weeping willows along it. At the back, square fruit-gardens and symmetrical coach houses with a big medieval barn. *Everywhere* was the activity this vibrant American female had called into existence, all going forward at once.

Plasterers and builders at work on scaffolding outside the building; plumbers, carpenters, builders, at the job inside, in almost every room and section; in the barn, more builders and fitters finishing the cottage being made out of one end for her to live in temporarily. Outside, a solitary woman planting pansies before the building was finished; in the courtyard, men laying drains; in the sunk garden, men planting and making paths; in the kitchen garden, the same.

None of them was taking any notice of the mistress, the dynamo that had set it going and planned it all: just getting forward with the work as an end in itself. It was an impressive spectacle. As she is impressive in her way, taking me round with it all planned: this end will be the library, the other a big drawing-room; here is a small dining-room; four guest bedrooms each with bathroom. Later, 'I mean this for my bedroom: I like a big room and a big bath' – taking the whole floor of the wing at the back.

It will be fine when she has finished it: such an eye, that saw at once that Bertie Abdy, instead of fiddling with the side of the valley at Newton Ferrers and making silly ponds, should have drowned the valley at the bottom and made a great lake to look down upon from the gorge.

Suddenly, after demonstrating her creation, she said in that maddening Nancy Astor way, 'But I don't want to live here. I don't want to live in England. I want to live in America.' I could have hit her, if I wasn't so tired with an over-active weekend and driving her fast and furious – while she complained that we weren't on the right road – from West Meon through Alton to Basingstoke, Pangbourne and Wallingford. Arrived at her own village green at Stadhampton, she didn't know where her house was, misled

1. Niece of Nancy Astor.

me so that we had to turn and go back again. Maddening woman. Restless. Too much—.

I wasn't best pleased when it was arranged over my head that I should drive her back. I didn't know the way; or whether the car would go. Besides, I was looking forward to chortling back happily, to being in the car by myself. Not a bit of it: clouds of smoke drifting across me, endless chatter, doubts as to where we were going, since she had gone through Reading and now missed it.

A good thing we had: we came straighter, faster; the little Minx went like a bird; I drove fast, but well (for once). But the morning was exhausting.

Hall Place a very different sort of beauty: a well-regulated atmosphere: lovely furniture and objects, evidences of taste: a Hellenistic head of a hetaira, seductive voluptuary; a tiny Chinese body on a seat lifting a hand in a half-deprecating gesture, head bent forward; Italian gilt stands, a Chinese Chippendale mirror, etc. Evidently a cultivated solitary lady, at home.

Not at home when I arrived: all off to see Hatchlands and Clandon. I arrived for tea, after leaving College meeting nattering angrily away about a Domestic Bursar. (My one interest is that he may not turn me out of my rooms.) Looking out of the drawing-room window, I saw at the end of the garden that a young bullock had got through and was pushing a sapling over. The butler and I sallied off to get him back. The old fool opened the gate and at once let a stampede of eight or nine bullocks into the garden. My God, I thought we'd never get them back. They were young steers with a wicked old leader to encourage them. They were out for a high old Saturday afternoon with the farm manager away – all over the garden, out for mischief. They broke in on the lawns at the side, then at the back, into the flower-beds; they scampered down the drive: I headed them back, tried to shut the drive gate – it was fixed wide open. I got my section of them back up the drive – but then there were the brutes at the back in the rose-garden, trampling the grass steps, snipping off everything. I managed to get that lot back into the long grass. They then made a deliberate break away down across to where a summer-house was being built: the young steers going down on their knees to plunge their faces into the heaps of yellow sand. They had a high old time. I never saw cattle before like a lot of naughty children. I despaired of our ever getting them back. At last the cowman arrived and the three of us with one woman got these bloody animals at last through the gate.

What an afternoon! bathed in sweat, sticky, smelly and hot, I went in to the delicious tea awaiting me on silver tea-tray – presentation to one of the

Cubitts – silver teapot and scone-dish, pretty pink cups and rich chocolate cake – apprehensive of what the Mistress would say when she came back to see the state of her lawns.

11 July

On my way, at last, to meet Sir Winston Churchill: he has bidden me to lunch at Chartwell. The reward of virtue, for never have I made such a sprint with a book – not even, I think, with *A Cornish Childhood*. I began to write about half-term – latter half of February. Since then I have written a book of 175,000 words – and that history, based on documents, sources, books – and finished last night at twenty-five minutes to midnight.

It has been achieved only by a rigorous routine: writing regularly every morning, 10 to 1; after lunch, to bed to replenish my energies; writing again from 4 or 4.30 to 7.30; and often from 8 or 8.30 to 10. In the last fortnight I have added some writing before breakfast, from 6.30 or 7 to 8. Only so have I managed to get the book out of the way before going to America.

Car announced at E.S.U. waiting for me.

10 p.m. in bed at A.S.C. What a day I have had! I came back in the train, all in: such a crowded exciting day on top of the strain of finishing the book just before midnight. Perhaps I should go to sleep now and not strain my tired brain any more today . . . Resume in the morning.

12 July

Before going down to Chartwell, I spent half an hour looking at the portraits of the Churchill women at Lancaster House: Henrietta and her sisters. When I got Winston's telegram summoning me, I felt as I had done years ago when I first visited Stratford or when, young, I went to tea with the Prime Minister, Ramsay MacDonald, at Chequers.

I was surprised by Chartwell: I expected a philistine house of not much taste, in suburban surroundings. I ought to have reflected that Winston is an artist: a beautiful valley, which he has much improved with a lake in the hollow, a sickle-shaped ridge of wood all down the opposite side, the house added on to wall-terraces making the most of the situation, looking sideways away to a distant view of the South Downs.

Arrived in the house, what surprised me was the stir of activity: not only a waxed-moustached ex-Guardsman of a butler, a Scot of ferocious aspect and whisky complexion, a private 'tec with fine eyes that took in everything, a lady-housekeeper mad about Lady Churchill's exquisite Siamese 'Gabriel', a pretty young secretary, but workmen moving books to and fro, clearing out and changing about rooms: a dynamo hum of activity.

I was shown into the library downstairs, a fair indication of the Man. There above the chimneypiece was a vivid Frank Salisbury of the wartime Prime Minister, zip-suit of R.A.F. colour. On the opposite wall the original big diagram of Port Arromanches, D ± 109, with all the ships, tracks, quays, etc. marked. On the table, a new biography of Anthony Eden uppermost. The books revealed the man: modern political history, biography, memoirs dominant. In one corner, all the original Correspondence of Lord Randolph Spencer-Churchill, two shelves full of bound folios; and eight or ten volumes of Marlborough's Letters, no doubt, from Blenheim. In addition, the historians and English classics, complete sets of Scott, Johnson, Macaulay and so on.

Before lunch I was bidden up to his bedroom, and there, at last, was the so familiar face, yet much aged: the face of a very old man who had gone back to babyhood. The eyes a cloudy blue, a little bloodshot, spectacles on snub nose, a large cigar rolled round in his mouth. Beside the bed a small aluminium pail for cigar-ash; before him on the bed a tray-desk, on which were the long printed slips of his *History of the English Peoples*.

He welcomed me kindly, courteously – evidently interested – and I sat down. We talked about his *History* and my book on the Churchills. I paid him some compliments, sincerely meant – that it was unfair of him to beat the professionals at their own game; that his Marlborough was, along with Trevelyan's *Age of Queen Anne*, an historical masterpiece. He said that he now had some time and was re-reading the History he had written before the war, but that he wasn't satisfied with it. There were people, however, who would read it, on account of 'my notoriety'. My compliment to Winston on his 'notoriety' – he paused; evidently I was expected to say something. I said, 'Just as in the emotion of love there is an element of volition, so in great fame there is an element of merit.' He was very pleased at this; I had passed the test: after that we got on very well – for he was easily bored with strangers.

He sent me off to read the chapters about Henry VII and Henry VIII while he got up and dressed. Twenty minutes or half-an-hour elapsed in the library, before I was summoned to the dining-room, with its Orpen of the young Parliamentarian. All the passages and corridors filled with his own paintings – less strong, more subdued than I expected.

The figure all the world knows now entered: stripy blue zip-suit, blue velvet slippers with W.S.C. worked in gold braid, outwards, for the world to read. He led me to the window, the view, the lake that he had made, the beautiful mare cropping with her foal below – was it Hyperion out of whom or what I didn't take in.

With the beginning of lunch *à deux* I detected what might become boredom: a stranger, with whom he had no experience in common. I knew his dislike of making the acquaintance of anybody new at his age. So I shifted the conversation away from history, which was beginning to stick, on to politics, politicians, the war. That engaged his interest: from that moment we got on and did not look back.

He told me all sorts of things, was quite uninhibited and released, instinctively generous. One thing I had never heard: he had it in mind, if the Germans had invaded the country and government had to scatter, to form a Triumvirate with Beaverbrook and Ernest Bevin. But then 'there was no danger in 1940. The Germans hadn't thought of ways and means of crossing the water, had nothing prepared.'

I asked if he thought that Hitler's idea was that we should surrender. It was in his mind, he said. I said that Hitler had a profound understanding of the forces of evil, but no understanding of the forces of good. Churchill then said that Hitler considered him representative of only a small minority in the country, that Britain was anti-Communist and should therefore go with him. I said he had behaved too criminally for that ever to be possible: Hitler never understood England.

He then told me that during the Great War (i.e. the first war), while L.G.[1] was working to reduce the Tory prejudice against him, before his return to office, he had written a private paper for L.G. advocating our seizure of the island of Borkum, as a base to bring the blockade nearer Germany, to obviate the strain of maintaining it hundreds of miles out at sea. – In this, he had put forward in embryo form the idea of landing tanks, the later methods of landing craft. By the mercy of Providence, he hadn't published this paper in *The World Crisis*, when he might well have done so: nothing against it; and the German General Staff scrutinized everything he wrote. When the war came, the Germans had nothing of the sort: they hadn't thought of it. He himself gave orders for building landing craft immediately after Dunkirk. Yet it was three years before we had enough to invade.

I told him how much I admired his chapter on the sinking of the Bismarck. He spoke of how bad it was to wake up in the morning and get the news of the sinking of the – '*Hood*' I supplied, he couldn't remember the name. We had to get the *Bismarck*: the nation expected it. One admiral said his ship hadn't enough oil to get to the spot and back again. 'I sent the telegram, "You get there and we'll tow you back."'

1. David Lloyd George.

He wished he could have had more time at the end of the war, a couple more years – this with great feeling and tears in his eyes. I asked him the explanation of the sudden change, at the formation of the Labour government, of Bevin to the Foreign Office, Dalton to the Treasury. Bevin, I know, expected to go to the Treasury. Sir Winston said that it was the King, who wouldn't have Dalton at the Foreign Office.* He spoke kindly of Dalton – said that of all the letters he had on leaving office in 1945, his was the nicest. I told him of Dalton's admiration for the weekly talks he used to give the Cabinet in the worst days of 1940, and that Dalton used to go away and write them all down. He had got them recorded. Churchill said he didn't know that.

I drew him on the subject of Chamberlain. He wouldn't say anything unkind, but didn't approve. It wasn't straight, that interview with his own Foreign Secretary in the presence of Grandi,[1] and saying one thing to one and another to another. And he knew another thing. At the end of Mr Baldwin's premiership, when he wanted to go, and various people said he couldn't – there was a by-election in a safe Tory seat – couldn't remember the name, near Westminster – completely blue. Moore-Brabazon said he wouldn't fight it so long as Baldwin remained P.M. 'That settles me,' said S.B. Duff Cooper was prepared to fight it, and went to Chamberlain, who was head of the Party Office, and told him that there would be no funds for *him* to fight the seat. Not straight. Take your chance – said the old sportsman.

But, equally, he spoke with feeling about Mrs Chamberlain – wonderful woman: twenty years and she's quite unchanged. I said I was glad he had asked her to his Farewell Dinner at 10 Downing Street – and delighted that he had asked the Attlees and Morrisons. That was not much after five years of comradeship in war, he said. He told me that the new Mrs Morrison is a strong Tory – though they're not advertising the fact.

Of Eden, he said that he and Anthony saw very much eye to eye: 'if you presented us both with a set of papers, we should take very much the same view'. I said the hand-over had taken place in the right way at the right time. He said he had been very lucky: he hadn't done anything, it was the people – he had been very fortunate.

The meal proceeded: a good one: fried fish, then lamb cutlets and peas, ice and fruit. I had to have some excellent hock. When it came to cheese, I wasn't going to have any – or port with it. I drew the line at port in the middle of the day; but since he was going to have cheese, I of course had

* George VI did express this prejudice. Nobody *liked* Dalton, not even his wife: she detested him.

1. The Italian Ambassador.

some. Then brandy? I had to have a liqueur with my coffee – 'Have some Cointreau; it's very soothing.' I had some: it was very soothing.

He tottered downstairs on his stick. Like to go round the corner? Some people coming to lunch – asked if they would like to wash their hands, said 'We did that at the gate.'

After lunch we went up some stairs to the big study next his bedroom. Over the fireplace a large eighteenth-century landscape of Blenheim.

I forgot to say that at lunch – the meal went on to 3.15! – he talked about the Labour Party, with no animus or even opposition: all that drossed away with the years. He asked what would happen to them now they were finding out that nationalization wasn't a solution. I said that it should mean that they would take the place of the old Liberal Party. He agreed and went on to say: you don't create wealth by just taking it away from other people. There should be minimum standards for people, and beyond that – Free Run.

One saw the old sporting feeling coming out in everything he said.

After lunch we spent half-an-hour or more in the upstairs study, going through my book. It was lucky I brought some of the typescript – I hadn't thought of boring him with it. He went through it carefully, making after-lunch noises, I thought he was going to fall asleep. Not a bit of it: he took in all the points of detail, and then made a most impressive general point. I had made a rather scathing condemnation of Charles I. He said that we don't consider how much more difficult things were for them in the past; so much easier for us, that earlier people had far less efficient instruments, they had to cope with everything themselves, where we have specialists, a machine upon which things move for us.

It was salutary to watch the generosity of mind of a great man of action, by contrast with the unimaginative, the supercilious condemnations of us academics and intellectuals, who think of things as happening '*comme sur le papier qui souffre tout*'.

He was particularly attentive to words: didn't like my describing the days of the Restoration as 'snobbish' (would he have liked 'class-conscious' any better?); nor my phrase about the Civil War 'degenerating' at the end – 'became spiteful', he suggested, 'I like the word spiteful.' When I said that someone 'pooh-poohed' something: 'I hope you don't say that,' he said mocking. It was like taking an essay to a tutor.

He sat in an armchair, back to his bedroom; a chair had been placed for me opposite him. There was a photograph of Roosevelt facing me, and high up on the wall behind the black-and-white portrait of a bulldog who was Winston. With touching, old-fashioned courtesy, he showed me everything:

the George I card-table some section of Conservatives had given him, an upright desk his children had given him, upon which the proofs of his *History* were laid out.

I noticed the gift for intense concentration Bill Deakin[1] had told me about: clue to his power of work. 'I like working,' he said. Also, there was the child-like desire for approbation, the self-centredness of a child, of an artist. But over all, there was an intense sadness: that of a great man whose powers were failing, who was passing out, his body failing him when there was still so much to interest him, to hold him here.

We went down into the broiling rose-garden, sitting on a deep seat together, the detective walking round unobtrusively, never leaving him out of eyesight, unless sent off on a mission – to get the gardener to put up an umbrella, to get the secretary to send *Marlborough* volume I, to fetch the stuff for feeding the fish.

Drinks were sent for – whisky and soda for him, orangeade for me. He went on reading my book with the same concentrated attention. I could not believe that he would be so interested until, partly out of nervous deprecation, I chipped in to comment something or other. And was ticked off: 'I can't read,' he said firmly. I laughed at myself – just the way I am with people – except that I haven't his gift of unselfconsciousness. I kept quiet after that, while *he* commented. 'Very good,' 'Quite right,' he would say. 'Quite right about James I's execution of Ralegh: I have always thought that one of the worst blots against that – extravagant – sodomite.' And *à propos* of John Churchill's relations with Lady Castlemaine, 'To have been seduced at sixteen (*sic*) by the King's mistress must have been interesting – and valuable experience.'

Reading my typescript reawakened his interest in his own book on Marlborough. He read some of it again with self-approbation and feeling: partly touched by regret for the vanished years. It was a little the mood, 'What a genius had I then!'; or the stricken Marlborough catching sight of a Kneller portrait of himself and saying, 'There was a man.' He had been to see all the battlefields – Blenheim, Ramillies, Oudenarde, Malplaquet. It was Rosebery who suggested that he should write Marlborough. Winston himself objected that he had never liked the Camaret Bay affair. Rosebery said, 'But you have never read Paget's *New Examen*.' Indeed, he had never heard of him. Rosebery lent him the book and that settled it.

The afternoon wore on, Sergeant Pride prowling among the rose-bushes.

1. Sir William Deakin, D.S.O., Oxford historian, parachuted into Yugoslavia as first liaison officer with Marshal Tito, had also assisted W.S.C. in his *Life* of Marlborough.

The time came for us to feed the fishes. First he showed me all round his creation: the little ponds, the stream, the cascade, looking down upon the swimming-pool, inviting in the heat. The hay was all cut and lying in bundles pretty thick in the upper half of the valley. The Churchill flag flew from the masthead over all. The goldfish were addressed as 'Darlings', as also had Rufus the poodle been. The old man tottered his way heavily up the slope to his spring, backed by the mixed blue and white of anchusa and white foxglove. ('Yes. That's just Clemmie.') So back to the Marlborough pavilion his nephew had decorated for him with a frieze in relief of Blenheim, roundels of Queen Anne, John and Sarah.

We went in. I had at various times made motions of taking my leave. No notice was taken: he intended to dedicate the day to me – that evening Beaverbrook was coming to dine. In my last moments he bade me into yet another study, much plainer and simpler – with all his mementoes of the first war, signed photographs of Pétain, Foch and Company; above them the better photographs of *this* war – Monty, Tedder, Eisenhower and the rest. He drew my attention to the Notice in Afrikaans advertising £25 reward for the escaped prisoner Churchill, dead or alive – spelt 'Prisioner'.

'That is all I am worth,' he said acting the part, sitting down like a weary Titan of an historic figure at the desk for me to observe.

We went out into the entrance hall, he taking off his shoes and having some difficulty in putting on a slipper. I dared to help; but he would not be helped. The same self-willed, self-reliant, self-centred spirit as from a child, lapsing back into childhood.

He would be going to bed now, until Beaverbrook came to dine. Sun poured from the west into the front door, upon the flowers, the head of Roosevelt sculpted in wood, the aged bulky figure waving goodbye in so friendly fashion.

It was infinitely sad and touching. One may never see or hear him again. At any moment the last stroke may come.

[London, 21 July, after addressing the Macmillan Sales Conference]

From there I went on to the Buckingham Palace garden party, almost the only man not in top hat and tails. I went in at the quietest entrance, at the back, when things were already in full swing. And made at once for some tea. Rather to my annoyance, I was hailed effusively by G. N. Clark, who didn't know anybody else there, and bade me to his table to talk to Barbara. Very nicely he went to get me some tea. (It would be even nicer if he exerted himself to propose me for the British Academy he presides over. But dear G.N., protesting affection and intimacy, has never exerted himself in any such way. Being rather a coward,* he backed Alan Taylor for the Modern History Professorship at Oxford: A.J.P.T. having pursued a vendetta against him for years. Result, an enthusiastic review by Taylor of G.N.'s contribution to the Modern Europe book, in the *New Statesman*. All very transparent, such is the way.)

I am rather cool with G.N. these days and take it out of him a bit. I rub in the circulation of my books. I did not fail to tell him about the Churchill book, now that it is finished. 'Ah, this is the secret weapon you have been preparing.' 'This is the time-bomb,' I said. Nor did I omit to tell him about the day with Winston . . . if these people won't behave generously to me I take it out of them. We parted less enthusiastically than (on his side) we met. But then, I hadn't wanted to join up with him, or anyone. I had come to look, observe unobserved, meet no-one, and have a good tea at the taxpayer's – i.e. my own – expense.

No-one accosted me after that, and among 7,000 people it is easy to pass unobserved. Edward Maufe the architect, with his noble appearance and plastic ear, put a hand on my shoulder, to introduce me to his son. He was regretful about the rebuilding of the Manciple's house at All Souls. Over thirty years we have had plans and plans for building, from Maxwell Fry, Elizabeth Scott, Newton, James and last (on my suggestion) Maufe. He produced distinguished plans, which were accepted. During the transition these were shelved and the College settled for reconditioning and adding on to the existing house, by the third-rate jobman the college employs for repairs.

I took, and take, no hand in the matter: I leave everything to them to do what they please.

I watched the mob, top-hatted, tail-coated, well-conducted, less idiotic than most mobs: all the same idiotic. The stupefied concentration on wherever groups of the Royal Family passed . . . I missed what had been going on until I had my tea. Then I joined in, to see the little Queen, fresh, dignified, going through the hoop; a hot and black-dressed Lord Chamberlain escorting her alone, a row of ladies-in-waiting like a gaggle of schoolgirls, led by Mowcher[1] giggling with a schoolgirl, came behind. The little Queen, in her flowered silk dress, went through it all as I have seen her mother doing it, the charm at will, the smile of dismissal, moving on to the next group of selected zanies. Later on, I saw her in the royal enclosure, engaged in real talk with Sir Winston, talking to him with force; laying down the

* Cold feet is his family's diagnosis of G.N.'s complaint.

1. Duchess of Devonshire.

law, emphasizing her points with firm gestures of the hand – evidently Queen Mary, chip off the old block, a personality in her own right; Winston quivering like a jelly, with pleasure.

In the Queen Mother's group, I caught a glimpse of Margaret: interesting to watch her face, bored, *mécontente*, ready to burst out against it all: a Duke of Windsor among the women of the Royal Family.

How German the background is! – the one thing the Germans have been successful at, exporting royalties all over Europe. And the energetic, long-limbed Duke has reinforced the German strain again, when diluted by the homely Scotch body of the Queen Mother. Going out through the Palace the Germanity of it all struck one: Duchesses of Hohenlohe-Langenburg, of Mecklenburg-Strelitz, Würtemburgs, Coburgs everywhere. In the gallery beyond the bow-fronted Garden drawing-room, only one Englishwoman appears, Queen Anne. She looked out of place there among all those Germans – and how she hated the Hanoverians who were to succeed her!

Next morning I packed feverishly and left Oxford with an uncomfortably overloaded car, two suitcases up-ended like sarcophagi beside me that slew over on top of me whenever I rounded a corner to the left. This made me drive carefully. I arrived at Salisbury in time for lunch, made a mistake about the approach to the Close, went on round it to the east and ended up in some water meadows to the west, where I had my picnic peaceably beside an elm-shadowed stream, Council houses fairly well curtained off on the other side.

On my way out, I took the opportunity to see Quidhampton for the benefit of my Simon Forman book –

'Simon Forman: Elizabethan Astrologer
Autobiography and Life.'*

Immediately outside the park walls of Wilton, the little village dominated by the spire of Salisbury across the water meadows. The farmhouse went back to Tudor days, possibly: nothing else. It gave me a picture.

Tired, exhausted with five months' intense concentration on the Churchills, during which I had written a book of 175,000 words, I could not face seeing a superb house like Wilton, lying open to the public, its grand gateway inviting among the leafy lines. Too hot, and too much like work.

* Contemplated all these years ago. 1973.

August 1956

I used to accept her[1] invitations to meet Elizabeth Eliot at their farmhouse made into a pleasant bachelor's residence (the house latterly overflown with women, old Harry having taken on his brother's widow and two daughters) behind Probus with a long view of the village, the large grey tower presiding phallically over the village goings-on – as to which Nancy informed me over a cup of tea encouragingly, suggestively. I had had to bring her back from lunch at Trewithen, her car being out of commission or some excuse. At their door I *heard* her forget her big gumboots in the back. Then I forgot, and subsequently remembered when on the high road, with all those gated fields behind me – and tumbled to the purpose.

Should I turn back? I detest people who give trouble: not time enough in life for that. I was busy: going to Plymouth to broadcast next day, shortly after back to Oxford. Before leaving I wrote a p.c. to say I had left the boots in the porch for her when passing by Trenarrer. A month later in Oxford I got a letter asking for her boots. I wrote shortly that the boots were waiting for her to collect.

When I came back after term, two or three months later, they were still waiting for me to deliver at Probus. She is a woman of very strong will. By this time an *impasse* was arrived at. Anthony Griffin down at Hallane – who had his own troubles with his wife – surprisingly piped up on Nancy's behalf: it was 'scandalous' that I didn't return Nancy's boots. (She must have informed him.) I was not going to move in the matter, let alone go down to Probus with them.

Friday, 24 August

Off at 10.30 a.m. for a day in Devon with the Studholmes. (With Peter on my knee it is rather difficult to write. I have to hold the book right up almost vertical above him.) I like zooming off into the void on my own, and it is touching to think that an experience so ordinary is now part of the irrevocable past, partakes of the same nature as history.* Up outside the gate Farmer Bovey delivering the milk, Beryl reminding me that I hadn't spoken to him – she likes telling me what I should do in front of other people. (To show on what intimate terms she is? or getting her own back, because not?) Anyway it irritated me along the road. The day already like autumn: the grey stillness before a storm of rain.

1. Nancy Tresawna, a Cornish neighbour who was a fellow luncheon-guest at Trewithen on this occasion.

* Yes, indeed: no more Farmer Bovey at the gate, no more Beryl, alas. Sept. 1973.

Traffic along the roads rather heavy in the St Austell neighbourhood; not till past Lostwithiel could I make any speed. For the first time I crossed by the Saltash Ferry. While waiting I noticed under the Bridge a house of 1584, date on the wide granite doorway, which Drake would have known, had probably entered, back garden conveniently on the water: evidently a prosperous merchant or shipper.

Following Judy Studholme's instructions I arrived at Wembury on time, to find the party assembled: her tall, distinguished self, her husband of well-bred looks, a couple called Lubbock and an old pansy called Fordham, evidently an earlier friend of Henry Studholme.

It is an attractive late Georgian house with wide-spaced single windows facing the castle walls of an earlier house, some kind of fort. Now it makes an admirable walled garden. The back of the house looks down its own fields to the cranny of the Yealm. Indoors properly furnished, pale gold wallpaper, needlework chairs, carpets, flowers: quiet, cultivated, moneyed.

After lunch Studholme and his old boy-friend and I sallied off across the spaces of South Devon to Ugbrooke to be shown Lord Clifford's treasures: I teasing Studholme with how much grander Devon is than Cornwall: to be bidden up is a case of 'Friend, come up higher'. Lavender-coloured church towers against green flanks of moor, twisting lanes leading to enviable small estates with their own trout streams, cream-washed Regency houses bowered in leafiness. We talked about Cecil Torr.[1]

Lord Clifford was all set for us and determined not to let us off his lecture. No longer living in the big house, they occupy a dower-house in view of Chudleigh Rocks ('my Rocks'), sideways to the hill sloping up to Ugbrooke Park. There was the familiar atmosphere of an old Catholic family: rather out of the world, unsmart, unbusinesslike, a bit untidy, their centre elsewhere.

Interesting things they had: Restoration portraits set the tone, not very good but authentic. An attractive one of Catherine of Braganza as St Catherine. I did my best for her appearance; Lord Clifford called her 'monkey-face'. An unexpected pose of the Lord Treasurer: the podgy face of the administrator, dressed in a loose silk coat, head resting on hand as it might be Tom Carew or Tom Killigrew.

Lord Clifford brought out the Lord Treasurer's dispatch-box: a substantial oak chest lined with walnut, with drawers, from which he abstracted a dozen or so folders containing the correspondence leading to the Secret Treaty of Dover, the original letters of Madame and Louis XIV and the Treaty itself, in both versions – that with the Catholic clauses for the Catholic members of the Cabal, that without it for the Protestant.

1. Author of *Small Talk at Wreyland*.

The old boy, wheezy and smelling of gin, improved the occasion, giving his version of events: the Secret Treaty was by no means a nefarious document, Holland was the enemy, the money Charles got was spent on the Navy, etc. It was really a patriotic affair. I said nothing. One was not expected to interrupt with a question or a comment. We were sat down on either side of a table while Lord Clifford handed up the documents from his ancestor's chest, the Lord Treasurer as a young man looking down upon the proceedings.

This brief eminence perpetuated itself in the family – its one moment, to which everything led up and from which it has declined. We were shown upstairs a portrait of the Lord Treasurer in peer's robes, reward of his devotion – though to it he seems to have sacrificed his life.

I wondered how displeased Lord Clifford might be when *The Early Churchills* comes out, with its unfavourable comments on his foolish ancestor, and assuming, as historians do, his suicide. Perhaps I oughtn't to have gone – though it was the Studholmes, not I, who suggested it.

On the way back quite a spirited argument with Studholme about Chamberlainism – I had drawn the parallel between Charles II's policy, letting down the interests of his country and enabling Louis XIV to get away with it, and Chamberlain's. As a Chamberlainite Tory M.P. throughout the period he was quite aroused; I was really rather bored, but was not going to let him off. In the end Studholme seems to have enjoyed the fight and Fordham in the back seat was riveted. I much preferred seeing Flete – vast Norman Shaw castle; Henry Studholme told me how well off Helen Mildmay was in spite of death duties. Some near millionaire relation had left her his money, also Miss Mildmay who died recently. I first met Helen when I was a young Fellow of All Souls – Barbara Buckler brought her: an unspoken possibility lay between us. I remember well the moment and the place – evening on the terrace outside the Common Room. But what was the point? I was preoccupied, a Left fanatic, poor and ill. She was the daughter of a Conservative peer. Years later, in different circumstances we have met: once staying with Nancy Astor at Plymouth; again when I had to propose Nimitz's health at the dinner in his honour in the Board Room at Devonport. She has several times pressed me to stay with her in Mothecombe. She did in fact marry beneath her: a nonentity of a naval officer, already married with a family, able to do the job and give her children. But she has not forgotten that moment on the terrace at All Souls.

Perhaps this vacation I will at length go and see her. I decided to as we went through the park where she was brought up, by the Victorian castle that is now a maternity home.

[September 1956]

Next day provided an experience; tea with Isaac Foot at Pencrebar: we[1] were not expecting one of the finest private libraries in the country. Some 70 or 80,000 volumes and many treasures: first editions of Milton and many of the poets, Wordsworth's with notes in his own hand, letters of Southey and his wife, manuscripts of Stevenson, a Bible that belonged to Thomas Butts, son of Henry VIII's physician, first editions of Victorian authors, books that had belonged to Carlyle, his own presentation copy of his *Cromwell* to 'Jane Welsh Carlyle from her own T.C.', letters of Carlyle, many of the prints and engravings from his study, the miniature of Cromwell he kept by him when writing about him, a Cromwell collection with two portraits of him, both by Walker, innumerable Civil War tracts and pamphlets – the most valuable in private hands, collections of first editions of many modern authors, Conrad, Hardy, Q., D. H. Lawrence, James Hanley, a special collection of rare Bibles, including an early Greek Testament of unique interest, Bibles in all languages – rarities like Borrow's Testament in the dialect of the Spanish Gypsies, the Commentaries of Erasmus – a special collection, of original editions, one of Melancthon with Luther's own notes, a Napoleon collection, a West Country collection, a library of standard history books, ditto for English literature. We were staggered. After perambulating library, drawing-room, dining-room, bedrooms, entire attic floor room after room, we descended to pantry, scullery, a whole range.

While we were there a comic crisis arose. It became clear that Isaac, aged eighty, has a fixation and that his second wife – John Leese's aunt – has a complex about the books. He keeps her short of money to buy more and more. Poor woman, she is desperate – has taken to burning books that have gone damp in the stables. After tea, though there is hardly an inch of space left in that roomy house, a large unplaceable bookcase arrived. Poor Mrs Foot blew up – and afterwards repenting, tried to make a place for it in the already full dining-room. He has the obstinacy of a senile fixation, and she is at her wits' end, *besought* me to intervene. But what can I do? What *locus standi* have I among all the Feet? Mrs Foot's daily help in that Temperance household said, 'Thank God, my old man's weakness is only drink.'

We came away convulsed and a bit upset. What an afternoon it had been!

1. Professor Jack Simmons was staying at Trenarren.

Sunday, 16 September

I had an old-fashioned lunch party, with two old-fashioned couples, the Kendalls of Pelyn and the Lloyds of Boscundle, who brought their girl-guest along: too many for my small table. We had a cheerful Sunday lunch. Nic Kendall, who is straight out of the eighteenth century, brought an old dog-eared manuscript, a squire's betting book of 1726, bets on cock fighting, with all sorts of technical words like 'norrell', 'hazzel', 'peckle', not in the *OED*, bets with the Bishop of Bristow that by next visit he would have his wife with child, etc. It was a very Cornish affair, looking up the history of farmhouses once manors, like Treveryan and Tredudwell, and the history of Frances Kendall's family, Herles of Prideaux and Vivians. I wanted Jack to get better acquainted with Jenefer Lloyd with a view to his penetrating Pencarrow and seeing their unexplored archives. But the baronet[1] was uninviting: 'If Mr Rowse wants to see my archives, why doesn't he write me himself?' I don't want to see his old archives, but Jack does. I also want him to see seventeenth-century Pelyn. Hence my lunch party: gay and cheerful, it did not break up till half-past three, when I went to bed for a bit.

Monday, 17 September

David family-bound, Jack and I went off to pay a visit to St Tudy. Church full of interest and slate monuments carved with figures in relief. But the place that possessed my mind was Advent. One sees the church tower alone on the shoulder of moor climbing up to Rowtor.

From the Camelford road we went down a steep lane to a bridge and up the other side. Only a few houses with cottage gardens gay with flowers: no road to the church, a track across the field. There was this lonely place, sacred once to the people, unvisited now save by the dead, who crowd the enclosure round. Inside damp, green mould, neglect. One primitive-looking granite slab to someone who died during the Commonwealth, that of a prominent M.P. of the time, Sir Henry Rolle, who sequestered himself in this remote place to avoid the embarrassments of Cromwell's regime. He could hardly have found a quieter corner, trout and salmon to fish in the stream, hares and foxes to hunt up on the moor, birds to hawk. In the churchyard, a New Zealand gunner has come to join the eighteenth-century dead.

In the quiet evening we went to Lanteglos-by-Camelford: large Victorian rectory, churchyard overgrown with ivy, nettles, weeds, several early Celtic crosses. One had the sense of an important early place: on the hill opposite

1. Sir John Molesworth-St Aubyn, Bart., was the brother of Jenefer Lloyd.

a primitive earthwork, in the valley below two deer parks of the earls of Cornwall, a Saxon place-name, the Duchy manor of Helstone-in-Trigg. There was a tablet to the rector I knew and used to call Canon (Perh) Apps – all my friends here in younger days gone their way.

Lanteglos had an eccentric eighteenth-century rector, Dr Lombard, who has left a memory and a library in the Victorian mausoleum. We went on to St Teath, which did not much speak to me: the atmosphere purged by a philistine parson with a flattened medieval face, neither scholar nor gentleman. He left me at the churchyard gate abruptly without saying goodbye. Thence up to Delabole, my first view of the immense quarry, 500 feet deep, whence comes the finest blue slate. Back by the wandering wooded valley of the river Allen to Wadebridge. 'Inland Cornwall has no interest.' Nonsense.

Sunday, 14 October

In bed at the Royal Station Hotel, Newcastle. Everybody advised me against making this journey into the industrial North by car and I had intended to come by train. But leaving it to the last to decide what I felt like doing I have come up by car and enjoyed every minute of it. The day before leaving, on Wednesday, I put in a tremendous spate of work, writing all day up to midnight; managing 5,000 words and finishing my second chapter of *The Later Churchills*. Then I put in all the notes and went to bed.

Next morning was distracted by shopping, engagements, interruptions; and Pierre Lefranc came to lunch to report more finds about Ralegh. Late, about three, tired and fussed, I took off into the wine-coloured, berried, afternoon of early autumn and never stopped until I got to Newark about 6 p.m.

The square recalled a memory of my wartime visit and the young sailor at night, in the dark and sexy crowded conditions of wartime, who was very worked up and wanted somebody to take him in hand. This evening not a sound, hardly anybody. Next morning I got up early to look at the magnificent church: fourteenth-century splendour, with some eighteenth-century monuments: one to a lady with a Northumberland Heron descent, who married a Newark Dr Taylor, physician to George II. I looked again at the medieval carved front of the White Hart, with its row of figures undisturbed in their niches with gilded canopies. The market square has several fine houses and Georgian market hall; also the earlier house with overhanging storeys that received Prince Rupert after his quarrel with the King in October 1645 – after Naseby, which I had passed on the road: then the Governor's house.

I set off about 9.30, Trent mist lifting, across Nottinghamshire and shortly into Yorkshire: the hard-bitten look of the landscape, the scraggy trees, told me I was in the North. I went through Doncaster and then a town filled with figures in dungarees – a Lowry world suddenly sprang to life: it must have been Darlington, past Sunderland Bridge, on a bend leading to an estate with park, I lunched at a lucky wayside inn at Croxdale. I arrived in Newcastle about 3 p.m. and spent a profitable afternoon in Steadman's bookshop raking out his treasures and setting aside a lot of eighteenth-century books. I fall for the eighteenth century more and more.

What should I do with my next morning? Let G. M. Trevelyan know I was here and disturb his seclusion, or try to see Wallington and Sir Charles[1] – perhaps my last chance? I rang up the latter, and got the frosty reception I half expected. Sir Charles had not much idea, if any, who I was. But he could hardly refuse me, having made such a dance about handing over Wallington to the public, being a Socialist, etc. So I went a roundabout way, under a leaden roof of sky about Morpeth, westward into fine country, through a small village with unspoiled architecture – Whalton – and beside a park at Belsay, along a straight Roman-looking road, off which I turned for Wallington.

I hadn't expected such a beautiful setting: the road descending among great beeches, silver-trunked, golden-leaved in the sun that came out to light up the William-and-Mary house on the hill above, the steep eighteenth-century bridge, by Payne, over the Wansbeck flowing away below.

What sort of reception should I have? I was prepared to take anything – even the nasty incident with which it began. A dog was nestling by the steps, came over, made himself friendly, rolled over on his back for me to stroke his belly. I did – and told him he was no good as a house-dog. I went up the steps and rang the bell. He followed me and put his nose beside my leg. I bent down to fondle his ears and at that he bit me on the thumb, very hard and quick. I had never been bitten by a dog before: it was quite a shock and my thumb started to bleed like mad. The door opened and in I went bleeding. I asked the maid to get a piece of plaster. Meanwhile, I could hear Sir Charles approaching: 'What does he want to see?' My name apparently meant nothing to him. I expected that it would, if only from my acquaintance with his brother. I had reckoned without the incommunicativeness of Trevelyans.

The plaster arrived. Lady Trevelyan took me to a tap, where I washed the wound, which was now pulsing and hurting, and put on the blissful plaster – which all bloody I have been wearing and driving the car with through the weekend.

'What does he want?' said Sir Charles, who vanished in disgust, leaving

1. G.M.T.'s elder brother.

his wife to do the regulation tour of the house. 'This is the china, or part of it, that the Blackett heiress brought with her as her dowry,' Lady T. said. She was a tall, hard-eyed, big-handed ancient blonde. I was too much amused by the situation to let my heart sink into my boots. At that moment their daughter arrived by the over-night train from London, having got a lift from Newcastle. She could have come with me, then I shouldn't have been bitten by the dog.

The dog was a stray and had been hanging about for several days. 'I shall shoot him,' said Sir Charles. I said that it was my own fault. Lady Trevelyan said that she would not have him shot, she would ring up the R.S.P.C.A. Then the cat appeared – a fine large ginger with big head, very loving and purring and anxious to be noticed – by way of proving, if it needed proof, how much nicer cats are than dogs. Lady T. said it had been a mad morning altogether – like Esther McCracken's Quiet Week-end.

For me it was an odd prelude to one of the most fascinating mornings I have spent.

Lady T. took me into the drawing-room, which at once revealed the quality of the house: such delicacy in the decoration, each small modillion in the cornice carved and rosetted, plasterwork of the ceiling later, end of the room with detached columns as at Trewithen and, behind, magnificent cases packed with more of the Blackett china. Lady T. said that the tradition was that two ships had gone down in the Tyne with the rest of it: this was what was saved. Two immense bowls of Bristol Delft celebrated Blackett and Fenwick's victory at an election. There was a portrait of the Sir John Trevelyan who made the fortunate marriage – a French-looking portrait; and a queer mix-up of his lady, said by Lady T. to be a unique example of a picture painted by both Reynolds and Gainsborough. It looked to me to have a Hudson sub-structure – typical fancy-dress, and broad hat painted out later, and a different style head provided; with a Gainsboroughish landscape background.

Next came a magnificent saloon, with raised coved ceiling: it reminded me of Corsham and Saltram. Fine pieces of furniture everywhere, mixed up with comfortable Victorian sofas to sit on and commonplace stuffs on them. It was very much a lived-in home: I'd have those comfortable armchairs and sofas out in no time, the piano removed and the William and Mary walnut bureau placed properly in the middle of the wall – and nowhere to sit down comfortably at all. The big portrait of Sir Walter Blackett, formidable tough, filled one end-wall, his three-cornered hat beetling sinister; Lady T.'s art-school needlework of the Trevelyans coming ashore from the waves of Lyonesse, the Mount in the background, filled the opposite wall.

Hospitably I was called into the library to coffee, which I must say I could do with, under the influence of various sensations. (Thumb still troublesome I put down the pen for tonight.)

Rarely have I enjoyed a morning's talk more.

We were in that southward-looking library, crisp northern sunlight lighting it up, the nineteenth-century collection of Sir George Otto Trevelyan surrounding us. Sir Charles, not much changed since I last saw him in the 1930s, for all his eighty-six years spry, springy, on wires. We sat close together, he in blue knickerbockers to match his wintry eyes, bright red morocco slippers; Lady T. and her daughter in the window taking their opportunity to chat. The last time I encountered that formidable daughter was when she was an angular undergraduate being examined for the third time for Responsions or Prelims; at the viva she turned the tables on me, but was ploughed all the same and went down from Oxford as she had from Cambridge – to marry some German. The marriage broke. Now she had become a rather handsome woman in early middle age. I wondered if she recollected me. I fear Oxford was no recommendation to her. However, 'Shug?' she said to me familiarly, handing me my coffee: the abbreviation surprised me in that environment.

By this time Sir Charles and I were getting on famously. We talked of G.M.T., his brother saying he was more than glum, in a curious state after his wife's death. He (Sir Charles) didn't approve of his giving himself up so entirely to some other person. He (George) was a great man and had a responsibility to the public. He should go on with his writing. I told him that I had urged him to write the history of the family, but he had answered that it fell into two parts and had no unity. All the same, Sir Charles vociferated passionately, 'How an historian like him who based himself on the French Revolution can have *no* understanding of the *Russian* Revolution beats me. It shows such a lack of *historical* understanding.' He spluttered with disagreement – having made a good point.

I came to the great man's aid. I said the fact was that he hated the modern world – to such an extent that I was surprised to discover that he detested the Industrial Revolution and everything since.

'But I don't at all,' said Sir Charles.

'I know you don't. You're a progressive – far more so than I am. I agree with your brother. But it is you who represent the real Whig tradition of your family. If Charles Fox were alive today, he would be where you are. Mind you, I don't agree with him. I'm with the younger Pitt: I think he was right. But you are the real Whig.'

'I'm more than that, I'm a Socialist,' said Sir Charles. He was vastly pleased; he was enjoying himself enormously. 'You must stay to lunch,' he said with an access of generosity quite contrary to his reputation. I knew better than that, however: I had to be in Newcastle soon after, had been enough of a nuisance already, but this was my one chance of coming. 'Oh no, you must stay,' laying a hand on mine. 'You did the right thing to come.'

I suddenly appreciated why he has always been an unpopular figure, and unfairly: because he has the directness and brusque candour of his family, no tact and doesn't bother to disguise what he thinks: an admirable wintry sincerity. I saw too that I had always had the conventional reaction, had been unjust to him without knowing him. In fact an original personality, sharp, humorous, full of character.

He told me that his brother intends to keep on his Cambridge house, that he can't stand the Northumbrian winter: 'four months of it, it goes on and on, the Spring never comes. But I like it,' he said. I believe him.

At that the family doctor came in with some pills. After overhearing some comic conversation about symptoms, I made myself scarce – looked at Macaulay's own books in the case (G.M.T. has the greater proportion), another bookcase entirely given up to books by members of the family, and back into the saloon.

I was recalled to be taken round the house by Sir Charles. We went into his study, where the desk was Macaulay's, upon which he had written the History. I was made to put my right hand on it to receive an accession of power. Next came the table on which Sir George Otto wrote *his* History, for out of reverence he would not write on Macaulay's desk. There was a collection of the counters, 100 guineas, 50 guineas, etc. with which Charles Fox used to gamble at Brooks's. I recalled that he and his brother, at sixteen, had lost £32,000 in three nights: 'They should have been horse-whipped.' This brought Sir Charles up short: 'Yes, if he hadn't horse-whipped George III afterwards, he *should* have been horse-whipped.' We laughed: I was delighted to see the strength of the family tradition.

There was an interesting collection of photographs: one of the Labour government of 1924, 'of which I am the sole survivor,'[1] another of the government of 1929–31; photographs of the Webbs, and a surprising one of Lenin. Sir Charles told me that his ancestor Sir John, on hearing of Louis XVI's execution, went straight off to Paris to cheer on the revolutionaries. Most touching to me was a snap of the two old brothers taken when out shooting together: a pause, each lying beside his gun side by side, in the shelter of a wall – as it might be the Roman Wall – unsmiling, unspeaking, each wrapped in his own thoughts.

This room gave me the feeling how fascinating it would be to belong to a family like that, rich in interest, intelligence, history – instead of belonging

1. He had been President of the Board of Education.

to no-one at all. All very well to create everything for one's self, but better to *belong*. I belong nowhere.

If I needed any reminder of that, it wasn't long in coming. Sir Charles was enjoying himself so hugely – family stories, politics, Winston (four years his junior at Harrow: both of them disloyal to their old school, Winston however having now made it up) – that he didn't want to let me go. Lady T. – not for nothing was she an ironmaster's daughter – arrived on the scene. I was trying to take my leave. 'He won't stay to lunch,' said Sir Charles. 'No, I must take my leave now,' I said, 'I don't want to tire him.' 'Yes, you must go,' said Lady Trevelyan.

Sir Charles clung on to my arm, as he had through the whole perambulation, still talking animatedly, through the Ruskinian-Renaissance hall that fills the old inner courtyard, with its pre-Raphaelite paintings of William Bell Scott, out into the staircase hall, with its portrait-bust of Macaulay and its memory of Sir William Harcourt taking no notice and, coming abreast with a marble owl, inquiring which member of the family that was. Out on to the steps where the horrid dog still was, quite unabashed; ensconced in my grand Humber Hawk I took leave of the two bleak old figures standing there, sped out into the coloured, leaf-strewn road, over the steep hump bridge, up among the beeches, silver and gold, and away along straight Roman roads into Newcastle.

In the afternoon my acquaintance from the beach at Hallane turned up and after tea we went out to Seaton Delaval. We missed our way and got tangled up in the coal-mining outskirts of Tyneside. Then, suddenly, we were there in the low avenue approaching the place: after the rows and rows of squalid miners' dwellings, the drabness and dreariness, there was the sombre magnificence of the noble house, in the sadness of oncoming night. My companion was responsive and felt the spell of the place. We drove up, left the car and prowled all round, even into the private garden with its watchful leaden figure. The roof had been renewed on the fired and gutted centre of the house, but the windows remained boarded up. No money for all that: it would take a fortune. Yet how many little *petit-bourgeoises* in Texas could do it with a flick of the wrist.

A chill wind of evening, to chill the marrow with memories, blew over the night-grey eastern sea running in to Seaton Sluice and Blyth lighthouse in the distance. The gaunt house rose like a forlorn menace, a wounded Samson behind us, full of force though in chains and rooted to the spot, a pale moon rising to reflect ghostliness on the sombre mass, wings extended behind our retreating backs.

*

Next morning was gay and golden, wine-coloured October Sunday morning, bells of St Nicholas ringing full tilt to church. We turned our backs and ran west for the Roman Wall. I had never seen it, and enjoyed driving along the straight military road General Wade made out of it, watching the vallum and works rising and falling to the left. My first contact with the civilization of the Wall was the little Mithraeum at Procolitia. We got out, skirted round the platform of the fort unexcavated under the turf, and down into a swampy depression where were the foundations of a tiny building, like an early Christian church. There were three altars set up at the east end by Batavians, Aquitanians and, I think, Tungrians. To think of these men moved about Europe by the authority of Rome to this remote outpost – making the most of the amenities they constructed in these outlandish places, subsequently, for so many centuries, uninhabited – while Rome's soldiers enjoyed their hypocausts and bath-houses, with their phallic symbols for luck, their Mithraic temples with male cults and rites! It was all very masculine and sexy.

In hot sunshine we got to Housesteads – a complete excavated fort on its escarpment with British town under the grass all down the southward slope to the stream. It was very exciting to the imagination, making our way uphill and in at the south gate, past the commander's house and the head-quarters, the open court with tribunal and shrine for the standards, past the granaries with stone piles to hip them up above the ground, to look out from the north gate upon the country towards Scotland, and to the east the Wall climbing the hill, rising and falling like a petrified snake. We went all round, identifying everything, corner watch-turret at highest point on the north-west, the west gate with guard-rooms on either side, the gate sub-sequently half-blocked. And so across the main street to the east gate, the bath-house in the south-east corner, latrines, water tank, drains – more sex in these very masculine quarters, given up to the exclusive life of men. Outside, going downhill was the British settlement, with shops and taverns and women; and a house, under the floor of which had been surreptitiously buried a man with a knife in his ribs. A mirage hung over the place for me: now so dead and empty, mere exposed walls on a remote hillside, yet thronged with the shadowy presence of so many men through centuries. I thought of Kipling.

We got back into the car and sung along, up hill down dale, to Chollerford, and in the afternoon Chesters: more bathing, more cult of the body, more phalluses beside the teeming river where the Roman bridge crossed and men came tramping and marched away – on one occasion, for ever.

After leaving Chesters the rest of the afternoon was in a different idiom – the Middle Ages. At Wark were the earthworks upon which stood the medieval castle; at Otterburn we were in the aura of the long struggle of the Borders with the Scots and of the Scots for independence. Thence we descended into the valley of the Coquet, rounding the mountain mass of Rothbury presenting its lion flanks as we followed the river round. And so, passing Brinkburn priory invisible among its trees, back in grey northern evening to Newcastle.

American Journal

Madison, Wisconsin, 31 January 1959

Here I am for the next four months, ensconced in my bare, but not altogether comfortless, little room in the University Club. It is like going back to being an undergraduate again. Yet I was quite happy to arrive, unpack my things, arrange my small library on the book-shelves, put away my clothes in the closet, underclothes neatly in order in the chest of drawers, writing materials, lecture notes, in and on the desk that looks out on snow-hard slush-covered Murray Street. (What Murray, if any?) Everything arranged – I remembered Beryl, 'You can see that you had to do everything for yourself' – I had a good hot bath and clean-up, after a night in the train (French pine-soap from Dolbear and Goodall at Oxford).

All the time I have been wondering if I have not been a fool to come – and I am not entirely clear in my mind why I have. Four months of my life in a place where I do not want to be, the raw Middle West, among strangers, and those predominantly German – when I might be getting on with my own work in my Hawksmoor rooms at All Souls, and at still more beautiful Trenarren. (How I shall miss Spring there, the bulbs and flowers I put in last autumn, and the dear little white shade figuring in the green landscape, sleeping on my knees in the study in the evenings, or in my bed at night!)

How to explain myself? Dollars, in the first instance. I wanted to come to America: here was a way of doing it. But not for quite so long, my God, not quite so long. I was despairingly lonely in Illinois for three months; this is a four months' sentence. I have been regarding it with apprehension. David Mathew said, when he came to dine, the one outburst of genuine kindness I have heard from him, 'This is the *last* time, Leslie, that you do it.'* I rather agree with him; a term of two months, yes, but not a whole, a terrible,

* I suspect this is what all my acquaintance thought about my absconding. Max Beloff: 'You have become the hyphen in the word Anglo-American.' Bob Brand: 'Your other country?' etc. They must all have talked at Oxford, as when Woodward deserted for Institute at Princeton. But they had made him a professor, and were madly envious of *him*.

semester again. It was the only way of fixing this. So here I am unpacked in the bare whitewashed room, No. 129, that is to be my home these next four months.

Even as I write the word, a picture of the terrace at Trenarren in winter sunshine, the japonica out, Beryl holding up Peter for me, comes into view: *there* is home, and I, as so often nowadays, a voluntary exile.

Why?

Too complex perhaps to fathom. There is the progressive alienation of my life, as from Cornwall so from Oxford and my literary situation in England; the impulse towards progressive withdrawal. Perhaps it is my form of T. E. Lawrence's self-immolation in the R.A.F., my form of self-punishment for dropping £15,000 on the Stock Exchange, my way of making a solitude for myself where no-one can get at me. Anyway, I never had much doubt about doing it, uncomfortable as I should make myself in the process. And it has been convenient for my work in New York, arranging about the publication of the book, *The Elizabethans and America* in *American Heritage*, seeing my literary friends there, renewing contacts, making new ones.

American Heritage has been made by a group of three young fellows returned from the war, Parton, Thorndike, Jensen. My contacts have been mainly with the last, who telephoned me in Cornwall one evening from New York and proceeded to have half-an-hour on the transatlantic telephone! A tall fellow, black hair just beginning to show grey, cut close in aggressively masculine fashion, grey eyes, Norwegian descent on one side, in old-fashioned crown-hat and long coat flapping round his long legs, he looks like a character out of *Rosmersholm*. He is the emotional one, unsubtle, humour rather crude and loud, good-hearted, full of enthusiasm. Thorndike the quiet, cautious, reserved one, rather mean little face. Jensen all for publishing the book in a big way, a fully illustrated edition; Thorndike against taking the risk.

It would be nice if the book turned out to have an appeal for the wide public. But one thing one has to accept – and I never can – these things go by favour and by luck. For all one slaves, bent on taking every chance and missing nothing, one cannot command luck or favour. (I have always regarded myself as doomed to never having a stroke of luck; everything has to be worked for, slaved for – one more reason why I am here.) For all Louis Quatorze's deliberation, industry, planning – one thing he could never command, the easy favour of his people. That kind of thing always falls to a Henri Quatre: John Betjeman to my painstaking Louis XIV. (Still more true. 1975.)

*

I feel, in America, the first stage of propitiatory apprehensiveness: getting used to it, the new environment, the new boy.

Equipped with my snow-galoshes I sallied forth for breakfast at the Students' Union. Bright, dazzling sun; biting clear air; Lake Mendota ahead, a large empty snowfield.

Too early and having to wait, I fell in company with a swarthy Indian from Patna, an historian who has written about East India Company administration and is now engaged on the rise of the Indian middle class.* He is surprisingly just about the character of British rule, and the role it played in India's economic and industrial development. A new boy, too, he did not much appreciate having breakfast at a cafeteria, the scrimmage and self-help. He thought it 'chaotic'; I praised the doughnuts.

I spent the morning in the Library reading an excellent critical account of Priestley's work – surely far better than it deserves? Young Mr Hughes is so sensitive and sensible that he half convinces me to give Priestley a try – when he is absolutely not my writer – the coarseness of texture, the obviousness, the commonplace competence: no real poetry or strangeness or distinction – always a certain commonness. The young man writes better than his master; and that almost persuades me to try what he regards as the best: *The Good Companions*, *Angel Pavement*, *Bright Day*. [No. I could *not*. 1975.]

But can I really see myself embarking on them? He always seems to me just a superb journalist.

In the afternoon I essayed the town, walking up the frozen ice of State Street to the Capitol – a passable imitation, at a tenth remove, via the Capitol in Washington, of Wren's dome, without any of the distinction, the airy floating perfection, at once mathematical and poetic.

Oh, the squalor of the town, the meaningless confusion of the buildings, the cheap shops and stores and bars and dives – evidently on a fine site with vistas of the lakes.

My ears already nipped – as the Duke of Marlborough warned me at Blenheim, 'or any other part of your person exposed' – I went in search of a warm woolly knitted turban to come down over my ears. No such object. The fur hats were all too small: nothing so large as my $7\frac{5}{8}$ obtainable. So I equipped myself with a pair of furry blue earphones and added one more to the spectacle of oddities in the streets. The Post Office closed too, I took the chance to look down on the other lake stretching away from the redbrick balcony of the Ladies' Club.

This lakeside town must have attractions in the summer, the looks of its

* Could this have been Chaudhuri?[1]

1. No, it was B. B. Misra. I owe this identification to Douglas Matthews.

population not among them. I have not seen so ill-favoured a population anywhere in America, German types predominating. A good-looking girl would make her fortune, I reflected sitting over coffee and sweet roll in a confectioner's. Opposite me was the regular type of *hausfrau*, fat, shapeless, enjoying her *küchen*. And Catholics, too, it seems, judging from the prominence of the Catholic Information Center, and the twaddle in the local paper about the enthronement of the new archbishop. It should be quoted to be believed. All about the various high points in the service, the Mass, the singing of the Ladies' Choir, the witty speech at the concluding dinner by the (Irish, of course) Vicar-General, and the pronouncement of the lady on the new archbishop – 'My, he's just like one of ourselves!' (Did she expect an archangel, or a cannibal?)

So far this place gives the impression of being even more provincial than Illinois – and less friendly a reception. I have been left entirely to my own devices these two days. But that suits me very well. As to the rest, we shall see.

An evening's work on the Portuguese voyages, a dip into Iris Murdoch's *The Bell* – dedicated to Norman's Magdalen friend, John Simopoulos, I see – an intermittent struggle with a leaky radiator, and now to bed, not unsatisfied with the day.

After an hour with Miss Murdoch, I go to bed and catch myself saying, 'I am in America, and it's very queer.'

2 February

Considering the apprehension and the neurotic state I bordered on about coming here – thinking of ticking off the days one by one, and then backward, 'only so many days before I am liberated', counting the weeks in proportion, is it one in sixteen gone by with the first week or one in twenty? etc. – my first day has passed off very well. In fact, I rather enjoyed it. I end the day moderately content.

Getting up early, I sallied out, earphones over ears, carrying my fortnight's washing to the Wee-Wash-It establishment down the street. The boss himself affixed the button off my heavy greatcoat. Conversation with a rough-neck Madisonian, who told me about the large perch that abound in the lake, and how it is 'kind o' dangerous' to skate on it because of holes – the fishermen know where they are and fish up a hundred perch in short time from them.

I crossed the street gingerly – snow and slush and scrunch iced up, bright sun, cold to bite your ears off, very beautiful – to the Students' Union for breakfast; the lake an immense plain of white, looking blueish in shadow. I took my tray and place in the cafeteria queue, horrid music playing all the while. The Americans abhor a vacuum and will always invent a noise to fill it.

Back across to the Club (at this moment a student passes my window whistling 'Over the sea to Skye' – one is not *so* far away: and I remember my chatting with the Queen Mother at Blenheim about going to Skye. Apparently she had only once been across to the Hebrides. I wondered about official visits: 'Oh, that's *different*,' she said, with distaste. One got the impression of a double life: the other was a job, something different from her own life, a curious disclaimer in those blue eyes and in her whole manner of putting it aside) to collect lecture notes I have been slaving away at, and then to toil up the slippery hill of ice and snow to Bascom Hall presiding with portico at the top, looking straight down and up to the dome of the Capitol, and sideways on Lake Mendota.

Inside, the usual scrimmage of nondescript students at an American university, milling round, beginning of the semester. Just like Urbana, just like a thousand such institutions in this most uniform of nations. Handshakes from temporary colleagues, a few formalities, half-an-hour more note-taking, and I face my class – the Chairman, Bill Sachse, nice man, shaking with nerves at introducing me. The class turned out to be quite responsive; I liked them and did my best. (Think what it would have been a few years later! – pandemonium.)

Departmental lunch at the Union to meet colleagues. I sat beside a Norwegian of second generation, Merrill Jensen, who talked American Revolution. He has formed a more favourable impression of George Grenville and George III, a *far* less favourable one of Pitt and Burke (how these people run in herds in their views!)

My afternoon class on the Tudors went more heavily: far too many people turned up for the room, we had to migrate about the building. Talked to some students after it, gathered up my papers, mail, books, etc. and got down off the hill, to a cup of coffee in the nearest drugstore and back to the warm solitude of my room, for an early dinner and an evening's work at the typescript of two of my Cambridge lectures for *American Heritage*, cutting and trimming and suggesting illustrations.

Now for a little more of Miss Murdoch's *The Bell*, and to bed. I am enjoying the silence.

4 February

Four o'clock rings out from the bell that dominates the campus, and the snow is coming down fast and furious, blanketing the cars that are left out in the street to accumulate bonnets, mufflers, mounds of snow over them, silting up the old-fashioned houses across the way that show one what America looked like before 1900, before the megalomaniac world of sky-scrapers laddering the skies.

Thank goodness my day's work is over, and I can give myself up to myself. Monday I quite overdid it, and Miss Murdoch's *Bell* was too much for me after midnight. Next morning I was so done up I could only rest on my chaste bed. I recovered with an afternoon walk to the Post Office, sending off the two *American Heritage* articles I had been slaving at. Some gentle reading, note-taking, and letters home completed the day.

Today much better. Early across to breakfast at my favourite view across the lake, though no sun and a snow-haze obscured the other side. Wisconsin is laying on an exceptionally testing winter for me. It would!

After breakfast I ran into Norman Gibbs from All Souls.* Resisting an impulse to steal behind a pillar and slap him on the back, I went back to help him with the breakfast drill around the cafeteria. He was pleased to learn that I had teaching to do here: 'You don't mean to say that they are making you work?' he said. And when I said goodbye to go to my class, 'It will be good for you.'

Rather patronizing, and it also expressed the envious voice of Oxford. Perhaps someday I'll explain to him how things came to be as they are. Or perhaps, for the record, I may have the time now I am here, to set it down along with a few other little things.

Up the hill I went to my morning class, which I am already rather fond of – so keen and interested, quick to take a joke. (An altogether brighter bunch than my Illinois class.) One member stands out: a handsome young fellow with a complete beard, out of the mask beautiful blue eyes search mine, as if for some assurance. Today I learned he is a Latvian: Andre Martinson. Believe it or not, I have a pupil called Anza Amen Lema. She must have been an answer to somebody's prayer.

Back down hill to the bank, where I was kept waiting while one bore of an official surveyed the universe and the news with a lady acquaintance. I took out my watch at him.

Lunch with a couple of professors. One, of part Scots descent, Becker, surprised me with his intimate knowledge of Ettrick, James Hogg, a four-

* Professor of Military History.

volumed eighteenth-century parallel to Scott's *Minstrelsy of the Scottish Border*, and an acquaintance with Bodmin Moor. So far I have hardly talked to my colleagues; this sociologist should be rewarding.

Afternoon back up the hill to my class on the Tudors, now got up to fifty – we had to move to a larger room. Down again to a cup of coffee and a doughnut in the drugstore, and back to solitude and snow-insulated bliss. I think I can manage this routine with the best.

It is wicked to allow oneself to be a fool; that is how all evil things come to walk in the world.

[Moral for *Auto*

9 February

I've just come in from hearing Eleanor Roosevelt speak in the Union Theater. A remarkable effort for an old lady nearing eighty. The auditorium was absolutely full – sold out at $2 to $3.50 a seat; it must hold two thousand. I suppose she is on a remunerative tour, snow or no. (It is snowing *again* tonight.) The audience was reverentially attentive: not a sound, not a cough, not a laugh – for there wasn't a joke. How these people can listen for an hour and a half in dead seriousness without a joke or a break – how anybody can deliver a lecture of such unalleviated solemnity without a crack – beats me.

She was worth hearing all the same. Not only for herself, Grand Old Lady, a considerable piece of history. The talk was well planned, though platitudinous to the last; of the utmost simplicity, slowness and repetitiveness, it had evidently been given a hundred times before across the States. Naively moral and ethical in tone, appeal and content, all about the United States having to face its responsibilities as leader of the non-Communist world – unexpected and unaccustomed, quite suddenly. They had grown up content to watch that leadership exercised by Great Britain. Now it was theirs. (I still cannot hear the fact of our situation in the world brought home by others without a fixed stare in my eyes, a certain tension, one finger betraying my inner feeling.)

She couldn't have been nicer, a good friend of Britain, described viewing the desolation of London with the King and Queen from the steps of St Paul's. This by way of introducing our need for help. Later there was a passage, a scrap of talk with a Russian peasant about the destruction of her village, the killing off of her family and her own struggle for survival in the forest living off roots. I wonder how many of the audience it struck that we owed those amenities to the Germans?

The theme of the lecture was the rivalry between the two giants, America and Russia, leaders of their two halves of the world, and the chances of World War III. Evidently nobody else counted much – except the potentialities of Communist China. Well, what a world the United States has succeeded to in the day of its power! We at least had it when the going was good.

All the same, I hand it out to her – a great lady, in her whole manner, the way she held herself, her cast of mind. Her speech might almost have been English; I asked the young man beside me, who said it didn't sound like an American accent. There were, however, American pronunciations – vurry for very; prodooce, though she said distribewtion. She was at her best in answering questions: experienced, gave all the right answers, shrewd.

The attitude of the audience was no less interesting: perfect politeness, with complete sense of equality they put their points. It was heartening in a way – a real democracy. Or it would be, if the background were not 1959, the nuclear age, the thought of World War III – one can never exclude the possibility.

I watched with my now accustomed ambivalence. In so far as I am here, with a small contribution to make, I wish them well and accept the assumptions of democracy. They are a people generous and of good-will towards the world. But it is not a world I can respond to, or have any care for: a world with all the quality taken out of it, a mass-civilization whether it is Russia *or* America, the world of the average man.

Mrs Roosevelt mentioned the Soviet concern for Culture, sending groups of young soldiers, or young people up from the country, to the Hermitage for the afternoon. And then look at the appalling painting they produce, or the architecture, or the literature! As Stuart Hampshire said to me at dinner my last Sunday – everything that comes out of Russia is so *appalling*: 'something has gone profoundly wrong with it all'.

How naif of him to expect any other! This is what to expect of a mass-civilization, mass-philistinism erected into a principle, an aggressive principle too that acts like an Inquisition and will not let anything sincere or original exist beside it.

I saw what it would be like long ago – with those political poems of the Thirties:

'These are they . . . Feed my lambs!'

Monday, 16 February

My life here is monastic, and I rather like it – the silence, the loneliness, no-one to speak to, the routine of work and self-communion. When I think of the unwillingness, the dread with which I regarded coming away – so far . . . so far all is well. Against everybody's judgement, it has been right to come . . . so far. *Pourvu que ça dure*!

It is a terribly monotonous routine: up the hill and back again twice a day on Monday, Wednesday and Friday; all day in the Library on Tuesday, Thursday, Saturday. Broken only on Sunday, when I write my letters and go out to lunch at an hotel (no meal to be had on the monastic premises on Sundays). How different from the domestic life of All Souls! Would I be back there, yet? – No.

I remember Eliot coming back from his year professoring at Harvard, saying in his quiet voice, 'But no-one to talk to! Just no-one to talk to.' If he found that – and after all he was a native – I might reasonably complain. But I don't though it is rare to find Americans with whom one can talk – some lack of subtlety, of irony, some incapacity for intimacy – a people oddly without a soul. But I don't repine. At any rate, not yet. At Urbana I went dotty with loneliness – and the heat. Here I have so far remained sane, for it is very cold. But this is only my third week, and I have a long way to go, all the way to June.

So far I make do by working hard, living very regularly, going to bed early; for want of anyone to talk to, I talk to myself and have odd dreams. One night I dreamed of Jack[1] in queer circumstances. He had unexpectedly taken the plunge and got himself a beautiful old house in the country. Everything laid on very plush: Aubusson carpets, lovely furniture, Georgian silver; and in addition to his mother, a staff – a most impressive butler, a kind of Jeeves. I was arriving for my first stay at this country villa, which I had some difficulty in finding – dark, mysterious country. I was much impressed by the turn-out, in admiring, congratulatory mood. In a second Jack dismissed it all, unscrambled the whole set-up. He had found something very disagreeable about the impeccable butler. Though nothing was visible to the eye – and both Jack's mother and I were most surprised – he knew that the excellent butler, to outward appearances all right, was really mad.

It later transpired that he was my illegitimate half-brother.*

A situation for a play: a farce.

Another dream was about Winston, who was coming up to honour

1. Professor Jack Simmons.

* The dream, I suppose, went back to the trauma.

some festival for which I was vaguely responsible. Great preparations and expectations, all very public – the whole community, as of village or town, keyed up and the great man was to make a speech. He arrived like a circus, and placed me beside him in the choir stalls, just like where I had seen him in the Abbey at the coronation.

And then – fiasco! He wouldn't play. He wouldn't make a speech. He just took himself off. Everything went flat. I wasn't much put out by this, took it philosophically, telling the people that this was just what great men were like, so very temperamental: one mustn't expect any other.

It occurs to me that this might be my subconscious expressing a certain disappointment at the reception of *The Churchills*. Not its critical reception, for that was excellent, but the sales. Those were nothing very special: no *Brideshead Revisited* or *Good Companions* for me.

Another was hardly a dream but more a nightmare about my mother. I often have nightmares about her, usually towards returning to consciousness in the mornings. Never anything kind or pleasant: either fear of her, or guilt at having treated her badly in her last years. Why, O why, should I have been treated to such an experience? In a way, I must have been deeply afraid of her: there was a real ferocity about her.

This time, as usual, I was having to look after her, eternal nuisance as she was, and somehow, somewhere I had mislaid her in the house. At once guilt: had she gone and killed herself? Then I found her, the shapeless huge mass she always was in bed, the clothes all huddled round her. But she was there, and alive. Inexpressible relief: the relief and the burden to face all over again immediately woke me up, my heart pounding with anxiety, my mind in misery.

One evening a memorable experience, not pleasant, but turned to good use. I went out to a dinner party at the Beckers'. He is an intelligent sociologist, part-German, part-Scots; intense, talkative, anxious to show off. Knows a lot about the Highlands, knows about me, too: has read *A Cornish Childhood*. He has a kindly *hausfrau* of a wife, beaming and intelligent. Beside me the Scots wife of a Welsh professor called Merritt Hughes: she had been at Edinburgh University. She surprised me at first by talking about Cockburn's *Memoirs* and James Hogg and Scott and Buchan.

Madeleine Doran was there, amused and amusing, with real charm, dark and engaging: she must have some Irish in her besides the German. Also Mark Eccles, whom I have long wanted to meet, for his work on Marlowe and Lodge and Middleton. And – a discovery I have made by coming here – he is just finishing a book on Shakespeare the Warwickshireman. I have long thought of writing a biography of Shakespeare under that title. But, so far, a disappointing man, who looks on the verge of a nervous breakdown, afraid to talk to one. A broad gnome-like man, with one eye perpetually blinking, who has obviously over-worked himself into this off-putting state.

After dinner Becker, anxious to dominate the scene, put on a fine performance. He read two stories of his father's life which had been taped and transcribed. And fine stories they made, of the rough life of Alaska in the nineties: logging on the Yukon amid the ice blocks, and sailing gold-diggers up through the Aleutians into the Behring Strait. Then he showed us fascinating photographs of the unchanging life of a Hessian village community, not far from Adam's[1] Imshausen. We talked about the Resistance movement, about which he knew a great deal. But I noticed that he never looked me straight in the eye. Has he a touch of the schizophrenic German?

Merritt Hughes, the Welsh American, I am not sure that I much take to: too much the upstage professor, paid deference to as a great authority on something (Milton); talks in a high, pulpit kind of voice, and no sense of humour. One has to explain to him when it is a joke; otherwise, all dead serious; no subtlety, everything either all one or the other.

He was giving me a lift back. We all got in. There was a slight turn in the drive, snowbanks on either side. Talking and not watching, impulsive and with no tactile sense, he at once backed into the snowbank and there we were stuck. (I might have done such a thing myself, through incompetence rather than inadvertence; but I recognized the Celtic type.) After futile scraping and sanding and spading in the cold, the rescue-tractor had to be called and we got away.

Once more we were on ice, and I found the horrid nerves my experience on the roads going back through Devon gave me – the skid and the crash – grip me. It shows how much that ghastly drive unnerved me that whenever we went downhill, I felt the horror. The insensitive fool went on yap-yap-yap while my nerves panicked; he was going fairly fast too. I just managed to control myself getting back to the city, and then the old fool announced that he wanted to go up the hill to Bascom Hall with some letters. It was already after eleven, no chance it would be open; the hill is quite steep and all iced up. I was on tenterhooks as we went up through ice-slush and dissolving snow – we had to go quite quick to get up the hill at all – and then swerved dizzily round into the terrace before the portico.

Of course the place was shut. But we had run into something that made my heart stand still. Under the full arc-light of the deserted portico, on a stage for all the world to see overlooking the city, absolutely statuesque and still, two lovers in unconscious ecstasy. A very tall, gold-headed young man,

1. Adam von Trott.

slender as a column, held his girl close to him, unmoving, unaware of the outer world. Then we drove on around the steepest corner downhill, the impercipient fool yap-yap-yap, 'This is the Home Economics Building; that is the new Girls' Dormitory.' '*Never mind about that*,' I heard myself say, terror making me desperate, '*Let us think about the road*.'

Mrs Hughes perceived that I was in complete panic and understood. The old fool had perceived nothing. Arriving at the Club, utterly shaken, I was profuse in my insincere thanks. But I was so upset that I couldn't possibly go to sleep until I had put a substantial hedge of reading between the experience and bed.

I am, however, now grateful. For the experience so shook me, penetrated something, that next day I wrote straight out the best poem for some time, 'Under the Pillared Portico'.

Friday, 20 February

4.30 in the afternoon: the week's work over, lectures, lunches, nobody to see, nobody to have to talk to: a moment of bliss. The world outside brilliant with sharp sun, the lines and shadows clean-cut, etched and chaste in the manner of the New World, hard snow lying, the wind biting. Inside the Club, warm; I have stocked myself up with books for the weekend, a book has come from the *New York Times* to review. All is, so far, well.

I like my classes, and I've got some keen research students in them, who keep me going. One of them is going to Magdalen: I expect that young man – Jewish? he knows Kronenberger and people at Brandeis – will have an academic future.*

I have been reading like mad, both for my classes and for myself. Yesterday a little book of Parry on Spanish Imperialism, a whole book on Music in Renaissance universities, and at night a fair slice of Edith Wharton's *A Backward Glance*. This in addition to taking part in entertaining Helen Cam, here to give two excruciatingly detailed lectures on the customs and courts of London in and around 1321. The first was not too bad, and I held up my head. The second was painful; but worth watching to see that the more specialist and boring it became, the more she lighted up: legal antiquarianism was her real passion, with her 'nice points', 'pretty little points'. I wondered whether this wasn't a deflection of the feminine, the way learned ladies are apt to go. I wonder why? losing touch with common-sense. It was also very Cambridge, academicism gone to her head.

And yet she is a woman with strong common-sense; I rather liked her as

* He came to nothing, threw everything up for a female, and left hot-foot.

a person: a masculine face, prominent nose, sharp chin. Twice she informed me she was a clergyman's daughter: she had the profile of a clergyman in the pulpit. The clerical upbringing was evident. She had a *warm* appreciation of Elizabeth Jenkins's book – far superior to the academic crabbing of G. R. Elton, the prejudice of A. J. P. Taylor. I dare say they pitched in to poor Elizabeth, simply because of my boost of the book helping its success.

Today another specimen of the English *virago intacta* loomed on the frozen scene: Miss Redmayne of Burford, Miss Redmayne of a little Spanish town near Segovia, Miss Redmayne of the Rhodes Trust and of American Rhodes Scholars, and taking 300 children to New Zealand, Miss Redmayne of everywhere. A thundering sort, replete, bounding with energy and zest, good causes, enjoyment of life – good family, woman of the world, an immense egoist. Conversation sizzled, boiled over, in Knaplund's pretty apartment looking over Lake Wingra with a little lagoon in the foreground.

Paul Knaplund is a remarkable man. Born in northern Norway, within the Arctic Circle, as a lad was much interested in the Boer War and very pro-Boer. I expect everybody outside Britain was; they now have some reason to reflect otherwise. In 1906 he came to America, and, very poor, worked on a farm, attending a little college when he could. He came to the university here in 1913, and for research took up Gladstone's attitude to the Empire, which he found to be much misunderstood. In 1922 he went to Britain to explore Colonial Office archives, since often the published accounts did not get the true situation right. For example, the Colonial Office under Stephen was much more liberal than Gibbon Wakefield. Much interested in the Stephen family – Sir James Stephen the biggest man of the lot – he had corresponded with Virginia Woolf, but found that she was not at all interested nor did he derive an impression of her that endeared her to him. I am not surprised: 'that dreadful woman',[1] according to G. M. Trevelyan. Apparently the original James Stephen had a neurotic strain and several times contemplated suicide. She accomplished it. I must read his strange autobiography, with its mixture of religiosity and eroticism: the two go together rather.

Knaplund is a shrewd old scholar, with the democratic bias of his peasant origins, very conscious of snobbery in others, but not displeased to be taken up and be in correspondence with the Gladstone family, Lady Victoria Hicks-Beach, etc.

What am I up to?

This evening, finishing Mrs Wharton's *A Backward Glance*, I read: 'Fate seemed to have conspired to fill those last years of peace with every charm

1. Quoted elsewhere by ALR as 'that horrid woman'.

and pleasure. "Eyes, look your last" – in and about Paris all things seemed to utter the same cry: the smiling suburbs unmarred by hideous advertisements, the unravaged cornfields of Millet and Monet, still spreading in sunny opulence to the city's edge, the Champs-Elysées in their last expiring elegance, and the great buildings, statues and fountains withdrawn at dusk into silence and secrecy, instead of being torn from their mystery by the vulgar intrusion of flood-lighting.'

Well, she had had the world when it still had its secrecies, and life itself was propitious to art, to one's efforts, to achievement.

For me, nothing is propitious, for oneself, one's art or any permanent achievement. From the external point of view, so far as people in general are concerned, it doesn't matter whether one achieves anything or no. A mass-civilization, herd-culture ('Culture Swap a Big Success' announced the *Wisconsin Journal* last week, *à propos* of an exchange between some Russian philistines with no standards and some American philistines with equal standards) has no idea what is good or what is bad, nor of the difference between first-rate or third-rate. Or rather it thinks the third-rate is first-rate, what is bad, good.

Though it is very difficult to accustom oneself not to mind, there is no point in caring, so far as the external world is concerned, what it thinks, whether it values or devalues, praises or dispraises. There is no value in its praise or its estimation. It is useful to have its estimation in cash,* but that is all the value it has – its utility.

I think then that this practically solipsistic way of life I have worked out, the isolation and insulation, moving out of people's reach, in the margin between one and the other, not sharing in other people's lives, except superficially as a visitor, a spectator – sad and the less fulfilled as it is, for it has little stimulus or inspiration from outside, no immersion and no love – is nevertheless, in the circumstances, the best line of defence, and even way of life in the world we have inherited.**

Most people in such a world consume not only their time in trivialities, but their lives. Everything they do is ephemeral. But in such a world even the good, with one's life-blood in it, can be no other than ephemeral, and that is hard to take. It almost makes the young men right to make no effort, their indifference about achieving anything. Most of them haven't it in them to achieve much anyway. That again makes it harder for me, who have had the energy to achieve almost anything – and, then, apart from the handicaps of both origins and illness, have never received any *real* encouragement to

* Even that is devalued.

** I still hold by this and have put it into practice. And said so in the Preface to *Collected Poems*, 1979.

my work or any real lift from circumstances. Except for the heroic, thrilling years of the war and tension and love: for a moment only, books and essays like *The English Spirit*, and *The Spirit of English History*, were in tune with the public mood.

Never, before or since, have I had that fortune, to be borne up by any wave of opinion or appreciation. It has always been a struggle, saying what I knew to be true – and nobody much wants to hear it, or finds it positively unwelcome.* Apart from the envies and enmities with which I am dogged – *New Statesman*, even *Spectator* (for nothing that I have done to them), BBC Third Programme, the Left Intellectuals, the academics, Oxford – a wall of misestimation surrounds me, in line with nothing, no party or body of opinion. It is a wonder that the *public* responds as it does. It has long seemed paradoxical to me: that the most unpopular of authors should be so popular a writer, a success with the public. (The *New Statesman* the other day got as far as to refer to me as 'an accepted author'.) David Hughes in his book about Priestley, written so much better than Priestley writes, started from the point that the integration of his work has never yet been established. The same thought could not but occur about mine. A more difficult task? Possibly – the history and the poetry, autobiography and politics, the Cornish and English, the ambivalence: no-one knows how to describe me, no-one has my length or height.** But it's odd that they make no attempt. When Wyndham suggested writing one of those British Council's brochures about my work – the thought came as a surprise to me – it was turned down by the British Council!

I do not fit into the accepted categories. But I do not make it any easier for them. On the other hand, though I do not relish being misconceived, misrepresented, I would rather that than be *rangé* with them, and not be free to escape, not have alternative avenues open to me – with the world as it is, and as things are.

I grew up with intense pride in England and her past, inspired by it, a strong motive always to do my best. It was an unquestioned assumption, the air one breathed, that England and the Empire were the greatest thing in the world. I came to maturity in a world where that has vanished at a touch. As a child I grew up on the fringe, at the park-gate, shut out, of the way of life of the gentry. Theirs was the life I always meant to share. When, by my own efforts, I arrived at the point of commanding such a life for myself, it was undermined or broken down.*** So with my effort to make contact with my own working class in the Labour Party: during all the years

* Whether about politics or literature.

** Still true. 1975.

*** Except for what I have salvaged with Trenarren.

when I was a hard-working candidate for it – out of power, in a hopeless minority. So with Oxford. So with All Souls – the most intimate contact of my life, for many years my cherished home.

Like Newman, I feel driven out – no doubt impelled partly by something in my own make-up, though, in my case, much more by the adverse circumstances of the time, really the end of a civilization.

In the civilization that is rising, a technological way of life with accompanying mass-culture, I have no interest whatever. I do not care what follows the world that was already vanishing when I glimpsed it through the park-gates: that was the only civilization I care for, though it was never mine and I did not belong to it. But it was what was in keeping with my innermost nature.

So what greater isolation could there be?

This uncommittedness has compensations in a time of universal break-up, decline of standards, of ever-present insecurity, living as we do, so ephemerally, on the edge of a precipice.

When I first came to America, within this decade, one idea was that of exploring the possibilities of an alternative life here. Britain lives perpetually on the verge of financial and economic breakdown. If there is a Labour victory it will unfailingly return, with a run on the pound, further depreciation of sterling, eroding one's hard-earned savings.

I have had more than enough of seeing my earnings go into the maw of the slackers of the Welfare State, wasted on the education of people largely uneducable (one is not allowed to say so in England or America – democratic dogma), commandeered for the upkeep of other people's perambulators – they should pay for their own pleasures. Driven beyond a certain point, I might be driven to leave all that I love – Trenarren, Oxford, Cornwall, my life in England – and go elsewhere. At present, I am still exploring, watching, betwixt and between. E. L. Woodward, a clever scrounger, who saw round two corners before anyone else – a continuous figure in this journal from early days in college – was there before me. From the Institute of Princeton he can say, and from no South American port of the poet's imagination: 'I already arrived am before you' . . . It is safer then to have an alternative, two planks across the abyss of our time.

Not that I am involved in this society, any more than that. I perform what I am paid for; I give good service, I do my best (or nearly my best) for my classes; I receive my wages. I am here to collect dollars. What else?

I am filled with rage, I could beat my head against the wall that things are as they are – never expected or intended by me. But then nothing in external circumstances ever goes as I wish: it always goes contrary. Reason for more rage. Other people had – and even now have – circumstances propitious for them.

Since they never go my way, perhaps I can settle for slipping between them, evading, escaping. Who'd have thought it of so obvious a type, so simple and so clearly in view, a target no-one could miss, in my home, in Cornwall, at Oxford or All Souls?

Now I play them a game. I have the laugh of them; I laugh indeed at them. But not too obviously. I dare say my escape vexes them now, my not being there, as much as my being there used to do. True, they can forget me. Books come out to remind them. But I should not taunt them too much. Too many already know my line – that I think the old country is done. That is still a weapon they can use against me.

It is difficult to keep silent. Especially for me, who have always been so talkative and open – though perhaps not quite so open as it seemed. It is something of a strain at All Souls to keep perpetual guard. I have come away from that: a good reason for being in America, and why, so far, I have found it something of a release. A release into an atmosphere of good-will, in place of envy and ill-will.

For that I have left those lovely Hawksmoor rooms, the view across gardens and to the Camera, the ordered routine, dinner in Common Room, the servants, my books and pictures, the furniture and rugs about, the desolation[1] of the atmosphere for these bare walls, this bed-sitting room, the rawness and the crudity. The job fits in very well with my literary plans to see to the articles coming out in *American Heritage*, arranging the publication of the book. A month would be enough, two months ample, four months may be a strain. But I have been away nearly a month, and beggars can't be choosers.

Shaw and Wells, Maugham and even Russell, all the generation before mine had the world while it was still good for the English. They came in on top of everything; they were important, attended to, their words waited upon, handsomely remunerated. They could keep the cash they made; invest it and it increased; go where they liked; everywhere they were made much of: they were the leading writers of the world's leading people. They were treated with a deference, the source of which they ungratefully did not recognize.

I have to take my chance, take a moderate place in the queue, make my way as a travelling scholar, go where I am asked and when, fitting in where I can. Well, I can take that. I can look after myself: one thing my origins fitted me for rather better than most middle-class academics. In the situation as it is, my country of reduced importance in the world, I can make do where not everyone else could.* I propose – all loyalties aside, which have

1. *sic* in ALR's corrected text: but one suspects a misreading; 'distinction' would make more sense.

* A. F. Pollard: 'What a man does depends on what he can do without.'

been so strong in my life, that have so rooted me to places, Cornwall and Oxford – I propose to use that talent.

I have some advantages. A Cornishman is not an Englishman. Cornwall is half-way between England and America. Most Cornish folk have kith and kin over here. I can fit in, rather better than people at home would believe. I have something to offer, something to sell. My country has shown itself no more anxious to take notice of my willingness to serve than my native town or county, school or college or university. It will be too late, like them. Richard Pares who, in spite of my looking after him, was terribly anxious lest the Regius Professorship should be offered to me, one day when I said that Namier was over-estimated as an historian now, replied, 'I'll bet when you are in your sixties you'll be over-estimated, too.' But that will be too late. I'll already have turned my back.

One day at the end of December I paid a visit to Newton Ferrers. I thought I should never see it again, what with the tragedy that hangs over that place with the curse on it. Nobody but me knows about the curse: the Elizabethan parricide, the Coryton eldest son who killed his father for opposing his love of some unsuitable girl. I found the deposition of an old priest a generation after confined in the Tower, who knew what had happened: I think the son took up a hay fork in the courtyard at the back and killed his father. Diane[1] knew that the place was haunted – she thought at the bottom of the drive. There she lived a life that was *supplice* enough with Bertie, bringing his mistresses through her bedroom. She was a most gallant, beautiful, talented creature, a profoundly well-bred nature – I cannot think of anything the least mean about her. And yet, no doubt spoiled, as so many of those women are. But who would have thought of such a ghastly fate? – that motor accident, and now a life-long invalid, stone-deaf, a vegetable in a bin. Perhaps she doesn't want to come out of her dream? She always drove about those narrow lanes too fast. I remember a difficult cross-country drive to Penheale with Garrett[2] and Joan Moore in the back, Diane and I talking furiously in the front, while Garrett was on tenterhooks. I was too nervous with them all to be afraid. During that weekend Diane immediately caught the point of the 'prophesied prison' in the poem I read to them by the piano in the bare beautiful salon with the Winterhalter and the Boldini.

That December day there was some nonsense to discuss with Simon Harcourt-Smith about a South-Western TV authority. We were to meet with Isaac Foot at Newton Ferrers. It was a day of torrential downpour, the

1. Abdy.
2. Lord Drogheda, chairman of the *Financial Times* and of the Royal Opera House, Covent Garden.

heavens opening. Infallibly I went wrong in the complicated lanes that lead away down from St Ives. I never can strike the right road and got hopelessly bogged down a farm lane, with only just room to turn round again. After that I went all round the compass and approached the place from the east downhill to the tiny bridges across the stream, and so in at the gate at the bottom, the drive in terrible disrepair, the land marshy, undrained – to Norman Colville's disapproval, while Bertie goes on with his 'works' in the world of fantasy he inhabits.

He says the place belongs to the bank. The expense of Diane's confinement, nurses, besides setting up Valentine in Paris – I cannot think how it goes on. He can no longer afford to keep a car, so he is marooned in this *pays du Grand Meaulnes*. No man-servant now. But a suspiciously pretty foreign young woman, who waited at table and gave me a look. There were still excellent wines – lost on me and old Isaac, whom I thought more 'totalish', as well as tee-totalish, than ever.

Simon Harcourt-Smith has all the manner, the affectations of a sissy, without apparently being one. At any rate he is married. Sufficiently confusing: I took him for one. Life in that house had come to a standstill. Nothing had changed, except that it looked a little barer, the blinds and curtains more drawn – Bertie can't bear the light – the atmosphere desolating.

He won't attend to his affairs – he never has done: Robert Heber-Percy told me he lost some enormous sum when a dock he owned was burned, and Bertie had neglected to sign the insurance policy. But he was still going on with his crotchets – bricks and mortar, stone and cement. Since I was last there he had built on a stone porch to the entrance door; and walled in the entrance to make a courtyard, so that you shall not see the breathtaking view of the terraces and the gorge, except from the house. He had planted camellias against the wall. With all his sense of beauty, his sensibility and responsiveness to objects, pictures, sculpture, women, he has in fact spoiled Newton Ferrers.

Isaac Foot was droning away about the resources of the Methodist Insurance or Provident Society he controlled as Chairman – some three millions. I found that sufficiently surprising – shows the financial pull of these canny Methodists. Myself outside of it all, I had no idea.

Bertie spirited me away upstairs, past the loveliest Hubert Robert I know, to his darkened, sinister bedroom. Turned on the light, got out a key and opened one of the superb *armoires* to show me his treasures: exquisite eighteenth-century *boiseries*, pieces of Sèvres, and an enormous eyeless Egyptian bird-god, as sinister and ominous as one could wish. I told Bertie of the panic I once had long ago in the basement of the Louvre, when it was closing time and I was left alone in a room full of these menacing, eyeless birds, and I thought I might have been locked in. If I had been, I'd have been picked up mad in the morning.

'A short story,' said Bertie.

He didn't guess that it was the sinister and ill-omened force of that bird, like something alive and full of power and evil, shut up in the cupboard, bringing a curse down upon the house and all within it, that was the story. One day I must write it: perhaps one day when it has worked itself out.

But I wonder what will be the end? It occurred to me as I went away from that house, haunted with ill-fate – perhaps Bertie's suicide. He said to me the house could never come to his son: he had made it all over to Diane. But I don't know what to believe.*

I said goodbye in the forecourt, and went down the heaped and rugged drive, bump, bump, bump, the rain pouring down, rustling down a million leaves, rhododendron, camellia, magnolia, eucryphia, bamboo; the whole place leaking tropically with the sound of water, and amid all the rain, the great *jets d'eau* were playing, spouting expensively away.

All at the Chicago Hilton was as before. Only the great pyramid of flowers in the lobby-hall had changed. Last time was Christmas, so there was some ineffable evocation of the Christmas spirit with, half-way up on the ballroom stairs, a crib with Mary plus Child and Shepherds. And Christmas carols played out from under the curtained shrine all night and all day.

This time being Easter we have a high-piled catafalque of annunciation-lilies built up in silver-papered pots; at the top a white cross that swivels round and ceases not night nor day. I watched it, fascinated, go round and round till I felt quite sick. The whole thing must have cost hundreds. All the while the chorales came dutifully out of the juke-box, with a lighted-up church that looked like sugar-cake icing on top. Higher up still, beneath the presiding portrait, which I took to be the President but turned out to be President Hilton himself (Harvard in the early 1900s: 'The President has gone down to Washington to see Mr Taft'), amid a jungle of white lilies was a long-eared white rabbit, winking and pawing and gesticulating away.

Really, the national genius of the Americans for reducing everything to the trivial, for debasing *everything* – love, literature, the arts, landscape, the sights of nature, the facts of nature, natural wonders, the element of wonder in life, of any romance or conviction or belief – is a subject to study. I wonder why?** It must be related to the impulse, on which the nation is founded, to bring everything down to the same dreary level, to pull everything down to sameness. (Max Lerner, my foot! with his rubbish about the

* It is Valentine's. 1975.

** It is the end-result of democracy.

superiority of American civilization: in itself a symptom of consciousness of inferiority.) This was bad enough in the days of Tocqueville and Dickens, of Henry James and Mrs Wharton – no wonder they found it unbearable; but in the days when the masses are on top, with all the mass-media of civilization, this is what one arrives at. Not much difference whether it is America or Russia. Look at Russian architecture! Russian painting! or Soviet literature!

This is the modern world, the characteristic civilization of our time. There is no question of putting up any resistance to it.

The question becomes, then, how to live one's life in such a civilization. The answer is – *to live it as an inner exile*. This has become more and more clear to me in the last few years. It is not just a problem how to escape from it physically, by withdrawing into my sanctum at All Souls and within the walls of Trenarren – though the way of life I have happened upon, and the rhythm between those two places, are as good as anything available – but there is the spiritual alienation wherever one may be, for *this* world is all around one. One becomes a constant watcher from outside, for which state all my life has been a preparation.

Easter Saturday

Yesterday was an interesting day, in spite of its slow start in the morning. In the afternoon I went to the Gauguin exhibition. It was a revelation. He has never been among my favourite painters: I had always thought of him as superficial and vulgar, a kind of poster-artist. But seeing him in bulk corrected that; for the first time I was in a position to enter his world. I could appreciate that the flat decoration was deliberate – to get the effect of fresco and a musical monumentality. It was not for want of skill to *approfondir*. In the headdress of the Breton peasant woman on the right of *The Yellow Christ* one can see through the lace to the modelled neck and form beneath. Similarly with some small landscapes, he allows himself to suggest vistas of depth beyond. Some of these mysterious landscapes recalled Watteau.

The colouring that had never attracted me I saw to be authentically expressive of his vision. No artist has more peculiarly a colour spectrum of his own, except perhaps Poussin. Though still not *attracted* by the ordering of his colour, I was impressed by the originality – the juxtaposition of steel-blue, and grey steel and lead with lavender, the acrid lemon and lime yellows and poison greens; or the explosive contiguity of ginger with scarlet, vermilion.

My surrender was begun by the splendid portrait of a cellist – of a classic firmness and power, monumental and authoritative. Things I noted: the enveloping movement of the arms; the scarlet form of the cello, like a great exotic fruit, again enveloped in the deep-sea blue of the suit enclosing it solidly. The hands that were formalized in the manner of Cézanne were yet sensitively articulated: one saw how the one wielded the bow, the other fingered the stops. Most striking, hypnotic in their effect, the slanted eyes of the intense blue of the suit, and absorbed in the inner dream of the music.*

The next to strike me was the self-portrait – Gauguin looking like a Venetian doge, a similar tall headdress; underneath again slanted blue eyes, watchful, predatory, lascivious; and that arrogant profile. A mobile pale hand holds the brush, while the painter watches and reflects a moment, with the intentness of the dedicated artist.

So my progress in revelation continued round the room.

The third picture to arrest me was quite different: the splendid 'Man with an Axe', full of the sense of arrested movement: the golden-brown of the young Tahitian, both arms uplifted in the rhythm of wielding the axe, the body beautifully constructed, broad at the shoulders and slendering to the waist. Behind him the upward diagonal thrust of the pale blue pirogue, in which his woman bends down with drooping dugs of sow or bitch – Gauguin's vision disguises nothing of the facts of nature. In the background another decorative native skiff with a sail, and beyond, the line of white foam on the reef curdling upon the sea.

All these pictures give an ominous, strangely threatening impression.

On my way back I stopped in that lobby-hall of the hotel. The Easter motets went on and on repeating themselves: I asked an attendant if the record couldn't be changed. No, they were on a non-stop tape. I now know these pieces as I got to know the chimes from the Amsterdam City Hall – at first fascinated, in the end nauseated.

There I ran into a young Canadian, good manners, Scotch name. We had coffee together. He turned out to be a professional skater, member of the company that gives an Ice Revue twice a night in the Boulevard Room. He was anxious for me to see the show, never having done so in my life. So I went. The result was a challenge: here were perfectly ordinary people, whom one wouldn't recognize in a crowd, displaying extraordinary talents on the ice. It put me in my place to reflect that I couldn't stand upright on the ice. These people glided about effortlessly like birds, wheeling and swerving, darting and leaping and dancing – to say nothing of the star performers, who were as good as ballet stars only faster and more acrobatic. I sat there

* Like Rostropovitch playing.

astonished, chastened, admiring, holding my breath at some of the feats, taking in the swift, evanescent beauty of it all.

Easter Monday

I awoke happily this morning with the dream that Jack had come over to join me. He had come by the CPR route – yes, had had an excellent sea-voyage, no sickness, no trouble. Yes, he had stopped in Quebec, and was duly impressed by the site of the city – wonderful. Complete corroboration. Other figures moved about on the edge of consciousness, among them Betty Stucley.[1]

Yesterday a quiet lazy morning, and slept after lunch. In late afternoon I took a bus-ride out along the South Shore – to see the dreary squalor of Chicago's housing away from the shining skyscrapers of the centre, the chromium glitter of State Street. Everywhere plenty of space – everywhere gaps where houses had been thrown down, the area flattened with the debris of bricks. Squalid saloons, squalid hoardings, whole derelict areas, streets and streets of hideous buildings, late nineteenth and early twentieth centuries. At one point tall new tenements to rehouse have been run up by the Medical Association. At another a hideous modern Lake Side Country Club with flat golf-course beside it and a few new trees growing in indignity. We passed the University area and the Lake Windermere Hotel where I went to visit Isaiah Berlin four years ago. 'Do come and see me: I am so lonely here,' he chanted. 'This was before we were married,' said his wife. So I went up: there he was in his virginal white bed-sitting room, opulent and comfortable, but nobody to talk to – as T.S.E. complained about his year as Professor at Harvard. Isaiah and I talked our old themes of Charles Henderson and Lightfoot and All Souls and Trevor-Roper, who had just perpetrated his caddish review of *The Expansion of Elizabethan England*, after an enthusiastic private letter. 'But he doesn't have any human perceptions,' said Isaiah, 'he's made of glass and rubber.'

Isaiah continues to be the cat's whiskers over here. William Appleton Williams wanted to know what it was all based on. He had read Isaiah's reports at Washington and couldn't see what there was in them. I said that Churchill was supposed to have been impressed. Williams wanted to know what I thought: I had no objection to telling him. Isaiah knows all these languages, is bilingual in English and Russian – knows everybody of importance in two continents, a great many people in Europe, especially France and Russia. But what have all these talents, these advantages, produced? A

1. A Cornish contemporary who believed herself in love with ALR and wrote a very bad novel about it.

couple of mice by way of books. The little book on Marx, quite inadequate and hopelessly proportioned: hardly goes further than 1848 and devotes more space to Marx's unimportant philosophical ideas than to his far more important views on economics and history. Then a little book, no more than an essay, is on Tolstoy's historical views, *The Hedgehog and the Fox*. A very sensible essay, badly written, for Isaiah writes sentences a page long; it reads as if dictated, in his verbose spoken style. And now another essay on Historical Inevitability, which I expect I should agree with. For I agree with him in scepticism with regard to doctrine and dogma, empiricism of approach and method, common-sense in the upshot.

But with Isaiah's gifts and facility, and at his time of life – allowing for the war years in Washington – he ought by this time to have produced a couple of big books. He *could* have given us a really solid and substantial history of Russian Social Thought. Instead of which he has given us a translation of an already translated Turgenev novel.

It is all bits and pieces; nothing solid, nothing substantial or in any way significant. And yet he remains not only a name, but the very whiskers of the cat Auden celebrated long ago.* Of course Isaiah has the Jewish claque behind him wherever he goes – as this in part accounts for the immense campaign on behalf of Pasternak. *Is Dr Zhivago* all that good?** Isaiah's review of it is quoted as a full – or half-page advertisement by (of course) the *New York Times* and the *Saturday Review*.

He is a fascinating (and inexhaustible) talker, a nice man, a great gossip with a good deal of (harmless) malice, essentially kind and good. So I wish him well. In addition to which, as dear Charles Henderson's discovery and protégé, he is one of my oldest, though never intimate, acquaintances. I strongly supported his election at All Souls. And, no doubt, now he has his troubles. His wife complained to me how much opposition he had to put up with from 'friends' and colleagues over his inaugural lecture on Two Views of Freedom. I said to her consolingly that they are just jealous.

As I am myself – with more reason. For there is no comparison between the solid body of my work, with its originality, and Isaiah's inadequate performance, with a couple of booklets and a couple of essays. His immense *réclame* is disproportionate.

In the evening I met good old Tom Davey, my pen-pal, of Palmer House.[1] He came up to my room for a sip of sherry, and showed me, with tears in his eyes, his apprenticeship indenture as a quarryman aged about eleven or

* And then to be given an O.M., Quite right for our time.

** I found it was not.

1. The famous hotel.

twelve, a boy of St Ann's Chapel at Calstock. 'This Indenture witnesseth that Thomas Knapman Davey doth put himself Apprentice to Bolt and Son, Granite Quarry Workers, of Hingston Quarry, Calstock, to learn with them their Art, and after the manner of an apprentice, to serve from 29 October 1895 unto the full term of four years . . . During which time the said Apprentice his Masters faithfully shall serve, their secrets keep, their lawful commands everywhere gladly do . . . He shall not waste his Masters' goods, or lend them.' All lost time to be made up, etc. The father's signature, barely able to write his name, was there with the others plentifully sealed. And at the end – 'This Indenture has been truly and faithfully served. Dated this 25/10/02. T. W. Bolt.'

Last night Tom told me that with knapsack and a few tools he walked down Gunnislake hill to the bridge with a few other fellows, not one of whom wished him good luck or said anything at all to the boy setting out in life, with one gold sovereign in his pocket. His wages were 6d a day the first year, 8d the second, 10d the third, 14d the fourth.

He took me all over Palmer House, which he has been identified with for the past twenty. I was deeply impressed – not so much by the vastness and lavishness of the equipment and the place, as by him. We went through immense basements, boiler-house, linen-rooms, several kitchens – one of them a Philippino kitchen serving a restaurant in a succession of dim-lighted Polynesian huts, carved posts, bamboo decoration, immense shells, exotic fish; kitchens for the staff of 2,000, cafeterias, palatial ballroom, fortunes in rings and chandeliers, etc.

But what impressed me was his own engineering office down in the basement. He had plans, drawn by himself, of every floor in the 24-storey building; plans of all the electric installations, every line of current and where they all connected up; designs and sections of the rooms with their plaster ceilings – no idea of beauty, naturally, but a complete mastery of the techniques. He had grown with this place, had a great deal to do with its designing, improvements, changes. In addition, by way of hobby, he is always scribbling for the *Chicago Tribune*, or the *Tavistock Times*, and lectures once a week to churches, veterans, 'anybody who will hear me' about the development and history of the United States.

He knew all the key-men in the place, and they knew him as Tom familiarly; he introduced me round as the Professor from Oxford who was a poor man's son, just a working-man's son, etc. It was a bit out of key in the environment of young America; however they and I knew how to take it.

No wonder Tom was naively proud of the way he had come from the youthful quarryman at Calstock – who knew how to ring the jumpers,[1] and

1. A term of art referring to Davey's training as a quarryman.

a fine upstanding lad he must have been – to becoming a key-man in this immense establishment. I noted the Cornish trait of naïveté in the egoism – the simplicity of the assumption that everyone would be as interested in his doings as himself; we all have the same guileless trait. More sophisticated types are not so keen. But I was filled with admiration for what the old boy had achieved with his life over here.

No wonder they came. No opportunities in impoverished Cornwall like these. He is a piece of history in himself. I pressed him, as I have before, to write a complete Cornish-American autobiography. By far the most interesting thing about him is his experience of life. He was looking a good deal older than when I last saw him. He may leave it till too late.

31 March

The news in the papers is of Easter churchgoing, chief prominence given to a photograph of Eisenhower – looking more than ever like a Presbyterian minister – being presented with a paper bag containing a little Easter chick, on his way to church, the usual inane guffaw, the mouth wide open, the rows of well-cared for presidential dentures.* The American genius for reducing everything to the trivial, once more. Imagine anyone trying to present the Queen with an Easter chick. Or, for that matter, George Washington, or Jefferson, Adams, or even Theodore Roosevelt or Woodrow Wilson. One sees how far we have progressed in democracy since then.

Yesterday afternoon I paid my first visit to the Newberry Library, where Pargellis, agreeable, avuncular – but a friend of the proselytizing Stanley Morison[1] – gave up the whole afternoon to showing me treasures.

And *what* treasures! A wonderful collection of maps, including one from Bologna 1566, by Zalterii, of New France; another from Leyden 1588 by Fr Raphelengius to illustrate Drake's West Indies expedition of 1585–6, a coloured map of Santo Domingo depicting the operations, the city in detail, the fleet with Drake's flagship grandly displaying the flag of St George. There was a beautiful Antwerp edition in Spanish and in colour of Ortelius' Atlas. We just picked out something here and there – the first sketch in colour of New Orleans, another of the plantations along the river there, with the large estate of Bieuville, now that fine exotic park by the bayou where I saw the camellia garden one November in full flower. From there we moved into the sixteenth-century section where we sat down to some

* Would I accept such infantile rubbish?

1. *Éminence grise* of *The Times*, himself an ardent convert to Roman Catholicism.

interesting new Elizabethan arrivals, including a book with a signature of interest.* Pargellis had read it as John Matthew, but it was Tobie Matthew, later Archbishop of York, friend of Bacon and everybody: a tract of 1589 describing the Lisbon expedition. And other charming tracts, about some of which I was able to make suggestions. One seems not have been reprinted, though there was a German and an Italian translation – Captain Robert Coverte's 'True and Almost Incredible Report of an Englishman (being cast away in the good ship *Ascension*)' on the fourth East Indian voyage, printed in 1614.

And so to a very rich collection of French political tracts of the sixteenth century, volumes and volumes of them mostly from the Wars of Religion. From the collection of Prayer Books one pulled out a good copy of the first Prayer Book of 1549, June impression – which sparked off the Prayer Book Rebellion in the West Country. This one had an advertisement of all the different prices according to the quality of the leather binding, whether calf's skin or forel (?) or whatnot.

'There is nothing sissy about Jesus Christ. He would be a star-athlete in Australia. He was every inch a man.' – The ineffable and vulgar Billy Graham to Australians, flattering their silliness.

1 May

Miles behind with my journal: only an Atlantic crossing will enable me to catch up now. So busy, so hot, summer has begun all at once: no Spring. Today is some sort of celebration, and with some dressing up. Since a dance is going on at the Presbyterian church across the way, with dance band, there is no going to bed yet, I may as well catch up on the last few days.

28 April: a frightful storm, torrential rain all night, floods out and a high wind: just my luck for my first air-flight. I was equally disturbed by a couple of letters at once from the odious Cornish Waif,[1] with the usual abuse about the money that should be hers, etc. She *says* that she has never received the 50/50 distribution of royalty I instructed Odhams to make between her and me. So there is that to look into.**

Rather upheaved and concerned I took my first flight from Madison to Minneapolis. Surprisingly unalarmed and interested by a belated new experience, I sat back and enjoyed the spectacle of Lake Mendota spread

* Denuding the old country, of course.

1. See above, p. 182.

** She ended up with more than 50 per cent – she made £425 she said, I £375. Her book was my property: I bought the mass of material and made a book of it.

out below, the rectangular pattern of fields and farms with white farmhouses and silver silos, the roads running straight for miles or in occasional curves, the light brushwood of the trees in patches. All the same, an alien landscape of this immense, immeasurable country stretching out flat, good cultivated farmland in every direction.

Soon it became cloudy and we went on through and above the low flying ones. Then fog and it became rough, so bumpy, the plane was riding the waves like a boat. Just my luck, for I have no head at all, and with the tremendous vibration was completely laid out: not sick, of course, for I had had nothing to eat since lunch, but the most frightful headache.

Louie Hill, whom I knew from the brief time he spent in Oxford – it is curious that we should have kept up, even sketchily, through all the years – was at the large busy ant-hill of an airport to meet me. In place of the handsome young fellow I had known, there was a broad middle-aged, grey-haired man, already somewhat wrinkled, hair balding along the forehead. I dare say he had a similar shock.

In his powerful Ford he took me off at terrific speed around the family town, made famous by his grandfather's activities, Jim Hill the Railway King, Empire Builder of the Great Northern, more than anybody else creator of the North-West. Feeling like death, hardly capable of attending, as sick as ever, I was whirled and swirled and swerved about those beastly roads, brought up with a jerk against Stop signs, while Louie talked with hundred horse-power voltage, hands off the wheel, turning round to demonstrate the beastly sights I could well dispense with for a lie-down and not a word from anybody, gesticulating, shouting as if he were addressing a meeting.

I had come to Madeleine Doran in my account of Madison and I found her the most charming person there. Her name was one of the few I knew before I went, from her book *Endeavours of Art*, which I possess but have not read. She is a native Californian and has the charm that goes with that. I shouldn't like to be exposed to it long – I might topple over. Especially on an afternoon like the farewell tea she gave me. It was a quiet Sunday afternoon – 24 May; she lives in an attractive loop across from a lagoon of Lake Wingra and the University Arboretum. Before tea we went across to one of the streams that feed the lake, a perfect halting ground for migrating birds in Spring. She showed me Canada violets, white with yellow centres, blue on the underside of the petal; delicate lavender water-leaf in blue clusters; wild woodland phlox in clumps in the glades; a tiny wild mint with blue flowers like diminutive skull-caps, perhaps a ground ivy. A clearing in the burr-oak copse was made for crab-apple and wild cherry, the blossom past its best now, though some was still out on the cherries, 'white along the bough'. Beyond, across the water, were the tall cotton-woods waving, and shimmering aspens here called popples. We went along the tracks by the marsh, paradise for birds, and back to her apartment for tea. The house was cushioned with bushes of bridal wreath out in full splendour; snow-balls of white blossom like hawthorn along the sprays, with leaves a Sung green.

We went in to tea. What more enticing than that feminine apartment, the tray laid with home-made preserves, apple jelly and cherry, home-made bread, fragrant tea – Lapsang – in the English manner. It was all enchanting – presided over by a charming woman in her Mexican dress, pink with white lace; intelligent, independent, with that beguiling clear voice. It wouldn't take much for me to fall for her.

But I expect she is as wary of falling as I. She gets what she can out of the birds. That too adds to the charm of the image – I see her, like a lady in a Japanese print, surrounded by sprays of flower-blossom and the birds of Spring.

After tea, and working through her library for suggestions for my Elizabethan studies, we went further afield into the Arboretum. Got out of the car and walked down through the wood, listening to the calls of wood-thrush and meadow lark. 'Ooh, I'm glad we came!' said Madeleine like a child. And, 'Oh, I wish I had brought my glasses.'

We made our way down to a delicious spring, where the birds visited. Other birds were there: extended beneath a tree were two lovers, very much in each other's arms, the young man practically on top of his girl, with a good deal of bird-play. Madeleine gave no sign of noticing; I of course was disturbed.

For her the birds are a substitute, if not a sufficient substitute. About the house Madeleine has a cardinal, a pair of them, superb blob of fiery crested red the male. When nesting, he solicitously feeds the female – 'his little *lady*'. She is a lady herself, and a gallant one. Apparently her father went broke on a citrus farm in California. So she keeps her mother, and goes dutifully back home to San Diego for her vacations. She is a very attractive woman, a fine one and I like her very much.

New York, 11 June

In the morning I wrote up my journal. And at twelve went down to the other end of the town to take Elizabeth Bowen out to lunch. She has been staying all winter in New York, and was now at the Grosvenor on 10th Street – Henry James and Mrs Wharton's New York. A more elegant hotel than mine – it looked expensive – I waited with something of the old social trepidation until Elizabeth came down. She stepped out of the lift in her stylish way, stammering her words in familiar fashion – a rush of clever words to the head. She still looked young, held herself like a girl, though the hair was greying now – no longer red-gold – skin stretched older on the forehead. Otherwise unchanged: the same amusing, distinguished but unaffected girl, at the same time unmistakably a lady of old Irish family. She had been accustoming herself to travelling up town in buses: I do not think the custom had gone very far.

A chain-smoker, as she described herself, she went straight to the complicated machine – 'I do this,' she said, and out dropped the right brand of cigarettes.

I don't know any restaurants at that end of the town, so, just like herself, she led me to a cheap restaurant around the corner, which wouldn't do at all, before we settled on the Breevoort, which she must have feared too expensive for my dollar resources. We settled down, Elizabeth looking very smart in her black-and-white check silk dress, and talked first about Madison, which she had liked so much she was sorry to leave after a month. I mentioned Jim Collins, the curious character in the Radio department, old Southern gentleman, French affectations, always talking in French clichés he had picked up in Paris – whom I saw a good deal of, who made up to me a lot, was kind and I not reluctant. He cherished a great devotion for Elizabeth – a highlight of his life when he entertained her to tea and radio. She dismissed him easily, 'a foolish absurd character'. And so indeed he is; yet I should never have found it in my heart to dismiss him out of hand like that. I added that he was kind, a Southern gentleman. Actually, since I saw so much more of him, he irritated me more. I marvelled at her being able to sum him up so quickly and ruthlessly.

Elizabeth told me about the book, impressions of Rome, she has just finished and was uproariously funny about the dialogue that comes in the middle, answering people's objections. 'Why Rome?' 'Why not Dublin?' 'Why not Greece?' etc. I mentioned Mary MacCarthy and Eleanor Clark. 'Oh, it's not going to be at all like *that*,' she said with distaste. 'Have you ever met Mary MacCarthy?' she said. I have decided that I don't care for her writing. She can only write about herself, and clever as it is, it is only the higher journalism. No wonder Cyril Connolly writes her up; she's a sort of American Connolly, hardly more feminine. One remembers the gushing female novelist Evelyn Waugh descried beneath Cyril's swelling bosom. I couldn't get through *The Groves of Academe*: too Mary MacCarthy.

Elizabeth said that she had complained that nobody listened to her at Oxford, and 'I should think not. There are the most brilliant men to listen to: better keep silent and listen to them.' But imagine an American woman keeping silent, and especially one of the MacCarthy sort! She must have had a disappointing time at Oxford.

Having finished the Roman book, Elizabeth is now engaged on a money-making article for *Holiday* on the Deep South, which fascinates her. She has several times stayed with her friend Eudora Welty, described her to me and her circumstances. The victim of her family, especially her mother, who is always threatening to go blind. Then Eudora has two brothers – handsome fellows, the younger of whom got some complaint and died quite young a year or two ago. Eudora was in the middle of a wonderful story, and the whole thing had to be packed up to look after the family. 'She is the nearest thing to a secular saint I know – and perhaps not so secular either.' She longs to come to New York, *loves* New York, but can hardly ever come. Elizabeth described her appearance: the beautiful ugliness, broad forehead and splendid eyes. She evidently admires Eudora's work while having no admiration for Mary MacCarthy and Eleanor Clark. In spite of Elizabeth herself being held fashionable, a friend of Cyril and Raymond, etc., what is interesting is that she does not really share their values: she is her own man.

We talked of Elizabeth Jenkins, who is another case: has never been fashionable or appreciated by that lot. We rejoiced at Elizabeth's triumph: she must have done well out of her *Elizabeth the Great*.* She has never made much money before. Elizabeth Bowen described the house in St John's Wood, the rather threadbare elegance, the pretty things Elizabeth Jenkins had picked up for five shillings, the things that wanted doing in the house and that she hoped to be able to do sometime, the good cooking she does all herself.

She told me about young Elizabeth's books, that *The Tortoise and the Hare* was a revenge novel. Young Elizabeth is so attractive that she could have been married twenty times. But it happened to her to have her young man taken off her – pretty, sensitive, gifted as she is – by a quite unattractive woman, ugly, thick legs etc. Elizabeth Jenkins saw the humour of it, but was also angry. She wrote it up in the novel and then blandly sent it to the offending couple: 'you may be interested to read my latest book'. No reaction, except for the husband writing to say that he 'looked forward' to reading it.

I said how much I dislike this formula and never use it myself. But Elizabeth Jenkins was rendered very unhappy by the affair. She never sent me the novel, though she sends me her other books. For example, her *Six Criminal Women*, *à propos* of which Elizabeth Bowen told me an amusing story. The publisher made a hash of the book, and Spencer Curtis Brown

* She did: £16,000.

weighed in to help Elizabeth dress him down. So they tracked him down and mounted the stairs: Elizabeth tiny and frail, very ladylike, diminutive hand in white glove resting on Curtis Brown's arm: an 1810 scene. When they got into the room Elizabeth left Curtis Brown's arm, stepped forward and said to the delinquent publisher, 'What the hell do you mean, making a mess of my book?' Everyone was astonished – from those lips and that presence. The hardened agent just sat back and let Elizabeth do the talking.

At this point I was interrupted in the train. A very young woman came and stood in the gangway by my seat – there was a vacant one inside. I was writing away and had no intention of being interrupted – plenty of vacant seats around. She went on standing, overlooking my writing, I took no notice, but went on writing. At this she said, 'Is there a seat vacant?' I said, 'Yes,' preparing to move reluctantly, without looking at her. Still without looking I made room and moved inside. And then, pointing with my pencil, '*There* is a vacant seat,' across the gangway.

'But I want the one by the window.'

'I am sitting by the window,' I replied, still not looking up.

'Oh, I see,' she said and moved on.

I took in that she was young and good-looking, evidently used to having everyone make way for her. Not so me. American bitches don't get their way with me by their bitchery.

Elizabeth talked about Bowenscourt,[1] evidently a problem, especially since Alan's death. Did I know anybody who would take it? She didn't really want to sell it, though there had been a financial crisis about it last year. People are moving to Ireland and that district is becoming quite fashionable. Eddy Sackville-West had settled there – handed over Knole, though he ought to have made an effort, to his next heir. He had always had a thing about Elizabeth – nothing romantic or amorous – and had come over to Ireland to be near her. Had spent all his money on making the place lovely. A sad defeated character, who should have stuck to his early promise – those first novels had talent; but he had allowed himself to be discouraged – largely by his literary friends. I said they wrote nothing themselves and hated it that others did. What he wanted was someone to love him. She said there was always someone in the background he was half in love with – it was all rather unhappy, devitalized.

By way of helping her with her background to the South and her general knowledge of America, I suggested one or two books for her – Morison and Commager, Henry's *Story of the Confederacy*. It is extraordinary how little

1. Her family house in Ireland, described by ALR (pp. 151–5).

Elizabeth knows about American history, for all the time she spends over here. I suggested she got in the way of reading in the New York Public Library – such a superb library; one doesn't need to buy the books. Then I told her what Mrs Masefield once said to me: 'It's wonderful how the Irish *contrive* to be so uneducated.'

Elizabeth laughed like anything at this. I told her about Lincoln – she had no idea that he was a Southerner by origin, or about Andrew Jackson. She was rather fascinated and kept saying that I ought to write a book about Lincoln and Lee! As if there aren't hundreds already, and anyway not at all my subject. It is true that most of them are written like mud, in the American manner; or think of the triviality and irrelevance of dear Mrs —, the silly woman at Urbana forever writing about Lincoln, his family, his wife, courtships, sons, his cats and his shoes. Is there one single, really first-class book written about him? Thomas's is the most sensible, though second-rate in its writing. Carl Sandburg's moneyspinner is a monstrous epic of self-identification. Sentimental old German, of very second-rate qualities.

Lunch drawing to a close, I wished Elizabeth good luck with the new book and said that I would review it, beginning with 'Miss Bowen's book forms a third on that eminent trinity along with Miss Mary MacCarthy and Eleanor Clark.' Elizabeth at once comically panicked. 'Oh *don't*, Leslie; *please*. Please don't mention me along with those dreadful American women.' Her agitation betrayed what she really thought.

'Of course not,' I said, 'I'm only teasing.'

Still panicky she said, 'I never know when I'm being teased. I'm Irish and have no sense of humour. I can't bear it.'

It was absurd and endearing that she should have been genuinely alarmed. I made to pour out some more of the excellent Breevoort coffee. The lid stuck, she rashly flicked it open and the coffee slopped over cup, saucer and table-cloth, and even made a spot – it seemed – on her dress. Then she really did panic, jumped up in alarm, saying, 'Every day I wash this dress out myself.' Actually I couldn't descry a single spot, but I discerned something of the background of Elizabeth's life over here.

At the end, 'You couldn't let me have two dollars in return for a cheque, could you?' I said, wouldn't she prefer twenty? 'Oh, of course, if you could. I don't want to appear as one of those hawks of English women for ever . . .' I said, would she like a hundred? 'But, *could* you manage it?' I said I was *rolling*, but she was not to mention it to anyone.

She said she would write a cheque, and would much rather that I gained from it. How much should it be? Wouldn't it be about £33? I said it might be £27. We might average it at £30. No, she would rather it was £33. Would I work it out? I took the back of the bill, and found that I was so nervous that I couldn't do this simple sum. I said, how odd: when I was an elementary schoolboy I could do arithmetic like anything; now I couldn't do it.

We walked back to her hotel, and she went up to her room to write her cheque. When she came down with it and said goodbye at the door, she said 'darling' – the first time I had earned such an endearment. It had been heavenly to see her; I was delighted with myself to think I had been able to come to her rescue – she was going away for a week – and that I had cleaned myself out of all my precious dollars for her.

I went across the street to see the gloomy Victorian church. On my way back in the bus I missed my dollars rather, but remained pleased that she had them. I found that I could do the sum $2.80 into $100 in my head, and that it made just over £33. When I looked at the cheque I found that it was for £30. I remained equally pleased and amused.

Queen Mary, 22 June

We are berthed here at Cherbourg for the afternoon: the journey that I feared would be hell has passed agreeably. The vast ship is completely packed. I suppose I was lucky to get a berth at all: I left it late. First thing I did was to go to the Purser to change from my upper berth in a cabin of four. Never travelled so before.

My companions turned out well enough. The first thing I noticed from his luggage was a Cornishman – James Pearce of Townshend, near Hayle. He proved to be an old naval man, who had made a success of his life. He learned electrical engineering at Falmouth, then joined the Navy. Was in various engagements, the first with the *Goeben*'s escort in the Straits of Messina. Then in the Dogger Bank action, and at Jutland in Beatty's battle-cruiser squadron. He shared Beatty's men's opinion that they should have been supported by Jellicoe. After the war he bought seven acres in his native village and settled down to market-gardening. He told me the story – it turned out to be excellent land, just right for the job. They built a long packing shed, one end of which they turned into a house for a time, laid on water from their own well, drainage; built up their connections with London, Manchester and Bradford shops; learned from experience the best routine of flower-crops to keep their land engaged all the year round – violets all through the winter; in the end, sold the whole thing at good profit, keeping an acre on which they had built their permanent house, made their own garden filled with flowering shrubs. The old boy was well pleased with himself and the way things had worked out, 'now very comfortable' he admitted; it was 'wonderful how one thing had led to another'. It was God who did it, he said. I let that pass without comment.

The second fellow had also been in the Navy during the war, a Mr Portsmouth travelling to Southampton.

The third intrigued me: a Mr Gabriel, with my initials, also skied like me in an upper berth. He went to bed very late and got up very late, so that one hardly saw him for the first few days. Who was he? Evidently a Continental, probably a Jew. I built up a regular fantasy about the Archangel, with which I amused myself and Mr Portsmouth. In the end it was the Archangel who surprised me. On the third morning I was shaving at the wash-basin, when he whom I had supposed dead to the world leaned out of Heaven and said 'Good Morning' – much as the original Archangel must have said to the Blessed Virgin. It then transpired that Gabriel knew a great deal about me and my books, about universities and libraries – a prodigious memory like a filing cabinet. We then became buddies: he would lie in wait for me in the mornings when the others had gone and conduct gossipy conversations while I shaved. An interesting man who has written about medieval universities.

Coming back to the irritations, provocations, backbitings, denigrations of life in England (if I feel like this about it, may not the time come when I decide to cut the painter), I have been thinking with the more regret of my pleasant life in Madison without these unpleasantnesses. Scenes of my routine there have come up in my mind: the pleasant University Club, Elizabethan red brick, with portico and steps to the square, which I would cross to Students' Union for some of my meals, University Library where I worked a good deal in the first half of the semester, the State Historical Library where I worked even harder the second. Then uphill beside the green swards extending down from Bascom Hall, where I lectured faithfully morning and afternoon on Mondays, Wednesdays, Fridays – never missing once on grounds of illness, but only on the two occasions of visits to Minnesota and Illinois. Never a cold; just solid, active work.

What luck I had! When I went over I had a very sketchy series of notes for the two courses I had to give. For the Tudors and Stuarts I had my Illinois notes up to 1570, as so much capital to begin with. I had at first to devote all my energies to accumulating a capital of notes on Portuguese, Spanish, French Expansion before I came to English, where I could hold my head above water up to 1620 or so; then there was English, Dutch and French Expansion after this to add.

It was by a narrow margin that I managed it. When I went over I had this on my mind, and worked away on the boat at Henry the Navigator, Parry's excellent textbook, etc. – though I am such an old hand now that I had a feeling of confidence underneath that I should *get through*.

I just managed it, with nothing to spare. For there were other assignments in addition to those six lectures (one couldn't possibly prepare each of six lectures every week). The egalitarian sentiment of the History Department was at work: I had come in on the ground floor (unlike my Illinois appointment, more honorific) and I wasn't going to be let off any assignments. There were two sets of examinations to correct for each course, mid-term and final. Two M.A. theses to examine, each of them good; while I read through Arthur Smith's for him out of friendship. George Mosse let me in for two sessions on Contemporary Trends before a large audience of 500 students, on Marxism, which were both amplified and recorded. These turned out successfully: all kinds of people spoke to me about them. I recorded a radio talk about Churchill; gave a public lecture, recorded, on 'Elizabeth I and America'; spoke to one or two undergraduate groups, and a University Extra-Mural class. Along with the routine seeing of pupils, answering their questions, giving them advice. Looking back on it all, I was fond of them, as they certainly gave every expression of their being for me. To operate in a group I need an atmosphere of good-will and affection. That does not exist at All Souls, or in Oxford; in Cornwall or in England. *Their* fault rather than mine – except that I am *too* sensitive, one skin too few. Hence vulnerable.

3 October. Afternoon at Hallington, Northumberland*

I have brought my chair out to a favourite spot on the lawn, on the edge of the deep dene, the still water of the barricaded burn spattered with fallen leaves, the noise of the water going through the weir coming up with the breeze that just stirs the beeches not yet turning. There is some colour about, lemon yellow of chestnut, crimson blush of dogwood, striped scarlet of sumach.

Walking here this morning the Master told me how it came to him. The creator of it was a fairly remote Trevelyan widow, left well-off, who put her money into improving this place. She increased the size of the house a good deal, Victorianizing it from its regular Georgian, and rather well, 'considering it was done in the 1860s – nothing Gothic about it'. But the essential thing she did was to buy the other bank on the other side of the burn, and plan the planting of the dene as a whole. It was just one bank, all jungle, pretty well impassable. She laid out paths on either side and blocked the stream to fill the bottom with water. Now the dene makes the whole charm of the place, purple and gold in high summer, lemon, russet, red in autumn. I have not seen it in Spring or under snow. It must be good at all times.

The Master's talk this morning was as sharp and unselfconscious as ever.

* Stopping with G. M. Trevelyan.

I read a bit to him from a new book about the Anglo-Florentines and, reminded of Browning, he suddenly began to quote from 'Old Pictures in Florence', and then went on for forty or fifty lines. His memory for verse is astonishing, and I said so. He said he had merely a good natural memory, but nothing out of the ordinary, like Macaulay who could recite the whole of *Paradise Lost*. He (G.M.T.) remembered poetry by the aid of the rhymes; it made it all the more remarkable to remember *Paradise Lost* in blank verse. I said that Edgeworth,[1] on his one crossing of the Atlantic, prostrated with seasickness, lay in his bunk reconstructing the *Odyssey* from memory and, I think, found he could do three-quarters of it.

What a pity it was my generation had such little memory for verse; the older generation at All Souls, people like Dougie Malcolm and Oman, had hundreds of lines by heart. G.M. said that a great mistake was made when they ceased to learn poetry by heart; it meant that the generation younger than mine didn't care for poetry. Except Shakespeare, since he was a dramatist and they liked plays. Shakespeare was the only poet they knew.

'Shakespeare and T. S. Eliot,' I said. 'Oomph,' he said with contempt.

Then, 'where should I be, incapable of reading or writing, if I hadn't reciting poetry to fall back on? I can recite Lycidas, L'Allegro, Il Penseroso, Wordsworth's "Intimations of Immortality" and "Tintern Abbey", Meredith's "Love in the Valley", and a score of sonnets by different people.'

Later, walking in the dene, he recited several stanzas of 'Love in the Valley', adding that he thought it the most beautiful poem of them all. He put more feeling into it than he usually recites poetry with. Perhaps he was thinking of Janet. I dare say, for shortly after he was loud in praise for Browning for the courage with which he took Elizabeth Barrett away from her possessive father, to the climate of Italy which cured her of her illness. In reciting poetry it is curious what little feeling he gives it, in that toneless Trevelyan voice.

His great-aunt left an only daughter, who 'had not much of what you and I call resources' and was utterly bored at Hallington. She asked G.M.'s grandfather's advice, who advised a six months' tour in Italy. She never came back: she lived in a palazzo in the centre of Taormina (where, he did not say, she married the local doctor). 'I only met her once. When I was there I called on her and had tea with her. She was touched by this attention and left me the estate. Fortunately I had the money to be able to look after it properly. For the last twenty years it had been let. That came to an end in 1927. I came here in 1928.'

It is now evening, the dene more shadowy, textured and tapestried. He

1. One of the very senior Fellows of All Souls when ALR was elected. See p. 9.

has just told me that the lady who created this place was the widow of Edward Spencer Trevelyan, brother of Sir Walter. Neither of them had a son, or Wallington would not have come to his grandfather, Sir Charles, whom G.M. speaks of as 'the greatest of us'.

This morning as we walked along the terrace, he admiring the colour of the dahlias against the stone, for there is little enough that he can see – though this morning in the walled garden he saw a Red Admiral feeding on a chrysanthemum – he was very modest about himself. He told me that in his will he had enjoined upon his son, to whom he had left all his copyrights, that there was to be no biography of him. One reason why he had written his *Autobiographical Essay* was to forestall anyone else writing it. I said he would not be able to prevent people writing about him. Look at the case of Thackeray, and Gordon Ray's too detailed biography, He asseverated strongly that Thackeray was in a totally different class – a man of genius, where he himself was only a man of talents who had done the best with his talents.

I said he was under-estimating the value of the historian's work as literature compared with the novelist's. And over-estimating Thackeray. Thackeray wasn't in the same class with Dickens. He agreed with that. But historians like Gibbon, Macaulay, Carlyle, were as important as writers as novelists were. He agreed about them, but did not compare himself with them.

At one point in the discussion he paid me an unlikely compliment. I said that I did not count. 'Oh, yes,' with conviction, 'you *count* – very much so.'

I said we historians had different things to contribute. There were two things present in G.M.'s work, which, much as we admired Gibbon's genius, were not present in *his*: the topographical sense, the sense of the bone-structure of England and her landscape, which I loved in his work and where he owed a lot to his life-long habit of walking. For another – the justice of mind which he had developed with the years, which was not present in Gibbon – or perhaps in his own earlier radicalism. He agreed that Gibbon had been essentially unjust to Christianity.

In his old age and increasing blindness, which has cut him off from work – always the main interest of his life – this reassurance was not unwelcome to him.

I admire his real liberalism, though I do not share it. Last evening, for instance, he did not complain of the decline of his income, owing to taxation, etc., as all writers do. He said, 'I agree with death-duties and supertax. I think it is right. I pay my taxes gladly.' He said his income had come down now to £6,000 a year. To pay tax on that, and maintain this place with all the dependants clustered round it, and the Cambridge house with his nurse-housekeeper, he must live on capital.

But then, when the going was good, what a good time *he* had! Like all the generation of successful writers before me. Like Cecil Roberts making a fortune of £300,000. Not to compete with bestsellers like Maugham who made a million.

*Every*thing has been against my making money: the constant upward drive of costs bringing my History series to an end, and paring down the margins on all my books. The slimming down and thinning out of newspapers and literary journals so that there is immeasurably less room to write in or demand for us to write. Let alone taxation. Let alone the decline in value of the pound, to one-third what it was before the second war – let alone what it was before the first! Let alone the instability, the ups and downs, of investments, the loss of our financial position in the world, the continuous inflation. Let alone the loss of freedom to do what one likes with one's own, the hard-earned product of one's toil.

All in all, *I* should have made a fortune of £200,000 or £250,000, in pre-war currency, had I had their conditions. I suppose one should be grateful to have done as inadequately as one has. It is now too dark to write any more. I must go in.

G.M.T. has very strict and upright Victorian moral principles. At tea he was approving of Nottingham[1] (Dismal) for, unlike the other cleverer ones, having no correspondence with St Germain.[2] I praised Marlborough's subtlety, to tease G.M.T. a bit; 'subtlety' is another word for 'treachery', he said. I was admiring the subtlest man of them all, Halifax. 'Yet he would not sign the invitation to William,' he said. I said that was very understandable, with his point of view. 'You mean to say that you wouldn't have signed the invitation?' I said, No. 'I think the less of you for that,' he said. 'You mean, you wouldn't?' I said that intellectually I should not have approved of signing it, emotionally I might have been carried away.

He was very disapproving. He said that Halifax was not disinterested. I said that the Whigs who signed were even less so; they had every interest in bringing William in. As for Halifax his position was a consistent one: he had saved the principle of the monarchy and James's succession by resisting the Exclusion Bill. He may have thought that the best thing would be to retain James as titular king, with William exercising power as Lieutenant of the Realm. G.M. said that Halifax had not realized, though he knew James for a fool, how *much* of a fool he was, nor that he would bunk from the country. I said precisely – if James hadn't fled, Halifax's more complex view of the situation might have been applicable. G.M. said that William would

1. Late seventeenth-century politician. The conversation revolves round the Revolution of 1688.

2. The exiled Court of James II.

not have accepted this subordinate role. And that at the critical moment, as with a lot of distinguished men, Halifax was NO USE.

This was so characteristic of G.M. – cutting through all the complicated cackle to the core of the matter. This is what I admire in him, though I do not share the point of view. When I was young and a fanatic I would have signed the party manifesto all right, or conceivably have gone to the stake for my convictions. Not so today. All that we have been through in our time, all that I have been through, has subverted any such simplicity. I wouldn't die for anyone, or any cause, any principle. Too many people in our time have been willing to.

'Why not?' said G.M. visibly moved.

'Because I despair of the futility of so much of human action.'

'Go away with you,' said he. 'Take the tea-things away and come back again.'

I came back at once for a renewed set-to. I made it clear that I do not share his simple moral standards, that I agree with Montaigne and Hume – and Gibbon.

Tonight his Cornish nurse told me something new about him. I always thought that Janet was all in all to him, that there never had been anybody but Janet. But not so. Only once did he fall in love, at nineteen, with a girl who refused him.[1] This was a great blow, but it turned out right: they were not really suited. The second time he met a girl he thought he would like to marry. Would she be suitable? He studied her mother, saw the kind of woman she might become and decided against. The third time he met Janet – over Meredith. Evidently not a love-match on his part; was it any more on hers? They lived their separate lives. She was not content to be just the wife of somebody; she had her own career, Foundling Site and all. Nor were they really close. And they were bad for each other in her years of illness, when each made the other worse.

Janet never liked Hallington, and in her last illness would never admit that she was there: she was always at Stocks,* or Welcombe, or somewhere abroad. Taken into the walled garden, where G.M.T. set up her initials with his along those of Edward Spencer Trevelyan and his wife who made it, Janet would say 'This *is* Stocks.' This hurt G.M., to whom Hallington meant a great deal. Though the most eminent member of the family, he was only the third son. He had to stand by and see Wallington go to his eldest brother, whom he strongly disapproved of ('He never had any morals'), while

1. Hester Lyttelton, who subsequently married Cyril Alington, Head Master of Eton and Dean of Durham. Evidently ALR did not know this. He was a friend of theirs and would certainly have had something to say.

* Her mother, Mrs Humphry Ward's place.

Welcombe went to the second son, R.C. Nothing for G.M., until out of the blue came this place – a substitute for Wallington, and his very own.* Hence all the loving care he lavished on it: planting belts of woodland, the coppices and spinneys he delighted to walk through, putting in the engine at the never-failing spring that feeds the burn to bring water to the house – 'Hallington water is very good'; thinning and planting and improving the dene; working up the gardens and lawns about the house; filling the house with good furniture and books.

I was surprised to hear him say that most of the antiques in the house he had got from the antique shops in Hexham, the books from Steadman's in Newcastle. There are good pieces of furniture in the house, though no overriding aesthetic sense to pull the thing together – unlike Trenarren: just disparate things – some Edward Lear watercolours, though none of the best; porcelain boxes, though shut up in a glass case in the Victorian manner; Georgian prints of Cambridge colleges, old wardrobes, chests, clocks. But the rugs, carpets, chair covers are very so-so.

However, the atmosphere of the house – hall-door open to the beds of snapdragons and dahlias, the curve of the drive with beeches as good as at Wallington, and way up on the horizon the Romans watching from their Wall – the whole atmosphere is authentic, generous and welcoming. Here the great historian is the Northumberland squire.

Sunday, 4 October

This morning we went for a walk up through one of the plantations he made thirty years ago, now trees tall enough for thinning and giving protection to the fields from north-east and south-west winds. 'I do hope I die before I go stone-blind,' he said in one of the those explosions of melancholy that afflict him. I tried vainly to console with, 'Your sight is better than it was three years ago. You can see to write a letter now.' In vain. 'I said I hope to die before I am stone-blind. And I say it again.'

On our way out he told me a story of Leslie Stephen, who made such an impression speaking for blind Henry Fawcett[1] that the constituency asked him to stand for the second seat. 'Damn you, don't you know that I am a clergyman?' he said. He and J. A. Froude were in the same case, being in deacon's orders.**

* After the success of his *History of England* made it possible.

1. Henry Fawcett (1833–1884), eminent Radical reformer, equally distinguished as a political theorist (he was the first Professor of Political Economy at Cambridge) and as an effective and popular speaker and politician.

** This disqualified them, until freed by Act of Parliament.

He had no opinion of Stephen's daughter, Virginia Woolf – 'a horrid woman'. He detested Bloomsbury and its works, making an exception for Keynes, who did not really belong. 'For one thing, he was infinitely public-spirited, and one of the things they discouraged was public spirit.' Then, 'they were all very angry with him for getting married. One of the things they had no use for was marriage. He married one of the nicest women possible.' He said that he detested Bloomsbury; when I said that they wrote very well, he replied, 'that made their influence all the more deplorable. A whole generation was ruined by them – gave them a debunking attitude towards great writers.' He once listened to a paper of Lytton Strachey's and registered, 'This is the end of all I care for. And it was.'

N.B. Wouldn't it be nice to give the Leslie Stephen lecture at Cambridge on 'Bloomsbury Considered'? (I was never asked.)

One little touch illumines his character. This evening we were talking of Firth's persecution by the history tutors at Oxford. He said that once A. L. Smith walked him, G.M., around the Parks and spoke of Firth in such terms as he would not have thought two dons could speak of one another. It reveals his own high Victorian standards, and also how little he knows how dons *do* speak of each other.

A story he got from Henry Jackson – at Madingley one day about 1860 with friends, well-read, educated. They were talking of Mrs Browning. One of them said, 'Hasn't she got a husband who writes poetry too?'

Mrs E.B.B. was far better known then. G.M.T.: all Browning's best poems were written in the forties and fifties. His *reputation* was the work of the sixties.

In G.M.'s copy of 'Bishop Blougram' he has marked the lines:

> Myself – by no immoderate exercise
> Of intellect and learning, but the fact
> To let external forces work for me.*

I see that he read the poem at Welcombe, 4 February 1903 – a date of interest to me: a couple of months before I was conceived.

5 October

We are both invalidish. I strained my back pulling and dragging those heavy logs and branches to the fires at Trenarren, and was waiting to get back to Oxford to have the blind masseur explore the trouble – bottom of the spine.

* They worked for G.M.T. all right; Baldwin, a Trinity man, gave him an O.M. in his fifties.

The day before I came up here I had a very heavy day in London, ending in giving the Shaftesbury Lecture to a crowded Fishmongers' Hall. I got back to Oxford at midnight. Next morning I had several chores before I got away at 10.30 to drive all the way to Northumberland, and added $\frac{3}{4}$ hour when I could ill spare it by mistaking a preliminary sign for the Ollerton by-pass and going back on my tracks into Nottingham and out again. All this added to a terribly exhausting journey of 280 miles, perhaps 300 – nine hours hardly stopping. I take too much out of my self.

Result – yesterday evening I developed suddenly an excruciating pain in my right leg, like a violent cramp that went on and on, would not stop, got worse when I went up to bed. I could hardly get up the stairs. I wondered what I could have done to myself, and still don't know. The nurse here suggests lumbago-sciatica from my straining the spine. I hope nothing worse. Nearly sick with pain I lay there worrying about this too-strenuous lecture tour that starts tomorrow: Barnsley Grammar School Parents' Association in the evening, the boys of the upper school next morning, at noon a large luncheon at Halifax; election day across Lancashire to Blackpool to a Girls' School, next day all the way back to Middlesbrough to speak to the embattled young scientists of the I.C.I.

I lay there groaning till, drugged, I went to sleep, mind filled with imaginings: being ill in somebody else's house, having to get the dear Manciple to come all this way and take me back, or an ambulance. And *what* was this terrible pain that gripped my leg, made it heavy as a log? Could it be a clot? or a spinal injury? – agonizingly painful. It has kept me in all day resting it and it gets better, though far from well, and it has pulled me down. Hubris, hubris, I thought during the wakeful hours of the night: I must put it away: I am never safe from accident, pain or just overdoing it.

I went to bed after lunch. G.M.'s real kindness has come out in my adversity, shuffled along the corridor to see how I was, kept me by the warm fireside in the drawing-room – charming this afternoon with the colours of the dahlias and Michaelmas daisies along the terrace, the room filled with October sunshine. No more dene for me!

When I came down he was lying on the sofa, very silvery and frail in full sun, half-dozing, nothing to do, almost blind, waiting for death. It was touching. We talked of dear Richard Pares[1] and what he died of. I remembered in the night that it began with a leg attack, like this. We talked of Namier. He said, 'He's a good historical researcher, but I don't think he's a good historian. He has no sense of the past.'

*

1. Pares had died of multiple sclerosis in March 1958.

This afternoon G.M. very interesting on the intellectuals of the twentieth century. 'The nineteenth century was better than the twentieth in a great many ways, and one of them was that it wasn't possessed with a passion for debunking . . . Roger Fry thought that Greek Art wasn't any good! Pshaw!'

He knew Henry James very well – 'lovable man' – then, in a low voice, 'adorable': the only time I have ever heard G.M. use such a strong expression of that kind. 'Underneath the complicated and subtle machine there were simple and direct feelings. No action was more characteristic of him than his taking British nationality, out of anger that the Americans were keeping out of the war. He saw that the world wouldn't be a better place if the German militarists won. President Wilson couldn't see it.'

Sister Thomas had somehow heard G. N. Clark denigrate Winston. And this I can corroborate from what I have heard him *beginning* to say – for I at once put a stop to that. But it is an indication of small-mindedness that it cannot appreciate large-mindedness. She said that these people had intellect without intelligence. Very true. G.M., who is in her hands and devoted to her – a remarkable Cornishwoman, with good judgement, intellectual as well as practical – cheered at this. He doesn't discuss *people* much. He is content with a brief mention: of Rupert Brooke, 'he was a charming fellow'; of Virginia Woolf, 'a horrid woman'; of Belloc, 'he was a liar'. Also true. But of David Knowles,[1] 'you can say anything to that man – so polite'.

He was vehement that the Civil War was not avoidable. 'For two reasons. One was that you could not trust Charles I. The other was that neither side had the idea of religious toleration. Bad as the Whigs at the end of the seventeenth century were, they had the idea of religious toleration. I'm a great believer in liberty. I'm glad I live in a country where everybody can express his own opinion.'

He is a man of absolutely firm and simple principles, which he applies consistently to history, and this gives him a grasp of and penetration into the essentials in a situation. I am left, as a Laodicean, to deplore the obstinacy of both sides that led to the Civil War, the consequent destruction of beautiful buildings, pictures, works of art, which I value more than I do people's principles.

It is interesting to look at the family photographs in his dressing-room, next my bedroom. There they are, Sir George Otto and Lady Trevelyan, quiet, silent, remote with their family grouped on the steps of Welcombe or Wallington. The eldest son Charles, handsome, sexy, looking rather slyly out of key with all that highmindedness; then the short-sighted closely-spectacled younger sons, R.C. the poet, and G.M. always looking somehow

1. The great historian of English monasticism.

discontented, and withdrawn. (I wonder why?) Apparently that was what he was like. Charles used to complain that out shooting he would break the line and wander away on his own. They would shout at him and he would come back sulky.

It is evidently only in the second half of his life that he broadened out, and only at the end that he has mellowed and developed a charm of his own. Largely under the influence of Sister Thomas. 'I have him where I want him now.'

13 October

I seem to be just squeezing through my crowded commitments on getting back. Today I have written my address for the Kipling Society luncheon tomorrow – a headache in the offing, while traipsing over a good deal of Northern England.

I came away from Hallington recovered from my attack, though with a leg rather heavy and queasy. I drove gingerly so as not to bring on cramp or another bout of sciatica – over those high moors, through desolate Tow Law, down into delightful Witton-le-Wear, and straight along blessed B6275 of Roman making. I lunched at the pleasant Bridge Inn at Wetherby, walked in the garden to exercise my leg, and reached Barnsley Grammar School in time for a cup of tea with inspectors and staff, and a tiresome Cambridge Hittite archaeologist, who was shocked by my speaking up about the Germans.

Trenarren, Sunday, 20 December

A night or two ago a not unpleasant dream. I was at a Cambridge college and learned it was Emmanuel. Never anything in the landscape of a dream is like the reality. I found myself in a crowded modern dining-hall, taken charge of by a number of the Fellows to see if I really thought their new building was as detestable as I had been saying. I gradually found that I had been entirely wrong (the truth is that I have been quite right: an *appalling* building, a disgrace to Cambridge). I began by noticing an interesting fusion of some eroded old arches with new masonry; I went on to find that the idiom of the new was excellent. Spontaneously I said, 'I must recant.' What should I do? a letter to *The Times*? a letter to the *Cambridge Review*? I decided on the latter. Leaving the college and going some distance down a steep hill (there are no hills in Cambridge) I looked back up the slope at the college with repentant admiration: I was particularly pleased by the articulation of the modern balconies and their blending with the classic building. (Nothing of that in fact.)

The Sixties

The sixties are the richest decade of these journals in spite of the fact that there are large gaps, some simply because the material does not exist, some the consequence of editorial selection.

The period is characterized by Rowse's transhumance from England to the U.S.A., following the pattern of the seasons as regularly as any mountain shepherd. He responds to the American experience with a critical sharpness and an appreciative warmth that, as in many other aspects of his character, contradict each other. His own personality, and certainly his understanding of it, expanded in the sunlight of his generous reception without losing its discriminating edge. He visited, as he was fond of claiming, more states than most native citizens of the Union and he enjoyed observing the differences in culture and ambiance *between them. Not that America dominates his consciousness or dims his vision of England, whose decline he repeatedly deplores. His account of his visit to Boconnoc, to take but one instance, is as brilliant as anything to be found in the pages of his friend and admirer, James Lees-Milne.*

But it is the portraiture of, and reflections on, his fellow writers that make this decade such absorbing reading. From popular novelists such as Daphne du Maurier, Agatha Christie and Howard Spring to Evelyn Waugh, Auden and T. S. Eliot there are illuminating sketches and succinct criticisms. The combination of the literary with the topographical, the specialité de la maison *so to speak, is at its most fascinating in the extended visit to D. H. Lawrence's shrine in New Mexico and his conversations with survivors of that strange circle.*

The world of affairs is represented by Churchill, Attlee and Beaverbrook: and music and the arts are well to the fore. Not the least of the riches of the New World that delighted the diarist were its splendid art galleries and private collections.

30 May 1960

Here I am at home in Cornwall in May for the first time for many years. Not since my boyhood days, not since I left home for Oxford in 1922, have I seen Cornwall in May time. It has been worth coming all the way down for. Even so, I should not have done it but for two things. I had to come down to Exeter to debate the Restoration with Isaac Foot on Thursday, 27th; and I've been feeling so fatigued that I thought I would come on and see what the sea air of Trenarren would do. It has been divine weather for me.

Entering Cornwall by the bridge over the Tamar at Launceston and crossing Bodmin Moor, I was excited to see the snowballs of may along the hedges, the sprays weighed down with blossom, like the bridal wreath in the Arboretum at Madison last year. White may running all along Cornish hedges – something I had forgotten; and from my bedroom window I see the white hedges running out to sea. I had never seen the ordinary purple ponticum in bloom at Trenarren; looking up from the lawn, one sees the grey stone of the house flanked by purple splendour, the mounded rhododendrons on either side. It reminded me of Portugal; I have kept going out to see the spectacle, up in the field on Sunday evening to look at the purple masses enclosing the house on the west, and through the beeches the blue of the bay. I had never seen the gold of broom in flower, the laburnum out or the rare tall shrub that has a flower like orange-blossom (drymis winteri), or the syringa the scent of which now fills the hall on entering.

But I'm still too tired to write any more.

I left Oxford on 26 May, Ascension Day, after taking part in the Ascension Day ritual of throwing pennies to the choirboys of St Mary's on the lawn, on their beating the parish bounds. The clergy, churchwardens, choirmen and women, the boys in red cassocks, come with willow wands in their hands since the parish boundary runs through All Souls. After the scramble they are given a handsome breakfast in hall.

It is a pretty spectacle and an old one. Young [ ] wouldn't turn out for the ceremony, sat sulkily on in the smoking-room – 'Let them have their pagan ceremony.' Ignorant – as if it *were* pagan; silly – it might give him an interesting scene in a future book. The Fellows remained, as usual, selfconsciously away from the St Mary's people. I went and chatted to them as always, made myself agreeable and enjoyed chaff with two good-looking curates, one dark, the other flaxen and fair.

Then I set off, happy to be by myself in the car sailing along the roads in May to Wantage. At the corner before coming into Wantage was that perfect Georgian house of red brick, about 1740, low-lying in the meads.

[On W. H. Auden]

There is a good saying of David Cecil's about the extraordinary landscape of Wystan's face, the thousand wrinkles and lines, the creases all running the wrong way up – 'Were a fly to attempt to cross it, it would break its leg.'

I ran into Wystan in Blackwell's at the beginning of term. We were in the English literature department and, looking down on Q.'s *Oxford Book of Victorian Verse*, he at once began to *run* it down. 'The worst anthology that ever was made,' etc. I listened to this with mounting impatience. No doubt it is the least good of Q.'s anthologies – he had a weakness for the sentimental and the facetious that went with his time. But these people never see *themselves* in perspective and that their weaknesses go with *their* time. The sense of historical perspective is wanting in them; it should induce a certain scepticism about their judgements. Wystan quoted a stanza from the book which he regarded as 'the most obscene' he had ever read. It certainly was a funny bit of unconscious Freudianism; the Victorians were marvellously unaware of that sort of thing.

At last loyalty to dear Q. uncoiled like a snake within me and I said hotly, No doubt Q. had his impercipiences, and was less good at some things than at others. Just like Wystan's own Introduction to Tennyson – which was such nonsense. Wystan was annoyed at this and protested, 'But I admire him so much.' I said, No doubt; but you wrote a lot of nonsense about him.

This ended the conversation. No doubt Wystan thinks I am a bore – I rather see that in his attitude, holding aloof when I am about. But, then, I have little enough in common with him. And, as usual, I did badly, by not responding physically, when we were young.

I cannot remember how or when we first met. As an undergraduate he used to come along to All Souls and read me the poems he was writing. I can see him now, sitting in a chair in the quad in summer, the pale flaxen hair unkempt, the muddy complexion, the pimpled skin. He was always rather unappetizing to look at. But I never had any doubt of his genius. For one thing, he had the providential good fortune of achieving a style of his own quite early; for another, he imposed *his* style and way of looking at things on the others.

But once I made a mistake. One summer afternoon he asked me along to his rooms in Peck.[1] He surprised me on arrival by sporting his oak,[2] pulling down the blinds and turning on the shaded green light of a reading lamp. He proceeded to read me extracts from letters of friends of his – one, in particular, in the Mexican Eagle Oil Company – describing the adventures they were having with boys. I listened noncommittally; a thought crossed my mind, vetoed by 'Fellows of All Souls don't do this kind of thing'. I was twenty-three and had no sense; or rather native sense was smothered by political fanaticism, and also there was the overriding necessity of the drug, tea at four. When four o'clock came, I said, 'Well, I must be getting back to All Souls for tea now'; and my relations with Wystan rather stopped at that point.

But I did hold his hand for him over his Schools – he had practically a nervous breakdown and emerged with a third. I didn't think very highly of that, though I didn't think the less of him as a poet. He left Oxford and went on to fulfil himself as a poet and to become, in time, internationally famous – to soar quite beyond my paddock.

A rather grand literary party was given for him by Faber's on 23 June. Since I was going to be in London for lunch with the Brinsley Fords and tea with Nancy Astor, I decided to go, really to see Eliot again after so many years.

It was all very nostalgic. I arrived very early. There was that nice girl with the welcoming smile at the door whom I used often to see in *Criterion* days in the thirties: today a middle-aged woman, and without her teeth. Upstairs a new generation welcomed me: Charles Monteith, a Magdalen contemporary of Norman's, whom I helped to elect at All Souls. Two sons were introduced to me – Janet Adam Smith's and Day Lewis's; I laid myself out to do my best with them. I had come up the stairs with a pleasant young man, who evidently knew me, though I couldn't remember who he was. He gave me a clue by recalling our last meeting with Veronica. Still mesmerized, I couldn't remember and, stupid as ever, didn't even try. It turned out to be George Rylands, two or three years older than I – hero of the story as he went on the operating table for the same naughty operation as Wystan had to have in Berlin, 'Sew me up, but don't sew me up too tight.'*

The word went round that Eliot and his wife had arrived; it was like the Royal Family arriving at a party. The hive had found its queen bee. Turning

1. Peckwater quad at Christ Church.
2. Closing the outer door of his rooms, which could only be opened from the inside.
* The subject of Wystan's 'The Wound'.

round, I saw the royal couple established in the centre of the room, everybody hiving round them. I was determined not to push myself, and felt a little unsure of my reception. By this time another literary enemy of mine had arrived, old Harold Nicolson, looking surprisingly young and undamaged by having fallen into his moat – such an unsocialist thing to do. I wasn't speaking to him. He was in a corner with Rylands (of course, I registered), commenting on the other members of the party. No doubt it will all go down in his diary, as in mine.

I chatted to Janet Adam Smith, who wanted to know about young David Caute, of whom I gave a good testimonial. The time had come for me to speak to Eliot, if at all. I had now half a mind to go without speaking to him. I was behind him and touched his sleeve. Very much accustomed to such things – in this, too, like Jesus Christ – he hardly perceptibly shrugged it off. I came round in front, said, 'My name is Rowse. How lovely to see you, after so many years.'

He was visibly delighted; the formal party-face vanished, the ageing eyes lit up and he beamed with genuine pleasure. 'You needn't have told me,' he said. 'I used to call you A.L.' – as he did to tease me, knowing it made me uncomfortable, most of his letters to me are written to A.L. 'I don't know what to call you now. They all call you Leslie.'[1]

He knew that I spent a good deal of time in America nowadays. I told him how pleased I had been, one day at the University of Kansas at Lawrence, to look up from talking to students to see the Epstein bust of him, large as life and as recognizable, brooding over the assembly – 'the agèd eagle'. With instinctive good manners, impeccable as ever, he wouldn't talk about himself, but said, 'But why not come to the universities in Missouri? – that was where I was born, you know. There are several of them.' As he has got older, he has allowed himself to become more American. What a story there is behind all that: his rejection of America and all things American – to the resentment of many American writers, old Carl Sandburg, for example – his approximation to English manners and standards, the cautious return to America, bridging the Atlantic, now a Colossus, a frail and tenuous one really bestriding both cultures. It is a marvellous acrobatic act. He has the most wonderful of autobiographies to write, if only he would write it. But he never will. Too prudent to say anything explicit now, too famous to break any eggs, almost to say anything at all – and therein lies the failure of his latest phase. There *is* evasion, prudence, in the astonishing structure of Eliot's fame, by which he is now bound hand and foot so that he cannot

1. ALR made a great fuss about disliking his Christian name Leslie, originally because it was common to both sexes, and urged his friends to address him as 'A.L.'. In fact after a brief period most of them reverted to calling him Leslie.

make a move in any direction. If only he could say, to hell with it and write his *Souvenirs d'Enfance et de Jeunesse*. But perhaps it is genuinely contrary to his nature.

I think the memories of the thirties were present to us both: too much to talk about. Of his unhappiness with his wife, the few times when we lunched together at the 'Etoile', his tentative proposal that we should set up house together, his unfailing kindness and avuncular help to me with my writing, my going back to Oxford and leaving Faber's for Cape, our ways parting – his, leading to this unparalleled, and quite unexpected (to him as well as to everybody else) world fame. One cannot but be a little jealous – not only of him, but of others now closer to him. I held aloof.

However, the one closest to him in all these years was one of the two notable absentees: John Hayward, who took Eliot as a lodger in the bleak back room of his flat – 'The Lodger' he used to call him. How Eliot could share with this picture of paralysis, the hunched-up figure in the wheelchair, the contorted claw-like hand reaching out to the telephone, the blubber lips sideways: it must have ministered to his masochism. It was certainly good for his grammar: the books of that period have acknowledgements to Hayward's scholarship, etc. But what sort of relationship can it have been? Hayward helped to mitigate Eliot's solitariness, told him what was going on at parties, kept him in touch with the literary gossip of London – and so helped with plays like *The Cocktail Party* and *The Confidential Clerk*. As I had helped years before by telling Eliot what to read, when he asked me, on Thomas Becket. *Murder in the Cathedral* is based on Dean Stanley's *Historical Memoirs of Canterbury*. An adept at covering his tracks, Eliot says nothing about that. He gives nothing away: it was Wyndham Lewis who said to me many years ago, 'Tom is so *sly*.'

Hayward cannot have shared Eliot's religious life, and there can have been no emotional relation – except possibly the sharing in misery. Misery is the great theme of this period in Eliot's work, and redemption through misery. I have never had any respect for this nonsense. But it was the *chic* thing to be miserable; you were just nobody at all if you didn't suffer from *Angst*. (*Pace* Cyril Connolly: he was at the party, in the centre of it. I mooched about the margin.)

The Sitwells were not there: too old and ill – and rival luminaries. Apparently they did for Eliot when young something of what they did for Walton, and helped to emancipate Eliot from working in a bank. Now so lofty and grand, Uncle Tom cannot bear to think of this obligation: another track covered up. Edith once spoke to me of him in friendly terms, 'he is so gentle'; but her motive for going Catholic was partly to go one better than Uncle Tom.

The other absentee was John Betjeman. Is he not on friendly terms with Eliot? – both so religious, so *angstvoll*, both Anglo-Catholics and prize darlings of the C. of E. – a large element in their success. When John was a boy at school at Highgate, Eliot was a master for a brief period and discouraged his early verses. It is certainly odd that they should not be friends.*

Some of this, and a good deal more, was present in my mind while we talked. Eliot was even eager to talk; I felt too moved to be at ease. It was like talking to the Queen on a formal occasion, or to Sir Winston – I couldn't help thinking how like it was, as I watched the goings-on. And noticed how very much Eliot had aged: he was now an old man, the head stooped forward on rounded shoulders. So I have forgotten what we talked about: eager, nervous nothings to cover the gap of the years. Some remark gave me the chance to quote sillily, *à propos* of what I had been doing, 'I have measured out my life with coffee-spoons.' He beamed; indeed he was beaming and gay throughout our talk.

'But you haven't met my wife – or have you?'

I said that I hadn't. I totally forgot that I must have exchanged letters with her when she was Eliot's secretary. Anyway, I was anxious to shake hands. 'She looks after me, in every way,' he said. I said, with conviction, how glad I was that he was happy.

He turned to get her by the arm; she was chatting gaily with people she evidently knew.

'I want you to meet Leslie Rowse,' he said. I greeted her with real pleasure, but felt that her reaction was cool. Not that I had said anything against her – unlike John Hayward. I was more than willing to be on friendly terms, so glad that Uncle Tom had found happiness at last. I put down her reaction to what others said of me. Plus, perhaps, the familiar objection for a late wife that I had known him years before she came into his life: always an awkward situation.

Immediately discouraged, I did not want to go on. Confused, I murmured something about knowing how much taken up they were, but how much I should like them to lunch with me one day. No response from her. Eliot did not want me to go, held on while I began to take my leave. 'Well, go on giving us good books,' he said eagerly, as I said farewell.

Transported, I left the room to the Connollys, Spenders, Day-Lewises, Nicolsons, etc., while the party was in full blow. I didn't want to remain a moment longer. Sadly, but glad to have seen him and talked with him again, I wandered down the familiar stairs – Geoffrey Faber himself, creator of it

* I must find out about this from John. I don't think he cares for T.S.E.'s poetry, and vice versa.

all, now an invalid beyond repair (his daughters were on guard upstairs: no wish to talk to them) – a word to the nice woman at the door and out into Russell Square. I wandered round for a moment looking up to the windows of No. 24, and then half-consciously followed the old route of twenty-five years ago to Brunswick Square.

Guilford Street, where the cheap tarts used to hang frequent along the pavements, as squalid as ever. Brunswick Square far more so: all the houses round the corner where Richard and I lived at No. 1 blown to bits, a large empty chasm. The garden was unchanged and I lingered at the gate.

Round the corner to the Foundling Hospital site; that Georgian palace had been deliberately pulled down before I came to live here. John Street more dilapidated than ever, and in my memory I had displaced Doughty Street, one further over. Into Mecklenburgh Square, once splendid, now ruined; the south side pulled down for a large Students' Hostel, the east side bombed. Only the north unchanged, where Tawney lived and, very infrequently, I looked in late at night to find him struggling with his letters, amid indescribable confusion and untidiness. Eileen Power lived charmingly on the east side, as near as may be to her adored mentor. We thought them in love; but it was C. K. Webster who made it with her. Tawney much too high-minded.

I remembered the night I stopped with Eileen, after an excellent dinner of roast duck, which made me ill all night. And the one and only dinner party Richard and I gave, in the Wharton room below his rooms (now mine), for Eileen – and the bobbling ear-rings she wore that shook and danced as she turned her pretty head this way and that. And then she went and married Postan – half her age, her pupil and creation; when we thought she might have married an earl. *Her* story was told me in jealousy of her by Mrs Mair[1] – of the criminal father who had been in prison and sponged on the three clever daughters, and Eileen's terror that it would all come out and his arriving on her, making a scene in public. Yet altogether she had an enjoyable life, so successful, good-looking and popular; travelling round the world, doing herself well, dressing stylishly – she told me that she never kept within her income – earning good money, never ill, happily married and then one day suddenly dropping down dead in Tottenham Court Road. At my age now.

All came back into mind as I walked down Doughty Street. There at the corner was the cheap bar at which I occasionally had an evening snack, kept by the woman with the extraordinary voice of a tired tart, husky, worn-out, minus a vocal chord. Somewhere I have a sketch of her.

1. Beveridge's secretary and subsequently wife.

Down to Gray's Inn Road, much rebuilt with office blocks, and into Kingsway along my old route to the L.S.E.

[A visit to Mr and Mrs Howard Spring, ?August 1960]

We entered the house. At once I took in the portrait of their son Michael, as he was when he came out of the Navy and I got him into Exeter College; so good-looking and sweet-natured. His mother said, 'His hair is grey now.' I remained rooted there, thinking of the years that had passed. Nothing has come of his artistic ambitions, his efforts as a sculptor. He teaches in a village school somewhere in the Home Counties. He has had no difficulty in knocking up a family. 'I don't think Michael is much interested in his old parents,' said Mrs Spring, with hardly a note of regret.

Archie[1] explained this very perceptively: the old couple so much wrapped up in each other, no need for the sons to go on inhabiting the nest. Howard Spring's large literary earnings – he told me some years ago that he accepted £3,000 a year from his English publishers, and £3,000 from his American – no doubt provide the wherewithal for both sons and their families. I was quite taken with Michael and could have captured him, if I had wanted to. What a charm these warm, sweet-natured young men possess – as my old friend, the vicar of Luxulyan, used to insist.

We went in to a well-cooked lunch – they have a Cornish cook-housekeeper, for Mrs Spring does every bit of Howard's typing and always has done: his permanent secretary, eyes visibly ageing. During lunch I missed a point: a prime example of the bestseller's innocent vanity. At Mylor church it appears that congregations have doubled this summer and collections more than doubled. It turned out that this was because of Spring's latest bestseller, which neither Archie nor I knew about, let alone had read. Considering that he is not my author, that I could hardly bear to read him, have in fact read nothing of him but his weekly reviews – and perhaps there is something of this in Michael's attitude to his father – Spring's attitude to me is friendlier than might be expected. Anyway I feel quite friendly disposed to him, and positively *fond* of her. She's a dear, if effusive, gifted too, an expert gardener, and has shown talent at making and decorating a big dolls' house upstairs.

We were piloted over the house, every room and every aspect of their joint achievement: the furniture they had collected through their long married life – and 'isn't it wonderful the way it has all fitted in?' As the royalties have rolled in, Spring's aspirations have gone up: he now buys expensive antiques

1. Graham Campbell, a colleague from All Souls who was staying at Trenarren.

from the Falmouth antique-shop. Upstairs on a mantelpiece were the photographs of three women – or a girl and two women. 'These are the three women in my life': Mrs Spring as a girl, young woman, and in middle age.

Archie was fascinated by such monogamous fidelity; it was rather touching – though restrictive, one would have thought, to a real knowledge of human nature. How unlike Flaubert, or Tolstoy, or Dickens, or Shakespeare. *Etwas verschiedenes*. 'To think,' said Archie, 'that that has been his life, and only that. Simplifies things a great deal.'

'Isn't it much better that way?' said Mrs Spring, looking at me with faithful ageing eyes. I could give her a hug, the old dear.

We were shown *everything*. And I am always interested in the way people write. His study is the long room on the ground floor right of the entrance. A good view out into that entrancing garden she has largely created, with half-a-dozen cats draping themselves over wall, terrace and steps. But he doesn't look out at the view. The hard-bitten journalist has always worked facing a wall. So his desk is in the corner bang up against it.

There he sits ensconced day in, day out for eighteen months on end when writing one of his long novels. He works to strict routine. From tea till dinner he gives himself up to reading his *Country Life* books: a conscientious reviewer. Then one day for the article. Friday morning is regularly devoted to business. I bet he is a far better business man than I. And he makes much more. The big difference is in outgoings: I expect he provides for three families, good paterfamilias. We were proudly shown the shelves and shelves of his books. And the translations! Translated into seventeen languages. Scores of thousands of his books are sold every year in Germany, where he is a bestseller no less than in Britain and America.

This is what it is to be a real professional author.

I wouldn't be that for all his royalties.

He took a perfectly simple and natural pride in his achievement, which, so far from being offensive, I found affecting. He told me that as a child in Cardiff there had been two bedrooms for a large family; one for all the children – divided by a curtain, I suppose, for girls and boys. He slept three in a bed, two down one way, the youngest with feet pointing up the other way. He thought it interesting that he had never been moved to write about his native town. Is he Jewish? He has a Jewish cast of countenance.

He was proud of having stood up to Beaverbrook – who had commanded him to dinner on one occasion. He was a regular journalist on his papers, then reviewer. Spring replied, 'But I have an engagement' – to the astonishment of the intermediaries. The engagement was to take 'this girl' to the pictures. If you let Beaverbrook possess you soul and body this way – as he did Bruce Lockhart – it would exhaust you, keeping you up all hours of the night, and having to start work early next morning. I admired his independence.

We were shown every inch of the garden, all of it occupied by fancy plants and flowers – all sorts of rarities, of which Mrs Spring knew the names both Latin and English. The garden ended at the railway embankment, whence they were visited by a nocturnal badger. I tried to take leave, but it was evidently intended that we should stay on for tea.

So we had a cup of tea brought out in the gold-leafed china I had admired, in the garden.

[Canada and U.S.A., September–December 1960]

I regarded it all with distaste; the docks, the boat, the mob on board, the human mass boxed up in the ship, the prospect of five days' hell: the linoleum corridors, the stewardesses waiting for seasickness, the sanitary atmosphere, the triangle playing 'Come to the cook-house door' along the heaving passages.

The first two days were roughish and the ship rolled. 'The long Atlantic swell' ran in my head as the cabin heaved and subsided, then made a long roll one way, then righted itself while the screw throbbed below, and the sickly motion began all over again. Everything tugged and creaked; the board to hold one in the bunk would fall forward, then back. A tie that my companion had hung on the mirror wagged to and fro. A door would unexpectedly open. My slippers slid quietly across the floor. Etc. – all the usual accompaniments of the long Atlantic swell.

I stayed in bed unable to lift my head from the pillow, slept the drugged sleep of Dramamine a good deal, sweated, changed my pillow and position a hundred times. And was obsessed by the thought of Peter – his endearing ways, nestled up in his favourite place at the foot of the big pine-tree, welcoming me with purrs and outstretched paws and turning over on his back; or waiting at the bottom of the garden for Beryl, or going up the back to meet me returning home in the car.

Dear little soul! and here was I where I didn't want to be, but had willed myself to be, when I might have been at Trenarren or in my rooms at Oxford. And suddenly, ungratefully – for it gives me so much work – I saw Trenarren as beautiful. As on that evening I dined with the Hartleys[1] down at Myrtle Cottage, the cottage pretty with red candles and flower decoration, sprigs of brambleberry mixed in – and oh, such a good dinner. Late, we came up the dark lane together with Apollo, their golden Labrador;

1. Kind neighbours for many years.

butter-coloured lights in the Boveys' farm windows, the mysterious groves around the house, owls hooting, and the span of the Plough over all.

Instead of that I am here with the zany antics of Saturday night dinner, everybody wearing paper hats and making fools of themselves, the little girls with pigtails twirling round to add to the horrid motion of the ship.

My first move consoled me a little: getting out of a full cabin of four, into one with only one – a good old German Jew, become American after living in London all through the war, very musical, friend of Myra Hess, knew Elena Gerhardt, Bruno Walter, etc. We filled in weary interstices by singing or whistling across at each other the themes of favourite pieces – me, the Elgar Cello Concerto, Brahms Intermezzi, chorales from the St Matthew Passion, the Agnus Dei from the B Minor Mass, etc. He had a much greater range and far better musical memory. It was clear how much music had meant in his life.

And what an interesting story! Had married a wife nineteen years younger, whom he found incompatible and from whom he was divorced (though a Catholic, not having been married in the eyes of the Church). Married her through having some financial obligation to the family. The moment he married, he knew it was a mistake. His uncle had been in business with her grandfather. The grandfather later married his housekeeper and, to prevent his money coming to her, the son had tied it up in inaccessible investments and lost half of it.

He himself had worked hard and earned well. Leaving Germany in 1939 he came to London and kept himself by a little photostat business which he worked from his bathroom; three nights a week served as fire-warden in the raids, used to go to the lunch-hour concerts of Myra Hess and others at the National Gallery. After the war he went to San Francisco with $7,500. In 1956 sold his business – had moved to Seattle – for $75,000, and went back to S.F. to live. Which he adores – *prachtvoll*. Good music, radio, and he has 500 records. Listens to music or whistles all day.

He has a fine son – the one good thing from his marriage – high up in the U.S.A.A.F. Makes a good income, now twenty-nine has just married. He will have $100,000 from his father. But his mother had married again, a rich manufacturer; they, having no children, brought up the son, who would inherit their money – $600,000.

(How American money talks!)

Himself – Dr Roland – a perfect dear: naif, kind, conscientious, religious. Goes into retreat with the Jesuits twice a year. Never misses Mass on Sunday. The spirit has its needs. I said, wasn't reason enough? He said, reason answered the mind's needs, but the heart had its spiritual needs.

He has Parkinson's disease in right arm and leg, but is cheerful about it.

In every other respect his health, heart, etc. are good. At seventy his sex is unimpaired and *es is erlaubt* – once, or once a night, or a week, as it falls out.

One sees how hopeless it is to expect reason, or any rational consistency, of human beings. Religious, and then – plenty of sex. I have noticed that lack of any principle of consistency again and again with Catholics. On the ship there is a sex-crazy young Irishman chasing every girl he sees, and has managed to have one every night except Saturday. He wears a cross next his skin under the shirt he takes off; does he keep the cross on for the job?

[Canada] Next morning, by inadvertence, I attended a Requiem at the big church of the French Canadians who form 80 per cent of the population of Lewiston. After the sea-fog, a brilliant autumn day, bright sun, cold wind, yellow leaves blowing. This French population is encisted within the mass of the state, enclosed within itself, like the Irish held together by the Catholic church, led and dominated by the priests.

It was rather touching to observe this piece of *Old* France in the midst of secular America: the priests vested in black, the coffin covered with a black pall, the lights, the Roman mutter and mummeries. It was not only anthropology, but so much sociology. With human beings in general the *truth* of the propositions they subscribe to has little importance. The comforting nonsense they have always been used to goes on – whether Shinto, or Confucianism, Buddhism or the Roman Church. All part of social observance. The corpse was surrounded by the family for the last time, while the incantations continued: adjurations, holy water thrown upon the coffin. The procession formed, the body carried on its way to the grave, while the bells tolled farewell.

Only one girl, not very near in relationship, was affected to tears. A tribute of youth. Swift's phrase was in my mind while I watched the procession forming outside: 'I have often observed that the merriest faces are to be seen in mourning coaches.' This, however, was not the case. Decorum was observed.

According to Donald Rickard[1] these French Canadians are an unattractive lot: sullen, intensely philistine, anti-education, speaking ghastly French and don't want to speak any better, under the thumb of their priests. To such an extent that when they have to confess an act of birth-control, their priests tell them, 'Go home to your wife and make a *complete* act and come to me again.' Emission before remission.

1. Cornish-American fan of ALR's writings who had volunteered to drive him about.

They keep so much to themselves that they make no effort to learn to speak English; they merely debase their own language – 'Ne vous botherez pas' for 'Ne vous dérangez pas'. At breakfast in the hotel there were several of them going to a wedding who could hardly speak any English. Plump, squat figures, both men and women, *very* French, not a tall person among them.

1 October

After my spying upon French-Canadian life, with a funeral and a wedding breakfast, we sailed off in brilliant Indian summer into Maine countryside. Full of lakes and woods, the maples already scarlet, bursts of flame upon the ground from scrub maples, the majority of the trees not yet turned. We made a half circle, lunching at Bridgeton, going by Long Lake and on to Lake Ossipee and thence to Wolfeboro, touching the large lake Winnepesaukee. In view were the White Mountains, blue in the distance; we skirted the foothills and so down into New Hampshire. At one point we got out and looked up the length of one cold lake, the wind blowing down the funnel of the hills. Rickard said that the canoe was made to carry freight: he wouldn't like to be holding a canoe against that wind. He described the skill of the woodsmen in navigating rapids: a long pole with steel head, with which they would hold or propel the canoe among the rocks. He lives in a Fenimore Cooper world and talks about it in the most natural way. I found him a great dear.

We came down from the lake-and-woods country into New Hampshire, quiet and English, to stop the night in Rickard's colonial house of about 1740, white panelling, low ceilings, good proportions. We sat in the porch exchanging Cornish information over tea.

[At a party on his visit, at Beaverbrook's invitation, to New Brunswick]

I suffered horribly from the heat: *all* the heating on, plus a wood fire on the hearth. I skirted round, keeping as clear of the fire as I could. Talked to a new head of the Women's Hall, a devoted gardener, bent on cultivation, adored the pure cold air of Canada in winter in the snow, came back from Switzerland longing for it, etc. Certain things, colours and scents spoke to her soul. Long-faced, long-nosed, silvery, perfect figure of a principal of a women's college, she dug her garden like a man, according to the women servants.

I moved on to banter and argument, chiefly politics, with the men. Toole, Vice-President, Irish gentleman, chemist, Catholic become rationalist, reads the *New Statesman*, bit of a Left doctrinaire with some of the illusions. I talked too much, but that was what I was there for. Came up against MacNutt's Loyalist anti-Americanism. Wish that I had not talked so much. Then hot coffee – at that hour and in that heat!

In the intervals of all this I had been reading Steven Watson's *Reign of George III* and neither got in touch with or been summoned by Beaverbrook. I rather enjoyed the Kafka *Castle*-like atmosphere, in the 'Lord Beaverbrook Hotel', somewhere on another floor this dynamo of energy, people coming and going; I needed a day or two's intermission before catching up with him. And was rather surprised that I was given it. No summons. One sunny morning I saw the little black dynamo stepping out along the river bank with his granddaughter. There were rumours of 'Lady Jean'[1] being here with him.

On the third day I went along to the Art Gallery, where he has a flat. Like Winston, who has had a marked influence on Beaverbrook's ways, he was in a whirl of activity. People were coming and going, carrying pictures to him to look at and away again; he was talking into a dictaphone or long-distance phone, dictating to a secretary, colloguing with the velvet-coated Director of his Gallery, and was prepared to receive me in this maelstrom.

He is a phenomenon – the speed of his mind, the quite abnormal memory, the pounce, and at eighty-two! Not a faculty is impaired; he is like a man of fifty-two or forty-two. At once he was *au fait* with my movements, and getting off the telephone and the dictation, cleared himself a space of fifteen minutes to take me into the vault and have the Hilliard miniature of Elizabeth I brought out for 'the Doctor'. I inspected it carefully: it looked to me like her in the later 1570s, rather young-looking and not faking her age. She must have remained young-looking until later middle age.

We walked out into the Gallery, where I was impressed by his phenomenal memory for people: one young man among the visitors he addressed by name and knew all about him. It was Churchillian; I noticed the courtesy with which he greeted people going round, also the magnetism of the man who had called it all into existence.

Next day, Sunday, 16 October, I finished Watson's *George III* in the morning, wrote my review in the afternoon, and dined with Beaverbrook in the Gallery flat. Toole was there, and a New Brunswicker from the West who is a member of the Senate, and last came Lady Jean Campbell. 'Guess who this is! Who is she?', he was as merry as a cricket. 'She's my grand-da'ter. Isn't she exactly like me?' Actually a good-looking girl, black hair, grey-blue eyes, pretty figure, all in black plus pearls.

1. Lady Jean Campbell, for long Beaverbrook's favourite granddaughter.

B. was in the gayest mood. Stories flowed. Asquith had said, 'Some men think while they talk [i.e. Lloyd George]; some men think while they write [i.e. himself]; some think both while they talk *and* while they write, and they are the salt of the earth.' We were all floored by this: whom did he mean? I thought of Morley and Balfour; but I should have guessed, from Beaverbrook's own predilections, it would be Birkenhead.

Comic stories flowed about Bottomley and Tim Healy – Beaverbrook thought them the best wits he had known. Bottomley protesting against some new parliamentary veto: 'What is a veto? It is a new kind of vegetable.' He threatened, against aristocrats, to follow the Cholmondeley example and call himself Bumley. Beaverbrook enjoyed having him to dinner, much to Bonar Law's disapproval who thought it a disgrace – Beaverbrook chuckled impishly. One evening he had Beerbohm Tree, who wanted to monopolize the conversation and wasn't going to let Bottomley in. He got the conversation around to the subject of the most beautiful woman he had ever seen. Nobody could guess. It turned out to be 'Lottie Collins'. – 'My A'nt,' shouted Bottomley, seizing his chance.

Then Healy. When Beaverbrook was Minister of Information in the first war, he got into some parliamentary trouble; Bonar Law wouldn't come to the rescue, advised him to try Tim Healy. B. got on the phone, and Healy said he would come across from Ireland by the Sunday boat after Mass. B. hoped Mass wouldn't last too long and would meet him for dinner. After dinner Tim was too tired to hear Beaverbrook's case, or decide on any line of defence. Next day at lunch he wouldn't think about it. When the debate came on in the House, Tim Healy said, 'This Minister of Information isn't so bad. The Minister before him was Carson' – and went over to the wrongs of Ireland. From that moment the name of Beaverbrook was no more heard in the debate.

And so on, all popping like the champagne served. An excellent dinner: Fredericton fish not being good enough for Beaverbrook, fish came fresh from St Andrew's. Artichokes in leaf, butter sauce, meringues, brandy. I was placed by the granddaughter, who took up most of my time. Stupidly I couldn't think who she was, but thought the Duke of Argyll's daughter. She expressed herself anxious to meet me, an admirer of my *Churchills*. When I said, *à propos* of Beaverbrook's praise of A. J. P. Taylor, 'Your favourite historian.' He said: 'No. You're my favourite historian. But I like Taylor. He's a brave man.' I didn't comment on this. Both irresponsible mischief-makers.

The young woman was engaging, spontaneity and vivacity under the sophistication of the society she lives in. She adores New York where she lives up on 94th Street among the Porto Ricans, has a job as *Daily Express* correspondent of U.N. Adores Krushchev, who has such a funny face, is a first-class comic and makes such fun of the solemn Americans and *their* U.N. I saw that she had the family anti-Americanism or, as she put it, a love-hate complex about the Americans. Her grandfather longed to bring Krushchev up to Fredericton. They both chuckled at the idea, the incursion into Fredericton's respectability.

We had some gossip about John Foster,[1] whom she had been consulting – 'my family has been much before the courts lately,' she said a little ashamedly. So she was the Argyll daughter? She was wearing a prehistoric gold bangle, grave-goods from Inveraray, which she had not returned to the Museum. I gave her my clue to John's sensual utilitarianism – the early rejection by his mother and his devotion to the old maid he calls his aunt; no aunt at all, but she had looked after him from a child when his mother rejected him. 'That fits in with the fact that he really hates women,' Lady Jean said. That had never occurred to me, for he is a tremendous performer with them. But no love, no ties, no emotion; just mutual pleasure. It gives him pleasure to meet his girl's lover coming to see her as he is leaving. Is he getting his own back – not vindictively, it makes him laugh so much. In the nineteenth century he'd be the victim of a *crime passionel*. Our society cares too little for that.

We turned to Colin Mackay,[2] so good-looking, so unattached, though several girls had done their best to no purpose. She had been studying him for years and come to the conclusion that there was no heart there; in the place of a heart, a stone. He wants money. Already rich, he wants to be richer. I caught some of the academic gossip of the others. Not one of the Faculty had wanted Mackay as President; Beaverbrook knew he was the right man and now they all agreed how successful he was. Mackay wouldn't leave N.B.U. now for anywhere, immersed in building it up, etc.

Once or twice I glimpsed Lady Jean laughing at my shyness or just my old-fashioned manner. But it seems she was a little taken with her elderly partner for, unasked, she gave me her address and telephone in New York and swore me to get in touch: she'd take me to see the U.N. building, which she was lyrical about. (Was she already married to Norman Mailer then?) Beaverbrook is undoubtedly fond of the girl – 'Doesn't she know that she is my favourite gran'child!' etc. The brandy circulated. She had two glasses, and wanted a third. Beaverbrook refused. 'But who taught me to drink, grand-pa?'

A good deal of talk about newspaper proprietorships. Only three newspaper groups *created* in the last thirty years, all by sons of the manse: the

1. All Souls friend, in whose sex life ALR found a vicarious excitement.
2. President of the University.

Express group, the Henry Luce group, and the Reader's Digest group created by Wallace. On religions at table, Beaverbrook declaimed that he was a Presbyterian Pagan, Toole that he was a Catholic Pagan who had discarded his Catholicism. I refrained from adding that I was an Anglican Pagan.

10.30 and Beaverbrook was anxious to break up. No more late night sessions, as with Winston in old days. The President says he 'watches himself like a ha'k'. Birkenhead, Beaverbrook told me, dying at sixty-two had expected to live another twenty years. Perhaps Beaverbrook at eighty-two will.

Monday morning, 17 October

I resumed my campaign with my heaviest chore: addressing the student body in a large hall with a gallery and difficult acoustics. My theme was 'The Use of History in Modern Society'. (Wesley recorded his sermon-texts; why shouldn't I?) Fortunately I managed to hold the big audience. The President took me to lunch, and then I got *his* perspective of Beaverbrook and his granddaughter. Mackay's view was that she hadn't had a chance, with the Beaver alternately spoiling and bullying her – he said nothing about her own unsatisfactory parents. She had no money of her own and no idea of money, but now had a job as *Express* correspondent of U.N. and perhaps things would go better. As for marrying, he opined, a little warily, that her grandfather would keep anybody off.

He told me his own experience with the Beaver. The Beaver's house looking on the river he had given for the use of the President. First year the Beaver had spent two weeks in it, the second two months; the third threatened to be more than Mackay could bear: he found his work added to by two or three hours a day. So during the seven weeks of vacation he himself ran up the odd little bungalow he occupies on the campus. The Beaver couldn't do anything about it – he had lost his caretaker – and took to staying in the hotel with a flat in the Gallery as a hide-out. Mackay thought of himself as a Catherine Parr to Henry VIII and sometimes wondered whether he would survive him.

25 October

In the afternoon I took the Greyhound bus and had an enjoyable ride through fine country to the Massachusetts border and into Connecticut. Big hilly country with forest, rocks and valleys, the road going on interminably as is the way in this immense country.

At Hartford – with Providence, R.I., one of the country's Insurance capitals – I was met by Lefty Lewis's[1] man-servant and luxurious car, and driven out to Farmington.[2] As distinguished as ever, even more rewarding, more pictures, more treasures – but this time Lefty alone, without wife, more cosy on a bachelor basis.

Every comfort on every side, waited on hand and foot by domestics, women and men; house, my room, bed, all delicious; everywhere books, and outside the additions containing thousands of manuscripts, books, prints, drawings, most of Horace Walpole's library and many of his possessions. I relaxed, at ease in Zion. Outside my windows the garden, beyond, the orchard, in which at times expensive dogs wandered, not allowed in, nor the poor little white cat.

Lefty is going to leave the whole place, as yet another foundation, to Yale, with half-a-dozen Fellows to research and be also at ease in Zion. Already he must employ a dozen staff at Farmington and at Yale, keeping the mss. and editing the Letters. It must all cost an enormous sum. Once more, brought home to me how agreeable to be rich; and how disagreeable not to be.

26 October

Lefty drove me on a honeyed morning, the trees full of light, into New Haven, where I spent the morning happily in the university library copying out Froude's letters to George Eliot, with eyes as usual on a far future book. I hadn't finished – and Lefty generously promised to give me a photostat of the remaining letters – when he carried me off to lunch at Wallace Notestein's[3] favourite table in the Club, carved with names of students a hundred years ago. A group of historians to meet me, but conversation with Wallace was best. He was pleased at my return to local history with the St Austell book and wanted a copy. We agreed about Robert Cecil being a much bigger man than he is usually considered – wouldn't he be the best person to take, instead of Leicester, for my 'Eminent Elizabethans'. Who were they to be? – Bess of Hardwick, Leicester or Robert Cecil, Lord Henry Howard, but who was the fourth, for my converse to Strachey? I have him in my notes. To be followed by 'Lesser Elizabethans'; Sir Richard Hawkins, Topcliffe, Henry Cuffe, etc. Life isn't long enough.*

Notestein said that he and Neale[4] agreed that we want more biographies

1. W. S. Lewis, scholar and collector of eighteenth-century English literature, notably of materials relating to Horace Walpole.
2. Lewis's country mansion.
3. The doyen of U.S. experts on English seventeenth-century parliamentary history.
* Most of this was accomplished years later.
4. Sir John Neale, the great Elizabethan historian, a consistent champion of ALR's work.

– very different from the discouraging attitude I met with over my *Grenville*. Dear Richard Pares could never bring himself to say a word in its favour, or in favour of historical biography at all. Discouraging, but wrong.

Wallace considered that the good Hurstfield wasn't really up to doing the biography of Robert Cecil. I should hope he could.* Notestein wants a biography of Lord Henry Howard – so do I. I said, what a snake! Wallace added innocently that he was a pervert and – what I didn't know – had relations with James's boy-friend, Carr. But is there evidence? Howard was very secretive – a crypto-Catholic, crypto-homo, crypto-everything. I wanted to write about him: 'Don't encourage anybody else to write about Lord Henry Howard: he's my skunk.' (Still not written. 1972.)

Outside in the streets loudspeakers were braying that Professor J. K. Galbraith of Harvard would be speaking that evening for Kennedy and Johnson. The young men about the streets provided familiar university atmosphere, some off for the afternoon's games, voices fresh and youthful, all their years before them.

A pleasant drive back through the afternoon, while Lefty talked quite intimately about Wyndham[1] and his *Walpole*. Also about Wyndham's relation to his family, which he thought one of love-hate; he recalled the emphasis with which Wyndham's mother said of the younger son, Dick: 'He's a *real* man.' On taking over Felbrigg, Wyndham ran her out of the house – actually, I was never allowed to meet her. He described the beginning of his friendship with Wyndham over Horace Walpole, Wyndham's coming to Farmington for months to work at the letters, and ending up by producing a book which was just scissors and paste. Should Lefty let this pass, or be a good friend and tell him the truth? He deciding on the latter, and Wyndham came back for another visit, rewrote his book and produced what is 'a competent, chronological account of Walpole's life and no more'. I said that it had not solved the enigma of Walpole's personality for me, that it presented the surface of his life, a life that was wanting a dimension.

That evening Lefty sat me down with the proofs of his own book, the Mellon Lectures at Washington, and by the end I saw that he had solved the enigma, added the dimension that has always been missing to Walpole and at length made him clear. Horace emerges as a good man, and I was touched by Lefty's summing-up of his virtues: constancy in friendship, contrition in regard to Gray, charity towards Lady Ossory, forbearance and patience with George Montagu, love and affection towards Conway, tolerance towards Mason, a good deal of kindness and generosity to many.

* But no sign of it after twenty years. QED.

1. Ketton-Cremer.

An admirable book, at length we shall have one of the most curious figures in our literature got right at last.

Conversation with Lefty was revealing. Twice he made the point what a triumph Walpole's life had been with that background and that inheritance, walking along the razor-edge he did, maintaining his balance, without toppling over into suicide. I knew that Lefty himself had once been off his head and maintained his balance in life with difficulty – a work of art, too.

I was glad to be helpful, not only psychologically, fortifying his confidence in the book, fruit of his strange life's work as a collector, but in reading his proofs and making corrections and suggestions. And I agree with him about the inhibiting attitude of Wyndham, who thought that 'when one ventures on psychology, one doesn't know where it will end'. The psychological perception of the book, sensitive and not at all strained, is convincing, one of the best things about it.

I reported to Lefty the portrait at the Boston Otis house, which I thought must be of Sir Charles Hanbury-Williams, holding a copy of his *Isabella, or the Morning*. He was thrilled by this, for he has the Hanbury-Williams Correspondence. In a farewell tour of the archives next morning, I noticed a dozen or more letters of Walter Harte, Vicar of St Austell,* one of the eighteenth-century clergymen I should like to write an essay about. Archdeacon Coxe, Thomas Birch, William Johnson Temple: *Four Georgian Clerics*.

So concluded a delightful visit, from which I greatly profited, did some work I had long wanted to do on Froude and much enjoyed myself.

4 November

One encounters a freer flow with Southerners: they think of themselves as more English, they are well-disposed to everything English, they come from Anglo-Scottish stocks. They are not so much on the defensive as people are apt to be in the Middle West, afraid of susceptibilities being hurt. Besides the pace of life is more English; Southerners are more relaxed, free to be themselves – except on one subject, slavery in the past, the coloured problem in the present.

Next day, Gunpowder Plot day, Randall[1] and I sallied off in summery sunshine in his tough little Volkswagen – he feeling a bit disloyal at its not being an English car – all the hundred miles to the capital, Montgomery. A noble highway cutting through endless forest all the colours of the Fall. At

* Eureka! I had forgotten. 1972.

1. Henry Randall, 'a gentle, Anglophile professor' who was doing the honours of Alabama.

Centerville the shapely pecan trees were dropping their nuts; beyond, we passed many peach-orchards, a buzzard with wide spread of wing over the Cahaba river, white tufts of cotton ungathered in a few fields, big golden globes of pumpkin heaped up for Thanksgiving. We lunched high up at the top of an hotel with a view all over the spreading town and away to the Alabama river. A carillon sprinkled its notes from the hideous Baptist church nearby, accompanied by the broadcast harmonies of a theatre organ. Bells without this nonsense would be better.

After lunch we visited the sights. The Historical Museum had a good Civil War flavour, though I noticed a powder horn that had belonged to Isaac May 1777, incised with carvings; Jefferson Davis' inauguration chair of red silk, appropriately askew. The wedding dress of Mrs Thomas Hill Watts, worn 10 January 1842 – her husband was the Civil War governor of Alabama, whose desperate appeal to defend Mobile to the last, 14 February 1864, was in another case: 'Those who love this city and the glorious *Cause* in which we fight will not hesitate to obey the calls which patriotism makes.' Twenty-two years before could they have seen what was in store for them? If human beings could, they would make no moves, or at any rate fewer.

Silk flags with the thirteen unlucky stars of the Confederate States, flags of the 117th and 334th Field Artillery, of the First Alabama Cavalry; homespun saddlebags, bullets and cannon ball made at Montgomery, ammunition and horseshoes at Devil's Run, an arsenal destroyed by a Federal raid and the stuff thrown in the Black Warrior river – boys would dive in early this century and bring up trophies. I noticed a small brass candlestick captured at Missionary Ridge, 1863, and a package of Virginia tobacco, 'The Soldier's Comfort', saved from a Federal raid in 1864.

Across the garden, looking to the large Capitol of about 1820, was Jefferson Davis' house as President: green shutters, red chimneys and porch, the crickets singing continuously all round. Everything within was well arranged to give an idea of Jeff. Davis' domestic life: dressing-gown and slippers, top hat-box, his bed, the family Bible taken away by a Northern soldier and restored years later by his brother, the school books and piano of the children, the bed in which Mrs Davis died and the things she left to the South. From the many photographs and engravings one sees what a Welsh type of face Davis had. He was less good at holding his team together than the English Lincoln.

After touring round the Regency Capitol, with its well-proportioned dome, I sat in the garden tired, watching the leaves as yet hardly turned, the November day warm as English summer, a light breeze in the acacias, looking across to the tall magnolia in front of Jefferson Davis' house.

[New York]

Spolia opima[1] – this is what the power of money can do. I try to console myself with the thought that it is one way of anchoring the New World to the Old, a powerful bond with the elect; that it is only right that there should be a fair share of the world's *significant* culture over here. Today, to keep my spirits up, I thought, these are the cultural products of the various elements that have gone to make America: the greatest of Europe's material creations.

But what has America achieved compared with it? A remarkable example of technical achievement, in government and social organization, no less than in industry, trade, mechanics, all geared to the average man. In this, as in other respects, I am torn in different ways: I *wish* to be just and even generous to them, but heart and mind are not there. Even with regard to their outstanding products like the congenial Franklin – Lefty Lewis spoke patriotically of him as a kind of Leonardo. What nonsense! Where is the poetry, the imagination, the divine illumination, the *spirit*? To have made a few elementary experiments with electricity, to have invented lightning conductors and written those prosy sentiments of *Poor Richard*, a pedestrian autobiography and a lot of inferior verse – and to compare that with Leonardo!

They are chiefly interested in themselves nowadays, and I have come into it, marginally, at a most discouraging moment. Every day there's a new book about their Civil War, the level of writing appalling, especially among the professors. I don't think they know what good writing is, or when or why it is good or bad. I have to pretend otherwise, but in fact I don't think their products, even their summits, other than second-rate: their Franklins, Washingtons, Jeffersons, Wilsons, Roosevelts, Prescotts, Parkmans, Hawthornes, Whitmans, Twains, Paul Joneses, compared with a Caesar, Napoleon, or a Nelson; a Gibbon or Montaigne, a Milton or Goethe. Let alone a Titian or Rembrandt, Shakespeare or Dante.

They try to hip up these second-rate figures. The biography of Whitman I was reading before coming over spoke of him along with the supreme poets, Shakespeare, Dante, Goethe. Ludicrous to speak of this *uneducated*, untutored spirit along with them; poetically speaking, repetitive and humourless – or he wouldn't have written such reams of absurd stuff, contemplating his own 'man-balls', 'O quivering jelly of love', etc.

To this I am inclined to make only two exceptions: Lincoln and Henry James. They *are* possibly on the summit.

*

1. Properly this means the arms and armour of a defeated general taken by his opposing commander in single combat.

I went to tea with a newly discovered fan, a Mrs Steel, at 1200 Fifth Avenue. Too enthusiastic, left a query in my mind; she engaged me for a dinner party to meet friends who would not forgive her if she kept me to herself, etc. The daughter of Charles Knight, the animal painter who frescoed so many museums with natural history scenes, contributed frequently to the *Illustrated London News*.

That evening I went to see *West Side Story*, and was most impressed: here was authentic American art, arising out of American life, even if wholly Jewish, libretto, music, choreography. It was extremely well acted and danced, the music good, the whole thing knit together. A modern version of *Romeo and Juliet*, the situation, theme, the tragedy (there is even an apothecary): all suggested by it. But the language, eloquence, poetry are all missing, because these people – Porto Ricans and immigrant Polacks – are morons who can only communicate in staccato phrases of broken American. The void is filled with cleverness and technical proficiency. But a genuine work of art: Authentic America.

19 November

I must withdraw one of my two Americans from the heights. I cannot think that Henry James, though the cleverest mind to have devoted itself to the novel, can really be placed on the same level as Tolstoy or Dostoievsky, or perhaps Dickens: too wanting in heart.

In his place I think I should reinstate Washington; not so much in himself, for he doesn't have the genius of Caesar or Napoleon, or even of Marlborough, Nelson, Wellington – but for his crucial part in the making of a nation.

[Baltimore]

Why this sadness? One rarely sees the American landscape positively *riant* like French landscape, or smiling like the English. I could not but think of it as I looked at the Pissarros and the Turner at the Walters Gallery at Baltimore. Why is it that I find the French landscape so much more affecting? There was the little path that wandered like a ribbon round the slope of the hill, the ordered poplars in the background, the village houses happily clustered amid their fruit trees, the church in the background, a couple of women arrested there on their afternoon walk sometime in the 1870s. Or a Sisley scene upon the Marne, a pleasant boating river fringed with rushes, the river-path waist-high in flowers, the trees so friendly and familiar.

The Turner was altogether more grand: the forbidding high moors and fells of Durham, yet in the middle distance, lit up by sun, was the historic splendour of Raby Castle, all towers and battlements, with smoke rising from the kitchen chimney – one could almost smell an old English breakfast cooking; for there in the foreground was the hunt, the hounds in full cry across the slope, the huntsmen galloping after. For all its grandeur – I dare say it was painted for Raby, and came from there – a congenial scene.

That's partly it: the landscapes of France and England are so largely man-made and have been so long inhabited, while those of America are still wild and untamed, and go on for ever like melancholia. Even when sunlit and gay with autumn colour, as the forests were in Alabama, Henry Randall complained that it was impossible to walk in them: they are trackless, full of snakes and poisonous insects or poison-ivy. You can't just walk carefree along and sit down anywhere. Besides everything is on so immense a scale, you'd be lost.

I suppose there are exceptions to this hostility of nature, in New England, in old settlements like Farmington and along the banks of the Merrimac.

[New York]

22 November was my big day, for which I had been nursing myself as well as I could. In the morning I finished preparing my Ralegh lecture, and at one met Robert Lowell at Cerutti's, where I was giving him lunch. I had been rather apprehensive from the tone of his voice over the telephone – 'Yah – Yah – Yah', just like Wystan Auden, off-putting. But he turned out to be *most* sympathetic, and we got on easily, without any trouble. We had no reserves with each other and came out with everything we thought. He, too, had a cold, a rather runny one, for which he stuffed menthol up his nose, rather unprepossessing, and recommended it to me. He was less bulky and shambling than I had been given to suppose, and less mad. In fact, he was sane, sensitive, perceptive and responsive, full of original thoughts, rather a dear, and obviously a man of genius. No-one in the United States came up to expectations as he did.

The talk was fascinating, though I can't hope to reproduce it. One thing that struck me was his unorthodox comment on Shakespeare's women. Apart from Cleopatra he hadn't created a full woman, like the women of French tragedy, Phèdre, for example. They were either boy-girls, like Rosalind, Beatrice, Portia, or else the innocent creature like Ophelia, Desdemona, Cordelia. But what about Cleopatra, or Lady Macbeth, or Hamlet's mother? Lady Macbeth is a monster, but Hamlet's mother is woman enough, frail and erring. There may be something in what Lowell said, and he related it to the range open to boy-actors. He thought that Shakespeare was very conscious of the daughter relationship, and clearly had a daughter. So has Lowell, and may be reading himself in this.

He said he was a lapsed Catholic, which made him more sympathetic to me. I quite understood the appeal of myth in religion, but didn't see why they had to put it over as true, in the sense in which 'H_2O = water' is true. To regard religious myth on the same level as poetry was not demeaning, since one regarded poetry as the highest of man's achievements.

Lowell was in sympathy with the suffering element in religion, the expression of the tragedy in life. I doubted if I were: there was so much unavoidable suffering in life that I hated it being added to, made a cult of – the side of Catholicism I am most allergic to, the bleeding wounds, the crown of thorns, the crucifixes, the pietás. Though there may be some element of catharsis to be allowed for here, possibly of sympathetic magic.

He told me a little about his life, shyly but without reserve: he had 'almost always been married'. I said he needed to be. But he had been divorced, and didn't go to church any more. Nothing short of Catholicism would do for him – Anglicanism, for instance; as for the family Unitarianism – too thin and etiolated, nothing of religion left in it. (How different from the great Boston days of William Ellery Channing!) He had left Boston for New York, finding Boston too restricted and provincial, hardly anybody to talk to. (Exactly what Eliot said to me long ago about his year at Harvard as Professor of Poetry.) Except one or two, like Edmund Wilson, I said. The Ford Foundation had given him a fellowship, just to go to the opera and study it – with a view to his writing an opera, if so moved.

We talked about Auden. He said his last volume of poems had had a poor reception in America. I said what a tragedy it was for Wystan, and for English literature, that he should have missed the inspiration of the heroic years, 1940–45, in England. There was so much passionate feeling for England in so many of the earlier poems, like 'Prologue':

> O love, itself the interest in thoughtless heaven,
> Make simpler daily the beating of man's heart . . .

Wystan once said to me that he couldn't go back over the ground of those early poems, the northern fells, Ingleborough, Sedbergh, the Lakes – that was Paradise, and he couldn't go back to it. Evidently Paradise Lost.

Lowell said that Wystan had lost inspiration by coming to America; it was always a mistake for Englishmen to come and live in America. *There* was a warning, and I instinctively know it to be true: cutting at the roots of one's inspiration, one's instinctual life. All right to visit, but to live there, make one's home there – one couldn't.

So our lunch passed and we went down Madison Avenue together still talking hard, though I was fearful for my voice.

Ambivalence is the line; Cornwall *is* half-way between England and America. I shall secure myself on the side of America, whatever happens in England. It means hard work, but I have always had to go the hard way, when things fall into the hands of others, who make the right connections, and are less determined on independence and honesty of mind. I often think of D. H. Lawrence's last words, 'I've had a hard life.' The same goes for me, too. D.H.L. and I never belonged, and would never pay the price of *belonging* – the suppression of our own individuality, in a word, conforming. So D. H. Lawrence's real triumph has come after his death. I suppose mine may come then, too, perhaps partly with this journal. But, hard as I have worked throughout my life, my work has not the human appeal of his, there is so much of life I am not interested in: relations between the sexes, heterosexual love, the family, so much of human involvement.* That need not prevent the revelation of a human being, by the same token *more* original.

New York, 24 November

Thanksgiving day; after giving up the morning to letters, I went down to Cass Canfield's pretty house on East Side for lunch. Of all the houses in New York this is the one I should like to inhabit: a small, narrow, Georgian house of three stories, back from the street, with patio, wall and iron gates before it, opened only from the house on ringing.

I arrived early for a business chat with Cass in that downstairs drawing-room, old furniture, flowers, sculpture by Mrs Canfield, admirable amateur. Cass drew out of his pocket, in his usual cool way, the information that *The Elizabethans and America* had sold in its second year a mere 500. I have to be content with that, for my sales never go beyond the academic barrier of 5 or 6,000. (Perhaps one day they will, but too late to give me pleasure, as with everything.) Cass was unmoved by my report of Houghton Mifflin's enthusiasm for the Ralegh book and offer of money for it.** So I suppose Harper will do it in the usual unenthusiastic way – though I must remember to check the terms. I gather that Maurois is an extremely hard bargainer with his books, actually gets more than the traffic can afford.

The Maurois now arrived. I had never met Madame before,*** and began with a compliment, about Maurois' devoting a couple of pages to my

* Considering all these limitations, I think I have made out very well. 1979.

** I should have accepted this.

*** Daughter of Mme Caillavet, Anatole France's celebrated mistress. Dynastic.

first book – 'like having one's name inscribed on the dome of St Paul's'. After that everything went swimmingly. We got on to the subject of Princess Bibesco, and this was not displeasing to Mme Maurois. She made a point of telling us how pleased she was at being remembered, after fifteen years, by the woman at the shop whence she had sent so many food parcels during the war. This was a useful line, I registered, in case I knew about her husband's bad break about England in 1940.

What made that still more inexplicable was something that Maurois told us – he had written the Queen's speech to the women of France, for which she had given him a pair of platinum cuff-links which they kept in the safe at home. In going through the speech with her they came to a phrase like 'tels hommes', which the Queen pronounced without the 's', said that her tutor had taught her that way, and why was it to be pronounced, in other instances not, etc. There was a pleasant anecdote of an occasion, one of many, when his work was confused with Mauriac's. The old King of the Belgians said he thought *Le Désert de l'Amour* a good book, wasn't it? Evidently he thought it was by Maurois. When Maurois said, Yes, it was a good book, the King looked surprised.

I didn't know that they had a country house in the Dordogne, and almost made the mistake of saying 'the Mauriac country', but saved myself by saying they were very near. 'Yes, he is in the Gironde: two principalities,' Maurois added. Actually he does not *belong*, as Mauriac does. When he was asked at the PEN Club which of his books he had most enjoyed writing, two of them were about Jews, Disraeli and Proust, the third was George Sand. Cecil Roberts wrote me of a visit to the Maurois' house at Neuilly, of the impression of luxury it gave. He has made a pile of money by his books – and invested it well. He relies on this, he is an industrious worker and has a first-class secretary – his wife. She does a great deal of research for his books and all his typing. I liked her, clever and perceptive, and not in the least overpowering. She asked me to be sure to let them know when coming to Paris.

Their house is next door to the Windsors', whom they know – they regard him as pathetic, a fish out of water. While the Duchess has recently written an article for the Paris press on how the English people treated her husband – she makes a lot of money by such stuff. She has a terrific anti-English complex. Talk was easy and agreeable, mainly historical and literary. I could not but admire the vitality of this elderly couple, who seemed not aged at all. The lunch was the best I had had in the States. Cass's wife runs the house like clockwork, in addition to being quite a good sculptor. I invited Mme Maurois to admire the pieces of sculpture about and, on behalf of Cass, prevailed on his wife to promise to do a head of him – which hitherto she wouldn't do.

26 November

I took the 11.45 train out to Haverford, where Boies Penrose and Helen met me and gave me lunch at the Country Club. To begin with, I feared it was going to be a difficult weekend, for Helen was exasperating with an attack on Wyndham, who used to be such a 'favourite' with her. She had greeted Wyndham on his arrival with an attack on Lefty Lewis, with whom he had just been staying. Wyndham had stuffily replied, 'I will not sit by and hear my old and valued friend attacked.' Then it was war, and Helen wondered how she was going to get through a week with him in the house. Apparently Wyndham was stuffy, too, about some Englishman who was a fellow guest he didn't take to. All this was poured out through lunch, whether Wyndham didn't take too much to drink, was 'Oh so *selfish* – the most selfish man she had ever met', while poor Boies sat there crestfallen and putting in a word to corroborate, not daring otherwise.

It was an inauspicious beginning, for I agree with Wyndham and privately thought it shocking manners to attack his friend on arrival, and now mine. But I had more sense than to say so. Without letting either Wyndham or Lefty down, indeed saying that I agreed with both of them, I turned it all into a tease and gently ragged her; Helen began to laugh and thaw. I said that *all* bachelors were well known to be selfish – I was one. This made her say, 'Oh no, you're not.' 'But I *am*, dear.' I pretended to be jealous: 'You have a love-hate complex – you love Wyndham more than you do me. Now *I'm* vexed,' etc. 'Oh, no I don't.' 'Oh, yes, you do.' Poor Boies was much relieved; it was really a great bore, but I had turned the corner and the weekend prospered.

27 November

At night I was glad to read, and in the morning to hear, about Boies Penrose,[1] the big boss. He was an immense fellow, six feet four and correspondingly broad. When young and down from Harvard, a fine figure of a man, out on the town looking for food, whisky and women. A gentleman born, he never associated with his own class, but with the streets, saloons and clubs, and for his women – for whom he had an equally voracious appetite – he went to brothels. The boys were brought up by their father, a well-known doctor and obstetrician, who lost his wife young, to be atheists; and when of the proper age, he took them along to the brothel to have them initiated. It must have given the cynical Boies pleasure to reply to a canting enquiry from

1. Father of his host.

President Eliot of Harvard why they had been placed in a private boarding house instead of in college – that their father was afraid for their morals.

The Boss was also a cynic about democracy. He realized early that the prime purpose of politics in the American late nineteenth century was *management* – with the lowering of standards since the early nineteenth century, the influx of immigrants, the milling about of the mob. In this right enough. He hated humbug and cant of every kind, believed that big business was best for the people since it promoted production and gave them work. Therefore, high tariffs, always push the interests of big business in politics – that was what it was mostly about, his job to deliver the vote. This he never failed to do with his control of the party machine, to which he dedicated his life; his prime motive – power, of which he was a great glutton, as of food, drink and women.

As for statesmanship, he had no ideas beyond those of big business. Not much of a speaker, and not bothering to make speeches, he was undefeated as a manager. Woe betide anyone who crossed him or the party machine – they felt 'the withering touch of Boies Penrose'. When asked once why he didn't marry, he replied, 'All right. Let the party machine choose the woman, and I'll marry her.' Never attended a dinner party in his life, couldn't bear the social graces or pretences. And yet was well-read. My Boies didn't know him till the last year of his life, when he was an invalid – from over-eating, more than over-drinking – and used to talk to young Boies about English literature, in which he was well-read. No-one would believe that.

What an extraordinary man, this great hulk of flesh, with his appetites and his tastes. Actually he respected Woodrow Wilson as a politician, though loathing his cant. But, the head of the G.O.P., he *did* make Harding President, to be a docile instrument in the hands of the party.

Helen told me that all the Penroses were as hard as nails. That our Boies had courted her for two years – both had been married before and their first marriages broken – and that she could not bear the hardness. When Boies's uncle, Richard, who made an immense fortune in mining in Colorado, leaving $45 million but nothing to Boies, the latter said: 'The son-of-a-bitch, it was good for him.' That Boies himself used to be so acid and cynical that people were afraid of his tongue and would go out of the room at his club when he came in. Now popular: she had softened him. I can believe it. Underneath the kindly-crusty manner, the dryness, sparing of words, the edge to tongue and temper, the no-nonsense about him, that make Boies, with his scholarship, his writing and collecting tastes, a distinguished man, I can see that what Helen said could be so.

Later that morning I was taken by Mrs Barnes out to their house to see her husband's library of books about old London. Hastily through that bumpy, hilly country, full of woods and hollows, to a house with the best view of all, like looking across Berkshire downs Hungerford way. It was a colonial house added on to, big panelled library taking in the view; terrace, loggia, swimming-pool, everything as usual that money can command.

These people were, exceptionally, not rich, but farmed the land, bred horses and sheep. All the same, a good estate to have and to hold, with another engaging house next door, let at present, for when the family grows up and may want it. Mr Barnes was a collector of John Buchan, much pleased and excited to hear about him. And had one or two books of mine, for me to autograph.

29 November

I was badgered by a silly woman who wanted to research about something, but didn't know how to set about it or how to explain herself. The answer to her problem was Caroline[1] on her doorstep. I sent her away short and sharp – she had bad 'domestic difficulties'. Then out to the Barnes Foundation to see the pictures – a great privilege which had taken more correspondence than I liked: I had almost thrown my hand in.

An extraordinary place out in a suburb at Merion on the Main Line, big gallery attached to the private house of the late Dr Barnes, who had made a fortune out of some drug and spent it on pictures. Laughed at by Philadelphians, a self-sufficient lot, looked down on as a parvenu with pretensions about his pictures, he was maddened by them and had taken every step to exclude them from his gallery. Serve them right. For what became visible after five minutes inside the building was that *this* man had extraordinary flair. He had not bought just everybody among the French impressionists, but the best of everybody. I remember Richard Pares telling me years ago about him, when he was in Philadelphia – a lifetime ago – and hadn't got in.

I was greeted by an ancient beldame, Miss Violette de Mazia, clad in the flowing frilly dress of a schoolgirl of fifteen, with silver rings on both her thumbs, a hooked Jewish nose and spectacles, and a free-limbed manner of walking that was more like swimming. She had inconveniently appointed the lunch hours, 12 to 2, for my visit; herself didn't lunch, that was why she was able to lecture from 3 to 5. I mustn't be left upstairs when she began, for the doors would be locked and I wouldn't be able to get out. Outside, the rain poured down; my hair was wet from my angry walk; I shot upstairs.

From there I could see the Matisse murals the Doctor had commissioned

1. Robbins.

to fill the attic spaces of the main hall. They were graceful nudes – his usual obsession with the female form, especially bottoms. But everywhere were treasures, with some insignificant ancient pictures, often German, heaped together and hung on an odd principle, with pieces of old steel strapwork decorating the dingy walls. In every room, any amount of artistic bric-à-brac, primitive Indian Christian daubs from New Mexico, textiles, Picasso tapestries, glass bottles, ceramics, bronzes, inferior but ancient furniture.

But what pictures when one came to them! The finest Renoirs, Cézannes, Manets, Rousseaus, Gauguins, Van Goghs. I cannot hope to remember one hundredth, I was so pressed for time. Plenty of the rosy-fleshed late Renoirs, with *his* obsession with the female form. Even so one of these, very lightly painted, almost unfinished, was superb: a woman with child at her breast, and another figure near, like a secular Holy Family; and a big picture from his blue period, of utmost magnificence: a Paris scene of two or three young men in evening clothes, tall hats, greeting two or three young women. Such character in the leading couple: a young dandy impressing his sex upon a young woman, impressed, while her girl-friend behind watches to see how she takes it – for all the world like the display of birds. As wonderfully painted, a crowded composition, comparable with 'Les Parapluies', the splendid horseman in the Bois de Boulogne that I remember from thirty years ago in Hamburg. One Manet at a first glance I took for a Renoir, from subject and treatment: a woman at the wash-tub in a garden with child on the other side, the whole flooded with light and gay garden colours.

And the Cézannes! – not only Mont St Victoires, and apples, but several of the monumental portraits: two of the severe, classic Madame Cézanne, a self-portrait, and a portrait of another man. Two or three early Cézannes and Van Goghs, painted in orthodox academic manner before they developed their individual styles. Of Van Gogh, there was his ebullient bristling portrait of the Postman, and splendid late landscapes. Good Gauguins, not specially noteworthy. Several Courbets, sombre and satisfying; a magnificent Daumier; an unnoteworthy Goya; good Utrillos, Pissarros, Sisleys, Seurats, Modiglianis – and of him Dr Barnes's choices were more varied, a nude lying face downwards for once, a young man instead of the eternal woman. A few Rouaults, some ugly Soutines, and a number of a painter I've never heard of, Pascin.

What an achievement out of the Doctor's discovery of a drug, which Philadelphia said was somebody else's discovery brought back from Germany. And how justified the Doctor stands, after his death, in his gallery. There were his books, written along with Miss de Mazia, which gave offence to the experts. I talked to an enthusiastic art student, who said there was no place where the appreciation of the picture was so expounded as here, everything extraneous like art-history and the biographical, kept subordinate. He swore by the beldame. She must be a remarkable woman to have survived the Doctor.

At 2 p.m. James Rawle came to fetch me. Of oldest Philadelphia family going back to Penn, he had never got inside. Of Cornish descent, he looks smashing in the uniform of the Philadelphia City Troop, a select recruitment from the best families. He knows Cornwall – especially about St Juliot where his family came from – and reads my books. Waiting in the car was a remarkable, ancient character, Harold Eberlein, aged eighty-five, leading antiquarian of Philadelphia who had laid on the ensuing pleasures for me.

Rawle drove us down to Newcastle, untouched and unspoiled, a prosperous little sea-going town in the eighteenth century, left high and dry when the later development took place at Wilmington, higher up the Delaware. All grouped around its green; Georgian church with spire, the arsenal, the early white Congregational church, town hall at the west end, perfect eighteenth-century houses along the streets.

[A visit to the Roosevelt family house, Hyde Park]

When he died – Gordon Ray told me, who was serving in the Pacific at the time – and the order went out to fly flags at half-mast, not one of the captains of those seven ships would obey the order. Unthinkable in England!

We went out by the little office along the front porch where F.D.R. worked, where he signed the agreement with Churchill for the making of the atomic bomb, where he made his broadcast as candidate for the fourth term as President. I went on alone to the grave in the rose-garden, the roses of the Roosevelts, surrounded by the high clipped hedge. There was the simple tomb

Franklin Delano Roosevelt
1882–1945
Anna Eleanor Roosevelt
1884–

with the grave in front, and one big wreath beside it.

Across to the library F.D.R. began building before his death, to accommodate the archives accumulated in so many years of office. He evidently contemplated retirement: there was his big study, in a grander manner than the house, with a ramp for him to wheel his chair into it. Since his death the building has grown into a museum, well arranged and set out.

One could watch F.D.R.'s life unfold from babyhood: with his christening clothes, and Eleanor's, the big Dutch family Bible on which he took his oaths of office, photographs of the boy on his pony in the grounds, with his elderly father, James Roosevelt, and young mother so long a widow; the relics of Harvard days, his Harvard Crimson sash; engagement to his cousin, another Roosevelt. His life-long interest in the Navy was displayed by a room devoted to models of ships, with scores of naval prints, including his favourite, the victorious fight of the *Constitution*. It seems he long entertained the idea of writing a biography of Paul Jones, and accumulated a lot of material – useful to Sam Morison in writing his book.

Another room was devoted to presents, interesting, some of them imbecile – like the personal attacks on him he collected: prints showing him as a grinning lunatic behind bars, attacks even on his little dog Fala; a photograph of the black Scottie perched up beside him in his car; another of the little creature doing tricks for the President, seated helplessly on the big sofa in the library. Fala died not long after his master.

The director, a Mr Kahn, came along to meet me and show me the archives: drafts of the speeches, some of them Robert Sherwood's, with interlineations and changes by F.D.R., including the last draft he was working on and his last pencilled words, 'We must go forward in strong and active faith', before he was struck down.

I was touched by it all, and came out in a dream, almost in tears, to a long drive back through superb country, the way he often came.

[California, 21 November 1962]

We climbed up the steep streets of Berkeley to the Nimitz house in Santa Barbara Road, with a superlative view across the Bay direct to the Golden Gate. A garden both in front and on the back slope, much tended by the Admiral and his wife; on the street a Mexican weeping pine, azaleas, an orange tree and around a little patio Mrs N.'s bonsais arranged. We had a cup of tea at the window overlooking the bay, thousands of lights coming out. Later, supper, and I went off to bed, to read the Japanese account of the battle of Midway Island, fascinated, until after midnight.

22 November, Thanksgiving Day

We drove off early, with the river fog from the Sacramento River obscuring the upper bay. It soon cleared as we drove into Marin County, still quite populous, for many miles suburbs from San Francisco; the name of Sir Francis Drake much in evidence on schools, hotels, shops, garages, whatnot. The country was beautiful and, when the houses cleared, became stock-raising ranches, country very like Somerset, especially when going through the hills, road narrowing, twists and turns, the redwoods thick on either side. Getting nearer the ocean the trees cleared and we came out into open country at Point Reyes, at the bottom of a long fiord – really an earthquake fault now an arm of the sea, superb for sailing and fishing for spearheads.

Here we met Captain Oko, gallant Jewish sailor, damaged by his war experiences and helping to run Jewish refugees into Palestine against the British embargo – yet a good friend of Britain, well-read in naval history, President of the Navigators' Guild, local realtor doing well in real estate in that neighbourhood, settled in a house at the parting of the roads. He had organized everything, including a Navy photographer to record the visit. As we drove out to the coast, the country became treeless and rocky, very like Dartmoor, but in spring covered with wild lupins. It became grander as we went out along the spine of the headland, the estuary or Estero on the left, open ocean on the right: like West Penwith, the Land's End country coming round to Zennor and St Ives.

At the end we came to Hall's Ranch, the real old America of the nineteenth century, timber-frame house, where Mrs Hall was cooking Thanksgiving Dinner for seventeen people. We trundled through the farmyard in our two cars and down the rough track to the Estero. On a little freshwater lagoon I saw a fleet of coots and a schooter duck; quail rose up under our feet as we tramped the last bit down.

Divine day, country, everything. There was the inlet, into which Drake could have come; a shoulder of hill cutting him off from any spying eyes at sea and giving shelter, at the foot of which the camp could have been made, where they stayed some thirty-eight days to careen the ship before setting off across the Pacific. The site is marked by a post and an anchor presented by Plymouth – nothing else to be seen, though they have dug around hopefully.

There are two schools of thought, bitter blows exchanged between them: one lot holding that Drake *did* anchor in San Francisco Bay, the other that it was here. Captain Oko is the leader of the local school, and this view seems more probable. We walked about, we imbibed the fresh Pacific air; we looked up the Estero that goes some ten or fifteen miles inland to a landing, where in old days they used to bring the butter and cheese for San Francisco.

When we got back, the Halls had laid on an out-of-doors party for us in the court, where they do the boiling of the crabs and lobsters they catch. Two splendid crabs were handed over to the Admiral, evidently adored by everyone – and there now turned up the farmer's husky son, a splendid fellow of six foot two, dark and winning, who stands behind me in the group photograph taken. This fine fellow had served under the Admiral in the *Missouri*.

Good cheer, good feeling, how friendly these farmer folk are – the salt of America. I sent them *A Cornish Childhood* for Christmas; one of the girls was a teacher.

We were driven back along the narrow West Country roads at speed by Captain Oko, talking to me all the time. We were given lunch in their house – old china that had come in through the Pacific trade, scholarly books, maps, antiques, good food and talk. Here at this uttermost point of land, near Inverness, a *finis terrae*. Where would one get the like in England? Well, one *might*: but there would be more constraint, more self-consciousness around an Admiral of the Fleet, also less scholarship, less education on the part of the Captain.

At the Halls' the Admiral told a story of his trial at Admiral Halsey's funeral, where he was representing the President and was pushed in front on the slippery edge of the grave; every now and then a few inches of soil would give, and the minister went on and on, while Nimitz thought if he goes on much longer – and a few more inches gave: it became a race between the live Nimitz and the dead Halsey which would get into the grave first. All very well acted, quite naturally – charming. But then, Nimitz has on top of everything great charm.

I got back tired out with sea air, talk, seeing everything, slept for a bit and went on reading about the war in the Pacific. The Admiral had piled me up with books and I read a great deal during my stay – came away much better informed. For Thanksgiving Dinner Admiral Watt and his wife came – a solid admiring engineer, slow of speech and story, but likable. He told me something valuable. When Nimitz took over the command after Pearl Harbor, morale was very low, fine fighting men really believed the war was lost. (Here Winston's speech to Congress must have been a tonic.) All the big ships lying on the bottom of the harbour, Nimitz had to hoist his flag on board a submarine. For the first five months his job was to build up, recover morale, always on the look-out for a second attack. After his day's work, he went to sleep all right at eleven, but always awoke at three and couldn't get to sleep again. To begin with, he worried whether this might not interfere with his efficiency; finding it did not, he made a habit of reading from 3 a.m. onwards, books about Japan, the coasts, shoals, weather, climate, etc. – all the things he would be up against. The morning after the battle of Midway Island,[1] he slept on so soundly that at 9.30 a.m. he had to be awakened by his man. The load of anxiety was relieved.

1. At which four Japanese aircraft-carriers were sunk: the turning-point in the war.

Present that evening was one of the four Hungarian girls the Nimitzes adopted and made members of their family after the Rising. The two younger girls have settled into American life and were married from the house – the Admiral giving one of them away and providing the wedding. The two elder girls not engrafted into American life – the younger of these kindly provided for my delectation: a good-looking, dark girl, anxious to make an impression, willing to contradict. She soon found that this did not interest me, though I did my duty by her. Next evening she was sharp enough to notice the 'tension' in me.

Meanwhile I was listening with all ears to everything the Admiral was telling – far too busy and absorbed to be able to write it down at the time. I have written notes in shortened form at the beginning of this volume of the fascinating Nimitz background, the famous old Ship hotel at Fredericksburg. The family wholly German on both sides, the Admiral didn't speak English until he was eight. Even today he speaks the language with care, thinking for the right word, extremely well, almost in a scholar's fashion. He told me a great deal about his life – in the most unegoistic manner: he is a great dear, with irresistible charm, innate goodness; duty and consideration the very air he breathes. Though Nelson is his hero, what Nimitz has is the Lincoln touch. He is well-read – when one thinks that most of his career was as an engineer and a submarine man, how many British sailors would be so well-read in history? He knows all about Drake, and especially about Nelson. In the drawing-room there hangs an original copy of the London newspaper, edged round in black, with Collingwood's account of Trafalgar and Nelson's death.

Nimitz was Chief of Naval Personnel at Washington when the summons to take over at Pearl Harbor came. He had been working all hours round the clock answering people's enquiries about the whereabouts of their boys – it was driving him frantic. But Pearl Harbor was no fault of Admiral Kimmel: he was a fighting admiral full of aggressive spirit – thought the spirit in the fleet was not keyed up with any expectation of what happened. On the other hand, if Kimmel had received warning of the Japanese approach he would have put to sea and been destroyed by overwhelming forces. Instead of losing 3,500 men as they did, they would have lost 25 or 30,000 men, including irreplaceable officers for the subsequent training of the men that defeated Japan.

I remember meeting Arthur Goodhart in the High, on the news of Pearl Harbor: '*Now* they are going to get what's coming to them,' he said. Meaning, first, the beastly Germans, of course. We were both in a highly emotional state after the long sickness of hope deferred, and the unspeakable things the Jews were enduring.

Obviously one of Nimitz's strongest suits was his sympathy with others – so very unlike a German. He had no difficulty in dealing with MacArthur, who was senior, so Nimitz deferred to him: always went to MacArthur's headquarters for conferences, MacArthur never came to his – only once to Hawaii when the President came there for a conference. I told Nimitz that Alanbrooke considered MacArthur the ablest soldier of the war. Nimitz said that he dare say he was. He kept on good terms with him, showed me a walking-stick that MacArthur had given him. He told me (*not* for the record: but how can anything told a historian not be for the record?) that, in the dispute between President Truman and MacArthur, Truman was right.

Nimitz has a great admiration for Truman, and relations between Trumans and Nimitzes were close. Mrs Nimitz told me an endearing thing as to the relations between the women. Poor Bess Truman had arthritis in her knees and found the formal parties at the White House with hours of standing unendurable: what was she to do? Mrs Nimitz had had trouble with her knees, so badly that she has had one of her knee-caps removed (and so rolls round like a true sailor's wife at sea). She offered Bess a rubber knee-cap, which was a godsend.

The Admiral keeps fit by a great deal of outdoor life, gardening, playing a game of throwing iron horse-shoes on a pitch at the foot of the garden, as he had done while at sea, and all in shorts, open shirt, no hat. He sleeps in the open on the upstairs balcony, with canvas sheets to keep out rain or wind, warm, for he has an electric blanket. In the morning he goes into the big double bedroom and rolls up and down the floor – he says it does good to the spine, the changing position top and bottom. I thought of Dr Johnson, who could never resist rolling down a slope.

When the Pacific war moved forwards nearer to Japan, and he moved his headquarters to Guam, he liked it. On his afternoon walks he used to fill his pockets with seeds of wild flowers and scatter them on the hillsides. This he and Mrs Nimitz used to do on their regular walks across the hills of Tilden Park behind Berkeley, trying to sow wild lupins, difficult to get to take. Angelic old couple! – this is the real heart of America, the salt of the earth, that the outside world knows nothing about. They know all the bores and platitudinarians, politicians and business executives, Hollywood and journalism; but they don't know the goodness of heart endemic in the true Americans, in Nimitzes and Nevinses, in Roosevelts and Browns of Providence and Rockefellers – though it should be obvious enough in the world-wide good works of the last.

Friday, 23 November

The Admiral took me for a drive round Tilden Park – an entire valley with hillside on either ridge, twenty miles long and only about a couple of miles wide, so that it is accessible from every part of Berkeley and Oakland. Everywhere were tall feathery clumps of eucalyptus, or in lines – what a success Old California made of that importation from Australia: one sees screens of them as windbreaks for the orange groves in the plains out towards Pomona and beyond, or in the fruit-growing plain of Ventura. Everywhere too were the white heathery bushes of rhus – of which one form is poison oak. (The Admiral and Mrs N. know a lot about trees, flowers, shrubs. Would that I did!) We stopped at Inspiration Point, and looked out in every direction. Here is another side to the American achievement: the dedication of these great open spaces to parks, the landscaping, planting, the care and pride – to offset the scars made by the population explosion.

The dog was Mrs S.'s child, she herself a psychiatrist – without much psychological perception. The dog was being sent solemnly to a Dogs' School, which he *just loved* – to learn reading and writing and probably to vote. If he was a naughty dog, he shouldn't go to school tomorrow – he would *just hate* that. The dog behaved like a spoiled child, all over the place, wouldn't keep quiet or do anything it was told – till George lost his temper and gave the creature a good hiding. After that the air cleared.

Saturday, 24 November

On the way to the airport the Admiral told me the story of Nehru's behaviour over Kashmir. After the hand-over in India, the U.N. proposed arbitration of the disputed boundary between India and Pakistan, and asked the Admiral to head an international commission to arbitrate. N. was willing and proud to undertake it, to perform a work of peace as the crown of his life's work. He worked at it conscientiously, as everything he undertakes; read up the history of the dispute, got the intelligence reports, British and American as well as Indian and Pakistani; he got together a strong body of international persons to conduct the plebiscite. But he found progress towards the objective blocked; and after two or three meetings with Nehru, he saw that Nehru never intended any plebiscite to be taken or justice done to Pakistan in the matter. Nimitz several times referred to him as no statesman. I had a harsher word for him.

[New York, September 1965]

Tea at Boconnoc

Before I left Jack swore me to write up the story of my visit to Boconnoc.[1] In all the years that I have lived within eight or ten miles of the place, a friend of the neighbouring Lanhydrock, a great friend of *their* – the Fortescues' – friend, Jenefer Lloyd, I had never been bidden or myself made any motion to penetrate the mysterious house in that lovely valley all to itself, hidden by beech-woods and a vast park. The whole place dripping with memories of the Civil War, of Braddock Down and Charles I sleeping in his coach by a hedge, the house itself asleep at the end of long drives in from the tangle of roads between the Fowey and Looe rivers. I have several times walked across it – once with Veronica, again with Jack and David Treffry – regularly looking down from the little church upon the inaccessible mansion, tenanted now by the Fortescues, in succession to Grenvilles and Pitts. Bought with the proceeds of the Pitt diamond from the Mohuns. In the fifteenth century the Courtenays had it. I have always longed to see it. Once and again I have suggested to Jenefer Lloyd to make a move – with no result.

Meanwhile I had heard something of the crackpottery of the old couple. Day, butler at All Souls, had been butler at Castle Hill, told me that the J. B. Fortescues of Dropmore and Boconnoc hadn't wanted the elder son to marry or succeed, had favoured the younger son who married and did have children. This couple, of course, none – the husband, George Grenville, not a likely father, crankish and impotent.

At last, at Prideaux Place, Padstow, I met them, standing in the middle of the room, hardly talking to anyone. I went out of my way to be introduced to them – he made himself agreeable, was evidently interested, talked intelligently about Sir John Fortescue's books, my books, Ebrington, Trenarren, which he said he had seen (Jenefer must have brought him in in my absence). Mrs F. stood her ground, with hot and angry eyes, hardly spoke.

Jenefer rang me up to say afterwards that if I wanted to see Boconnoc it would be quite all right if I wrote; that they were a rather formal old-fashioned couple.

That was on Saturday, 21 August. I did nothing for a week. Came Sunday, 29 August, when I had Alison and Elizabeth Johnstone to lunch, with the Kendalls of Pelyn. The Johnstones had just been to tea at Boconnoc for the first time and Alison was full of the treasures there. Then I wondered. Should I never see the place? The eccentric couple were getting old. I had lived all my life nearby and never penetrated it. Perhaps here was a last chance. It

1. Boconnoc was the great house of the Fortescues; Lanhydrock that of the Robartes, who had always made ALR welcome.

was absurd that a leading historian living nearby all his life should never see it. I changed my mind, and in the week wrote George Fortescue a polite letter putting the point. *At once* he telephoned asking me over that day – 2.30 on Saturday, 4 September.

It was grey and showery as I entered the upper gate on the Lostwithiel road and drove down a couple of miles of drive. At first open brackeny country with furze clumps and sparse trees, a few pines – good pheasant country. John Bevil Fortescue, the old man, 1850–1939, came down to Boconnoc from grand Dropmore only for the shooting. A party would descend once in the year, for the rest it was closed – though the clay-dues of the Boconnoc estate rolled in their hundreds of thousands, constantly increasing, to the Fortescues. When George and his wife occupied the house for a bit they had to provide everything, linen, cutlery, even their own brooms and mops.

Then the great beeches began, silvery, columnar, the finest beeches in Cornwall. I passed another lodge-gate into the deer-park. There were the stags gathered under a tree, antlers held high. A third lodge and I was in the bowl of a valley dominated by the long south wing of the house, eighteenth-century but plate-glassed and Victorianized by J.B.F. I passed a couple of estate-folk and in at the gate I had gazed down upon disconsolately over the years.

The bell clanged, the dogs barked, the door was opened by Geo. Fortescue himself, in the shabbiest old suit – not a servant – he would have been cleaning up after lunch. Behind him Mrs F. extended a hand, reddened, coarsened by much washing-up – with all their money, they do the work of that house themselves. No wonder they don't know where to begin – Elizabeth Johnstone said that they were bewitched by the house. They are. And no wonder. The place made an extraordinary impact on my mind; for the next twenty-four hours I could think of nothing else.

The front hall was not large, the stone hall of a Queen Anne house, a couple of columns at the back screening the passage right and left. The hall had marble tables *à la* Kent, busts, hall chairs; two country portraits of Reginald, first Lord Mohun and his wife, painted in 1629, perhaps to celebrate his marriage. Both were in their finery, ivory silk or satin, she with pink love-knots all over her dress, he a square masculine head, black hair and eyes. Convincing and attractive portraits by an unsophisticated hand.

In the state dining-room on the right were the previous generation of Mohuns, the father by Cornelius Jansen with a large sweep of hat. State dining-room! – it looked more like an auction-room. The tables and chairs of at least two dining-rooms – Boconnoc and Dropmore – were crowded into it, chairs stacked in rows, tables loaded with Sèvres, books and bric-à-brac, one couldn't get round to look at the pictures. The Mohun portraits had been bought with the house by Governor Pitt. There he was, a heavy, forceful man, by Kneller, black hat with the Pitt diamond in it. Mrs F. showed me a replica – I have never seen the original in the Louvre: bought for the French crown by the Regent Orleans. I have never seen so large a diamond. The old couple had paid it a visit in the Louvre.

Four portrait busts on pedestals around the room – the family prime ministers. George Grenville of the Stamp Act, to whom we owe the loss of America; Lord Grenville, Foreign Secretary, of the innumerable Dropmore Papers; Chatham with hawk nose larger than normal, and the younger Pitt, more of a Grenville than a Pitt. Governor Pitt bought Boconnoc as convenient for Cornish rotten boroughs. He thought he had made a poor bargain and didn't care for the remote place. Little did he realize that it would be a goldmine for his descendants with all those china-clay dues and royalties making them richer than ever. The Fortescue estate must be the richest in Cornwall, except for Lord Falmouth's. But how the Governor's plans bore fruit in the figure his family cut in the next generations!

We went up the staircase, painted *à la* Laguerre in the early eighteenth century – not large, just the staircase of a Queen Anne Cornish house. But it led into the long gallery – at either end a square room: at the eastern end the library with tall Venetian window, ruined by Victorian plate-glass, at the western end a pretty sitting-room. In between the olive-painted gallery looking south towards the river Lerryn, with all the family portraits on the walls, Pitts, Grenvilles, Lytteltons: Reynoldses, Gainsboroughs, Romneys.

All the carpets were up, the furniture crowded and stacked along the middle, one couldn't get *through* it, one had to skirt gingerly round. I couldn't take in all the portraits; not many were of the first quality – not a very good one of Chatham. Not to be compared with the William Hoare of him I have just seen at Raleigh, North Carolina – this one brings home the force of that large horsey face, the immense nose, the blazing eyes.

The old couple brought out their treasures for me. One of the four heads of Tippoo Sahib's throne, a lion's head of gold, the eyes rubies – loot from India; four altogether, one was given to the Royal Family, the whereabouts of the other two I have forgotten. They showed me the two volumes of Chatham's original letters to his nephew, Lord Camelford, at school – of which I have a first printed edition. In the library they pulled out the big family Bible in two volumes, splendid French binding, with the entries of Chatham's birth and his brothers and sisters. This room, too, like the drawing-room at the other end, cluttered with furniture, books, priceless china – I have never seen a house with so much Sèvres lying about.

The old couple had never got the place in order since the war. They took pride to themselves for the improvements they were making – fixing a basket handle here, going to put in a door there. On a sofa lay the red silk from a room at Dropmore which Mrs F. intended to put up on the drawing-room walls. But they must have sold Dropmore in the 1940s – and the silk there waiting on the sofa ever since. Mrs F. took pride in having removed the heavy plush curtains that hung in the gallery – 'the first thing we did'; but now there were no curtains up at all. Everything was on the floor, the doors they intended to restore between library and gallery – they had them on the place – not put in twenty years after!

Elizabeth was right: they were bewitched. Such a house was beyond them, with not a servant living in to look after it or them. The poor old couple just go round in circles. Downstairs they had got a large sitting-room in some order, though here too were *two* fine mahogany tables (Boconnoc and Dropmore) loaded with books and china. In one corner stood the splendid Charles II cabinet I had heard about twenty years ago from Charles Oman – one of the finest in existence, with long figures in chased silver down the panels, the doors off and put away, black ebony, silver, glass mirrors. In another corner was a pyramid of Lord Grenville's travelling-cases, fine black leather turned out with brass edges and fittings. A tiny repair had been made, but the wood not yet repainted. One sees the eldering couple mesmerized, unable to see the wood for the trees.

As they saw me out they asked, fearsomely, if I would stay to tea. Of course, I said I had to be back. Much relieved, Mrs F. insisted on going down the drive to open the gate for me. It was beginning to rain. I protested. She said, 'Let me into the car. We're quite hardy,' got out, opened and shut the gate and made her way back to that melancholy house. As I drove down the valley I looked back at the long plate-glass of the gallery catching the grey gleams of westering light.*

When I got back I was really ill. At lunch I had eaten two onions, though I know I cannot digest them. It was Beryl's half-day off, no-one in the house. For seven long hours I endured frightful pains and retching, was sick again and again. Crept to bed thoroughly frightened lest I had aroused the old ulcer trouble. All through this nightmare evening my mind was possessed by Boconnoc. I went over every detail, planning what I would do, how I would live in it if I were the lucky heir.

Lucky heir! – heir to nothing. I do not even own my own name – a cuckoo

* The gallery was designed by the connoisseur first Lord Camelford, one of Horace Walpole's group at Strawberry Hill. Now demolished – and Desmond Fortescue would like to pull the whole house down.

in every nest, not belonging anywhere. Hence it is that I peregrinate about the world (I write these words at Akron, Ohio). *Le Vagabond.*

– While I fantasy what I *would* do with Boconnoc *if* . . . I should live in it as Wyndham lives in Felbrigg. Actually the associations of Boconnoc, resuming Dropmore, are grander, its treasures greater. I should have a proper complement of servants, even in these days: a butler, a housekeeper, a couple of maids, possibly a footman, certainly a secretary. I should call in Fowler to put the house, especially the long gallery, in order, restore the small-paned glass throughout, paint the walls some heavenly colour, rich golden terracotta or egg-shell blue, hang up the silks, lay the carpets, arrange the furniture, display the wonderful Sèvres and Meissen now stacked as if awaiting the auctioneer.

Then one could *begin.* With all that money and all that space I should collect pictures. The splendid William Hoare of Chatham would not be in America. Or the fine Romney(?) of the younger Pitt I also saw at Raleigh. I should make a collection of landscapes and others, go in for watercolours for the corridors and bedrooms. One wouldn't need to collect any more furniture, but what fun it would be to replace the worn carpets of the gallery with brilliant honey-coloured savonnerie, to drape the windows with silks, fill the rooms with rugs and *objets d'art.*

I fear, however, that living at Boconnoc would be a full-time job. No time for writing, lecture-tours, visits to America or anywhere else for long. This age witnesses the end of everything such – and it speaks all the more eloquently in its present condition – not kept going as a living thing, but part-temple, part-junk-house of the departed glories of English history.*

I have done some research into the way of life of the old couple. The clue is miserliness. Jenefer told me of their tea-party for the Howes (Loveday Hext) – they never ask anyone to anything other than tea. Mrs F. told George to boil the kettle. He came back from the kitchen saying that there was a hole in the bottom. Lady Howe said, Boil the water in a saucepan, it's just the same. What a brilliant idea, they said. Mrs F. said, George, haven't you got a cake? Yes, he had, put away in a cupboard. When brought out it was covered in mould. When Lady Howe had surreptitiously fed bits to the dog, Mrs F., spotting her, said that the cake was quite all right if you cut off the outside.

As a cleaning woman came in only every other day, the dining-room table had six places laid: for breakfast, lunch and supper for two days while Mr and Mrs F. moved round the table. Now they do more for themselves: George having to cook bubble-and-squeak for lunch and supper. They are

* Further loss: the gallery pulled down 1973.

addicts of the Saturday edition of the *Telegraph*, as it has advertisements of cheap bargains. So they give themselves up to an evening's orgy of what they *could* buy and what bargains they would get.

All in some contrast to the extravagance of Chatham and the younger Pitt's unconcern about money.* This is what the descendants of the Pitts and Grenvilles, the Fortescues and the Russells (she was a Frankland-Astley-Russell) have descended to! – a close-up of our time.

Though cranks, they know what is due to them. Some neighbour asked permission to fish in the river. When he got back there was no-one at home, so he hung two of his catch on the knob of the front door for them. This gave great offence. Similarly the nephew and heir – old J.B. and his wife prognosticated right – to whom George has turned over most of the estate – has annoyed them by putting up a tennis-court at the Stewardry where he lives.

In the end they did show me all that they have to show; without going so far as to make tea, they put themselves out. And they have a good name as landlords all round their estates.

Saratoga Springs, 13 October 1965

– nearly sixty-two years away from 4 December 1903. A few days after my unforgettable visit to Boconnoc I went over to lunch at Lanhydrock: 7 September. I had the feeling that it might be the last time I should see my old friend, Lord Clifden, who has always been so kind to me. I really should have gone to see them at Belgrave Square when in London: he chided me for passing his door.

I made my way round to the side door – no more young footman to send down to open the Barbican gate. Faithful George Archer – who worked with our George[1] in Devonport Dockyard during the war – was on duty, but complaining as everybody complains nowadays. The third manservant was away on holiday, and it took one man's whole time to look after 'Lordie' nowadays. I found him so frail physically, though his voice was good. He can't move without help, and so deaf I knelt beside him to make him hear. There has always been such a *rapport* between us that he has been able to hear me; though he is very incommunicable nowadays, he still could hear me and make jokes with me.

They put on an excellent luncheon as always and I drank a little red wine to please him. But now Everilda is another invalid. Falling and breaking a leg has put her neck out – a sight to see – and with it her balance. When we

* He left debts of £40,000, neglecting his own affairs for the country's, which paid them.

1. ALR's brother.

moved to lunch I had to take her on my arm, while George practically carried Gerald.

He cheered up immensely at chatting with me – so George told me – talking about old times with Gerald Berners chiefly, his days at the House when he was a member of the Bullingdon, when Tommy Strong was Dean. Before I went he said the most emotional thing I have ever heard him say. 'I want to tell you how much I admire you for what you have achieved.' I had to go down on my knees to receive a kind of accolade.

When I went to say goodbye to Eva – usually a mixture of kindness and acidulation – she once said when she had got me over to meet John Betjeman, 'I suppose you know *every*body?' – she was now all kindness. She held out both hands with real affection, and wrote me the warmest letter in reply to mine. Violet was rather out of the emotional atmosphere. They have *always* been so good to me, from early days, the 1930s when we were together against Chamberlain. The Robarteses have always been Liberals, but Gerald had been a Foreign Office man and was opposed to Appeasement.

I had the saddest premonition that I shouldn't see them, all three together, again. Sadder still was to see how ugly a thing growing old can be, in my kind old friends. And what a contrast they afforded with their neighbours, the Fortescues, across the Lostwithiel road.

I made my way out by the great double avenue and the gateway built by John, 2nd Lord Robartes, in 1657 in his withdrawal from affairs during Cromwell's rule. Over beautiful Respryn bridge.

[A conversation with T. S. Eliot's widow, 24 November]

She told me a couple of stories. Tom was being driven in someone else's car one day, and they were all talking somewhat snobbishly about their dogs, their breeds, etc. The chauffeur was fond of dogs too; but he said apologetically that his was only a mongrel – 'he wasn't a consequential dog'. Tom was enchanted by this, and intended it for the title of his sequel to the book of Practical Cats. I asked why he had never written it, was he more fond of cats? No, he was more fond of dogs (how right for a hetero!) – they used to breed Yorkshire terriers. She said it was just one of the many books that didn't get written.

Yes. He should have written that, and the last play he had it in mind to write – and an autobiography. That could have been the most wonderful autobiography of our time, if he had only spoken out – told the story of his personal life, which he was so reserved about. Above all, what a significant autobiography it could have been, the young American coming to England and becoming the acknowledged leader in English literary life. Even more so than Henry James, who had greater competitors in Hardy, Meredith, Shaw, Kipling. It was not only a pity that T.S.E. would never write it, would never give himself away – and that was deliberate too. Wyndham Lewis said to me early on 'Tom is so sly – he's so *sly*.' He meant only that he was so fly – he certainly was pretty wary, no pitfalls for him (always excepting that first marriage).

In a way, it shows that literature was not the ultimate and *only* thing with him that it is with me. This may appear a paradox. But in fact he thought that life and love, and the exigencies of reserve they impose, are more important. With me, conversely, literature has always come first. I don't sufficiently respect people to restrict the overriding claims of literature. I am with Boswell. The lost works of literature I mourn are Byron's Memoirs, Dr Johnson's Autobiography, Heywood's Lives of the Elizabethan Dramatists, and the autobiography Eliot could have written, so central to the literary life of our time, symptomatic of the relationship between Britain and America. Shall I have time to write about it from the other way on? I at least am willing: I have no reserves. And I have the far more difficult problem: am I willing to write about a homo life? I believe that I am not afraid – I can always write in such a way that those who do understand *will* understand, and those who don't won't.

I remember that working-class use of the word 'consequential', meaning 'of consequence' (why not?). My mother used to say of Mamie Rowe, who took *our* place in Uncle and Aunt Rowe's affections and inheritance: 'some consequential little old thing'.

There was another story – of the admirer of Eliot's, who followed him out of church in Kensington hoping to hear the great man say something remarkable. What he heard when Eliot got to his car was: 'That bloody bird's done it again.'

I told her in return the story of T.S.E.'s little practical joke in the 1930s, when I was staying in Arthur Salter's flat, to ring up the Vicar of St Mary's Kensington. I half-knew something was afoot for the address to the postman was in verse: to the effect

> Postman, do not falter
> Till you come to the house
> Of Sir Arthur Salter
> Where you'll find A. L. Rowse etc.

When I rang up, the Vicar didn't know what it was about, nor who I was, any more than I knew who he was. T.S.E.'s little joke came off. Gerald

Berners told me of an early party of Eliot's while he was with his first wife – at which Tom had put soap in the éclairs so that the guests foamed at the mouth. It was, as A. P. Ryan said to me of Tom's cutting his name in a desk at Harvard, the only criminal act recorded of him.

[Decatur, Georgia, December 1965]

Walter B. Posey is very much a Southern gentleman. In earlier years an admirer of Henry Wallace,[1] evidently liberal and progressive. But was finished by the following story. A boyhood friend of Wallace was given the job of collecting subscriptions for a college. Called on Wallace, had a nice chat about boyhood memories, local people, etc. At last told Wallace what he had come for. Wallace said, 'I'll show you something.' Opened a drawer in his desk and took out a list of names of prominent college-presidents, etc. who had voted against F.D.R. and Wallace. Wallace said, 'You see your name down there among them? Not one of them will ever get a dime from me.'

Walter B., nice man that he is, was shocked by this. It was just what I would have done.

Friday, 10 December

At an airport again – named for the fatuous demagogue Patrick Henry – at Newport News for Baltimore *en route* for Los Angeles to pick up the threads of work again. The hiatus is over, my tour of Virginia – a fascinating way of seeing it all on the cheap, lecturing my way, working my passage. It has enabled me at last to penetrate beyond the Blue Ridge, into the Great Valley of Stonewall Jackson's campaigns – and of his birth at Lexington.

What fools the English have been – to fight each other over the American Revolution, when together they could have ruled the world! Then they did it all over again with the Civil War, killing each other off in hundreds of thousands, while Germans poured in to populate the Middle West, Italians the Eastern cities.

This morning I walked along to William and Mary College, to look into hall and chapel modelled after an Oxford college. The hall was hung with inferior portraits of the Bolling family, through the eighteenth century into the nineteenth. (I believe that Woodrow Wilson's second wife was a Bolling.) The chapel had memorials to Commissary Blair, the Bishop of London's Commissary and President of the College; a Cumberland Dawson, who

1. Ran as Vice-President on Roosevelt's first winning ticket.

went to Queen's College, Oxford, and became a professor out here; a Madison, President of the College. Outside was a memorial to various students of the place who had taken a part in forcing the breach with England. One who wrote the first pamphlet arguing that England and the Colonies were co-ordinate kingdoms; another who first proposed Committees of Correspondence; then Jefferson who was a student 1760–62, just before the Stamp Act stirred up the hornets' nest. Just like a lot of students agitating today. –

Not too pleased with my visit to William and Mary. Everywhere else my visit was properly advertised and full houses. Not so at W. and M. So they got a lecture with rather an edge to it. It went down all right, but the professors could appreciate the undertone. Fancy at the Jamestown 350th celebrations inviting G. N. Clark, and not me – what had he to do with Jamestown, early Virginia history, etc.? Perhaps he went as President of the British Academy. But I remember noticing at the time . . . Then there was D. B. Quinn's personal attack on my *Ralegh* book in their *Quarterly*. I intended to tick off Kappon, the Editor, for that. He was to take the chair – but was 'called out of town'. No copy of *Southampton*[1] goes to them for review. (This broke off relations with that group.)

A dreary cocktail period before dinner was attended by a well-read Eng. Lit. professor, who thought that Tennyson wrote no good poetry after *In Memoriam*. His wife at dinner called something or other I had said 'ridiculous' – she couldn't see the point. When I was having a high-spirited exchange with Colonel Fitzroy, who had taken the trouble to come down from Richmond, she interjected, 'Tell us what you think about C. P. Snow.' I went on with the point I was making with Fitzroy. She repeated her interruption. I thought of something to continue on with the Colonel. Put in her place, she subsided. (I expect she had been drinking.)

Baltimore airport: I forgot to mention among the memorials at William and Mary – almost like an Oxford college – that to the French soldiers who died in the College and other Virginia hospitals during the siege of Yorktown. There were their forgotten names – from the Regiments of Saintonge, Picardie, Deux-Ponts, Agenais, Bourbonnais, Touraine. This was unveiled to commemorate the 150th anniversary of Cornwallis's surrender at Yorktown. As I looked, a half-unconscious image formed in my mind of Lord North pacing the dining-room of 10 Downing Street – 'My God! so it is all over.'

Silly idiots, to have let themselves in for it! Human beings *will* not take trouble to nip things in their early stages, *not* allow themselves bit by bit to

1. *Shakespeare's Southampton* (1965), ALR's first excursion into sonnet country.

be inveigled into a fatal course of action. Like the South in 1861. Like the Rhodesians today – asking for still more trouble.

Wednesday 8th,[1] I had an agitating drive – for we were half-an-hour late in starting with carburettor trouble – through beautiful Blue Ridge country. Vexed and headaching as I was with engagement-anxiety, so that I could not enjoy the drive, I did catch sight of Nancy Astor's Mirador, where she was born. A Colonial red-brick square house on a bluff above the road, with its appurtenances – outside kitchens, stables, etc. The back of the house looks sideways across to the green-clothed Blue Ridge; and across the road to an eighteenth-century brick church with little cloister (I'll bet the arcade was put up by Waldorf). An English Georgian grouping in this horsey hunting countryside.

In spite of my anxiety and irritation with the other occupants of the car, we arrived just in time. The boring Professor of Education from Chicago wanted to talk to me about Advertising. 'I'm not in the least interested in Advertising,' I said. Every road out of Richmond is ruined by hideous and enormous billboards. Especially the road from Richmond to Williamsburg. One can hardly see the historical markers – of the 1781 campaign, or of McClellan's lines, etc. – for Howard Johnson's Motels, Have a Pepsi, Have a Coca-Cola, etc. The perpetual solicitation of eye and ear beats me.

After lecture and lunch and class I *was* interested to see the manse Woodrow Wilson was born in in 1856, a pleasant late Georgian type of house practically on Mary Baldwin Campus. Inside on the left the room he was born in, with portraits of father and long-nosed mother – after both of whom he took – immigrants from Carlisle to Ohio. So really Wilson was hardly a Virginian, except by accident. He was taken away at the age of two by his parents – his father a Presbyterian minister – to Georgia. Most interesting were two portraits – one of Gladstone, the other of Burke: the two poles of Wilson's political thought. *Those* were the days when we called all the tunes. Now! . . . my mind has been haunted by the retort.

'I was passionately interested in a Britain that was the centre of a world – Empire and Commonwealth. I am not interested in a second-rate country in decline.' – Retort to what? When will the opportunity come to make the retort on TV or radio?

Interesting bits and pieces: the metal carriage the child had for a toy, his crib and chair, in the nursery next door. In one room a bed the Wilsons occupied when he was President of Princeton. Downstairs the old Bible in

1. ALR is here following his practice of writing up entries from rough notes, perhaps while waiting in Baltimore airport. Hence that for December 8th follows that for the 10th.

which his birth was noted – '12¾ at night'. In a shed at the bottom of the garden the ex-President's old Pierce-Arrow motor-car, high in the step.

Everything worked out well for him, the fortunate son of a Presbyterian minister! The gates opened easily: professor when quite young, dean, President of Princeton, Governor of New Jersey, President of the United States. There he was, as President, addressing Congress for the first time; the spruce, prim don, tail-coat, smart tie with pin, prim pince-nez – the old professionals lolling around, not best pleased – Boies Penrose and other reprobates among them. They can't have liked the unwelcome apparition at the rostrum. (He had unmitigated contempt for them – they did him in the end.)

Last day in the year 1965

Another evening of extreme beauty – rain clouds this time are banked up thunder-blue edged with white over the mountains: heavy black-blue with under clouds of blue-white. The strange light emphasizes the white of the Mediterranean-looking houses. A tall palm in front rocks to and fro, scarecrow fronds at top fretting, while a pale pink flushes the trousered dead fronds. As we came in, earlier, breaks in the cloud-massif exposed areas of Poussin or even Tiepolo blue, against the general Turneresque scene. Now the whole arena is blackening – frightening. In the distance the lights of Arcadia and Santa Anita sparkle with sinister sharpness. Storm is on the way.

Sunday, 20 February 1966

Today a picnic[1] in the mountains up at Chantry Flats. Exquisite Californian spring. As we went along Sierra Madre Boulevard, explosions of pink and red blossom, peach or prunus, a shower of white, or here a carpet of canary yellow and gold, some succulent in flower. Going up the Santa Anita highway was a bit queasy – such falls of rock from the heavy rains. A pale blue haze hung over the mountains, not detracting from visibility but softening lines and colours, making a blue haze through the live oaks and pines.

A slight contretemps blew up between dear Mary Nevins and blooming Mabel Billington. Each had brought enough to feed the whole party. Mary was determined on lighting a fire and roasting steaks – it couldn't be a picnic without a fire. Mabel had bought enough cooked cold chicken for us all.

1. The party included Allan Nevins, Ray Billington and Marcellus Steadman, ALR's favourite colleagues at the Huntington. Mary Isabel Fry was Steadman's constant companion.

Mary Isabel (Fry) and I walked off up the mountainside and struck a cart-track. Wild gooseberry and elder were pushing out green shoots; a strong aromatic scent of sage-brush came up from below. We got up to where a path carries on up over the saddle-back to Mount Wilson, seven miles off. We paused at the corner, to listen to the stream plashing deep in the glen. Going back, a nice young fellow in blue jeans was leading his horse up the trail.

When we got back, peace had descended on the scene. Mary had got her fire going, the steaks were cooking, and in a contented state of greed I assailed Mabel's cold chicken and Mary's avocado salad. Ray (Billington) photographed the proceedings; then Mabel, with her mechanical genius – the only woman in America who can't drive a car – broke her camera. Soon we attracted the attention of half-a-dozen blue jays, of the crested kind with darker colouring than the common sort. Then a couple of the latter joined the rest, with their lighter, more flashing, kingfisher blue; with their skittering up and down the branches, their flapping and pouncing, it made a decorative scene against the green screen of trees, the grey and sand-coloured rocks.

After lunch, and after we had got Marcellus (Steadman) away from the fruit on the table, we walked down the mountain side, I acting, under Mary's instructions, as a brake on Allan. On the way back we passed a boy of fifteen with his girl – quite small, he already had an enormous bulge in his trousers.

Herbert Davis* told me a fascinating thing he had found in Swift's marginal notes in Baronius' Church History at Christ Church, in Dublin. A comment on the Nicene Creed, which he must have recited every time he attended communion – the ordinary western Creed offered to the Russian Orthodox Church: 'Confessio fidei digna barbaris'.

Tonight I had E. V. Lucas's daughter to supper here.[1] She told me that her father when young once met a deaf old lady who had known Dickens. Immensely excited young E.V.L. asked if this were so. 'Yes, I knew them very well. *They were both vulgar.*' That was all the old lady had to offer on a man of genius.

I said, How like ordinary human fools. It had often happened to me, when I asked someone who knew a remarkable person – he or she can *never* describe the person to you. Not even physically, what the great man looked like, let alone the lines and quirks of personality.

* A leading Swift scholar.

1. At Pasadena.

2 March

O, how exquisite the Californian spring! There is a Sant' Anna wind, crisp and cleansing, never has the landscape been so pencil-fine, sharp and clear. From the garden this morning we could see the outline of Catalina Island on the horizon, and the mountains to the south of the Great Valley. This evening the slopes of the San Gabriel Mountains from my window are of an indescribable shadow – velvety colour, and rippling downward like some unfolding tumbled cloth. The lights of Arcadia sparkle brilliantly, green emeralds through the tousled trees. And over all is the unearthly beauty of the mountain peak of Old Baldy, behind the dark mass of the mountain range between, a withdrawn white radiance drawing to itself what light remains.

I am so grateful to be here in the Californian spring. This morning Marcellus and I walked down through the magnolia walk – stellata scattering its petals under the breeze – to the lower road. There has been too drastic a removal of trees from the eucalyptus grove. Jack Pomfret says that Crotty, Chairman of Trustees, is too restless, like a child with a toy, forever upheaving and changing. Marcellus adds – But not the right change, e.g. the Japanese garden needs reconstructing to get it right. The bridges are too clamant in colour; one ought not to have a *cement* path through the grass, but fine-combed sand, real, not synthetic rocks, etc. It is not for me to speak. I am content to enjoy what there is.

[Back in England] Huddersfield, 4 May

My hotel bedroom looks out on a Victorian scene of factories, chimneys, coagulated rows of houses, a few pricking spires, and a long spine of Yorkshire moors – the Pennines – under grey sky and drifting mist. It is May-time, it is grey and already beginning to sprinkle. The Victorian town makes not a bad appearance. The splendid porticoed railway station with its long wings is a masterpiece. It needs cleaning, and shooting the sparrows and/or pigeons. They have cleaned some of the early Victorian buildings, shaped sandstone or limestone. Whole stretches of 1840–60 building are uninterfered with; the streets keep their layout. On my way through Queen's Street I passed the house where the Reverend Mr Macdonald was minister, 1847–50, father of those celebrated daughters who mothered Kipling and Baldwin, while two more married Sir Edward Poynter and Burne-Jones, while a fifth, Edith, was reduced to becoming a writer. There must have been something in the genes, and how successfully those girls pounced!

I looked in at the early nineteenth-century church, complete with black-oak galleries and the shaming works of C. S. Lewis. I read his *A Grief Observed* – title imitated from Fry's *Venus Observed*. Imagine observing his wife's death from cancer in order to turn it into Christian journalism. The self-exposure for Christian profit is nauseating; so is the pushful candour, not much better than Buchman.[1] 'This book is about myself, and her, and God in that order; when of course it should have been in the opposite order.' I like that 'of course' – bogus-humble. His wife's deathbed is taken advantage of to conclude with Dante, *Poi si tornó al'eterna fontana*. Upon which the appropriate comment is – whose? – '*C'est de la littérature*.'

I must give him what should be coming to him one day – a book like Barrès' *Leurs Figures*? The angelic T.S.E. confronting C.S.L.; Powicke confronting Namier, etc.

I went along the pavement outside the decent 1840-ish façades – there must have been some good architects working hereabouts then – to the Art Gallery. Almost wholly Royal Academy art – depressing in its monotony. Evidently what the Art Committee of the Town Council likes – or what could be got across it. I wouldn't burden my memory with it. But there was a splendid pencil drawing of Conway Castle by Turner; an exquisite drawing of mountain scenery with castles, by Ruskin, and a little watercolour study of oak leaves. What a fine artist he was! – he knew from experience what was involved: in itself a major qualification for writing about the subject. A delicate fine-pointed drawing of Sion – I suppose an architectural fantasy – was by Bonington. Among the moderns a David Jones pencil portrait of a man in an armchair, from an odd angle, downward sloping and rightward looking. I wish I might have had a portrait painted by him – is he too mad now to paint? Or that I had one of his intricate calligraphical drawings of Arthurian figures. A Piper 'Portmadoc' in that spotty later technique of his didn't hold me.

On my way through London yesterday I had a busy three-quarters of an hour at Macmillan's dealing with various questions, books etc. arising out of my now considerable literary estate. My translation of Romier's *History of France* is going into a seventh or eighth printing. It has made thousands for me. Yet Bruce McFarlane: 'I can't think why you did it.' A. J. P. Taylor – then a friend – 'Why should Dr Rowse have wasted his time on such a job?' That was in an unfriendly review in the *Manchester Guardian*. When I was going to protest to him, quite gently, walking round Magdalen, he cut me dead! We were friends – he used to suck up to me with 'my oldest Oxford

1. Dr Frank Buchman, founder of the movement first known as the Oxford Group and subsequently as Moral Rearmament.

friend'. Bruce said that to behave like that was characteristic of him. I hadn't attacked *him* – he had written an unfriendly review of me in the first chance he had; when he cut me.* From that day to this, nearly twenty years, we haven't spoken to each other.

And now he is a major figure in the English firmament – along with his friend Malcolm Muggeridge, his friend Kingsley Martin, Michael Foot, etc. With his irresponsibility – Hitler not much more responsible for the war than Britain was! – his constant playing to the gallery, his not caring whether what he says is true or not (the ultimate sin for an historian). It is all part of the decline of Britain.

[Reflecting on T. S. Eliot]

I suppose it was with him as with the Victorian Fellows of All Souls – above noticing furnishings, décor. They never minded; nor can he have done. He must have been content with comfort, after the squalor of living with John Hayward. He had never had any domesticity, and his whole nature longed for just a happy domestic life.

The room[1] was dominated by the large, lanky, masculine portrait by Gerald Kelly – very material and unspiritual, a good likeness, but without the sweetness of Tom's nature. It rendered the large, loose-limbed Yankee, hands authoritatively placed on arms of the chair, signet ring – a Royal Academy portrait, the O.M. 'He was a wonderful mixer of salad-dressing,' said Bob Howard to me at Cape's on Monday. 'Whether he should have been an O.M., I am not so sure.'

Valerie told me a surprising thing – that he didn't really like writing, that he would probably not have written if it hadn't been for the unhappiness in his life, not only over his first marriage but before that – as if there must have been some malaise in his family background. That he owed his writing to that – it drove him to self-expression for relief or consolation. He once said to me that in order to write he had to persuade himself that it was a technical problem to be solved. A curious attitude for a writer. No *great* writer has ever had it. They have all been driven by their daimon.

Sunday, 19 June

Tired and stale as I get in Oxford in summer, immediately after lunch I drove off to Hungerford, in my comfortable little new Morris Oxford

* His friend Barraclough says that this was in keeping – he is a coward.

1. ALR was dining with Eliot's widow in their flat ('a large Victorian ground-floor flat').

with the automatic drive. I enjoy having a car again, this one so easily manoeuvrable that I can think as I flip along the leafy summer lanes. I felt happy to get away from my complexes, the complexes of College, of Oxford, of literary life – indeed of life with others – to be cruising along the dry stone-walls of Besselsleigh, the elderly lanes towards Frilford, the flats of Wantage and up into the fresh airy downs above Hungerford and along the Kennet valley.

Only once before had I glimpsed this long gabled Elizabethan house across its water meadows: Littlecote. I went steeply up from Froxfield and shortly was looking down upon the elongated front, beautifully disposed in a curve, red brick and grey flint upon acres of green lawn. It was all that I had hoped for – filled with fine English furniture, Queen Anne walnut chests, Georgian mahogany, refectory oak, elegant Regency – and the china! – best Worcester, Bow, Chelsea, Ming, Sèvres, Dresden.

What it was to be a Wills and be able to command it all up to the Second War! The bedrooms had their four-posters – Elizabethan, William and Mary – red damask, chintz, tapestry, etc.; the Long Gallery packed with good furniture, portraits of Pophams; a pretty library with the old Lord Chief Justice's books, Chippendale side-tables, whatnot; fine hall with quantities of armour and yellow buff coats good as new;[1] an admirable Cromwellian chapel, pulpit in place of altar, black-oak gallery and pews.

Just what I should like to have inherited.

Not even Willses can afford to live in it today: they live in a small house; this is for the public. After viewing it, I walked about the lawns, down to the canal bordering the garden, with moat outside the wall, and sat looking back at the immense range of building, stable cupola and all, regretting all that vanished life. Though the public grounds were kept up, the big walled kitchen-gardens were empty and uncultivated – too sad, such good loamy soil. I grieve for a way of life that was never mine. Would it had been!

I stopped to see the church at Chilton Foliat, with Popham and Leybourne Popham monuments. Beside it the exquisite red-brick rectory (for sale the other day), Georgian front with big bay extended. I played with the thought of how nice to inhabit it. Then up the steep hill and over the downs again, silver-trunked beeches, waving barley, acres of wheat and grass, down into Lambourn. I got out to see the improbably large church – with Tudor alabaster tomb of Sir Thomas Essex and wife – their manor house vanished. So up over more downs by the Letcombes and Childrey – familiar from Swift's letters in 1714 – to Wantage and back to Oxford with bells ringing for evensong, well content.

*

1. From the Civil War.

We[1] went on to see Comper's lovely St Mary's, Wellingborough again, and found an even more pathetic figure – the Vicar alone, keeping his watch in church. He was glad of our company, stuck to us and made us go down to his vicarage and late for our next port of call. He was sad that there was no prospect of ever finishing the church – so many windows still wanted their glass, so much of the roof unpainted. Nobody comes to church any more, so what is the point of finishing it? Is there any sense in my dream of putting the roof on St Thomas' Chapel at Bodmin as a memorial, or replacing the spire, or completing the rood screen? Or of finishing Truro Cathedral, with its cloister, deanery and all?

I wouldn't leave a penny of my money to advance anything in the contemporary world. Only for the benefit of the past. I hate the guts of the modern world, everything about it, even its good points. I am furious that things have gone this way. They *would*! after all the efforts I made earlier to achieve a way of life that accords with my tastes and my nature, the whole thing collapses on me and Suburbia wins – shiftless, tasteless, characterless, trivial, wasting money on the pointless, the hideous – the inhabitants of the fuck-hutches in millions don't know what to do to spend it. As one working-class woman said in the shopping centre, heaving everything she could lay hands on in range into her shopping-bag, 'It's terribly difficult to get rid of £30 a week.' At home George Rowse's wife has no difficulty. Every time she comes to see Beryl, she has a new handbag, costing £5 a time. Every month, new clothes: after she has worn them a few times she gives them to my housekeeper.

The inhabitants of really beautiful houses are hard put to it to keep the roof on, keep the rain out, or hold on to things of real value – pictures, china, good furniture, objects of art.

Not that the Idiot People shouldn't enjoy a decent standard of living – one takes that for granted, totally without taste, value, interest as it is. But that things of real beauty and significance – churches, country houses great and small, are so hard put to it to survive. That is all I care for. Not the Idiot People. They are all too easily replaceable. But things of beauty from the past with the associations of a vanished way of life of a once-great country, which they carry into a seedy present and dubious future. Nothing to be proud of here – a People without pride of ancestry and all too much hope of posterity. The past of this country is far more interesting than its future is likely to be.

That lovely unfinished church, with its glimpse of opulent Edwardian devotion, the three sisters who left their money for it – the rood-loft with

1. ALR was accompanied by an old friend who taught at Ripon.

gilded angels and wings folded and unfolded, the glass blue and gold, many windows still unfilled though the designs are all ready and waiting – the Vicar teased me about devoting my money to finishing it. I played with the thought a little. I *could*, if I wished. Why should I wish it? Nobody comes to church any more, it is really all dead. Besides, what have I to do with Northampton? – what I have should go to Cornwall.

There's Bodmin church, there's finishing Truro. Think what could have been done there! – the interior of the cathedral was being decorated all through the long lifetime of Comper. Not a thing by him! The glass by Clayton and Bell not bad, but the altars, woodwork, furnishings all second-rate – like the succession of people who had the doing of it. In all Cornwall only the tiny church of Little Petherick has Comper's work in it.

No, I don't think my money will go to finishing St Mary's, Wellingborough. (Though father worked in the iron mines nearby during the first war – I remember Irthlingborough, Rushden, Wellingborough on his lips. Wouldn't it be nice to complete those windows in the aisles in his unknown memory, with a secret cipher: 'RR — AR'?)

This episode made us late on the roads for our last port of call, Elton Hall. We were just in time to get in and go round. Larger, more straggling, less beautiful than Hinwick, it had much more of interest. The Probys had Irish estates, and from their castle burned down – by the People – in the Troubles, they had brought over some Renaissance panelling in the hall. The finest thing was a splendid library – evidently a reading family; books in several rooms, including a pretty Regency octagon upstairs with contemporary books, all very Jane Austen – one could see the cultivated leisured life of the time. Now the tramp of the hordes, including us.

One fabulous treasure was a little book of Psalms and Prayers bound with the Litany of 1544 which Henry VIII gave to Catherine Parr.

29 July

Bruce[1] died on Saturday, 16 July: one whole quarter of my life goes out with him. Karl Leiser[2] rang me just before dinner at All Souls. Told me that Bruce had been out in the car with Helena at Quainton, went over the hedge into a field, stumbled over a root, fell heavily. Helena heard a gasp, went and found him dead.

I have been numbed by it – unable to write, either about him or about Gerald Clifden here at home, whose obituary appeared alongside of Bruce's.

1. K. B. McFarlane.
2. *sic*, *recte* Leyser.

Two friends gone – one of them a pleasant part of my life in Cornwall, the other part of life itself.

As I realized on an inexpressibly beautiful and sad drive down to Cornwall on the Sunday. I was glad to be leaving Oxford. I walked down along the pavement between All Souls and Queen's, where we have so often walked together – the High was quiet and grey in the early summer morning – to see if the flag was flying at half-mast on Magdalen tower. Years ago when I once saw it, I had a sudden fear that it might be Bruce, and couldn't rest until I had satisfied myself that it wasn't. That Sunday there wasn't a flag – perhaps they hadn't heard the news yet.

I thought of Bruce's poor little cat, Jasper, who adored him, all his possessions, the china cats crowded about his rooms, the large collection of books, the bric-à-brac, boxes of manuscripts, notes, letters – all piled up at Magdalen and at Quainton, now awaiting dispersal, Bruce taken away in the middle of it; the so familiar rooms, full of the memories of years, of so many intimacies exchanged, so many confidences, awaiting a new occupant. So much of my life gone out with Bruce.

[30 July]

A fortnight ago Bruce died. I haven't been able to come to terms with it yet. I have been going through a curious experience: in the numbness and grief for him I have been reading a book that counterpointed the grief – the *Memoirs of Hadrian*. The book has moved me too, full of understanding of grief, the transience of life and love, the thought of death. Bruce's death has brought home thoughts of my own, naturally enough. Hitherto, I have been accustomed to thinking of my span in terms of my parents, each dying in their eighties, and giving me time to complete my work – the third volume of *The Elizabethan Age*, successive volumes of Autobiography, more Cornish books. Bruce, dying at sixty-two, had far from completed his – if he ever would have done. He was deeply inhibited about writing.

I hardly knew him as an undergraduate, met him two or three times at Exeter with John Garrett.[1] (He had put himself down for New College, but had to be content with a scholarship at Exeter and the tuition of the martinet Atkinson, which he supported very well.) He had frightful ill-luck the year of his Schools: his mother was dying of cancer. He grew up to be a big man, over six feet and broad, well-developed, not unattractive, fairly muscular, big well-shaped hands.

I hardly knew him at the time of the Fellowship Examination at All Souls,

1. Subsequently a great headmaster.

where I don't think he made much of an impression. He got some sort of Senior Scholarship, went a great deal to the P.R.O. and had attic rooms above Cornmarket Street. He must have asked me up there, for I remember climbing all those stairs and being regaled on chocolate liqueurs. In earlier years he had a mania for these – very ungrown-up and bad for his complexion. He himself thought that he had a soft centre – the years hardened him, made him notably crotchety and difficult, but he always remained warm at heart.

He put in his Cardinal Beaufort thesis for the Prize Fellowship at Magdalen and got it. He was then the big baby of the College, a favourite with old Warren,[1] Fletcher,[2] Craig, Benecke,[3] Thompson[4] and those who formed the inner circle. (So much nicer than today.) Bruce played his cards well – the canny middle-class Scot in him – and, when the chance of a permanent tutorial Fellowship turned up, grasped it with both hands. I was a bit surprised – I always thought research and writing better than becoming a teaching hack. But Bruce was right to make sure.

With him entrenched at Magdalen we came to know each other better, Bruce taking the lead. The first time we ever stayed together was early one summer vac. when he proposed we should stop at Chipping Campden. Jimmy Crowther[5] descended on me that weekend and I awkwardly brought him along too. Bruce took it in good part, though they had nothing in common. When Charles Henderson came back to Oxford as Fellow of Corpus I made him and Bruce acquainted. They had the Middle Ages in common and Charles asked Bruce to stay at Penmount, when I couldn't ask him to stay at Robartes Place – not a room, nor a bed.

Bruce played a characteristic trick on Charles in a Cornish church, the uncrowned king of Cornish ecclesiastical lore. When some incumbent contradicted something Charlie said, he cited the great Charles Henderson as his authority. Bruce wouldn't say, as I should have done at once, 'This *is* Mr Henderson.' Charlie was very much huffed. It was the kind of thing that amused Boo-boo. When I asked a question, hoping for the answer Yes, he would say No. And vice versa. He was as contra-suggestive as the Abbé Woodward – whose father was an Admiralty civil servant along with Bruce's.

From early on Bruce was homo. When an adolescent he once in a train put his hand on a sailor's prick, the sailor took it well but discouragingly.

1. Sir Herbert Warren, then President of the College.
2. C. R. L. Fletcher, who collaborated with Kipling in a popular history of England.
3. The Nestor of the College: he was a great-nephew of Mendelssohn.
4. J. M. Thompson, authority on the French Revolution.
5. Popular writer on Economics who had been one of ALR's schoolmasters.

Boo-boo blushed for himself. For years he let me go on in an innocent state of half-realization of the facts of life, not coming to grips until a visit to the Continent – because he thought it 'rather sweet' that I should remain innocent.

But how much I owed to him in knowledge of the Middle Ages, medieval architecture and history, churches and places. It was he who took the initiative, made the arrangements. How many walks and bus-rides to villages and churches around Oxford, how many excursions to cathedrals and historic towns he organized! Obsessed with politics, literature and illness, I gave only half an eye to the architecture, while Bruce would stand and study it, go over it with the attentiveness of a professional, memorizing it. I remember his doing this at Lincoln, York, Wells – while I contented myself with impressions of everything. Bruce had a most observant eye for detail – in regard to people, plants, flowers, birds, animals (particularly cats – another bond between us). It was Bruce who introduced me to the best of the old country-town hotels, the White Hart at Lincoln, the Swan at Wells. I never had time to pick up such knowledge on my own.

While I went dutifully home to Cornwall nearly every vacation, Bruce had no home to go to and was free to explore. He had no liking for his Scotch father, who married again. Bruce regarded his stepmother as a 'silly woman', but treated her not badly, in fact generously – refusing to accept the money that had come to her through his father. The places he discovered for himself he would then introduce me to – when I had time. We walked about the Oxfordshire countryside in those days. It was Bruce who first took me to Rycote, as I describe it in the essay in *The English Spirit*, to Thame and walked me across the beech-woods of Stokenchurch, Christmas Common, Fingest and into the Stonor valley, in the dower-house of which he later lived.

[Back in the U.S.A.] Detroit, 27 September

Feeling a bit better once I have got across and am firmly fixed to the conveyor-belt. Never have I been so reluctant to uproot myself and leave, from Trenarren after the enjoyable summer I've had there; or from Oxford, so affecting in the oncoming of autumn – with the Michaelmas term about to begin, and all the young men arriving to make or mar: their Oxford life before them as Bruce's and mine were forty-four years ago.

Fog delayed my start five hours on Sunday, but the crossing was good. A very busy day here yesterday – a couple of hours doing a press conference, being interviewed, photographed; a hurried walk round the Art Institute; dinner with a Jesuit professor, Fr Hughes, Peter Stanlis, and Rabe, the Public

Relations man at the University. All in preparation for my visit here, 13 and 14 October.

Wellington Hotel, New York, 4 October

Back in my old quarters after a fine trip laid on for me around the Upper Peninsula of Michigan. All went well, and it was indispensable for my book:* I now feel that I can tackle the second half with better confidence. It was a surprise to find the Cornish in thousands all through that country, not just concentrated in the twin towns of Houghton and Hancock, across the convenient inlet of Portage Lake. Very beautiful too just at this moment, with the trees every colour of fruit, peach, strawberry, grape-bloom purple of sumach, cherry, then flame-colour and rose. Most touching was to stand among the graves in lonely Pine Grove Cemetery, the wind of Lake Superior in the trees and the noise of water on the shore, and read the names on the headstones. Many of them died so young – the hardships must have been terrific – many were children; two Berryman brothers killed together in Central Mine. At Copper Harbor at the tip of the peninsula a Cousin Jack ran a country store – a Phillips, his father came from Penzance.

At Marquette a very recognizable Cornishman is editor or public relations man for the local newspapers: a Treloar. I couldn't fall for him much, though he was helpful – too like the Rowses, full of himself. It was interesting to see the Cornish temperament all there, in the third generation (his grandfather had died young of pneumonia in Arizona), putting too much energy into what he was saying, gestures, etc. – as Robert Traver describes in *Laughing Whitefish* – underneath the unattractive American heartiness of a Rotarian sort everyone has to affect to survive. *How* recognizable he was! – he might well have been one of the Rowses.

The exposed bleak country on those mining ranges: around Quincy mine and Calumet and Hecla must have been familiar enough in one way – like the exposed mining country of West Cornwall, or St Austell, Caradon or Calstock. But how did they take to those winters, five months of snow? – *The Long Winter Never Ends*. Insupportable, except that the miners were warm enough underground. What a life to have escaped! – the life of my family only two generations back.

* *The Cornish in America.*

Oxford, Sunday, 18 September[1]

I had Horatia Durant – Nelson's great-great-granddaughter, through whom one can see Nelson's blue eyes, colouring, shape of head and way of holding it on one side – and Queen Mary's niece, Duchess of Beaufort, to lunch. We were a hilarious little party at the small table in my green room, in which we included Louth[2] and made him laugh. They very much appreciated the chef's *oeufs aurores* and we sent Louth back for a second go at the dish. They didn't leave till 4.20, so that I was late with the real business of the day: which was to go over to Quainton, where Bruce died, and hear the whole story from Helena.[3]

For all the gaiety of the day, I set off sadly in the overcast evening, my mind full of Bruce, the way he often went from Oxford. I went wrong about Stanton St John and this made me later and more miserable. I got to Brill, passed Wotton Underwood – to which B. and I walked that Sunday from Nether Winchendon many years ago (Mrs Barnard entertaining Air Marshal Brooke-Popham to lunch) – no time to look in on Arthur Bryant. I went out of my way once more, cursing Helena for suggesting this route; then came out on the Bicester–Aylesbury main road, and left it to go up the hill to Quainton, a straggling village.

I found the Old Rectory next the church, and a fine Georgian brick house it is; double bays in front and good spread of Tudor panelled hall between. It was a splendid find of Helena's, Bruce thought too expensive. It cost only £6,000, but another £6,000 to put it right, the place was derelict, big garden an overgrown wilderness.

For me the place where B. had lived and meant to retire was infinitely sad, on this sad day, grey and miserable. Helena took me all round the garden she has rehabilitated. Twenty years older, as vigorous, matter-of-fact, prosaic, on the mark, as ever. I have never liked her, and I don't suppose she has ever liked me. I have always liked Peter – to whose surgery I owe my life – and Peter me. What *was* Helena and Bruce's relationship? Inscrutable. I don't believe Karl's theory that they ever were lovers:* Bruce had *no* feeling for women. Helena realized his plight, his alienation from life; in 1930 on the verge of a breakdown when she met him at lunch at All Souls, and grafted him into her family. B. certainly had both Tish and Michael, of the four boys; no girls to bother anyone.

1. The date is that on which ALR was writing up his journal, some weeks after the events described.
2. ALR's scout who served the lunch.
3. Helena Wright, wife of Peter, the surgeon who had saved ALR's life just before the war.
* Helena was in love with him, and made him sleep with her, though not his thing. He was indebted to her, not in love with 'the Empress'.

In the garden Helena told me in her matter-of-fact, unsentimental, almost unfeeling way about her being in contact with Bruce by automatic writing. Normally, all my life, I should have dismissed this as nonsense. Now, one simply doesn't know. Life is so mysterious and I have been so upset by B.'s death that I was prepared to keep an open mind. We went in and she showed me all over the fine house – too big for me – and a grand job she has made of it. Bruce's things were about the place: the Moroccan carpets he brought back from his visit to Tangier with her (when they had rather a choppy crossing in a little boat); his big radiogram; in the corridor outside his wing the Chinese vases I gave him for a house-warming present at Stonor. I never made time to go and see him at either Stonor or Quainton – I never wanted to encounter Helena.

We went into Bruce's wing – the whole north wing: at least two studies or book-rooms, his bedroom and large bathroom looking up to Quainton Hill. We settled into his library with the big bookcases, into which he had moved his most valuable fifteenth-century books for future work – to complete his life's work by writing his books at last. Too late.

The house is shrouded by trees – a cedar, sequoias and other funereal trees: not much light or sun. I observed that Norman had given Bruce a white mulberry tree – Helena told me that Norman and Paul had been to stay two or three times, there and at Stonor. This gave an understandable tug at the heart: Bruce wasn't good to Norman while he was *my* friend;* only after our breach that they linked up.

From the darkening room one could see the church tower and bells were ringing for late evensong. Helena proceeded to read to me her communications with dear Bruce. I was in tears. I never knew that her son Tish had died, at the age of forty-two. She said from heart failure, too. Karl told me it was suicide, and that drugs were involved. One simply cannot trust human beings' sense of truth. Could one trust Helena's? One always could Bruce's. She spoke without feeling, in that extraordinary matter-of-fact way. A friend of Tish, John, had also died, and a friend of Helena, Betty. So she put them all in touch with Bruce when he 'passed over' – how he would have derided the phrase – to help him, especially John, as being more reliable than Tish (an indication of her attitude).

At last she had got through to Bruce and was in regular touch with him at the weekends in his room with all his things around. Did I feel his presence? Actually I did not, in this room where I had never seen him. I always saw him in his rooms at Magdalen.

When Bruce had his fatal stroke he felt a 'terrific' (a Helena word, not a

* Bruce was psychotically jealous of me, and resented my friends, Jack Simmons, David Treffry. Revealing that he took up Norman only after our breach.

Bruce word) pain in his chest; he gave out two loud noises like coughs. He found himself bewildered, nothing like this having entered his experience. Helena called on John and Betty and Tish to help him, who brought him back to sleep for a long while in the house. Helena gave him a word from me, said that I was anxious and upset. Bruce gave her a message for me, with an equivocal 'quite' in it that was just like him and a convincing touch. 'Yes, I should *quite* like you to.' Now, that was either Bruce, or else Helena knew very well B.'s ambivalent attitude towards me – good to me when I was down and needed help, envious when I was up and didn't need him or depend on him – which was the case in all these last years since the war and I had become too successful for him.

Helena asked if he had met with Hodge, the black cat Bruce had in Combe Wood days, in the 1930s – a bond between him and me. One day B. came back into his rooms at Magdalen and found Hodge and me lying full length on the carpet – I had mesmerized Hodge. Bruce replied that he hadn't – it had been a long time since he passed over and no doubt had found other friends, but that he would keep a look-out for him.

Then there was something complicated about history. Bruce said how fascinating it was to see the events of the past – '*it's all true*'. Helena explained that this was unintelligible to us, as if there were a recording that could be scrutinized in that other world, and that Bruce had added '*as you know*'. She said that Bruce did not know that she had long experience of automatic writing. This I do not believe: it would be quite unlike Bruce not to know. Any more than I believe what she told me about not knowing Bruce's heart condition. I will ask Peter: both Peter and she knew that Bruce depended on a drug to keep his heart down from inflating. How could she, his most intimate friend, not know that? We all knew it. The looseness with which people sit to the truth is unforgivable – in them.

I raised no objections, I made myself as receptive as I could, I kept an open mind. I was anxious to learn all I could. One thing I did not learn. In the middle of the séance I took the opportunity to insert Karl's suggestion, 'Were you in love with Bruce?'

She was more than a match for that. 'What does that mean?' she said: 'Of course we all loved Bruce.' That line of enquiry was dismissed. She found the ending of thirty-six years of such intellectual companionship unbearable, until she re-established communication, and I could do the same. My conclusion is that she was in love with Bruce, fifteen or more years younger; I do not believe that he was ever in love with her or with any woman.

From over here[1] I have written her a letter with some questions to put to

1. In America. ALR was writing up notes of his journal made before he had left England.

Bruce. Simple-seeming as they are, only he could know the answers. If the answers came out right, it would have some effect on my mind. (They did not.)

The youngest of the Wright boys came up into the room to say goodbye. This was the spastic, Adrian, whom Bruce managed to get admitted to Magdalen – whom he thought the nicest of the boys. Michael was there in the background, too – whom Norman was taken up with one term. How important are these things? Karl says that Helena deliberately closed her eyes to them. How far does this invalidate her objective view? Karl says that she is an extreme extrovert, therefore everything has to be objectivised, whereas her view is really a subjective one extrapolated. She is an intelligent and admirable woman – why do people have to be such fools? Why can't they stick to what is true?

Downstairs in the hall, where Brucie ordinarily sat, she told me the facts of his death. Poor woman, I felt sorry for her then – such a terrible experience, caring for him as she did. This was at any rate the realm of fact. Upstairs I had been given an extraordinary sense of Bruce's continuing in some way – it was just as if he were alive, in another mode, though not present at the time.

[U.S.A.] I break off to go and hear Lili Kraus – I didn't know she would be still alive. My appreciation of her I owe to Jack; but Mozart was Bruce's favourite – Mozart and Haydn.

As far as Karl was concerned, a gallant young officer in the Black Watch, Bruce wrote him hundreds of letters using every kind of argument and persuasion, – intellectual, aesthetic, philosophical, moral.

On my very last walk around Magdalen I said to Bruce, teasing him: 'I've got something terrible to tell you: I'm ceasing to be *interested*.' He laughed and said that that wasn't so for him. He found the young workers at Quainton very teasing – of course, it wouldn't do to take any notice. He always had himself well in hand – the Scotch side to him. Yet they all looked up to him and treated him as the Master. Very few dons can have had so devoted a body of pupils. Partly because he was a dedicated tutor: he gave himself and his work to them. He would hand over a budget of valuable notes from original sources to one of them to go on with, instead of working them up (better) himself. But, like Richard, he had an inhibiting effect on his pupils. John Bromley[1] told me that it was owing to Richard, whom he deeply admired, that he hadn't been able to get forward with a book. The

1. Professor of History at Southampton.

same with Bruce's pupils – not one of them has produced a book yet. It is all very well to put it down to perfectionism – everybody knows that one's work can be improved upon afterwards: the point is to get it out. Bruce himself would say to me, of his chapter on 'The Lancastrians' in the *Cambridge Medieval History*, 'It's all wrong.'

That was the chapter that nearly caused a breakdown over thirty years ago. I went down to Magdalen one afternoon and saw the first page of the chapter spread out on his refectory table – twelve or thirteen versions of it, with the slightest verbal variations and alternatives. It was after that, I think, that Helena took him in hand.

How strange their relationship! Helena, though a great authority on sex, doesn't appear to be sexy.* She is an impersonal and, in a way, objective woman, decidedly prosy. That was what made [I recognize the deep notes of the *Queen Mary* or *Queen Elizabeth* making down the Hudson for home] the relationship possible. What Helena, a Jewess, appreciated was 'thirty-six years of wonderful intellectual companionship' – she could never get that with dear Peter, her husband.

I learned all the time from Bruce: he wouldn't take anything from me. Except my early proselytizing politics – fat lot of good it did him or me. But he became a Labour man, and in the miserable election of 1931 he came down to Penryn and Falmouth to drive round and pick up Labour voters – we had hardly any cars on the road. I forget where he stayed – no room at 24 Robartes Place, with its three bedrooms. He was sent up with his roomy car to Carslake, an exposed place on the spine of Cornwall, remote, rough china-clay Higher Quarters people. The women crowded in on top of him, one of the girls making very free with him. 'If you do that, I shall drive you into the ditch,' he said with that uncompromising glare Karl mentioned in *The Times* obituary. And he would have done. No more trouble from that quarter.

One by-product of my left-wing fanaticism was unfortunate. I was partly responsible for getting B. to have A. J. P. Taylor appointed as the second History tutor at Magdalen. It turned out badly for B., for though Taylor was a stimulating tutor for those tough enough to stand it, he put off others (Leo Butler, for one) and never pulled his weight, was always getting a term off or getting sabbatical leave. Bruce hardly ever: he would rather see that the work was properly done. As years went on and latterly A.J.P.T. became a TV star, historian to the Beaverbrook newspapers and public charlatan,

* She began by getting him to give her semen in a test-tube for professional use. Bruce was amused by the idea of having unknown progeny. *Ich nicht.*

he positively neglected his tutorial work and, Bruce said, was hardly ever there.

It fell to A.J.P.T.'s lot to prevent Bruce from becoming President of Magdalen. Bruce was Vice-President throughout the war and ran the College; first, because George Gordon was Vice-Chancellor and, when he died, the College postponed electing until the war was over. Bruce ran the College well, since he was both methodical and orderly, and just-minded. I think he enjoyed having all the affairs and papers in his hands. He told me the story of J. A. Symonds' dismissal from his Fellowship over some 'scandal'. He also found that his original injustice towards Gordon as President was hardly justified – I never thought so – 'Gentleman George', as they called him (because he was a policeman's son), worked at the job more than they gave him credit for.

Karl made the point that Bruce had a marked capacity for eliciting the common purpose of a meeting and then giving a lead. B. told me that at Magdalen every Fellow lived in a separate cage glaring out at the others. He certainly had some eccentrics, not to say crackpots, to deal with: Weldon, Chapman, Driver, Alan Taylor himself. All the responsible elements and the loyal old Magdalen men wanted Bruce for President. This was enough to put Taylor against him – he organized the campaign that got Sir Henry Tizard elected, and by only one vote! The one vote that prevented Bruce from becoming President was that of the person he had had made Fellow. Characteristic of human beings, and what I hate them for – I don't find it 'interesting': too bored with their ways and monkey-tricks.

Bruce took it philosophically, told me that in the end he was so sickened by the whole thing that he didn't want to become President. But he certainly took swift action when the chance came – with maximum effect.

I once reproached A.J.P.T. with his part in the matter. He said, brazenly enough, that Bruce was too neurotic to be President – this from him, a crackpot! – and that Sir Henry Tizard was the man the College needed. Also a paradox from this nuclear disarmer of the Left – Tizard was wholly interested in war, radar, defence, the R.A.F., Whitehall, government. He had no conception of running a college, and at once began to run it as a department, interfering in everything, treating the Fellows as his subordinates. After two years he made a fatal mistake. Always more interested in Whitehall than Oxford, he accepted a prime government appointment in Defence, hoping to run it together with Magdalen – but without getting the sanction of the College first.

He had reckoned without Bruce, who made himself the pivot of the College opposition to Tizard doubling the job and made him choose between the two. He could only choose Whitehall. Tizard went. It was a wonderful *revanche* for Bruce. He took it all coolly enough but said to me, with that stony look in the eye, 'You don't think that I would miss that opportunity, do you?' He didn't miss a move in the game. He then had easy-going Tom Boase made President, and sat back relaxed.

Bruce's last move in the game with A.J.P.T. was muffed by Boase. A.J.P.T. knew how much more dangerous an opponent B. was: 'he sits up there in his room like a spider spinning his nets of intrigue'. B. gave Taylor enough rope to hang himself: terms off work, two terms off, T. away more than half the week in London or the Isle of Wight, with one or the other of his two *ménages*, Margaret whom he was divorced from but lived with, Tony Crosland's sister, his second marriage which also broke down. In the end, the College got fed up: the other History tutors were doing his work. At the same moment A.J.P.T.'s University lectureship – he had become the sensation of the History School, lecturing on his head like his TV stunts – came to an end and was not renewed. Neither was his tutorial Fellowship: Bruce saw to that. He had waited patiently, without complaining, and done the work himself.

But Tom Boase as President was so anxious to get rid of Taylor that he made a mistake. He suppressed a letter Taylor had written putting his point of view, urging in his defence the books he had written and presumably suggesting that his tutorial Fellowship might be turned into a research Fellowship. Bruce had intended that the nuisance be got rid of from Magdalen altogether – as he would have been, and from Oxford too, if Boase hadn't slipped up. Bruce would never have made a mistake like that. A sentimental appeal for sympathy can always collect a majority in an Oxford college. Taylor got his research Fellowship, and is freer than before to do more damage than ever with his books, his journalism, his TV stardom – the leading academic in the mind of the British public, totally irresponsible, brilliant and cracked, not α but αγ.[1]

Bruce said to me after this episode, with contempt for Tom Boase for fumbling it: 'I shall never take the same interest in Magdalen again.' He had arrived at the same point at which I had arrived with All Souls years before, in 1952.

But it is Bruce who is dead, and A. J. P. Taylor who goes on and who counts in the mind, if that is the word for it, of Britain today.

And this is a reason why I leave the scene and turn my back on it.

1. The Oxford system of marking essays and exam papers employs the first three letters of the Greek alphabet: Alpha (α) for real quality; Beta (β) for decent work; Gamma (γ) for inadequacy. The symbols could be combined, as here, to indicate marginal estimation.

L.[os] A.[ngeles] airport, 20 January 1967

Almost the only opportunity I have of writing a scrap of journal, working as hard as usual at the book, and much pulled down, as each year, by flu. However, I am staggering towards the end of *The Cornish in America*: a big book, a sort of twentieth-century successor to *Tudor Cornwall*. Terribly exhausted, I can tell it in writing – without *élan* and sometimes hung up for a word. Curiously enough, it never seems to make much difference to the writing of the book. I find, like Bertrand Russell, that the first words that come to mind are usually the best; sometimes I alter them, then have to change them back.

Actually, underneath the intense concentration on work, the engagements to lecture and very few social engagements, *underneath* this has been the most unhappy, harried, worrying of my visits. I am being pursued – like all successful authors – for arrears of tax. There is the latent threat that ferrets into my subconscious, wakens me at night. Along with it is the worry whether to leave Britain and become an American citizen. I don't want to live anywhere other than Cornwall and Oxford, at least to have my base there for visits to U.S., but I deeply resent having my hard-earned earnings confiscated for the benefit of the slackers of the Slacker State. I don't want to have my money scalped off me to maintain other people's children. I don't like other people; I particularly don't like their children; I deeply disapprove of their proliferation making the globe uninhabitable. The fucking idiots – I don't want to pay for their fucking. I am tolerant enough not to disapprove of their enjoying themselves, but in this scientific age it need not have the deplorable consequences of the population explosion. I realize that I am outside of society (I am the real Outsider, not Colin Wilson) – it is *their* society, with their families, their children, their enjoyments, their pathetic ties. I don't belong; it's nothing to do with me. And I particularly do not want to be fleeced for what I do not approve of.

I agree with Evelyn Waugh, who in the end was maddened by the society we have lived into and which we detest (he couldn't have detested it more than I do, after all he was a family man, rooted in it: I am not) – he objected to being told by others how he was to spend his own money. That is putting it mildly. I *hate* everything about contemporary society. And I do not belong to it.

What to do about it?

I have no sentimental feeling about giving up England. After all, I am a Cornishman; and I don't like the modern English – the soft, easy-going, flaccid, slack, lazy, eleemosynary English, a disgrace to their history, the finest of any people's in the past four centuries. But it was the work of the governing class, and it is *past*. There will be no future. And the present is contemptible. I have really dissociated myself at last: like Edmund Wilson in regard to *his* country, I feel an inner alienation.

The American people? I like the Americans – they're a very decent sort of people, kindly, friendly, generous. Their menfolk are finer specimens, at any rate one sees handsomer types among them. In any case, I am not involved; I don't have any responsibility for what they do – it's none of my business.

Whereas the English have in every respect gone counter to what I wanted. In the 1920s the rule of the hard-faced men who looked as if they had done well out of the war; the humbugging Baldwin, the stupid return to the gold standard, the coal strike in consequence, the obstinacy of coal-owners and trade-union leaders alike, the fatuous A. J. Cook (no wonder the intelligent Frank Hodges did just what I have done and opted out), the disastrous General Strike. The fraudulent General Elections, 1924 (the Red Letter Scare – we now know that the Zinoviev letter was a forgery, well paid for by Conservative Party Headquarters); the superfluous idiocy of 1931; Baldwin's fraudulent election in 1935.* And, all the time, the crazy lunacy of Appeasing Hitler going on.

The British took every wrong turning they could up to 1939. And after the heroic interlude of the war that should never have been necessary and ruined the country, they again insisted on taking every wrong turning after it. Lost their chance of going in with Europe and taking the leadership of it – both Labour and Conservatives to blame; and see what France has been able to achieve under a truly great man, and after the humiliations of her war record, of losing both Indo-China and Algeria! It shows what *can* be done, with will, determination, thrift, hard work, hard-fistedness, no illusions about oneself or anybody else – all the values I believe in, totally disregarded in decadent, declining Britain.

28 February

Here at last I am in Albuquerque, New Mexico. (I must ask Isaiah Berlin to remind me of the rhyme about 'several persons of the same sex living in Albuquerque, New Mex . . .'). I have always wanted to see Taos, and the other end of D.H.L.'s pilgrimage from bleak Eastwood, the grimy coal-mining village in Nottinghamshire, the cemetery where his parents are buried. This afternoon Matt Pearce's wife showed me her coloured slides of the ranch about Taos, where Lawrence and Frieda lived and fought. First

* L. S. Amery admitted as much to me. [And was understandably annoyed when ALR used this private conversation in a printed article.]

came a little one-storey house, with a tiny grassy enclosure among the pines, a burst of gold chamisa in bloom at the entrance. Then the second house they built, a kind of New England farmhouse with the trees right up to the windows. Last the chapel, a shrine for them. Within, an altar-table with D.H.L. inscribed, his ashes brought from France within; above, a golden window with sun-rays. Outside, Frieda lies under a large stone, large enough to keep her down – Frieda Lawrence Ravagli (for she married Angelino, before she died). He went back to Italy. She married him so that he might stay in the country during the war. She had trouble getting him in, since she declared his status as her 'lover', instead of her 'chauffeur'. From the little chapel there is a wonderful view west to the Nacimiento Mountains. Frieda thought that D.H. would have lived, if only he had remained at Taos. Many consumptives who have come here to die have lived thirty years.

What an *épopée* it all was! even though we have heard too much about it. It is all so well documented. *Every*body in the group was so literate.

I came over yesterday to lecture at the University. This morning young Professor Beer took me down to the old plaza – pleasant Spanish adobes, earth-coloured, the colour of the pale pink earth hereabouts, with shaded arcades and balconies – and a blaring loudspeaker to ruin the peace of the place. Into the church with its tawdry ugliness, all the Spanish names of the men from the parish in the U.S. forces.

Thence to the older Indian pueblo of Isleta, with its story: the church closed and under interdict by the Archbishop, because the Indian community handcuffed and threw out their priest: a tactless German who tried to repress the Indian rites underneath their Catholicism. From time immemorial they had danced their fertility-rite spring-dance inside the churchyard. They dance themselves into contact with the spirits of the earth that give growth to the crops. I expect the church was built by the Spaniards (in 1613) on what was already the ground sacred to these rites. These have always gone on from long before. But the German ended the matter brutally, by cementing over the dancing place, so that the spirits of the earth are cemented down and the parish can no more get into touch with them.

So the Indian governor of the pueblo had him handcuffed and dumped in a truck outside their land and never to come back. Now the rectory is empty, furniture removed, the yard derelict and deserted, the rose-trees dying for want of watering. The church locked, we couldn't get in.

Pearce told me that in one of the Lawrences' quarrels D.H. was calling her a slut – I suppose for her going to bed with other men – when she replied 'if you go on like that I shall tell the world about your private parts'. That effectively shut him up. For, of course, he was quite inadequate. He was really a feminine type, who wanted to be had – by the eldest Chambers son at the Haggs, then by Murry. All that harshness (as with Milton) came from the incessant effort to assert masculinity. He should have been content to be what he was. A generation later he would have done so. Then there would have been no Frieda, no Savage Pilgrimage – and perhaps no writing.

Frieda told Pearce that life with him was hell. I expect life with her was even more so.

The lovely Sangre de Cristo Mountains are just coming out of morning-blue shadow to show lighted surfaces and ribs of rock, the horizontal crest like a striated Chinese wall. Further north a little snow dusted on the mountains. Those to the south, the Manzanas, are out of sight towards Texas – the Little Texas part of New Mexico beyond.

[L.A. airport, on way to Charleston, S.C., 14 March]

I *was* lucky in my visit to New Mexico – without any preparation or forethought, everything worked out it could not have been better. Matt Pearce telephoned ahead to Santa Fé. When I arrived there – driven through that haunted country the other side of the Sangre Mountains, like a rust-red, juniper and piñon parkland – a lunch party was awaiting me. Winfield Towneley Scott, the local poet – a better poet, Witter Binner was dying (what a name, sounds like a bird). Scott, a good-hearted man of no pretensions, had got together a group of intelligent fellows from St John's College, Annapolis, which has thrown out a shoot in the uplands above Santa Fé. A noisy lunch in a reverberating Spanish-style cavern of a restaurant. I barely had time to look into the cathedral of *Death Comes for the Archbishop* – his statue, Archbishop Lamy, outside it – before I was swept off by George Miller up the hill to St John's for the afternoon.

Goodness, how well-to-do Americans are spoiled – just as at St Andrew's, Middletown at the beginning of this trip. Beautiful buildings artfully displayed about the hillside, water introduced into a desert patio, every conceivable convenience and spectacular views on every side. To the north the snow-dusted Sangre de Cristo that dominate Taos, towards which I have looked longingly from the train. I didn't know in what fortunate circumstances I should one day see them close by. Everything comes to him who waits.* To the south, the Manzanas, to the west the Nacimientos. Miller came back to tea with me at the hotel – dark, good-looking, inclining to fat, had been a professional actor.

* Does it? 1974. No. 1990.

In the evening Mabel Dodge Luhan's daughter, Mrs Rossin, gave a dinner for me. Her parents had been partners with Harriet Monroe in the Poetry Bookshop. Then not much money, but her long one-storey house was packed with books. She married a rich New York Jewish lawyer, who left her very well-off: a no doubt good-hearted woman, but noisy and assertive after the manner of American women; this made her unattractive in spite of her possessions. The dinner was a bore – too long a wait over endless drinks until we adjourned to the restaurant next door for the (noisy) meal. One way and another I met a great deal of noise in Santa Fé. The only thing I learned from her was that Mabel Dodge was petrified when D.H.L. turned up in New Mexico, she had so built him up as prophet and soothsayer. Little Alice had to cook him his first breakfast – that was apparently her role, before she married money.

Next day I sallied off on my own to Taos, not knowing what to expect or whether I should get to D.H.L.'s ranch at all – there has been a recent fall of snow and it is 6,000 feet up. I boarded the bus, my mind haunted all day by Hardy's lines.

> When I set out for Lyonesse . . .
> Nor did the wisest wizard guess
> What should betide at Lyonesse.

The bus mounted up and up the whole way, another thousand feet. I kept regular notes as it went along of how the country looked – red and rust-coloured to begin with, the Rio Grande muddy in the plain it irrigated. The Sangre de Cristo range, partly snow-covered, lay to the east; a large military cemetery outside Santa Fé (how can so many fellows have died there? Perhaps their bodies had been brought back). Once we entered the canyon going up through the mountains the river changed colour to the ice-green of melting snow. I watched it the whole way rushing down fast, tumbling over rocks, full of vivacity. All the way up, wherever there was a patch of soil there were apple orchards. The colours winter-subdued, the trees looked dead and leafless; actually the cottonwoods were pale rust and silver, only the willows a vivid raspberry. When I left the cosy security of the bus and got out with suitcase to walk up the hill all alone, I felt a bit apprehensive. Would it work out?

I made for the little plaza and the Fonda hotel, went in; the proprietor said that the coffee shop was closed for redecoration. No lunch: my spirits sank. Where had I got to? I said, 'Do you know if Miss Brett is still alive?' 'Yes, I know her well.' 'Would you telephone her for me?' When I told her that I was a friend of her brother, Oliver Esher, the gallant old girl replied that she would come into town from three or four miles out and get me.

The hotel proprietor cottoned on and asked if *he* might take me to lunch across the plaza. Meanwhile he let me in to see the Lawrence pictures which were banned from England. Impossible to understand the fuss now: not very good, but they were not bawdy, and certainly not pornographic. The figures were mostly nude, rather two-dimensional, like frescoes. I made notes of some of them. The kind Greek, a bachelor of forty with sympathetic eyes, took me up to his bedroom, showed me his collection of highbrow English books – Cecil Beaton, David Garnett, Maurice Bowra – and insisted on my stopping the night as his guest, arranged a room, put my suitcase in it.

After lunch Dorothy Brett – the famous Brett, of the D.H.L. circle – arrived. She had been a name to me for years, though I hadn't realized that she was Esher's sister. By this time a splendid monument, large, capacious, very deaf (with a hearing-aid), every ounce a great lady, was there. As we rattled and bumped along in her station-wagon we gathered acquaintance. She found that I was quite aware of the difficulties of writing her father's life – a life-long homo, about whom everybody knew – not a breath of scandal. For herself, she gave it as her opinion, let the truth be told, only Oliver minded, and he was dead. She also let me know that Victorian brothers didn't treat their sisters very well. I said what luck she had escaped it all and led a far more interesting life of her own abroad.

She took me into the Taos pueblo, inhabited unchanged for several hundred years, every year the stucco renewed afresh, ladders in place of stairs to the upper storeys. The whole dominated by magical Taos mountain, up which the Indians don't allow whites to go: it is *their* mountain, where in the caves they still perform the rites of their real religion, the Catholic church below for their surface observances.

Extricating ourselves from the pueblo, we arrived at a cabin not far along the road, with an amphitheatre of mountains lying before. A scene of extraordinary untidiness and squalor – dilapidated chairs strewn about the porch; we had to step over a dog-gate (for Reggie – after her father) and into a painter's studio in fantastic confusion, paints, paint-boxes, brushes, pots, pans, endless litter, I couldn't see where, let alone how, anybody could live there. Yet there was a stove. And ahead was a bay-windowed space which was Miss Brett's bedroom. Her bed was neatly made, with her dachshund at the foot, wooden steps for him to get up and down, for the bed was high, the floor littered with fairly clean dry bones. In the window were some beautiful figures made of glass, a cockerel, a lion, eighteenth-century glass from Old Mexico. No doubt whatever I was in the apartment of an old English lady – I have seen that kind of mess before: they were not brought up to look after themselves or do any sort of housekeeping.

We went across to the Manchester Art Gallery – the door opened by Mr Manchester upon a scene in great contrast. His was a fine adobe house with big rooms, good furniture, carpets, pictures, everything in great taste. Including the beautiful young man from San Francisco whom Mr Manchester was entertaining and putting himself across. Mr M. – who fancies himself as descended from the Dukes of Manchester, in spite of the fact that their name is Montagu – was himself a good piece: greying fair, getting on for fifty and six feet, well-equipped and sexy, predatory look in the seagull grey eyes. The boy was very handsome, tall and slender, over six feet, long legs, beautiful head of auburn hair. He had a sulky look, but ravishing when he smiled. Mr M. was obviously greatly disturbed, the young man holding himself in reserve. How had he arrived? Who was he? – Mr M. was careful not to tell me his name, other than Donald and that he was Scottish. I was careful not to enter into any rivalry, and anyway was much more interested by Brett.

As we drank our coffee out of cups of modern earthenware – as it might be St Ives – Miss Brett and I talked of old days in England. Mr M. went on with his game: he was very hospitable, the young man could have his spare bed for the night up in the loft at the end of the studio. I left Mr M. to it, though I noticed that, like all homos, he had the feminine capacity of taking in two conversations at once. Miss Brett went on with her dancing classes at Windsor in the reign of Queen Victoria, attended by the old Queen herself. Once the clumsy little girl, petrified, tripped over her footstool. 'Don't worry little girl, it doesn't matter at all,' said the old lady. But a wife of one of the Windsor ecclesiastics told her that, if she did that again, the Queen would cut off her head. This sent the little girl into hysterics. When, at home, the reason for her fright was got out of her, her mother told her father, who told someone, who told the Queen, who really was cross then. For many a day the cleric's wife wasn't allowed inside the Castle.

Mr Manchester kindly proposed to take us all to the ranch. I sat in the uncomfortable back seat with the ravishing young man as we rattled along nearly twenty miles to the ranch. At length we came to a dirt track, with snow still lying in the ruts, and into heavenly piñon country along a ridge, a cultivated valley on one side, the other dominated by Taos mountain. It was a haunting presence. Mr M. said that it either liked you or it didn't; if it didn't, it spewed you out. At a turn we left even the track, and as we stuck in a quagmire I got rather alarmed and asked if this *détour* was necessary. Apparently it was, to drop Brett at the cabin of farmer friends she would visit with while we went up to the shrine. Mr M. was no sissy, but a tough driver and air-pilot, who flew all over this country taking pictures. He calmly let down his extra wheels in front, jolted us out of the rut we had sunk in and dropped Brett with her old friends. She did not like going up to the shrine, the house where they had all lived hugger-mugger together.

Just my lot, I reflected, to arrive when it was all long over. But this is what I like – not to be involved at the time, to be in on it when it is over, the poetry of what is past, the grief, the nostalgia: The Historian.

We arrived at the comfortable Swiss chalet or New England framehouse Frieda was able to build when D.H.L.'s books began to make her comfortably off. Behind was the bungalow where they lived in the heroic days, with the two porches they built on themselves to sit out in, the tiny one-roomed cabin Brett inhabited behind. What a life! But lived a good deal out of doors. Frieda was a home-keeping *hausfrau*, while D.H.L. and Brett roamed the countryside, rode and fished. L. had his little vegetable garden. Brett liked fishing, but found the Rio Grande, which had good fish, a treacherous river, sudden deep pools and swift currents that carried people away.

We went up to the shrine, rather German in inspiration, which Mr M. found in execrable taste. Frieda had planted an avenue leading up to it; the chapel had a kind of altar with D.H.L. inscribed and his ashes supposed to be in it. Mr M. told me that in fact he believed that L.'s ashes were scattered over the mountainside; for Brett was so very insistent that hers should be and at a certain definite spot. Frieda is buried outside the chapel under a suitably massive stone, with the arms of the Richthofens above. Above the little chapel stood D.H.L.'s phoenix.

However tasteless Mr M. thought it, I found it very moving – here was the end of the astonishing pilgrimage that had brought D.H.L. all the way from raw Eastwood. Of the group I was the only one who knew the Nottinghamshire beginnings: perhaps I should complete my Eastwood essay with one on 'The End of the Pilgrimage'. Or perhaps a little book, with another on 'Lawrence in Cornwall', one on Lady Chatterley, one on Leavis as Critic.*

Mr M. told me that Brett was a great healer. I am not surprised: there is something monumental and calm about her. When D.H.L. was dying in Vence, Frieda cabled urgently to Brett to come and heal him 'as you did before'. But it was too late: he was dead before she got there. One of her pictures shows the three devoted women, Frieda in the centre, Mabel Dodge and Brett on either side at a table, D.H.L. a little man like a satyr in the background – les Trois-Maries, one might say. In her studio was a painting

* A good idea for Cornwall. 1974.

of the two sides of Lawrence – the Christ side (which he was afraid of, Brett said), and the capering satyr, or Devil. What an extraordinary circle, united in worship of him and his genius! Even Mabel Dodge, whom I had thought of as a silly woman with a fixation on L.: Brett – who is beyond malice – told me that Dodge was an intelligent woman, though rather given to making mischief.

Brett* was noble too about Frieda: my visit rather altered my picture of her. I had always detested the thought of Frieda as a German bitch. But Brett was above any rivalry and told me that Frieda had a wonderful way of making D.H.L. feel more of a man, when in fact he was inadequate. (The *German frau* in her, making up to a man.)

John Manchester told me that Brett believed that she was in touch with him: I should have loved to speak with her about that – especially after my feelings about Bruce since his death – but wouldn't have dared to touch on anything so intimate on so slight an acquaintance. Still, she is the faithful guardian of D.H.L.'s memory. A pity that Frieda didn't leave the chalet to her, instead of to Angelino. This Italian peasant whom she lived with, then married – no doubt he gave her what Lawrence could not – has gone back to his family in Italy, with one half of the D.H.L. estate. Frieda left the rest to her Weekley daughters. Apparently D.H.L.'s family wanted no part in his books – too ignorant. Just like working people. I thought of the occasion at Nottingham when I attended the luncheon in his honour, the exhibition of his work, and his niece – 'I am Ada's daughter' – came up to speak to me. Now his literary estate brings in scores of thousands – Laurence Pollinger the literary executor.

Brett also corrected for me the Matt Pearce view that Frieda and D.H.'s life together was Hell. 'It wasn't as bad as that,' she said; 'they had their quarrels, but that was from time to time.' My view that D.H. should have married Jessie Chambers and would have been happier is rectified then: there certainly wouldn't have been such a story, the savage pilgrimage.

John M. was informative too – understood perfectly how strong the homo strain was in D.H.L., but told me that he fought against it. Hence the harsh assertion of masculinity – silly. (How obtuse of John Sparrow not to be able to see *anything* homo in D.H.L. – the Lawyer in Literature.)** There was a Swedish painter who came to Taos, with whom there was a passage – *he* may have been in love with D.H. Then there was the William Henry passage at Zennor, and L.'s feeling for Murry, besides Jessie's eldest brother at the Haggs. I had better write all about it – it would be something new. e.g.

* One most important thing – Brett told me that L.'s autobiography is in Lady Chatterley. And that is perfectly clear – the real clue to the book.

** No wonder he can't see that Emilia was the Dark Lady. QED.

1. D.H.L. and Eastwood: The Beginning of the Pilgrimage.
2. Lawrence in Cornwall.
3. L.'s Ambivalence – the Homosexual Element.
4. Lady Chatterley's Lover – as Autobiography.
5. Criticism of the Work.
6. Taos – The End of the Pilgrimage.

As the result of this brief visit I have got the whole picture clear – in fact, at last I have got it right. Of course, if I write I must read the books the three Marys wrote about him.

All the while John M. and I talked the beautiful lanky boy was listening in, a disturbance to us both. M. was able to inform me (and him, *pour l'encourager*) that Brett's father had lived with a succession of boy-friends from his Eton days. Brett herself told me that he was discreet about it. But Arthur Bryant's father, Sir Frederick, Comptroller of the Royal Household knew, for he warned young Arthur – not that there was the slightest need: 'Never trust a man who uses scent, my boy!' But – did Edward VII know?

Brett told me a wonderful story of Edward James's eccentricity – Mrs Willie James's offspring, over whom Lulu Harcourt killed himself (what cruel and wicked nonsense!) – who now lives in Los Angeles, very rich. He was staying at Taos, and in the middle of the night wrote a poem – was so excited about it that he got up to go over to Mabel Dodge's house to read it. So as not to lose his way back, he gathered up all the candles in the house and lit them along the path. When he got to the house Mabel Dodge's Indian husband, Luhan, answered out of the bedroom window, 'We are sleeping, and don't want to hear your poem.' – In the morning, when the maid came to the house to make breakfast, with all the guttering candles in the path, she was sure that the witches had been there.

Brett told me too about Robinson Jeffers' marriage. His wife completely cured him of his alcoholism. Then one day a beautiful girl came to the little peel-tower of a house Jeffers built with his own hands at Carmel, with tiny rooms you could scarcely move in them. Out of the window the wife saw the poet go off into the undergrowth with the girl. So Mrs Jeffers went upstairs, got into the bath and carefully shot herself, so as to give herself a graze of a wound. When the erring couple came back, the poet went up, to find his wife in a pool of blood. He shouted to the girl to come up, who rushed up the stairs and concussed herself against the low doorway. Both women were laid out. What was he to do with them? he asked the local hospital, telephoning to collect them. His son was more philosophical. 'So Mother has been acting up again,' he said.

But was Jeffers any good as a poet? Richard Pares introduced me to him in the late 1920s; but I never really cottoned on to him.

However, there *was* a circle out in those remote outposts in the 1920s. Not much in the way of automobiles, they went about by horse. They were all young, full of their work and each other. It must be a sad and empty world for Brett these days. She did not give that impression – a tower of strength and calm. A wonderful woman; above everything, a great lady.

The only note of regret was when we were looking at photographs, when we saw her slim and long-necked. Now she is monumental – very fine-looking but massive, blue eyes, white hair, very deaf, a hearing-aid. 'What time does!' she said. Yes, indeed!

We went down the little avenue with its wonderful views away to the mountains in the west, and then along the farm track with Taos mountain crouching like a watching monster to the south-east, to collect Brett who had spent the afternoon with her friends at the farm – a rustic, humorous type of old American farmer, so raucous-voiced he could hardly speak, friendly and welcoming. We picked up the grand old lady; I took my seat in the back beside the handsome boy; we rattled and bumped and jolted along the track to the ranch so familiar to D.H.L., Frieda, Mabel and Brett in former days when they were all young – now all but one dead.

That evening I entertained them all to dinner at a restaurant, La Cordova, outside Taos. The lighted houses among the trees by the river showed the countryside more populous along that narrow ribbon than I had supposed. Miss Brett was arrayed like a lady for dinner, if rather exotically, silk Indian trousers and decorative Indian leather boots. My preoccupation with her enabled Mr M. to go on with his pursuit of the young man. The poor young fellow was famished, having had nothing to eat all day. Where had he come from? Who was he?

When I arrived back at La Fonda, there was my bedroom awaiting me. I awoke in the night with the thought – I have totally forgotten to ask Brett what Lawrence's voice was like. Suppose if she were to die, the last person to have known? The reply came to me in a letter from Saki Karavas.[1] 'It was soft and insinuating – except when he was angry with Frieda, when his voice was shrill and harsh with the Midland accent of his childhood.'

I should have asked her many more questions. She had typed and re-typed many of his stories. 'The Rocking Horse' was based on an incident she had told him about her little nieces. She liked very much 'The Man Who Died'. 'The Woman Who Rode Away' is about Mabel Dodge. I must ask if there

1. Greek proprietor of the hotel at Taos who showed ALR much kindness.

is one about Brett. We talked of the poems; I reminded her of some she had forgotten, 'Pipistrello' for example.

John M. told me, a painter himself, that he considered her the best painter of Indian life. She has certainly entered into it, and they both have a great respect for the Indians' religious ideas. She showed me the drawing for her next picture, 'The Religious Clowns' – those who make clowns of themselves for the love of God – like 'Le Jongleur de Notre Dame'.

Saki Karavas mentioned to me people's curiosity about Mr M.'s relation to Brett: what was he, an unknown quantity, doing with this aristocratic lady with her grand English connections? Would he possess himself of all, etc.? There was malice in the curiosity. I felt that Mr M. was a cool customer, who did not much take to me – he had something else to preoccupy him; but that he was indispensable to Brett. What would she do there without him, cooking for her, waiting on her, caring for her? It looked as if he had the money: he certainly had the possessions. He told me that she had healed *him*. He did not go into it, evidently from a psychological breakdown of some sort. I had no difficulty in understanding the relationship – of a homo to an older woman: quite familiar. He also said that he was the third great love of Brett's life, D.H.L. being the first, I have forgotten the second.

Another thing Brett told me: D.H.L. and Aldous Huxley. The two men detested the thought of each other before meeting. On meeting they immediately fell for each other. (Can this be quite right? They must have met each other in Garsington days.)

D.H.L. said that Katherine Mansfield would not have died, if she had come to Taos. Nor would D.H.L. have done, if he had stayed there. They were actually going to come back to Taos when he died in France. When I write Brett I must ask which are the books or stories she comes into. And get Simon Brett to do a portrait of me – he has done a fine one of the Old Lady of Taos.

Next morning, 3 March, Saki Karavas would take no money for my room, took me out to breakfast and to the bus. Of course, he *is*: fine, honey-brown, seeking eyes, wanting to be loved, perhaps still more, wanting to be made a friend of. He was extraordinarily almost suspiciously kind. Before I left California he sent me Cecil Beaton's Diaries and Leigh Fermor's Journey in Northern Greece. Not a clever man, he kept calling me a Phil-Hellene. He introduced me to his mother: a little old lady dressed perpetually in black Greek costume. Late in life she took to painting, and painted some remarkable flower pieces in his collection.

The hotel was full of paintings, including D.H.L.'s – not good and quite inoffensive. Saki has placed a price of $150,000 upon them! Perhaps he may get it from the University of Texas. He is evidently collecting paintings of the Taos circle, including Brett's and Simon Brett's portraits of her. Perhaps he knows a thing or two, and I fit into his picture. All the same I could not get over how everything had come together on my visit – providentially, almost predeterminedly. All the way down the mountains the lines kept singing in my mind:

> Nor would the wisest wizard guess
> What should betide at Lyonesse
> When I set out for Lyonesse . . .
> A hundred miles away.

The journey down from the mountains was very provoking. A handsome driver, quite a character, had chaffed with me in the bus-office. But in the bus was an attractive sexy bitch, with seductive breasts, very dark, Spanish-Indian looking. He got off with her; it was provoking to watch the whole process from the second seat behind her.

27 March

I have tidied up my affairs in New York; the house is swept, but not garnished; my belongings all packed up for tomorrow's flight. Two visits to Curtis Brown for mail and tax problems; to Scribner's with typescript of my Foreword, then a long journey down to Broad Street, skirting the East River with the mammoth housing projects for the proliferating people. A bit early I walked up to the Doric portico of the original U.S. Treasury, where Washington took his oath of office, and along Wall Street, following the line of the original stockade from the Hudson to the East River. Then lunch with the Editor of the *Wall Street Journal*, an agreeable Southerner who rejoices in the name of Vermont Connecticut Royster. Lunch was at the Recess Club, of a conservative flavour with Nixon among its members, with a wonderful high view over the Narrows, Governor's Island in the foreground, Staten Island in the distance, skyscrapers of downtown disposed about. Conversation agreeable, with a Southern flavouring. I hope nothing happens to break my connection with the *W.S.J.*, so much more friendly than *N.Y.T.*

At the Wyeth exhibition this week Brendan Gill of the *New Yorker* sprang up behind me with oaths against the show. 'I *hate* it. I detest everything about it. Look at that picture over there. *Cheesy*.' I said that I didn't know what that cliché meant. He said. 'No good.' He added, 'Vulgar. Look at it. Photography can do better.' I said it could not: Wyeth's painting was not photographic, but selective and poetic. An austere, Puritan poetry, deliberately low-toned and restricted, chaste and unvoluptuous, authentically American. I turned on him. Why couldn't he *give* himself to the experience and try to appreciate, instead of reacting with journalistic clichés?

He was surprised and taken aback. I said that the astonishing public response to the show was a phenomenon that should interest him as a journalist. The public was sick and tired of being *bombarded* by paint; that was not what paint was for. Of course, there was sometimes a poetry in the moderns, Paul Klee, for example. He did not recognize the German pronunciation. But, for the most part, they couldn't draw. I took him across to the superb pencil drawing of carts and cartwheels. This annoyed him, he never gave it a look.

And another thing, I added for good measure, so many modern artists are indistinguishable from each other. Wyeth's work, so far from being photographic, was immediately recognizable as his, with his own personality. This was already a sign. As Auden used to say – a recognizable style was one sign of genius.

Mr Gill had met more than his match; he went away displeased, quite unconvinced. These people have nothing to learn – and everything to learn. They have false standards, and now cannot tell good work when it stares them in the face. Imagine the brutality of treating the life's work of a genuine, dedicated artist like that. But this is what the contemporary journalist world is like. It is just like what I have to put up with from them too.

New York, Sunday, 24 September

Really this should follow in the little blue book in which I entered at haphazard some of this summer's doings in England – a most varied and enjoyable summer: not much work done.

Thursday, 21 September

After an appalling morning with the Income Tax authorities, louring like a cloud over the scene for months, I went up to tea with Joan Wake in Charlbury Road. Indomitable old girl, crippled and arthritic, she is just back from Rhodesia. The worse for her journey because at the last moment the blacks altered the plane schedules, and instead of being able to lie down at night at two stops and rest, she had to sit up, grin and bear it. Result – dizzy head holding up her editing of a Northamptonshire journal, which she says gives a fascinating picture of the activities of an eighteenth-century country squire. Blissful civilization! – if most people were outside its full enjoyments, what matter? – they always will be.

She told me that Edith Sitwell was her cousin and used to come and stay at Courteenhall. When Joan was about twenty-five and Edith twenty-two they used to play duets. One day out on a walk upon which Joan had dragged her – Edith loathed country walks – she came out with long quotations of poetry she remembered. Joan was impressed and asked her if she wrote any herself. Edith reluctantly produced a line of her own. Joan said, 'That's all right,' and added, 'I really think poetry is your line, not music. Why don't you go in for it properly?'

So that Joan regards herself as having propelled Edith on her way. She has a bundle of her early letters* – they afterwards got out of touch. What spirit and initiative Joan Wake has! – it probably comes from her Cornish temperament, forthright, tactless, full of energy and drive. When one considers what she has achieved, in saving archives, alerting people all over the country to their value, starting the Northamptonshire Record Society, saving and equipping Delapré Abbey for its centre!

She is a grand piece of the past in herself, a remoter past than I knew comes alive in talking to her. She used to stop at Morval in its valley with the hanging woods and the lane that led to bathing at Vellandreath. Those were the days of the old Miss Tremaynes, only one of whom married. She wanted to know how things were. I told her: all going to ruin through the folly of the heir to it. Quite well off, came into a good deal of money, Charles Henderson's cousin, whom I met once at Oxford, tall, gangling, plenty of sex. He ruined his marriage to beautiful Penelope, who took to Bertie Abdy's welcoming arms, from whom Paul Getty took her, having at command all the money in the world.

Prince Bibesco, a great connoisseur of women, to Marthe: 'I've often wondered what it is that women want . . .' (Musing) 'I've come to the conclusion that the one thing they all want is – Money.' Betty Stucley candid soul, agreed.

La Guardia airport, 25 September, to the strains of the usual ghastly airport music

Last night I went to hear the Vienna Philharmonic play Bruckner's 8th Symphony, round the corner at Carnegie Hall. I have always wanted to know his music better, since thirty years ago I heard No. 4, the 'Romantic',

* What has become of them, I wonder?

with its opening horn sounding *im wald*. In the intervening years I missed a chance to hear his *Te Deum* at Notre Dame. Now was my chance to hear his 'masterpiece'.

It wasn't a masterpiece or, if so, a masterpiece of the second class. But it gave me the chance to come to terms with Bruckner. One sees the point of the critics – the German nimiety, the too-muchness (Germans never know when enough is enough). Plenty of fine music in the work – he is incapable of making an ugly sound. Like Elgar, he is episodic and repetitive, even obsessive, in place of intellectual construction. Perhaps there was a block in his mind, at some point – bachelor, celibate, religious, not a hint of the erotic – descriptive and repetitive. Having got a theme he will repeat it a few notes up, and then again – too naif. Or give it a different colouring with different orchestration. Then *too* emphatic in the German manner, hammering out a chord again and again. Only the simple can respond to that – and the audience did – as the critic Hanslick admitted at the original performance in Vienna. What a contrast with the perfection of Mozart's G minor symphony that preceded it. I was glad to hear the traditional Viennese rendering of this – everything kept in proportion, no drawing it out of shape to emphasize particular effects, as often happens with the return in the first movement.

Boston, 11 October [Reflections prompted by hearing of Attlee's death]

I have often thought, when Bevin and Attlee became great names in the land, how often they have addressed meetings in the clay area when only a dozen or so people would turn up to hear them. Attlee was unimpressive in those years. My closest contact with him was on the evening he became leader of the party – on the withdrawal of George Lansbury. We sat together alone that evening in the hotel at Brighton, saying little, though he must have been thinking hard as to what it might lead to. I don't think anybody was really in his confidence: Bevin was the only person he listened to at party conferences – quite rightly too. I wanted Morrison; no-one could have seen how Attlee would increase in stature. Winston: 'A wasp that is fed on royal honey becomes a queen-bee.' Actually he had confidence in himself, and developed complete assurance. Lord Strang told me he was a master at running the machine of government, had an instinct for it, in a wholly different class from Neville Chamberlain. Montgomery regarded him as a far better chairman of the Cabinet than Winston, who talked too much. Clem ran through paperwork like a paper-knife, with fewest possible words, excellent at summing up the sense of a meeting.

I must jot down a few stories of him from Douglas Jay, who worked in proximity with him 1945–51. Dick Crossman was always giving trouble, no sense of direction or loyalty, no sense. (Bevin: 'I won't 'ave these university men in the Cabinet: you can't trust 'em.') Dick took an opportunity in the smoking-room of the Commons to beard Attlee, 'Mr Attlee, I think the new foreign policy statement of the party was very good.' Dick told the story himself. 'And, do you know, he never said anything at all. I thought he hadn't heard me. So I said again. "Mr Attlee, you know, I thought the party's new statement of its foreign policy very good." And all he said to me was: "Did you?"'

He had a way of arousing the least opposition, where bigger men, Bevin and Winston and Lloyd George, aroused as much opposition as support.

Another story was of Attlee and Aneurin Bevan's visit to U.S.S.R. – he didn't want to go, just went to keep an eye on Aneurin. I saw him on Ava Waverley's P.L.A.* yacht-cruise down the Thames (*every*body was on board, from the Archbishop of Canterbury downwards, politicians of all colour – or rather of the same uniform drab colour – Diana Duff Cooper draping herself gracefully against a mast under a shady hat – and deaf old Thames-side H. M. Tomlinson to whom I talked). Clem said that he had been inoculated against everything for his visit.

At the party William Hayter gave for them at the Embassy there was Aneurin in closest contact with Malenkov on a sofa, Clem standing alone in the middle of the room, looking on the ground, not speaking a word.

Bill Hayter: 'Mr Attlee, would you like to come over and talk to Mr Malenkov? Or Mr Krushchev? Or there's Mr Mikoyan over there . . .'

Clem: 'No, sick of the lot of them.'

He was only there to keep an eye on Aneurin. When they came out of the country at the other end, at Vladivostok, they were met by the world press for their impressions. Aneurin held forth on the importance of Malenkov, a *most* intelligent and understanding man; Aneurin felt that it was possible to do business with him, etc. Then, 'Mr Attlee, what were *your* impressions?'

Clem, crisply, 'A very capable man.'

Within three weeks Malenkov had fallen from power.

One time after the war there was a crisis within the Parliamentary Party whether to support the armaments programme thought necessary. A combination of elements made the vote a very near thing, and nobody knew whether the leadership could carry it. The debate went on and on. When the vote was taken the leadership got a majority of only two. Attlee, in the chair, read the result and at once snapped, 'The meeting's closed.'

* Port of London Authority.

Astonishment reigned, everybody was caught aback, protests – but the meeting was closed, Attlee gone.

In the underground passage leading out of the House Douglas Jay caught up with the little man padding along with briefcase on his way home. It had been such a narrow squeak – the party's policy would have been overthrown if Attlee had not just scraped through – that Douglas expected him to say something about it. All he said was: 'My wife has been left a small sum of money. What would your advice be as to how to invest it?'

Really, a conventional upper middle-class man of the best type, background of public service, loyal, reliable, old public-school standards, dedicated to duty, brought up with an orthodox Church of England tradition; officer-class, but with an inner idealism, bent on helping the underdog, no humbug, no nonsense, no exhibitionism, allergic to prima donna-ism whether in Ramsay MacDonald or Winston, great common-sense and good judgement, not bothered by self though aware of his position and well capable of holding it, happy family life unhampered by private complications (unlike Eden and Macmillan), sharp as a needle, but rather colourless – excellent camouflage: it made a strong combination, of all politicians the least open to attack. He had no personal quarrels – sheer waste of time – though of course he had his likes and dislikes.

His great attachment was to Ernest Bevin, whom he greatly admired. Exceptionally, I don't think he *enjoyed* politics, as most professionals do: it was all a matter of duty, like serving in the Army.

I remember early in the war a meeting in my rooms at A.S.C., packed, people sitting on the floor, Clem sitting with them, back against the closed door leading into the Old Library. One was hardly conscious of his presence and he said nothing (how wise – saving his breath). I registered – he was then the second man in the government, after Winston: if the second man in Hitler's government, Göring, had been there should we have been unconscious of his presence? He had no *presence*, unlike most political leaders, MacDonald, Winston, Bevin. That again was a potent factor in reducing others' envy, along with the adulation aroused by others – L.G., MacDonald, Churchill. Attlee looked anonymous. This made it easy to under-estimate him. Especially for us intellectuals, with occupational bad judgement.

G. D. H. Cole, for example, was a far more important figure in our eyes, and actually was so in the Labour Movement right up into the 1930s. In some ways he did more for the Labour Movement, for the W.E.A. in education, at Oxford, in training up the next generation now at the head of the party. Harold Wilson was his pupil, so were Hugh Gaitskell and Evan Durbin, and many others.

Attlee hadn't much use for intellectuals, though too shrewd to attack the hornets' nest. He said of Cole that he was the perpetual undergraduate. This was rather hard, coming from a University man to whom old Grant Robertson had awarded a sound Second in the Schools. Cole was a brilliant Balliol man, a First in Schools, a prize Fellowship, prolific of books, articles, lectures all over the country; a striking personality, handsome and glittering, a better speaker. But Attlee, as usual, was right; Douglas Cole remained the brilliant undergraduate (like Trevor-Roper today), who never grew up into maturity. Still, Attlee should have awarded Cole something, some recognition for all the work he had done. But he knew that Douglas would make trouble, so he never did. The result was that – though Clem liked coming back to University College and coming down for a weekend (I recall a weekend at A.S.C. when he persuaded Oliver Franks to take on the embassy in Washington) – Douglas Cole came to detest him, and spoke ill of him. I well understood its source.*

Attlee despised Laski. This was more justified, though Laski too rendered considerable service to the Labour Movement. His judgement was even worse than Cole's, and he was more of a liability, a trouble-maker. He agitated for Morrison to take Attlee's place as Prime Minister – though a decade before, at the Leicester conference, he had been such a fool as to fall for the resolution rigged up by the Trade Unionists purposely to exclude Morrison from becoming Treasurer, which would have brought him the succession. Even I saw through that one; Laski fell into the trap. I never knew that Laski wrote to Attlee proposing himself for ambassador to Washington. The reply was, 'Letter received. Contents noted.' Attlee's public rebuke later – 'A period of silence from you would be welcome' – was singularly effective. Shortly afterwards Laski cracked up. No loss to the Labour Movement.

Only Attlee, unegoistic, colourless, and devoted to service, could have presided over that snake-pit. Bevin was a bigger man – a truly great man – but he hadn't the politician's finesse for the job and, though he had the power and the say-so, he aroused as much opposition as support. Bevin and Morrison detested each other, largely Bevin's fault. Morrison refused always, in particular as leader of the London County Council, to treat trade unions with favouritism. Anyway he was the leader of the constituency parties, the political side. Bevin fixed it that he didn't succeed Arthur Henderson as Treasurer – as he certainly should have done. I well remember the strained white look on Herbert's face as this fix-up was put through. Another tribute to Attlee's judgement was that he switched Bevin from

* So too with Dick Crossman.

his original choice of Chancellor of the Exchequer to the Foreign Office, where he wouldn't have to work closely with Morrison as Leader of the House.

It fell to Attlee to have to get rid of Bevin in the end, when he was visibly dying, and he had to appoint Morrison in his place. The old man said, 'The little bugger has got rid of me at last.' Morrison was far less successful at it: it proved a trap for him and lost him his chance of succeeding Attlee. He ended a soured and disappointed man. Hugh Molson said, while staying with me at A.S.C. last summer, that he had never known a retired politician who was not an unhappy man. Can't do without the drug, I suppose, the limelight, the sense of being at the centre of affairs. The great exception here again was Attlee: when he retired he continued a happy relationship with his party – unlike Macmillan.

I never describe my life over here [U.S.A.], but yesterday, 12 October, may have a certain importance: I have probably ceased to be a Harper author, to become a Scribner one. Alan Collins described it as a big decision, and the right one. He has cool judgement, takes as much trouble with my small affairs as with Svetlana Stalin's. I hate making irrevocable decisions, breaks of that sort. And I am too much bothered by tax persecution to care very much one way or the other. However, today I am on my way out to meet and lunch with these new Scribner people, who are anxious to have me.

Here's my day. Breakfast down below, squalidly, at the drugstore counter. When I first came to the Wellington there was a quiet dining-room, gold curtains and old prints; I breakfasted there respectably in the English manner, plus the *N. Y. Times*. Now this place has gone down in the world, the dining-room has been rendered hideous.

I am a familiar figure at the drugstore counter, run by a taciturn good fellow, Elmer, surrounded by appetizing placards: 'Have a liverwurst with a Coke'; 'Sugar free Diet-Rite Cola'; 'Cheeseburger with Float', etc. The men who work behind the counter I have now known by sight for years – the dark Jewish fellow with good teeth and tuft of hair on chest; the poor little Porto Rican drudge with hands in water perpetually washing dishes. They are all competent, good-tempered, respectable fellows, though none so quick as Elmer at making a sandwich, a hamburger, cooking eggs, carving beef, turkey, making up a package 'to go' – a hundred operations, reduced to routine, enough to drive one dotty, all in good temper, a deflating, slightly sardonic humour.

I know some of the familiar residents of the hotel – pathetic old ladies, some wispy, some solid, with out-of-date hats, who have lived in their bed-sitters for years. An elderly Englishwoman teaches in a school – linguistics, how to speak the language; she perks up with me, I have offered to take her out to tea at the English-speaking Union. She has been here for years, has never been home. Then a faded elderly woman, who must have been pretty once, has a fearful facial tic: her whole face, neck and arms convulse every few seconds.

We all are together at the counter – the grey-haired English professor they can't make out, along with the rest: the sometimes handsome airmen and women of the Scandinavian airline, the Czechs, Germans, Austrians of visiting orchestras at the Carnegie Hall next door; the French tourists; the Spanish-speaking Central and South Americans; the Jews, the blacks, their women arrayed in all colours. Hardly ever an Englishman, for they have no money to go abroad: prisoners of the Slacker State, just as much as in U.S.S.R.

The bell-boys, blacks, all of whom I know by sight and most for years – are a decent lot of fellows, the bell-captain a good-looking one, who was seriously ill a couple of years ago. I think these fellows like me: they know I like them – I save on my meals to give them good tips. Here too the hotel is going down. When I first came there was a handsome coloured fellow for doorman. He moved down the street to the Americana. So with others. The coloured maid who looks after this room told me that the proprietors used to be a family, who looked after the place; now a company.

Monday, 16 October

I have run into the fortnight dedicated to a Retrospect of Rouben Mamoulian's films after all. Yesterday I went along to the Huntington Hartford theatre to see 'Queen Christina' and him. After the film he came on to the platform, and when he saw me came, surprised, to the edge to greet me. Mild sensation: good salesmanship. He then gave me a glowing testimonial as a 'great historian', etc., and I had to turn round and say a few words to the audience.

20 October

A dash to remote south-western Virginia, to a little offshoot of the university in the coal-mining mountainous part of the Clinch Valley, to lecture 18–19th. Why do I do these things? Money. To see the country. To help to circulate my books. For, of lecturing as of other carnal pleasures I should at length have had a satiety – to adapt old Grant Robertson on examining. It was a grey louring day, not very rewarding visually in the plain, mostly ploughing away above mist. Arrived at Tri-Cities Airport, Tennessee, I was met by a fine fellow of a Virginian, of good family, six feet four or so, who had fought in the war and done graduate work under C. K. Webster at the L.S.E. His subject was Appeasement, so for two hours as we drove slowly into the mountains I did my best to tell him all I knew. The country was rather beautiful in spite of the rain, hills and valleys, forested with deciduous trees all turning, leaves fluttering down red and gold. We motored sixty miles, across the Clinch river and valley, named for an early explorer, up the Coeburn mountain to a splendid view of the Cumberlands, looking towards the famous Gap through which Southerners (including Lincoln's parents) poured to populate the West, Kentucky, Illinois. It was rather like the Lake District without the lakes.

Here I was in the heart of authentic rustic America. Hardly any blacks, plenty of poor whites, original Anglo-Saxon stock, that have got left behind. The forest country pullulating with Fundamentalist religious sects, as with rattlers and copperheads. Church of God, Church of Christ, primitive Baptists who won't have music in their churches. Terrifying fanatics. Like this odious Mississippi Baptist minister, chaplain of the Ku Klux Klan that murdered three Civil Rights workers, then turned state's evidence on his accomplices. ('I can always kill me one'!) One of the sects combine their religion with snakes – the Snake Handlers. Because the Bible says, Ye shall handle snakes without fear, if ye have faith, etc. So the fools have their ritual festival at the height of the snake season in summer, fondle them round their arms, etc. And afterwards set them free in the woods. Of course, some get bitten – but that is owing to a failure in faith. Once bitten, one would have thought sufficient to let a little reason in. But, no: the idiots are incapable of that.

A biology professor asked for a snake for his anatomy class. A student brought him a bag full – 'You didn't say which sort you wanted, so I have brought you specimens of different kinds.' Even the Dean's little boy of ten goes catching them, knows all about the different varieties, came one day into his father's study holding one by the neck – to his father's horror.

The little place did its utmost to make an occasion of my visit, or get the most credit for the large fee it cost them. (I must send their new library some of my books.) A couple of old ladies, fans of mine, told me that they had driven seventy miles that morning to my lecture. (So perhaps I am getting known over here.) Various delegations from other schools kept arriving late all through the first half of my lecture. Held in a large gymnasium. The microphone was appalling, kept grumbling away and making comments on its own, until we turned it off. Then I had to strain my voice to reach 750 or 800 people. (Result, a cold.)

I maintained an angelic disposition throughout – deliberately: the poor little place had put itself out to raise such a large fee.

Then the long drive to the airport in pouring rain.

After Charleston, West Va., we ran into the tail-end of a tornado, in a small slow jet-prop. The pilot played for safety and made a wide sweep off our route into western Pa., over Pittsburgh, to cross the Alleghenies, and land in upper New York State to refuel. It was agonizingly boring, dreadfully bumpy, the plane also wobbling and plunging as we tried to get above the clouds, no visibility, flying by radar. (Thank God for a British invention, I thought.) A handsome Virginian soldier, fair with gold silk hair, slept blissfully all through it in front of me. I didn't know what to do to occupy my mind. I finished a paperback of Hemingway's indifferent journalism – revealing of conditions and atmosphere in the 1920s. I talked to dear Peter (dead) as always when I want to induce sleep. I thought of John Betjeman's teddy-bear, which he always took to bed with him and Penelope once threw out of the window after a quarrel. I tried counting the prime numbers: 1, 3, 5, 7, 11, 13, 17, 19, 23, 29, 31, 37, 41, 43, 47, 53, 57, 61, 67, 71, 73, 79, 83, 87, 91, 97? When alerted that we were fourteen minutes from Rochester I began counting the seconds and ticking off the minutes. Of course I was several minutes in hand when we eventually landed at Rochester. We waited a whole hour until we got the All Clear to proceed. Several people left the plane, some to get a fast jet to New York. I stuck it – going to the gangway to get several breaths of fresh air. Still a storm of wind and rain. The last leg was better: the storm had moved east out over the ocean. The moon rose clear; sometimes we were in clear moonlight above the low rounded clouds, sometimes flying through them.

I got back $4\frac{1}{2}$ hours late, with today my first cold.

27 October

Before the Salters left I went over to tea with them in their expensive suite looking over the East River. Arthur in his eighty-seventh year, Ethel not far behind. He was anxious about his book, *Slave of the Lamp*, which had had no notice whatever in England and no prospect of publication over here. Nor would it if I didn't weigh in. He had given me a copy of it, from which I saw what a crucial job he had done to save Britain in 1940–41 as head of the Shipping Mission in Washington.

Pasadena, New Year's Day, 1968

Not a word in my journal since arriving here at the beginning of November. For one thing, I work too hard all day at the Library; for another local entertainments (and people) are too dull.

I am greatly enjoying my return to the Elizabethan Age, in the Art Gallery reading up the art and architecture; in the basement, at music, medicine and science; in the rare-book room looking up original scores. But all to an obbligato of worry about the declining country at home, what to do about it? Leave it all? Cornwall, Trenarren – I don't mind so much about All Souls now – not the old College I loved. It is *maddening* to live in a time when one's country is going down the drain. I do not know what to decide.

All night there has been the swish of the hundreds of thousands of cars that pour into Pasadena for today's Rose Parade, salute taken by Senator Dirksen. I closed up my windows looking out on South Hill and up towards Colorado. Now I have to wait for Allan (Nevins) who, contrary to wont, has decided to come and see the Parade with me. Just like him: I hadn't intended to go, but stay in and try to get those infernal *Birmingham Post* articles written about the state of the country. But I am so sick with the thought of it that, for once, I have great difficulty in making myself do it.

3 January

Every night I worry in my sleep – about the state of the country and my own situation in regard to it. Every night I dream, but forget my dreams. One night I dreamed that I saw Oliver Cromwell, pale and long-haired. Another night I saw Ezra Pound slap Eliot's face, and then kiss him 'to make it better', as children do; and Eliot solemnly kissed him back. Another night I dreamed I was making a poem and was aware of each line – the last line perished as I awoke, but the last word was 'escaped'.

Last night's dream was very visual. I dreamed that I had taken on a dilapidated castle – evidently my memory of Pengersick. When I saw it my heart failed me: a big Perpendicular barrack, stone staircase, stone floors, no conveniences, no furniture – all was to do. What had I taken it on for? I already had a perfectly convenient little house of my own and couldn't think why I had saddled myself with this white elephant: Trenarren Castle. Moreover, the woman I had taken it from had planted a lot of snakes – grass snakes in the garden: they were for the rabbits. (Were the rabbits to eat them? I wondered; or were they to improve the grass for the rabbits?) With my horror of snakes, though harmless, I was furious. I would tell her off when I saw her. Somebody said, Don't make a fuss just when you are taking over. I said, You know what I'm like – if somebody displeases me they are for it. Nothing would stop me from saying what I thought. I went through the dishevelled grass to the castle: to enter it, by a door half-way up the face of the peel-tower, one had to climb a ladder. How can I possibly manage such a place? I thought. How can I have taken it on, when I was perfectly well provided before? And woke – worrying.

May–September 1967

Since this was kept as a separate journal it seemed better to make a slight interruption in the chronological sequence than to mix up passages written at different distances from the scenes described. The visits to Combe Florey to examine Evelyn Waugh's books and papers and to Menabilly to talk to Daphne du Maurier are particularly interesting.

Trinity Sunday, 1967

A wild day of wind and blustering rain, unlike the fine early-summery days Trinity Sundays usually are. In all day, I wrote letters, and then most of the day have spent living in Charlie's company, copying out from the two diaries I have brought down to hand over to the R.I.C.[1] They have brought him back so vividly to me: a poignant pleasure being with him again. Rather humbling in a way, his vitality was so intense, his interests so wide, his nature kind and good. Evidently there was much of his life I didn't share, didn't want to share. He was extraordinarily extrovert – in this respect his diaries read like Elizabethan diaries, factual, concise, hardly any introvert expressions. Even then they are chiefly of regret at parting from friends, from his undergraduate pupil, Fred Maxse, Sir Ivor's son, with whom Charles travelled ten weeks in Italy in 1925 and had him to stay at Penmount. Charles became extremely fond of this backward boy. I wonder what became of him? And if he remembers Charlie? And who was Ian Macalister with whom Charles travelled to Salzburg in the summer of 1932? By then I knew Charles well, and remember the fixation he had on bathing and learning to swim in those last years. I remember a sulky journey down from Oxford for summer vacation, with Charles, an elongated trout swimming in the Avon at Amesbury, and again in the icy Dart at Fingle Bridge. He wanted to try himself out physically, to make up for lost time, to compensate for his bookish youth. It was as if he couldn't gulp down life fast enough – God knows he had little time left: the summer after the Austrian holiday of 1932 he was dead.

But the amount of life he got through! the number of people he knew and met, the places he went to, at home and abroad, the amount of travelling! He evidently had immense energy, but I wonder if he didn't exhaust himself – with six feet six inches to provide for. The earlier diary, 1925–6, is the more interesting: all new to me, before I knew him. It contains his Cornish life in that year, as well as the Italian travel. Every day, almost, he would be

1. Royal Institution of Cornwall, to whom ALR was presenting the Diaries of Charles Henderson.

sallying forth from Penmount on some excursion, historical jaunt or lecture to give; very much given to dropping in on people for lunch or tea or to stop the night. So much the opposite of my introvert life, not wanting even to know people in those years, struggling with illness and living an inner life of the mind. Charles must have had some inner life, but there is no evidence of it in his diaries. They are all about what he is *doing*. He certainly had plenty of fun, a time crowded with every sort of interest, sightseeing, people, places.

Not much evidence of reading either. When we first became acquainted, I took his *general* reading in hand and told him to read the contemporary authors, Virginia Woolf, D. H. Lawrence, Strachey, Eliot. He had never read any of them. He had other talents – his gift for drawing figures and scenes. Several of his sketchbooks exist. Chrys must have the long saga of the Sobeys of Truro that gave them so much fun. At Antony they have an amusing sketchbook of life there – the Community for Unmarried Fathers, for the Unclerical Clergymen, and so on. He was an *original*; a humorous character in the old-fashioned sense; a unique figure, awkwardly but advantageously placed socially. His background was upper-class, country gentry rather than middle-class. This opened all kinds of doors to him, as with Joan Wake, that would not have been opened in those days to lower-class academics. On the other hand, he was odd-man-out with the latter, becoming dominant in the educational profession.

All the same, I am surprised at the width of his social contacts, in Europe no less than in England: the advantage of having stayed with his people in Rome and Florence in earlier years. To these Italian contacts he added Austrian and German friends later – Adam von Trott, through me.

His diaries show how very much of a piece he was, how much a gentleman. Small-minded local people resented his standing out – but they couldn't do much about that in his case. And he was such fun, a gangling great boy, an innocent, guileless, with a gallumphing sense of humour, ready to keep everyone amused and in good temper. Brought up well, he knew how to behave: it could not be said of him that he had 'no sense' (G. M. Trevelyan on *him*self).

Sometime I must fill in the gaps in his life. He was humbly in love with Sandy Rendall in those last years – as the diary shows him deeply fond of Fred Maxse earlier. When Sandy was taking his Schools, Charles would get up at 6 a.m. to lay a fire for him to work by before breakfast! (He got his inevitable Second.) There was that little dinner party in Charles's room at Corpus for his mother, Chrys,[1] Sandy and me; after which he took the two

1. Charles Henderson's sister.

women on ahead around Christ Church Meadow, in the bowery, scented, sexy summer evening, while I was to find out whether Sandy were, or ever could be, in love with Charles. Not that Charles meant to go to bed with him – 'I'd rather shoot myself': it was all platonic. Receiving a negative – so familiar a situation with the young, irresistible and second-rate – Charles decided to try himself out with women.

Part of his growing up, at thirty, trying to develop in all directions, he took to attending an art school. There he fell in with an art student, Cecilia. Deliberately, as part of his apprenticeship, he got her to fall for him; purchased a French-letter and had her on the floor of his room in college. 'Poor little Cecilia was the butterfly that was broken on the wheel.' (I didn't quite like that patronizing attitude towards the poor butterfly.) Charlie didn't much care for the experience either. But it gave him the confidence that he was capable of marrying; then he found a socially suitable person to marry in Isobel. (Funnily enough, she didn't much care for sex either: it always made her feel sick, she once told me, and her real emotion was for Honor Smith, as befitted a Somerville girl.)

All this happened the moment I moved away to London, to L.S.E. and P.R.O. Charlie was in a hurry – and then it all folded up in one fell stroke at Monte Gargano on his honeymoon. Of course, I was jealous at his marrying, of course I resented losing him – even worse with Richard Pares. His death brought him back to me, and I fell in behind Isobel loyally, to keep his memory green.

Here I have been still at it – thirty-four years after – this past fortnight, since her memorial service. And there is more to be done. I must now raise the question and organize an appeal for a tablet to him in the Cathedral. I can't think why we didn't think of it before.*

1 July

Yesterday, 30 June, I had to devote, according to promise, to looking after Andrew Rolle's[1] (of Occidental College) wife and two children. A day of family life was more than I could stand. However, I took them to lunch expensively at the Bear at Woodstock, and after lunch into Blenheim Park.

After the Palace and Park, we went on to Bladon. There, on the rose-tree-lined churchyard were these people I had known. I saw Consuelo Vanderbilt's grave first, and thought of my visit to her apartment in Sutton Place, and her invitation to lunch afterwards, which I was such a fool as to refuse

* So much in America, I have never found time to do this.

1. A member of ALR's circle at the Huntington.

for a lecture engagement at some women's college. I missed her a last time when she was to have been staying at Blenheim for a family party. Very good of the Duchess to have asked me. Then, not long after, *she* died. I went to her Memorial Service at Christ Church: not a member of the University: not David Cecil, nor the Trevor-Ropers, who had accepted her hospitality. The nurse who had nursed her all during the fearful pains of cancer wept a little. Next came Winston's brother, Jack Churchill, Clarissa's father, whom I met in London during the war. Then Consuelo's favourite son, Ivor, talented homo, unmarried, who made a fine collection of pictures, and died agonizingly of brain tumour. Then there was Winston's grave, solid and square-set: 'Winston Leonard Spencer Churchill'. Behind him his gay[1] parents, sad souls really, Lord Randolph and Jennie. All simple and touching. It made me feel now elderly, that here were people I had known a little – my own life passing over, and its interest. Nothing interesting to come or to expect.

I next made for Chipping Norton and Chastleton. In earlier days there used to be a last old Miss Jones, of the family of Walter Jones of Witney, wool merchant, who built the house in 1603. It would have been building when Shakespeare rode by on his way over the hill to or from Oxford and London.

This time there was another seedy end of the family, unmistakably a gentleman, long-visaged seventeenth-century face, dirty, stained, ragged trousers, a bit sodden, pipe in ill-kept hands, well-spoken, knowledgeable, defeated. The house was sour-smelling, as of dogs' piss, or cats', or mice: it needed windows open, scented wax upon wood panelling, acres of polish, £10,000 or even £20,000 spent upon it.[2] Since last here, there was some rearrangement: the long refectory table that stood in the centre of the hall now moved to the side, the Charles I Bible with some interesting association disappeared – perhaps sold for more death duties. These enchanting houses will be skinned at last, the rest pickled, in the interest of more perambulators for unwanted population, more colleges for the uneducable. The little Queen Anne parlour behind the dais, with its old china, no longer shown, the china perhaps sold. Fine pieces of Sheldon tapestry have long ago been sold. So, too, most of the pictures that were any good: peeling daubs and copies all that remained, the top pictures left a couple of not bad Hudsons. In the library a foolish man turned over the Italian melodies written by Eliza Wood, about Jane Austen's time. 'She was my great-grandmother,' he said resignedly, that book her only claim to fame.

1. ALR never used this adjective in its recently imposed sense.
2. Now well looked after by the National Trust.

There were still a few bits of old china about: one fine eighteenth-century bureau full of coloured Worcester; the dining-room set with rare salt-ware. And some of the musty, fusty rooms were charming, big Elizabethan windows, plenty of light and views in every direction. The house is set half-way down a steep hill: from the back, the park (most of it sold away) slopes upward, with Renaissance stone dovecote; to the east, formal garden with cut box and roses; the north looks out over the Vale of the Red Horse and all South Warwickshire, verdant, plumy trees, rich agriculture and July briar-roses, green lovers' lanes, all very Shakespearean.

The enchanting house made a desolating impression. If only it had Cynthia Carew-Pole's[1] drive and care, above all her money – think how the haunting old place could be made to come alive! But it *needs* luxury. It needs fine rugs and carpets on the threadbare floors, it asks for polished furniture glowing in varied hues; it needs pictures and tapestries – like the splendid Pegasus for sale in John's shop next door for £400; wallpapers and fresh chintzes and books. The place could be made to live and glow, where now it is faded and drooping, a defeated invalid like the pathetic man who took us round. But now, never is it likely to happen, never again come alive and wake from its haunted sleep.

I wandered across to the tiny church – I half felt that there was someone there I knew to call on. There were only the modest Jones monuments, mostly of the eighteenth century. Only later did I realize that there *was* somebody else in the aisle: Anthony Throckmorton who had the house before Walter Jones rebuilt it.*

Sir Richard Westmacott, the Victorian sculptor, is buried in the churchyard. But I didn't see his grave: I was intercepted by an upstanding old boy, who was helping to get the grass in trim: the church-warden. A gentleman: he was sporting a Guards tie, and imparted to me that he had been a land-agent and so was paid to be observant. This twice over: what he had been so observant about was that the gutter of the little chancel was blocked, for the rain was running down the wall. At one time he worked a 400-acre farm here, now no longer. He had had a fall in the hunting field and lost a piece out of his head. He too was boozey – and had a deformation of the nail of the right thumb. (Not the only one to be observant.) It transpired that he was first cousin to old Lord Macclesfield; Chairman of the Rural District Council and other things. His father a North Oxfordshire Parker, I suppose planted out from Shirburn in the last century. He certainly had his share of the prosiness that is a characteristic of the Parkers.

1. ALR's frequent hostess at Antony.

* See my *Ralegh and the Throckmortons*.

Playing round the corners of my mind as I speeded back along the lanes was the half-conscious game of what I would have done with Chastleton if it were mine. A tormenting game to play. If I had my time over again *not* to make the mistakes I have made. Chiefly over money: if I had had a good stockbroker in the 1930s and 1940s I should have been very well-off, before America came in to rectify the balance. I should have bought that lovely Mierevelt of Henrietta Maria for only £150 in the sale room at Newport, the fine Moonlit Waterfall by Wright of Derby which I saw in London for another £150 only, the Christopher Wood White Cottage for £40, the Tilly Kettle portrait* I once considered at Spinks' in King Street, the eighteenth-century painted bed I could have had at Monmouth for £25, the set of early-Victorian chairs with blue velvet covers for £27.10 at Truro, the Pegasus tapestry now at John's. I could bring the poor old house alive with all my furniture, rugs, china, silver, books from Trenarren. But then I wouldn't want to open the place to the public, like the people being taken round it that sad summer afternoon.

Sunday, 2 July

A perfect morning of high summer, sun, breeze blowing the blustering bells of Christ Church into the quad – and not a soul there. In spite of Franks Reports and new Visiting Fellows from overseas, the haunted place is lonelier than ever – and full of ghosts. I love having it all, sadly, luxuriously to myself. This morning before properly working I couldn't bear the thought of going on my travels again; after reading the morning papers, that fill me with apprehension and the decline of our country, my head tells me that I ought to go, should do what I ought to do, not what I should like.

Yesterday, 1 July, I went in the afternoon to a house in complete contrast to pathetic Chastleton – to Lord Bearsted's Upton, between Banbury and Stratford. Last year Heather Bearsted took to me at a lunch – I cannot recall where – and was insistent I should go over to lunch at Upton. I couldn't be bothered to. Shortly after she left him.

This year I reckoned I ought to see the pictures – which I couldn't have seen comfortably at a lunch. So I went over on my own.

Here was a house done up and restored, any amount of Jewish money spent on it, lovely furniture (Chinese Chippendale!) all polished you could lick it, woodwork waxed and shining, rich rugs, dripping with china – mainly Chelsea – no expense spared. The whole place had been re-done and added to by Morley Horder in the 1920s in correct taste – and robbed of all

* Later I managed to acquire this.

character. If only some of the idiosyncrasies of the old house had been allowed to remain – as so delightfully at Tom Upcher's Sheringham Hall, where there could not be a more Victorian living-room, or a more charming. I kept wondering what one could do to Upton to give it more allure. The smaller rooms of the old house, William and Mary, had been thrown into one disproportionately long saloon, without character, like Clarence House, Elizabeth II's middle-class taste. The best one could do would be something exotic, such as Lutyens did at Renishaw – not that one would want a black ceiling. Fowler or even David Hicks might be called in – perhaps something chichi would give the place character. *All* the rooms in this largeish house have plain colour-washed walls. Too bourgeois. They need variegated wall papers, more challenging colours instead of pale greens and pale yellows, strong mauve, grape purple, rose-red; flaming curtains and autumnal tapestries. Even so, nothing could redeem the standardized correctness of the interior: a London stockbroker's abode.

The contents are magnificent. It must be the only English house with an El Greco – a beauty too: sketch for the splendid Christ on Calvary in Toledo. Imagine a house with a Jean Fouquet, not to mention Hieronymus Bosch, two Guardis, a Tintoretto, a Tiepolo! But the house is chiefly rich in sporting pictures – enchanting Stubbses, many Devises, two fine Hogarth scenes, Ben Marshalls, Francis Wheatleys, Matthew Peters. I shall not forget the splendid life-size Romney of William Beckford, so revealing of that forever dissatisfied man. Everything betrayed him: the relaxed pose, one shapely leg behind the other, leaning against a sculpted pedestal, the delicate fingers, feminine curved lips, small sharp nose, eyes with a glint of fixation in them, the haughty expression with a suggestion of disdain – as well he might have. Everything gives him away and foretells the unhappiness to come.

I went round by myself, free to take everything in.

[From a discussion of men's and women's attitudes to marriage]

The chief objection is that it is *distracting* from the main objective – work, one's own fulfilment in life. For their fulfilment in life they need a partner; we don't – at any rate, remarkable men don't. Ordinary humans, yes; but who cares two hoots about them? They recur – and are gone. Those few of us – I make an absolute distinction between us and them (completely contrary to everything in contemporary society) – who have something in us to fulfil have a primary duty to fulfil that; 90 per cent of men can fulfil the other, nature's purposes, thinking them to be their own.

[In Kilvert[1] country]

There was a question of his settling for the chaplaincy at Cannes, on grounds of health. The parish was more populous in his time, certainly more *country* life. But there couldn't have been five hundred people at the reopening of Clifford church – not more than a couple hundred at most. A great deal of parish and county activity, much coming and going, his father and mother (at seventy-five) coming to stay with him, sister Dora keeping house for him, the furnishing of the vicarage costing some £260, the Wye and its doings constantly in view, iced over and people skating on it in winter, or breaking its banks and flooding. Never a dull moment in this sequestered country parish in the depths of the Victorian age.

Evidently Kilvert knew his predecessor John Houseman, who also died young. Then at Hay Castle were the Beavans, where now is Mr Booth the second-hand book-seller with his large stores. I shan't forget that couple of days lost in the lush lanes of South Herefordshire, exploring for myself alone, yet accompanied by the sense of the presence of Bruce – *his* country, just over the mountain at Llanthony.

I mustn't forget to record a few of the things Hugh Molson told me about his early friendship with Evelyn Waugh. They were at Lancing together (with Max Mallowan),[2] and were close friends without really liking each other. Evelyn had a nasty nature (though also charm when he chose). Molson used to stay in the Hampstead house with the Waughs. Old Mr Waugh was a caricature of a Victorian, with a rhetorical, sentimental way of speaking. Evelyn couldn't bear it, or him, and made no bones about expressing it at table or in the presence of his parent. (Compare the family tensions with the Betjemans: Betjeman *père* was an appalling vulgarian.) Old Arthur Waugh would complain to young Molson, asking for sympathy, wondering what he had done to deserve this treatment from his son. Evelyn couldn't stand the canting way his father had of expressing himself.

I learned that Richard Pares's great love affair was with Evelyn. They were inseparable in Evelyn's first year (Richard's second); what separated them was that Richard did not share Evelyn's craze for drink. Hugh Molson did. But theirs was not a homo relationship. On the other hand, Hugh confided his portentous political ambitions to Evelyn, who promptly made fun of them in the *Cherwell*. Hugh, always pompous, at once broke with Evelyn. (He told Max Mallowan that Evelyn wasn't 'respectable'.)

1. A curate in the Welsh borders during the 1870s. His enchanting *Diary* was discovered and edited (1938–40) by William Plomer.
2. A professorial colleague at All Souls, married to Agatha Christie.

Hugh wasn't homo, but neither was there any evidence of hetero inclination. He was all political ambition. The pompous manner was originally an affectation, taken up, according to Evelyn, out of mockery. Once taken up, Molson never let it drop. When we were undergraduates I couldn't believe in it – the portentous air: 'I really mour-rn Lord Davidson', etc., patronizing as he was, I never disliked him. The pomposity did not spoil a decent nature underneath, unmalicious and a good sort.

Molson had wished himself on me for a weekend: I hadn't invited him. But he made himself agreeable to everyone, and it was interesting to see what the years had done to him – I hadn't seen him in forty years. In middle life he had married a rich widow, chairman of his local constituency party. That was a consolation prize for him: it means a flat in Wilton Crescent, and a country farm in Scotland (difficult to run, however, impossible to get anybody to work, etc.).

He has, however, missed being important in politics – not even a Minister, let alone a Cabinet Minister. So he is a disappointed man – as Alan Lennox-Boyd is not. After all, with his looks and *his* s.a., he was able to marry a Guinness, and that in itself made him a Colonial Secretary.[1] Molson has consoled himself a bit with drink, too, and has grown deaf and absent-minded. When he returned to London, he sent me the letter he had written to condole with some fellow peer on an operation; and sent *him* his bread-and-butter Collins. He appeared purple in the face, and slow in mind. I flatter myself on looking ten years younger.

[Visit to Combe Florey]

One of the most memorable jaunts of this crowded summer was to Combe Florey, taking Robert Dougan and Margaret to inspect Evelyn Waugh's *Nachlass* for the Huntington. I called for them at the 'Golden Cross' at 9.30, Thursday, 8 June, and made good speed in time for lunch at Combe Florey a few miles the other side of Taunton: a pretty village where Sydney Smith was parson. We circled round it, paused to eye the summer flowers, cottages festooned with roses and clematis, at last made the Elizabethan gate-house with pathetic sale-notice outside, up the rugged slope to the square Georgian house with fine door-case I had seen advertised in *Country Life*. Welcomed in by Evelyn's widow, Laura, no beauty, inured to work and struggling with a family, had obviously had a hard life and been through a good deal.

The house made an impression of sadness on me, of the strong personality

1. An uncharacteristically ungenerous judgement of a remarkably able politician.

that had made it – the interior, all the possessions so characteristic – so recently inhabited it, leaving it now deserted, rather down-at-heel, a bit shabby, not too much money to spare for repairs, or even to keep things shipshape. In fact the comfortable untidiness of a Catholic household, averse to money values. For all the money Evelyn made – 750,000 of *Brideshead Revisited* sold in America – he lived up to every penny of it, a largeish family, children to educate, nothing spared them, lashings of drink, generous entertaining. Like Belloc, model and mentor. (What a model, what a mentor!)

The front parlour was dilapidated, smelt of drink, the table with drinks already liberally partaken of, so that, when offered sherry, there wasn't a clean glass available. What surprised me was Evelyn's cult of Victorianism – all his life he had collected Victoriana. The walls were covered with pictures by Augustus Egg and Arthur Hughes, Victorian landscapes and *genre* pieces, Victorian chandeliers, carpets and furniture; a stupendous Burgess settle, painted and parapeted, given him by John Betjeman. I had no idea their tastes were so close. Before lunch Laura's mother, Mrs Herbert, looked in: more drinks for her, and then the Taunton solicitor came to meet us.

We went in to lunch. Fine hall, uglified by Victoriana – I wouldn't have such a collection in a fine Georgian house – Evelyn's bowler hat placed on a marble group above a bookcase filled with treasures of a lifetime's collecting. How sensible of him to have bought from undergraduate days lovely books like John Martin's *Illustrated Milton*, landscape books with illustrations by Turner, Daniell, Prout; the Pre-Raphaelite *Tennyson* and so on. Superb books. We passed into the hospitable, family dining-room also rather the worse for wear, Evelyn's Captain's cap with red band placed firmly on the youthful bust of the Master. His presence was everywhere.

I felt sadder and sadder for Laura, and made myself useful helping her with the waiting. She had cooked the lunch herself – a simple affair of steak-and-kidney pie, no trimmings. I followed her out into the large old-fashioned kitchen, and into the pantry, where the cat had already got at the remains of the pie. I chatted to her as we waited, leaving Robert to his slow-timed conversation with the lawyer. The dining-room had a pleasant sequence of pictures by Augustus Egg, 'The Pleasures of Travel', stage-coach in 1750, railway compartment in 1850; Evelyn had commissioned Richard Eurich to paint the discomforts of railway travel in 1950.[1]

We moved on to the library, with elaborate bookshelves coming out into the room installed by Evelyn (and putting off to inquiring purchasers, I

1. Of air, not railway, travel.

gathered). The atmosphere was discouraging. But the books and papers were fascinating.

Characteristic of Evelyn – a man's books give a portrait of him – were the serried ranks of the *Catholic Encyclopedia*, Burke's *Peerage and Landed Gentry* (of whom he fancied himself one). There were earlier books from Arthur Waugh's library and, in a Belloc-inscribed volume, Maurice Bowra's typed verses on Betjeman receiving the Duff Cooper award from the hands of Princess Margaret. Maurice's private verses, brilliant and bawdy, are an extraordinary production. His friend Sparrow says what a pity it is that Maurice's genius is intransmissible to posterity, for his 'verse is unprintable, and his prose unreadable'.

Evelyn had been *collecting* books all the way along, and I was interested to see the inscriptions of old friends: Harold Acton (in part Anthony Blanche of *Brideshead*), inscribing *Humdrum* in 1928 – 'To dear Evelyn praying it will not bore, with much love from Harold.' Then *Peonies and Ponies*, 1941, has 'To gallant Evelyn for a chuckle betwixt commandoes, from his unrepentant old crony Harold.' Quite recently, *Old Lamps for New*, 1965, has: 'To my old friend Evelyn who so patiently read some of these chapters and encouraged me to persevere, with much affection from Harold.' Evelyn had fixed his book-plate: *Industria Ditat* with his arms quartered with the Herberts'!

A lifetime's friendships showed up in these inscriptions, since we were all young together at Oxford. Now Evelyn is dead, and Harold has been operated on for cancer. What absorbing lives they had! I had never heard of these books by Harold – an ineffective literary career, in contrast to Evelyn's: a triumph. But Evelyn had genius; Harold, just talent.

Quite recently came Edith Sitwell's *Collected Poems*: 'For dearest Evelyn with great admiration and much love from his god-daughter Edith.' So he had a hand in her conversion – I don't fancy that he was much of a friend of the Sitwells before. But he was a fanatical proselytiser – responsible for converting Penelope Betjeman away from John. And then was disillusioned with the Catholic Church himself at the end, succumbing to the modern movement, Anglicizing the Mass, making up with the other Christian sects. Evelyn thought that there was the one institution that was changeless and beyond time. He was wrong: even that failed him in the end.

While Robert endlessly chaffered and haggled with the lawyer – I have never seen anyone so slow, and I am certain that he never saw into the quality or appreciated the literary value of Evelyn's papers – I looked into them. I was astonished at their richness and at his conscientiousness. The manuscripts of all his novels were in his own hand with corrections all the way through – an accomplished, stylish hand. The typescripts were also corrected, and I believe proofs. And some unpublished stories. Best of all, were the unpublished journals, frank and candid, as one would expect. I looked into them here and there, noting a comment on his friend Betjeman's later TV career – showing people over the stately homes of England: was that any better than succeeding to old Ernie Betjeman's business in *papier-mâche* objects for the Middle East? Evelyn had to resist – as I have – the temptation to write a letter to *The Times* every day about some new folly. But he complains that his memory is going – like his friend Molson, too much drink all through life, and (in Evelyn's case) drugs.

Molson told me of Evelyn's anxiety to keep his homosexuality from his son, Auberon. But it is all written across his work, written into *Brideshead*, and reappears in the voices he hears in *The Ordeal of Gilbert Pinfold*. As if one could keep it from the contemporary generation! – naif of Molson to think it possible.

At last, after several efforts, I managed to get a move on – it was getting well on in the afternoon, and we had to get to Exeter – and unstick the haggling Robert. Before we left, Mrs Waugh showed us the big back drawing-room, with carpet specially woven after a Great Exhibition carpet, on the proceeds of winning a *Daily Express* libel case in the 1930s.[1] It had an odd effect to furnish so fine a Georgian house with Victorian carpets and furniture. *My* furniture would have looked better in the house. At the foot of the staircase an admirable Holman Hunt portrait of Evelyn's grandmother. Upstairs an extraordinary Burgess washstand, painted, with cistern and tap, and an elaborate clothes cupboard. Outside I noted a touch of Evelyn: a small enclosure in the garden, with a couple of Victorian sphinxes couchant on the wall, placed looking away from each other.

Mrs Waugh came down to show us the Elizabethan gate-house, a fine affair of 1593, built by John Frauncis, with his coat-of-arms in the living-chamber over the gate, his cartouche in plaster in the long loft. The original house ran a court back from here. Just like the Georgians to site their house so much better, up the slope with pretty Somerset views in each direction.

The house made a deep impression on me – I was overwhelmed by the sense of loss and desertion, the glimpse into the life and mind of the man of genius who had called it into being. I looked for his grave in the churchyard below the house; but of course he wouldn't be there, uncompromising to the last. Where is he buried?[2] At Downside?

1. According to the *D.N.B.* it was the proceeds of *two* lawsuits in the *1950s*.
2. In the churchyard at Combe Florey. ALR must have missed it.

Friday, 8 September

My last visit from home – to Daphne du Maurier, after twenty years. I took Andrew Rolle, staying with me from California, to Fowey and left him to go sightseeing, while I took the familiar road back to the turn for Kilmarth,[1] where I used to visit the Singers over a couple of decades. The landscape fills with memories. I hadn't been along the Rashleigh country for years. Here were the gates, one of the fine pillars crashed into by a lorry and left unsafe; the lodge empty, stinging nettles grown up in the yard. The park landscape beautiful as ever, but fallen trunks uncleared away.

When I arrived Daphne came nervously around the corner of the house, as over twenty years before when I was there last. Then, myself nervous, I had brought Phyllis Bottome, a war-horse of a bestseller. Phyllis, a masculine type, half-American, took the offensive.

'I suppose you don't go to America?'

'No, I couldn't bear to. I don't really like leaving this place.'

'I suppose you wouldn't like lecturing in America?'

'Oh, no. I couldn't bear to lecture.'

Daphne was pathologically shy, could hardly bring herself to face visitors, or leave Menabilly. Phyllis, a veteran of women's guilds and lunches and platforms, could face anything. She had reduced poor Ernan – suggestively named – to the status of lady-in-waiting. I thought these two bestsellers were hating each other. I was wrong: it was the beginning of a friendly correspondence between them.

After nearly a quarter of a century – so much of life had gone by for us both, into the void. Daphne's husband, Boy Browning, brave Commando officer, died two years ago. She was alone in that big house. Phyllis is dead and forgotten. We were alone, and I knew Daphne wanted to talk to me, so I didn't take a stranger. She was not much changed: fair hair now grey and pale complexion dusty, later middle age; her figure lithe and youthful as ever. She had just come back from a swim, the beach at Pridmouth full of people (something new: there used to be no-one).

She showed me all over the house in which she has lived her fantasy life. Three times the size of Trenarren, far more sophisticated, built in the reign of Queen Anne, the date of Utrecht 1713 on the launder-heads, a fine staircase with plasterwork ceiling, panelling. What surprised me was that Daphne was no aesthete, had not much taste. It was a family house, lived in, fine rooms devoted to play-rooms, the untidiness of having children about the house. That is what the money has gone into – no furniture worth

1. The house to which Daphne du Maurier finally moved.

noticing, worn carpets, toys, TV, radio, games. Such a contrast to John Tremayne's Croan, or Trenarren. With all that money, and all the years there, I'd have made it a treasure-house. Daphne had it comfortable and shabby. It revealed her – interested only in writing.

We went upstairs along both corridors and wings – even the double guest-room had nothing much in the way of furniture – so different from the Johnstones' Trewithen, or Helen Mildmay's Mothecombe, let alone the *chic* of Easton Neston or Evangeline Bruce's embassy. Daphne was where she always had been: a bourgeois background. It was I who had moved on.

We came down to tea in the long library – which used to have a fine William and Mary bureau with mirrored panels at the end. I remember at the sale it made a few hundreds, now it would be thousands. She had lost interest in writing novels, hadn't written one for several years; hence the book on *Vanishing Cornwall*. Which I can't much like, and envy its sales, but have written two generous reviews of, in the *Wall Street Journal* and *Financial Times*. She ought to be pleased: I think she was. She had two or three ideas for short stories, but even these wouldn't 'gell' (horrid word). She couldn't write unless the whole thing came clear in her head and possessed her.

This made me feel sorry for her, and I suggested a biography of her gallant husband. No, that was too dull – soldiering! This surprises me – he was something of a hero, trained the Commandos, Comptroller of Prince Philip's Household, etc. I suggested some reading in the hope that it might inspire her: the two greatest of Tolstoy's short stories, 'The Death of Ivan Ilyitch', and 'Father Sergius'; Kipling's 'The Gardener'. She hadn't read any of them, living so solitary, so unintellectual a life, not really educated.

This is part of the trouble, I suspect: she has nobody to tell her, no pace-makers, nobody to correct her style. When I told her the end of 'The Gardener' she was thrilled, 'Brilliant,' she responded. It is much more than that – it is heartbreaking.

By this time she was coiled up on her sofa like a girl, legs under her: her eyes giving themselves to me completely: I noticed that they were a rare blue, Colette's favourite periwinkle. Upstairs, as we went round the bedrooms I thought 'How would it be? Nobody in the house.' But it would have been a mistake; no passions aroused. We went quickly through the General's room – a boy's room: full of caps and cups and racquets and odds and ends of sports and tackle – like the bedroom of a school prefect or captain of boats at a university. 'I hadn't the heart to touch it,' she said. How would it be if she married someone more sophisticated, more complex, less of a boy, and less of a man? She might get a new lease of inspiration. But she is a solitary; and so am I, too old to turn over a new leaf and make new adjustments now.

But she as certainly needs more intelligent society. What about Raleigh Trevelyan? I must talk to him about it when he comes tomorrow.

Daphne claimed that her essential life was solitary, that family life – which was so much in evidence all round, the children and grandchildren having shortly gone back from their holiday – had not meant much to her.

She wondered if she had been a good wife to Boy Browning – never going up to London with him, attending all those dinners, Prince Philip's circle and the Royal Family. I think she has been over this ground before, and didn't need me to reassure her. I politely did – said that what men liked was change, difference of interest. She said he liked the contrast, liked coming home, the sea and boats, never talked about the other life. I said that she had accompanied him on his sailing. She said, 'really a fair weather sailor, though'. Anyway, she swims – there were the wet bathing things drying out of the upstairs window.

She asked me what I thought about survival after death – as one gets older one thinks more about such things. I told her my experiences about Bruce and Helena's spiritualism, her belief that she was in touch with him. One simply doesn't know. All Helena's 'messages' were within the realm of her knowledge of him; when a question of mine related to something she did not know the answer was dubious. 'Exactly,' said Daphne, 'the promptings of her unconscious: just what I think.' I said that the human tragedy was that one could not know.

I disguised nothing from her. It was obvious that she wanted a heart-to-heart talk, and we had it. We didn't talk about my work, though afterwards I wished I had asked her about the stories, the ones she wished I had reserved for full-length treatment as novels.

We talked about our friends, Clara Vyvyan and Foy Q.,[1] and dear old Q. Daphne told me again the story of Q. summoning her to his presence after her second book, about a young man and woman living together in Paris. Q. was most upset. Daphne, aged twenty-two, sat trembling on the edge of her chair. 'But, Daphne, people don't say such things.' A book no-one would notice compared with what they say now. 'People don't do such things.' 'But, Sir Arthur,' protested Daphne, who knew, 'they *do*.' The old boy couldn't face this. 'All I can say is that if that is the case I can't have my daughter introduce you to her friends, Lady Vyvyan', and so on. The attitude of that Lesbian circle towards sex would have been an eye-opener to dear Q.

From that to the inhibiting effect on Foy Q. – like Chrys Henderson, a not fully developed human being, something constricted, inhibited. I told

1. Quiller-Couch.

Daphne Foy's last words to me a day or two before, 'One has such standards to live up to.'

Really, rather absurd, from a woman nearing seventy.

I went into Q.'s make-up, Clifton, the second generation on from Matthew Arnold, the belief in public service, writing as only a part of life. No great writer has ever thought that. Q. once said there were things in life too deep to write about – he meant the death of his son. He couldn't face it. But Kipling faced it, and out of it came 'The Gardener'.

She told me she had seen two people die – her mother and her husband – and what a shock it was! only a moment before, speaking – and then silence. I said I had never yet seen anyone die, and didn't think I could face it: women were brave about the basic facts of life.

We went out into the garden. She told me all her problems about the house. Some of the Rashleigh family wanted to come back and live there. So as a precaution she had taken on Kilmarth and was doing it up – neglected by the Singers, practically falling down. It was costing the earth. I said that she and Agatha[1] were principal supports of the British Treasury. She said a lot of her money had gone into trusts. I knew that. Shrewd old Walter Graham of Fowey had done better for her in time than the grandest London lawyers.

There was a question about pulling down the large Victorian wing at the back – immensely expensive. Let it become a creeper-covered ruin. The path along the garden front on the east had become part of the lawn. No borders, few flowers, less work to do than Trenarren. We went round to the front: she said that I had told her to restore the smaller Queen Anne panes in place of the Victorian plate-glass windows. 'Then the money ran out' – she hadn't continued it on the garden front.

The view of the sea that there used to be had been obliterated by encroaching rhododendrons on either side. I wondered that the General hadn't cut them back. No, he was interested only in boats – his upturned boat was there as his monument out at the edge of the fence towards the sea. We walked round the field-walk where I had trespassed as a youth, and where she used to come to peer in through the shuttered windows of the house – inspiration of her work. I said that Kilmarth, if she should have to go, might prove another inspiration, another phase. She was aware of that, but didn't want to leave – she looked at the place that is her life, has become a fixation, so that she doesn't mind inhabiting it entirely alone. As an old lady of seventy she wouldn't mind going further up the road, but not yet.

1. Christie.

At the front door we scrutinized the Rashleigh coat-of-arms on the pediment – the crescent moon, the curious T (for Torridge). Taking my leave I took leave to kiss her, which she took in good part – though she doesn't like to be touched. I may be as wrong about this as about Phyllis Bottome twenty years before! But she does want to come and see me at Trenarren. And I must send her the Kipling story.

I scooted off up the bedraggled park, great trunks lying about, out at the gate with the rickety stone pillar, past Tregaminion church, built by old Victorian Jonathan – I have one of his prayer books with Tregaminion on it, along with other books and furniture from Menabilly at Trenarren – and up the road past the turning to Polkerris, with the silvery light of autumn upon all the landscape and the evening bay.

17 September

I drove out via Cowley – huge and awful – past the corner where I last saw Ottoline, by Chiselhampton church and house (once lived in by Sir Charles Peers who used to come to lunch with Oman), to Stadhampton and Cuxham, where I stopped to look at the little church, like a medieval barn. Then to Watlington and out to Brightwell to see Douglas Jay.[1] Having time on hand I went up the slopes to the Icknield Way, where a troop of young women were pleasantly riding. Back to Monument Cottage, empty of occupants. I walked down the chalk lane, to look through the hedge at the kind of scene that makes one so sad at leaving England. A splendid red-brick mansion of George II or George III, about 1760, with outspread wings, tall elegant column in front, looking down the green slope of its park and across the autumn stubbles up the slopes to the ridgeway along the horizon.

The scene gripped mind and heart as I looked at it, the unspoiled dignity and content, quiet Sunday afternoon with people walking the upper slopes, under a marvellous cloudscape of puffed sails of white, pastel blues and sun-haze. In the golden stubbles the cock pheasants were preening and sparring.

The party arrived back from their walk and we had tea in the sun at the back of the cottage, looking across the Lady Pamela Mountbatten's pastures, black-and-white cattle flicking tails under the oaks. After tea Douglas and I walked down the lane and he told me the inner story of his dismissal from the Cabinet. The inconsiderateness of it – without a word of warning during Bank Holiday weekend. Douglas was always a close friend of Hugh Gaitskell

1. Considered by ALR one of the most brilliant Fellows of All Souls elected in his time. A long-serving Labour M.P. and briefly a Cabinet Minister.

and no admirer of Harold Wilson. Apparently Wilson will have no opposition to his attempt to get into E.E.C. Of course, if it comes off he will have been right. If de Gaulle vetoes us again, it may act as a boomerang: Douglas will have been right. Douglas considers it only right that members of the Cabinet should express their views on the subject, instead of being shut up by notes from Wilson stopping any discussion.*

Wilson himself is under pressure. George Brown is a Cecil King man, who paid him a retainer when out of office. Both are determined to get into the Common Market. Douglas suspects that George Brown presented an ultimatum: if he has to take charge of the negotiations he wants no dissidents. Cecil King says, 'I made Harold Prime Minister, and he has to do what I tell him.' This led on to relations between Cabinet members and the Press, those who purchase popular writing-up by their favourite journalists in return for titbits of political information – always leading to rows in the Cabinet. Unthinkable in Attlee's day. What a contrast between that government, with four big men: Attlee, Bevin, Cripps and Morrison. The present a government of second-raters.

[U.S.A.] 17 March 1968

It is St Patrick's Day in New York, also the third Sunday in Lent – an appalling day of ceaseless rain, as it might be any day in the Emerald Isle itself, or an excruciating Sunday in Victorian Liverpool, grimy, smutty windows, looking out on the unsavoury prospect of Seventh Avenue. The hotel is full of young hooligans from various schools, taking part in the entertainments of yesterday, the St Patrick's Day Parade up Fifth Avenue, banners of dear old County Carlow and all – I wish they might have had today's weather on them – football matches in some series or other, I wouldn't know what.

They have turned the hotel into a bear-garden. They began yesterday by playing about with the elevators so that the whole traffic of the hotel was slowed up, one could hardly get up or down. They stopped the lift at every floor – there are twenty-seven floors – and held it at each floor as long as possible. Result, lifts jammed to dangerous overcapacity, inside one could scream from claustrophobia. In the hotel lobby a patient crowd of resigned older people waiting to get about their business. I have several times walked down the stairs from my eighth-floor room.

In the night they made every kind of clatter, ringing fire and burglar alarms, throwing objects out of windows, smashing glass. When I went out

* My instinct would have been with Wilson.

into the corridor this morning it was strewn with broken glass, in addition to every other kind of object, cigarettes, cigarette-packets, cartons, mess. At the foot of the elevators the mailing box had been messed up so that it was Out of Order – no posting of letters possible; outside the deluge continues: one has the sense of being marooned.

At breakfast at the drugstore counter the patient old inhabitants were gently full of the inconveniences they had suffered – some of them had had windows smashed (in such weather!). On my return I heard a loud report in the corner of my room – innocently I thought a pipe burst, or a piece of the waterworks come through the ceiling. It was a heavy can thrown from above inwards against my window, failing to smash it, but lodged against the air-conditioning apparatus. Meanwhile, there is a fusillade of drink-cans being exploded into the street – it would be unsafe to go out just at present. It is like a besieged city, under siege by the younger generation – *but the enemy are within.*

The shot at Fort Sumter may have been the shot that rang around the world (or what was?), but that shot at my window has crystallized my resolution to go ahead and say what I think about the siege conditions under which we live, the breakdown of civilized standards with the advance of 'democracy', to strip the humbug away from the truth as to how things are and say quite nakedly what is what.

Most people are afraid to, or live in such a state of muddle that they hardly realize what is going on around them, or don't like to think, let alone speak out about what they have to put up with – most people are the most frightful fools anyway, and don't know it. So what price democracy? (The clatter of cans into the street continues.) What price their education?

They are, strictly speaking, uneducable – in any significant sense of the term 'education'. One thing I have been wanting to get off my chest anyway – one thing you are not allowed to say under the contemporary rule of humbug. In fact, in all the palaver about education in Britain one wouldn't be allowed to say that over any of the mass-media of communication, B.B.C. or TV or whatnot. I have never been allowed to speak my mind on such matters on any of them – though concerned all my life with education at every level and having won my way (when it was difficult!) from elementary school through grammar school to Oxford. But what I have to say about people's educability is *true*, based on long experience and wide observation in two continents. But that is why they won't have it expressed: it is too true. It cuts at their cherished illusions. We live in a world of make-believe, in which the make-believe has all the say-so. I am going to strip it away. I have never had any use for illusions, and despise those who shore themselves up with them. I am going to tell the truth and nothing but the truth. People won't like it. Fat lot I care.

In any case *they* have been saying what they think about us long enough, without any of us telling them what we think about them. Not that I speak from any Establishment point of view. I don't belong to any Establishment – a plague on both their houses that have brought our country into such disrespect (Football hooligans!) I have won the right the hard way, coming up from the bottom, to speak independently for myself.

In fact those very people who won such kudos by attacking the Establishment are themselves the Establishment today. Take such types as those old fellow Trotskyists, Malcolm Muggeridge and A. J. P. Taylor, entrenched in B.B.C., TV and the Beaverbrook press, with their audience of millions.

When I say 'They' I mean those people who have made a career out of attacking and undermining all that made Britain great, all the achievements of her history, the work of past generations with their energy and initiative to which they gave their lives. I mean those mean, scrabbling little people who can't bear anything larger than themselves, let alone anything really great – it's natural enough in them – who have not only eaten the heartstrings of Empire and Commonwealth away but brought our society down into confusion and chaos.

Take Muggeridge as a precise example – a cultural idol of the society of which he is such a tell-tale expression (he knows it is worthless, none better and nowadays tells them so). Whatever asset Britain had, he would be sure to attack it, to discredit it, denigrate it and demean it. True, he had his living to make, but need he make it this way, or be supported by public institutions in doing it?

I am no more sold on monarchy than he is – but it happens to have been an asset of Britain's, particularly overseas, particularly in the United States where it matters most. Anything that helps to keep things together, especially at a time when things are falling apart. It was a good thing, in the bleak and gloomy post-war years, to have a radiant young woman coming to the throne, against the background of elderly bald-pated generals and presidents on the international scene. But the young woman was shy and had yet to gain confidence. It was above all important that she should make a good impression on her first state-visit to the United States.

She was greeted on her arrival by a much-publicized article by one of her own people, Muggeridge of course, attacking her personally, her personal appearance, her style of dress, her very voice and accent. I hope he was well paid for it, the cad. He should have been horse-whipped for it, not promoted by the B.B.C.

Then, too, when Churchill died, the last of our world-assets, the pipsqueak piped up: 'I have always thought Churchill a much over-estimated figure, trying to make up by his rhetoric about the past for his fantasies about the present.' In fact Churchill proved to be more realistic about the present, about Germany and Hitler, Stalin and Russia, the importance war would have in the twentieth century from the very beginning, than any other democratic statesman. Here is this skunk decrying him. It is not worth arguing the matter, it is just that people of that type and size hate anyone larger than themselves. Egalitarian society gives full rein to those envies: never was there a society so reeking with envy as Welfare State Britain. (A. J. P. Taylor is another of the same feather about Churchill. He would be.)

When Muggeridge took the same line about President Kennedy, a much over-estimated man who had achieved nothing very much, couldn't manage Congress, etc., the Americans gave him the cold shoulder. Anything you like to say against the British goes, the British won't mind – they'll make you their cultural mascot (Shaw), or award you an O.M. (Bertrand Russell). The Americans are not so easy-going about mud thrown in their faces. Muggeridge used to be given a fair show of attention in U.S. before that. After that, they rather closed down on him. The cruellest attack on him, i.e. the most appropriate, flaying the skin off his back – all about Muggeridge's technique of 'mugging' people – was by Conor Cruise O'Brien in the *New York Review of Books*.

Perhaps Noel Coward on some women is in order: 'Some *men* should be tied up, put in a bath-tub, and pissed on regularly for hours.'

All Souls, 24 October

An unexpected visit from a *revenant* – old Robert Sencourt *alias* George of New Zealand – from Oxford of the 1930s has given me some new information about T.S.E.'s first marriage. In spite of Sencourt's eccentricity I believe it is reliable – and in spite of his being in and out of the Warneford,[1] etc. Vivien Haigh-Wood's brother is still alive, a successful stockbroker with whom Sencourt is in touch, to whom he says he has shown all that he has written about the marriage – while Valerie (understandably) has closed down on him. When she came down to my lunch party on 12 October, she imparted to me the secret that the full typescript of 'The Waste Land' has turned up. How lucky T.S.E. is! It will make a sensation when the news

1. The Oxford hospital for the mentally disturbed.

breaks in New York next week – I haven't said a word to a soul, though sorely tempted when talking about T.S.E. to one or two people lately. Even if people play it down – as may happen, the Kermodes and the like regarding him as now 'out of the centre' – it will nevertheless keep him in the news, keep him alive, even if *they* want to regard him as no longer vital.

Then, too, though T.S.E. took such pains to suppress knowledge of his private life, destroyed a whole chest of papers and documents before he married Valerie, he won't have succeeded. Robert Sencourt knew Vivien, and regarded her as under-sexed. It was news to me that she should have been had by Bertie Russell – not that he would not have been capable of it, but B.R. assured S. in a letter that it was not so.* From T.S.E.'s line about

> O golden foot I may not touch, etc.

one would suppose that she didn't want to be had.

He was in love with her: S. has seen letters to his 'Dearest' and 'Darling, who are at the centre of my heart', etc. But no-one could live with her for any time. When sharing a bedroom with her T.S.E. would have broken or sleepless nights. And when, in the end, after long trial and thought he decided on a separation, he never would see her again. She would come to the office and hang about the door; poor Tom would have to escape by the back way. Her brother said to him, 'Does it have to be this way?' Tom replied – 'What other way can there be?' He was right: he was far too sensitive and gentle to be able to stand a confrontation. I knew that she made public scenes and tried to humiliate him.

Once, when I asked T.S.E. to lunch with me at the E.S.U., he explained to me that he couldn't, for his wife was a member, and he might meet her. She behaved as a psychotic female would: (as the cracked nurse Mahood used to do with me at Polmear): Vivien kept his name on her telephone number so that his calls came through to her; she kept his books, and wouldn't give them up.

I never knew what happened to her after. In later years she got somewhat better, with the new drugs and tranquillizers. Comfortably off with £8 or £900 a year left her by her father, she moved about from guest-house to guest-house, not in a loony-bin, as I surmised, until she died of a syncope.

It will be curious to see what Sencourt has made of it all, in spite of his own mental divagations. He suddenly came in on me, when I hadn't seen him for years, used to cold shoulder him in the 1940s: he was regarded as a hanger-on, as he certainly was a sucker-up of the eminent. He had changed

* That great moralist was not above lying.

his name; he hadn't any footing in the University; he was a Catholic convert and proselytizer; he was always hanging round with some too obvious young man. Woodward spoke of him with disdain. I disapproved of him as a Catholic Appeaser and pro-Fascist, and regarded his writings with contempt. In the end I barely spoke to him.

Twenty years later he arrives unannounced in my rooms – nobody else would have got through without telephoning. Aged seventy-eight, unchanged, wearing a medal to show that he was a Benedictine lay-brother, on his way to lunch with the intolerable Lady Gater ('a very old friend'). He wanted to know the true story of T.S.E.'s rejection for the Fellowship here – he got *that* wrong and didn't seem to want to know the true version.

He repeated to me how much T.S.E. was disconsidered as a poet by the old Harvard clique – Berenson, for instance, regarded him as 'a charlatan'! Edith Wharton was no better. Sencourt spoke highly of *her* poetry unpublished – is it among her mss. At Yale?

3 November

Sunday 10.30 a.m. in the discomfort, the demotic squalor of a plane filling up, the odd smells and creaks of baggage, handbags, holdalls, people, old bags, black, white, grey, to the sickening accompaniment of airport music. As usual gloomy at uprooting myself and starting on my travels again, exchanging the comforts, the service, of All Souls for the questionable down-at-heel Wellington, the noises of 7th Avenue. A female bickering is going on in the seat ahead about one of the three who wasn't in some place where they were waiting for her. 'She said she'd be there, and we waited,' etc. A man tried to pacify them – 'She won't miss the plane.' When she turns up, reproaches, recriminations. These subside with 'Who's worried? I'm here, and I'm glad I'm going home.' The word 'home', I register, I've never heard on American lips before.

Today the plane is jam-packed. My plan of travelling on Sundays no longer holds: all the world is travelling. We're off.

Everything laid on very kindly for my departure this morning. Rowe brought my breakfast on a tray in bed; the dear Manciple (a charming boy bent on courting when we were young) arranged for his now grown-up son (courting in turn) to drive me to the airport. A heavenly autumn day, delicate, feathered and clear, colours subdued, not like the riot of colour in America I missed this October.

We've just passed Windsor Castle spread out in all its grey magnificence. I proudly draw the attention of the talented American girl drawing beside me, as if I had any part in Windsor, or any reason to be proud of it. Then

Reading, and I look up the Thames Valley towards Oxford, as far as the huge electricity generators now disfiguring the valley, competing with Wittenham Clumps.

Swiftly this morning through the familiar places: pretty Nuneham Courtenay in autumn array, grouped eighteenth-century cottages two by two, past the turning to Burcot where John Masefield lived his last years. Then Dorchester, abbey church of the monks of ill-fame, past the antique shop where I bought the late Georgian chimney-piece for the library at Trenarren (where I might now comfortably be). Down the sweeping valley at Bix, Stonor on the left, with all the Stonors in it – poison-tongue Jeanne, nice oppressed Sherman, archiepiscopal David Mathew. Through Henley-on-Thames, and dear Charles Henderson's phrase, 'what a *bourgeois* river!' – at Henley regatta. Up through the woods of the Chilterns and through the thickets mentioned in some Tudor book of mine, about Bisham – two miles by the signpost. Bisham, with all its memories: the body of Clarence's son, poor young Warwick, being dispatched up the Thames to lie with his Montagu ancestors; then the Tudor translator of the *Cortegiano*, young Thomas Hoby and his elder brother, more of a father to him; much later the All Souls civil lawyer, Vansittart and his line, that continued up to today, until impossible to live in the house any longer. And poor old Geoffrey Baskerville, who had an estate up in these hills, where I went to lunch once with his mother – one more mother-victim, with the usual effect. Tragic in his case – he spent a couple of years in prison for a choirboy. He was walking up the High with Weaver[1] of Trinity, when the policeman came and put a heavy hand on his shoulder. I once repeated that, wickedly, in the same spot: he winced. Kind old Robertson's explanation of his fall was that it came from reading too much early Renaissance literature.

The last promontories and inlets of south-western Ireland are passing below: mapped greens rising out of cerulean blue, up to crests of white under early snow – I think of those mountains as the refuges of the Munster clansmen in the 1580s, or the scenes of Froude's *Two Chiefs of Dunboy*[2] – the Shannon winding lengthily along the northern horizon. Elizabeth Bowen's country.

Robertson, too, was a mother's victim, though it didn't take him that way: it merely prevented him from marrying. In his youth an Edwardian 'masher' with kid gloves, he went to dances and all – had Marie Corelli for his guest at Encaenia, wrote a novel *Love, the Judge*, under the romantic name of Wymond Carew. His mother maintained a firm hand on him, kept

1. J. R. H. Weaver, President of the College.
2. A historical novel which ALR edited and abridged.

house for him all through his time as Vice-Chancellor at Birmingham, and – too bad – saw him out at seventy! She herself lasted to ninety-five.

I stayed on this October to examine for the Fellowship and, though a small field, I never remember better work. One very clever fellow from St Edmund Hall, apparently a hard-up Rhodesian: Robert Jackson. Exceptionally intelligent, powerful and original, wide vocabulary in which to express ranging thoughts. What will become of him? At the viva I was able to help him, save him months of work, for he proposed to work at Sir Thomas Roe – whom two other people are already at work on. He at once cottoned on, with quick initiative, got in touch with Michael Brown at Agnes Scott College. Then his supervisor, John Stoye, got on to me to find another subject for him. At last I have found someone equal to tackling the great John Selden. He – Jackson – is interested in seventeenth-century intellectual history.* I shall watch him with great interest and expectation.

The second, a Balliol man, called Clark, reminded me of Richard Pares: a feminine type.** A Greats man, good classic, stylish, with a sense of irony and even humour – in an examination paper! Writes poetry.

Ernest Jacob couldn't get it right: revealed himself as the second-rater he is, wanting to stand out against both Rohan Butler and me, at one in that Clark was a whole head above the historian Jacob wanted to run, a man called Hannah. (Some Ur-Judaism, quite unconscious?) Stuck to this against all the rest of the examiners, Max Beloff, Ford, Frere, Christopher Makins, Jeremy Lever, Stern – with the obstinacy of a weak man (and not without a revealing edge towards me. I don't complain. I treated him with contempt ever after the Wardenship Election. Underneath the camouflage the worm had turned.)

Ernest's ponderous silliness – playing the wise elder, anxious to 'see justice done', must 'consult Matthews' on Hannah's economics – led him to a fiasco. In the last lap he ratted, and on a second reading rated Hannah lower than Rohan and I had done. Pure waste of time – but it exposed him. It did no harm, merely gave an opportunity for two entire asses – Michael Dummett and Roy Stuart, never happy unless in a minority – to dissent from what should have been a unanimous report. Nevertheless, under my pressure, the College was given a clear lead, and the Election went through without a hitch.

The first hour of the Election meeting was taken up by John Sparrow on the absurd subject of a threatened sit-in by students. He should have made

* Nothing has come of this. 1973.

** Feminine to look at, but madly hetero, now already married. Hippie-ish. Not written anything yet. 1973.

a brief statement to the College on the measures he thought necessary and left it at that. But it was too good an opportunity to waste time: he has no sense of time – like Warden Pember, a similar combination of classics with the law, of courtly gentleman with an essential negativeness. While John talked and made clever jokes – at which sixty clever men guffawed and whiled the time away – I read a whole book, Jack Simmons' *St Pancras* (admirable job, full of detailed Victorian scholarship). Meantime the College was locked against any intrusion on the part of undergraduates.

After tea I went out to the post and was rather surprised – since I hadn't bothered to listen to the morning's palaver – to find a screen of students barring the entrance. 'What are you doing here? – wasting your time, when you should be working. You are here to work, not waste your time and other people's!'

The poor young men were quite taken aback at this onslaught. After a stunned silence the ringleader, holding his banner like a crozier, fell into the trap. 'What about *your* work?' he said.

'My name is A. L. Rowse; I've written thirty books. What have you done?'

They were quite *ébahi* – until one of them said weakly, 'What about the others?'

Not my business to defend the others – it is evidently Sparrow who has elicited the attack. I said 'You don't know what you're talking about.' I told them that the Fellows were elected by examination. As for them, I pointed out the ringleader as a middle-class type whose way to Oxford had been made easy, the public paying for it – and contrasted the struggle I had from a working-class background, with only one scholarship for the whole of Cornwall, etc.

They were utterly silenced, and I flounced off with 'fatuous fools' – into the arms of Arthur Goodhart, after running the gauntlet of the High. The young men had been so polite and respectful to me – I took no notice of their bill-board, 'Who killed Cock Sparrow?' – that I quite fell for them and wished I could have asked them in to tea.

[Cornwall] 20 April, 1969

Norman [Colville] and his sister have contributed a large sum – £3,000 – to restore the pre-Reformation painted pulpit in Launceston church in memory of his son and heir, Gavin, killed in the R.A.F.: a decorative affair of Renaissance floral design buried under coats of brown varnish.

He told me something of the financial burden of running Penheale – his wages and insurance bill runs to £500 a fortnight. I don't see how anyone can keep that up indefinitely. He has trustified all he can, for the upkeep of the grounds and the education of 'the boy'.[1]

There came to lunch Desmond Fortescue and wife, who have just succeeded to Boconnoc in the most discouraging conditions. Old George left everything he could to Joan[2] – a lot was not entailed – library, silver, china, furniture. A long feud within the family has meant that Joan has denuded the big house of its furniture, not even allowing her nephew to *buy* objects that went with the house. She has decamped to Ethy with the Dropmore Papers – somebody called in on her there with them all heaped around her on the floor. She will live at Ethy as she did at Boconnoc – as in a sale-room.

So Desmond Fortescue feels no duty to do anything for or by Boconnoc. The house had been a good deal spoiled by the Victorians, who put in a Mansard roof and plate-glass. Claud Phillimore had pronounced against it architecturally, so I suppose it will be left to moulder away – it is full of dry rot, the wall of the long gallery giving way, etc. All the same, the gallery was impressive, a long range of Georgian windows bright with sun looking southward down the valley, with a square room at either end, one of them the library.

Who has bought the books? The Pitt family Bible, with all the entries of their births; the manuscript of Chatham's letters to his nephew, Lord Camelford, and so on. One more historic accumulation dispersed, one more wreck of a great house – first Dropmore,* then Boconnoc.

Newton Ferrers is already derelict, after the fire, with one wing gutted and never restored. Bertie Abdy has handed everything over to Valentine, who thinks of decamping to Switzerland. So all the art-objects there have labels attached to them, as if already in the sale-room.

It is the end of civilization – at any rate the only civilization I care for.

9 July [Visit to Stratfield Saye]

The approach was distinctly disappointing. I had imagined a big, imposing, ugly nineteenth-century *château*. Not a bit: a not very big country gentleman's mansion, attractive, Dutch gables, looking across an unimpressive stable-court to symmetrical stable-buildings and down the drive to a small-scale monument of the Duke, not much larger than a churchyard monument. Similarly with the entrance, small, rather shabby porch, stand filled with a medley of ancient carriage umbrellas.

1. His second son, James.
2. His widow. For ALR's visit to them, see pp. 351–4.
* Now Dropmore, apple of Lord Grenville's eye, his creation, in Arab occupation has been burned down, 1989.

The entrance hall improved the impression: floored with mosaics from Silchester[1] 'on the estate'; marble busts of Wellington's contemporaries, Blücher, Alexander I and an extraordinarily handsome one of Nicholas I – not only a noble head, but sensitive sensuous lips: hard to imagine the rigidity of his character. Perhaps he ossified into it.

I needed a wash and something more. Shown into a garden-room to the left, I couldn't see a wash-basin, let alone a WC. The butler had to show me the latter, enclosed in a large cupboard – never seen such a contraption before. The room was largely filled with the big billiard table the great Duke thought the most beautiful piece of furniture. Bookcases all round the walls contained the splendid architectural books his connoisseur descendant had collected in Rome.

Thence along the gallery into a greenish sitting-room where two men were awaiting me. The Duke at eighty-two, looking a spry sixty-two, though deaf; the other a dilapidated contemporary of mine at Christ Church, who said he had met me but whom I too obviously hadn't remembered: Francis Needham, the Duke's librarian. Anything else? I suspect factotum and door-mat. My, but he did look seedy, fifteen years younger than the Duke – looked as if he drank too much. He remained very mum, never spoke unless spoken to, has evidently devoted his life to the books and possessions of the Duke.

The Duke pointed out that I shouldn't find much of the atmosphere of the great Duke – I should find that more in his private rooms at Apsley House and Walmer: he hadn't greatly cared for Stratfield Saye, came there chiefly in the autumn for the hunting. His correspondence shows him there sometimes in winter. The present interior is largely this Duke's creation – and what a successful job he has made of it: it makes a most livable house, not too large, and not at all grand: though deprecating about it, he has made it beautiful. Rich carpets along the ground-floor gallery and all the living rooms, specially woven in Madrid, as I knew. Ceilings sparingly gilded, wallpapers in keeping: each room made an harmonious whole. The pictures did not much attract me, and indeed nothing special: a fresh and unusual baroque portrait by Nicholas Maes, some pleasant Pillements, looking like Vernets; the family portraits rather boring – apart from the great Duke and the Marquis Wellesley, not an interesting family.

The Duke cleared up for me that there was no connection whatever between Wellesley and Wesley – obviously quite right.

We were given an excellent lunch, and fresh raspberries for dessert. The Duke was cross with David Cecil for misrepresenting the great Duke over Catholic Emancipation – and was again right. Quite inaccurate of David

1. The Roman city of Silurnum.

to say 'suddenly reversing the conviction of a lifetime' Wellington plumped for Catholic Emancipation: he had long favoured it. And indeed he wasn't an Ultra at all: was rather independent in his attitude to his own Tory party.

After lunch the Duke was ready to take me round, had got out of the safe the George[1] that Charles I wore on the scaffold – it had come down through the Young Pretender's daughter, I think, by Clementina Sobieski. It was wonderful to hold this object in my hand and think of its associations. We walked through the pleasant rooms, low and well-proportioned, the core being a house of the 1630s, with larger eighteenth-century rooms at either end. The gallery had a series of fine marble busts of Roman emperors, and so through several rooms which the first Duke had papered with his prints – one of the Russian ones the deathbed scene at Taganrog. In the library I was shown Napoleon's copy of a French biography of Marlborough, printed by the Imprimerie Impériale in 1808 – before Napoleon involved himself fatally in Spain, Austria, Russia. The volumes were taken from St Cloud by Colonel Gurwood – I suppose fair spoil, like the pictures captured in Joseph's coach at Vittoria. Two cases contained the present Duke's collection of fine bindings – it is he who has made the whole interior so *gemütlich* and pleasant. I held in my hand the great Duke's George, restored to Queen Victoria after his death, and given to this Duke by the present Queen one evening at Windsor. The most splendid George of all – Marlborough's, which came to Wellington, was one of the things stolen from the Victoria and Albert Museum, with the two diamond swords, the very night after I was allowed in to see them.

More intimate and touching, in a way, was to see the complete toilet-case with all accessories, which Wellington carried round with him on the Continent, which he bought for himself; the iron and canvas folding-up bed which accompanied him abroad; and *in situ* the capacious bath with the big hot-water can, with mustard-filtering contraption. Also one of the Duke's heavy umbrellas he had made, with, screwed inside the ferrule, a knife like a small bayonet – for the Duke was twice attacked in London. Rather touching, too, was the little painting the Duke carried round with him on his campaigns of his two sons as babies, whom he never saw for years – worn with being carried about.

The first thing he did on buying Stratfield Saye was to build on a large conservatory, which used to be filled with greenery and plants and flowers, when there were servants to do the watering required – now turned into a gallery of marbles. – Indeed the only thing I missed in this house of so much taste was the presence of flowers, which a woman in the house would have

1. The insignia of the Order of the Garter.

seen to: those two elderly bachelor types not. The Duke is by nature a bachelor, I suspect, in spite of his marriage to Dorothy, who earned the name 'Dotty Wellesley', eccentric and dypso poetess.

On the way out the Italian marble table in the hall had belonged to Cardinal Fesch. Two portraits from Encaenia proceedings at Oxford this Duke had bought from Lord Eldon's sale for £2 and £3. What fun he has had! What a good job he has made of it! Though this has been a minor job compared with Apsley House, where he says the best things are.

He saw me kindly off at the door, explaining a better way back to Oxford via Aldermaston and Pangbourne, escaping the hideous ganglia of Reading. I sailed off down by the little Wellington Monument, my head happily full of all I had seen and heard.

All that, followed up by reading the excellent Selection of Wellington's Letters, has given me a much better idea of the man he was, especially of the older Wellington in politics, after the wars were over, with England sitting securely in her island, on top of the world. He was a man of principle, but not an Ultra-Tory – indeed he detested the odious Cumberland – and on the whole kept in harness with Peel, reasonable about the Repeal of the Corn Laws. A man of great practical common-sense, always looking for expedients, the best way to get things done. His one defect – that he was always expecting Revolution just round the corner – understandably when he had grown up in the world of the French Revolution. That he was a nice man comes out in his relations with the Arbuthnots, Lady Wilton and even Miss Burdett-Coutts, whose infatuation for him he did not return. Extraordinary to find this (I thought, hard-headed) young woman appearing in his private rooms at an early hour of the morning, as if she had passed the night there – and he had to remonstrate with her twice. As an elderly man a real vein of kindness and consideration for others comes out. No wonder the young Victoria always refers to him as 'the good old Duke', or the extraordinary George IV – with his astonishing entourage like an Oriental Pasha – felt towards him an emotion 'which could be described only as love'.

I hurtled back in time to greet —, over from New York for a few days, to whom *I* was a bad host. He arrived pickled in drink – perfectly sober and nice and agreeable; but whenever he came near me I detected the detestable odour that people who soak themselves in gin give out – like methylated spirits. Just like people who have eaten garlic, unaware of it themselves. Every time he came near me I moved away: he couldn't understand it and I didn't like to tell him. But, sensitive and intelligent as he is, he persisted in coming near, or walking near, until it became almost a game: I skipped aside, or manoeuvred to get behind a piece of furniture; when he was safely on a path, I walked on the grass. He invariably followed on to the grass; I then returned to the gravel. He must have thought I was mad.

7 December

At last the English winter has caught up with me – I haven't seen it for seven or eight years. Today sleet and snow, and the Warden of New College's garden below my bedroom a pretty Christmas card – white along ledges of walls and buildings and sketching out the black edges of boughs, at last stripped and bare.

It has been a *golden* autumn, and I have loved every moment of it, the leaves, russet and gold, staying on the trees right up to December: no winds, no frost. I have often been transported with delight, while slaving at my book at the table in the centre of the room, looking up to see the towering copper beech in Queen's garden, honey-coloured with afternoon light, or sepia and brown, or a cage of variegated lights through the glow of the setting sun. All round me this beauty in this room – soon to leave it. I did not make a mistake in deciding to stay here this autumn. And I have got forward with the book.

Last Sunday, 23 November, a crisp golden day, out to Wallingford to lunch with Max and Agatha:[1] a cosy, warm, hospitable, middle-class interior, with all the comforts and amenities, the pretty china and good furniture that Agatha's prosperity has brought. Better still the warm, kindly atmosphere both radiate. Max has (Austrian) charm and kindness; Agatha full-bosomed English comfortableness, plus the American strain of generosity. Better still, the wine-coloured autumn light as it came flooding into the blowsy, cosy room – too large, billowing chairs (like Agatha), the lavender colour of the slagware on the chimney-piece. She brought out piece after piece of old china for me – nothing spectacular, like Jack Plumb's Sèvres, just pleasant Victorian pieces (again like Agatha herself).

I have always been curious to know the truth of *her* detective story – that of her first marriage, her background, whether the episode of her losing her memory and being identified at Harrogate was true – for after that she never looked back.

Last week, lunching in London, I learned the truth from an old friend, a Cambridge girl – had been a friend of Arthur Goodhart, but found him too ugly to marry, in spite of his money. I knew that Agatha's father was an American expatriate, who lived at Torquay where he married. Agatha is patriotic about Devon and, when the millions began to roll in, bought Mary

1. Christie. Her husband, Max Mallowan, was a professorial colleague and friend at All Souls.

Bolitho's Greenway on the Dart (long before Sir Humphrey Gilbert's). She married a Lieut.-Col. Christie, and had one girl – was happily married, living in London, not well-off. She went back to Torquay for a few weeks to look after her dying mother. When she came back she was met by husband demanding a divorce to marry the woman friend who was looking after her husband for her while away.

Agatha *did* practically lose her reason – after the strain of her mother's illness, then this betrayal. She was apparently prevented from throwing herself off the balcony upstairs, but had a nervous breakdown and genuinely lost her memory.

I just remember the furore in the newspapers in the 1930s at her disappearance for several days, and being identified in a hotel. 'You are Agatha Christie,' someone said. 'Am I?' Everybody thought it a publicity stunt; but it was genuine – like all the best jobs. For, after that, she never looked back – *every* book was a bestseller, everything fell into her hands. Unexpected. Like what Shakespeare says about good often coming out of ill.

Mrs Polgreen[1] said, how the original Christie must have regretted what he lost. She was very much in love with him – a contented wife, geared to domestic happiness. It must have been then that Max turned up to console her – so that that was genuine too, before her tremendous fame and success. He also has had the reward of his niceness. Everything genuine about the old couple. Actually Max is my age, but he has had a stroke, left hand and arm dragging and a bit helpless. I fancy he has done himself well these last twenty years – no asceticism in that quarter!

Mrs Polgreen was witness to Agatha's innate modesty. She hadn't thought highly of her play *The Mousetrap* – it surprised her that it goes on year after year, now for seventeen years, bringing in £4,000 a year to her grandson. No wonder he can afford to collect pictures. I was sitting beside this (to me unknown) youth one evening at dinner in hall; we were talking about painting. He said he had bought a Sidney Nolan. 'That must have cost a lot,' I said. He said, 'It did.' 'How did you manage that?' 'I have a rich grandmother,' he replied.

As Max tells me, 'Money means nothing to her.' It pours in in millions – and goes to the tax people. She is trustified and companyfied, trusts in every direction for her family – she is very much a family woman (poor foolish Mr Christie – what a story he would make, looking at it from his point of view!) – and latterly joined some tax-evasion corporation. Still the money pours in. Still she writes the books. She has given me her latest, *Hallowe'en Party*. (I'm no reader of detective novels.) I read about a third of this one –

1. ALR's luncheon informant.

good middle-brow stuff; no literary distinction. The famous trick – really a kind of O. Henry trick, something unexpected at the end – one detects almost from the beginning. Yet – still the rapturous reviews, when books of mine, with all the work that goes into them, the originality and literary quality, are scurvily reviewed, if at all.

The Cornish in America is a *new* contribution to American history, based on unpublished material – all the people who write to me about it respond to it and are enthusiastic about it. It has never been reviewed by the *New York Times Book Review* or the *New York Review of Books*. Nor in London by *any* of the literary weeklies, *Spectator* or *New Statesman*, *Observer* or *Sunday Times*. It wouldn't have been reviewed in the *Telegraph* or *Sunday Telegraph*, if I hadn't seen to it myself. It was sabotaged by an old acquaintance, Brogan, in a nasty notice in *T.L.S.* – a shocking performance.

Is it any wonder that I am mentally sick at this treatment? I know as well as the next man the penalties attaching to exaggerated self-esteem, that I am thought an egoist – aren't they? I also know that there is no justice of mind among them; that this is a still more sick and diseased society, and that the centre of the sickness is the Leftist, liberal establishment. That it is still unrepresentative of the country: wherever I have been this autumn, Preston, Stroud, Eastbourne, Newton Abbot, I have had enthusiastic reception and response. The London establishment regards me as an enemy. They would strangle me if they could – and have succeeded, so far as reviewing and being reviewed are concerned.

Sunday, 28 June

Back from an interesting expedition to lunch with Lees-Milne,[1] his wife and Rosamond Lehmann[2] at Alderley on the western edge of the Cotswolds looking towards Bristol. A swishing summer-drive, under coloured rain-clouds along the Roman road from Cirencester to Tetbury, where I went wrong – along the Bath Road, until I found myself passing the gates of Westonbirt and Worcester Lodge at Badminton. However, I had time in hand, found the right turning and scooted down a ridge road through Tresham, with Stroud-like views opening west, to the stone village of Alderley. A characterful Georgian house behind its dry-walling, little closes filled with lawns, pleached alleys, flowers, mostly roses. Inside, just the house

1. James Lees-Milne, architectural historian, for many years on the staff of the National Trust. His volumes of memoirs (*Another Self*, *Ancestral Voices*, etc.), witty, waspish and well-written, are among the most vivid of the mid to late twentieth century.

2. Author of *Dusty Answer* (1927) and other novels. The subject of an acclaimed recent biography by Selina Hastings.

for me. Largeish stone-flagged hall with fine eighteenth-century staircase, on either side a big beautifully furnished room.

In front of a wood fire was Rosamond whom I hadn't seen since the thirties, when we were all young together and who belonged to a set I didn't much like – Wogan Phillips' Jewish wife, Goronwy Rees's[1] mistress. Still beautiful, dark eyes, white hair, round as a barrel. I was able to fill in gaps in her story since then. She left Wogan Phillips, with whom she lived in the Reade house at Ipsden, where I once visited, for Cecil Day-Lewis.[2] He wouldn't marry her, said he was already married and his wife wouldn't give him a divorce. One day he left Rosamond at the drop of a hat for a chit of a girl, within months got a divorce and married her. Rosamond was passionately in love with Goronwy – I learned that he was very good in bed, as I expected. So was Elizabeth Bowen, but I don't think she had much, if any, of Goronwy's juice. However, she got her own back in her portrait of him as the cad he was in *Death of the Heart*.

I gathered that the clue to Elizabeth was her mother's death when she was fourteen: her heart's world somehow ended then. She married Alan Cameron not out of love, but for a stable relationship with a good fellow, and got it – better than Rosamond did in falling in love with her men, and then what? What is she doing now? – her writing has petered out. She must have money from various sources, and she is connected (surprisingly) with the Makinses by marriage – not by their wish, I suspect, they are such snobs . . . I ragged Rosamond mercilessly for the phrase 'emotionally immature', said that all the Fellows of All Souls were emotionally immature: I knew I was. But I liked her, as I never had in her glamorous days: there she sprawled, a fat loving Jewess with all that life having passed through that tub of a body. We were in absolute agreement about Goronwy, spoiled by Oxford, everybody in love with him, behaving like a cad to everybody and like a shit over those dreadful articles spilling the beans about his friends. Guy Burgess (the sod), who had always loved Goronwy and whom Goronwy *sold*, said 'Poor Goronwy! he must have wanted money badly.' I got one of his enchanting smiles when he last dined here:[3] I nodded and passed on.

Mrs Lees-Milne was rather out of all this literary chatter – but after all, I had been only on the margin. In return for Rosamond's candour I owned up that I had been in love with Adam von Trott. With Mrs Lees-Milne I had chat about Badminton and the Duchess.

It was evident how much J.L.-M. loved his house, though she had found it a bit too much – he loved it in winter, the feeling of being shut in, snow

1. Goronwy Rees, one of ALR's least favourite colleagues at All Souls.
2. Cecil Day-Lewis, poet laureate, detective novelist and, latterly, publisher.
3. Presumably ALR is recalling an evening at All Souls, not in the Lees-Milne house.

on the heights above. (But would one like being shut up alone with her?) Full of beautiful objects everywhere, books, rugs, pictures (not very valuable), a small bronze hand on the hall-table, agate eggs in a marble dish, even the WC handle was a beautiful coloured cord with tassel, the décor was completed by two small exquisite greyhounds, heraldic creatures as J.L.-M. said.

I sailed back well content with my foray to the western edge of the Cotswolds.

Saturday 27th I lunched at St Antony's with Geoffrey Hudson and his Japanese wife. Rebecca West was looking younger than for years with her attractive grey wig (and really ugly fat legs). She told me surprising information about Henry Andrews – that he was really Jewish, his people Lithuanian Jews, who made a lot of money. They must have had some in Mexico, for Rebecca has been over there for three months arranging her late Henry's affairs. Henry *adored* Rebecca and was exceedingly watchful and jealous – a regular Jewish husband. Once, when I suggested to Rebecca that she come down to see me at All Souls – 'I couldn't trust myself,' she said naively. She also told me the story of the Cazalets – that before 1914 they had millions upon millions in Russia (like the Duke of Bedford); that even though all that was wiped out they were still far from impoverished. She thought Thelma Cazalet a dull woman – I thought her vivacious and intelligent. While she doted on the platitudinous American at her lunch, wildly rich on alimony – I found her the usual American woman, with unbearable flat voice. Rebecca doesn't have much taste for people, let alone for pictures or objects – what a contrast her interior and the Lees-Milnes!

From Basil Gray I got much more of an insight into Helen Sutherland,[1] who left his wife, Nicolete Binyon, most of her money, and the remarkable place in Cumberland she once tempted me with – it was only a try-on: the fish didn't bite. Her shipping-magnate father did not leave her his large fortune: he left over a million to the King Edward VII hospitals. Helen: 'I could have spent it much better.' And she would have done. However, she got her mother's money and spent that well. Her father, a conventional Victorian, didn't approve: her marriage was a failure, ending in an annulment, though the husband subsequently married and had children. Helen was always tiresome with her airs: perhaps he couldn't make it with her. I always thought she was a Lesbian, with her intense friendship with Violet Holdsworth, her crush on the girls Nicolete Binyon and Kathleen Raine. But no – there were other men she fancied, including Bill Beveridge!

1. Generous patron and friend of painters and musicians. David Jones, in particular, has recorded his admiration and gratitude to her.

Her great days were the thirties, when she entertained generously at Rock, of the Hodgkins, in Northumberland. Then Charles Bosanquet was sticky about the lease and ended her tenancy – that was the end of Rock, now tenantless and mouldering into decay. (He was an obstinate fool. She was obstinate too. The house suffered.) Her real love had been for a Fellow of All Souls, Lionel Smith, but he had never responded – like so many of the Fellows, 'emotionally immature'. She had a flat in London and collected pictures – I remember her Seurat, which she sold for £5,000, now in the Newcastle gallery, and the Turner and Newall scrip-offer lying on the table in the music-room with all the books and flowers. And those horrible spoiled dogs, one of which would snap! The last time I saw her was at the T. S. Eliot *feier-fest*, where she was sitting right behind me. She caught me out: 'You thought I was dead.' The fact was I did think so. Shortly after, she was.

Saturday, 18 July

Morning spent in writing a quatercentenary article for *The Times* on John Felton, who fixed the Papal Bull of Deposition of Elizabeth I on the Bishop of London's gate in 1570. Then I sailed off to lunch with Julian and Igor Vinogradoff at Broughton Grange. Up nearly to Banbury, turning west through Bodicote, across the Chipping Norton road, down a country road to a white gate, a long downwards drive, there was the house. I was charmed by the summer situation of the grange, a pleasant slope down to its own trout-stream, up the other side to the horizon, not a house in sight, a couple of brown stone barns; the hay lying in swathes, farm land on either side, with beeches, a Wellingtonia obviously planted by Julian's Morrell grandfather. That was what brewing could do in the Victorian age: the Morrell estate at Headington, the big house now occupied by Robert Maxwell; lovely Garsington, which I knew briefly under Ottoline and Philip; Blackhall in Oxford, where retired grandmother Morrell held state; and then this attractive grange *in villegiatura*, to which granddaughter has retired from the strain of the house in Gower Street. On the proceeds of the small fortune she made out of the much-publicized group around Ottoline – letters of Russell, Strachey, K. Mansfield, Eliot and all.

I was warmly welcomed by Igor, even more by two cats, London strays, who made for me, mewed to me, recognized me for *unus ex istibus*. It was exciting to link up with Julian again after more than forty years. A lifetime has gone by in between. When I went out to Garsington (Ottoline to Julian: 'But he's a *genius*!') Julian was a girl of eighteen or nineteen being pursued with ardour by the very hetero Russian bear, son of the famous professor,

Wykehamist friend of Richard Pares. The affair was on and off, they bickered and quarrelled, Igor was very sexy, very Slav, temperamental, intolerable. When he got a junior lectureship at Edinburgh, he announced that he would give an Inaugural. Then he drank. She married somebody else and had three children; he married somebody else and had one child. Then, later in life, they married, had no joint children, but altogether have twelve or fourteen grandchildren. Thank God none was there on my visit. I could enjoy the place in peace.

It was exceedingly attractive, even more livable, utterly sequestered and agreeably Victorianized. Now the family relics could be roomily displayed: rare cabinets, one of tortoiseshell, another of ebony with painted panels; plenty of Chinese china, *famille rose*, and blue and white; paintings and drawings of Ottoline – the famous John head under the baroque hat, an unfinished full length by John, pencil and pen sketches.

Such an agreeable house, long corridors running right through it with cabinets, tables, heaped with *objets d'art*; a biggish library walled with books, over it a large study for Igor, littered with Russian *débris* and a sideways view to the fields. But he has done nothing with his life, failed at Edinburgh, took to drink, has never written a book – with all his chances, all his education, all his virile strength and sex – now an elderly stooped man mooching about somewhat unsteadily. They have come together after the long breach, and they seem to be happy – though Julian is very much the heiress and he waits on her. She has fattened with the years (she loves cooking and cooked an excellent tasty salmon, with a special American mayonnaise).

After lunch we settled down to look over the old photographs. Ottoline in every conceivable attitude, and dress; Garsington in sun and snow – lovely that, outlining ledges and gates and gables. One photograph showed Russell, Keynes and Strachey together on a garden seat; several of Strachey looming about; separate ones of girlish Katherine Mansfield and Middleton Murry (Muddleton Moral), strange ones of Virginia Woolf, several of E. M. Forster and Goldie Dickinson, whom Ottoline was so anxious for me to meet – with special intention? Surprisingly there was one of tall Roger Makins and Evelyn Baring, with me between them, on the steps of the house, all of us mere boys and laughing delightedly. I was surprised to see that I looked healthy and happy, no sign of the ravages of ulcer as yet. (It ought to have been arrested *then* – if only I had had a decent doctor. It was after that first ghastly peritonitis that I dropped contact with Ottoline and her circle. I wonder now if it was she who raised the money for my operation?)

It was all rather touching to find how undimmed memories were – hers as well as mine – after forty-four years. I came back transported through the country roads of Oxfordshire in high summer, meadowsweet out in the hedges. I stopped at Bloxham in memory of my poor old father, who worked here in the ironstone quarries, along with wicked Uncle Joe who deserted Aunt Emily for a bitch from there. I went into the church Father went to occasionally on Sundays, where he could hear the sermon only if he sat by a certain pillar in the nave.

Index

Note : Works by Rowse (ALR) appear directly under title; works by others under author's name